D1469150

SPECIAL EDUCATION SERIES
Peter Knoblock, *Editor*

ACHIEVING THE COMPLETE SCHOOL:
STRATEGIES FOR EFFECTIVE MAINSTREAMING
Douglas Biklen
with Robert Bogdan, Dianne L. Ferguson,
Stanford J. Searl, Jr., and Steven J. Taylor

CLASSIC READINGS IN AUTISM
Anne M. Donnellan, *Editor*

Classic Readings in Autism

Edited by
ANNE M. DONNELLAN

This book is made possible by a grant
from the National Football League Charities
to the National Society for Children and Adults with Autism.

Teachers College, Columbia University
New York and London

Published by Teachers College Press, 1234 Amsterdam Avenue,
New York, N.Y. 10027

Library of Congress Cataloging in Publication Data

Main entry under title:

Classic readings in autism.

  (Special education series)
  Includes index.
  1. Autism—Addresses, essays, lectures.
I. Donnellan, Anne M., 1943–   . II. Series:
Special education series (New York, N.Y.)
RJ506.A9C53 1985   618.92'8982   85-2695

ISBN 0-8077-2774-1

Manufactured in the United States of America

90 89 88 87 86   2 3 4 5 6

Contents

Foreword

Since 1981, NFL Charities has been funding the establishment of library "Research Collections on Autism" in home cities of our National Football League teams. The purpose has been twofold: first, to make available a wide range of accurate information to families with autistic children and to the professionals who work with them; second, to provide comprehensive, one-stop reference centers on autism for the benefit of educators, diagnosticians, program developers, and researchers whose efforts focus on prevention, cure, and amelioration of the negative effects of this tragic disorder.

It is only natural that we of NFL Charities would expand our efforts to include *Classic Readings in Autism*, a compendium of many of the most important papers about autism that have ever been written. We will be proud to include this volume in libraries that presently house NFL Autism Research Collections.

Pete Rozelle
President, NFL Charities

Acknowledgments

David Park, as publications committee chairman of the National Society for Children and Adults with Autism (NSAC), had the original idea for this book and throughout its inception was its strong supporter and advocate. From the beginning, Victor Winston was a supporter and provided invaluable advice regarding the mysteries of publication. Donald Cohen, chair of the Professional Advisory Board of NSAC, was always available to answer complex questions about these articles and to offer encouragement and assistance. Daniel A. Torisky, secretary of NSAC, made the book a reality through his efforts to find financial support. His contribution to this project, along with that of National Football League Charities, is incalculable.

All the contributors to this volume were unfailingly generous with their time and their talent. The selection process began with the development of a panel of international experts to serve as an editorial board. The panel members, listed in the back of this book, recommended those articles they believed to be "classic," that is, articles that have withstood the test of time or had major impact on the field for a period of time. Because several hundred articles were suggested, the gleaning of the twenty-one included in this volume was very difficult. Several panel members, particularly Beverly Kilman, assisted in this process. We read every article that was suggested and was available. The decision was made to include where possible, a representative sample of noteworthy medical, educational, psychological, and linguistic papers.

Once the articles were chosen, they were sent to the panel members who had volunteered to write the brief commentaries to place each paper in historical perspective. The commentators did an admirable job under very rigid space restrictions. Several scholars wrote excellent commentaries on fine articles that, because of severe cuts required for publication, had to be deleted at the last moment. They are Jerry Sloan commenting on DSM-III; Donald J. Cohen and George Anderson commenting on Ritvo, Yuwiler, Geller, Ornitz, Saeger, and Plotkin, 1970; Barbara Cutler commenting on Kozloff, 1973; Saul Harrison commenting on Fish, 1977; Peter Knoblock commenting on Fenichel, Freedman, and Klapper, 1960; Gerald Groden commenting on Creak, 1961; Gregory Olley commenting on Rutter, 1967; Nannette Negri-Shoultz commenting on Dewey and Everard, 1974; and Catherine Lord commenting on Cox, Rutter, Newman, and Bartak, 1975 (these articles are referenced at the end of chapter 1).

I must especially acknowledge the very generous assistance of Gary LaVigna, Marie Ruiz, Peter Tanguay, and Frank Warren. All these fine professionals deserve credit for their contribution to this effort. The responsibility for final selection, however, and thus for any unwitting slights or errors, rests with me.

As always, I acknowledge the loving support of my son, John Douglas Donnellan Walsh, who patiently gives up so much of his mother for the benefit of other children, and my mother, Mary Casey Donnellan, who is always there with love and encouragement.

The proceeds of *Classic Readings in Autism* will go to further the work of NSAC, which is "dedicated to the education and welfare of children and adults with severe disorders of communication and behavior." To all those who made this book possible, therefore, I offer a mighty "thank you" on my own behalf and on behalf of all the individuals and families who live with the challenges associated with autism. May our efforts contribute to a time in which their burdens are lifted through greater understanding.

Classic Readings
in
Autism

1

Introduction

ANNE M. DONNELLAN

Forty years ago Leo Kanner published an article about eleven children whom he had seen in his clinical practice over the course of five years. Since the publication of "Autistic Disturbances of Affective Contact" (see chapter 2[1]), his name has been synonymous with this most perplexing of developmental disorders. Although in his unpublished autobiography[2] he credits his fame to "a piece of serendipity" (1977), it was Kanner's superb skill at both observing and recording behavior that has allowed his original description to withstand the test of time and empirical verification (see chapter 2, commentary, Rutter).

As John Wing (1976) has noted, large numbers of cases and sophisticated statistical analysis are not necessary for all advances in psychiatry and Kanner's eleven case histories attracted professional attention despite the small sample. The first reactions did not appear in print for several years, but the situation changed abruptly after 1950.

> At least 52 articles and one book were concerned specifically with the subject of autism between then and 1959. The first European confirmations of the existence of the syndrome came in 1952 from Van Krevelen in Holland and from Stern in France. (Kanner, 1977)

Since that time, it is hard to imagine another behavioral phenomenon of relative rarity that has attracted such attention among professionals and has fueled so much passionate discussion and disagreement. Much of the controversy from the earliest days concerned itself with the cause of the disorder. In his first paper on the subject (see chapter 2), Kanner concluded the discussion with a clear position about the biological cause of autism:

> We must, then, assume that these children have come into the world with an innate inability to form the usual, biologically provided affective con-

---

[1]Chapters cited in this Introduction are chapters in this book.

[2]Excerpts from Dr. Kanner's unpublished autobiography appear here through the kind permission of his family. Portions of this material appear in a 1977 videotape interview (Donnellan & LaVigna, 1977).

1

tact with people, just as other children come into the world with innate physical or intellectual handicaps. If this assumption is correct, a further study of our children may help to furnish concrete criteria regarding the still diffuse notions about the constitutional components of emotional reactivity. For here we seem to have pure-culture examples of *inborn autistic disturbances of affective contact*.

Unfortunately, the "further study" to which Kanner referred was long in coming, as many of the early writers were more concerned with explaining the psychopathology of the maternal-child interaction that brought about the autistic withdrawal (e.g., Bettelheim, 1959; Szurek & Berlin, 1956) than with finding out whether any such pathology existed at all. Although he clearly recognized an innate biological deficit in 1943, Kanner himself may have prompted the schizophrenegenic detour through his comments on parental coldness and, more significantly, through his choice of the term "autism." Apparently, he chose the word reluctantly because of the connotation of withdrawal:

> The term autism was introduced by Eugen Bleuler who wrote: "Naturally some withdrawal from reality is implicit in the wishful thinking of normal people. . . . Here, however, it is mainly an act of will by which they surrender themselves to a fantasy. . . . I would not call the effects of these mechanisms 'autism' unless they are coupled with a definite withdrawal from the external world."
>
> All this does not seem to fit in with Bleuler's criteria for autism. There is not withdrawal in the accepted sense of this word and a specific kind of contact with the external world is a cardinal feature of the illness. Nevertheless, in full recognition of all this, I was unable to find a concise expression that would be equally or more suitably applicable. After all, these children do start out in a state that resembles the end result of later-life withdrawal and there is a remoteness at least from the human portion of the external world. An identifying designation appeared to me to be definitely desirable because, as later events proved, there was danger of having this distinct syndrome lumped together with a variety of general categories. (Kanner, 1977)

Concise though the term "autism" might be, it was soon confused with other concepts such as Bleuler's autism and Minkowski's (1953) "autism riche." This was most unfortunate as the autism of Kanner's syndrome is quite distinct from what Bleuler and Minkowski described. In fact, as John Wing (1976) notes, "The lack of fantasy and creative inner life demonstrated by children with Kanner's syndrome, and so clearly expounded by Kanner himself, cannot possibly be explained by an escape into fantasy." (For reviews of literature regarding cognitive, linguistic, and symbolic deficits in autism, see chapter 10, Hermelin & Frith, and commentary, Schuler; chapter 13, Shapiro et al., and commentary, Kilman; and chapter 18, Wing et al., and commentary, Groden and Groden.) Nevertheless, the confusion about definition gave impetus to the "psychogenic" literature on autism that so dominated the field through the fifties and into the early sixties. According to Kanner, autism became quite "fashionable" in the 1950s and psychotherapy was the treatment of choice:

> While the majority of the Europeans were satisfied with a sharp delineation of infantile autism as an illness "sui generis," there was a tendency in this country to view it as a developmental anomaly ascribed exclusively to maternal emotional determinants. Moreover, it became a habit to dilute the original concept of infantile autism by diagnosing it in many disparate conditions which show one or another isolated symptom found as a part feature of the overall syndrome. Almost overnight, the country seemed to be populated by a multitude of autistic children, and somehow this trend became noticeable overseas as well. Mentally defective children who displayed bizarre behavior were promptly labeled autistic and, in accordance with preconceived notions, both parents were urged to undergo protracted psychotherapy in addition to treatment directed toward the defective child's own supposedly underlying emotional problem. (Kanner, 1977)

Kanner's description of the state of the art in the fifties was confirmed during the preparation of this book. Only two of the more than 150 articles recommended by various members of the editorial panel as "classic," that is, significant for their time or having withstood the test of time, were from that decade.

One of the two recommended articles was "Joey, a 'Mechanical Boy' " (Bettelheim, 1959). Although not as famous as some of Bettelheim's books, the article received a great deal of popular attention. Several editorial panel members felt it had a significant impact on professional and lay attitudes about autism for many years. Certainly, it merits inclusion as a well-written and imaginative example of a genre that continues to intrigue a lay audience (e.g., Axline, 1964; Kaufman, 1976; McCracken, 1973). Unfortunately, at the request of the author, "Joey, a 'Mechanical Boy' " will not be reprinted in this volume. However, as this approach to autism had such a profound influence on notions about cause and treatment, and because the myths about the "hidden genius" inside the "withdrawn" autistic child continue to appear in the popular media, a comment appears in order. Lorna Wing suggests that in light of present-day understanding of the syndrome, Joey's behavior can be more parsimoniously and usefully explained as the highly circumscribed interest of a child with limited imagination:

> Most autistic children lack imaginative play, but among those of higher levels of ability there are some with limited, repetitive symbolic activities.

A few, like Joey, have remarkably elaborate circumscribed interests. Seen in isolation, such children are bewildering but fascinating, and an invitation to theorize for those who prefer speculation to fact. Bettelheim was one of the group who adopted this approach to child psychology and whose ideas once dominated the field. Their publications comprised individual case studies, with no attempt to use scientific methodology. They wrote persuasively and were instrumental in popularizing the (untested) belief that autistic children are of normal intelligence but have chosen to withdraw into their own world because of emotional problems due to the abnormal child rearing practices of their parents.

As data from clinical, psychological, and epidemiological research have accumulated, autism has come to be seen as a developmental disorder with organic causes. The behavior of children like Joey can best be understood as a limited, uneven development of the imagination. The bizarre stereotyped activities represent the child's maladaptive strivings to cope with his patchy and distorted picture of the world.

In my clinical experience, the view of autism as an emotional disturbance interferes with attempts to estimate each child's level of function and to plan a sensible program of management and teaching. The theories concerning the parents tend to compound the distress of having a handicapped child and undermine confidence in ability to cope.

No independent evaluation of Bettelheim's results has ever been published. (L. Wing, personal communication, January 16, 1985)

Certainly, in the fifties there was other fine work available, such as that described by Fenichel, Freedman, & Klapper (1960), Bender (1956), and Kanner himself (Eisenberg & Kanner, 1956), but it was not until the sixties that the subject of autism began to attract a wide variety of serious investigators. Kanner credits some of the change to the shifting winds of fashion:

The 1960's witnessed a considerable sobering up. The fashion . . . had gradually subsided. This is perhaps caused in part by the fact that those who go in for the summary adoption of diagnostic clichés found another handy label. . . . Instead of the many would-be autistic children who are not autistic, there was the ever-ready rubber stamp of the "brain injured child" and [this] left the serious study of autism to those pledged to diagnostic accuracy. (Kanner, 1977)

One of the first efforts to clarify the diagnosis was the work of Creak (1961) and her colleagues who attempted to establish criteria for separating the diagnosis of autism from the myriad of other labels for mental impairments. Although the label they eventually chose was "schizophrenic syndrome of childhood," their descriptions of the characteristics have been often cited in other definitions of autism, such as that of the National Society for Autistic Children (Ritvo & Freeman, 1981). However, twenty years after

Creak and her colleagues attempted to describe the syndrome, the matter of differential diagnosis of autism remains unsettled and somewhat controversial (see Deckner, Soraci, Deckner, & Blanton, 1981).

In fairness, of course, it must be said that very little about autism is ever noncontroversial. One article from the sixties is, perhaps, the exception that proves the rule. Lotter's 1966 (see chapter 6) epidemiological data indicating an incidence of 4.5 per 10,000 has been supported by subsequent studies. The more recent work of Wing (1981) and Wing, Yeates, Brierley, and Gould (1976) expands upon rather than contradicts Lotter's findings except as regards sex ratios (see chapter 6, commentary, Rumsey). On the other hand, one author deliberately created a controversy that he then effectively if not immediately settled. Rimland (see chapter 5) took issue with Eisenberg and Kanner's (1956) efforts to diminish the importance of the "heredity versus environmental" question in autism and with other efforts to attribute the genesis of autism to family dynamics. In his award-winning book, *Infantile Autism*, Rimland laid to rest the ghost of psychogenesis so persuasively that no serious behavioral scientist has raised it again. His work has, of course, been supported by further research (see Cox, Rutter, Newman, & Bartak, 1975; McAdoo & DeMyer, 1978; chapter 9, Rutter). The most direct beneficiaries of this change in attitude were the parents, who were no longer scapegoats (see chapter 12, Schopler) but rather were recognized as important advocates and partners in treatment efforts (Donnellan & Mirenda, 1984; Kozloff, 1973; Schopler & Reichler, 1971). Indirectly, everyone concerned benefited from the recognition that autism is a profound developmental disorder with a physiological basis. The studies of physiological causes that began in the sixties (e.g., see chapter 4, Schain & Freedman; and chapter 8, Ornitz & Ritvo) are part of the changing pattern of research that resulted from a shift in the attitude about causation.

It was also in the sixties that psychologists interested in applied behavior analysis first began to turn their attention to the problems of children with autism. Certainly no area of expertise has had a more dramatic impact on the lives of these children and their families. Ferster (see chapter 3) was the first behavioral "purist" to write on the topic. Some colleagues argued that he should not be included in this volume because of his radical position in analyzing autism as a function of the individual's reinforcement history. However, as Gary LaVigna notes in his commentary, Ferster was also ahead of his time in ascribing communicative function to some of the seemingly random aberrant behaviors he observed. Recently, other investigators (e.g., see chapter 16, Carr) have begun to reexamine communicative functions of problem behaviors in an effort to more effectively match the intervention with possible cause (see also Donnellan, Mirenda, Mesaros, & Fassbender, 1984, for a review of the pragmatic analysis of aberrant behavior).

Though Ferster's work remains important, it was Lovaas and his colleagues (see chapter 7 including commentary, Woods) who dominated behavioral analysis of autism with their repeated demonstrations that these children could learn under appropriate stimulus conditions. It was, however, the parents who made the critical difference as they were quick to set up programs to utilize methods with proven efficacy. Their success and the support of other researchers (Rutter, 1967) attested to the value of appropriate schooling, and provided considerable impetus to advocacy and research efforts of the sixties and seventies.

By the seventies the situation had changed substantially. Through the efforts of parent-professional coalitions in national societies for autistic children in North America, England, and elsewhere, researchers and educators from a wide variety of disciplines were drawn to study these children and their needs. As Kanner (1977) commented, "Indeed, in the past few years, the diagnoses have been more uniformly reliable and the discussion has been considerably less obfuscated by the smuggling in of irrelevant materials."

Hundreds of papers have been published on the topic of autism in the past decade or so. Those included in this volume from that period are among the most significant. It should be noted, however, that where two or more were recommended of similar value, the paper was chosen that would be most difficult for future scholars to locate. Thus, many otherwise deserving articles from the *Journal of Autism and Developmental Disorders*, such as Dewey and Everard's (1974) paper on near-normal adolescents, were not included here.

Looking back from the perspective of the eighties, it is not really possible to judge what is "classic" from a previous decade. The articles presented from the seventies, however, do address issues about autism that are likely to be important for many years to come. Among these are questions regarding specific aspects of the syndrome: cognitive (see chapter 10, Hermelin & Frith); linguistic (see chapter 13, Shapiro et al.); symbolic (see chapter 18, Wing et al.); and communicative (see chapter 15, Schuler & Donnellan-Walsh). Some recent literature on social interaction is too new to have been included (e.g., Hermelin, 1982; Knoblock, 1982; McHale, 1983; Prior, 1984; Rutter, 1982; Strain, 1983), but as noted by Rutter (see chapter 2, commentary), this aspect of autism is likely to become a major focus of future research.

While it is heartening to see expanded interest in the syndrome, by and large, research efforts are severely limited by lack of necessary resources. The complex interaction of cognitive, linguistic, and social deficits in autism are even now barely understood, and researchers are no closer to understanding the cause or to finding a cure than twenty years ago. Papers included here address factors that are neurological (chapter 21, Damasio & Maurer); genetic (chapter 17, Folstein & Rutter); and chemical (chapter 19, Cohen et al.; and chapter 22, Rimland et al.), but as the commentators attest, there is still more controversy than conclusion.

It appears that even this brief collection of classic papers has more to teach than a history lesson. Although the richness of phenomenological description provided by many of these earlier works is impressive, present-day scholars can learn a lesson or two about humility in noting the certitude with which some theories that have not withstood the test of time were asserted. Most humbling of all is the knowledge of how far we have to go. Coleman (see chapter 20) put it quite succinctly: "At our present level of knowledge, we do not know either the etiology, neuropathology or neurophysiological mechanisms causing autistic systems. Much research lies ahead."

Fortunately because of the efforts of earlier scholars, those who are part of the fifth decade of study about autism do start with some certainties. They know that parents are not culprits but are essential to the success of almost any intervention. Earlier notions of autistic children as "normal" or even "gifted" with their retardation seen as secondary have given way to an acceptance of the high incidence of retardation among this population of learners (Rutter, 1970). Moreover, it is well understood that the disability is lifelong. Thus, there has been a transition from reliance on treatment to an understanding of the critical importance of education and training.

There have been attitudinal changes as well. Parents and professionals alike are far less tolerant of painful aversive behavioral interventions and dangerous levels of drugs designed to reduce or eliminate "autistic" behaviors. Rather, there is an awareness of the need for individualized, appropriate, comprehensive, preparatory, and longitudinal educational programs (Donnellan, 1981). And, there is not likely to be a cure or "magic bullet," either medical or psychological. There is a realization of the need to develop better support systems, more effective educational and vocational options, and more residential alternatives geared to meet the widely variant needs of persons disabled by the problems of autism (see Cohen & Donnellan, in press). Otherwise, the grim data regarding the large number of institutionalized persons with autism will not change. And, at least in North America, the results of institutionalization are about the same today as they were for the original group of children that Kanner wrote about in his 1971 follow-up (see chapter 11): "One cannot help but gain the impression that State Hospital admission was tantamount to a life sentence . . . a total retreat to near-nothingness."

Fortunately, though this is a low-incidence population, there is much to recommend support for the development of more creative and flexible programs and expanded budgets for basic research in autism. For example, if educational and social service systems are developed that are responsive to the extraordinary problems often found in autism, these systems are likely to be appropriate for other special learner populations as well. Moreover, basic research into the physical and psychological phenomena associated with autism will undoubtedly yield valuable information about the development of other forms of mental disorders (Fish, 1977; Rutter, 1982) as well as normal growth and development. John Wing (1976) stated it well:

> Autistic children do have a fascination which lies partly in the feeling that somewhere there must be a key which will unlock hidden treasures. The skilled researcher will indeed find the treasure . . . but the currency will be everyday and human, not fairy gold. In return for our attention, these children may give us the key to human language which is the key to humanity itself. (p. 14)

Let us hope that this volume will contribute to the search for that knowledge.

REFERENCES

Axline, V.M. (1964). *Dibs in Search of Self.* New York: Balantine.

Bender, L. (1956). Schizophrenia in childhood. *American Journal of Orthopsychiatry, 26,* 499.

Bettelheim, B. (1959). Joey: A "mechanical boy." *Scientific American, 200,* 116–127.

Cohen, D.J., & Donnellan, A.M. *Handbook of autism and disorders of atypical development.* New York: John Wiley, in press.

Cox, A., Rutter, M., Newman, S., & Bartak, L. (1975). A comparative study of infantile autism and specific developmental receptive language disorder: II. Parental characteristics. *British Journal of Psychiatry, 126,* 146–159.

Creak, M. (1961). Schizophrenic syndrome in childhood: Progress of a working party. *Cerebral Palsy Bulletin, 3,* 501–504.

Deckner, C.W., Soraci, S.A., Deckner, P.D., & Blanton, R.L. (1981). Consistency among commonly used procedures for assessment of abnormal children. *Journal of Clinical Psychology, 37,* 856–862.

Dewey, M., & Everard, M. (1974). The near normal autistic adolescent. *Journal of Autism and Childhood Schizophrenia, 4,* 348–356.

Donnellan, A. (1981). An educational perspective of autism: Implications for curriculum development and personnel development. In B. Wilcox & A. Thompson (Eds.), *Critical issues in educating autistic children and youth* (pp. 53–88). Washington, DC: National Society for Children and Adults with Autism.

Donnellan, A.M., & LaVigna, G.W. (1977). An interview with Leo Kanner. In G.W. LaVigna & A.M. Donnellan (Eds.), *Educating persons with autism.* California Department of Health/Telecommunications Service, Camarillo.

Donnellan, A.M., & Mirenda, P.L. (1984). Issues related to professional involvement with families of individuals with autism and other severe handicaps. *Journal of the Association for Persons with Severe Handicaps, 9,* 16–24.

Donnellan, A.M., Mirenda, P.L., Mesaros, R.A., & Fassbender, L.L. (1984). A strategy for analyzing the communicative functions of behavior. *Journal of the Association for Persons with Severe Handicaps.*

Eisenberg, L., & Kanner, L. (1956). Early infantile autism, 1943–1955. *American Journal of Orthopsychiatry, 26,* 556–566.

Fenichel, C., Freedman, A.M., & Klapper, Z. (1960). A day school for schizophrenic children. *American Journal of Orthopsychiatry, 30,* 130–143.

Fish, B. (1977). Neurobiologic antecedents of schizophrenia in children. *Archives of General Psychiatry, 34,* 1297–1313.

Hermelin, B. (1982). Thoughts and feelings. *Australia Autism Review, 1,* 10–19.

Kanner, L. (1977). *Autobiographical notes.* Unpublished manuscript.

Kaufman, B.N. (1976). *Son Rise.* New York: Warner.

Knoblock, P. (1982). *Teaching and mainstreaming autistic children.* Denver: Love Publishing.

Kozloff, M.A. (1973). *Reaching the autistic child: A parent training program.* Champaign, IL: Research Press.

McAdoo, W.G., & DeMyer, M.K. (1978). Personality characteristics of parents. In M. Rutter & E. Schopler (Eds.), *Autism: A reappraisal of concepts and treatment* (pp. 251–267). New York: Plenum Publishing.

McCracken, M. (1973). *A Circus of Children.* New York: Lippincott.

McHale, S. (1983). Social interactions of autistic and non-handicapped children during free play. *American Journal of Orthopsychiatry, 53,* 81–89.

Minkowski, E. (1953). *La schizophrenie.* Paris: Desclee de Brouwer.

Prior, M. (1984). Developing concepts of childhood autism: The influence of experimental cognitive research. *Journal of Consulting and Clinical Psychology, 52,* 4–16.

Ritvo, E.R., & Freeman, B.J. (1981). Definition of the syndrome of autism. In B. Wilcox & A. Thompson (Eds.), *Critical issues in educating autistic children and youth* (pp. 316–332). Washington, DC: National Society for Children and Adults with Autism.

Ritvo, E.R., Yuwiler, A., Geller, E., Ornitz, E.M., Saeger, K., & Plotkin, S. (1970). Increased blood serotonin and platelets in early infantile autism. *Archives of General Psychiatry, 23,* 566–572.

Rutter, M. (1967). Schooling and the autistic child. *Special Education, 6,* 19–24.

Rutter, M. (1970). Autistic children—Infancy to childhood. *Seminars in Psychiatry, 2,* 435–450.

Rutter, M. (1982). Cognitive deficits in the pathogenesis of autism. *Journal of Child Psychology and Psychiatry, 24,* 513–531.

Schopler, E., & Mesibov, G.B. (Eds.). *Social behavior and autism.* New York: Plenum Publishing, in preparation.

Schopler, E., & Reichler, R.J. (1971). Parents as co-therapists in the treatment of psychotic children. *Journal of Autism and Childhood Schizophrenia, 1,* 87.

Strain, P.S. (1983). Generalization of autistic children's social behavior change: Effects of developmentally integrated and segregated settings. *Analysis and Intervention in Developmental Disabilities, 3,* 23–34.

Szurek, S.A., & Berlin, I.N. (1956). Elements of psychotherapeutics with the schizophrenic child and his parents. *Psychiatry, 19,* 1–9.

Wing, J. (1976). Kanner's syndrome: A historical perspective. In L. Wing (Ed.), *Early childhood autism*. Oxford: Pergamon Press.

Wing, L. (1981). Sex ratios in early childhood autism and related conditions. *Psychiatry Research, 5,* 129–137.

Wing, L., Yeates, S.R., Brierley, L.M., & Gould, J. (1976). The prevalence of early childhood autism: A comparison of administrative and epidemiological studies. *Psychological Medicine, 6,* 89–100.

2

Autistic Disturbances
of Affective Contact

LEO KANNER

Since 1938, there have come to our attention a number of children whose condition differs so markedly and uniquely from anything reported so far, that each case merits—and, I hope, will eventually receive—a detailed consideration of its fascinating peculiarities. In this place, the limitations necessarily imposed by space call for a condensed presentation of the case material. For the same reason, photographs have also been omitted. Since none of the children of this group has as yet attained an age beyond 11 years, this must be considered a preliminary report, to be enlarged upon as the patients grow older and further observation of their development is made.

Case 1

Donald T. was first seen in October, 1938, at the age of 5 years, 1 month. Before the family's arrival from their home town, the father sent a thirty-three-page typewritten history that, though filled with much obsessive detail, gave an excellent account of Donald's background. Donald was born at full term on September 8, 1933. He weighed nearly 7 pounds at birth. He was breast fed, with supplementary feeding, until the end of the eighth month; there were frequent changes of formulas. "Eating," the report said, "has always been a problem with him. He has never shown a normal appetite. Seeing children eating candy and ice cream has never been a temptation to him." Dentition proceeded satisfactorily. He walked at 13 months.

At the age of 1 year "he could hum and sing many tunes accurately." Before he was 2 years old, he had "an unusual memory for faces and names, knew the names of a great number of houses" in his home town. "He was encouraged by the family in learning and reciting short poems, and even learned the Twenty-third Psalm and twenty-five questions and answers of the Presbyterian Catechism." The parents observed that "he was not learning to ask questions or to answer questions unless they pertained to rhymes

Reprinted with permission of the publisher from *Childhood Psychosis: Initial Studies and New Insights*, ed. Leo Kanner (Washington, D.C.: V. H. Winston, 1973), 1–43. First published in *Nervous Child* 2 (1943): 217–250.

or things of this nature, and often then he would ask no question except in single words." His enunciation was clear. He became interested in pictures "and very soon knew an inordinate number of the pictures in a set of *Compton's Encyclopedia*." He knew the pictures of the presidents "and knew most of the pictures of his ancestors and kinfolks on both sides of the house." He quickly learned the whole alphabet "backward as well as forward" and to count to 100.

It was observed at an early time that he was happiest when left alone, almost never cried to go with his mother, did not seem to notice his father's homecomings, and was indifferent to visiting relatives. The father made a special point of mentioning that Donald even failed to pay the slightest attention to Santa Claus in full regalia.

> He seems to be self-satisfied. He has no apparent affection when petted. He does not observe the fact that anyone comes or goes, and never seems glad to see father or mother or any playmate. He seems almost to draw into his shell and live within himself. We once secured a most attractive little boy of the same age from an orphanage and brought him home to spend the summer with Donald, but Donald has never asked him a question nor answered a question and has never romped with him in play. He seldom comes to anyone when called but has to be picked up and carried or led wherever he ought to go.

In his second year, he "developed a mania for spinning blocks and pans and other round objects." At the same time, he had

> a dislike for self-propelling vehicles, such as Taylor-tots, tricycles, and swings. He is still fearful of tricycles and seems to have almost a horror of them when he is forced to ride, at which time he will try to hold onto the person assisting him. This summer [1937] we bought him a playground slide and on the first afternoon when other children were sliding on it he would not get about it, and when we put him up to slide down it he seemed horror-struck. The next morning when nobody was present, however, he walked out, climbed the ladder, and slid down, and he has slid on it frequently since, but slides only when no other child is present to join him in sliding. . . . He was always constantly happy and busy entertaining himself, but resented being urged to play with certain things.

When interfered with, he had temper tantrums, during which he was destructive. He was "dreadfully fearful of being spanked or switched" but "could not associate his misconduct with his punishment."

In August, 1937, Donald was placed in a tuberculosis preventorium in order to provide for him "a change of environment." While there, he had a "disinclination to play with children and do things children his age usually take an interest in." He gained weight but developed the habit of shaking his head from side to side. He continued spinning objects and jumped up and down in ecstasy as he watched them spin. He displayed

> an abstraction of mind which made him perfectly oblivious to everything about him. He appears to be always thinking and thinking, and to get his attention almost requires one to break down a mental barrier between his inner consciousness and the outside world.

The father, whom Donald resembles physically, is a successful, meticulous, hard-working lawyer who has had two "breakdowns" under strain of work. He always took every ailment seriously, taking to his bed and following doctors' orders punctiliously even for the slightest cold. "When he walks down the street, he is so absorbed in thinking that he sees nothing and nobody and cannot remember anything about the walk." The mother, a college graduate, is a calm, capable woman, to whom her husband feels vastly superior. A second child, a boy, was born to them on May 22, 1938.

Donald, when examined at the Harriet Lane Home in October, 1938, was found to be in good physical condition. During the initial observation and in a two-week study by Drs. Eugenia S. Cameron and George Frankl at the Child Study Home of Maryland, the following picture was obtained:

There was a marked limitation of spontaneous activity. He wandered about smiling, making stereotyped movements with his fingers, crossing them about in the air. He shook his head from side to side, whispering or humming the same three-note tune. He spun with great pleasure anything he could seize upon to spin. He kept throwing things on the floor, seeming to delight in the sounds they made. He arranged beads, sticks, or blocks in groups of different series of colors. Whenever he finished one of these performances, he squealed and jumped up and down. Beyond this he showed no initiative, requiring constant instruction (from his mother) in any form of activity other than the limited ones in which he was absorbed.

Most of his actions were repetitions carried out in exactly the same way in which they had been performed originally. If he spun a block, he must always start with the same face uppermost. When he threaded buttons, he arranged them in a certain sequence that had no pattern to it but happened to be the order used by the father when he first had shown them to Donald.

There were also innumerable verbal rituals recurring all day long. When he desired to get down after his nap, he said, "Boo [his word for his mother], say 'Don, do you want to get down?' "

His mother would comply, and Don would say: "Now say 'All right.' "

The mother did, and Don got down. At mealtime, repeating something that had obviously been said to him often, he said to his mother, "Say 'Eat it or I won't give you tomatoes, but if you don't eat it I will give you tomatoes,' " or "Say 'If you drink to there, I'll laugh and I'll smile.' "

And his mother had to conform or else he squealed, cried, and strained every muscle in his neck in tension. This happened all day long about one thing or another. He seemed to have much pleasure in ejaculating words or phrases, such as "Chrysanthemum"; "Dahlia, dahlia, dahlia"; "Business"; "Trumpet vine"; "The right one is on, the left one off"; "Through the dark clouds shining." Irrelevant utterances such as these were his ordinary mode of speech. He always seemed to be parroting what he had heard said to him at one time or another. He used the personal pronouns for the persons he was quoting, even imitating the intonation. When he wanted his mother to pull his shoe off, he said: "Pull off your shoe." When he wanted a bath, he said: "Do you want a bath?"

Words to him had a specifically literal, inflexible meaning. He seemed unable to generalize, to transfer an expression to another similar object or situation. If he did so occasionally, it was a substitution, which then "stood" definitely for the original meaning. Thus he christened each of his water color bottles by the name of one of the Dionne quintuplets—Annette for blue, Cécile for red, etc. Then, going through a series of color mixtures, he proceeded in this manner: "Annette and Cécile make purple."

The colloquial request to "put that *down*" meant to him that he was to put the thing on the floor. He had a "milk glass" and a "water glass." When he spit some milk into the "water glass," the milk thereby became "white water."

The word "yes" for a long time meant that he wanted his father to put him up on his shoulder. This had a definite origin. His father, trying to teach him to say "yes" and "no," once asked him, "Do you want me to put you on my shoulder?"

Don expressed his agreement by repeating the question literally, echolalia-like. His father said, "If you want me to, say 'Yes'; if you don't want me to, say 'No.' "

Don said "yes" when asked. But thereafter "yes" came to mean that he desired to be put up on his father's shoulder.

He paid no attention to persons around him. When taken into a room, he completely disregarded the people and instantly went for objects, preferably those that could be spun. Commands or actions that could not possibly be disregarded were resented as unwelcome intrusions. But he was never angry at the interfering *person*. He angrily shoved away the *hand* that was in his way or the *foot* that stepped on one of his blocks, at one time referring to the foot on the block as "umbrella." Once the obstacle was removed, he forgot the whole affair. He gave no heed to the presence of other children but went about his favorite pastimes, walking off from the children if they were so bold as to join him. If a child took a toy from him, he passively permitted it. He scrawled lines on the picture books the other children were coloring, retreating or putting his hands over his ears if they threatened him in anger. His mother was the only person with whom he had any contact at all, and even she spent all of her time developing ways of keeping him at play with her.

After his return home, the mother sent periodic reports about his development. He quickly learned to read fluently and to play simple tunes on the piano. He began, whenever his attention could be obtained, to respond to questions "which require yes or no for an answer." Though he occasionally began to speak of himself as "I" and of the person addressed as "you," he continued for quite some time the pattern of pronominal reversals. When, for instance, in February, 1939, he stumbled and nearly fell, he said of himself, "*You* did not fall down."

He expressed puzzlement about the inconsistencies of spelling: "bite" should be spelled "bight" to correspond to the spelling of "light." He could spend hours writing on the blackboard. His play became more imaginative and varied, though still quite ritualistic.

He was brought back for a check-up in May, 1939. His attention and concentration were improved. He was in better contact with his environment, and there were some direct reactions to people and situations. He showed disappointment when thwarted, demanded bribes promised him, gave evidence of pleasure when praised. It was possible, at the Child Study Home, to obtain with constant insistence some conformity to daily routine and some degree of proper handling of objects. But he still went on writing letters with his fingers in the air, ejaculating words—"Semicolon"; "Capital"; "Twelve, twelve"; "Slain, slain"; "I could put a little comma or semicolon"—chewing on paper, putting food on his hair, throwing books into the toilet, putting a key down the water drain, climbing onto the table and bureau, having temper tantrums, giggling and whispering autistically. He got hold of an encyclopedia and learned about fifteen words in the index and kept repeating them over and over again. His mother was helped in trying to develop his interest and participation in ordinary life situations.

The following are abstracts from letters sent subsequently by Donald's mother:

> *September, 1939.* He continues to eat and to wash and dress himself only at my insistence and with my help. He is becoming resourceful, builds things with his blocks, dramatizes stories, attempts to wash the car, waters the flowers with the hose, plays store with the grocery supply, tries to cut out pictures with the scissors. Numbers still have a great attraction for him. While his play is definitely improving, he has never asked questions about people and shows no interest in our conversation. . . .
>
> *October, 1939* [a school principal friend of the mother's had agreed to try Donald in the first grade of her school]. The first day was very trying for them but each succeeding day he has improved very much. Don is

much more independent, wants to do many things for himself. He marches in line nicely, answers when called upon, and is more biddable and obedient. He never voluntarily relates any of his experiences at school and never objects to going. . . .

November, 1939. I visited his room this morning and was amazed to see how nicely he cooperated and responded. He was very quiet and calm and listened to what the teacher was saying about half the time. He does not squeal or run around but takes his place like the other children. The teacher began writing on the board. That immediately attracted his attention. She wrote:

> Betty may feed a fish.
> Don may feed a fish.
> Jerry may feed a fish.

In his turn he walked up and drew a circle around his name. Then he fed a goldfish. Next, each child was given his weekly reader, and he turned to the proper page as the teacher directed and read when called upon. He also answered a question about one of the pictures. Several times, when pleased, he jumped up and down and shook his head once while answering. . . .

March, 1940. The greatest improvement I notice is his awareness of things about him. He talks very much more and asks a good many questions. Not often does he voluntarily tell me of happenings at school, but if I ask leading questions, he answers them correctly. He really enters into the games with other children. One day he enlisted the family in one game he had just learned, telling each of us just exactly what to do. He feeds himself better and is better able to do things for himself.

March, 1941. He has improved greatly, but the basic difficulties are still evident. . . .

Donald was brought for another check-up in April, 1941. An invitation to enter the office was disregarded, but he had himself led willingly. Once inside, he did not even glance at the three physicians present (two of whom he well remembered from his previous visits) but immediately made for the desk and handled papers and books. Questions at first were met with the stereotyped reply, "I don't know." He then helped himself to pencil and paper and wrote and drew pages and pages full of letters of the alphabet and a few simple designs. He arranged the letters in two or three lines, reading them in vertical rather than horizontal succession, and was very much pleased with the result. Occasionally he volunteered a statement or question: "I am going to stay for two days at the Child Study Home." Later he said, "Where is my mother?"

"Why do you want her?" he was asked.

"I want to hug her around the neck."

He used pronouns adequately and his sentences were grammatically correct.

The major part of his "conversation" consisted of questions of an obsessive nature. He was inexhaustible in bringing up variations: "How many days in a week, years in a century, hours in a day, hours in half a day, weeks in a century, centuries in half a millennium," etc., etc.; "How many pints in a gallon, how many gallons to fill four gallons?" Sometimes he asked, "How many hours in a minute, how many days in an hour?" etc. He looked thoughtful and always wanted an answer. At times he temporarily compromised by responding quickly to some other question or request but promptly returned to the same type of behavior. Many of his replies were metaphorical or otherwise peculiar. When asked to subtract 4 from 10, he answered: "I'll draw a hexagon."

He was still extremely autistic. His relation to people had developed only insofar as he addressed them when he needed or wanted to know something. He never looked at the person while talking and did not use communicative gestures. Even this type of contact ceased the moment he was told or given what he had asked for.

A letter from the mother stated in October, 1942:

> Don is still indifferent to much that is around him. His interests change often, but always he is absorbed in some kind of silly, unrelated subject. His literal-mindedness is still very marked, he wants to spell words as they sound and to pronounce letters consistently. Recently I have been able to have Don do a few chores around the place to earn picture show money. He really enjoys the movies now but not with any idea of a connected story. He remembers them in the order in which he sees them. Another of his recent hobbies is with old issues of *Time* magazine. He found a copy of the first issue of March 3, 1923, and has attempted to make a list of the dates of publication of each issue since that time. So far he has gotten to April, 1934. He has figured the number of issues in a volume and similar nonsense.

Case 2

Frederick W. was referred on May 27, 1942, at the age of 6 years, with the physician's complaint that his "adaptive behavior in a social setting is characterized by attacking as well as withdrawing behavior." His mother stated:

> The child has always been self-sufficient. I could leave him alone and he'd entertain himself very happily, walking around, singing. I have never known him to cry in demanding attention. He was never interested in hide-and-seek, but he'd roll a ball back and forth, watch his father shave, hold the razor box and put the razor back in, put the lid on the soap box. He never was very good with cooperative play. He doesn't care to play with the ordinary things that other children play with, anything with wheels on.

He is afraid of mechanical things; he runs from them. He used to be afraid of my egg beater, is perfectly pertrified of my vacuum cleaner. Elevators are simply a terrifying experience to him. He is afraid of spinning tops.

Until the last year, he mostly ignored other people. When we had guests, he just wouldn't pay any attention. He looked curiously at small children and then would go off all alone. He acted as if people weren't there at all, even with his grandparents. About a year ago, he began showing more interest in observing them, would even go up to them. But usually people are an interference. He'll push people away from him. If people come too close to him, he'll push them away. He doesn't want me to touch him or put my arm around him, but he'll come and touch *me*.

To a certain extent, he likes to stick to the same thing. On one of the bookshelves we had three pieces in a certain arrangement. Whenever this was changed, he always rearranged it in the old pattern. He won't try new things, apparently. After watching for a long time, he does it all of a sudden. He wants to be sure he does it right.

He had said at least two words ["Daddy" and "Dora," the mother's first name] before he was 2 years old. From then on, between 2 and 3 years, he would say words that seemed to come as a surprise to himself. He'd say them once and never repeat them. One of the first words he said was "overalls." [The parents never expected him to answer any of their questions, were *once* surprised when he did give an answer—"Yes".] At about 2½ years, he began to sing. He sang about twenty or thirty songs, including a little French lullaby. In his fourth year, I tried to make him ask for things before he'd get them. He was stronger-willed than I was and held out longer, and he would not get it but he never gave in about it. Now he can count up to into the hundreds and can read numbers, but he is not interested in numbers as they apply to objects. He has great difficulty in learning the proper use of personal pronouns. When receiving a gift, he would say of himself: "You say 'Thank you.' "

He bowls, and when he sees the pins go down, he'll jump up and down in great glee.

Frederick was born May 23, 1936, in breech presentation. The mother had "some kidney trouble" and an elective cesarean section was performed about two weeks before term. He was well after birth; feeding presented no problem. The mother recalled that he was never observed to assume an anticipatory posture when she prepared to pick him up. He sat up at 7 months, walked at about 18 months. He had occasional colds but no other illness. Attempts to have him attend nursery school were unsuccessful: "he would either be retiring and hide in a corner or would push himself into the middle of a group and be very aggressive."

The boy is an only child. The father, aged 44, a university graduate and a plant pathologist, has traveled a great deal in connection with his work. He is a patient, even-tempered man, mildly obsessive; as a child he did not talk "until late" and was delicate, supposedly "from lack of vitamin in diet allowed in Africa." The mother, aged 40, a college graduate, successively a secretary to physicians, a purchasing agent, director of secretarial studies in a girls' school, and at one time a teacher of history, is described as healthy and even-tempered.

The paternal grandfather organized medical missions in Africa, studied tropical medicine in England, became an authority on manganese mining in Brazil, was at the same time dean of a medical school and director of an art museum in an American city, and is listed in *Who's Who* under two different names. He disappeared in 1911, his whereabouts remaining obscure for twenty-five years. It was then learned that he had gone to Europe and married a novelist, without obtaining a divorce from his first wife. The family considers him "a very strong character of the genius type, who wanted to do as much good as he could."

The paternal grandmother is described as "a dyed-in-the-wool missionary if ever there was one, quite dominating and hard to get along with, at present pioneering in the South at a college for mountaineers."

The father is the second of five children. The oldest is a well known newspaper man and author of a best-seller. A married sister, "high-strung and quite precocious," is a singer. Next comes a brother who writes for adventure magazines. The youngest, a painter, writer and radio commentator, "did not talk until he was about 6 years old," and the first words he is reported to have spoken were, "When a lion can't talk he can whistle."

The mother said of her own relatives, "Mine are very ordinary people." Her family is settled in a Wisconsin town, where her father is a banker; her mother is "mildly interested" in church work, and her three sisters, all younger than herself, are average middle-class matrons.

Frederick was admitted to the Harriet Lane Home on May 27, 1942. He appeared to be well nourished. The circumference of his head was 21 inches, of his chest 22 inches, of his abdomen 21 inches. His occiput and frontal region was markedly prominent. There was a supernumerary nipple in the left axilla. Reflexes were sluggish but present. All other findings, including laboratory examinations and X-ray of his skull, were normal, except for large and ragged tonsils.

He was led into the psychiatrist's office by a nurse, who left the room immediately afterward. His facial expression was tense, somewhat apprehensive, and gave the impression of intelligence. He wandered aimlessly about for a few moments, showing no sign of awareness of the three adults present. He then sat down on the couch, ejaculating unintelligible sounds, and then abruptly lay down, wearing throughout a dreamy-like smile. When he responded to questions or commands at all, he did so by repeating them echolalia fashion. The most striking feature in his behavior was the difference in his reactions to objects and to people. Objects absorbed him easily and he showed good attention and perseverance in playing with them. He seemed to regard people as unwelcome intruders to whom he paid as little attention as they would permit. When forced to respond, he did so briefly and returned to his absorption in things. When a hand was held out before him so that he could not possibly ignore it, he played with it briefly as if were a detached object. He blew out a match with an expression of satisfaction with the achievement, but did not look up to the person who had lit the match. When a fourth person entered the room, he retreated for a minute or two behind the bookcase, saying, "I don't want you," and waving him away, then resumed his play, paying no further attention to him or anyone else.

Test results (Grace Arthur performance scale) were difficult to evaluate because of his lack of cooperation. He did best with the Seguin form board (shortest time, 58 seconds). In the mare and foal completion test he seemed to be guided by form entirely, to the extent that it made no difference whether the pieces were right side up or not. He completed the triangle but not the rectangle. With all the form boards he showed good perseverance and concentration, working at them spontaneously and interestedly. Between tests, he wandered about the room examining various objects or fishing in the wastebasket without regard for the persons present. He made frequent sucking noises and occasionally kissed the dorsal surface of his hand. He became fascinated with the circle from the form board, rolling it on the desk and attempting, with occasional success, to catch it just before it rolled off.

Frederick was enrolled at the Devereux Schools on September 26, 1942.

Case 3

Richard M. was referred to the Johns Hopkins Hospital on February 5, 1941, at 3 years, 3 months of age, with the complaint of deafness because he did not talk and did not respond to questions. Following his admission, the interne made this observation:

> The child seems quite intelligent, playing with the toys in his bed and being adequately curious about instruments used in the examination. He seems quite self-sufficient in his play. It is difficult to tell definitely whether he hears, but it seems that he does. He will obey commands, such as "Sit up" or "Lie down," even when he does not see the speaker. He does not pay attention to conversation going on around him, and although he does make noises, he says no recognizable words.

His mother brought with her copious notes that indicated obsessive preoccupation with details and a tendency to read all sorts of peculiar interpretations into the child's performances. She watched (and recorded) every gesture and every "look," trying to find their specific significance and finally deciding on a particular, sometimes very farfetched explanation. She thus accumulated an account that, though very elaborate and richly illustrated, on the whole revealed more of her own version of what had happened in each instance than it told of what had actually occurred.

Richard's father is a professor of forestry in a southern university. He is very much immersed in his work, almost entirely to the exclusion of social contacts. The mother is a college graduate. The maternal grandfather is a physician, and the rest of the family, in both branches, consists of intelligent professional people. Richard's brother, thirty-one months his junior, is described as a normal, well-developed child.

Richard was born on November 17, 1937. Pregnancy and birth were normal. He sat up at 8 months and walked at 1 year. His mother began to "train" him at the age of 3 weeks, giving him a suppository every morning "so his bowels would move by the clock." The mother, in comparing her two children, recalled that while her younger child showed an active anticipatory reaction to being picked up, Richard had not shown any physiognomic or postural sign of preparedness and had failed to adjust his body to being held by her or the nurse. Nutrition and physical growth proceeded satisfactorily. Following smallpox vaccination at 12 months, he had an attack of diarrhea and fever, from which he recovered in somewhat less than a week.

In September, 1940, the mother, in commenting on Richard's failure to talk, remarked in her notes:

> I can't be sure just when he stopped the imitation of word sounds. It seems that he has gone backward mentally gradually for the last two years. We have thought it was because he did not disclose what was in his head, that it was there all right. Now that he is making so many sounds, it is disconcerting because it is now evident that he can't talk. Before, I thought he could if he only would. *He gave the impression of silent wisdom to me.* . . . . One puzzling and discouraging thing is the great difficulty one has in getting his attention.

On physical examination, Richard was found to be healthy except for large tonsils and adenoids, which were removed on February 8, 1941. His head circumference was 54½ cm. His electroencephalogram was normal.

He had himself led willingly to the psychiatrist's office and engaged at once in active play with the toys, paying no attention to the persons in the room. Occasionally, he looked up at the walls, smiled and uttered short staccato forceful sounds—"Ee! Ee! Ee!" He complied with a spoken and gestural command of his mother to take off his slippers. When the command was changed to another, this time without gestures, he repeated the original request and again took off his slippers (which had been put on again). He performed well with the unrotated form board but not with the rotated form board.

Richard was again seen at the age of 4 years, 4 months. He had grown considerably and gained weight. When started for the examination room, he screamed and made a great fuss, but once he yielded he went along willingly. He immediately proceeded to turn the lights on and off. He showed no interest in the examiner or any other person but was attracted to a small box that he threw as if it were a ball.

At 4 years, 11 months, his first move in entering the office (or any other room) was to turn the lights on and off. He climbed on a chair, and from the chair to the desk in order to reach the switch of the wall lamp. He did not communicate his wishes but went into a rage until his mother guessed and procured what he wanted. He had no contact with people, whom he definitely regarded as an interference when they talked to him or otherwise tried to gain his attention.

The mother felt that she was no longer capable of handling him, and he was placed in a foster home near Annapolis with a woman who had shown a remarkable talent for dealing with difficult children. Recently, this woman heard him say clearly his first intelligible words. They were, "Good night."

Case 4

Paul G. was referred in March, 1941, at the age of 5 years, for psychometric assessment of what was thought to be a severe intellectual defect. He had attended a private nursery school, where his incoherent speech, inability to conform, and reaction with temper outbursts to any interference created the impression of feeblemindedness.

Paul, an only child, had come to this country from England with his mother at nearly 2 years of age. The father, a mining engineer, believed to be in Australia now, had left his wife shortly before that time after several years of an unhappy marriage. The mother, supposedly a college graduate, a restless, unstable, excitable woman, gave a vague and blatantly conflicting history of the family background and the child's development. She spent much time emphasizing and illustrating her efforts to make Paul clever by teaching him to memorize poems and songs. At 3 years, he knew the words of not less than thirty-seven songs and various and sundry nursery rhymes.

He was born normally. He vomited a great deal during his first year, and feeding formulas were changed frequently with little success. He ceased vomiting when he was started on solid food. He cut his teeth, held up his head, sat up, walked, and established bowel and bladder control at the usual age. He had measles, chickenpox, and pertussis without complications. His tonsils were removed when he was 3 years old. On physical examination, phimosis was found to be the only deviation from otherwise good health.

The following features emerged from observation on his visits to the clinic, during five weeks' residence in a boarding home, and during a few days stay in the hospital.

Paul was a slender, well-built, attractive child, whose face looked intelligent and animated. He had good manual dexterity. He rarely responded to any form of address, even to the calling of his name. At one time he picked up a block from the floor on request. Once he copied a circle immediately after it had been drawn before him. Sometimes an energetic "Don't!" caused him to interrupt his activity of the moment. But usually, when spoken to, he went on with whatever he was doing as if nothing had been said. Yet one never had the feeling that he was willingly disobedient or contrary. He was obviously so remote that the remarks did not reach him. He was always vivaciously occupied with something and seemed to be highly satisfied, unless someone made a persistent attempt to interfere with his self-chosen actions. Then he first tried impatiently to get out of the way and, when this met with no success, screamed and kicked in a full-fledged tantrum.

There was a marked contrast between his relations to people and to objects. Upon entering the room, he instantly went after objects and used them correctly. He was not destructive and treated the objects with care and even affection. He picked up a pencil and scribbled on paper that he found on the table. He opened a box, took out a toy telephone, singing again and again: "He wants the telephone," and went around the room with the mouthpiece and receiver in proper position. He got hold of a pair of scissors and patiently and skillfully cut a sheet of paper into small bits, singing the phrase "Cutting paper," many times. He helped himself to a toy engine, ran around the room holding it up high and singing over and over again, "The engine is flying." While these utterances, made always with the same inflection, were clearly connected with his actions, he ejaculated others that could not be linked up with immediate situations. These are a few examples: "The people in the hotel"; "Did you hurt your leg?" "Candy is all gone, candy is empty"; "You'll fall off the bicycle and bump your head." However, some of those exclamations could be definitely traced to previous experiences. He was in the habit of saying almost every day, "Don't throw the dog off the balcony." His mother recalled that she had said those words to him about a toy dog while they were still in England. At the sight of a saucepan he would invariably exclaim, "Peter-eater." The mother remembered that this particular association had begun when he was 2 years old and she happened to drop a saucepan while reciting to him the nursery rhyme about "Peter, Peter, pumpkin eater." Reproductions of warnings of bodily injury constituted a major portion of his utterances.

None of these remarks was meant to have communicative value. There was, on his side, no affective tie to people. He behaved as if people as such did not matter or even exist. It made no difference whether one spoke to him in a friendly or a harsh way. He never looked up at people's faces. When he had any dealings with persons at all, he treated them, or rather parts of them, as if they were objects. He would use a hand to lead him. He would, in playing, butt his head against his mother as at other times he did against a pillow. He allowed his boarding mother's hands to dress him, paying not the slightest attention to *her*. When with other children, he ignored them and went after their toys.

His enunciation was clear and he had a good vocabulary. His sentence construction was satisfactory, with one significant exception. He never used the pronoun of the first person, nor did he refer to himself as Paul. All statements pertaining to himself were made in the second person, as literal repetitions of things that had been said to him before. He would express his desire for candy by saying, "*You* want candy." He would pull his hand away from a hot radiator and say, "*You* get hurt." Occasionally there were parrot-like repetitions of things said to him.

Formal testing could not be carried out, but he certainly could not be regarded as feebleminded in the ordinary sense. After hearing his boarding mother say grace three times, he repeated it without a flaw and has retained it since then. He could count and name colors. He learned quickly to identify his favorite victrola records from a large stack and knew how to mount and play them.

His boarding mother reported a number of observations that indicated compulsive behavior. He often masturbated with complete abandon. He ran around in circles emitting phrases in an ecstatic-like fashion. He took a small blanket and kept shaking it, delightedly shouting, "Ee! Ee!" He could continue in this manner for a long time and showed great irritation when he was interfered with. All these and many other things were not only repetitions but recurred day after day with almost photographic sameness.

Case 5

Barbara K. was referred in February, 1942, at 8 years, 3 months of age. Her father's written note stated:

> First child, born normally October 30, 1933. She nursed very poorly and was put on bottle after about a week. She quit taking any kind of nourishment at 3 months. She was tube-fed five times daily up to 1 year of age. She began to eat then, though there was much difficulty until she was about 18 months old. Since then she has been a good eater, likes to experiment with food, tasting, and now fond of cooking.

Ordinary vocabulary at 2 years, but always slow at putting words into sentences. Phenomenal ability to spell, read, and a good writer, but still has difficulty with verbal expression. Written language has helped the verbal. Can't get arithmetic except as a memory feat.

Repetitious as a baby, and obsessive now: holds things in hands, takes things to bed with her, repeats phrases, gets stuck on an idea, game, etc., and rides it hard, then goes to something else. She used to talk using "you" for herself and "I" for her mother or me, as if she were saying things as we would in talking to her.

Very timid, fearful of various and changing things, wind, large animals, etc. Mostly passive, but passively stubborn at times. Inattentive to the point where one wonders if she hears. (She does!) No competitive spirit, no desire to please her teacher. If she knew more than any other member in the class about something, she would give no hint of it, just keep quiet, maybe not even listen.

In camp last summer she was well liked, learned to swim, is graceful in water (had always appeared awkward in her motility before), overcame fear of ponies, played best with children of 5 years of age. At camp she slid into avitaminosis and malnutrition but offered almost no verbal complaints.

Barbara's father is a prominent psychiatrist. Her mother is a well-educated, kindly woman. A younger brother, born in 1937, is healthy, alert, and well developed.

Barbara "shook hands" upon request (offering the left upon coming, the right upon leaving) by merely raising a limp hand in the approximate direction of the examiner's proffered hand; the motion definitely lacked the implication of greeting. During the entire interview there was no indication of any kind of affective contact. A pin prick resulted in withdrawal of her arm, a fearful glance at the pin (not the examiner), and utterance of the word "Hurt!" not addressed to anyone in particular.

She showed no interest in test performances. The concept of test, of sharing an experience or situation, seemed foreign to her. She protruded her tongue and played with her hand as one would with a toy. Attracted by a pen on the desk stand, she said: "Pen like yours at home." Then, seeing a pencil, she inquired: "May I take this home?"

When told that she might, she made no move to take it. The pencil was given to her, but she shoved it away, saying, "It's not my pencil."

She did the same thing repeatedly in regard to other objects. Several times she said, "Let's see Mother" (who was in the waiting room).

She read excellently, finishing the 10-year Binet fire story in thirty-three seconds and with no errors, but was unable to reproduce from memory anything she had read. In the Binet pictures, she saw (or at least reported) no action or relatedness between the single items, which she had no difficulty enumerating. Her handwriting was legible. Her drawing (man, house, cat sitting on six legs, pumpkin, engine) was unimaginative and stereotyped. She used her right hand for writing, her left for everything else; she was left-footed and right-eyed.

She knew the days of the week. She began to name them: "Saturday, Sunday, Monday," then said, "You go to school" (meaning, "on Monday"), then stopped as if the performance were completed.

Throughout all these procedures, in which—often after several repetitions of the question or command—she complied almost automatically, she scribbled words spontaneously: "oranges"; "lemons"; "bananas"; "grapes"; "cherries"; "apples"; "apricots"; "tangerine"; "grapefruits"; "watermelon juice"; the words sometimes ran into each other and were obviously not meant for others to read.

She frequently interrupted whatever "conversation" there was with references to "motor transports" and "piggy-back," both of which—according to her father—had preoccupied her for quite some time. She said, for instance, "I saw motor transports"; "I saw piggy-back when I went to school."

Her mother remarked, "Appendages fascinate her, like a smoke stack or a pendulum." Her father had previously stated: "Recent interest in sexual matters, hanging about when we take a bath, and obsessive interest in toilets."

Barbara was placed at the Devereux Schools, where she is making some progress in learning to relate herself to people.

Case 6

Virginia S., born September 13, 1931, has resided at a state training school for the feebleminded since 1936, with the exception of one month in 1938, when she was paroled to a school for the deaf "for educational opportunity." Dr. Esther L. Richards, who saw her several times, clearly recognized that she was neither deaf nor feebleminded and wrote in May, 1941:

> Virginia stands out from other children [at the training school] because she is absolutely different from any of the others. She is neat and tidy, does not play with other children, and does not seem to be deaf from gross tests, but does not talk. The child will amuse herself by the hour putting picture puzzles together, sticking to them until they are done. I have seen her with a box filled with the parts of two puzzles gradually work out the pieces for each. All findings seem to be in the nature of a congenital abnormality which looks as if it were more of a personality abnormality than an organic defect.

Virginia, the younger of two siblings, was the daughter of a psychiatrist, who said of himself (in December, 1941): "I have never liked children, probably a reaction on my part to the restraint from movement (travel), the minor interruptions and commotions."

Of Virginia's mother, her husband said: "She is not by any means the mother type. Her attitude [toward a child] is more like toward a doll or pet than anything else."

Virginia's brother, Philip, five years her senior, when referred to us because of severe stuttering at 15 years of age, burst out in tears when asked how things were at home and he sobbed: "The only time my father has ever had anything to do with me was when he scolded me for doing something wrong."

His mother did not contribute even that much. He felt that all his life he had lived in "a frosty atmosphere" with two inapproachable strangers.

In August, 1938, the psychologist at the training school observed that Virginia could respond to sounds, the calling of her name, and the command, "Look!"

> She pays no attention to what is said to her but quickly comprehends whatever is expected. Her performance reflects discrimination, care, and precision.

With the nonlanguage items of the Binet and Merrill-Palmer tests, she achieved an IQ of 94. "Without a doubt," commented the psychologist,

> her intelligence is superior to this. . . . She is quiet, solemn, composed. Not once have I seen her smile. She retires within herself, segregating herself from others. She seems to be in a world of her own, oblivious to all but the center of interest in the presiding situation. She is mostly self-sufficient and independent. When others encroach upon her integrity, she tolerates them with indifference. There was no manifestation of friendliness or interest in persons. On the other hand, she finds pleasure in dealing with things, about which she shows imagination and initiative. Typically, there is no display of affection. . . .
>
> *Psychologist's note, October, 1939.* Today Virginia was much more at home in the office. She remembered (after more than a year) where the toys were kept and helped herself. She could not be persuaded to participate in test procedures, would not wait for demonstrations when they were required. Quick, skilled moves. Trial and error plus insight. Very few futile moves. Immediate retesting reduced the time and error by more than half. There are times, more often than not, in which she is completely oblivious to all but her immediate focus of attention. . . .
>
> *January, 1940.* Mostly she is quiet, as she has always worked and played alone. She has not resisted authority or caused any special trouble. During group activities, she soon becomes restless, squirms, and wants to leave

to satisfy her curiosity about something elsewhere. She does make some vocal sounds, crying out if repressed or opposed too much by another child. She hums to herself, and in December I heard her hum the perfect tune of a Christmas hymn while she was pasting paper chains.

June, 1940. The school girls have said that Virginia says some words when at the cottage. They remember that she loves candy so much and says "Chocolate," "Marshmallow," also "Mama" and "Baby."

When seen on October 11, 1942, Virginia was a tall, slender, very neatly dressed 11-year-old girl. She responded when called by getting up and coming nearer, without ever looking up to the person who called her. She just stood listlessly, looking into space. Occasionally, in answer to questions, she muttered, "Mamma, baby." When a group was formed around the piano, one child playing and the others singing, Virginia sat among the children, seemingly not even noticing what went on, and gave the impression of being self-absorbed. She did not seem to notice when the children stopped singing. When the group dispersed she did not change her position and appeared not to be aware of the change of scene. She had an intelligent physiognomy, though her eyes had a blank expression.

Case 7

Herbert B. was referred on February 5, 1941, at 3 years, 2 months of age. He was thought to be seriously retarded in intellectual development. There were no physical abnormalities except for undescended testicles. His electroencephalogram was normal.

Herbert was born November 16, 1937, two weeks before term by elective cesarean section; his birth weight was 6¼ pounds. He vomited all food from birth through the third month. Then vomiting ceased almost abruptly and, except for occasional regurgitation, feeding proceeded satisfactorily. According to his mother, he was "always slow and quiet." For a time he was believed to be deaf because "he did not register any change of expression when spoken to or when in the presence of other people; also, he made no attempt to speak or to form words." He held up his head at 4 months and sat at 8 months, but did not try to walk until 2 years old, when suddenly "he began to walk without any preliminary crawling or assistance by chairs." He persistently refused to take fluid in any but an all-glass container. Once, while at a hospital, he went three days without fluid because it was offered in tin cups. He was "tremendously frightened by running water, gas burners, and many other things." He became upset by any change of an accustomed pattern: "if he notices change, he is very fussy and cries." But he himself liked to pull blinds up and down, to tear cardboard boxes into small pieces and play with them for hours, and to close and open the wings of doors.

Herbert's parents separated shortly after his birth. The father, a psychiatrist, is described as "a man of unusual intelligence, sensitive, restless, introspective, taking himself very seriously, not interested in people, mostly living within himself, at times alcoholic." The mother, a physician, speaks of herself as "energetic and outgoing, fond of people and children but having little insight into their problems, finding it a great deal easier to accept people rather than try to understand them." Herbert is the youngest of three children. The second is a normal, healthy boy. The oldest, Dorothy, born in June, 1934, after thirty-six hours of hard labor, seemed alert and responsive as an infant and said many words at 18 months, but toward the end of the second year she "did not show much progression in her play relationships or in contacts with other people." She wanted to be left alone, danced about in circles, made queer noises with her mouth, and *ignored persons completely* except for her mother, to whom she clung "in panic and general agitation." (Her father hated her ostensibly.) "Her speech was very meager and expression of ideas completely lacking. She had *difficulties with her pronouns* and would repeat 'you' and 'I' instead of using them for the proper persons." She was first declared to be feebleminded, then schizophrenic, but after the parents separated (the children remaining with their mother), she "blossomed out." She now attends school, where she makes good progress; she talks well, has an IQ of 108, and—though sensitive and moderately apprehensive—is interested in people and gets along reasonably well with them.

Herbert, when examined on his first visit, showed a remarkably intelligent physiognomy and good motor coordination. Within certain limits, he displayed astounding purposefulness in the pursuit of self-selected goals. Among a group of blocks, he instantly recognized those that were glued to a board and those that were detachable. He could build a tower of blocks as skillfully and as high as any child of his age or even older. He could not be diverted from his self-chosen occupations. He was annoyed by any interference, shoving intruders away (without ever looking at them), or screaming when the shoving had no effect.

He was again seen at 4 years, 7 months, and again at 5 years, 2 months of age. He still did not speak. Both times he entered the office without paying the slightest attention to the people present. He went after the Seguin form board and instantly busied himself putting the figures into their proper spaces and taking them out again adroitly and quickly. When interfered with he whined impatiently. When one figure was stealthily removed, he immediately noticed its absence, became disturbed, but promptly forgot all about it when it was put back. At times, after he had finally quieted down following the upset caused by the removal of the form board, he jumped up and

down on the couch with an ecstatic expression on his face. He did not respond to being called or to any other words addressed to him. He was completely absorbed in whatever he did. He never smiled. He sometimes uttered
inarticulate sounds in a monotonous singsong manner. At one time he gently
stroked his mother's leg and touched it with his lips. He very frequently
brought blocks and other objects to his lips. There was an almost photographic likeness of his behavior during the two visits, with the main exception that at 4 years he showed apprehension and shrank back when a match
was lighted, while at 5 years he reacted by jumping up and down ecstati-
cally.

Case 8

Alfred L. was brought by his mother in November, 1935, at 3½ years of
age with this complaint:

> He has gradually shown a marked tendency toward developing one special
> interest which will completely dominate his day's activities. He talks of little
> else while the interest exists, he frets when he is not able to indulge in it
> (by seeing it, coming in contact with it, drawing pictures of it), and it is
> difficult to get his attention because of his preoccupation. . . . There has
> also been the problem of an overattachment to the world of objects and
> failure to develop the usual amount of social awareness.

Alfred was born in May, 1932, three weeks before term. For the first two
months, "the feeding formula caused considerable concern but then he
gained rapidly and became an unusually large and vigorous baby." He sat
up at 5 months and walked at 14.

> Language developed slowly; he seemed to have no interest in it. He sel-
> dom tells experience. He still confuses pronouns. He never asks questions
> in the form of questions (with the appropriate inflection). Since he talked,
> there has been a tendency to repeat over and over one word or statement.
> He almost never says a sentence without repeating it. Yesterday, when
> looking at a picture, he said many times, "Some cows standing in the
> water." We counted fifty repetitions, then he stopped after several more
> and then began over and over.

He had a good deal of "worrying":

> He frets when the bread is put in the oven to be made into toast, and is
> afraid it will get burned and be hurt. He is upset when the sun sets. He
> is upset because the moon does not always appear in the sky at night. He
> prefers to play alone; he will get down from a piece of apparatus as soon

as another child approaches. He likes to work out some project with large boxes (make a trolley, for instance) and does not want anyone to get on it or interfere.

When infantile thumb sucking was prevented by mechanical devices, he gave it up and instead put various objects into his mouth. On several occasions pebbles were found in his stools. Shortly before his second birthday, he swallowed cotton from an Easter rabbit, aspirating some of the cotton, so that tracheotomy became necessary. A few months later, he swallowed some kerosene "with no ill effects."

Alfred was an only child. His father, 30 years old at the time of his birth, "does not get along well with people, is suspicious, easily hurt, easily roused to anger, has to be dragged out to visit friends, spends his spare time reading, gardening, and fishing." He is a chemist and a law school graduate. The mother, of the same age, is a "clinical psychologist," very obsessive and excitable. The paternal grandparents died early; the father was adopted by a minister. The maternal grandfather, a psychologist, was severely obsessive, had numerous tics, was given to "repeated hand washing, protracted thinking along one line, fear of being alone, cardiac fears." The grandmother, "an excitable, explosive person, has done public speaking, published several books, is an incessant solitaire player, greatly worried over money matters." A maternal uncle frequently ran away from home and school, joined the marines, and later "made a splendid adjustment in commercial life."

The mother left her husband two months after Alfred's birth. The child has lived with his mother and maternal grandparents. "In the home is a nursery school and kindergarten (run by the mother), which creates some confusion for the child." Alfred did not see his father until he was 3 years, 4 months old, when the mother decided that "he should know his father" and "took steps to have the father come to the home to see the child."

Alfred, upon entering the office, paid no attention to the examiner. He immediately spotted a train in the toy cabinet, took it out, and connected and disconnected the cars in a slow, monotonous manner. He kept saying many times, "More train—more train—more train." He repeatedly "counted" the car windows: "One, two windows—one, two windows—one, two windows—four window, eight window, eight windows." He could not in any way be distracted from the trains. A Binet test was attempted in a room in which there were no trains. It was possible with much difficulty to pierce from time to time through his preoccupations. He finally complied in most instances in a manner that clearly indicated that he wanted to get through with the particular intrusion; this was repeated with each individual item of the task. In the end he achieved an *IQ of 140*.

The mother did not bring him back after this first visit because of "his continued distress when confronted with a member of the medical profession." In August, 1938, she sent upon request a written report of his development. From this report, the following passages are quoted:

> He is called a lone wolf. He prefers to play alone and avoids groups of children at play. He does not pay much attention to adults except when demanding stories. He avoids competition. He reads simple stories to himself. He is very fearful of being hurt, talks a great deal about the use of the electric chair. He is thrown into a panic when anyone accidentally covers his face.

Alfred was again referred in June, 1941. His parents had decided to live together. Prior to that the boy had been in eleven different schools. He had been kept in bed often because of colds, bronchitis, chickenpox, streptococcus infection, impetigo, and a vaguely described condition which the mother—the assurances of various pediatricians to the contrary notwithstanding—insisted was "rheumatic fever." While in the hospital, he is said to have behaved "like a manic patient." The mother liked to call herself a psychiatrist and to make "psychiatric" diagnoses of the child. From the mother's report, which combined obsessive enumeration of detailed instances with "explanations" trying to prove Alfred's "normalcy," the following information was gathered.

He had begun to play with children younger than himself, "using them as puppets—that's all." He had been stuffed with music, dramatics, and recitals, and had an excellent rote memory. He still was "terribly engrossed" in his play, didn't want people around, just couldn't relax:

> He had many fears, almost always connected with mechanical noise (meat grinders, vacuum cleaners, streetcars, trains, etc.). Usually he winds up with an obsessed interest in the things he was afraid of. Now he is afraid of the shrillness of the dog's barking.

Alfred was extremely tense during the entire interview, and very serious-minded, to such an extent that had it not been for his juvenile voice, he might have given the impression of a worried and preoccupied little old man. At the same time, he was very restless and showed considerable pressure of talk, which had nothing personal in it but consisted of obsessive questions about windows, shades, dark rooms, especially the X-ray room. He never smiled. No change of topic could get him away from the topic of light and darkness. But in between he answered the examiner's questions, which often had to be repeated several times, and to which he sometimes responded as the result of a bargain—"You answer my question, and I'll answer yours." He was painstakingly specific in his definitions. A balloon "is made out of lined rubber and has air in it and some have gas and sometimes they go up in the air and sometimes they can hold up and when they got a hole in it they'll bust up; if people squeeze they'll bust. Isn't it right?" A tiger "is a thing, animal, striped, like a cat, can scratch, eats people up, wild, lives in the jungle sometimes and in the forests, mostly in the jungle. Isn't it right?" This question "Isn't it right?" was definitely meant to be answered; there was a serious desire to be assured that the definition was sufficiently complete.

He was often confused about the meaning of words. When shown a picture and asked, "What is this picture about?" he replied, "People are moving *about*."

He once stopped and asked, very much perplexed, why there was "The Johns Hopkins Hospital" printed on the history sheets: "Why do they have to say it?" This, to him, was a real problem of major importance, calling for a great deal of thought and discussion. Since the histories were taken at the hospital, why should it be necessary to have the name on every sheet, though the person writing on it knew where he was writing? The examiner, whom he remembered very well from his visit six years previously, was to him nothing more nor less than a person who was expected to answer his obsessive questions about darkness and light.

Case 9

Charles N. was brought by his mother on February 2, 1943, at 4½ years of age, with the chief complaint, "The thing that upsets me most is that I can't reach my baby." She introduced her report by saying: "I am trying hard not to govern my remarks by professional knowledge which has intruded in my own way of thinking by now."

As a baby, the boy was inactive, "slow and phlegmatic." He would lie in the crib, just staring. He would act almost as if hypnotized. He seemed to concentrate on doing one thing at a time. Hypothyroidism was suspected, and he was given thyroid extract, without any change of the general condition.

> His enjoyment and appreciation of music encouraged me to play records. When he was 1½ years old, he could discriminate between eighteen symphonies. He recognized the composer as soon as the first movement started. He would say "Beethoven." At about the same age, he began to spin toys and lids of bottles and jars by the hour. He had a lot of manual dexterity in ability to spin cylinders. He would watch it and get severely excited and jump up and down in ecstasy. Now he is interested in reflecting light from mirrors and catching reflections. When he is interested in a thing, you cannot change it. He would pay no attention to me and show no recognition of me if I enter the room. . . .

The most impressive thing is his detachment and his inaccessibility. He walks as if he is in a shadow, lives in a world of his own where he cannot be reached. No sense of relationship to persons. He went through a period of quoting another person; never offers anything himself. His entire conversation is a replica of whatever has been said to him. He used to speak of himself in the second person, now he uses the third person at times; he would say, "He wants"—never "I want."

He is destructive; the furniture in his room looks like it has hunks out of it. He will break a purple crayon into two parts and say, "*You* had a beautiful purple crayon and now it's two pieces. Look what *you* did."

He developed an obsession about feces, would hide it anywhere (for instance, in drawers), would tease me if I walked into the room: "You soiled your pants, now you can't have your crayons!"

As a result, he is still not toilet trained. He never soils himself in the nursery school, always does it when he comes home. The same is true of wetting. He is proud of wetting, jumps up and down with ecstasy, says, "Look at the big puddle *he* made."

When he is with other people, he doesn't look up at them. Last July, we had a group of people. When Charles came in, it was just like a foal who'd been let out of an enclosure. He did not pay attention to them but their presence was felt. He will mimic a voice and he sings and some people would not notice any abnormality in the child. At school, he never envelops himself in a group, he is detached from the rest of the children, except when he is in the assembly; if there is music, he will go to the front row and sing.

He has a wonderful memory for words. Vocabulary is good, except for pronouns. He never initiates conversation, and conversation is limited, extensive only as far as objects go.

Charles was born normally, a planned and wanted child. He sat up at 6 months and walked at less than 15 months—"just stood up and walked one day—no preliminary creeping." He has had none of the usual children's diseases.

Charles is the oldest of three children. The father, a high-school graduate and a clothing merchant, is described as a "self-made, gentle, calm, and placid person." The mother has "a successful business record, theatrical booking office in New York, of remarkable equanimity." The other two children were 28 and 14 months old at the time of Charles' visit to the Clinic. The maternal grandmother, "very dynamic, forceful, hyperactive, almost hypomanic," has done some writing and composing. A maternal aunt, "psychoneurotic, very brilliant, given to hysterics," has written poems and songs. Another aunt was referred to as "the amazon of the family." A maternal uncle, a psychiatrist, has considerable musical talent. The paternal relatives are described as "ordinary simple people."

Charles was a well-developed, intelligent-looking boy, who was in good physical health. He wore glasses. When he entered the office, he paid not the slightest attention to the people present (three physicians, his mother, and his uncle). Without looking at anyone, he said, "Give me a pencil!" and took a piece of paper from the desk and wrote something resembling a figure 2 (a large desk calendar prominently displayed a figure 2; the day was February 2). He had brought with him a copy of *Readers Digest* and was fascinated by a picture of a baby. He said, "Look at the funny baby," innumerable times, occasionally adding, "Is he not funny? Is he not sweet?"

When the book was taken away from him, he struggled with the hand that held it, without looking at the *person* who had taken the book. When he was pricked with a pin, he said, "What's this?"and answered his own question: "It is a needle."

He looked timidly at the pin, shrank from further pricks, but at no time did he seem to connect the pricking with the *person* who held the pin. When the *Readers Digest* was taken from him and thrown on the floor and a foot placed over it, he tried to remove the foot as if it were another detached and interfering object, again with no concern for the *person* to whom the foot belonged. He once turned to his mother and excitedly said, "Give it to you!"

When confronted with the Seguin form board, he was mainly interested in the names of the forms, before putting them into their appropriate holes. He often spun the forms around, jumping up and down excitedly while they were in motion. The whole performance was very repetitious. He never used language as a means of communicating with people. He remembered names, such as "octagon," "diamond," "oblong block," but nevertheless kept asking, "What is this?"

He did not respond to being called and did not look at his mother when she spoke to him. When the blocks were removed, he screamed, stamped his feet, and cried, "I'll give it to you!" (meaning "You give it to me"). He was very skillful in his movements.

Charles was placed at the Devereux Schools.

Case 10

John F. was first seen on February 13, 1940, at 2 years, 4 months of age.

The father said: "The main thing that worries me is the difficulty in feeding. That is the essential thing, and secondly his slowness in development. During the first days of life he did not take the breast satisfactorily. After fifteen days he was changed from breast to bottle but did not take the bottle satisfactorily. There is a long story of trying to get food down. We have tried everything under the sun. He has been immature all along. At 20 months he first started to walk. He sucks his thumb and grinds his teeth quite frequently and rolls from side to side before sleeping. If we don't do what he wants, he will scream and yell."

John was born September 19, 1937; his birth weight was 7½ pounds. There were frequent hospitalizations because of the feeding problem. No physical disorder was ever found, except that the anterior fontanelle did not close until he was 2½ years of age. He suffered from repeated colds and otitis media, which necessitated bilateral myringotomy.

John was an only child until February, 1943. The father, a psychiatrist, is "a very calm, placid, emotionally stable person, who is the soothing element in the family." The mother, a high school graduate, worked as secretary in a pathology laboratory before marriage—"a hypomanic type of person; sees everything as a pathological specimen rather than well; throughout the pregnancy she was very apprehensive, afraid she would not live through the labor." The paternal grandmother is "obsessive about religion and washes her hands every few minutes." The maternal grandfather was an accountant.

John was brought to the office by both parents. He wandered about the room constantly and aimlessly. Except for spontaneous scribbling, he never brought two objects into relation to each other. He did not respond to the simplest commands, except that his parents with much difficulty elicited bye-bye, pat-a-cake, and peek-a-boo gestures, performed clumsily. His typical attitude toward objects was to throw them on the floor.

Three months later, his vocabulary showed remarkable improvement, though his articulation was defective. Mild obsessive trends were reported, such as pushing aside the first spoonful of every dish. His excursions about the office were slightly more purposeful.

At the end of his fourth year, he was able to form a very limited kind of affective contact, and even that only with a very limited number of people. Once such a relationship had been established, it had to continue in exactly the same channels. He was capable of forming elaborate and grammatically correct sentences, but he used the pronoun of the second person when referring to himself. He used language not as a means of communication but mainly as a repetition of things he had heard, without alteration of the personal pronoun. There was very marked obsessiveness. Daily routine must be adhered to rigidly; any slightest change of the pattern called forth outbursts of panic. There was endless repetition of sentences. He had an excellent rote memory and could recite many prayers, nursery rhymes, and songs "in different languages"; the mother did a great deal of stuffing in this respect and was very proud of these "achievements": "He can tell victrola records by their color and if one side of the record is identified, he remembers what is on the other side."

At 4½ years, he began gradually to use pronouns adequately. Even though his direct interest was in objects only, he took great pains in attracting the attention of the examiner (Dr. Hilde Bruch) and in gaining her praise.

However, he never addressed her directly and spontaneously. He wanted to make sure of the sameness of the environment literally by keeping doors and windows closed. When his mother opened the door "to pierce through his obsession," he became violent in closing it again and finally, when again interfered with, burst helplessly into tears, utterly frustrated.

He was extremely upset upon seeing anything broken or incomplete. He noticed two dolls to which he had paid no attention before. He saw that one of them had no hat and became very much agitated, wandering about the room to look for the hat. When the hat was retrieved from another room, he instantly lost all interest in the dolls.

At 5½ years, he had good mastery of the use of pronouns. He had begun to feed himself satisfactorily. He saw a group photograph in the office and asked his father, "When are they coming out of the picture and coming in here?"

He was very serious about this. His father said something about the pictures they have at home on the wall. This disturbed John somewhat. He corrected his father: "We have them *near* the wall" ("on" apparently meaning to him "above" or "on top").

When he saw a penny, he said, "Penny. That's where you play tenpins." He had been given pennies when he knocked over tenpins while playing with his father at home.

He saw a dictionary and said to his father, "That's where you left the money?"

Once his father had left some money in a dictionary and asked John to tell his mother about it.

His father whistled a tune and John instantly and correctly identified it as "Mendelssohn's violin concerto." Though he could speak of things as big or pretty, he was utterly incapable of making comparisons ("Which is the bigger line? Prettier face?" etc.).

In December, 1942, and January, 1943, he had two series of predominantly right-sided *convulsions*, with conjugate deviation of the eyes to the right and transient paresis of the right arm. Neurologic examination showed no abnormalities. His eyegrounds were normal. An electroencephalogram indicated "focal disturbance in the left occipital region," but "a good part of the record could not be read because of the continuous marked artefacts due to the child's lack of cooperation."

Case 11

Elaine C. was brought by her parents on April 12, 1939, at the age of 7 years, 2 months, because of "unusual development": "She doesn't adjust. She stops at all abstractions. She doesn't understand other children's games, doesn't retain interest in stories read to her, wanders off and walks by herself, is especially fond of animals of all kinds, occasionally mimics them by walking on all fours and making strange noises."

Elaine was born on February 3, 1932, at term. She appeared healthy, took feedings well, stood up at 7 months and walked at less than a year. She could say four words at the end of her first year but made no progress in linguistic development for the following four years. Deafness was suspected but ruled out. Because of a febrile illness at 13 months, her increasing difficulties were interpreted as possible postencephalitic behavior disorder. Others blamed the mother, who was accused of inadequate handling of the child. Feeblemindedness was another diagnosis. For eighteen months, she was given anterior pituitary and thyroid preparations. "Some doctors," struck by Elaine's intelligent physiognomy, "thought she was a normal child and said that she would outgrow this."

At 2 years, she was sent to a nursery school, where "she independently went her way, not doing what the others did. She, for instance, drank the water and ate the plant when they were being taught to handle flowers." She developed an early interest in pictures of animals. Though generally restless, she could for hours concentrate on looking at such pictures, "especially engravings."

When she began to speak at about 5 years, she started out with complete though simple sentences that were "mechanical phrases" not related to the situation of the moment or related to it in a peculiar metaphorical way. She had an excellent vocabulary, knew especially the names and "classifications" of animals. She did not use pronouns correctly, but used plurals and tenses well. She "could not use negatives but recognized their meaning when others used them."

There were many peculiarities in her relation to situations:

> She can count by rote. She can set the table for numbers of people if the names are given her or enumerated in any way, but she cannot set the table "for three." If sent for a specific object in a certain place, she cannot bring it if it is somewhere else but still visible.

She was "frightened" by noises and anything moving toward her. She was so afraid of the vacuum cleaner that she would not even go near the closet where it was kept, and when it was used, ran out into the garage, covering her ears with her hands.

Elaine was the older of two children. Her father, aged 36, studied law and the liberal arts in three universities (including the Sorbonne), was an advertising copy writer, "one of those chronically thin persons, nervous energy readily expended." He was at one time editor of a magazine. The mother, aged 32, a "self-controlled, placid, logical person," had done editorial work for a magazine before marriage. The maternal grandfather was a newspaper editor, the grandmother was "emotionally unstable."

Elaine had been examined by a Boston psychologist at nearly 7 years of age. The report stated among other things:

> Her attitude toward the examiner remained vague and detached. Even when annoyed by restraint, she might vigorously push aside a table or restraining hand with a scream, but she made no personal appeal for help or sympathy. At favorable moments she was competent in handling her crayons or assembling pieces to form pictures of animals. She could name a wide variety of pictures, including elephants, alligators, and dinosaurs. She used language in simple sentence structure, but rarely answered a direct question. As she plays, she repeats over and over phrases which are irrelevant to the immediate situation.

Physically the child was in good health. Her electroencephalogram was normal.

When examined in April, 1939, she shook hands with the physician upon request, without looking at him, then ran to the window and looked out. She automatically heeded the invitation to sit down. Her reaction to questions—after several repetitions—was an echolalia type reproduction of the whole question or, if it was too lengthy, of the end portion. She had no real contact with the persons in the office. Her expression was bland, though not unintelligent, and there were no communicative gestures. At one time, without changing her physiognomy, she said suddenly: "Fishes don't cry." After a time, she got up and left the room without asking or showing fear.

She was placed at the Child Study Home of Maryland, where she remained for three weeks and was studied by Drs. Eugenia S. Cameron and George Frankl. While there, she soon learned the names of all the children, knew the color of their eyes, the bed in which each slept, and many other details about them, but never entered into any relationship with them. When taken to the playgrounds, she was extremely upset and ran back to her room. She was very restless but when allowed to look at pictures, play alone with blocks, draw, or string beads, she could entertain herself contentedly for hours. Any noise, any interruption disturbed her. Once, when on the toilet seat, she heard a knocking in the pipes; for several days thereafter, even when put on a chamber pot in her own room, she did not move her bowels, anxiously listening for the noise. She frequently ejaculated stereotyped phrases, such as, "Dinosaurs don't cry"; "Crayfish, sharks, fish, and rocks"; "Crayfish and forks live in children's tummies"; "Butterflies live in children's stomachs, and in their panties, too"; "Fish have sharp teeth and bite little children"; "There is war in the sky"; "Rocks and crags, I will kill" (grabbing her blanket and kicking it about the bed); "Gargoyles bite children and drink oil"; "I will crush old angle worm, he bites children" (gritting her teeth

and spinning around in a circle, very excited); "Gargoyles have milk bags";
"Needle head. Pink wee-wee. Has a yellow leg. Cutting the dead deer. Poison deer. Poor Elaine. No tadpoles in the house. Men broke deer's leg"
(while cutting the picture of a deer from a book); "Tigers and cats"; "Seals
and salamanders"; "Bears and foxes."

A few excerpts from the observations follow:

> Her language always has the same quality. Her speech is never accompanied by facial expression or gestures. She does not look into one's face.
> Her voice is peculiarly unmodulated, somewhat hoarse; she utters her
> words in an abrupt manner.
>
> Her utterances are impersonal. She never uses the personal pronouns
> of the first and second persons correctly. She does not seem able to conceive the real meaning of these words.
>
> Her grammar is inflexible. She uses sentences just as she has heard
> them, without adapting them grammatically to the situation of the moment. When she says, "Want me to draw a spider," she means, "I want
> you to draw a spider."
>
> She affirms by repeating a question literally, and she negates by not
> complying.
>
> Her speech is rarely communicative. She has no relation to children,
> has never talked to them, to be friendly with them, or to play with them.
> She moves among them like a strange being, as one moves between the
> pieces of furniture of a room.
>
> She insists on the repetition of the same routine always. Interruption
> of the routine is one of the most frequent occasions for her outbursts. Her
> own activities are simple and repetitious. She is able to spend hours in some
> form of daydreaming and seems to be very happy with it. She is inclined
> to rhythmical movements which always are masturbatory. She masturbates more in periods of excitement than during calm happiness. . . . Her
> movements are quick and skillful.

Elaine was placed in a private school in Pennsylvania. In a recent letter,
the father reported "rather amazing changes":

> She is a tall, husky girl with clear eyes that have long since lost any trace
> of that animal wildness they periodically showed in the time you knew her.
> She speaks well on almost any subject, though with something of an odd
> intonation. Her conversation is still rambling talk, frequently with an
> amusing point, and it is only occasional, deliberate, and announced. She
> reads very well, but she reads fast, jumbling words, not pronouncing
> clearly, and not making proper emphases. Her range of information is really
> quite wide, and her memory almost infallible. It is obvious that Elaine is
> not "normal." Failure in anything leads to a feeling of defeat, of despair,
> and to a momentary fit of depression.

DISCUSSION

The eleven children (eight boys and three girls) whose histories have been briefly presented offer, as is to be expected, individual differences in the degree of their disturbance, the manifestation of specific features, the family constellation, and the step-by-step development in the course of years. But even a quick review of the material makes the emergence of a number of essential common characteristics appear inevitable. These characteristics form a unique "syndrome," not heretofore reported, which seems to be rare enough, yet is probably more frequent than is indicated by the paucity of observed cases. It is quite possible that some such children have been viewed as feebleminded or schizophrenic. In fact, several children of our group were introduced to us as idiots or imbeciles, one still resides in a state school for the feebleminded, and two had been previously considered as schizophrenic.

The outstanding, "pathognomonic," fundamental disorder is the children's *inability to relate themselves* in the ordinary way to people and situations from the beginning of life. Their parents referred to them as having always been "self-sufficient"; "like in a shell"; "happiest when left alone"; "acting as if people weren't there"; "perfectly oblivious to everything about him"; "giving the impression of silent wisdom"; "failing to develop the usual amount of social awareness"; "acting almost as if hypnotized." This is not, as in schizophrenic children or adults, a departure from an initially present relationship; it is not a "withdrawal" from formerly existing participation. There is from the start an *extreme autistic aloneness* that, whenever possible, disregards, ignores, shuts out anything that comes to the child from the outside. Direct physical contact or such motion or noise as threatens to disrupt the aloneness is either treated "as if it weren't there" or, if this is no longer sufficient, resented painfully as distressing interference.

According to Gesell, the average child at 4 months of age makes an anticipatory motor adjustment by facial tension and shrugging attitude of the shoulders when lifted from a table or placed on a table. Gesell commented:

> It is possible that a less definite evidence of such adjustment may be found as low down as the neonatal period. Although a habit must be conditioned by experience, the opportunity for experience is almost universal and the response is sufficiently objective to merit further observation and record.

This universal experience is supplied by the frequency with which an infant is picked up by his mother and other persons. It is therefore highly significant that almost all mothers of our patients recalled their astonishment at the children's *failure to assume at any time an anticipatory posture* preparatory to being picked up. One father recalled that his daughter (Barbara) did not for years change her physiognomy or position in the least when the parents, upon coming home after a few hours' absence, approached her crib talking to her and making ready to pick her up.

The average infant learns during the first few months to adjust his body to the posture of the person who holds him. Our children were not able to do so for two or three years. We had an opportunity to observe 38-month-old Herbert in such a situation. His mother informed him in appropriate terms that she was going to lift him up, extending her arms in his direction. There was no response. She proceeded to take him up, and he allowed her to do so, remaining completely passive as if he were a sack of flour. It was the mother who had to do all the adjusting. Herbert was at that time capable of sitting, standing, and walking.

Eight of the eleven children acquired the *ability to speak* either at the usual age or after some delay. Three (Richard, Herbert, Virginia) have so far remained "mute." In none of the eight "speaking" children has language over a period of years served to convey meaning to others. They were, with the exception of John F., capable of clear articulation and phonation. Naming of objects presented no difficulty; even long and unusual words were learned and retained with remarkable facility. Almost all the parents reported, usually with much pride, that the children had learned at an early age to repeat an inordinate number of nursery rhymes, prayers, lists of animals, the roster of presidents, the alphabet forward and backward, even foreign-language (French) lullabies. Aside from the recital of sentences contained in the ready-made poems or other remembered pieces, it took a long time before they began to put words together. Other than that, "language" consisted mainly of "naming," of nouns identifying objects, adjectives indicating colors, and numbers indicating nothing specific.

Their *excellent rote memory,* coupled with the inability to use language in any other way, often led the parents to stuff them with more and more verses, zoologic and botanic names, titles and composers of victrola record pieces, and the like. Thus, from the start, language—which the children did not use for the purpose of communication—was deflected in a considerable measure to a self-sufficient, semantically and conversationally valueless or grossly distorted memory exercise. To a child 2 or 3 years old, all these words, numbers, and poems ("questions and answers of the Presbyterian Catechism"; "Mendelssohn's violin concerto"; the "Twenty-third Psalm"; a French lullaby; an encyclopedia index page) could hardly have more meaning than sets of nonsense syllables to adults. It is difficult to know for certain whether the stuffing as such has contributed essentially to the course of the psychopathologic condition. But it is also difficult to imagine that it did not cut deeply into the development of language as a tool for receiving and imparting meaningful messages.

As far as the communicative functions of speech are concerned, there is no fundamental difference between the eight speaking and the three mute children. Richard was once overheard by his boarding mother to say distinctly, "Good night." Justified skepticism about this observation was later dispelled when this "mute" child was seen in the office shaping his mouth in silent repetition of words when asked to say certain things. "Mute" Virginia—so her cottage mates insisted—was heard repeatedly to say, "Chocolate"; "Marshmallow"; "Mama"; "Baby."

When sentences are finally formed, they are for a long time mostly parrot-like repetitions of heard word combinations. They are sometimes echoed immediately, but they are just as often "stored" by the child and uttered at a later date. One may, if one wishes, speak of *delayed echolalia*. Affirmation is indicated by literal repetition of a question. "Yes" is a concept that it takes the children many years to acquire. They are incapable of using it as a general symbol of assent. Donald learned to say "Yes" when his father told him that he would put him on his shoulders if he said "Yes." This word then came to "mean" only the desire to be put on his father's shoulders. It took many months before he could detach the word "yes" from this specific situation, and it took much longer before he was able to use it as a general term of affirmation.

The same type of *literalness* exists also with regard to prepositions. Alfred, when asked, "What is this picture about?" replied: "People are moving *about.*"

John F. corrected his father's statement about pictures on the wall; the pictures were "*near* the wall." Donald T., requested to put something *down*, promptly put it on the floor. Apparently the meaning of a word becomes inflexible and cannot be used with any but the originally acquired connotation.

There is no difficulty with plurals and tenses. But the absence of spontaneous sentence formation and the echolalia type reproduction has, in every one of the eight speaking children, given rise to a peculiar grammatical phenomenon. *Personal pronouns are repeated just as heard,* with no change to suit the altered situation. The child, once told by his mother, "Now I will give you your milk," expresses the desire for milk in exactly the same words. Consequently, he comes to speak of himself always as "you," and of the person addressed as "I." Not only the words, but even the intonation is retained. If the mother's original remark has been made in form of a question, it is reproduced with the grammatical form and the inflection of a question. The repetition "Are you ready for your dessert?" means that the child is ready for his dessert. There is a set, not-to-be-changed phrase for every specific occasion. The pronominal fixation remains until about the sixth year of life, when the child gradually learns to speak of himself in the first person, and of the individual addressed in the second person. In the transitional period, he sometimes still reverts to the earlier form or at times refers to himself in the third person.

The fact that the children echo things heard does not signify that they "attend" when spoken to. It often takes numerous reiterations of a question or command before there is even so much as an echoed response. Not less than seven of the children were therefore considered as deaf or hard of hearing. There is an all-powerful need for being left undisturbed. Everything that is brought to the child from the outside, everything that changes his external or even internal environment, represents a dreaded intrusion.

Food is the earliest intrusion that is brought to the child from the outside. David Levy observed that affect-hungry children, when placed in foster homes where they are well treated, at first demand excessive quantities of food. Hilde Bruch, in her studies of obese children, found that overeating often resulted when affectionate offerings from the parents were lacking or considered unsatisfactory. Our patients, reversely, anxious to keep the outside world away, indicated this by the refusal of food. Donald, Paul ("vomited a great deal during the first year"), Barbara ("had to be tube-fed until 1 year of age"), Herbert, Alfred, and John presented severe feeding difficulty from the beginning of life. Most of them, after an unsuccessful struggle, constantly interfered with, finally gave up the struggle and all of a sudden began eating satisfactorily.

Another intrusion comes from *loud noises and moving objects,* which are therefore reacted to with horror. Tricycles, swings, elevators, vacuum cleaners, running water, gas burners, mechanical toys, egg beaters, even the wind could on occasions bring about a major panic. One of the children was even afraid to go near the closet in which the vacuum cleaner was kept. Injections and examinations with stethoscope or otoscope created a grave emotional crisis. Yet it is not the noise or motion itself that is dreaded. The disturbance comes from the noise or motion that intrudes itself, or threatens to intrude itself, upon the child's aloneness. The child himself can happily make as great a noise as any that he dreads and move objects about to his heart's desire.

But the child's noises and motions and all of his performances are as *monotonously repetitious* as are his verbal utterances. There is a marked limitation in the variety of his spontaneous activities. The child's behavior is governed by an *anxiously obsessive desire for the maintenance of sameness* that nobody but the child himself may disrupt on rare occasions. Changes of routine, of furniture arrangement, of a pattern, of the order in which everyday acts are carried out, can drive him to despair. When John's parents got ready to move to a new home, the child was frantic when he saw the moving men roll up the rug in his room. He was acutely upset until the moment when, in the new home, he saw his furniture arranged in the same manner as before. He looked pleased, all anxiety was suddenly gone, and he went around affectionately patting each piece. Once blocks, beads, sticks have been put together in a certain way, they are always regrouped in exactly the same way, even though there was no definite design. The children's memory was phenomenal in this respect. After the lapse of several days, a multitude of blocks could be rearranged in precisely the same unorganized pattern, with the same color of each block turned up, with each picture or letter on the upper surface of each block facing in the same direction as before. The absence of a block or the presence of a supernumerary block was noticed immediately, and there was an imperative demand for the restoration of the missing piece. If someone removed a block, the child struggled to get it back, going into a panic tantrum until he regained it, and then promptly and with sudden calm after the storm returned to the design and replaced the block.

This insistence on sameness led several of the children to become greatly disturbed upon the sight of anything broken or incomplete. A great part of the day was spent in demanding not only the sameness of the wording of a request but also the sameness of the sequence of events. Donald would not leave his bed after his nap until after he had said. "Boo, say 'Don, do you want to get down?' " and the mother had complied. But this was not all. The act was still not considered completed. Donald would continue, "Now say 'All right.' " Again the mother had to comply, or there was screaming until the performance was completed. All of this ritual was an indispensable part of the act of getting up after a nap. Every other activity had to be completed from beginning to end in the manner in which it had been started originally. It was impossible to return from a walk without having covered the same ground as had been covered before. The sight of a broken crossbar on a garage door on his regular daily tour so upset Charles that he kept talking and asking about it for weeks on end, even while spending a few days in a distant city. One of the children noticed a crack in the office ceiling and kept asking anxiously and repeatedly who had cracked the ceiling, not calmed by any answer given her. Another child, seeing one doll with a hat and another without a hat, could not be placated until the other hat was found and put on the doll's head. He then immediately lost interest in the two dolls; sameness and completeness had been restored, and all was well again.

The dread of change and incompleteness seems to be a major factor in the explanation of the monotonous repetitiousness and the resulting *limitation in the variety of spontaneous activity*. A situation, a performance, a sentence is not regarded as complete if it is not made up of exactly the same elements that were present at the time the child was first confronted with it. If the slightest ingredient is altered or removed, the total situation is no longer the same and therefore is not accepted as such, or it is resented with impatience or even with a reaction of profound frustration. The inability to experience wholes without full attention to the constituent parts is somewhat reminiscent of the plight of children with specific reading disability who do not respond to the modern system of configurational reading instruction but must be taught to build up words from their alphabetic elements. This is perhaps one of the reasons why those children of our group who were old enough to be instructed in reading immediately became excessively preoccupied with the "spelling" of words, or why Donald, for example, was so disturbed over the fact that "light" and "bite," having the same phonetic quality, should be spelled differently.

Objects that do not change their appearance and position, that retain their sameness and never threaten to interfere with the child's aloneness, are readily accepted by the autistic child. He has a good *relation to objects*; he is interested in them, can play with them happily for hours. He can be very fond of them, or get angry at them if, for instance, he cannot fit them into a certain space. When with them, he has a gratifying sense of undisputed power and control. Donald and Charles began in the second year of life to exercise this power by spinning everything that could be possibly spun and jumping up and down in ecstasy when they watched the objects whirl about. Frederick "jumped up and down in great glee" when he bowled and saw the pins go down. The children sensed and exercised the same power over their own bodies by rolling and other rhythmic movements. These actions and the accompanying ecstatic fervor strongly indicate the presence of *masturbatory orgastic gratification*.

The children's *relation to people* is altogether different. Every one of the children, upon entering the office, immediately went after blocks, toys, or other objects, without paying the least attention to the persons present. It would be wrong to say that they were not aware of the presence of persons. But the people, so long as they left the child alone, figured in about the same manner as did the desk, the bookshelf, or the filing cabinet. When the child was addressed, he was not bothered. He had the choice between not responding at all or, if a question was repeated too insistently, "getting it over with" and continuing with whatever he had been doing. Comings and goings, even of the mother, did not seem to register. Conversation going on in the room elicited no interest. If the adults did not try to enter the child's domain, he would at times, while moving between them, gently touch a hand or a knee as on other occasions he patted the desk or the couch. But he never looked into anyone's face. If an adult forcibly intruded himself by taking a block away or stepping on an object that the child needed, the child struggled and became angry with the hand or the foot, which was dealt with per se and not as a part of a person. He never addressed a word or a look to the owner of the hand or foot. When the object was retrieved, the child's mood changed abruptly to one of placidity. When pricked, he showed fear of the *pin* but not of the person who pricked him.

The relation to the members of the household or to other children did not differ from that to the people at the office. Profound aloneness dominates all behavior. The father or mother or both may have been away for an hour or a month; at their homecoming, there is no indication that the child has been even aware of their absence. After many outbursts of frustration, he gradually and reluctantly learns to compromise when he finds no way out, obeys certain orders, complies in matters of daily routine, but always strictly insists on the observance of his rituals. When there is company, he moves among the people "like a stranger" or, as one mother put it, "like a foal who had been let out of an enclosure." When with other children, he does not play with them. He plays alone while they are around, maintaining no bodily, physiognomic, or verbal contact with them. He does not take part in competitive games. He just is there, and if sometimes he happens to stroll as far as the periphery of a group, he soon removes himself and remains alone. At the same time, he quickly becomes familiar with the names of all the children of the group, may know the color of each child's hair, and other details about each child.

There is a far better relationship with pictures of people than with people themselves. Pictures, after all, cannot interfere. Charles was affectionately interested in the picture of a child in a magazine advertisement. He remarked repeatedly about the child's sweetness and beauty. Elaine was fascinated by pictures of animals but would not go near a live animal. John made no distinction between real and depicted people. When he saw a group photograph, he asked seriously when the people would step out of the picture and come into the room.

Even though most of these children were at one time or another looked upon as feebleminded, they are all unquestionably endowed with good *cognitive potentialities*. They all have strikingly intelligent physiognomies. Their faces at the same time give the impression of *serious-mindedness* and, in the presence of others, an anxious *tenseness*, probably because of the uneasy anticipation of possible interference. When alone with objects, there is often a placid smile and an expression of beatitude, sometimes accompanied by happy though monotonous humming and singing. The astounding vocabulary of the speaking children, the excellent memory for events of several years before, the phenomenal rote memory for poems and names, and the precise recollection of complex patterns and sequences, bespeak good intelligence in the sense in which this word is commonly used. Binet or similar testing could not be carried out because of limited accessibility. But all the children did well with the Seguin form board.

Physically, the children were essentially normal. Five had relatively large heads. Several of the children were somewhat clumsy in gait and gross motor performances, but all were very skillful in terms of finer muscle coordination. Electroencephalograms were normal in the case of all but John, whose anterior fontanelle did not close until he was 2½ years old, and who at 5¼ years had two series of predominantly right-sided convulsions. Frederick had a supernumerary nipple in the left axilla; there were no other instances of congenital anomalies.

There is one other very interesting common denominator in the backgrounds of these children. *They all come of highly intelligent families.* Four fathers are psychiatrists, one is a brilliant lawyer, one a chemist and law school graduate employed in the government Patent Office, one a plant pathologist, one a professor of forestry, one an advertising copy writer who has a degree in law and has studied in three universities, one is a mining engineer, and one a successful business man. Nine of the eleven mothers are college graduates. Of the two who have only high school education, one was secretary in a pathology laboratory, and the other ran a theatrical booking office in New York City before marriage. Among the others, there was a free-lance writer, a physician, a psychologist, a graduate nurse, and Frederick's mother was successively a purchasing agent, the director of secretarial studies in a girls' school, and a teacher of history. Among the grandparents and collaterals there are many physicians, scientists, writers, journalists, and students of art. All but three of the families are represented either in *Who's Who in America* or in *American Men of Science*, or in both.

Two of the children are Jewish, the others are all of Anglo-Saxon descent. Three are "only" children, five are the first-born of two children in their respective families, one is the oldest of three children, one is the younger of two, and one the youngest of three.

COMMENT

The combination of extreme autism, obsessiveness, stereotypy, and echo-lalia brings the total picture into relationship with some of the basic schizophrenic phenomena. Some of the children have indeed been diagnosed as of this type at one time or another. But in spite of the remarkable similarities, the condition differs in many respects from all other known instances of childhood schizophrenia.

First of all, even in cases with the earliest recorded onset of schizophrenia, including those of De Sanctis' dementia praecocissima and of Heller's dementia infantilis, the first observable manifestations were preceded by at least two years of essentially average development; the histories specifically emphasize a more or less gradual *change* in the patients' behavior. The children of our group have all shown their extreme aloneness from the very beginning of life, not responding to anything that comes to them from the outside world. This is most characteristically expressed in the recurrent report of failure of the child to assume an anticipatory posture upon being picked up, and of failure to adjust the body to that of the person holding him.

Second, our children are able to establish and maintain an excellent, purposeful, and "intelligent" relation to objects that do not threaten to interfere with their aloneness, but are from the start anxiously and tensely impervious to people, with whom for a long time they do not have any kind of direct affective contact. If dealing with another person becomes inevitable, then a temporary relationship is formed with the person's hand or foot as a definitely detached object, but not with the person himself.

All of the children's activities and utterances are governed rigidly and consistently by the powerful desire for aloneness and sameness. Their world must seem to them to be made up of elements that, once they have been experienced in a certain setting or sequence, cannot be tolerated in any other setting or sequence; nor can the setting or sequence be tolerated without all the original ingredients in the identical spatial or chronologic order. Hence the obsessive repetitiousness. Hence the reproduction of sentences without altering the pronouns to suit the occasion. Hence, perhaps, also the development of a truly phenomenal memory that enables the child to recall and reproduce complex "nonsense" patterns, no matter how unorganized they are, in exactly the same form as originally construed.

Five of our children have by now reached ages between 9 and 11 years. Except for Vivian S., who has been dumped in a school for the feebleminded, they show a very interesting course. The basic desire for aloneness and sameness has remained essentially unchanged, but there has been a varying degree of emergence from solitude, an acceptance of at least some people as being within the child's sphere of consideration, and a sufficient increase in the number of experienced patterns to refute the earlier impression of extreme limitation of the child's ideational content. One might perhaps put it this way: While the schizophrenic tries to solve his problem by stepping out of a world of which he has been a part and with which he has been in touch, our children gradually *compromise* by extending cautious feelers into a world in which they have been total strangers from the beginning. Between the ages of 5 and 6 years, they gradually abandon the echolalia and learn spontaneously to use personal pronouns with adequate reference. Language becomes more communicative, at first in the sense of a question-and-answer exercise, and then in the sense of greater spontaneity of sentence formation. Food is accepted without difficulty. Noises and motions are tolerated more than previously. The panic tantrums subside. The repetitiousness assumes the form of obsessive preoccupations. Contact with a limited number of people is established in a twofold way: people are included in the child's world to the extent to which they satisfy his needs, answer his obsessive questions, teach him how to read and to do things. Second, though people are still regarded as nuisances, their questions are answered and their commands are obeyed reluctantly, with the implication that it would be best to get these interferences over with, the sooner to be able to return to the still much desired aloneness. Between the ages of 6 and 8 years, the children begin to play in a group, still never *with* the other members of the play group, but at least on the periphery *alongside* the group. Reading skill is acquired quickly, but the children read monotonously, and a story or a moving picture is experienced in unrelated portions rather than in its coherent totality. All of this makes the family feel that, in spite of recognized "difference" from other children, there is progress and improvement.

It is not easy to evaluate the fact that all of our patients have come of highly intelligent parents. This much is certain, that there is a great deal of obsessiveness in the family background. The very detailed diaries and reports and the frequent remembrance, after several years, that the children had learned to recite twenty-five questions and answers of the Presbyterian Catechism, to sing thirty-seven nursery songs, or to discriminate between eighteen symphonies, furnish a telling illustration of parental obsessiveness.

One other fact stands out prominently. In the whole group, there are very few really warmhearted fathers and mothers. For the most part, the parents, grandparents, and collaterals are persons strongly preoccupied with abstractions of a scientific, literary, or artistic nature, and limited in genuine interest in people. Even some of the happiest marriages are rather cold and formal affairs. Three of the marriages were dismal failures. The question arises whether or to what extent this fact has contributed to the condition of the children. The children's aloneness from the beginning of life makes it difficult to attribute the whole picture exclusively to the type of the early parental relations with our patients.

We must, then, assume that these children have come into the world with innate inability to form the usual, biologically provided affective contact with people, just as other children come into the world with innate physical or intellectual handicaps. If this assumption is correct, a further study of our children may help to furnish concrete criteria regarding the still diffuse notions about the constitutional components of emotional reactivity. For here we seem to have pure-culture examples of *inborn autistic disturbances of affective contact.*

COMMENTARY by Michael Rutter

There are few scientific papers that have stood the test of time as well as Leo Kanner's first description of the syndrome that came to bear his name. The fact that he was the first person to recognize that this constellation of behaviors constituted a condition that was different from the general run of problems grouped under "mental retardation" or "schizophrenia" was quite enough for the paper to receive an honored place in the history of psychiatry. It was indeed a reflection of Kanner's remarkable clinical acumen that he was able to see so clearly that which had escaped the notice of his many distinguished contemporaries and predecessors. There can be no doubt that Kanner was a clinician of quite exceptional quality. But Kanner's description of the syndrome of autism is far more important than simply that which happened to be written first. The fact of the matter is that it is still read with profit by students today. The reasons are not difficult to find.

In the first place, it is a mark of Kanner's greatness that his observations were not only amply confirmed by subsequent investigations but, also, further research demonstrated that he had been correct in his identification of the key features that held the syndrome together. As Leon Eisenberg commented in his preface to the 1973 collection of Kanner's papers on autism, "The genius of the discovery was to detect the cardinal traits . . . in the midst of phenomenology as diverse as muteness in one child and verbal precocity in another."

Better still, Kanner described these phenomena in language that is a joy to read. All too often syndromes are described in pretentiously obfuscating jargon, with theoretical ideas intruding into the clinical descriptions so that the reader cannot tell what was observed and what was inferred. But not Kanner! His descriptions of the 11 children with autism were vivid and personal but written with a care to stick close to the behavior as seen. As a result, his account of those first 11 children remains as good a description of the syndrome as is to be found. DSM-III (American Psychiatric Association, 1980) provides the operational criteria for the behaviors that must be present for the diagnosis of autism to be made. However, for an appreciation of what the children with these symptoms are like, one cannot do better than return to Kanner.

It is striking, too, that from the outset Kanner described autism in developmental terms: "Between the ages of 5 and 6 years they gradually abandon the echolalia and learn spontaneously to use personal pronouns with adequate reference. Language becomes more communicative, at first in the sense of a question-and-answer exercise, and then in the sense of greater spontaneity of sentence formation." In the years that followed the 1943 paper, other writers sought to place autism in the field of psychoses, with the course described in terms such as "remission" or other terms derived from the literature on psychotic symptomatology. Kanner had the foresight to see that a developmental approach made more sense. The current DSM-III terminology of "pervasive developmental disorders" constitutes a recognition that Kanner was years ahead of his time in that regard.

There are two other respects in which Kanner's account showed a prescience of a remarkable degree: the genetic basis of autism and the emphasis on lack of affective contact. For a long time it was concluded that genetic factors probably played little or no part in the etiology of autism: the rarity with which two cases of autism occurred in the same family seemed to attest to that conclusion. However, it has become clear over the last few years that our logic was at fault and, moreover, the evidence from twin and sibling studies now strongly suggests an important genetic component. For years Kanner's insistence that the key abnormality in autism concerned the lack of affective contact was rather neglected; research focused instead on the cognitive and language abnormalities. Unquestionably, the findings confirmed the reality of cognitive deficits but it has become apparent that the socio/emotional abnormalities had still to be explained. The research focus has turned at last to an analysis of the abnormalities that underlie autistic children's lack of empathic awareness. Adequate answers have yet to be obtained but, some 40 years behind Kanner, his concluding words to the 1943 paper have come to be recognized as the prophetic insights that they were: "We must, then, assume that these children have come into the world with innate inability to form the usual, biologically provided affective contact with people, just as other children come into the world with innate physical or intellectual handicaps. If this assumption is correct, a further study of our children may help to furnish concrete criteria regarding the still diffuse notions about the constitutional components of emotional reactivity." How right he was!

REFERENCE

American Psychiatric Association. *Diagnostic and statistical manual of mental disorders* (3rd ed.). Washington, D.C.: American Psychiatric Association, 1980.

3

Positive Reinforcement and Behavioral Deficits of Autistic Children

C. B. FERSTER

Infantile autism, first described by Kanner (6), is a very severe psychotic disturbance occurring in children as young as 2 years. At least outwardly, this childhood schizophrenia is a model of adult schizophrenia. Speech and control by the social environment are limited or absent; tantrums and atavistic behaviors are frequent and of high intensity; and most activities are of a simple sort, such as smearing, lying about, rubbing a surface, playing with a finger, and so forth. Infantile autism is a relatively rare form of schizophrenia and is not important from an epidemiological point of view. The analysis of the autistic child may be of theoretical use, however, since his psychosis may be a prototype of the adult's; but the causal factors could not be so complicated, because of the briefer environmental history. In this paper, I should like to analyze how the basic variables determining the child's behavior might operate to produce the particular kinds of behavioral deficits seen in the autistic child. To analyze the autistic child's behavioral deficits, I shall proceed from the general principles of behavior, derived from a variety of species, which describe the kinds of factors that alter the frequency of any arbitrary act (3, 10). The general principles of behavior applied to the specific situations presumably present during the child's developmental period will lead to hypotheses as to specific factors in the autistic child's home life which could produce the severe changes in frequency as well as in the form of his behavior. As an example, consider the effect of intermittent reinforcement, many of the properties of which are comparatively well known from animal experiments. To find how intermittent reinforcement of the autistic child's behavior might produce deficits, we would first determine, in the general case, what specific orders of magnitude and kinds of schedules produce weakened behavioral repertoires. The factors in the child's home life could be examined to determine estimates of what kind of circumstances could conceivably cause schedules of reinforcement capable of the

Reprinted with permission from *Child Development* 32 (1961): 437–456. © The Society for Research in Child Development, Inc.

required attenuation of the child's behavior. The analysis will emphasize the child's performance as it is changed by, and affected in, social and nonsocial environment. As in most problems of human behavior, the major datum is the frequency of occurrence of the child's behavior. Although the account of the autistic child's development and performance is not derived by manipulative experiments, it may still be useful to the extent that all of the terms of the analysis refer to potentially manipulable conditions in the child's environment and directly measurable aspects of his performance. Such an analysis is even more useful if the performances and their effects on the environment were described in the same general terms used in systematic accounts of behavior of experimental psychology.

Some of our knowledge of the autistic child's repertoire must necessarily come from anecdotal accounts of the child's performance through direct observation. Although such data are not so useful as data from controlled experiments, they can be relatively objective if these performances are directly observable and potentially manipulable. A limited amount of experimental knowledge of the dynamics of the autistic child's repertoire is available through a program of experiments in which the autistic child has developed a new repertoire under the control of an experimental environment (5). These experiments help reveal the range and dynamics of the autistic child's current and potential repertoires. In general, the autistic child's behavior will be analyzed by the functional consequences of the child's behavior rather than the specific form. The major attempt will be to determine what specific effects the autistic child's performance has on that environment and how the specific effects maintain the performance.

SPECIFICATION OF THE AUTISTIC CHILD'S PERFORMANCE

We must first describe the current repertoire of the autistic child before we can describe possible environmental conditions that might produce gross behavioral deficits. A topographic description of the individual items of the autistic child's repertoire would not, in general, distinguish it from the repertoires of a large number of functioning and nonhospitalized children, except perhaps in the degree of loss of verbal behavior. The autistic child's behavior becomes unique only when the relative frequency of occurrence of all the performances in the child's repertoire is considered. In general, the usual diagnostic categories do not adequately characterize the children in the terms of a functional analysis of behavior. Hospitalization of a child usually depends upon whether the parent can keep the child in the home, rather than a functional description of the role of the parental environment in sustaining or weakening the child's performance.

Range of Performances

Although the autistic child may have a narrower range of performances than the normal child, the major difference between them is in the relative frequencies of the various kinds of performances. The autistic child does many things of a simple sort—riding a bicycle, climbing, walking, tugging on someone's sleeve, running, etc. Nevertheless, the autistic child spends large amounts of time sitting or standing quietly. Performances which have only simple and slight effects on the child's environment occur frequently and make up a large percentage of the entire repertoire, for example, chewing on a rubber balloon, rubbing a piece of gum back and forth on the floor, flipping a shoelace, or turning the left hand with the right. Almost all of the characteristic performances of the autistic child may be observed in nonhospitalized children, but the main difference lies in the relative importance of each of these performances in terms of the total repertoire. Conversely, isolated instances of quite "normal" performances may be seen in the autistic child. Again, the relative frequency of the performances defines the autistic child.

Social Control over the Child's Performance

The major performance deficits of the autistic child are in the degree of social control: The kinds of performances which have their major effects through the mediation of other individuals.

The main avenue of social control in a normal repertoire is usually through speech, a kind of performance that is unique because it produces the consequences maintaining it through the mediation of a second person (12). Autistic children almost always have an inadequately developed speech repertoire, varying from mutism to a repertoire of a few words. Even when large numbers of words are emitted, the speech is not normal in the sense that it is not maintained by its effect on a social environment. When normal speech is present, it usually is in the form of a *mand* (12). This is a simple verbal response which is maintained because of its direct reinforcement, e.g., "Candy!" "Let me out." The main variable is usually the level of deprivation of the speaker. It lacks the sensitive interchange between the speaker and listener characteristic of much human verbal behavior, as for example, the *tact* (*see* below). The reinforcement of the mand largely benefits only the speaker. In the case of the autistic child, it frequently affects the listener (parent), who escapes from the aversive stimulus by presenting a reinforcing stimulus relevant to the child's mand. At suppertime, the child stands at the door screaming loudly and kicking the door because the ward attendants in the past have taken the child to supper when this situation became aversive enough. Sometimes, the form of the mand is nonvocal, although still verbal, as when the mand involves tugging at a sleeve, pushing, or jostling. The dynamic conditions which could distort the form of a mand into forms most aversive to a listener will be described below. In contrast to the mand, the tact (12) is almost completely absent. This form of verbal behavior benefits the listener rather than the speaker and is not usually relevant to the current deprivations of the speaker. This is the form of verbal behavior by which the child describes his environment, as, for example, "This is a chair"; "The mailman is coming." This latter kind of verbal control is generally absent or weak, as with other kinds of verbal behavior except an occasional mand.

Atavisms

Tantrums, self-destructive behavior, and performances generally aversive to an adult audience are relatively frequent in the autistic child's repertoire. Most autistic mands depend on an aversive effect of the listener for their reinforcement. To the extent that social behavior is present at all, its major mode is through the production of stimuli or situations which are aversive enough so that the relevant audience will escape or avoid the aversive stimulus (often with a reinforcer). For example, on the occasion of candy in the immediate vicinity, the child screams, flails about on the floor, perhaps striking his head, until he is given some candy. There is evidence that much of the atavistic performance of the autistic child is operant, that is, controlled by its consequence in the social environment. The operant nature of the autistic child's atavisms is borne out by experiments where a child was locked in an experimental space daily for over a year. There was no social intervention, and the experimental session was usually prolonged if a tantrum was underway. Under these conditions, the frequency of tantrums and atavisms declined continuously in the experimental room until they all but disappeared. Severe tantrums and attempts at self-destruction still occurred when sudden changes in the conditions of the experiment produced a sudden change in the direction of nonreinforcement of the child's performances. Severe changes in the reinforcement contingencies of the experiment produced a much larger reaction in the autistic than in the normal child. Consequently, we learned to change experimental conditions very slowly, so that the frequency of reinforcement remained high at each stage of the experiment. Much of the atavistic behavior of the autistic child is maintained because of its effect on the listener.

Reinforcing Stimuli

The reinforcers maintaining the autistic child's performance are difficult to determine without explicit experimentation. Small changes in the physical environment as, for example, direct stimulation of the mouth, splashing water, smearing a sticky substance on the floor, breaking a toy, or repeated tactile sensations, appear to sustain the largest part of the autistic child's repertoire. Nevertheless, these may be weak reinforcing stimuli which appear to be strong, because the response produces its reinforcement continuously and because alternative modes of responding are also maintained by weak reinforcers. The durability and effectiveness of a reinforcer can usually be determined best by reinforcing the behavior intermittently or by providing a strong alternative which could interfere with the behavior in question. In the controlled experiments with autistic children, most of the consequences we supplied to sustain the children's performance, such as color wheels, moving pictures, music, and so forth, were very weak reinforcers compared with food or candy. Food generally appeared to be an effective reinforcer, and most of the performances associated with going to the dining room and eating are frequently intact. In contrast, the normal children could sustain very large amounts of behavior through the nonfood reinforcements. It is difficult to guess the potential effectiveness of new reinforcers, because the estimate depends upon some performance being maintained by that reinforcer.

In the everyday activities of the autistic children, little behavior was sustained by conditioned or delayed reinforcers. But, in a controlled experimental situation, such activities could be sustained by explicit training. For example, (a) The sound of the candy dispenser preceding the delivery of candy served as a conditioned reinforcer. The fine-grain effects of the schedules of reinforcement show this. The difference in performance produced by two different schedules of reinforcement could have occurred only if the effective reinforcer were the sound of the magazine rather than the delivery of a coin. The actual receipt of the coin or food is much too delayed to produce the differences in performances under the two schedules without the conditioned reinforcer coming instantly after a response. (b) With further training, the delivery of a coin (conditioned reinforcer) sustained the child's performances. The coin, in turn, could be used to operate the food or nonfood devices in the experimental room. (c) Still later, coins sustained the child's performance even though they had to be held for a period of time before they could be cashed in. The child worked until he accumulated five coins, then he deposited them in the reinforcing devices. (d) Even longer delays of reinforcement were arranged by sustaining behavior in the experimental room with a conditioned reinforcer as, for example, a towel or a life jacket which could be used later in the swimming pool or in water play after the experimental session terminated. The experimental development of these performances shows that, even though the usual autistic repertoire is generally deficient in performances sustained by conditioned reinforcement and with delay in reinforcement, the children are potentially capable of developing this kind of control.

Little of the autistic child's behavior is likely to be maintained by generalized reinforcement, that is, reinforcement which is effective in the absence of any specific deprivation. A smile or parental approval are examples. The coins delivered as reinforcements in the experimental room are potentially generalized reinforcers, since they make possible several performances under the control of many different deprivations. However, we do not know whether the coin has actually acquired the properties of a generalized reinforcer.

Stimulus Control of Behavior

It is very difficult to determine the stimulus and perceptual repertoire of autistic children. When a child responds to a complex situation, it is not usually clear what aspect of the situation is controlling the child's behavior. In most cases, it is difficult to determine to what extent these children can respond to speech discriminatively, since the situations are usually complex and many stimuli may provide the basis for the simple performances. Similarly with visual repertoires. Controlled experiments showed unequivocally that behavior can come under the control of simple stimuli when differential effects of the performances were correlated with the different stimuli. When a coin was deposited in a lighted coin slot, it operated the reinforcing device. Coins deposited in unlighted slots were wasted. The children soon stopped putting coins in the unlighted slots. The previously developed stimulus control broke down completely when these stimuli were placed in a more complicated context, however. A new vending machine was installed with eight columns, eight coin lights, and eight coin slots, so the child could choose a preferred kind of candy. The slight increase in complexity disrupted the control by the coin light, and it took several months and many experimental procedures before the stimulus control was reestablished. A better designed procedure, in view of the minimal perceptual repertoire of these children, would have been a gradual program by which variations in the specific dimensions of the coin slot and coin light were changed while the reinforcement contingency was held constant in respect to the essential property.

In summary, the repertoire of the autistic child is an impoverished one. Little is known about the perceptual repertoire, but the available evidence suggests that it is minimal. The absolute amount of activity is low, but this deficit is even more profound if the specific items of activity are evaluated in terms of whether they are maintained by significant effects on a social or even nonsocial environment. Most of the child's performances are of a simple sort, such as rubbing a spot of gum back and forth, softening and twisting a crayon, pacing, or flipping a shoelace. Those performances in the child's repertoire having social effects frequently do so because of their effects on the listener as aversive stimuli. Atavisms and tantrums are frequent.

THE EMERGENCE OF PERFORMANCE DEFICITS
DURING THE EARLY DEVELOPMENT OF THE AUTISTIC CHILD

Having characterized the autistic child's repertoire, the next step is to determine the kinds of circumstances in the early life of these children which could bring about the behavioral deficits. The general plan is to state how the major behavioral processes and classes of variables can drastically reduce the frequency of occurrence of the various behaviors in the repertoire of any organism. Then, the parental environment will be examined to determine circumstances under which the actual contingencies applied by the parental environment to the child's behavior could weaken the child's performance similarly. The datum is the frequency of occurrence of all of the acts in the child's repertoire, and the independent variables are the consequences of these acts on the child's environment, particularly the parental environment. All of the terms in such a functional analysis are actually or potentially directly observable and manipulable. In general, the performances in the child's repertoire will be simultaneously a function of many factors, each contributing to changes in the frequency of the relevant performances. It is important, therefore, to consider relative changes in frequency rather than simple presence or absence of various performances. The datum is the frequency of occurrence of the behavior. In the same vein, singly identifiable factors may be interrelated and functioning simultaneously.

The major paradigm for describing the behavior of an organism is to specify the consequences of the act (reinforcement) which are responsible for its frequency. In this sense, the major cause of an instance of behavior is the immediate effect on the environment (reinforcement). The continued emission of the verbal response "Toast" depends on its effect on the parent in producing toast. Every known behavioral process influencing the frequency of a positively reinforced performance is relevant to the problem of defining conditions under which we may produce a behavioral deficit. Given the variables which maintain it, a performance may be weakened by their absence or by changing the order of magnitude. It is perhaps surprising to discover that large behavioral deficits are plausible without any major appeal to punishment or suppression of behavior by aversive stimuli.

Intermittent Reinforcement and Extinction

Intermittent reinforcement and extinction are the major techniques for removing or weakening behavior in a repertoire. The most fundamental way to eliminate a kind of behavior from an organism's repertoire is to discontinue the effect the behavior has on the environment (extinction). A performance may also be weakened if its maintaining effect on the environment occurs intermittently (intermittent reinforcement).[1] Behaviors occurring because of their effects on the parent are especially likely to be weaken by intermittent reinforcement and extinction, because the parental reinforcements are a function of other variables and behavioral processes usually not directly under the control of the child. The reinforcement of the verbal response, "Give me the book," may go unreinforced because of many factors which determine the behavior of the listener. He may be preoccupied, listening to someone else, disinclined to reinforce, momentarily inattentive, etc. In contrast, the physical environment reinforces continuously and reliably. Reaching for a book is usually followed by the tactile stimulation from the book. Verbal behavior, particularly, depends entirely for its development and maintenance on reinforcements supplied by an audience (usually a parent). Because of the possibility of prolonged extinction and infrequent, intermittent reinforcement, speech and social behavior are the most vulnerable aspects of the child's repertoire. The young child is particularly vulnerable to the extinction and intermittent reinforcement occurring in social reinforcement because only the parental environment mediates nearly all of the major reinforcers relevant to his repertoire. Large parts of the child's repertoire are reinforced by first affecting a parent who in turn produces the reinforcer for the child. The 2-year-old child who asks for a cookie from a parent and gets no response usually has no alternative audience who will reinforce this vocal behavior. The result will either be the extinction of the child's verbal behavior or the reinforcement of nonvocal verbal forms when the child produces a cookie by a tantrum from which the parent escapes by giving the cookie.

Factors in the Parental Repertoire Affecting the Frequency of Reinforcement of the Child's Performances

To find the conditions under which the child's repertoire will be weakened, therefore, we must look for conditions influencing the parents' behavior, which will alter the parental performances, in turn providing reinforcement of the child's performances. These might be:

1. The general disruption of the parental repertoire. Any severe disruption of the parental repertoire will severely affect the frequency with which the parent reinforces the behavior of the child. Consider, for example, the

---

[1]The reader may suggest at this point an apparent contradiction with the fact that extinction after intermittent reinforcement is more prolonged than after continuous reinforcement. This aspect of intermittently reinforced behavior's durability is not a general proposition, however, and does not hold for behavior which is still being maintained. Behavior reinforced intermittently will, in general, be emitted less frequently and be more easily weakened by emotional factors, changes in deprivation, punishment, and physiological disturbances than continuously reinforced behavior.

depressed parent whose general level of behavior is very low. One consequence of this low level of behaving will be a lessened frequency of reacting to the child. Therefore, many items in the child's repertoire will be less frequently reinforced in the depressed than the normal parent. The verbal responses, "May I have some bread" or "I want to go outside," might go unreinforced or be emitted many times without reinforcement. Various kinds of somatic disturbances, such as alcoholic "hangover," drug addiction, severe headache, somatic diseases, etc., could also produce large changes in the over-all reactivity of the parent to a child. To the extent that the child's performances occur because of their effect on the parent, the severely weakened parental repertoire may correspondingly weaken the child's behavior. If the parental extinction of the child's behavior is systematic and periodic, much of a child's behavior could be eliminated.

2. Prepotency of other performances. Whether or not a parent reinforces a child's performance also depends upon the alternative repertoire available to the parent. For example, the parent who is absorbed in various kinds of activities such as housecleaning, a home business, social activities and clubs, active telephoning, and so forth, may at various times allow many usually reinforced performances to go unreinforced. In general, the likelihood of omitting reinforcement would depend upon the strength of the prepotent repertoire. As an example of a prepotent repertoire, the housewife absorbed in a telephone conversation will not be inclined to answer a child or comply with a request. Housecleaning might be another repertoire controlling some parents' behavior so strongly that it is prepotent over behavior in respect to the child. In both cases, the essential result is the nonreinforcement of the child's behavior in competition with the prepotent parental repertoire. Mothers of autistic children often appear to have strong repertoires prepotent over the child. This may be at least a partial reason why mothers of autistic children are so often well-educated, verbal, and at least superficially adequate people.

3. A third factor producing intermittent reinforcement of the child's behavior is related to the first two factors listed above. If the parent finds other reinforcers outside of the home more rewarding than dealing with the child, the child becomes an occasion on which the significant elements of the parental repertoire cannot be reinforced. A parent changing diapers, or otherwise taking care of a child, cannot telephone a friend, be out socializing, be on a job, or doing whatever the autistic mother finds rewarding. The child acquires the properties of a conditioned aversive stimulus because it is an occasion which is incompatible with the parents' normal repertoire. This is of course the major method of aversive control in human behavior—the discontinuation of positive reinforcement. Another basis for establishing the child as a conditioned aversive stimulus to the parent is the emergence of

atavisms and a large degree of aversive control of the parent by the child. To the extent that the parent is reinforced by escaping from the child because of his conditioned aversive properties, the frequency of the parental reinforcement of the child's behavior is further reduced.

The development of the atavistic behavior in the child by the parent is necessarily a very gradual program in which the beginning steps involve small magnitudes of behavior such as whining, whimpering, and crying. As the parent adapts to these or becomes indifferent to them because of the prepotence of other kinds of activity, then progressively larger orders of magnitude become reinforced. The large-magnitude tantrum may be approximated or "shaped" by gradual differential reinforcement. The parents of one autistic child, for example, at one period took turns all night standing in the child's room because one step out of the room would immediately produce a severe tantrum in the child. When the child functions as a conditioned aversive stimulus for the parent, the parent is less likely to reinforce the child's behavior positively. This lack of positive reinforcement, in turn, emphasizes the atavistic responses on the child's part as the major mode of affecting the parent.

The usual limiting factor in preventing excessive development of tantrums is the emergence of self-control on the part of the parent in escaping from the aversive control by the child rather than reinforcing it. Here, again, the repertoire of the parent is relevant. The development of self-control requires a highly developed repertoire which depends for its development on the ultimate aversive consequences of the child's control of the parent. The child's control becomes more aversive to the parent if it interrupts strong repertoires. Specifically, a parent engrossed in a conversation will find a child's interruption more aversive than a parent who is simply resting. If, in fact, there is no strong behavior in the parent, then the child's control is not likely to be aversive, and there is no basis for developing self-control.

All three of the above factors—over-all disturbances in the parental repertoire, prepotent activities, and escape from the child because of his aversiveness—reduce the amount of parental reinforcement of the child's performances. The over-all effect of the nonreinforcement on the repertoire of the child will depend upon the length of time and number of items of the child's repertoire that go unreinforced, as well as the existence of other possible social environments that can alternatively maintain the child's behavior (*see* below).

Differential Reinforcement of Atavistic Forms of Behavior by the Parent

The schedule by which the parent reacts to the child is also relevant to the development of atavistic behavior. Initially, a tantrum may be an unconditioned consequence of parental control as, for example, sudden nonreinforcement or punishment. Eventually, however, the child's tantrums may come to be maintained by their effect on the parental environment, because they present an aversive situation that can be terminated if the parent supplies some reinforcer to the child. The reinforcer presented by the parent to escape from the aversive consequences of the tantrum also increases the subsequent frequency of atavistic responses.

The effect on the parent of the given form and intensity of tantrums will vary from time to time, depending on the conditions maintaining the parents' behavior. This variation in sensitivity of the parent to aversive control by the child results in a variable-ratio schedule of reinforcement of the child's tantrum by the parent—a schedule of reinforcement potentially capable of maximizing the disposition to engage in tantrums. This is the schedule of reinforcement that produces the high frequencies of performances as in gambling (10). The sensitivity of the parent to aversive control by the child will depend on the general condition of the parental repertoire as discussed above. The same factors in the parental repertoire that tend to produce non-reinforcement of the child's behavior—general disruption of the parent or other behaviors prepotent over the child—correspondingly produce reinforcement of large-order-of-magnitude tantrums. The parent whose total repertoire is severely enough disrupted to interfere with the normal reinforcement of the child's behavior will also react only to tantrums that are of large order of magnitude of aversiveness. A range of sensitivity of the parent to aversive control by the child produces ideal conditions for progressively increasing the intensity or frequency of tantrums. A high sensitivity to aversive control guarantees that some tantrums will be reinforced at least periodically. A low sensitivity differentially reinforces tantrums of large orders of magnitude. At one extreme, the parent may be hypersensitive to the child and, at other times, so depressed that only physical violence will produce a reaction. The schedule by which the parent's behavior terminates the tantrum is a second factor which will increase the range of reactivity of the parent. As more behavior is required of the parent to terminate the tantrum, the parent's inclination to do so will fall. When the parent is less inclined to reinforce a given intensity of tantrum, any variation in tantrum intensity is tantamount to differential reinforcement of extreme forms, if the parent now reacts to the larger-order-of-magnitude tantrum.

How much the parent differentially reinforces tantrums in the child depends, in part, upon the child's other positively reinforced repertoires. When, for example, a child's performance suddenly goes unreinforced, as when a parent may refuse a request, the likelihood and severity of a tantrum will in part depend on the parent's ability to "distract" the child. This, in turn, depends upon whether alternative modes of behavior are in fact available to the child. When conditions are present for the progressive reinforcement of more and more severe tantrums, the process is potentially non-self-limiting. Autocatalysis is likely to occur, particularly if the parent has little disposition to reinforce the general items in the child's repertoire for reasons other than terminating the aversive demands of the child.

Nonsocial Reinforcers

Some of the child's behavior is maintained by his direct effect on the physical environment without the intervention of other individuals. In general, very small effects on the environment will sustain performances with which the parent usually has little reason to interfere. For example, the child plays with his own shoelace, moves his fingers in his own visual field, emits minimal nonverbal, vocal responses, and so forth. Larger effects on the physical environment as, for example, moving objects about the house, speaking to the parent, playing with toys, touching and handling usual household objects, are more likely to enter upon the parental repertoire and so may produce a response whose effect is to discontinue the behavior or interfere with its reinforcement. The punishment aspect of the parental interference with the child's activities will be dealt with separately below. The relative possibility of parental interference and nonreinforcement of the hierarchy of performances may account for the large part of the autistic child's repertoire, which consists of behaviors having small, limited effects on the physical environment. Occasionally, even behaviors that are maintained by the most simple effects on the environment are extinguished or punished when they occur in the presence of a parent. For example, the father of one autistic child reports that the child reached for a chandelier while he was holding him. The father instantly dropped the child, with a reaction of considerable disapproval because "You should pay attention to me when you're with me." Aside from the secondary effect on the child, the immediate result of the incident is the nonreinforcement of the child reaching for a common physical object.

The existence of "nonverbal" vocal behavior in some autistic children may be related to forms of vocal behavior with which the parent will or will not interfere. Vocal behavior maintained by its effect on a parent (verbal) is susceptible to weakening by parental extinction. A parent interferes less easily with vocal behavior maintained by its direct effect (nonverbal) comparable with making noise by rubbing a stick over a rough surface. Further, such nonverbal vocal responses can emerge readily at any stage of the child's life, unlike verbal behavior, because it does not depend on a generalized reinforcement.

Failure to Develop Conditioned and Generalized Reinforcers

The normal repertoire of the child consists almost entirely of sequences of behavior that are maintained, in a chain or sequence, by conditioned and generalized reinforcers (10). An example of a chain of responses would be the behavior of a child moving a chair across the room and using it to climb to a table top to reach a key which in turn opens a cupboard containing candy. This complicated sequence of behavior is linked together by critical stimuli which have the dual function of sustaining the behavior they follow (conditioned reinforcement) and setting the occasion for the subsequent response. The chair in the above example is an occasion on which climbing onto it will bring the child into a position where reaching for food on the table top will be reinforced by obtaining food. Once this behavior is established, the chair in position in front of the table may now be a reinforcer, and any of the child's behavior which results in moving the chair into position will be reinforced because of the subsequent role of the chair in the later chain of behaviors. A minimal amount of behavior is necessary before a chain of responses can develop. The development of the control by the various stimuli in the chain, both as discriminative stimuli setting the occasion for the reinforcement of behavior and as reinforcers, depends upon a high level of activity, so that the responses will occur and come under the control of the stimuli. This is even more true for the development of the generalized reinforcer. When the child has moved enough objects about the house and achieved a variety of effects on his environment relative to a range of deprivations and reinforcers, simply manipulating the physical environment may become a reinforcer without reference to a specific level of deprivation. This, of course, is the uniquely human reinforcer that makes possible much of verbal behavior, education in general, and self-control. Again, large amounts of behavior—many chains of behavior with many different kinds of conditioned reinforcers—are a necessary condition for the emergence of a generalized reinforcer. To the extent that the child's repertoire becomes weakened by intermittent reinforcement and extinction, as mentioned above, and punishment and aversive control (*see* below), the possibility of the development of generalized reinforcers, and hence more complex behavior, becomes less and less likely. Parental "attention" is probably one of the most important generalized reinforcers normally maintaining the child's behavior. Parental attention is an occasion upon which the child's performances may have an important effect on the parent. Inattention is an occasion on which the child's responses are likely to have little effect. Hence, the parents' performances in smiling, saying, "Right," "Good boy," or "Thank you," all come to function as conditioned reinforcers. Their emergence as generalized reinforcers again depends upon the existence of a large behavioral repertoire. A large number of chains of responses will produce important positive effects when the parent smiles or says, "Good boy." Lower frequencies of reinforcement follow for these same activities when the parent is frowning or says, "Bad boy."

Any large reduction in the child's over-all performance will interfere with the initial development of conditioned reinforcers or their continued effectiveness. The control by the environment over the child's behavior depends first upon the emission of the behavior. This follows from the manner in which the environment comes to control the child's performance: the successful execution of an act on one occasion, coupled with the unsuccessful act in its absence. Until a child climbs on chairs, as in the previous example, a chair has little chance of becoming a discriminative stimulus. Without the development of stimulus control, conditioned reinforcers cannot develop. The reinforcing effect of the chair in the above example depends upon its being the occasion on which further performances may be reinforced. In this way, a low general level of behavior may impede the enlargement of the child's repertoire because it does not allow stimulus control and in turn prevents reinforcement of new behavior. A limited development of simple conditioned reinforcers in turn prevents the development of a generalized reinforcer. Parental responses, such as smiling, "Good," or "Right," can have little effect on the child if there is not a history by which many different forms of the child's performance have produced various reinforcers on these occasions. Without parental generalized reinforcement, educational processes and positive parental control are all but impossible. This control is normally carried out by the use of praise and parental attention, coupled with mild forms of threats of discontinuing the reinforcers. Even after a generalized reinforcer has acquired its function, its continued effectiveness depends on the various stimuli continuing to stand in a significant relation to the child's performance. The actual form of the parents' generalized reinforcer is not nearly as important as the parents' subsequent reinforcement practices with the child. The reinforcing effects of the smile derive from the reinforcing practices associated with it. A smile usually functions as a generalized reinforcer in most people because a smiling person is more likely to reinforce. The correlation between smiling and reinforcement is by no means inevitable, however. Some individuals may be more disposed to punish than reinforce when smiling in some situations. In a similar vein, if the child has no behavior in his repertoire that will be more likely to be reinforced on the occasion of a parental smile, it matters little what the parent's reinforcing practices are when smiling as against when frowning.

STIMULUS CONTROL

The specific occasions on which a child's performances have their characteristic effects on the environment will subsequently determine whether the child acts. In the absence of the characteristic circumstances under which the behavior is normally reinforced, the child will be less disposed to act in proportion to the degree of similarity with the original situation. Changing a stimulus to one which has not been correlated with reinforcement is another way of weakening a repertoire. New stimuli also elicit emotional responses and general autonomic effects that may interfere with established performances. Here, simply repeated exposure to the stimuli may produce adaptation to the stimuli and eliminate their emotional effects. Ordinarily, the infants' performances are under the control of a limited range of stimuli, usually one or two parents in a limited part of a specific home environment. The discriminative repertoire broadens as the child grows older and other individuals come to be occasions on which his performances have significant effects. The parental environment of the very young child narrows the control of the child's performance to a limited range of stimuli, largely because the parent mediates almost all of the important events affecting the child. A major factor which brings the child's behavior more narrowly under the control of the parent is the nonreinforcement of much of the child's behavior in the absence of the parent. The close control of the child's behavior by the parent weakens the child's repertoire in the absence of a parent much more when there has been explicit differential reinforcement than when there has been simply a limited reinforcing environment.

Sudden shifts in the child's environment may or may not produce major performance deficits. At one extreme, a sudden shift of the stimuli in the child's controlling environment will have little influence if the child already has been reinforced on the occasion of a wide range of circumstances and individuals. At another extreme, a repertoire can be eliminated almost completely if the child has had a history in which major kinds of performances have gone unreinforced except on the occasion of a single person in a specific environment. The sudden shifts in the situations and persons controlling the child's behavior may occur under a variety of circumstances, such as a sudden change in a constant companion, death of a parent, or a sudden shift in the physical environment. A sudden shift in the environment of one of the subjects reported in the previously mentioned experiment could conceivably have been the major factor in her autistic development. Many of the activities of the child's mother were prepotent over dealing with the child, and she solved the problem by hiring a teenage babysitter as a constant companion and nursemaid. After a year, the babysitter left, suddenly and abruptly, leaving the child with the mother. Within four months, the child began to behave less in general, lost speech, and showed increasing frequency of atavisms. The child's repertoire possibly was under such close control of the babysitter that the very sudden change to the mother created an environment which in the past had been correlated with nonreinforcement. If the child's behavior were under very narrow control by the babysitter, because of the nonreinforcement on all other occasions, a sudden shift, as in the loss of the babysitter, could produce a dramatic deficit in the child's repertoire.

Disruptive Effect of Sudden Stimulus Changes and the Amount, Durability, and Range of Behavior

A novel reinforcing environment will not sustain a child's performance unless the repertoire contains behavior of a sufficient range and durability. The new environment weakens the performance because it nearly always requires slightly different forms of behavior. For example, a new person entering a child's home is not so likely to respond successfully to the incompletely developed verbal behavior of a child as the parent. The possibility of the child's affecting the stranger will depend upon his having verbal responses different from those usually reinforced by the parent and, also, durable verbal behavior that will continue to be emitted under the intermittent reinforcement that is likely to occur. If the child's repertoire is durable and extensive enough so that the verbal response may be repeated several times and supplemented by auxiliary behavior, the child has a greater chance of affecting the new person or of being shaped by him. Similarly with other kinds of social behavior. The wider the range of behavior and the greater the disposition to emit it the more likely that the child's performance will be within the range of responses potentially reinforcible by the new environment.

For a stimulus to acquire control over behavior, the child must first emit behavior in the presence of the stimulus. Consider, for example, the performance of a child at a children's party at which there are lots of toys and games, such as bicycles, swings, and so forth. The likelihood of the child's behavior coming under the control of any of the other children as reinforcers is minimal if the new environment suppresses or makes the child's entire repertoire unavailable because it is a novel stimulus and is an occasion on which the child's behavior has never been reinforced. If the behavior of playing with a swing or riding a tricycle is sufficiently strong that it may be emitted even under the adverse conditions of the very strange party environment, then the simple emission of the previously developed behavior provides a situation under which other children at the party may potentially reinforce or otherwise affect the child's repertoire. Simply the acts of eating cake, candy, or ice cream, or picking up a toy put some of the child's behavior under the control of the new environment. Each new performance which can potentially occur at the party provides a basis for the child's reinforcing some behavior of other children at the party or of his coming under the control of the other children's reinforcers. On the other hand, a sudden exposure to a new environment with a weak and narrow repertoire may produce a severe behavioral deficit. In any case, the child will be much less disposed to go to the party if he had behaved unsuccessfully in the new environment. This lower disposition to attend and engage in the party would in turn make it less likely that the child will emit behavior that would be reinforced in the party environment.

Adaptation

The emotional and elicited autonomic effects of novel environments may also interfere with a child's performances. Adaptation to new environments occurs with gradual exposure. A sudden exposure to a new environment will produce gross emotional and autonomic responses which will in turn interfere with, or even completely suppress, the emission of possible operant behavior potentially reinforcible by the new environment. The rate at which the child is exposed to the new environments will determine the magnitude of disturbance. Exposure to a new environment and adaptation of the emotional responses do not necessarily create the potential basis for responding, however. A repertoire that will make contact with the new environment is also necessary.

Amount of Prior Nonreinforcement

The more closely controlled the child's performances are by specific stimuli, the more likely a sudden shift in the environment will produce a cessation of responding. For example, the child receiving minimal care from a parent probably will be less affected by a sudden shift in environment than a child closely affected and controlled by parental response. It is paradoxical that the parent who responds sensitively to the child's performance may be potentially weakening it more than the parent who exerts little control over the child. It is the alternate reinforcement and nonreinforcement that place the child's behavior narrowly under the control of very specific stimuli so that it is much more vulnerable to sudden changes. The range of stimuli in whose presence the child's behavior goes unreinforced will determine the narrowness of the stimulus control.

CUMULATIVE EFFECTS OF A BEHAVIORAL DEFICIT

The continuous development of more and more complex forms of a child's behavior is normally achieved because the parents and community approximate the required performances. At each stage of the child's development, the community reinforces the child's current repertoire even though it is more disposed to react to small increments in the child's performance in the direction of the required complex performances. Should any of the above processes produce a deficit in performance or an arrest in the development of the child's performance, further development of a repertoire would depend upon the community's relaxing its requirements and reinforcing performances in an older child that it normally accepts only from a younger one. Ordinarily, the reinforcing practices of the community are based on the chronological age and physical development of the child.

Only between the ages of 1½ to 4 years does the parent have sufficient control of the child to weaken his performance to the degree seen in infantile autism. This is a critical period in the child's development during which his behavior is especially susceptible to extinction, because the traditional social pattern in the usual family restricts the child's experience to one or two parents. Before the age of 1½, the child has few performances with which the parent will interfere or that have important effects on the parent. Much of the infant's behavior is maintained by simple and direct effects on its environment. As the child approaches 2 years, the rapid development of a behavioral repertoire, particularly social and verbal behavior, makes possible extinction and other forms of weakening. The effectiveness of the parental environment in weakening the child's repertoire depends upon the availability of concurrent audiences for the child's behavior. In general, the 2-year-old child is limited to the home and comes into increasing contact with other environments as he grows older, perhaps reaching a maximum at school age. The presence of an older sibling might appear to preempt the possibility of a sufficient degree of isolation to account for an aversive behavioral deficit. A sibling could provide an alternative to the parent as a reinforcing environment. The behavioral or functional influence of a sibling would depend on the amount and nature of interaction between the children. For example, an older child might possibly completely avoid the younger one or tend to have the same patterns of reaction as the parent. In many cases, the older sibling has playmates outside the home to the complete exclusion of the younger child. The older sibling, in many circumstances, punishes as well as extinguishes the younger child for any attempted participation in his play. There are very few facts as to the exact nature of the interactions in most cases.

The parent as the sole maintainer of the child's behavior is perhaps even more likely when the child is raised in a rural or isolated community, and perhaps with one of the parents largely absent. The above analysis suggests that a survey of severely autistic children would, in general, show them to be first-born children; or, if other siblings were available, they would have provided little interaction with the child. It also suggests that the child would be raised in a house physically or socially isolated from other families or children such that there were no alternative social environments that could provide reinforcement for the child's behavior. When the child was exposed to both parents, it would be expected that both parents were consistent in their nonreinforcement of the child's performances.

AVERSIVE CONTROL AND PUNISHMENT

It has been possible to describe conditions which might produce major behavioral deficits without dealing with punishment or aversive control. A similar account might present a functional analysis of how performance deficits might occur as a result of aversive control. Many writers have already described some of these factors by extending general principles of aversive control to human behavior (7, 8, 11). For the purposes of the analysis presented in this paper, I should like to restrict the discussion of aversive control to its relation to positive reinforcement. Much of human aversive control is carried out by discontinuing or withdrawing reinforcement (3, 10). For example, a frown or criticism may function as an aversive stimulus because these are occasions on which reinforcements are less likely to occur. Even when corporal punishment is given, it is not clear as to whether the resulting effect on the child's behavior is due to a slap or to the lower inclination of a punishing parent to reinforce. Most parents who spank a child will be indisposed to act favorably toward the child for some period of time subsequently. As a result, one major by-product of frequent punishment may be a larger order of interference with the child's normal repertoire along the lines of the positive reinforcement deficits described above.

The obvious effectiveness of punishment in some kinds of human control appears to contradict experimental findings with animals which show punishment to have only a temporary effect on behavior (1, 2, 9). The role of positive reinforcement factors helps resolve the dilemma. The effectiveness of punishment depends on how strongly the punished behavior is maintained by positive reinforcement. The apparent effectiveness of punishment in the control of children may occur when weak repertoires are punished or when the punishment indirectly produces extinction. Most animal experiments using electric shock as an aversive stimulus have used strongly maintained positively reinforced operant behavior as the base-line performance to be punished. The aversive control might be more effective when the performances to be punished are less strongly maintained.

CONCLUSION

As might be expected from the relatively low frequency of infantile autism, the combination of circumstances hypothesized above would occur only rarely. The above hypothesis provides a framework for investigating the circumstances surrounding the development of the autistic child. All of the variables that might weaken the behavior of a child are directly or potentially observable. The data required are the actual parental and child performances and their specific effects on each other, rather than global statements such as dependency, hostility, or socialization. Not all of the factors responsible for a child's performance may be present currently. Using retrospective accounts, however, makes it difficult to determine the actual correspondence between the verbal statements of the parent and their actual practices in raising the child. The alternatives are, first, an objective assessment of the child's repertoire in a wide enough range of environments so as to allow an assessment of the nature of the environmental control of the child's current behavior; and, second, actual home observations of the specific social consequences of the child's performances early in the development of the disease.

The same kind of functional analysis can be made for the performance of the adult psychotic although the specific deficits observed in autistic children and their manner of occurrence may not be relevant. In particular, the analysis of the adult's behavior would be more concerned with the factors which weaken behavior already in the repertoire rather than the development of new repertoires as with the analysis of the autistic child's behavior. Maintaining already-established behavior is more at issue in the adult than the initial development of a performance as in the case of the child (3).

REFERENCES

1. Azrin, N.H. Punishment and recovery during fixed-ratio performance. *J. exp. anal. Behav.*, 1959, 2, 301-305.
2. Estes, W.K. An experimental study of punishment. *Psychol. Monogr.*, 1944, 57, No. 3 (Whole No. 623).
3. Ferster, C.B. Reinforcement and punishment in the control of human behavior by social agencies. *Psychiat. Res. Repts. 10,* 1958, 12, 101-118.
4. Ferster, C.B., & DeMyer, M.K. A method for the experimental analysis of the behavior of autistic children. *Amer. J. Orthopsychiat.*, in press (1962).
5. Ferster, C.B., & DeMyer, M.K. The development of performances in autistic children in an automatically controlled environment. *J. chronic Dis.*, 1961, 13, 312-345.
6. Kanner, L. Early infantile autism. *J. Pediat.*, 1944, 25, 211-217.
7. Miller, N.E., & Dollard, S. *Personality and psychotherapy.* McGraw-Hill, 1950.
8. Rotter, Julian. *Social learning and clinical psychology.* Prentice-Hall, 1954.
9. Skinner, B.F. *The behavior of organisms.* Appleton-Century-Crofts, 1938.
10. Skinner, B.F. *Science and human behavior.* Macmillan, 1953.
11. Skinner, B.F. Some contributions of an experimental analysis of behavior to psychology as a whole. *Amer. Psychologist*, 1953, 8, 69-78.
12. Skinner, B.F. *Verbal behavior.* Appleton-Century-Crofts, 1957.

COMMENTARY by Gary W. LaVigna

This controversial paper earns its place in a book of classic readings on autism because it represents the first significant publication that viewed the problem of autism within a behavioral framework. As such, it signalled the unparalleled contribution the field of applied behavior analysis would make to the treatment of this devastating disorder. In fact, aside from the dated view of autism as a childhood form of schizophrenia, this paper, along with the two he published with DeMyer (1961 and 1962), provide a careful analysis from which we can still learn. For example, Ferster's view of behavior problems serving a social interactive, communicative function has yet to receive the full attention it deserves from behavioral researchers. The controversy surrounding this paper concerns Ferster's attempt to understand how environmental factors could have caused the characteristic behavioral deficits and excesses associated with autism. Some have interpreted Ferster's statement of the possible parental role in this behavioral process as another version of the theme of parental causation of autism itself, a view more typically attributed to the psychogenic school of thought. Fortunately, Ferster's work with DeMyer lends clarification to his opinion, which appears to have been that independent of their parents, children with autism *are* fundamentally "different" from children considered normal, at least in the rate they learn and, to an undetermined extent, at least in their basic constitutional and physiological make-up. This view has since, of course, been substantiated. In reading this article today's young researcher may yet find fertile ground for future investigations.

REFERENCES

Ferster, C. B., & DeMyer, M. K. The development of performances in autistic children in an automatically controlled environment. *Journal of Chronic Disorders,* 1961, *13,* 312-345.

Ferster, C. B., & DeMyer, M. K. A method for the experimental analysis of the behavior of autistic children. *American Journal of Orthopsychiatry,* 1962, *32*(1), 89-98. Reprinted in Bijou, S. W., & Baer, D. M. (Eds.), *Child Development: Readings in Experimental Analysis.* New York: Appleton-Century-Crofts, 1967.

4

Studies on 5-Hydroxyindole Metabolism in Autistic and Other Mentally Retarded Children

RICHARD J. SCHAIN
DANIEL X. FREEDMAN

There is little doubt that the biogenic indolealkylamine, 5-hydroxytryptamine (5-HT, serotonin), plays some role in neuronal function in the brain, although the nature of this role is still unclear. Various theories have been developed regarding the mechanism of action of 5-HT, and of its possible relationships to mental disease,[1-3] but there has been no widespread acceptance of any of these hypotheses.[4-6]

The search for evidence of abnormal 5-hydroxyindole metabolism in schizophrenia has been vigorously pursued for the past 6 years without producing any clear-cut evidence of such an abnormality. Most investigators now agree that there is no evidence of a generalized disturbance in the metabolism of 5-HT in schizophrenia.[7-9] Recently, Pare and colleagues[10-11] have published data on blood 5-HT and urine 5-hydroxyindole acetic acid (5-HIAA) levels in mentally defective children. They initially reported that persons with phenylketonuria have low blood 5-HT levels; they have subsequently confirmed this observation and have also provided data indicating that other defectives have abnormally *high* 5-HT levels.[12] These workers are presently attempting to make meaningful correlations between specific diagnoses and elevations of blood 5-HT.[13]

Sutton and Read[14] have reported evidence of the decreased ability of one child with infantile autism to convert tryptophan to urinary indole acids. On the other hand, Shaw and co-workers[15] have administered 3 Gm. of L-tryptophan to schizophrenic and nonschizophrenic children. They found no difference in the increase of 5-HIAA excreted by either group.

One of us had been engaged in the clinical characterization of a group of 50 children with the diagnosis of infantile autism who had been committed to the Southbury Training School.[16] Blood levels of 5-HT determined on a

Reprinted with permission from the *Journal of Pediatrics* 58 (March 1961): 315–320.

This investigation was supported in part by Traineeship NBI-EP BT-507 from the National Institute of Neurological Diseases and Blindness and by United States Public Health Service Grant M-1204, National Institute of Mental Health.

few of these children were considerably higher than those heretofore obtained in our laboratory from a heterogeneous group of patients (excluding those with carcinoid syndrome). On the basis of these findings and in view of the suggestive data previously mentioned, it was decided to study some aspects of 5-hydroxyindole metabolism in these children.

Experimental Methods

Blood 5-hydroxytryptamine and urine 5-hydroxyindoleacetic acid were determined on 23 children whose clinical diagnosis was infantile autism. Their ages at the time of the investigation were 6 to 18 years with an average age of 10.8 years. The criteria for establishing this diagnosis and the clinical data are discussed elsewhere.[16] Briefly, these criteria can be outlined as follows:

1. Evidence of a severe personality disorder characterized by preoccupation with self and unrelatedness to people in the environment.
2. Presence of a history indicating the onset of this disorder during the first 2 years of life as manifested by the failure to develop the expected patterns of relationships to parents or other guardians.
3. Absence of a history of serious motor retardation which is associated with most forms of gross brain defect.

Other defective children roughly matched for age and sex were also studied. Multiple determinations were made on all children.

Tryptophan loads consisting of 1 Gm. of L-tryptophan daily for 3 days were given to some of the children. This amount was estimated to·be approximately twice the average daily intake of L-tryptophan in the diet. Blood 5-HT was estimated before and after this procedure.

Blood samples were uniformly drawn in the early afternoon and kept frozen for periods of up to 24 hours until extractions were performed. The clotted blood was homogenized and 5-HT extracted with 20 volumes of acetone.[17] The acetone extract was dried in vacuo and kept at $-18°$ C. prior to assay. Estimations of 5-HT were performed by bioassay on the heart of the clam *(Venus mercenaria)* or on the rat uterus in estrus. The recovery of added 5-HT from whole blood has been a difficult problem for many investigators concerned with the absolute significance of their data. Hardisty and Stacey[20] reported an average of 30 per cent recovery of 5-HT from human red blood cell suspensions with the use of 95 per cent acetone for extraction. Kärki and Paasonen[21] mention a consistent 35 to 45 per cent recovery from rat blood with 95 per cent acetone. Cargill-Thompson and associates[22] have obtained extremely variable recoveries using buffered butanol as the solvent (39 to 96 per cent; average 56 per cent). They report much better recoveries in certain animal species (cat, dog, goat, ox, and rat). Humans, along with guinea pigs, rabbits, sheep, and pigs, yielded poor recoveries. Correale[23] has stated that 80 per cent acetone gives much better recoveries of 5-HT from brain than 95 per cent acetone. Recently, evidence has been presented indicating that free 5-HT in blood is rapidly oxidized by oxyhemoglobin in vitro.[24] It has been noted that the addition of EDTA[25] or ascorbic acid[26] improves the recovery of added 5-HT from blood.

We also have found great variability in the recovery of added 5-HT from blood (25 to 75 per cent). 2-Mercaptoethanol, a potent reducing and chelating agent, in 0.0001 to 0.01 molar concentration in blood did not improve recovery. The use of 80 per cent acetone in two experiments gave the same recovery as 95 per cent acetone. Ascorbic acid interfered with the function of the test object and could not be used. EDTA was not tested in these experiments.

In spite of these poor recovery rates based on addition of exogenous 5-HT, we have found that the levels of endogenous 5-HT measured in blood have not shown the same extreme degree of fluctuation. Twelve determinations done at different times on one normal adult gave a mean 5-HT level of 0.090 gamma per cubic centimeter with a standard deviation of 0.018. The multiple determinations on children with mean blood 5-HT values over 0.200 gamma per cubic centimeter showed consistent elevations. Waalkes,[25] using EDTA with a fluorimetric method (which always yields higher numerical values than those derived by bioassay), has reported average blood 5-HT levels of 0.130 gamma per cubic centimeter with a range of 0.090 to 0.180.

We believe 5-HT artificially added to blood is more susceptible to destruction than endogenous 5-HT. Although we do not regard our data as indicative of absolute levels of blood 5-HT (our data are probably lower), we have found our results to be more consistent than the highly variable recovery data would indicate.

Urine samples were collected in the morning, and 5-HIAA assayed according to the method of McFarlane and co-workers.[18] The ether used for extraction was washed with 2 per cent ferrous sulfate, and acidified distilled water was used throughout. Urinary creatinine was determined by use of the Jaffé reaction,[19] and results were expressed as micrograms of 5-HIAA per milligram of creatinine.

Results

The patients studied can be roughly divided into three groups:

A. Mildly retarded children with intelligence quotients of 60 to 80 obtained with the revised Stanford-Binet test, e.g., familial "subcultural" defective children, high-grade Mongols.

B. Children with the diagnosis of infantile autism who function on a severely retarded level. These children are usually not trainable and are segregated with other low-grade retarded children. Features of this syndrome are described in detail in the study of Schain and Yannet.[16]

C. Severely retarded children without a diagnosis of autism (I.Q. under 20), e.g., congenital cerebral defect, diffuse encephalopathy. These children live in the same cottages as the autistic children.

The mildly retarded children (Group A) had blood 5-HT levels averaging 0.072 gamma per cubic centimeter with a range of 0.042 to 0.156, which is similar to the normal values obtained in this laboratory. The autistic children had average blood 5-HT levels of 0.141 gamma per cubic centimeter with a range of 0.033 to 0.540. When the data from this group are studied individually, it can be seen that certain of the autistic children have particularly high levels (Fig. 1). Six of the 23 autistic children had mean levels over 0.200 gamma per cubic centimeter, a figure which is well above the range of normal for our laboratory (0.02 to 0.15 gamma per cubic centimeter). One of these cases had 11 determinations ranging from 0.210 to 0.540 gamma per cubic centimeter with an average of 0.342 gamma per cubic centimeter. Values for adult chronic schizophrenic patients are within the normal range.

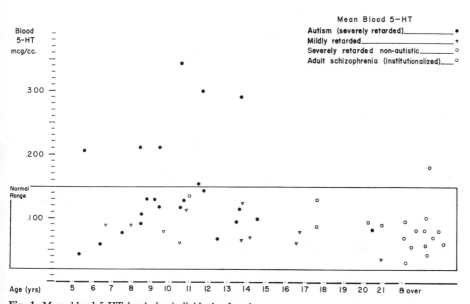

Fig. 1. Mean blood 5-HT levels for individuals of each group.

A small group of nonautistic low-grade defective children were also studied. Their average blood concentration of 5-HT was 0.128 gamma per cubic centimeter. This is not significantly different from the autistic group as a whole, although one of the individual values of one child was over 0.200 gamma per cubic centimeter (Table I).

Tryptophan loads were given to 4 autistic children. This was followed by no consistent change in blood 5-HT.

Some children were receiving phenobarbital, Dilantin, or chlorpromazine at the time of this study. None of these drugs seemed to be associated with any changes in blood 5-HT. Three children on reserpine had no detectable blood 5-HT. This is in accord with the well-known observation of Brodie,[1] subsequently confirmed by many investigators, that reserpine depletes most tissues of 5-HT.[27] Consequently, patients on reserpine were not included in this study.

Urine 5-HIAA values were distinctly higher in the autistic group than in the mildly retarded group when expressed as gamma per milligram of creatinine (Table II). The absolute amount of 5-HIAA per milliliter of urine was similar in both groups; creatinine values, however, were much lower in the autistic children, indicating greater dilution of urine. None of the 5-HIAA

Table I. Comparison of blood serotonin levels in autistic and nonautistic retarded children, t-tests (mean difference)*

	Normal control	*Autistic*	*Non-autistic low-grade*	*Middle and high-grade*
Normal control	—	4.04‡	3.02†	1.00
Autistic		—	1.00	3.57†
Nonautistic low-grade			—	2.67†
Middle and high-grade				—
Mean blood 5-HT	.065	.141	.128	.072
Standard deviation	.017	.078	.045	.033
Number	4	23	7	12

*t's calculated by the Cochran-Cox method of testing the significance of the hypothesis of equality of means, weighted in terms of their respective variance.

†Significant at or beyond the 5 per cent level of confidence.

‡Significant at or beyond the 1 per cent level of confidence.

Table II. Comparison of urinary 5-HIAA and blood 5-HT in 12 autistic and 6 mildly retarded children

Autistic children		Mildly retarded children	
5-HIAA (gamma/ mg. of creatinine)	Mean blood 5-HT (gamma/ ml.)	5-HIAA (gamma/ mg. of creatinine)	Mean blood 5-HT (gamma/ ml.)
8.3	.148	2.2	.068
10.0	.343	1.6	.126
0.9	.079	0.8	.080
2.2	.202	2.1	.073
5.7	.125	1.8	.077
5.2	.283	1.2	—
4.5	.097		
8.6	.119		
6.6	.290		
4.4	.065		
8.4	.202		
4.8	.205		
Mean 5.9	.141	1.6	.072

results can be considered as significantly abnormal. The 24-hour excretion of 5-HIAA probably falls in most cases within the generally accepted values of 2 to 9 milligrams.

Discussion

These results confirm the impressions of Pare, Sandler, and Stacey[12] that mentally defective children have elevated levels of 5-HT in blood. Our data would indicate that the elevations tend to be present only in some of the more severely defective children. Consistent unusual elevations of blood 5-HT were found only in children with the diagnosis of autism, although the mean blood 5-HT level of other severely retarded children was higher than that of the mildly retarded group. Sandler[13] has apparently found high levels in various clinical groups; details of this study are not available as yet. We have analyzed the histories of the 6 autistic children with the highest blood 5-HT levels and have been unable to find any specific correlative signs. The presenting symptomatology of these 6 children did not differ from that of the other autistic children who had normal 5-HT levels. The only feature that appeared at all noteworthy was the absence of seizure disorders in any of the 6 autistic children with elevated 5-HT. The frequent occurrence of seizures in autistic children was one of the most significant results of the clinical study of these children.[16] Only 1 of the 6 children with elevated blood 5-HT had had even one questionable seizure.

It is difficult to decide at this time whether the elevation of blood 5-HT is meaningfully related to the behavioral disorders of these children. Diet and exercise are two important factors that may affect the levels of metabolites in body fluids. The lack of an effect of a 3-day tryptophan load on blood 5-HT in our studies would seem to indicate that this parameter is not immediately influenced by dietary changes. We do not know the effect of prolonged dietary variations on blood levels of 5-HT. Sandler has not been able to correlate physical activity with 5-hydroxyindole production in mentally defective spastic persons. We have not studied the factor of exercise. In general, the autistic children are much less active than those in the mildly retarded group.

It may be that as biochemical factors are more intensively studied in children presenting with mental retardation, the same kind of problem will appear that is well known in investigations of adult schizophrenia, viz., the increased variability in many biochemical and physiologic parameters in this disease. This feature has provided frequent false leads in the search for a specific metabolic defeat associated with schizophrenia.[8] The reasons for this variability are not readily apparent, but its repeated occurrence has made most investigators of the biology of schizophrenia highly skeptical about the significance of changes in specific biochemical parameters. It is quite possible that the same kind of variability will be noted in mentally defective children. We do not know, as yet, if the abnormally elevated blood concentrations of 5-HT in some of these children will be an example of this phenomenon. The elevations do occur consistently within individuals, and the possibility of identifying a specific subgroup by the measurement of 5-HT remains to be explored.

Severely retarded children receiving custodial care in even the best of institutions live radically different lives as compared to their normal peers. It is difficult to assess the effect of these differences on parameters measured. It would seem worth while in investigating developmental disorders to pursue studies in younger children who are still living at home. This would have the advantage of investigating problems at a time before the secondary effects of prolonged institutionalization unduly complicate the picture. We are presently hoping to survey blood 5-HT levels of children with major developmental lags who appear in the clinics during the first few years of life.

Summary

Aspects of 5-hydroxyindole metabolism have been studied in some groups of mentally retarded children. Six of 23 children with the diagnosis of infantile autism had consistently elevated blood 5-HT levels. The mean level of blood 5-HT of other severely retarded children was higher than that of the mildly retarded group. No specific clinical signs could be found in these children.

REFERENCES

1. Brodie, B.B., and Shore, P.A.: A Concept for a Role of Serotonin and Norepinephrine as Chemical Mediators in the Brain, *Ann. New York Acad. Sc.* 66: 631, 1956.
2. Wooley, D.W.: Serotonin in Mental Disorders, in The Brain and Human Behavior, *A. Res. Nerv. & Ment. Dis. Proc.* 36: 381, 1958.
3. Marrazzi, A.S.: The Action of Psychotogens and a Neurophysiological Theory of Hallucination, *Am. J. Psychiat.* 116: 911, 1960.
4. Stacey, R.S.: 5-Hydroxytryptamine and Other Pharmacologically Active Substances in the Central Nervous System, *Acta physiol. et. pharmacol. neerl.* 8: 222, 1959.
5. Giarman, N.J.: Neurohumors in the Brain, *Yale J. Biol & Med.* 32: 73, 1959.
6. Crossland, J.: Chemical Transmission in the Central Nervous System, *J. Pharm. & Pharmacol.* 12: 1, 1960.
7. Feldstein, A., Hoagland, H., and Freeman, H.: Blood and Urinary Serotonin and 5-HIAA Levels in Schizophrenic Subjects and Normal Subjects. *J. Nerv. & Ment. Dis.* 129: 62, 1959.
8. Kety, S.S.: Biochemical Theories of Schizophrenia, *Science* 129: 1590, 1959.
9. Sjoerdsma, A.: Serotonin, *New England J. Med.* 261: 231, 1959.
10. Pare, C.M.B., Sandler, M., and Stacey, R.S.: 5-Hydroxytryptamine Deficiency in Phenylketonuria. *Lancet* 1: 551, 1957.
11. Pare, C.M.B., Sandler, M., and Stacey, R.S.: Decreased 5-Hydroxytryptophan Decarboxylase Activity in Phenylketonuria, *Lancet* 2: 1099, 1958.
12. Pare, C.M.B., Sandler, M., and Stacey, R.S.: The Relationship Between Decreased 5-Hydroxyindole Metabolism and Mental Defect in Phenylketonuria, *Arch. Dis. Childhood* 34: 422, 1959.
13. Sandler, M.: Personal communication, 1960.
14. Sutton, H.E., and Read, J.H.: Abnormal Amino Acid Metabolism in a Case Suggesting Autism, *A.M.A. J. Dis. Child.* 96: 23, 1958.
15. Shaw, C.R., Lucas, J., and Rabinovitch, R.D.: Metabolic Studies in Childhood Schizophrenia, *Arch. Gen Psychiat.* 1: 366, 1959.
16. Schain, R.J., and Yannet, H.: Infantile Autism; an Analysis of 50 Cases and a Consideration of Certain Relevant Neurophysiologic Concepts. *J. Pediat.* 57: 560, 1960.
17. Amin, A.H., Crawford, T.B.B., and Gaddum, J.H.: Distribution of Substance P and 5-Hydroxytryptamine in the Central Nervous System of the Dog, *J. Physiol.* 126: 603, 1954.
18. McFarlane, P.S., Dalgliesh, C.E., Button, R.W., Lennox, B., Nyhus, L.M., and Smith, A.N.: Endocrine Aspects of Argentaffinoma, *Scottish M.J.* 1: 148, 1956.

19. Hawk, P.B., Oser, B.C., and Summerson, W.H.: *Practical Physiological Chemistry*, New York, 1954, Blakiston Company, p. 889.
20. Hardisty, R.M., and Stacey, R.S.: 5-Hydroxytryptamine Concentration in Normal Human Platelets, *J. Physiol.* 130: 711, 1955.
21. Kärki, N.T., and Paasonen, M.K.: The Influence of Iproniazid and Raunescine on the Penetration of 5-Hydroxytryptamine Into Brain Tissue From the Circulation, *Acta pharmacol. et toxicol.* 16: 20, 1959.
22. Cargill-Thompson, E.C., Hardwick, D.C., and Wiseman, J.M.: Estimation of 5-Hydroxytryptamine in Blood and Serum, *J. Physiol.* 140: 10P, 1958.
23. Correale, P.: The Occurrence and Distribution of 5-Hydroxytryptamine in the Central Nervous System of Vertebrates, *J. Neurochem.* 1: 22, 1956.
24. Blum, J.J., and Ling, N.S.: Oxidation of Serotonin and 5-Hydroxyindoles During Denaturation of Oxyhemoglobin, *J. Biochem.* 73: 530, 1959.
25. Waalkes, T.P.: The Determination of Serotonin (5-Hydroxytryptamine) in Human Blood, *J. Lab & Clin. Med.* 53: 824, 1959.
26. Davis, R.B.: The Concentration of Serotonin in Normal Human-Serum as Determined by an Improved Method, *J. Lab & Clin. Med.* 54: 344, 1959.
27. Freedman, D.X., and Benton, A.J.: Persisting Effects of Reserpine in Man, *New England J. Med.* (in press).

COMMENTARY by Arthur Yuwiler

The discovery that the vasoconstrictor substance from the gut, serotonin, also occurred in the brain; that it was structurally similar to the psychotominetics psilocybin, bufotenine, dimethyltryptamine, and LSD-25; and that its metabolism, storage, or actions were affected by the psychotherapeutic agents, reserpine, chlorpromazine, and the monoamine oxidase inhibitors had the effect of galvanizing interest in the possibility that serotonin was involved in abnormal human behavior. The possibility still exists but the problem then, as now, was how to test it. Since abnormal behavior implies an abnormality in brain function, it would be logical to look for associated abnormalities in the serotonin system of the brain. But a syndrome like autism can only be defined in man and the living human brain is, and should be, inviolate. With the direct approach precluded, investigators resorted to the indirect one of searching for abnormalities in serotonin concentration and metabolism in those tissues that are clinically accessible, primarily blood and urine, in the hope that a fundamental defect in the serotonin system would be reflected in both peripheral and central serotonin even though they differ in aspects of serotonin metabolism and physiology.

The paper by Schain and Freedman exemplifies this indirect approach. Several things are notable. First, their finding of an increased incidence of hyperserotonemia among autistics has now been confirmed by a number of laboratories even though the precise criteria used to define the syndrome has varied somewhat over time and between authors, and even though the early bioassay system used by Schain and Freedman to quantitate serotonin has now been supplanted by more specific fluorometric, radioenzymatic, and chromatographic procedures. Second, blood serotonin is almost wholly confined to platelets and it is still unclear if the hyperserotonemia in autism reflects a disturbance in platelet physiology or in serotonin metabolism. Third, the incidence of hyperserotonemia is neither confined to autistics nor present in all autistics. Only 20–40% of autistics show hyperserotonemia (as compared to about 1% of "normals") and its incidence in mental retardates (exclusive of those with Down's syndrome or the aminoacidemias like phenylketonuria who have abnormally low blood serotonin) is similar to that found among autistics. Finally, while blood serotonin concentrations in adult humans are sufficiently consistent over time to suggest it is a trait-dependent rather than state-dependent marker, data from other species call this into question.

Nonetheless, the paper by Schain and Freedman has stimulated much of the current biochemical studies on autism. The questions it raised, however, have yet to be answered.

5

The Etiology of Infantile Autism: The Problem of Biological versus Psychological Causation

BERNARD RIMLAND

The literature on autism contains many papers in which it is asserted rather than suggested that psychogenic factors play a major part in the etiology of the disease. Indeed, a substantial proportion of these papers carry no indication that biological factors may play even a minor part in the disease.

This chapter will be devoted to a detailed consideration of the problem of the etiology of infantile autism. The present writer disagrees with Eisenberg and Kanner's assertion that "Arguments that counterpose 'hereditary' versus 'environmental' as antithetical terms are fundamentally in error. Operationally defined, they are interpenetrating concepts" (1956, p. 563). That heredity and environment are "interpenetrating" cannot be denied. But the conclusion that their interpenetration precludes analysis does not follow. Complex problems require that we *increase*, not diminish our analytical efforts, if we are to have hope of solving the problems confronting us (Burt, 1958; Cattell, 1960).

There are several reasons for drawing close attention to the consideration of etiology in infantile autism.

1. The welfare of individual autistic children and their families hinges closely upon the problem of specific etiology, as van Krevelen has amply demonstrated (e.g., 1958, 1960). If the disease is psychogenic, the causative factors need to be identified. On the other hand, if autism is determined solely by organic factors, there is no need for the parents of these children to suffer the shame, guilt, inconvenience, financial expense, and marital discord which so often accompany the assumption of psychogenic etiology. (For examples of this, see May, 1958; Peck, Rabinovitch, and Cramer, 1949. Oppenheim, 1961; and Stuart, 1960 are also germane.)

2. So long as the practitioners who actually deal with autistic children

Adapted with permission of the author from *Infantile Autism,* Bernard P. Rimland (New York: Appleton-Century-Crofts, 1964), 39-66. This book has been reprinted by the author and is available from him. To save space here, he has deleted portions of the chapter including the reference list.

feel satisfied that the disease is largely or entirely psychogenic, biologically trained research workers will feel disinclined to concentrate their efforts on the problem. It should be added at this point, in all frankness, that while the purpose of the review which follows was to investigate the specific etiology of early infantile autism, the issue is a broad one and a good deal of the material covered relates closely to the problem of causation of childhood behavioral disorders in general. The results of this work were surprising to the present writer and discordant with his previous beliefs. They may also be so to the reader. It is largely because of the large discrepancy between research findings and the remainder of the published literature that such detailed consideration is given the problem of etiology in this chapter.

Failing to find any adequate formulations of many of the inexplicit assumptions on both sides of the issue, the writer has attempted to articulate these, in his belief that a good part of the unique function of the psychologist is to try to articulate what seems ineffable.[1] No doubt much of this formulation will be challenged, and additional points will need to be added to those listed. We can do no better on this issue than to refer to Bacon's assertion that truth is more likely to emerge from error than from confusion.

The Arguments for Psychogenesis of Infantile Autism

The case for psychogenesis of autism would appear to rest on the following arguments and assumptions:

1. No consistent physical or neurological abnormalities have been found in autistic children which could account for their condition.
2. Many autistic children have been raised by parents apparently deficient in emotional responsiveness, which could have pathogenic effects on the child.
3. Certain children raised in hospitals or orphanages where maternal contact was sparse have been reported to show an undue frequency of emotional difficulties.
4. The behaviors of the child—his indifference or aggressiveness, his refusal to speak (or "elective mutism"), his apparent withdrawal from the outside world—are interpreted as signs of "punishment" or "retaliation" against the parents.
5. Certain incidents in the life of the autistic child appear to be pathogenic and permit the disorder to be traced to them.

---

[1] There are certain arguments, however, that defy our attempt to reformulate them in any testable way: "I believe that the child who shows autistic behavior has been traumatized in the early months of life since he symbolizes to the mother so definitely the hated sibling" (Ribble, in discussion of Despert, 1951, p. 350).

6. Psychotherapy or otherwise placing the child in a kind and under-standing environment has beneficial effects.
7. The high incidence of first-born and only children suggests that pa-rental attitudes may be causative.

Let us consider these points in turn:

1. *The absence of signs of organic impairment.* While the presence of phys-ical symptoms is ordinarily regarded as conclusive proof of organicity, as in mongolism or phenylketonuria, the absence of such symptoms cannot be considered indicative of functional determination. This is so because "Neu-rological science thus far has been quite unable to furnish an adequate de-scription of the neural processes involved in even the very simplest forms of mental activity" (Sperry, 1952, p. 292). Eisenberg and Kanner have said of autism, "neurologic investigations of the integrity of central function re-main as yet in their clinical infancy and a negative result with current meth-ods cannot be regarded as a conclusive demonstration of the lack of central nervous system pathology" (1956, p. 560).

There are numerous cases in the literature where even gross brain dis-ease which eventually caused the death of the child had escaped intensive repeated neurological examination and was found only post-mortem (e.g., Ross, 1959). Heller's disease and phenylketonuria were both considered "functional" childhood psychoses until their organicity was determined (Benda, 1960; Kanner, 1949). Nevertheless writers such as Despert (1947) and Bettelheim (1959b) have written that the possibility of organic damage in the cases they cite was "ruled out" by physical and neurological exami-nation. May (1958) and van Krevelen (1960) have cited cases in which the possibility of organic damage was ruled out without even examining the children.

2. *Parental personalities.* Eisenberg and Kanner are among the many writers who subscribe to the notion that parental behavior is a factor in pro-ducing autism in the child, although, unlike many others, they are careful to qualify their position:

> It is difficult to escape the conclusion that this emotional configuration in the home plays a dynamic role in the genesis of autism. But it seems to us equally clear that this factor, while important in the development of the syndrome, is not sufficient in itself to result in its appearance. There ap-pears to be some way in which the children are different from the begin-ning of their extrauterine existence (1956, p. 563).

Kanner and Eisenberg do not specify *why* it is hard to escape the con-clusion. They cite no supporting evidence. Plausible as the hypothesis may seem, there is no reason for accepting it in favor of competing hypotheses.

This is a clear case of subscription to the fallacies that *post hoc ergo propter hoc,* and that "correlation implies causation."

How can one say that both the child's and the parent's behavior are not related consequences of the same genetic factors? Granted, it may be *possible* that psychological factors contribute, but it has not yet been demonstrated that they do, to even a minor extent; nor has it been demonstrated that any familial environment, no matter how favorable, would have prevented the emergence of the disease.

Perhaps it is in relation to the "parental personalities" that reference should be made to the recent work on "affectional systems" in monkeys (e.g., Harlow and Harlow, 1962a; 1962b). These points appear to be most relevant: The behavior of infant monkeys is relatively independent of the personality (or response repertoire) of the mother. Infant monkeys raised by cruel, rejecting, unsympathetic and indifferent mothers reacted not by "autistic" withdrawal but by persistent and vigorous attempts to obtain the mother's attention. Even infant monkeys brutally beaten by mothers attempting to discourage contact showed no signs of maladjustment. Infant monkeys raised only with inanimate cloth-covered "mother surrogate" effigies showed no signs of maladjustment until adulthood, when their sexual functioning was found to be severely impaired.

The only way in which any of Harlow's infant monkeys could be treated to cause them to simulate "autistic" withdrawal was through total social deprivation for extended periods. But even twenty minutes a day of contact with other infant monkeys seemed sufficient to produce normal development.

With regard to the problem of *absence* of maternal contact, as differentiated from the nature of those with whom the subject is in contact, there is ample evidence at the human infant level.

3. *Maternal deprivation and hospitalism.* The works of Goldfarb, Spitz, Ribble, Bowlby, and others on the syndrome of "hospitalism" or "maternal deprivation" are frequently cited as analogous evidence that early infantile autism is psychogenic. The analogy with autism is a poor one, since the symptoms which characterize these infants do not resemble autism, as noted by Eisenberg and Kanner (1956), Keeler (1957), and others, and do not begin to approach autism in severity. Additionally, the special circumstances relating to the sampling and physical environment of these maternally-deprived infants make them a poor basis on which to construct a psychogenic theory.

In 1951 Bowlby wrote that there was "no room for doubt . . . the prolonged deprivation of the young child of maternal care may have grave and far-reaching effects on his character" (p. 46).

Despite Bowlby's assurance on the matter, psychologists have been very skeptical and critical of the hypothesis. The hospitalism studies have been subjected to criticisms of the gravest nature. Pinneau (1955), who earlier pointed out severe deficiencies in the work of Ribble in this area, has also called attention to what appear to be disqualifying errors in the work of Spitz and Fischer. Pinneau notes, to cite one example, that of the 59-point drop in the Development Quotient Spitz reported for his "maternally deprived" group of infants, 55 points were lost *prior* to the time at which most of the children were separated from their mothers! Stevenson (1957) has observed that the screened-off cribs Spitz has described may have resulted in the infants being deprived of adequate physical sensory stimulation, rather than of maternal affection.

With regard to Fischer's study of hospitalism, Pinneau noted that Fischer selected for study, at a home for unwed mothers, those infants with IQs under 90. Then, after observing their behavior in much the same way as is done in *arriving* at IQ scores for infants, she concluded that their poor performance was due to "hospitalism"!

Pasamanick and Knobloch have recently noted that the maternal deprivation hypothesis may turn out to be simply another instance of misdirection by the *"post hoc ergo propter hoc"* fallacy:

> Further, since a large number of children exhibit no significant difficulties after hospitalization, we must consider the possibility that it may be largely those children having some brain injury, with a consequent lowering of thresholds to stress, who are affected by hospitalization during infancy (1961, p. 87).

They also note that a number of the hospitalized children included in Goldfarb's study were grossly defective or brain-damaged and suggest that this was why the children remained hospitalized rather than being placed in foster homes. This could readily account for the so-called "symptoms of hospitalism."

Faced with a rising tide of evidence disconfirming the maternal deprivation hypothesis from both his own subsequent work and the reports of other investigators, *Bowlby reversed his stand.* In 1956 he concluded that some of the workers who drew attention to the dangers of deprivation, including himself, had tended to "overstate their case." "In particular, statements implying that children who experience institutionalization . . . early in life *commonly* develop psychopathic or affectionless characters are incorrect" (Bowlby, Ainsworth, Boston, and Rosenbluth, 1956, p. 242). He noted that "only a small minority develop those very severe disabilities of personality which first drew attention to the pathogenic nature of the experiences" (p. 240).

Inasmuch as a small minority of *any* group of infants will show personality disorders, especially if they had been selected because of adverse circumstances surrounding pregnancy or birth, it does not seem that the proponents of the psychogenic view may look to the maternal deprivation hypothesis for support.

Actually, our attention to the maternal deprivation studies results not from their actual relevance to the problem of etiology of autism, but only from their having frequently been cited as analogous evidence favoring psychogenesis of autism. In actuality, the case history materials supplied by Kanner and others show very little reason for believing the children were neglected. Kanner observes that very few of the children were at least overtly rejected (1949). The mothers "were anxious to do a good job," and they performed like "overconscientious gasoline station attendants." The mother of Donald T., Kanner's first case of autism, for instance, tried to help her son by spending "all her time developing ways of keeping him at play with her" (1943, p. 217). The verbal behavior of the children is also suggestive of a good deal of contact with adults.

Bowlby's original statement that there was "no room for doubt" about the adverse effects of maternal deprivation is very similar to a statement made with equal assurance more than half a century before by the noted Langdon Down (Down, 1887, p. 89)—except that Down was sure that the *opposite* conclusion was correct—maternal emotionality causes idiocy!

4. *Child's behavior as suggestive of etiology.* Many writers consider th child's hostility or indifference to his parents as evidence that the parents ˙ ˍe guilty of causing the disease. Noting that many autistic children were exposed to parental "coldness, obsessiveness, and a mechanical type of attention," Kanner observed that the children's "withdrawal seems to be an act of turning away from such a situation" (1949, p. 425). Elsewhere Kanner uses the term "retaliation." Others also have written in this vein.

It would seem more reasonable to regard the child's actions as *symptoms,* not as indications of etiology. In the case of the adult who insists that he is being persecuted by the Communists, the F.B.I. or by little green men from Mars, one does not take his statements at face value but only as an indication that he is ill. Unless there is a reason for believing otherwise, it seems best also to regard the autistic child's symptoms solely as symptoms, even if "the patient acts as if his mother is the source of his psychotic fears, and he attributes the potentiality of the same responses onto other humans" (Weiland & Rudnik, 1961, p. 552).

Does "elective mutism" really represent the child's *refusal* to speak? One cannot conclude this unless one is willing also to conclude that adult aphasics who are virtually mute until an emergency arises (Brian, 1960, p. 180) also had "elected" their disability.

Is the fact that many autistic children ignore humans and are interested solely in objects indicative only of some sort of "willful" rejection of mankind, or can this result from organic pathology? Nielsen (1951, p. 185 ff.) describes a fully conscious patient who, after occipital lobe damage, was apparently blind with respect to "animate" objects, including the surgeon's fingers, a doll, and her own artificial teeth, but had no trouble in perceiving non-living objects. Another patient could perceive *only* animate objects after occipital and temporal lobe damage. Autos and mountains were not recognized, but flowers and an animal grazing near the autos were readily identified.

Nor does it seem to be widely appreciated that brain pathology can influence affection as well as cognition. Those who believe that an autistic child's behavior represents withdrawal from his parents should also believe, it would seem, that the sweet disposition and loving nature that is almost universal among Mongoloid children stems from the pleasure the parents of these children must experience on viewing their offsprings' malady.

5. *Pathogenic incidents.* Many discussions of etiology of autism refer to certain specific events which are said to be traumatic to the child and thus causative of his disorder. The birth of a sibling, a stay in the hospital, the absence of one or both parents are examples of the incidents cited.

That such incidents can produce disorder has not been demonstrated. Many infants and children suffer exceedingly traumatic lives with no evidence of autism or other disorder, while some autistic children have backgrounds free of at least obvious pathogenic incidents.

Renaud and Estess (1961) have published a study of the "pathogenic incidents of childhood" as derived from intensive interviews with 100 above-average young men (military officers). Renaud and Estess discovered, to their considerable surprise, that there was just as much material of a supposedly "pathogenic" sort in the childhoods of these men as would have been expected in a clinically abnormal group. The implications of this finding are clear.

Stevenson (1957) explored the literature relevant to the proposition that personality is "plastic" in infancy and came to the conclusion that "if the experiences of childhood importantly influence the later personality, we should expect to find some correlation between such experiences and the later occurrence of mental disorders. In fact, no such correlations have ever been shown" (p. 153).

6. *Psychotherapy.* Indirect support for the psychogenic hypothesis is often inferred by writers who point to the improvement wrought through psychotherapy or by other means of modifying the child's social environment. As Kuten and Kuten (1958) point out, such evidence for psychogenesis typically comes from writers who cite only very small numbers of cases. Control groups are not used.

Kanner has discussed the results of psychotherapy for the first 42 of his cases with infantile autism, and has observed that: "29 did not get anywhere," including some who had "what is regarded as good psychotherapy." On the other hand, the 13 who recovered sufficiently to go to school "are children who have not had anything that is regarded as good psychotherapy or as psychotherapy at all" (1954b, p. 471).

It might be argued that Kanner's group is too small to provide conclusive evidence that psychotherapy is ineffective in infantile autism, but taken in aggregate, the evidence relating to the efficacy of psychotherapy in childhood (or adulthood, for that matter) is generally quite negative and thus lends no support for the psychogenic hypothesis (Astin, 1961; Eysenck, 1961; Hood-Williams, 1960; Levitt, 1957, 1960).

It should be noted that the force of this argument does not rest on the adequacy of the studies of the utility of psychotherapy, since it is not asserted here that the efficacy of psychotherapy has been disproven, but only that it is unproven.

In the absence of evidence that psychotherapy produces improvement in excess of base rate, writers who cite improvement in individual case studies as evidence that autism was psychogenically induced are taking an untenable position. This untenability is underlined by the further point that even if psychotherapy *could* be proven to be effective, it could not be taken as indicative of psychogenic causation any more than the efficacy of oxygen in heart failure proves that the heart failure was caused by a lack of oxygen.

7. *Birth order.* The high frequency of the first-born with autism is sometimes taken as evidence of psychogenicity. There are two obvious objections to this line of reasoning. First, there are many children with autism who have both younger and older normal siblings. Second, a high frequency of first-borns is also consistent with organic causation, since there are many physical disorders associated with primogeniture, especially in male infants. Pyloric stenosis, a digestive system disorder which becomes evident shortly after birth, has long been known to occur primarily in first-born male infants.

Among specific conditions having "mental" involvement, mongolism and anencephaly are reported to be disproportionately represented among the first-born (MacMahon and Sowa, 1961; Stott, 1960) as is epilepsy (Colver and Kerridge, 1962).

Studies which have attempted to relate birth order to parental behaviors and attitudes have far more often produced negative than positive results (Lasko, 1954). In view of these considerations, one can hardly argue that birth order data support psychogenesis in autism.

I have discussed the various factors that I have been able to identify or isolate as having been offered as evidence that early infantile autism is psychogenic in origin. In no case can it be argued that the psychogenic aspect of the factor is more potent than the biological aspect, nor, in fact that the psychogenic factor can be shown to have *any* potency at all in the causation of infantile autism. We are not saying that psychogenesis is an imaginary influence; we are merely saying that there appears to be no evidence that it is anything but imaginary.

It may appear that the case for psychogenic hypothesis has been understated. Yet the present writer is only one of many who have made a search for evidence and come to the conclusion that evidence is lacking. Stevenson (1957) has observed that:

> The literature of psychiatry abounds in articles asserting causal connections between the early experiences of life (especially training practices) and the later personality. The far fewer articles reporting objective studies of such relationships fail to support the assertions made (p. 152).

In addition to his own well-documented review, Stevenson cites three previous review articles. More recently, Hebb (1958b) and O'Connor and Franks (1961) have come to similar conclusions after reviewing the relevant research.

The Case for Biological Causation

Unlike the hypothesis that autism is psychogenically determined, there are a number of points of information which support the hypothesis that autism may result from a rare recessive trait, or be otherwise determined by biological factors. Kanner, in his various publications (especially with Eisenberg, 1956), has cited the first five points listed below as evidence against the psychogenic view. The remaining points have been identified by the present writer or others who have concerned themselves with this problem.

1. Some clearly autistic children are born of parents who do not fit the autistic parent personality pattern.
2. Parents who do fit the description of the supposedly pathogenic parent almost invariably have normal, non-autistic children.
3. With very few exceptions, the siblings of autistic children are normal.
4. Autistic children are behaviorally unusual "from the moment of birth."
5. There is a consistent ratio of three or four boys to one girl.
6. Virtually all cases of twins reported in the literature have been identical, with both twins afflicted.
7. Autism can occur or be closely simulated in children with known organic brain damage.
8. The symptomatology is highly unique and specific.
9. There is an absence of gradations of infantile autism which would create "blends" from normal to severely afflicted.

1. *Parents who do not fit the pattern.* "Some 10 per cent" of parents of autistic children are warm and friendly and do not fit the personality stereotype reported so commonly for these parents (Eisenberg and Kanner, 1956). This point is also made in Eisenberg's article on the fathers of autistic children (1957). Keeler (1957) reports autism in a child adopted by warm and loving foster parents within ten days after birth. No mention of the natural parents was made. The parents of van Krevelen's case are specifically described as warm and affectionate, as are those mentioned by Chapman (1957), Schachter (1958), and others. The father described by van Krevelen does fit the "intelligent-driving personality" stereotype, however. While the physician and lawyer described by Polan and Spencer fit Kanner's pattern of intelligence and seriousness, the mothers did not. One was a "warm and gentle person" and the other was an "intelligent and efficient individual of normal emotional spontaneity." There are numerous other examples in the literature.

2. *"Autistic-type parents" with only normal children.* Many parents who do fit the personality stereotype exactly and therefore might be expected to have autistic children if the psychogenic theory were correct, instead have perfectly normal children, as noted by Kanner and others (see especially Kanner, 1957), and as very probably can be verified from the reader's own experience.

The experiment conducted by Dennis (1941) on the development of infants under conditions of "minimum social stimulation" seems relevant to this point. Dennis raised fraternal twins from the end of their first month to the end of the fourteenth month by attending strictly to their material needs only. He gave no encouragement or approval of any sort. Despite this systematic attempt to serve the child in what must undoubtedly be a more detached and indifferent manner than Kanner's parents could have achieved inadvertently, Dennis concluded from his experiment that if the child's well-being was assured, his behavioral development would take its normal course.

Dennis' experimental treatment of children is certainly not to be recommended as routine. No one would willfully run the risk of injuring the child's sense of security, or any other aspect of his personality, even though the available research suggests that adverse effects, if there are any, may be too small to be detected by presently available methods. One is cautious even with a gun one has good reason to believe is not loaded. But Dennis' work certainly does suggest that the case for psychogenically induced adverse effect has been greatly overstated.

3. *Siblings are normal.* Kanner and a number of others have noted that many normal children are raised as siblings to an autistic child. It is a rarity to have more than one autistic child in a family, except in the case of twins. Of 131 siblings to Kanner's first 100 autistic children, only three could be

regarded as probably autistic. Seven others showed evidence of emotional disturbance (Kanner and Lesser, 1958). This is a small proportion, especially when it is considered that these siblings were probably under closer scrutiny than normal and under severe stress as well (Creak & Ini, 1960). Rattner & Chapman (1959) have reported an autistic child in the middle of a series of eleven normal children. Polan & Spencer (1959) reported two normal siblings for each of the three cases of autism they described. Phillips (1957) reports all siblings of his cases to be normal. Both siblings of van Krevelen's (1952) case were normal, as were also both siblings of the girl described by Poppella (1955) and by Sutton & Read (1958). Similar instances are plentiful.

4. *Autistic children unusual from the "moment of birth."* Kanner has often referred to autism as "inborn" and "innate." Even the psychogenically oriented writers do not appear to question this point. It is difficult to understand why pathology severe enough to be recognized so early is not considered severe enough to cause later behavior disorder without the compounding of it with psychogenic factors which have yet to be demonstated to be other than fictional.

5. *The high sex ratio.* That males are less viable than females from conception to old age is common knowledge. The attrition of males before birth is even greater than after. Males are susceptible not only to a great variety of sex-linked hereditary diseases, but also to later acquired infections and other adverse somatic conditions. Thus the occurrence of autism in three or four times as many boys as girls is consistent with the known greater vulnerability of males to organic damage. It would be hard to find a convincing psychogenically oriented explanation for this ratio, especially since boys tend to be more often welcome in our culture than girls, and especially so as first children.

6. *Twins with autism.* One of the strongest lines of evidence against psychogenic etiology of autism has come to light only in recent years. Keeler (1957, 1958) sems to have been the first to call attention to the incidence of autism in identical twins. He did not tabulate the cases of such twins known to him, but in a later personal communication to the writer (1960) Keeler referred to a set of identical twins in addition to the blind twins he had mentioned in 1958. Keeler pointed out that there were no known cases where only one of monozygotic twins was afflicted, nor where both of dizygotic twins exhibited autism. His 1957 paper refers to a set of fraternal twins where only one child was afflicted.

Kallman, Barrera, and Metzger (1940) also reported blind identical twins. These twin boys, congenitally blind with microphthalmia, showed motility patterns "strikingly similar" to those displayed by the blind children Keeler (1958) described as manifesting the syndrome of infantile autism. The verbal behavior of the twins described by Kallman et al. would also warrant their being considered as possibly autistic. They could, for example, repeat anything said to them, but showed little comprehension of the meaning. This is very typical of autism.

Chapman (1957), in reporting a case of identical autistic twin girls, also raised the issue of twinness, and called attention to the cases of identical twin boys reported earlier by Sherwin (1953) and Bakwin (1954).

Polan and Spencer (1959) reported still another set of identical twin boys. They referred to this set as the fifth known to them.

The present writer, who had independently become impressed with the frequency with which twins with autism were being reported, has attempted to tabulate all cases of probable autism in the literature involving multiple births. The list follows:

1. Kallman, et al. (1940) identical twin boys.
2. Sherwin (1953) reported identical twin boys.
3. Bakwin (1954), another case of identical twin boys.
4. Eisenberg & Kanner (1956) described a set of twin boys, one of whom died in infancy before it could be discovered whether he was autistic like his brother. No reference to zygosity.
5. Keeler's (1957) fraternals, only one being autistic.
6. Chapman's (1957) identical twin girls.
7. Lehman, Haber & Lesser (1957) reported identical twin boys.
8. Keeler's (1958) blind twins. Presumably, from Keeler's report, these are boys.
9. Polan & Spencer's (1959) identical boys.
10. Bruch (1959) referred to twin Negro boys with autism. In personal communication to the writer (1961), she identified these as identical twins.
11. & 12. Chapman (1960) reported knowledge of two additional sets of identical twins.
13. Keeler (1960, personal communication) one other set of identical autistic twins. Sex not stated.
14. Ward & Hoddinott (1962) described a set of concordant fraternal twin girls who were "typical examples of early infantile autism."

This compilation raises the number of known multiple births involving at least one case of autism to fourteen. Known cases involving twins reported to be monozygotic is thus raised from five (Polan and Spencer) to a new total of eleven (excluding sets numbered 4, 5, and 14). Each of these sets is concordant (i.e., both twins similar with regard to affliction-nonaffliction). Kallman's set, reported prior to Kanner's delineation of autism, is the only one not so classified by the original author.

The identical autistic twin sons described by May (1958) in his book, *A*

Physician Looks at Psychiatry, have been included in the above list.

Kanner has made no specific mention of twins in his group, with the exception of set 4, above, referred to incidentally in illustrating a point concerning the twin's parents. No mention was made of this or other multiple births in either Kanner's 1954a listing nor Kanner & Lesser's 1958 detailed listing of the birth conditions and order of the first 100 cases, nor in the listing of the mental status of his autistic patients' siblings. (Correspondence has determined that the twins referred to by Eisenberg and Kanner were contained in separate sacs. Although dichorionic twins are usually fraternal, zygosity cannot be stated with certainty in this case.)

In general, only one of three twin births is monozygotic, so one would expect to find 22 cases of dizygotic twins for each eleven monozygotic cases reported. Even allowing for errors in establishing zygosity, this appears to represent a strong overloading of monozygotic twins with autism, as opposed to dizygotic. Additionally, since only about one birth in 285 is of monozygotic twins (Allen & Kallman, 1955), there would also appear to be an overloading of such twins in the absolute total number of cases of reported autism. Including the fewer than 150 cases Kanner has reported (1958b), there are probably no more than about 200 bona-fide cases of autism referred to in the literature, not nearly enough to support finding eleven twin cases, let alone eleven monozygotic twin cases, on a chance-only basis.

Luxenburger (cited by Rosanoff, Handy, & Plesset, 1937) has demonstrated that one may expect to find a disproportionately high incidence of monozygotic and concordant twins in twin studies based on search of the literature. The degree of overloading reported by Luxenburger (which was considerably greater than that reported by Rosanoff et al.) would not begin to account for the high incidence of twins with autism reported above. Autism seems especially likely to be reported, seen in single births, not only because its manifestations are so striking, but because the parents frequently take the child from clinic to clinic in the hope of finding someone who understands the disease (May, 1958; Rothenberg, 1960). Additionally, the early age of onset of autism, before irrevocable separation of twins is likely to take place, as well as an increased understanding of the importance of twin data to etiological research, make it appear unlikely that Luxenburger-type bias is an overriding or even important variable in the present instance.

The finding of at least eleven sets of monozygotic twins, all concordant, seems highly significant in terms of the biological etiology of the disease. Kety (1959) has remarked that Chapman's (1957) reference to three sets of identical autistic twins was suggestive. Ward & Hoddinott (1962), in describing their set of concordant fraternal twins, observe that for infantile autism, "to appear in twins, particularly fraternal twins, is an event beyond statistical probability" (p. 191). That one of the two cases of reported fraternal twins is discordant (set Number 5) serves only to enhance this finding. (The twin who died at five months in set 4, probably fraternal, was reported only as "more responsive" than his definitely autistic brother.)

The high susceptibility of twins to neurological defects does not adequately account for the high incidence of *identical* twins with autism. While the ratio of *defective* monozygotic to dizygotic twins is lower than the one-to-one ratio found for nondefective twins (Rosanoff, et al., 1937; Allen & Kallman, 1955), the preponderance of monozygotic twins with autism is none the less striking.

Kallman's data (1953, 1956), widely accepted by the scientific community as providing the clearest evidence of the strong hereditary component in mental disorder (e.g., Knobloch & Pasamanick, 1961; Rosenthal, 1961; Meehl, 1962), show 9 per cent of non-twin siblings to be schizophrenic when one sibling is affected, 15 per cent of dizygotic twins to be concordant if one twin is schizophrenic and 86 per cent concordance if one of monozygotic twins is schizophrenic. When schizophrenia was diagnosed at an early age, between five and eleven years, only 71 per cent of identical twins were concordant. Judged by these standards, the genetic element in autism would appear to be unusually strong.

It is of interest that in several cases of identical twins stricken with autism, the degree of affliction, while invariably severe, is not quite identical (Sherwin; Lehman et al.; Polan & Spencer). This suggests that while genetic factors may predispose toward autism post-conceptional factors could be operative (see Burt, 1958; and Price, cited by Rosenthal, 1961, for references on prenatal identical twin differences).

7. *Austim caused or simulated by known organic disease.* A line of evidence which suggests the organicity of early infantile autism stems from the many cases in which the symptomatology may be traceable to a postencephalitic condition or other form of central nervous system injury. Some of these cases are those described by Anthony (1958), Rattner and Chapman (1959), Frankl (1943; see Sarason & Gladwin, 1958, p. 216); Ross (1959), Sutton and Read (1958), van Krevelen (1960), and possibly the cases of Anastasi and Levce (1960), Kallman et al. (1940), Poppella (1955), Schacter (1958), and Vaillant (1962). The appearance of the syndrome in children given oxygen shortly after birth is also germane to this point.

These cases do not prove autism is *invariably* organic, but they at least indicate that the symptoms *can* be caused by organic agents. It is not believed that there is parallel evidence supporting the view that the symptoms of autism *can* be produced by sociopsychological factors.

8. *Uniqueness and specificity.* The high degree of interindividual similarity in the symptomatology of autism would seem to identify it as biological. As May (personal communication, 1959) has observed:

> I do not know any one of these children who did not have the rocking and banging of head . . . the particular interest in some machinery . . . the

typical speech patterns . . . This identity of symptomatology pleads strongly for a well-localized lesion . . . .

Much experimental research in genetics has shown that what appears to be a complicated and varied syndrome can be traced back to a single initial fault in development (Roberts, 1959). It should be noted, however, that while a single abnormal gene may produce a remarkable variety of symptoms *within* an individual, the syndrome from individual to individual tends to be highly uniform, especially when it is a recessive gene that is at fault. In phenylketonuria, for example, there is a characteristic diversity of problems: motor involvement, seizures, eye and skin pigmentation effects, and skin sensitivity in addition to mental retardation. Yet each victim exhibits the *same* syndrome, because there is but a single recessive underlying defect.

That gene effects within the nervous system can be highly specific does not seem to be widely appreciated. C. E. Keeler (1940) has described an interesting study in which the exact locus of the inherited nerve lesion causing "waltzing" in guinea pigs was located. It was then possible to duplicate the inherited waltzing tendency by making carefully placed surgical lesions in normal animals. Keeler observed that, "So steady is the hand of genetics and so accurate in repeating these operations that you may have a thousand identically operated specimens to study quite as readily as one" (p. 97).

Moorhead, Mellman, and Wenar (1961) have recently made a related finding in humans by tracing a family defect involving speech and mental retardation to a heritable chromosome translocation.

It may be of interest to note the many similarities in the symptoms of autism with those described for "brain-injured" children by Lewis, Strauss, and Lehtinen (1951); and by Strauss and Lehtinen in other publications. The similarities between autism and the symptomatology of brain injury should not permit the confusion of autism with the general brain-injured syndrome. The more general term "brain-injured" encompasses many cases whose lesions apparently include involvement of the brain areas in which profound but localized dysfunction, usually in genetically sensitive infants, may produce true early infantile autism.

Kanner has observed that some autisticlike symptoms are found in brain-injured (and innately retarded) children (1958b). However, the "brain-injured" in this sense will rarely show the *composite* of symptoms which defines autism. In Kanner's words, "The symptom combination in most instances warrants an unequivocal diagnostic formulation" (1951, p. 23).

9. *The absence of "blends."* If autism were a reaction to environmental factors we would expect it to exhibit not only the diversity of manifestations from case to case as a consequence of situational differences (above), but, in addition, the usual gradation in intensity, depending on the adverseness of the environment. Environmental adversity would ordinarily be assumed to

follow a continuous, probably Gaussian distribution, rather than a dichotomous one. While there is variation in severity and in prognosis, the degree of variation does not account for the large void between autism and normal behavior. There have been few serious attempts to deny the existence of this void.

Psychogenesis as an Inadequate and Pernicious Hypothesis

Perhaps it should be made explicit at this point that the writer does not presume to have shown that autism is biologically determined and that the psycho-social environment plays no part in its etiology. What the writer *does* assert is that a careful review of the evidence has revealed no support for the psychogenic point of view. The evidence is instead highly consistent with expectation based on organic pathology.

Our finding with regard to autism coincides with the more general view formulated by the participants of a recent conference on the causes of mental disorder (Milbank Memorial Fund, 1961):

> There seems to be no clearly demonstrated instance of either a cultural or social factor being known to be a predisposing factor in mental illness. . . . The absence of clear-cut evidence does not show that the hypothesis is incorrect but only that it has not been demonstrated even once (p. 379).

Neither Creak and Ini (1960), who intensively studied 100 sets of parents of psychotic children, nor Peck, Rabinovitch, and Cramer (1949), who studied 50 sets of parents, were able to find evidence of a psychogenic nature. What they did find was a good deal of suffering brought on by the child's behavior and a good deal of intense (and we might add unnecessary) feelings of guilt.

It is probably too early to suggest that psychogenesis as a *hypothesis* no longer be considered. ("Hypothesis" is used advisedly, because there appears to be too little evidence to support use of the term "theory.") No avenue for learning all that we can about the etiology of mental disorder should be unexplored. The detailed explication in this chapter of the arguments concerning the etiology of autism was in part intended to facilitate, and perhaps even to provoke, some long-overdue, rational, and articulate consideration of the problem, even at the expense of jointly provoking a measure of articulate and inarticulate wrath.

It is not questioned that distinction should be maintained between a disproven and an unproven hypothesis, but neither should there be a failure to distinguish between an unproven and an uninvestigated hypothesis. The psychogenic hypothesis is by no means uninvestigated.

Whatever may be the merit in being patient with psychogenesis as a hypothesis, there is much less in being patient with it as an assumed force-in-fact. The all too common practice of blatantly assuming that psychogenic etiology *can* exist or *does* exist in any individual case or in any given class of disorders is not only unwarranted but actively pernicious.

It is perhaps permissible for writers such as Weiland & Rudnik (1961) to "postulate" that "the expectation of murderous attack or of symbiotic engulfment by a psychotogenic mother results in a failure to progress beyond autism and in panicky attempts to escape from symbiosis into autism" (p. 552), especially when they add (in a footnote) "We do not believe this has been demonstrated conclusively. . . ." It is something else again when the implications of this view are translated into action, and psychogenic causation is assumed to be a reality rather than merely a hypothetical possibility.

Ross (1959) presents an interesting and instructive case history of an autistic girl whose mother had been held to be responsible for her child's plight because the mother's affection was considered "intellectualized and objectified." Only when the child died did the fact of extensive brain damage become evident. Intensive neurological examination had failed to reveal the difficulty before the child's death, which interrupted intensive psychotherapy. It was fortunate for the mother that the brain damage was of a sort that present-day techniques could disclose, else she would to this day be held responsible for her daughter's death.

Consider the case of "Jonny" (Rothenberg, 1960). After stating that Jonny, at 1½ pounds, was one of the smallest premature babies ever born in the United States to survive, and after noting that 3½ months spent in an incubator under high oxygen tension and heat lamps had turned the infant's hair orange and his skin chocolate brown, the author attributed his later severe behavior disturbance to lack of mothering while being incubated. "Cure" was said to be greatly facilitated by suddenly confronting Jonny with a model of the incubator—a personification of the mother who supplies only material needs and no nourishment of the ego. The possibility that organic brain damage might have resulted from such adverse physical conditions was apparently not seriously considered, yet it had been known for some time that a high concentration of oxygen is able to cause destruction of nerve tissue in infants.

Bettelheim (1959a) interpreted the psychosis of "Joey, the Mechanical Boy" as a reaction to his mother's hostility when the evidence was also quite consistent with hereditary determination, since the mother appeared to be severely mentally disturbed herself. (See also the reply by May to this article.) In this case, as in Rothenberg's, the appeal of the psychogenic concept appeared to preclude consideration of concealed organic defect. Somehow the adherents of the psychogenic hypothesis tend to overlook the possibility that the complex and little understood cerebrum could be structurally or chemically impaired.

In another case Bettelheim (1959b) found emotional isolation to have caused the psychosis of a girl who had been conceived, born, and raised by her Jewish parents in World War II in a small hole beneath a farm building in Poland. The hole was too cramped to permit an adult to stretch out. German soldiers were nearby (sometimes firing shots into the building) so that the mother had to smother the infant's cries. Not considered by Bettelheim was research showing the adverse effects on the offspring's emotionality of prenatal stress in the mother (e.g., Thompson, 1957), nor of sensory deprivation in the child.

It should not be thought, however, that workers in this field are universal in accepting environmental determination. Some writers have been frank in rejecting the psychogenic hypothesis. Keeler (1957), for example, has said, "I certainly do not adhere to the opinion put forth by some that infantile autism stems from a very specific type of pathological parent-child (especially mother-child) relationship." Anthony (1958) notes, "I do not think that traumata which sometimes seem to precipitate a psychosis in childhood are anything greater than normal developmental hazards (sibling birth, etc.). It is the predisposition that makes them vulnerable." Chapman (1960) also believes the role of the psycho-social environment has been overestimated: "the degree of interpersonal pathology between parents and child rarely seems sufficient to explain the catastrophic interpersonal disorder of the child." Goldstein (1959), in his very illuminating discussion of autism, has pointed out clearly the gratuitousness of assuming psychogenesis as an etiologic factor in the disease.

In discussing the obvious prejudice against the hereditary viewpoint, Nolan Lewis (1954) points out, "It would seem that most of the prejudice against genetic inheritance stems from a feeling in the realm of wish fulfillment, based on the idea that acceptance of genetic factors would create an attitude of therapeutic hopelessness." Williams (1956) cites this point among others in his attempt to penetrate the prejudice against heredity. He notes that hopelessness is by no means justified by the evidence, and cites the ready correction of the effects of diabetes, phenylketonuria, and hypothydroidism as examples.

It should not be necessary to ask for recognition of the role played by genetic factors among persons trained in scientific thinking, but Williams has seen the need to do so:

> We therefore make a plea for an unprejudiced facing of the facts of heredity. We urge that such facts be accepted with as great readiness as any others. This plea seems necessary in view of the attitude which we have

repeatedly noted, namely, that of willingness to arrive at "environmental-
istic" conclusions on the basis of slender evidence while rejecting points
of view which would emphasize the role of heredity, even though the
weight of the evidence, viewed without prejudice, appears overwhelming
(p. 16).

When dark-haired and dark-eyed parents produce a dark-complexioned
child, we all are quick to agree, "Mendel was right!" But when introverted
parents produce a child who similarly shows little interest in socialization,
the refrain inexplicably changes to "Aha, Freud was right!"

In arguing for more critical use of the diagnosis of autism, Kanner says:

> The misuse of the diagnosis of autism has played havoc with the comfort
> and finances of many parents of retarded children, who were made to feel
> that their attitudes and practices were primarily responsible for their off-
> spring's problems, were made to submit themselves and the child to
> lengthy, expensive, and futile therapy, and were pauperized and misera-
> ble to the time the true state of affairs was brought to light (1958a, p. 111).

Kanner's appeal for the protection of the parents of children misdiagnosed as autistic is certainly to be commended, but what of the parents of
accurately diagnosed cases? In view of the present status of research on the
efficacy of psychotherapy, and of the fact that the evidence for psychogenic
etiology of autism is not, to use Kanner's term, "unequivocal" (1958a), it
would seem that the parents of properly diagnosed autistic children might
also be deferred from being made "pauperized and miserable," for the time
being.

In a court of law it is impermissible to convict a person solely on evidence consistent with the hypothesis that he is guilty—the evidence must also
be inconsistent with the hypothesis that he is innocent. This simple point of
justice has been neglected, consistently, by those who deal with families
having children afflicted with autism, and the damage and torment this
practice has wrought upon parents whose lives and hopes have already been
shattered by their child's illness is not easy to imagine nor pleasant to con-
template. To add a heavy burden of shame and guilt to the distress of people whose hopes, social life, finances, well-being, and feelings of worth have
been all but destroyed seems heartless and inconsiderate in the extreme. Yet
it is done, as May (1958), Oppenheim (1961), Stuart (1960), and van Krevelen (1960) amply illustrate.

In view of these pernicious implications and the absence of scientific evidence, the wide acceptance of the psychogenic view is difficult to understand. A partial explanation for the prevalence of this view may be found in
Kanner's unguarded admission that he is perplexed by the fact that the great

majority of the parents of autistic children have been able to rear non-autistic children, while other parents who fit the parental typology perfectly, raised children who responded aggressively rather than by withdrawal: "the existence of these exceptions is puzzling. . . . It is not easy to account for this difference of reaction" (1949, p. 426). The same "puzzling" inconsistency is clearly present in other childhood mental disorders, such as mongolism, Tay-Sachs disease, and phenylketonuria, and is readily explained in terms of recessive inheritance.

Despert provides another example of a child psychiatrist who does not apply what she must certainly know of genetics to her thoughts on etiology:

> It is sometimes argued that these mothers had other children who were normal or relatively normal, but it must be remembered that a mother, biogenetically identical for all her children, may nevertheless psychogenetically differ widely from one child to the other (1951, p. 345).

"Biogenetically identical"—100 years after Mendel!

Perhaps we are painting too dark a picture. There are signs of a growing recognition that the failure to find support for psychogenesis may possibly lie in the inadequacy of the concept rather than in a lack of resourcefulness among its investigators. Despert, whose 1951 view was quoted immediately above and who in 1947 wrote of cases in which neurological disorders had been "ruled out" by examination, has written in 1958 that the possibility of finding constitutional factors in infantile autism was particularly strong (Despert & Sherwin, 1958). Ekstein, Bryant, and Friedman (1958) show a willingness to question "our prejudiced, one-sided consideration of etiological factors" (p. 653); and Bettelheim, for years a leader of the psychogenic school, was recently willing to "reserve judgment" about what causes autism, although he is still "pretty sure" that psychogenic factors "contribute" (1959b, p. 463).

Szurek, who started in 1946 "to test the hypothesis that the etiology of psychotic disorders of childhood are entirely psychogenic" (Boatman & Szurek, 1960; p. 389) takes a much weaker stand today in stating that certain "facts" "seem to lend weight to the possibility that psychogenic factors are at least important" (p. 430). (The reader may wish to see these "facts.")

To the present writer these indications of a retreat from the psychogenic hypothesis, like Bowlby's previously cited disavowal of the maternal deprivation hypothesis, represent a timely and welcome willingness to let conviction be subordinated to evidence. The history of science proves this to be the first step toward progress.

COMMENTARY by David L. Holmes

Rimland's chapter, "The Etiology of Infantile Autism: The Problem of Biological Versus Psychological Causation," in his book, *Infantile Autism* (1964), is probably the most significant statement on the psychogenic versus biogenic causation of autism. This treatise set the tone for more critical analysis of the etiology of autism, resulting in reduced credibility of the psychogenic theory of causation, and increased interest in viewing autism from a biogenic vantage point. Although criticized at the time of its publication as the subjective ravings of a distraught father, Rimland held to his posture that the evidence is lacking for a psychogenic causation of autism, and that there is far more support for the hypothesis that autism is a biologically determined disorder.

Rimland's hypothesis of a biogenic causation of autism has held the test of time, and, in fact, is the foundation upon which research into the biophysical nature of autism has followed from the late 1960s through the present. Further, Rimland's chapter was also successful in stimulating work with parents, viewing them not as causative agents in autism, but rather, as potential members of a helping team to reduce the effects of the syndrome on the child.

It is this reviewer's opinion that Rimland's work, "The Etiology of Infantile Autism: The Problem of Biological Versus Psychological Causation," is one of the most significant treatises in the development of current research trends into the etiology of autism, as well as being an effective training source for parents who act as cotherapists in the treatment of their children with autism.

6

Epidemiology of Autistic Conditions in Young Children

VICTOR LOTTER

PART 1. PREVALENCE

Introduction

In spite of an increasingly voluminous literature about "psychotic" disturbances in children, etiology remains obscure (Kanner, 1957), the lack of agreed behavioural criteria reflects the nosological uncertainties and prevents the useful comparison of findings (Despert and Sherwin, 1958; Tramer, 1962; Rimland, 1964) and prevalence is unknown (Bellak, 1958).

Adequate behavioural descriptions are rare. The most detailed are still those made for "early infantile autism" by Kanner over 20 years ago, and in a number of papers since then (e.g., Kanner, 1943, 1946, 1951, 1954; Eisenberg and Kanner, 1956; Kanner and Lesser, 1958). In addition, detailed descriptions of certain aspects of behaviour were made by Norman (1954, 1955) for a group of 25 "schizophrenic" children. In 1936, Earl described in some detail the behaviour of a small group with what he called "the catatonic psychosis of idiocy," while three children with Heller's syndrome (classified as a "schizophrenic" reaction) were reported in detail by Yakovlev et al. (1948). Since the present survey was completed, two detailed behavioural studies of "psychotic" children (Rutter, 1966) and "schizophrenic" children (Wolff and Chess, 1964) have been reported.

The differences between the behaviour manifested in "psychotic" children who become ill during early childhood and those whose illness is of later onset have usually been attributed to the immaturity of the former (Potter, 1933; Kanner, 1957). However, from Kanner's study of "infantile autism" much other evidence may be derived to suggest that the disturbances in the

Reprinted with permission from *Social Psychiatry* 1 (1966): 124–137. Copyright 1966, Springer-Verlag.

This survey was supported by a grant from the Health Department of the Middlesex County Council, England.

earliest years might warrant separate investigation. In a growing number of cases he has reported a great preponderance of middle-class parents and has consistently failed to find a raised incidence of serious mental illness in the families (Kanner, 1954; Kanner and Lesser, 1958). Although Kanner has emphasized the importance of distinguishing his cases on the basis of onset and behaviour from other cases of "childhood schizophrenia," the confirmation of some of his findings in large groups of young "psychotic" children by workers who did not make this separation (Creak and Ini, 1960; Rutter, 1964) suggests that "psychotic" disturbances in young children may be different in important respects from those occurring later. These findings are in marked contrast to those reported by Kallman and Roth (1956), whose group included only older children, and Bender (e.g., Bender and Grugett, 1956), whose groups usually included older children, although at any age her diagnoses may not be comparable with the other groups quoted (Kanner, 1958; Despert and Sherwin, 1958; Bruch, 1959).

All the groups on which the reported findings were based were, however, clinic or hospital admissions; referral bias cannot therefore be excluded as a possible explanation for some of the results (Creak and Ini, 1960; Bender, 1959).

"Psychotic" conditions in children have traditionally been reported as rare. A few early reports suggested the numbers might be greater than had long been thought because of the confusion of some cases with "feeblemindedness" (Potter, 1933; Despert, 1938). In more recent years diagnoses have been much more readily made although with greatly varying frequency. Thus of 7,000 children aged 2 to 12 years admitted over a period of 20 years to the Bellevue Hospital in New York, 850 (12%) were given the diagnosis "prepubertal schizophrenia"; however, only 105 were under 6 years old (Bender, 1958). Kanner (1958) reported having seen 150 cases of "infantile autism" in 19 years, i.e., about 8 cases a year, while Creak (1963) saw 100 cases of the "schizophrenic syndrome of childhood" in about 18 years, i.e., about 6 cases a year. Fontes (1958) in Lisbon reported 4 cases of "infantile schizophrenia" in 8,300 clinic admissions. In a population survey, Jaeggi (1964) found 50 cases of "infantile psychosis" among the 50–60,000 persons under 20 years old in Geneva, a rate of between 8 and 9 per 10,000, while Rutter (1966) discovered 4 "psychotic" children in the whole 8 to 10 year old population of Aberdeen, Scotland; a rate of 4.4 per 10,000.

Estimates of prevalence range therefore from about 4 to nearly 10 per 10,000 but the criteria used to select cases are seldom stated in such a way as to permit useful comparison. No study aimed at discovering prevalence according to stated criteria in a sufficiently large, general population has been reported.

In spite of the very considerable difficulties of definition and case finding in psychiatric disorders (Reid, 1960) and in children's behaviour disturbances in particular (Shepherd and Cooper, 1964), epidemiological methods may produce data which indicate fruitful directions for further research (Pasamanick, 1954), as well as providing useful administrative information (Tizard, 1963) and permitting the examination of clinical hypotheses. A cross-sectional survey was therefore made in the County of Middlesex during 1963/64 with the main aim of estimating the age-specific prevalence of behaviourally defined "autistic conditions" in young children. In this paper the survey is described and rates of prevalence as well as certain characteristics of the identified children are reported. The results of the analysis of further descriptive and epidemiological data will be the subject of a second report.

Method

1. *A note on terminology.* Because of the probable heterogeneity of the disorders included amongst young children classified generally as "psychotic" or "schizophrenic" (Kanner, 1957), and because an impairment in their relations with people, sometimes called "autism," appears to be the most commonly reported symptom, the adjective "autistic" was used in this study as a convenient descriptive label. It is important to note that the term was *not* intended to refer only to Kanner's syndrome of "infantile autism," and in what follows is used without qualification to refer to all children who met the behavioural criteria used to select cases. References to "autistic behaviour" are to be similarly interpreted.

2. *Definition of a case.* The most comprehensive behavioural criteria for the recognition of young autistic children are those of Creak et al. (1961). Based mainly on the descriptions of Kanner and Norman, they include the principal aspects of behaviour emphasized also by other writers, such as a marked unevenness in intellectual retardation (Scheerer et al., 1945), bizarre motility (Earl, 1936; Yakovlev et al., 1948), gross anxiety reactions and "clinging" social behaviour (Mahler et al., 1949), and unusual sensory sensitivities (Bergman and Escalona, 1949). The criteria were used in a version prepared by Wing (1966) which aimed to clarify the behavioural descriptions and avoid interpretation of behaviours.

The number of behaviour categories was reduced by subsuming into other categories the behaviour referred to as indicating an "unawareness of self-identity" and, in the final selection of cases, performance on tests replaced the subjective assessment of "islets of ability." Only behaviour which had been persistently present for a prolonged period was accepted, so that transient episodes and normal developmental patterns simulating the disorders were excluded. The presence of ascertained brain damage or other handicaps did not automatically exclude a case. No one aspect or combination of behaviours was considered to be of special significance, except that emphasis was placed upon the presence of behaviour indicating impaired social relationships.

The few cases expected, and the need for developmental description, determined both the choice of population and the method.

3. *The population.* Because it has a dense mainly urban population, extensive social services, a co-operative local authority, and was accessible and large enough to yield an adequate number of cases, the County of Middlesex, with a population of about 2¼ million, contiguous with the west and north boundaries of the County of London, was chosen for the survey. In order to gain the maximum advantage from accumulated medical and school records, and to avoid case finding difficulties resulting from school transfer at 11 years, the enquiry was limited to the approximately 78,000 children born in 1953–55, and thus aged 8–10 years on the survey census date, January 1, 1964, whose homes were in Middlesex on the date.

4. *Case selection.* The survey population comprised two main administrative groups: normal and handicapped children. Most children ascertained handicapped according to the 10 categories defined by the Education Act 1944 (blind, partially sighted, deaf, partially deaf, educationally subnormal, epileptic, maladjusted, physically handicapped, those with speech defects, and the delicate) attended special schools, and for all of them there existed detailed case records containing medical, psychological and educational reports. For the normal school population, amongst whom it was thought there might be a few unrecognized autistic children, the only sources of information were the schoolteachers, and in some cases, child guidance clinics.

A 22-item behaviour questionnaire was therefore constructed, aimed mainly at screening the ordinary school population. The items covered speech, movements, social behaviour, and repetitive-ritualistic behaviour, and were to be marked as applying to the child definitely, somewhat or not at all.

Discussions with teachers following two pilot studies involving 910 normal school-children, 107 educationally subnormal and 20 maladjusted, in altogether 9 schools, showed that while they had submitted returns for many children without autistic symptoms, no child showing marked autistic behaviour excluded. Two independent judges examining the pilot questionnaires, according to the same criteria, to select those describing behaviour which required further examination, achieved 84.3% agreement in the first pilot, and 87.5% in the second. Of the 7 questionnaires returned for diagnosed "psychotic" children in a school for maladjusted (not in the survey area), 6 were selected by both judges. The one child not chosen no longer showed any of the listed behaviour. Language problems raised by a high proportion of foreign children (in some schools as high as 50%) were not found to present the teachers with the difficulties that had been anticipated.

The main conclusions arising from these preliminary surveys were that while teachers returned forms for all children who exhibited at all markedly the behaviour specified, over-inclusion would require careful screening of completed questionnaires; when the teachers gave detailed examples in the questionnaire of the behaviour being rated, selection of "possible" cases was easier and more reliable. In the revised form finally used the importance of detailed examples of behaviour was stressed and more space was provided for them (see appendix 1).

In the survey itself the population was screened in several stages:

a) *Stage I*. A preliminary letter was sent to every possible source of Middlesex children both within and outside the county, including private schools, asking how many aged 8–10 were under their care. The total number reported was 76,388. The revised questionnaire was then sent to all these "sources" with a letter explaining that the survey was concerned with unusual children showing "certain kinds of behaviour," and accompanied by a sheet of instructions containing a description and examples of the kinds of behaviour sought. Replies were received for 75,930, or 99% of the total reported population. Of the 458 children in "sources" which failed to cooperate after being sent the questionnaire, 457 were in ordinary schools. The number for whom returns were made thus represented 97% of the total population of 78,000, estimated from the latest (1961) national census returns. Altogether 2,154 questionnaires were completed. Most of these contained little or no evidence of abnormal behaviour apart from "backwardness" and were excluded by a minimum criterion of acceptability. The remaining 666 were submitted to the two judges familiar with the syndrome, who had participated in the earlier stages of the survey (N.O. and J.W.). Using different methods they independently agreed that 578 (87%) could be confidently excluded. Disagreed cases and those both judges agreed were "possible" were retained, a total of 88 names.

Independent screening of the local authority case records of all handicapped children aged 8–10 years by two other workers familiar with autistic children and with previous experience of case record examination according to agreed rules (A.L. and V.L.), produced 82 "possible" cases. A reliability check on a 10% sample of case records showed complete agreement between the workers as to which cases should be rated as having "strong" or "moderately strong" indications, but there was some disagreement about those who should be rated "weak," because the policy of over-including doubtful cases was differently interpreted by the two examiners. These disagreements however were slight. Thirty-five of these possible cases were already included in the list of 88 names described in the previous paragraph. The remaining 47 names were added to the list, making 135 possible cases in all.

b) *Stage II*. Each of these 135 children was seen by the investigator (V.L.), either in ordinary school, special school or junior training school, hospital or at home. An attempt was made to test each child on the Peabody Picture Vocabulary Scale (Dunn, 1959), the Séguin formboard and the Draw-a-man test (Goodenough, 1926), and a detailed description of current behaviour was obtained on a standard form from an informant, usually a teacher, nurse or training school supervisor, who knew the child well. Items of observed and reported behaviour were rated (0–absent; 1–present but very mildly or only intermittently; 2–definitely present but in moderate degree; 3–unmistakeably and strongly present) in five categories: speech, social behaviour, motor peculiarities, repetitive-ritualistic behaviour, and "other." Of the 135 children interviewed, only 61 satisfied the following criteria and were therefore retained for the next stage:

—Case records contained evidence rated "strong" or "moderately strong," whether or not the present behaviour was autistic.

—Current behaviour was rated (3) in any of the five categories (non-speaking children not noted during the case record examination were retained only if the behaviour rating concerned some other category than speech or social behaviour), or for whom the sum of the ratings amounted to 4 or more.

c) *Stage III*. A social and medical history and a detailed behavioural description of the development of these 61 children was then obtained from their mothers according to a standard interview guide. One interviewer (V.L.) saw all the mothers. In addition the Vineland Social Maturity Scale (Doll, 1947) was completed for each proband, details were obtained about the mental health of the parents and siblings, and both parents were tested on the Standard Progressive Matrices and the Mill Hill Vocabulary Scale (form 1, Senior: Raven, 1962).

d) *Stage IV*. Finally, all available medical records were examined for details of behaviour, the results of clinical investigations, and the circumstances of the birth of both probands and siblings. Wherever possible, descriptions were obtained also from previous schools attended by the probands, and from the records and recollections of child guidance clinic staff.

e) *The selection of autistic children*. All information was then combined in a single file for each child. These files were examined in turn and 24 items of behaviour were rated: 0–absent, 1–present but not markedly, or 2–markedly present. (Note: ratings of mood disturbances were not included because almost every child was reported to have or have had tantrums, and finer discrimination was difficult.)

The sums of the individual ratings constituting the total "score" for each child were then ranked. A cut-off point was chosen by inspection below the lowest scoring child who, on clinical grounds, it was thought should be included. (When "speakers" and "non-speakers" were ranked separately, the same cases were included.) The 32 children with total scores above the cut-off point were called autistic (cases 1–32); those with smaller scores (non-autistic) were retained for comparison (cases 33–54). (It should be noted here that all the survey interviews, the extracts from the hospital case notes, and the final behaviour ratings were made by the same worker.)

5. *The selection of a "nuclear" sub-group*. Amongst the autistic children a subgroup was formed of those with the highest scores in the two categories "social" and "repetitive-ritualistic" behaviour (see Table 1). The co-existence of symptoms in these two behaviour areas is characteristic of "infantile autism" but, because very similar behaviour was found in some of the survey children who became ill only after the age of 2 or 3 years, the subgrouping was made independently of the age of onset. The categories were defined as follows:

a) *"Social" behaviour*. Abnormality in their relationships with people is the most commonly reported characteristic of autistic children. Although described by different terms such as "autism," "withdrawal," "lack of object relations," "defect in emotional rapport," "disturbed social contact," or, as in the Creak criteria, "a gross . . . impairment in emotional relations with people," a common element is a failure to *respond* in a normal way to people. This characteristic was present in all the autistic children in the survey, at some time, in varying degrees; the kinds of behaviour by which it was

Table 1. *Scores allocated to the 32 autistic probands in the areas "social" and "repetitive-ritualistic" behaviour, illustrating the score criterion for the selection of Group A*

GROUP A Case No.	Total score, all items	Social behav. score	Repet-rit. score	GROUP B Case No.	Total score, all items	Social behav. score	Repet-rit. score
1	22	6	9	16	12	6	2
2	24	5	5	17	23	5	4
3	17	5	7	18	13	5	2
4	23	7	6	19	18	5	4
5	22	8	9	20	17	5	4
6	26	9	6	21	12	2	2
7	20	7	5	22	19	6	3
8	33	10	7	23*	13	4	3
9	28	7	6	24	11	5	1
10*	27	10	5	25*	14	7	2
11*	28	8	9	26*	12	8	2
12	24	6	6	27	15	6	0
13	25	5	6	28	15	4	2
14	22	8	6	29*	13	6	4
15*	27	8	10	30	13	5	0
				31	13	6	0
				32*	16	6	3

Maximum total score: speaking children = 48   Maximum score on social behaviour = 14
                   non-speaking = 40   Maximum score on repetitive-ritualistic behaviour = 10
* Non-speaking children

recognized varied among the children according to the severity of their apparent mental subnormality, and can best be described by examples.

Children with I.Q. over 55

Amongst the children with I.Q.'s above 55 none at the time of the survey played ordinarily with other children, and most paid little or no attention to them; all had some useful speech so that a refusal to use it, or bizarre content, or visual avoidance while speaking, accentuated the peculiar quality of their relationships. In some, behaviour was appropriate in a face-to-face situation (e.g., during testing) but was markedly solitary and bizarre in the playground. A few children with good speech seemed almost "normal" at interview and for them assessment was based mainly on descriptions of earlier behaviour. Examples are:

Case 5, age 9–6, untestable, previous Terman-Merrill I.Q. 57 at age 7–0. *Present social behaviour abnormal:* Seen in special unit. Repeatedly filling and emptying a container with sand: violently pushed away a child who approached his activity. Reported to speak rarely, and only to his teacher; usual response to questions is "No." Screamed when certain words were said by others. Will engage in rough play with adults but entirely ignores other children. Seen again, at his home, refused to enter the room, remained alone in the kitchen (for 2½ hours) playing an elaborate water game.

Case 1, age 11–3, Verbal I.Q. 101, previous Merrill-Palmer I.Q. 89 at age 7–4. *Present social behaviour almost normal:* Seen at his home; he met me at the door. Long sensible conversation possible. Has no friends, is "uninterested in children," never goes out alone. *Previous social behaviour:* Referred at the age of three for lack of speech; "behaving like a deaf child," ignored anyone speaking to him; at age 3½, showed "A complete lack of affect" and was "happy in his own world"; he ignored people coming into the room.

Case 17, age 9–5, Verbal I.Q. 126 (overestimate), previous Binet I.Q. 90 at age 9–5. *Present behaviour almost normal:* Seen at his home, greeted me, conversed sensibly at a rather immature level. Avoids other children—never goes out alone. *Previous social behaviour:* At 3, refused to be cuddled or touched or helped in dressing, "We couldn't get near him." By 5, "very aloof, a life apart," never any spontaneous affection. Refused to talk about school. At 6, a psychiatrist reported him to be "very anti-social, grossly over-dependent, emotionally fixated at an infantile level." At 6½, a psychologist reported "he can now look me in the eye"; at school (age 7), "frightened of other children, spent his time tapping things—never joined in class activities, sometimes jumped up and shouted irrelevant commands." For years refused to allow any other children into his house.

Children with I.Q. below 55

When they were seen, most of the more severely subnormal children (I.Q. under 55) had little speech and many failed to respond to words. Only a few were intensely self-isolating, sometimes shutting themselves in cupboards or occupying themselves solitarily in corners. None had any contact with other children and some deliberately avoided them. None made spontaneous approaches to strange adults (e.g., visitors) but many seemed to enjoy physical contact with their parents or familiar adults. Those who were seen in mental subnormality hospitals could not readily be distinguished by observed or reported contemporary behaviour from some other children in the same wards so that assessment rested mainly on descriptions of their earlier behaviour. Examples are:

Case 10, age 11–0, formboard 32 secs., no previous tests. *Present social behaviour abnormal:* Seen in training school. He was sitting at a sand tray, facing the wall, filling and emptying a bucket, an habitual activity. He ignored several attempts to interest him in the formboard. Eventually completed the test obliquely, resolutely facing the sand tray and the wall while doing so; after each trial pushed the formboard away. He acknowledged our presence in no way, nor did he once look at us. He had no speech.

Case 11, age 10–3, formboard 44 secs.—many errors. No previous tests. *Present social behaviour abnormal:* In mental subnormality hospital since age 5. Refused to look at tester. Pushed tester away but enjoyed being tickled. Interested in formboard, tried to manipulate by using tester's hand as a tool. Solitary, mute. *Previous social behaviour:* He has never responded to his name; family called him by whistling. Behaved "like a deaf and dumb child"; never came to mother for comforting, has always "ignored strangers" and never took any notice of children. Began early to use mother's hand to manipulate even those things he could do himself. He has never spoken.

Case 14, age 10–6. Untestable, no previous tests. *Present social behaviour abnormal:* In mental subnormality hospital since age 9. Would not sit down, looked at tester from a distance but turned away when spoken to. Moved aimlessly about, rocking and waving a sweet paper, occasionally masturbating. Screamed "No" to questions, otherwise paid no apparent attention to the interviewer. Can say few parrot phrases only. *Previous social behaviour:* From before age 12 months "she never looked at us" (mother). By 18 months, people asked if she was deaf, she failed to respond to their attempts to "amuse" her. (Diagnosed "mentally defective" at age 3.) Always extremely solitary; lack of speech comprehension led to her being "herded about the house like an animal." Severely disturbed behaviour led to the intervention of the police and admission to hospital.

b) *"Repetitive-ritualistic" behaviour*. Evidence for an "obsessive insistence on the preservation of sameness" was observed by Kanner (1943) in a wide variety of behaviours, many involving an elaborately repetitious manipulation of objects. The two categories of the Creak criteria concerning a "pathological preoccupation with particular objects" and "an insistence on the preservation of sameness" were therefore combined. The items within the combined "repetitive-ritualistic behaviour" category represented behaviour which is easily reported and recognized; detailed descriptions are therefore not presented. It should, however, be noted that Item 23 (see Table 2) refers to a resistance to certain changes in the *physical* environment (e.g., the arrangement of articles of furniture, or the wearing of certain clothes), while Item 24 refers to *activities* (e.g., the temporal ordering of events, the direction of a usual walk, the use of verbal formulae and similar rituals). Resist-

Table 2. *Mean percentage scores on 24 behaviour items in groups A, B, and C*

Item	Behaviour rated	Mean percentage scores and types of children		
		Autistic		Non-Autistic
		Group A (N=15)	Group B (N=17)	Group C (N=22)
	All speech items *	54	38	12
1.	Speech not used for communication	63	33	0
2.	Reversal of pronouns	21	12	8
3.	Echolalia	67	46	25
4.	Repetition of phrases	67	58	13
	All social behaviour items	72	53	14
5.	Visual avoidance	53	38	2
6.	Solitary	97	70	32
7.	Ignores children	87	79	15
8.	Aloof and distant	97	70	18
9.	Walks/looks through people	30	6	0
	All movement peculiarity items	40	28	8
10.	Self spinning	47	14	0
11.	Jumping	43	44	14
12.	Flapping	33	14	14
13.	Toe walking	13	18	9
14.	Other marked mannerisms	63	47	5
	All "auditory" items	45	34	10
15.	Behaves as if deaf	67	50	5
16.	Covers ears	47	26	11
17.	Distress at noise	23	26	14
	All repetitive/ritualistic items	49	16	7
18.	Elaborate food fads	27	6	2
19.	Lines and patterns with objects	43	9	0
20.	Spinning objects	17	9	5
21.	Other elaborate ritual play	83	35	11
22.	Carrying, banging, twirling etc. objects	37	38	9
23.	Insistence on sameness (objects)	53	9	15
24.	Insistence on sameness (events)	80	12	9

° Speaking children only

ance was by screaming or temper tantrums; these reduced in frequency as the demands were understood and acceded to by parents.

Fifteen children who had high scores in both these categories were called group A (cases 1–15); they tended also to have the highest over-all scores

(Table 1). Autistic children who did not show this marked *combination* of behaviours and who generally had fewer, less marked, and more heterogeneous symptoms, were called group B (N = 17, cases 16–32). The remaining, non-autistic, handicapped children, many of whom nevertheless had some behaviour similar to the autistic children, were called group C (N = 22, cases 33–54). Percentage scores were calculated for each of the 24 items and for the category totals; these are shown separated for groups A, B, and C, in Table 2.

6. *Limitations of the material*. For 11 children, data were incomplete. Three mothers refused to be interviewed, 6 were either dead, ill, or could not be traced, or the children were illegitimate and no substitute informant was available; the parents of 1 child were abroad and returned by post a detailed behaviour questionnaire only. One child could not be seen. Because of inadequate alternative data, 7 of these 11 children were excluded from the behaviour rating. In a report of the survey made to the Middlesex County Council (Lotter, 1966) 3 of these children were included in group B and 4 in group C, on the basis of the limited information available. In order to simplify presentation of the comparative analysis, all 7 were excluded from the group reported here. (The 3 autistic children originally included in group B are however included in the calculation of prevalence in the Results section that follows.)

7. *Reliability*.
a) *The selection of cases*. An estimate of the reliability of the questionnaire returns, and the selection of questionnaires by the independent judges, was made by comparison with the cases selected from local authority case records. Complete agreement was not expected, since the case records contained more detailed information about the children, including their early development, whereas questionnaires were completed on the basis of present behaviour only.
  —Questionnaire returns versus case records: Of 82 cases selected from the records, questionnaires were expected for 76 (6 children were at home and no questionnaire was possible), and 58 were received; of the 18 which teachers failed to return, 4 were included as autistic on the final behaviour ratings. One of these was in a special school, having lost many of his earlier behaviour peculiarities, and 3 were in junior training schools where many of the children have peculiar behaviour and selection by the teachers was especially difficult.
  —Case records versus judges: Of the 666 children whose questionnaires were submitted to the judges, 52 were chosen also from case records, and 35 of these were included amongst the 88 questionnaires selected by the judges. Of the 17 they failed to select, only 1 was included as autistic in the final behaviour ratings.

b) Behaviour rating. All the interviews and the final ratings were made by the same worker (V.L.). To check the possibility of a consistent bias in the allocation of scores to the items, all the information in each case file was rated independently by a psychiatrist (J.W.). Of the 32 children rated as autistic by the interviewer, 28 were amongst the 32 given highest scores by the independent rater.

c) Mothers' reports. The accuracy of retrospective data derived from mothers' reports has often been questioned, and most recently by Robbins (1963). However several authors have shown that data which are objective, well-defined and based on questions about *whether* certain events took place rather than *when* they did, or their duration, are relatively more accurately recalled (Lapouse and Monk, 1958; Haagard et al., 1960; Robbins, 1963). Since most of the descriptive data in the survey were obtained retrospectively from mothers, an attempt was made to estimate their reliability. Three indices were used: birth weight, age of first walking unaided, and the presence or absence of certain behaviours.

Birth weights reported by mothers were compared with those recorded in maternity hospital case notes; age of walking reported by the mother during the survey was compared with her earlier reports to a clinic or hospital which, in most cases, were recorded not longer than 2 to 3 years after the event. The discrepancy in the mean birth weight reported by mothers ($N = 28$, 114.1 ounces) was $+0.9$ ounce and in the mean age of walking ($N = 22$, 18.7 months), was -0.2 months. These are very similar to the discrepancies reported by Robbins (birth weight $+0.02$ ounce, age of walking -1.1 month) in reports made about children when they were only 3 years old. A lower correlation found for reports of walking-age ($r = .86$) than for birth weight ($r = .98$) was probably caused partly by the difficulty of reporting a precise age at which an emerging ability becomes established.

In order to estimate accuracy of the mothers' descriptions of behaviour, their reports on 4 behaviour items in each of 4 areas (social, motor, auditory, and repetitive-ritualistic behaviour) were compared with observations made in clinics or hospitals at various times previously. Of the autistic children with detailed hospital records, 21 were included in the comparison; 11 from social classes I and II, and 10 from classes III–V. Fifteen were boys and 6 girls. Each of the individual behaviour items noted as "present" or "absent" according to the hospital descriptions, was then compared with the mothers' reports of the same item. In 77 of the 84 items (92%) the mothers' descriptions agreed with the earlier records.

The recall of birth weights and motor milestones may not be comparable with the recall of abnormal behaviour. Nevertheless mothers are able to recall birth weights with great accuracy, and to report similarly about motor milestones at interviews widely separated in time. The high level of agreement between behaviour previously reported by mothers, or independently observed, and reports by the mothers at the survey interviews probably results partly from the early onset of behaviour which in autistic children may show similar patterns over long periods (see Kanner, 1943). Anxiety about their childrens' development, frequent medical consultations requiring rehearsal of the symptoms, and the strangeness of much of the behaviour may all have contributed to the accuracy of the mothers' descriptions of behaviour for the autistic children in the survey. None of the comparisons described above revealed marked differences in the accuracy of recall between mothers from different social classes.

Results

1. *Prevalence*. Including the 3 autistic children for whom only incomplete data could be obtained, the total of 35 children represents a rate of 4.5 per 10,000 at age 8–10 in the County of Middlesex. Fifteen of these (2.0 per 10,000) had the marked symptom-combination defining group A. If only the 32 children included in the behaviour analysis are considered, the over-all rate is 4.1 per 10,000, with 2.0 per 10,000 defined as group A.

2. *Age and Sex*. The mean age of the 32 autistic children on the survey census date 1.1.1964 was 9.5 years. The mean age for sub-group A was 1 month less than the mean for the other two groups.

There was an excess of boys in all three groups. The largest excess occurred in group A (11 boys, 4 girls, a ratio of 2.75:1), the next in group B (12 boys, 5 girls, =2.40:1), and the smallest in the non-autistic handicapped group C (13 boys, 9 girls, =1.44:1). All the autistic children above I.Q. 55 were boys; amongst the low I.Q. autistic children therefore the boy/girl ratio was no higher than amongst the non-autistic children.

3. *Onset*. The autistic probands were classified according to the type and age of onset. Ten (4 of them in Group A) had an onset involving a "setback"[1] in development, while 22 (11 in Group A) had a gradual onset without evident loss of abilities, or were always backward. Of these 22, 17 had *some* retardation in motor milestones and 18 said their first words late or have never spoken.

For most of the children with a setback, there was little difficulty in establishing the age of the child when the changes in behaviour were taking place since they were usually severe. Of 3 children with a setback between age 18–27 months, 2 became mute by about 24 months, and one was referred to specialists at 27 months because of a failure in speech development

---

[1] By "setback" was meant either a) the loss of some ability, for example, speech, or b) the failure to progress after a satisfactory beginning. A child had a "satisfactory beginning" if he learned to sit unsupported by 10 months, walked unaided by 17 months, and said his first intelligible word by 16 months.

and odd behaviour following a promising early development. In a further 7 children, the setback occurred after 27 months: in 4 before age 3 years, and in 3 between 3–4½ years. In 3 of these later onset children, setback was severe and fairly rapid.

Attempts to establish an age of onset in retrospect for autistic children without a setback are difficult and probably unreliable; most of them, however, were more or less retarded in development and in this sense were "abnormal" from an early age. Often early peculiar behaviour was attributed by parents to slowness in learning to speak. All these 22 children were recognised as retarded or peculiar by age 3 years, and 7 had some autistic behaviour by 27 months.

4. *Intelligence.* Only a single attempt to obtain a test result for each child was possible in the survey. Where a satisfactory estimate could not be obtained the results of other tests made after age 5 were used. Four of the 32 autistic children refused all the survey tests and had not been successfully tested before; all four were in mental subnormality hospitals or homes, and there was no evidence to suggest they were not severely subnormal.

Altogether about two-thirds of the autistic children were functioning at a severely subnormal level, i.e. with I.Q.'s below 55 (Table 3). Where a score slightly above I.Q. 55 was achieved on the Séguin formboard only, a few children were classified as "below I.Q. 55" on the basis of a consistently lower performance in all other tests. Eight of the 10 children with I.Q.'s above 55 were classified according to their scores on the vocabulary test; one other child had a verbal I.Q. of 53, but 80 on the Séguin, 87 on the Draw-a-man, and at age 6 had a Binet I.Q. of 69, while the other, untestable at the survey, had a Binet I.Q. of 57 at age 7.

A consistent feature of the autistic children was their social immaturity. Of 15 low I.Q. (below 55) children for whom social quotients could be obtained, only 2 scored over S.Q. 45. Of the 9 higher I.Q. children for whom comparative data were available, all had S.Q.'s below their other test scores, 5 of them below S.Q. 62.

Because many of the children were severely disturbed and had marked abnormalities in their use of speech, and because the non-verbal test used

Table 3. *Frequency and percentage distribution of I.Q. scores for autistic children in Groups A and B*

	I.Q. Range		
Group	80 plus $N^0/_0$	55—79 $N^0/_0$	under 55 $N^0/_0$
Autistic, Group A	2 (13.3)	3 (20)	10 (66.7)
Autistic, Group B	3 (17.6)	2 (11.8)	12 (70.6)
Totals	5 (15.6)	5 (15.6)	22 (68.8)
Incomplete data	—	1	2

Table 4. *Summary of the type of onset in 32 autistic children according to the level of tested intelligence and early developmental status*

Developmental status	Number of children				
	with setback			without setback	
	Total	I.Q. 55+	I.Q. < 55	I.Q. 55+	I.Q. < 55
No marked retardation					
1. All milestones average	12	2	7	3	—
2. Sitting and/or walking and/or talking "late": none "very late"	4	—	—	2	2
Some marked retardation					
3. Sitting "average", and					
(a) Walking, talking "very late"	2	—	—	2	—
(b) Walking "late", talking "very late"	4	—	—	—	4
(c) Walking "average", talking "very late"	1	—	—	—	1
Marked retardation					
4. Sitting "very late", walking and talking "late" or "very late"	9	—	1	1	7
Totals	32	2	8	8	14

Key to milestones:	"average" (months)	"late" (months)	"very late" (months)
Sitting unsupported	up to 10	11—12	after 12
Walking unaided	up to 17	18—20	after 20
Age of first words	up to 16	17—20	after 20

(the Séguin) is a timed test assuming a certain motivation, the results obtained must be regarded as representing a present level of functioning rather than a measure of capacity. It is possible that more careful testing, perhaps with different tests, might demonstrate a somewhat better ability than was apparent during the survey in a few of the low I.Q. group, 5 of whom had formboard scores in the I.Q. 45–55 range. In this sense, the test results represent the relative severity of the existing handicaps, whether these are considered to be primarily "mental illness" or "mental subnormality." For the comparisons described below, a single division was made at I.Q. 55 between a "high" and a "low" I.Q. group.

5. *The relation of onset to status at the time of the Survey.* Because the clinical severity of autistic disorders and intelligence test results are related (Rutter, 1964; Wolff and Chess, 1964), the low and high I.Q. groups represented children who were relatively more or less severely affected at the survey mean age of 9.9 years. Improvement is usually evident at an earlier age (Eisenberg, 1956) so the condition of the children at the time of the survey was possibly an indicator of what their eventual social and intellectual condition would be.

Early development, type of onset and I.Q. were compared (Table 4). One child, normal until 2½ years, shared with her normal siblings a "family trait" of walking late; she was classified as having average milestones.

All but 2 children with a setback had a low I.Q.; although a setback was partly defined by average early milestones, one child with generally retarded development had a clear setback at 18–24 months. In neither of the 2 children with a high I.Q. was the setback severe.

Outcome following an onset without a setback was variable, children with the most consistently retarded milestones tending to be of low I.Q. at the survey. All but 3 of the 15 children in whom late talking was associated with retarded motor milestones (groups 3 a, b, and 4 in the Table) had low I.Q.'s.

Toilet training was not included as a milestone in Table 4. Some mothers are probably more tolerant than others of difficulties of this kind, so that only reports that a serious problem existed are likely to be comparable. A "serious" problem was defined as present if a child became dirty after becoming trained, or if bowel training was acquired only after age 4 years, or was associated with behaviour (such as persistent playing with faeces) making it a special problem, or if bowel training was never established. Of the 16 children with any marked retardation (groups 3 and 4, in Table 4), 6 presented serious toilet problems; however, neither of the children with I.Q. 55+ (group 3 a in the Table) had such difficulties. In the 7 low I.Q. children with average milestones and a setback, onset was accompanied in 5 by serious toilet problems such as loss of control, severe constipation, bowel prolapse, or playing with faeces and "spreading it all over the room."

6. *Speech.* Communicative speech (Eisenberg, 1956), as well as the functioning level of intelligence, is an indicator of the relative severity of the disorder in autistic children. In autistic groups A and B, the ability to use speech communicatively, and estimates of intelligence, varied together (Table 5). Thus, all the mute children were of low I.Q. and all those with the most nearly normal use of speech as language had I.Q.'s classified as relatively high.

Discussion

In the present survey it was assumed that accumulation of individual behaviour items would distinguish a "case" and that the greater the number and severity of the symptoms the closer the behaviour of the child would approximate to the clinical case descriptions from which the items were derived. All interviews and ratings were made by the same worker in order to minimise differences in the interpretation of symptoms. For an autistic group defined in this way, the point where a line is drawn separating it from the population of "non-autistic" children is arbitrary. The possibility of error in the delineation of so small a group according to rather imprecise criteria in a large population is considerable. However only about 3% of the estimated total population were not screened, the reliability of the selection procedures seemed reasonably satisfactory and there appeared to be no systematic bias in the rating of the behaviour descriptions.

Table 5. *Comparison of speech in Groups A and B according to intelligence level at the survey*

	I.Q. 55+ Group A	I.Q. 55+ Group B	I.Q. < 55 Group A	I.Q. < 55 Group B
1. Speech freely and adequately used	2	3	—	—
2. Use of speech limited to some extent	3	2	2	1
3. Use of speech very limited	—	—	5	5
4. Mute	—	—	3	6*
All children	5	5	10	12

* One child was deaf.

Definitions of categories: 1. Speech is freely used for spontaneous communication; although the content may be concentrated on their own interests, there is no unwillingness to talk and what is said is sensible. 2. The children can speak sensibly, but speech may be reluctantly used, or refused in certain situations, or although articulation and quantity of spontaneous speech may be nearly normal, content may usually be repetitive and of limited value communicatively. 3. In this group were included children whose only speech was parrot phrases and echolalia, or who spoke so seldom that the usefulness of speech for them was drastically reduced, or whose more complex speech was addressed primarily to dolls or to themselves. It was not possible to have a conversation however simple with these children. One of these had a very severe articulation difficulty. 4. Children who at the survey were mute: 5 had never spoken (one was deaf), the others had lost an earlier ability to say single words, or in one case simple phrases.

The 35 autistic children selected probably therefore include nearly all those in the chosen age group with the kinds and severity of behaviour here called "autistic," and the 32 included in the analyses may be considered representative of the population of "autistic" disorders. All the 35 had at some time been known to the local authority as handicapped. Only one autistic child was discovered in a school for normal children; his parents refused to be interviewed and available information about his early behaviour was scanty. This boy was one of the 7 children excluded from the behaviour ratings because of insufficient data.

The survey estimate of the prevalence of the conditions characterised by the behaviour described is thus probably a close approximation to their true frequency in the age-group studied. However, "true" prevalence may not be a useful concept in the case of a syndrome (or syndromes) so poorly defined. In addition, any children who died before age 8 years would not have been included in the survey and any who, at age 8–10, were symptom-free and who for any reason did not appear in the local authority records, would probably not have been found. There may very well be a higher prevalence at an earlier age.

Although they are not common, autistic disorders cannot be considered "rare." Applying our rates to the school-age population of the County of Middlesex (about 279,000 aged 5–14 years) there would be about 126 autistic children of all grades; 59 of them would have the marked symptom combination of group A and at least 53 would have testable I.Q.'s above 55. For administrative purposes, useful comparisons may be made with certain other severe handicaps for which published figures are probably reliable. Thus, in 1963, there were 57 blind and 175 deaf children in special schools in Middlesex (some of whom would have been over the age of 14). If the number of autistic children with I.Q.'s over 55 is taken as the minimum number who would be considered eligible for "special schooling," there would be nearly as many educable autistic children in the County as there are blind children in special schools. Since several of those allocated to the low I.Q. group in the survey may improve, or by more intensive testing be shown to have better abilities than were elicited by the survey tests, there may well be many more autistic than blind children suitable for special education.

Goodman and Tizard (1962) estimated the prevalence in Middlesex of imbeciles and idiots (I.Q. below 50) aged 10–14 years to be 3.61/1,000; applying this rate to the 5–14-year-old population there would be about 1,000 school-age idiots and imbeciles in the County. In the same population there would be 73 autistic children with I.Q.'s under 55, representing about 7 per cent of the severely subnormal population.

Even allowing for the unreliability inherent in the use of poorly defined criteria, the number of autistic children found, in comparison with the number of children in the County known to have other serious handicaps such as blindness, is substantial and raises challenging problems of educational assessment and provision.

The over-all excess of boys amongst the 32 autistic children is lower than the 4:1 ratio reported for some other groups (e.g. Kanner, 1954; Creak and Ini, 1960) but was much higher than the 1.6 or 1.7:1 found, for example, in large populations of "mental defectives" (Malzberg, 1953; Hallgren and Sjögren, 1959).

An unexpected finding was that all the higher I.Q. children in both autistic sub-groups were boys. Previous reports have not suggested that boys are less severely affected nor that they tend more often to recover. The absence of autistic girls with higher scores is difficult to account for. The possible inclusion among the higher I.Q. children in group B of one or two children who might be classified as having, instead of autistic disorders, some "developmental speech disorder" (in which according to Ingram and Reid (1956) the proportion of affected boys may be very high) does not explain the absence of girls. The numbers in the survey are very small, however, and chance variations may easily affect the proportions found.

One-third of the survey cases had an onset involving a setback in development. Large proportions of cases with an onset of this kind have been reported. Creak (1962) found about one-quarter, and Wolff and Chess (1964) found one-half. To some extent the differences may be due to a lack of uniformity in the definition of a "setback."

Children with a setback occurring at any time during their early years are usually severely affected. This was the case in all but two of the survey children with a setback at any age from before 2 to just over 4 years. All Wolff and Chess's cases with a setback before 2 years were severely affected; a sinister prognosis for such an early setback was reported also by Eisenberg and Kanner (1956), and for setback at 3–5 years by Anthony (1958). Creak (1962), however, found no such association between the type of onset and prognosis in a group of 108 "psychotic" children.

Although it may be difficult, especially in children in whom autistic symptoms develop gradually, to discover the precise age at which they started, all the survey children were markedly abnormal by the age of 5. The child with the latest onset had a severe setback at 4½ years. No child was found who first developed autistic symptoms after this age. The absence of later onset suggests that whatever the underlying disorders may be, autistic behaviour as described here is peculiar to disturbances beginning in the first few years of life.

The low I.Q. autistic children whose early milestones had shown marked evidence of retardation were more severely handicapped at the time of the survey than those without such early retardation. Using inability to speak or to produce a scoreable performance on the formboard, and the fact of hospital placement, as indices of the severity of their present handicaps, the differences in present status between children who had retarded milestones and those who had not may be illustrated as shown in Table 6.

Table 6.	All autistic children classified as "below I.Q. 55" (N=22)	
	No marked early retardation (N=9)	Some marked retardation in early milestones (N=13)
Mute	1	8
Untestable or unscoreable on the formboard	3	11
In subnormality hospital or on waiting list	1	10

(See Table 4 for definition of milestones)

Any conclusion from these figures is complicated by the possible effects of institutional life (Creak, 1963; Rutter, 1964; Tizard, 1964). However, all but 2 of the institutionalised children were placed after the age of 8 years, by which time their condition had shown no sign of amelioration.

The comparison of attempts to identify factors which predict social and intellectual prognosis is complicated by differences in case selection as well as by differences in the criteria used to assess outcome. Thus, amongst cases of "infantile autism" for whom Eisenberg and Kanner (1956) identify the presence of useful speech at age 5 as the most important prognostic feature, very few cases appear to have been retarded in early development, or to have shown evidence of neurological abnormalities (Kanner, 1943; Kanner and Lesser, 1958). On the other hand, amongst the "psychotic" children in whom Rutter (1964) finds poor performance on I.Q. tests to predict outcome most usefully, a large proportion had definite evidence of brain dysfunction.

Rutter has not provided developmental data for his series; however, it may be assumed as likely (in view of the high incidence of "organic" disorders) that many of his "subnormal" cases were developmentally retarded. If this assumption is correct, the present survey finding that amongst autistic children with low I.Q.'s those who were developmentally retarded are relatively more severely affected, suggests that more meaningful comparisons as to outcome may be made by specifying these cases separately. The most useful prognostic indicator may not be the same in all cases.

REFERENCES

Anthony, E. J.: An aetiological approach to the diagnosis of psychosis in childhood. Acta paedopsychiat. 1/2, 89–100 (1958).

Bellak, L. (ed.): Schizophrenia: a review of the syndrome. New York: Logos Press, 1958.

Benda, C. E., M. J. Farrel, and C. Chipman: The inadequacy of present day concepts of mental illness in child psychiatry. Amer. J. Psychiat. 107, 721–729 (1951).

Bender, L.: Genesis in schizophrenia during childhood. Acta paedopsychiat. 1/2, 101–107 (1958).

———: Autism in children with mental deficiency. Amer. J. ment. Def. 64, 81–86 (1959).

———: Mental illness in childhood and heredity. Eugenics quart. 10, 1–11 (1963).

———, and A. E. Grugett: A study of certain epidemiological factors in a group of children with childhood schizophrenia. Amer. J. Ortho-psychiat. 26, 131–144 (1956).

Bergman, P., and S. Escalona: Unusual sensitivities in very young children. Psychoanal. St. Child 3/4, 333–352 (1949).

Bruch, H.: The various developments in the approach to childhood schizophrenia. Acta psychiat. neurol. scand. 34, 1–48 (1959).

Creak, M.: Juvenile psychosis and mental deficiency. In Proceedings of the London Conference on the scientific study of mental deficiency. B. Richards (ed.), Vol. 2, 389–397. London: May and Baker 1962.

———: Follow-up of cases (100) of schizophrenic syndrome of childhood. Second European Paedopsychiatric Congress, Rome, 1963.

———: Childhood psychosis—a review of 100 cases. Br. J. Psychiat. 109, 84–89 (1963) (a).

———, and S. Ini: Families of psychotic children. J. Child Psychol. Psychiat. 1, 156–175 (1960).

———, et al.: Schizophrenic syndrome in childhood. Dev. Med. Child Neurol. 3, 501–504 (1961).

———, et al.: Schizophrenic syndrome in childhood: further progress report of a working party. Dev. Med. Child Neurol. 4, 530–535 (1964).

Despert, J. L.: Schizophrenia in children. Psychiat. Quart. 12, 366–371 (1938).

———: Differential diagnosis between obsessive-compulsive neurosis and schizophrenia in children. In Psychopathology of childhood, (ed. P. H. Hoch and J. Zubin). New York: Grune and Stratton 1955, pp. 240–253.

———, and A. C. Sherwin: Further examination of diagnostic criteria in schizophrenic illness and psychoses of infancy and early childhood. Amer. J. Psychiat. 114/9, 784–790 (1958).

Doll, E. A.: Vineland Social Maturity Scale: manual of directions. Minneapolis: Ed. Test Bureau 1947.

Dunn, L. M.: Manual for the Peabody Picture Vocabulary Test. Minneapolis: American Guidance Service 1959.

Earl, C. J. C.: The primitive catatonic psychoses of idiocy. Br. J. Med. Psychol. 14, 230–251 (1936).

Eisenberg, L.: The autistic child in adolescence. Amer. J. Psychiat. 112, 607–612 (1956).

———, and L. Kanner: Early infantile autism: 1943–1955. Symposium on childhood schizophrenia. Amer. J. Orthopsychiat. 56, 556–566 (1956).

Fontes, V.: Schizophrenic infantile. Acta paedopsychiat. 25, 183–190 (1958).

Goodenough, F. L.: The measurement of intelligence by drawing. New York: Yonkers-Hudson, World Book Co. 1926.

Goodman, N., and J. Tizard: Prevalence of imbecility and idiocy among children. Br. Med. J. 1, 216–219 (1962).

Haagard, E. A., A. Brekstad, and Å. Skard: On the reliability of the amnestic interview. J. Abn. Soc. Psychol. 61, 311–318 (1960).

Hallgren, B., and T. Sjögren: Clinical and genetics—statistical study of schizophrenia and low grade mental deficiency in a large Swedish rural population. Acta Psychiat. et Neurol. Scand., 35, Suppl. 140 (1959).

Ingram, T. T. S., and J. F. Reid: Developmental aphasia observed in a department of child psychiatry. Arch. Dis. Childhood 31, 161–172 (1956).

Jaeggi, F.: Personal communication (1963).

Kallman, F. J., and B. Roth: Genetic aspects of preadolescent schizophrenia. Amer. J. Psychiat. 112, 599–606 (1956).

Kanner, L.: Autistic disturbances of affective contact. Nerv. Child 2, 217–250 (1943).

————: Irrelevant and metaphorical language in early infantile autism. Amer. J. Psychiat. 103, 242–246 (1946).

————: Child psychiatry. Third edition. Oxford: Blackwell 1957.

————: The conception of wholes and parts in early infantile autism. Amer. J. Psychiat. 108, 23–26 (1951).

————: To what extent is early infantile autism determined by constitutional inadequacies. Res. Publ. Ass. Nerv. Ment. Dis. 33, 378–385 (1954).

————: History and present status of childhood schizophrenia in the U.S.A. Acta Paedopsychiat. 25, 138–149 (1958).

————, and L. I. Lesser: Early infantile autism. Ped. Clin. N. America 5, 711–730 (1958).

Lapouse, R., and M. A. Monk: An epidemiological study of behaviour characteristics in children. Amer. J. Publ. Hlth. 48, 1134–1144 (1958).

Lotter, V.: Report of a survey of the prevalence of autistic conditions in childhood in the County of Middlesex. Unpublished report to the Greater London Council, 1966.

Mahler, M., J. R. Ross, and Z. de Fries: Clinical studies in benign and malignant cases of childhood psychosis. Amer. J. Orthopsychiat. 19, 295–305 (1949).

Malzberg, B.: Sex differences in the prevalence of mental deficiency. Amer. J. Ment. Def. 58, 301–305 (1953).

Norman, E.: Reality relationships of schizophrenic children. Br. J. Med. Psychol. 27, 126–141 (1954).

————: Affect and withdrawal in schizophrenic children. Br. J. Med. Psychol. 28, 1–17 (1955).

Pasamanick, B.: Epidemiology of behaviour disorders in childhood. Res. Publ. Ass. Nerv. Ment. Dis. 24, 297–403 (1954).

Potter, H. W.: Schizophrenia in children. Amer. J. Psychiat. 12, 1253 (1933).

Raven, J. C.: Guide to using the Mill Hill Vocabulary Scale with the progressive Matrices Scales. London: H. K. Lewis 1958.

Reid, D. D.: Epidemiological methods in the study of mental disorders. Geneva: W. H. O. papers, No. 2, 1960.

Rimland, B.: Infantile autism. New York: Appleton-Century-Crofts, 1964.

Robbins, L. C.: The accuracy of parental recall of aspects of child development and of child rearing practices. J. Abn. Soc. Psych. 66, 261–270 (1963).

Rutter, M.: Diagnosis and general aspects of child psychosis. Address to the conference on the educational needs of psychotic children. London: Ministry of Education, 1964.

————: Behavioural and cognitive characteristics of a series of psychotic children. In Early childhood autism. (ed.) J. K. Wing, Oxford: Pergamon (1966).

Scheerer, M., E. Rothman, and K. Goldstein: A case of idiot savant: an experimental study of personality organisation. Psychol. Monogr., 58, (whole No. 269) (1945).

Shepherd, M., and B. Cooper: Epidemiology and mental disorder: a review. J. Neurol. Neurosurg. Psychiat. 27, 277–290 (1964).

Tizard, J.: Community services for the mentally handicapped. London: O.U.P. 1964.

————: The epidemiology and genetics of mental deficiency. Dev. Med. Ch. Neurol. 5, 287–291 (1963).

Tramer, M.: Childhood schizophrenia as a problem of nosology. Acta Paedopsychiat. 29, 337–368 (1962).

Wing, J. K.: Diagnosis, epidemiology, aetiology. In Early childhood autism. Oxford: Pergamon, 1966.

Wolff, S., and S. Chess: A behavioural study of schizophrenic children. Acta Psychiat. Scand. 40, 438–466 (1964).

Yakovlev, P. I., M. Weinberger, and C. Chipman: Heller's syndrome as a pattern of schizophrenic behaviour disturbance in early childhood. Amer. J. Ment. Def. 53, 318–337 (1948).

(Commentary for this article on page 134.)

Appendix 1

After each of the following statements there are three columns — 'D', 'S' and 'A'. If the child shows the behaviour described by the statement to a marked degree, circle 'A'. If the child behaves somewhat according to the statement but to a lesser extent or less often, circle 'S'. If, as far as you are aware, the child does not show the behaviour, circle 'D'. Please circle *one* letter for *each* statement. *Please note: it is very important that examples be given wherever possible.* Thank you.

Statement	Doesn't Apply	Applies Somewhat	Certainly Applies
1. Unable to speak; uses only grunts or noises	D	S	A
2. Speech very muddled (but *not* due to difficulty in pronunciation) .	D	S	A
3. Speaks only in single words or short phrases	D	S	A
4. Usually refers to him or herself as 'you', 'he', 'she' or by name, rather than 'I' or 'me' *(Give example:*	D	S	A
5. Frequently repeats phrases without regard to their proper meaning (e.g. echoes part of phrases said to him or her). . . . . *(Give example:* . . . .)	D	S	A
6. Although able to speak, usually uses mime or demonstration instead (e.g. leading by the hand)	D	S	A
7. Often uses a 'special' or peculiar voice (e.g. sing-song, gruff, or squeaky, etc.) . . *(Give example:* . . . .)	D	S	A
8. Very restless. Often running about or jumping up and down. Hardly ever still .	D	S	A
9. Squirmy, fidgety child — always in and out of his/her seat	D	S	A
10. Frequently shows odd movements (tick which), e.g. flapping of arms . . .	D	S	A
spinning, round and round			
odd walk or posture			
twisting movements of hands in front of face			
facial grimacing			
other ( )			
11. Is solitary; spends most of the time on his/her own	D	S	A
12. Makes little or no attempt to mix with other children	D	S	A
13. Avoids looking at others directly, looks past or through them . . .	D	S	A

14. Abnormally preoccupied with a fixed idea to the exclusion of ordinary behaviour (e.g. constantly pretending to be a train or always drawing the same things over long periods) . . . . D   S   A
(*Give example:* . . . .)

15. Will do certain things only according to a special routine (e.g. *has* to do things in a particular order or *has* to put things in piles or rows, etc.) . . . . D   S   A
(*Give example:* . . . .)

16. Tends to examine things in odd ways (e.g. by sniffing or biting them) . . . . . D   S   A
(*Give example:* . . . .)

17. Carries or collects *curious* objects such as stones or tins . . . . D   S   A
(*Give example:* . . . .)

18. Preoccupied with certain aspects of things (e.g. their shininess, texture or colour) . . . D   S   A
(*Give example:* . . . .)

19. Very clumsy or awkward in bodily movements, co-ordinates poorly . . . . D   S   A

20. Has marked difficulty with his/her hands (e.g. using a pencil or doing up buttons or shoe laces) . . . . D   S   A

21. Markedly backward in school work . . . . D   S   A

22. Although backward generally, is particularly good at some things (such as maths. or music). (Specify which: . . . .) D   S   A

Are there any other things about this child which strike you as unusual?

Appendix 2

Three standard case-histories, on each from groups A, B and C, are given in order to illustrate the material collected about all children in the series.

Case 8 — Group A

Early development and medical history

Female, born 7-12-55. Birth weight 6½ lbs. Illegitimate; adopted 6 weeks. Seemed normal in first 12—18 months. Sat 6 months, walked 12 months, first words began 12 months. Good child, laughed and smiled; she often woke and cried, and was then very hard to comfort. No serious illnesses.

Social behaviour

By 2, mother sure "something wrong". Little response to strangers talking to her, but liked tickling. At 2—3, liked cuddling on lap, but passive, no spontaneous gestures like putting arm round mother's neck. By 3, would sit on mother's lap, gazing out of window; mother convinced the child was not seeing anything — "a Buddha-like communing with herself". Had spells until 8—9 years when family would say "she's gone away". Up to about 5 years would fail to recognize father in the street; ran right past him. Would "look through" well-meaning strangers in a way the family found embarrassing. Until recently ignored other children entirely.

Speech

By 2, could say "dandelion", "buttercup", "want a biscuit". At 2—3, knew some rhymes and songs. From 2½, seemed not to develop further. Simple speech, ignores pronouns, no reversal of "you" and "I". Spoke very seldom, and only in odd phrases. By 3—4, would use adult's hand to achieve an object; still does this sometimes. Now talks more, but mainly in learned phrases to doll. No conversation possible. Understands ordinary commands etc. Much more vocal when in a temper, or when *driven* to speak.

Motor

At 2—2½, over-active; always on the go, turning on taps, emptying containers. Rocked in cot briefly from 12—18 months. In screaming fits, would bang head on cupboard at 3—3½ years, the "worst" period. Began at 4 jumping up and down when excited, still occasionally does so, and may flap her arms. Fine finger control was good, but at 3½ walking was a "lope"; much on her toes, and she tended to trip over any unevenness.

Sensory

In pram, no response to loud noises (e.g. backfire); she is not deaf; can hear sweet paper rustle. At 3—4, would eat sawdust, dogs' excreta. Since about 5, covers ears at loud noises or when avoiding some situation.

Mood

From age 2, much screaming at frustration. Impossible to wait for a bus, or on a walk to hesitate between alternative routes — screamed unless she kept moving. Sometimes no discoverable reason for screaming which could be extremely violent.

Repetitive-Ritualistic

Before 5, she was making patterns with pencils, toy bricks; no play except these activities. Play with water taps and repetitively and incessantly emptying kitchen containers. For years certain ornaments in the home could not be changed about. Many rituals — refused to turn right when leaving the house, insisted on order of "going to bed"; changes or attempts to break the routine resulted in tantrums and screaming.

Other

Bowel control for 1 month at age 2; then became dirty and for years presented a difficult problem. Medical attention at 3 for retention and bowel prolapse. She would play with faeces and smear the walls and herself. Apart from early crying no special sleep disturbance. Unselfconscious exposure embarrassed her older brother (adoptive) and his friends; public masturbation occasionally noticed at about 8 years.

Medical Investigations

Single out-patient examination aet. 2 years 7 months. Suggested diagnosis: "Behaviour disturbance". Psychotherapy from 4 to 5 years of age.

Psychometric Examinations

Untestable.

Placement

Special boarding school since 5 years.

Case 23 — Group B

Early development and medical history

Female, born 27-3-54. Birth weight 4³/₄ lbs. at term. Two older sibs. Seemed normal in first year, sat 12 mos, walked 20 months. Good baby, first words about 18 months. Mumps, chicken-pox and measles "all in a row" at 18 months. Odd head shaking, "Spasms" since about 12 months.

Social behaviour

Slow speech and lack of response to words led to suspicion of deafness; but child thought to have "looked at" mother normally. Often seemed to "walk over" people, pushing them out of the way. Has always been "affectionate", she likes people, will go to anyone who is "sympathetic". Distractable and overactive since 2¹/₂—3 years and might be rough with people; not aloof. Loves being tickled and will then laugh ordinarily. She liked being with other children but could not play. At school (age 4) observed to wander about by herself; was very aggressive toward other children.

Speech

Acquired about 8 words (never clear) "Jelly", "Mum", "Dad", "Bye-bye", "No"; all were lost by about 2¹/₂ years. Learned to sing recognizable tunes by 3—4 years, and can still do so.

Motor

Has rocked since about 12 months, very marked since 2¹/₂; she still does so. Severe head banging when frustrated, since about 3 years. Always wildly overactive, has run away. Jumps up and down when pleased or excited; has always twisted hands by her face, opening and shutting her hands "spasmodically". Gross motor ability good, she is quick and nimble, can climb anything, and never seems to tire.

Sensory

Given hearing aid at about 3 for suspected hearing loss; but could hear "sweetie" in a whisper. Always indiscriminate about what she ate; school (age 4) refers to her eating earth. At loud noises (dog barking) she would at 3—4 cover her ears with her hands.

Repetitive-ritualistic

Never played with toys, fleeting attention to jig-saw puzzles which she was "quite good at". Very destructive. For months at a time became attached to odd objects, such as a metal bottle label; if lost she screamed and was uncontrollably violent. Constantly flicked lights on and off, so bulbs had to be removed. Recently screams if a different route is taken to the hospital; "any day that is unpatterned would be absolute hell".

Other

Bowel control slow, never complete; prolapsed bowel appears from time to time. Since 2½ often awake at night, climbing about, shouting; drugs ineffective.
Main interest appears to be in food: "she will eat and eat", voraciously.
Public masturbation since "quite young", still engaged in.
At school (age 4) reported that "she will often shudder and shake from head to feet".

Medical Investigations

Age 2—3: Hospital: EEG: no definite abnormality. No fits, not microcephalic.
Diagnosis: Autistic, likely to prove retarded, may be partially deaf.
Age 5—8: Hospital: No clinical abnormality found.
Diagnosis: Psychosis, probably on a defective background.

Psychometric Examinations

Age 4—9: Merrill-Palmers: Mental Age 2—1, I.Q. = 44; uncooperative.
Age 10—4: Séguin formboard unscorable attempt.

Placement

Subnormality hospital since 5 years.

Case 39 — Group C

Early Development and Medical History

Male, born 11-2-53. 8 weeks premature; Birth weight 3—0 lbs. Concurrent maternal T.B.; child reared in an institution until 8 months. No information about first 18 months available, but early development very slow; by 19 months could stand but not crawl or walk. Convergent squint. Two younger siblings.

Social Behaviour

Seemed normal, responsive, when returned to his mother at 18 months. Has always been "affectionate", now plays with other children, would always go indiscriminately to anyone. Excluded from school (age 4—9) after 1 day for unmanageable behaviour and aggression. Related "poorly" to the psychiatrist at 5 years. When seen he was friendly and cooperative (age 11—0).

Speech Said 2 or 3 words by 18—19 months — speech developed slowly, sentences appearing only at $3^{1}/_{2}$—4 years. By 11 years his speech had improved greatly: then his verbal ability was "much higher" than his general level of attainment. No speech mannerisms noted.

Motor Since very young jumped up and down, flapping his hands, in a frenzy of excitement. Most noticeable when spinning his wheels. Jumping behaviour a persistent mannerism, frequently noted still at age 10 years. Manual dexterity considered to be "poor on the whole", but can model wheels extraordinarily well in clay.

Sensory No peculiarities noted.

Mood Twice before age 5 sent home from school for unmanageable behaviour, having been admitted under age to relieve the mother. Decribed by school as "destructive, spiteful, disobedient; he screams at frequent intervals and for no apparent reason". Aggressiveness less but still present at 11 years.

Repetitive-Ritualistic Shortly after 2 began twiddling things; soon started spinning them, jar lids, coins, wheels, with great skill. Wheel-spinning persisted strongly for next 8 years; he made wheel collections, talked constantly about them, and while spinning them jumped spasmodically, grimacing "horribly" and seeming out of touch.

Other At 5 operated on for squint. Separation to an aunt at age 3 for 8 months (mother's T.B.). Bowel control by 3, still occasionally wets. Sleep always good.

Medical Investigations No abnormalities reported apart from squint. Psychiatric diagnosis (age 11) "psychotic amentia of hereditary origin".

Psychometric Examinations
Age 5—3 Binet Mental Age 3—5: I.Q. 65
Age 6—6 Binet Mental Age 5—1: I.Q. 78
Age 10—10 Binet Mental Age 9—4: I.Q. 85
Age 11—5 Peabody P.V.T. I.Q. 103
Age 11—5 Vineland S.Q. 74.

Placement $5^{1}/_{2}$— $7^{1}/_{2}$ excluded from school: attended junior training school. 8 —$10^{1}/_{2}$ special unit for severely disturbed children. Now in special boarding school.

COMMENTARY by Judith M. Rumsey

This is the first epidemiological study of autism and autistic-like conditions. The entire eight- to ten-year-old population of the County of Middlesex, England, was screened by a behavioral questionnaire sent to schools and other agencies dealing with children from the county. Records of handicapped children were also screened as part of a thorough case-finding effort. Suspected cases were then personally examined, mothers were given a standard interview, and all available medical records were examined.

Major findings include: (1) a prevalence rate of 4.5 cases per 10,000; (2) an overabundance of males (the male–female ratio fell between 2:1 and 3:1), which was limited to a higher functioning (IQ >55) subgroup; (3) substantial retardation (IQ >55) in two-thirds of this autistic population; and (4) onsets under three years in the majority, although a few cases showed onsets with marked regressions between three and four years of age.

Dr. Lorna Wing has since conducted similar epidemiological work on children through 14 years of age in the London borough of Camberwell. Most of Lotter's findings have been replicated with one notable exception—the finding of a more extreme male–female ratio of 15:1 for classic autism (Wing, 1981). The interested reader may want to review Dr. Wing's epidemiology-based hypotheses about possible etiologies.

REFERENCE

Wing, L. Sex ratios in early childhood autism and related conditions. *Psychiatry Research*, 1981, 5, 129–137.

7

Acquisition of Imitative Speech
by Schizophrenic Children

O. IVAR LOVAAS
JOHN P. BERBERICH
BERNARD F. PERLOFF
BENSON SCHAEFFER

With the great majority of children, the problem of teaching speech never arises. Speech develops within each child's particular environment without parents and teachers having to know a great deal about how it occurs. Yet, in some children, because of deviations in organic structure or prior experience, speech fails to develop. Children with the diagnosis of childhood schizophrenia, especially autistic children, often show little in the way of speech development.[1] The literature on childhood schizophrenia suggests two conclusions regarding speech in such children: first, that the usual treatment setting (psychotherapy) in which these children are placed might not be conducive to speech development[2]; and second, that a child failing to develop speech by the age of 5 years remains withdrawn and does not improve clinically.[2] That is, the presence or absence of speech is an important prognostic indicator. It is perhaps obvious that a child who can speak can engage in a much more therapeutic interchange with his environment than the child who has no speech.

The failure of some children to develop speech as a "natural" consequence of growing up poses the need for an increased knowledge of how language is acquired. A procedure for the development of speech in previously mute children would not only be of practical importance but might also illuminate the development of speech in normal children. Although several theoretical attempts have been made to account for language development, the empirical basis for these theoretical formulations is probably inadequate. In fact, there are no published, systematic studies on how to go about developing speech in a person who has never spoken. We now outline a procedure by which speech can be made to occur. Undoubtedly there are or will be other ways by which speech can be acquired. Furthermore, our proce-

Reprinted from *Science* 151 (February 11, 1966): 705–707. Copyright 1966 by the American Association for the Advancement of Science.
This study was supported by grants from Margaret Sabl.

dure centers on the acquisition of only one aspect of speech, the acquisition of vocal responses. The development of speech also requires the acquisition of a context for the occurrence of such responses ("meaning").

Casual observation suggests that normal children acquire words by hearing speech; that is, children learn to speak by imitation. The mute schizophrenic children with whom we worked were not imitative. Thus the establishment of imitation in these children appeared to be the most beneficial and practical starting point for building speech. The first step in creating speech, then, was to establish conditions in which imitation of vocal sounds would be learned.

The method that we eventually found most feasible for establishing verbal imitation involved a discrimination training procedure. Early in training the child was rewarded only if he emitted a sound within a certain time after an adult had emitted a sound. Next he was rewarded only if the sound he emitted within the prescribed interval resembled the adult's sound. Toward the end of training, he was rewarded only if his vocalization very closely matched the adult's vocalization—that is, if it was, in effect, imitative. Thus verbal imitation was taught through the development of a series of increasingly fine discriminations.

The first two children exposed to this program are discussed here. Chuck and Billy were 6-year-old in-patients at the Neuropsychiatric Institute at UCLA. These children were selected for the program because they did not speak. At the onset of the program, vocal behavior in both children was restricted to occasional vowel productions with no discernible communicative intent. These vowel sounds occurred infrequently, except when the children were tantrumous, and did not resemble the pre-speech babbling of infants. In addition, the children evidenced no appropriate play (for example, they would spin toys or mouth them). They engaged in a considerable amount of self-stimulatory behavior such as rocking and twirling. They did not initiate social contacts and became tantrumous when such contact was initiated by others. They evidenced occasional self-destructive behavior (biting self, headbanging, and so forth). Symbolic rewards such as social approval were inoperative, so biological rewards such as food were substituted. In short, they were profoundly schizophrenic.

Training was conducted 6 days a week, 7 hours a day, with a 15-minute rest period accompanying each hour of training. During the training sessions the child and the adult sat facing each other, their heads about 30 cm apart. The adult physically prevented the child from leaving the training situation by holding the child's legs between his own legs. Rewards, in the form of single spoonsful of the child's meal, were delivered immediately after correct responses. Punishment (spanking, shouting by the adult) was delivered for inattentive, self-destructive, and tantrumous behavior which interfered with the training, and most of these behaviors were thereby suppressed within 1 week. Incorrect vocal behavior was never punished.

Four distinct steps were required to establish verbal imitation. In step 1, the child was rewarded for all vocalizations. We frequently would fondle the children and we avoided aversive stimulation. This was done in order to increase the frequency of vocal responses. During this stage in training the child was also rewarded for visually fixating on the adult's mouth. When the child reached an achievement level of about one verbal response every 5 seconds and was visually fixating on the adult's mouth more than 50 percent of the time, step 2 of training was introduced.

Step 2 marked our initial attempt to bring the child's verbal behavior under our verbal control in such a manner that our speech would ultimately stimulate speech in the child. Mastery of this second step involved acquisition of a temporal discrimination by the child. The adult emitted a vocal response—for example, "baby"—about once on the average of every 10th second. The child was rewarded only if he vocalized within 6 seconds after the adult's vocalization. However, any vocal response of the child would be rewarded in that time interval. Step 3 was introduced when the frequency of the child's vocal responses within the 6-second interval was three times what it had been initially.

Step 3 was structurally similar to the preceding step, but it included the additional requirement that the child actually match the adult's vocalization before receiving the reward. In this and in following steps the adult selected the verbalization to be placed in imitative training from a pool of possible verbalizations that had met one or more of the following criteria. First, we selected vocal behaviors that could be prompted, that is, vocal behaviors that could be elicited by a cue prior to any experimental training, such as by manually moving the child through the behavior.

An example of training with the use of a prompt is afforded in teaching the sound "b." The training would proceed in three stages: (i) the adult emitted "b" and simultaneously prompted the child to emit "b" by holding the child's lips closed with his fingers and quickly removing them when the child exhaled; (ii) the prompt would be gradually faded, by the adult's moving his fingers away from the child's mouth, to his cheek, and finally gently touching the child's jaw; (iii) the adult emitted the vocalization "b" only, withholding all prompts. The rate of fading was determined by the child; the sooner the child's verbal behavior came under control of the adult's without the use of the prompt, the better. The second criterion for selection of words or sounds in the early stages of training centered on their concomitant visual components (which we exaggerated when we pronounced them), such as those of the labial consonant "m" and of open-mouthed vowels like "a." We selected such sounds after having previously found that the children could discriminate words with visual components more easily than those with only auditory components (the guttural consonants, "k" and "g," proved extremely difficult and, like "l" and "s," were mastered later than other sounds). Third, we selected for training sounds which the child emitted most frequently in step 1.

Step 4 was a recycling of step 3, with the addition of a new sound. We selected a sound that was very different from those presented in step 3, so that the child could discriminate between the new and old sounds more easily. To make certain that the child was in fact imitating, we randomly interspersed the sounds of step 3 with the sound of step 4, in a randomized ratio of about 1 to 3. This random presentation "forced" (or enabled) the child to discriminate the particular sounds involved, in order to be rewarded. There was no requirement placed upon the child in step 3 to discriminate specific aspects such as vowels, consonants, and order of the adult's speech; a child might master step 3 without attending to the specific properties of the adult's speech. Each new introduction of sounds and words required increasingly fine discrimination by the child and hence provided evidence that the child was in fact matching the adult's speech. All steps beyond step 4 consisted of replications of step 3, but new sounds, words, and phrases were used. In each new step the previously mastered words and sounds were rehearsed on a randomized ratio of 1 to 3. The next step was introduced when the child had mastered the previous steps—that is, when he had made ten consecutive correct replications of the adult's utterances.

One hour of each day's training was tape-recorded. Two independent observers scored the child's correct vocal responses from these sessions. A correct response was defined as a recognizable reproduction of the adult's utterance. The observers showed better than 90 percent agreement over sessions. When the child's correct responses are plotted against days of training, and the resulting function is positively accelerated, it can be said that the child has learned to imitate.

The results of the first 26 days of imitation training, starting from introduction of step 3, have been plotted for Billy (Figure 1). The abscissa denotes training days. The words and sounds are printed in lower case letters on the days they were introduced and in capital letters on the days they were mastered. It can be seen that as training progressed the rate of mastery increased. Billy took several days to learn a single word during the first 2 weeks of the program, but a single day to master several words during the last 2 weeks. Chuck's performance was very similar to Billy's.

After 26 days of training both children had learned to imitate new words with such ease and rapidity that merely adding verbal responses to their imitative repertoire seemed pointless. Hence the children were then introduced to the second part of the language training program, wherein they were taught to use language appropriately.

Fig. 1. Acquisition of verbal imitation by Billy. The abscissa denotes training days. Words and sounds are printed in lower case letters on the days they were introduced, and in capital letters on the days they were mastered.

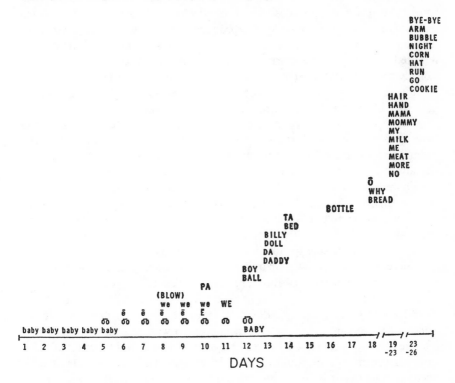

The imitation training took place in a rather complex environment, with many events happening concurrently. We hypothesized that it was the reward, given for imitative behavior, which was crucial to the learning. To test this hypothesis, the adult uttered the sounds as during the training and the children received the same number of rewards as before. However, the rewards were contingent upon time elapsed since the last reward, regardless of the child's behavior.

The data show a deterioration in imitation behavior whenever rewards are shifted from response-contingent to time-contingent delivery. It is concluded, therefore, that reward immediately following correct, imitative behavior (and withholding of reward following incorrect responding) is a crucial variable in maintaining imitative behavior in these children. The same finding has been reported by Baer and Sherman,[3] who worked with imitative behavior in normal children.

Since the child was rewarded whenever he responded like the adult, *sim-*

ilarity was consistently associated with food. Because of such association, similarity should become symbolic of reward. In other words, imitative behavior, being symbolic of reward, should eventually provide its own reward.[3] To test this hypothesis, both children were exposed to Norwegian words which they were unable to reproduce perfectly when first presented. The adult simply stated the Norwegian word and the child always attempted to repeat it; no extrinsic rewards were delivered. However, occasionally the child was presented with English words which the adult rewarded when correctly imitated. This procedure was necessary to maintain the hypothesized symbolic (learned) reward function of imitation.

The children improved in the imitation of the Norwegian words over time. It is as if they were rewarded for correct behavior. In view of the data pointing to the need for rewards in maintaining imitative behavior, and in the absence of extrinsic rewards, we would argue that the reward was intrinsic and a function of the prior imitation training. There is one implication of this finding which is of particular interest for therapeutic reasons: children may be able to acquire new behaviors on their own. (This finding contrasts with the frequent stereotype of a conditioning product, namely, that of an automaton unable to function independently.)

Currently, three new schizophrenic children are undergoing the same speech training program as Billy and Chuck. After 3 days of training, one of these children achieved a level of imitative behavior similar to that shown by Billy and Chuck after 26 days. It should be pointed out that schizophrenic children are a very heterogeneous group with respect to their speech histories and symptomatology in general, and that Billy and Chuck had failed in development to a profound degree. Insofar as one works with such a diverse population, it is likely that numerous procedures could be helpful in establishing speech.

REFERENCES

1. B. Rimland, *Infantile Autism* (Appleton-Century-Crofts, New York, 1964).
2. J. Brown, *Amer. J. Orthopsychiat. 30*, 382 (1960).
3. D. Baer and J. Sherman, *J. Exp. Child Psychol. 1*, 37 (1964).

COMMENTARY by Thomas S. Woods

The article by Lovaas, Berberich, Perloff and Schaeffer (1966) represents a significant turning point in the development of behavioral and educational services for children with autism and other developmentally handicapping conditions. It directed the attention of an entire generation of graduate students, practitioners, and parents to the implications of the operant conditioning paradigm for remedial intervention with all children demonstrating delayed development. This research showed that the methods of a science of human behavior could be taken out of the laboratory and applied to problems of real significance in the lives of autistic children. Specifically, the paper recounts how speech responses were carefully operationalized, and then strengthened and extended by the application of contingencies of reinforcement—a well-researched and well-documented approach to behavior change that heretofore had seldom been seen outside the laboratory. Furthermore, Lovaas and his colleagues then used the data to inform their decision making as programming advanced through levels of greater accuracy in child performance. Although our methodology in all these areas has grown substantially, the appearance of this degree of scientific rigor in clinical research and practice was nothing short of revolutionary in 1966.

We may still ask why this particular research was the catalyst for such rapid growth in psychology and education. Perhaps a clue to the answer to that question can be found in the paper itself. The authors state that according to then prevailing psychiatric opinion, the presence of speech in the repertoire of a schizophrenic (sic) child was a good prognostic indicator. It follows from this that any significant changes that one might make here would provoke considerable interest, as indeed they did. Importantly, those significant changes were also verifiable as such by empirical means, derived from a knowledge base with genuine scientific integrity, and accessible to the professional community for replication and extension.

It is true that a reading of this paper from the perspective we now hold calls to mind some of the many advances the field has undergone in the nearly two decades since its publication. There has been quantum change in our research methodology, in our concerns with the functional value of that which is taught, in our standards of practice with respect to the use of nonintrusive suppression strategies, and in our focus upon the long-term maintenance and generalization of the speech repertoires we build for children. Yet it was this seminal paper, perhaps more than any other, that set that growth process in motion.

8

Perceptual Inconstancy
in Early Infantile Autism

EDWARD M. ORNITZ
EDWARD R. RITVO

Within the decade since the syndrome of early infantile autism was first described by Kanner,[1-2] terms such as childhood schizophrenia,[3] atypical children,[4] children with unusual sensitivities,[5] and symbiotic psychosis[6] were used to conceptualize similar, yet apparently distinctive clinical entities. The tendency to create separate entities was reinforced by a desire for diagnostic specificity and accuracy and etiologic preference. As the symptomatology in these children varies both with the severity of the illness and age, it has been possible to emphasize distinctive clusters of symptoms and relate these to particular theories of causation. For instance, the predominance of disturbances of relating coupled with the prevailing belief in the 1940s and 1950s that specific syndromes in children must be outgrowths of specific parental behaviors or attitudes[7] led to attempts to implicate the parents in the development of early infantile autism. The notion that something noxious was done to the children, presumably by the parents, led to a teleological view of the disturbed behavior. Thus, disturbances of relating, perception, and motility have been described as defensive or protective, as a warding off or withdrawal from adverse stimulation or as compensatory self-stimulation.

The purpose of this paper is to describe a single pathologic process common to early infantile autism, certain cases of childhood schizophrenia, the atypical child, symbiotic psychosis, and children with unusual sensitivities. It will be shown that these descriptive categories are variants of a unitary disease. First, we shall describe a specific syndrome of abnormal development which is defined by observable behavior patterns that occur as clusters of symptoms. These clusters of symptoms involve the areas of: (1) perceptual integration, (2) motility patterns, (3) capacity to relate, (4) language, and (5) developmental rate. Secondly, we shall show that a pathologic mechanism underlying the syndrome can be inferred from the nature of the symptom clusters. While this pathologic mechanism may be associated with

Reprinted with permission from *Archives of General Psychiatry* 18 (January 1968): 76–98. Copyright 1968, American Medical Association.

This work was supported by United States Public Health Service grants No. MH-12575-01 and No. MH-13517-01.

multivariant etiologic factors, it is operative at birth and makes it impossible for the child to utilize external and internal stimuli to properly organize further development. If maturational or as yet unknown self-corrective factors do not mitigate the influence of this pathologic process, a relatively complete clinical picture of the syndrome develops and persists. If maturational or self-corrective factors do mitigate the influence of this pathologic process, symptoms may wane or shift in predominance resulting in a varying clinical picture. In all such cases the child's later development will show residuals of varying severity. The relationship of these residuals to the primary pathology common to all the symptom clusters will be elaborated.

It will also be emphasized that while early infantile autism must be defined as a behavioral syndrome, it is at the same time a disease. The symptomatology will, therefore, be interpreted as primarily expressive of the underlying pathophysiology rather than being purposeful in the intrapsychic life of the child.

DIAGNOSTIC TERMINOLOGY

The different diagnostic labels that have been used to characterize the large group of young children whose symptomatology has varied from Kanner's criteria for early infantile autism have included pseudoretardation, atypical development, symbiotic psychosis, childhood schizophrenia, and infantile psychosis.

The major criteria for the diagnosis of early infantile autism were the inability to relate to people in the expected manner, failure to use language for communication, an apparent desire to be alone and to preserve sameness in the environment, and preoccupation with certain objects.[1-2]

The term pseudoretardation has been used because many of these children appear retarded while showing intellectual potential which differentiates them from the general group of retarded children.

The term atypical development was originally used to describe children[8] with histories and behavior indicative of grossly uneven ego development. Later, when it became apparent that these children shared some of the features of early infantile autism, the term atypical development became used to denote children in whom relatedness was not quite so disturbed as to make the term autistic appropriate.

The term symbiotic psychosis[6] was used to describe children whose behavior appeared to be the opposite of those with autism. That is, the child rather than being aloof, remote, and emotionally isolated was found to be emotionally fused and physically clinging to the mother.

The term childhood schizophrenia has been used by some authors as a synonym for early infantile autism,[9] by others to describe a presumed separate syndrome,[10] and by some to describe symptoms which others accept as those of early infantile autism without reference to that terminology.[11-12] While some authors[11] describe a continuum of abnormality in which infants and very young children with the symptoms of the autistic child represent the earliest manifestations of schizophrenia, others [10,13] attempt to maintain a distinction between the two conditions wherein the term childhood schizophrenia is reserved for those cases in which the pathologic process appears to begin after the age of 4 to 5. They postulate that in childhood schizophrenia, a prior stage of intact psychic organization has decompensated, whereas in the autistic child, psychic organization failed to develop. However, in our experience, follow-up of some children who were diagnosed autistic prior to the age of 5 reveals the development over the years of a picture indistinguishable from schizophrenia. Brown and Reiser,[14] apparently observing similar changes, reported eight different clinical outcomes (after 9 years of age) of atypical children and included a "schizophrenic" group. Also, in some cases, if detailed retrospective histories of children diagnosed as being schizophrenic after the age of 5 are taken, previously overlooked but diagnostically significant behavioral deviancies can often be elicited. For example, behaviors such as hand-flapping, hypersensitivity to noise, and the failure to adapt to solid foods may be overlooked in ordinary history taking.

Although neither Eisenberg[15] nor Rutter[10] observed paranoid ideas, hallucinations, or delusions in follow-up studies of autistic children, one would not necessarily expect to see these classical symptoms of adult schizophrenia in children. However, in our clinical experience with children, we have observed clear transitions from early infantile autism to the thought disorder characteristic of adult schizophrenia. Similarly, Eisenberg[15] found "peculiarities of language and thought" possibly characteristic of schizophrenia. The case reported by Darr and Worden[16] illustrates an acute schizophrenic reaction in a marginally adjusted adult who had been autistic as a child. When 4 years old, this patient had been examined (Dr. Adolph Meyer) and the classic symptoms of early infantile autism were recorded. At 32 years of age, this woman complained that people would be killed by the poison that was in her, that she would die because she was urinating cider, etc. Tolor and Rafferty[17] found that adolescents diagnosed as schizophrenic scored high on a checklist of symptoms of early infantile autism. While the delineation of early infantile autism from childhood schizophrenia may have prognostic and therapeutic value, available evidence suggests that the former condition can develop into the latter and that so many transitional states occur as to imply a fundamentally similar underlying mechanism in many of the cases. Difference in age of manifest onset rather than separating the two conditions, demonstrates the effect of maturational and developmental level on the way the disease process is expressed.

Reiser[13] has suggested the term infantile psychosis to describe the period from birth to 5 years of age in which the pathologic process develops.

He suggests this term as encompassing and, therefore, replacing all of the other terminology just discussed. He feels that the designation "psychotic" is merited by virtue of impairment in perception, failure to test reality, social isolation and withdrawal, impaired control of instinctual energies, and disturbances of feeling, thinking, and behavior. This description overlaps the syndrome and subclusters of symptoms which will be described in the following sections of this paper. However, the terms *psychosis* and *psychotic* are also commonly used in a broader sense than is applicable to these conditions. Therefore, the terms *early infantile autism* and *autistic child* will be used in this paper as representative of the group of clinical states under study. Early infantile autism and the other conditions will be further considered as variants or sequelae of a basic disease.

NATURAL HISTORY

Family

When the syndrome of early infantile autism was first described by Kanner,[1] it was thought that these children came from highly intellectual families in the upper socioeconomic levels. In fact, the parents were from the academic and professional communities and their family life was characterized by obsessive meticulousness and intellectualism. The corollary of these attributes was an emotional coldness often described as "refrigeration."[2] In the subsequent two decades a broader clinical experience with autistic children and their families has revealed that these children come from every socioeconomic class and that the parents may, or may not, be professionally employed. The fathers may indeed be university professors, psychiatrists, electronic engineers, or mathematicians. We have observed, however, that they may be common laborers or artists. Wolff and Chess[9] have made similar observations. While some of the parents are reported to be cold, isolated, or refrigerated individuals, others have proven to be warm, loving, and quite capable of raising normally affectionate siblings of their autistic child. A condition of family disruption and emotional turmoil may surround the infancy or childhood of autistic children[13] or the disease process may develop in a normal emotional climate.[10]

A relative sparcity of schizophrenic parents has been noted by some observers. However, Rutter's[10] failure to find a single schizophrenic parent in his population of autistic children was not confirmed by Goldfarb,[12] Wolff and Chess,[9] or O'Gorman.[18]

It is rare to find more than one nontwin sibling with the disease,[13] and we have seen only one such case. However, J. Simmons (oral communication, June 1967) has followed five families with two nontwin autistic siblings. Dizygotic twins are discordant for early infantile autism. With one exception,[19] all reported cases of monozygotic twins are concordant for the disease when monozygocity has been adequately demonstrated and the disease is not associated with perinatal trauma to one twin.[20-21]

Pregnancy and Delivery

Available surveys provide conflicting evidence as to the relative incidence of complications during pregnancy and delivery in the mothers of these children as compared to other diagnostic groups. Schain and Yannet[22] and Kanner[23] reported no increase in prenatal and perinatal complications. However, in a well-controlled study, Taft and Goldfarb[24] reviewed hospital charts of autistic children, their siblings, and normal controls. They reported a significantly greater incidence of prenatal and perinatal difficulties in the autistic group.

Postnatal

In the immediate postnatal period, some autistic children have been described as unusually quiet, motorically inactive, and emotionally unresponsive or, conversely, as unusually irritable and extremely sensitive to auditory, tactile, and visual stimuli. The same infant may alternately manifest both types of disturbance.

Following the immediate postnatal period two general courses of development may be reported. In the first, the baby shows early signs of deviant development. In the second, relatively normal development is described by the parents until the age of 18 to 26 months, at which time an apparent regression in all areas of behavior rapidly occurs. These children then look identical to the children whose development has been deviant from birth. In many cases, parents report that the "regression" is associated with some concurrent event such as the birth of a sibling, marital rift, economic reversal, or a move to a new home. In other cases, the behavioral changes are associated with factors influencing the child directly, such as illness, hospitalization, or separation from a parent. We have found in several cases where "normal" development was reported during the first 18 months, detailed history taking revealed evidence of deviant development which had gone unnoticed.

Neonatal Period

Most frequently it is reported that the autistic infant was: "a good baby"; "he never cried"; "he seemed not to need companionship or stimulation"; and "he did not want to be held." Concomitant with being "good," he may have shown a reduced activity level, torpor, and a tendency to cry rarely, if at all. When picked up, he may have been limp with peculiar posturing and flaccid muscle tone. This data obtained from retrospective questioning of parents of autistic children has been confirmed by one prospective study.[25]

First Six Months

During the early months of development the mothers often report being perplexed by the baby's lack of crying or by their difficulty in relating crying to hunger or to discomfort from other specific needs. These babies seem content to be left alone a great deal. In some family constellations these factors are very disturbing to the mothers, resulting in anxiety and bewilderment which then leads to either compensatory overinvolvement or withdrawal. Either response may result in the mother's loss of self-esteem in her role as mother. In other families, the advent of such an "undemanding" baby is welcomed by a harrassed mother who then leaves the baby alone.

The first definite signs of deviant development may be the baby's failure to notice the coming and going of the mother, a lack or delay of the smiling response, or the lack of the anticipatory response to being picked up. Concomitantly, underreactivity (failure to play with the crib gym or show an interest in toys) and paradoxical overreactivity to stimulation (panic at the sound of a vacuum cleaner or telephone) may occur. Finally, failure to vocalize during the first half year may also be noted.

Second Six Months

An ominous sign of later pathology may appear when solid foods are introduced. A baby who had fed well at breast or bottle and adapted easily to strained foods may show severe distress when rough textured "junior" and table foods are introduced. Several types of response occur, including refusal to hold food in mouth, refusal to chew or swallow, or intense gagging. After dentition appears, it may become apparent that the infant avoids chewing food. Some of these children actually remain on pureed baby foods and the bottle until their 6th or 7th year.

The disinterest in toys noted during the first six months may precede the active casting or flicking away of toys. Objects placed in the hand may be simply dropped. This behavior may contrast markedly with an alternate tendency to hold an object such as a piece of string, a broken pencil, or a marble. Such a child often is panicked and upset if the object disappears. He may persist in holding onto it for years.

The sequence of motor development may be precocious or retarded or may be characterized by accelerated achievement of one motor skill followed by a lag before development of the next. Also characteristic is the tendency to give up a previously acquired motor skill; the parents often describe the child as not wanting to use an acquired ability.

Mothers frequently describe their autistic children as being unaffection-
ate. When picked up and held, they may either go limp or stiffen. When put
down by the mother, they do not seem to notice. At this point the busy or
bewildered mother may leave the baby alone because her feeling that he does
not need her is reinforced. By the age of 10 or 11 months these babies do
not play "peek-a-boo" and "patty-cake" games and do not imitate waving
"bye-bye." The mother's bewilderment at her baby's lack of responsiveness
may be further reinforced by his failure to develop communicative speech.
The baby who did not "coo" or "babble" earlier may now show a crucial
failure to imitate sounds and words. As with motor function, speech development may be retarded or may show precocious advances followed by failure to use words previously learned. Nonverbal communication also lags: the
child does not point toward what he wants and does not look toward a desired object.

At this stage of development and later, these children are frequently
thought to be deaf. This possibility is often belied by unusual sensitivity to
and awareness of certain unexpected or loud sounds. A similar type of sensitivity may also be observed in the visual modality. Sudden changes in illumination may evoke panic. Often the earlier tendency of babies to regard
their own writhing hand and finger movements becomes a consuming
preoccupation. Other sensory modalities may also be affected. For example,
unusual tactile discrimination with adverse reactions to rough wool fabrics
and preference for smooth surfaces occurs. Proprioceptive and antigravity
responses may be similarly involved and come to attention when the father
who enjoys tossing the child in the air is rebuffed by the baby's distress.

Second and Third Years

After 12 months, unusual sensitivity to auditory, visual, tactile, and labyrinthine stimulation is often accompanied paradoxically by peculiar and
bizarrely expressed pursuit of sensations in these modalities. Noisy, vigorous, and sustained tooth grinding occurs. Some of the children scratch surfaces and listen intently to the sounds they have created. They may pass their
eyes along surfaces apparently attending to patterns. They may rub surfaces
with their hands, apparently reacting to textural differences. Contrasting with
these behaviors, they seem to ignore more meaningful, environmentally determined stimuli.

Between 1 and 3 years of age, repetitive habits, mannerisms, and gestures may begin to develop. They suddenly cease activity, posture, and stare
off into space. Frequently, this posturing involves hyperextension of the
neck. Such children may begin to whirl themselves and characteristically
flutter or flap their arms, hands, or fingers. The fingers may flick against
stable objects or in the air. A variant of flapping is an oscillatory motion of
the hand and forearm. As the child learns to walk and run, he frequently

does so almost exclusively on his toes. Toe walking, whirling, and flapping may be seen as slow, consistent, repetitive mannerisms which may be suddenly interrupted by peculiar darting or lunging movements accompanied by excited gesticulation of the arms. Certain external stimuli, such as spinning objects (children's tops), may set off these explosive, yet organized patterns of activity. Continuous body rocking and head rolling are also frequently observed. These behaviors may become organized into complex repetitive sequences. Long hours may be spent spinning tops, wheels, jar lids, coins, or any available object, running back and forth across a room, switching the overhead lights repetitively on and off, and dancing around an object while flapping the hands.

By this age, it may become apparent that there is a lack of eye contact. They seem to look beyond or through people as if looking through a window. Other people can be used as extensions of the child's self, e.g., taking the arm of the adult and placing it on a doorknob. In doing this, they do not look at the adult but only at the desired object. Although they may seek out objects for repetitive stereotyped activity, e.g., light switches or tops, they usually show an utter lack of interest in toys offered to them.

Fourth and Fifth Years

By the time the child is between 3 and 5 years old, the unusual sensitivities to external stimulation noted above may decrease. Motor retardation, when it has occurred, is usually overcome and the child becomes capable of physical activities appropriate to his age. Yet, he may not actually engage in such activities as jungle-gym climbing or riding a tricycle because of his lack of social awareness of the activity itself. The tendency to walk on toes, flap arms, and whirl may decrease but in some cases continues for many years.

A major problem in the 3 to 5-year-old child is found in the area of language development. Speech may not have developed at all or if present may be characterized by parroting (echolalia), the parroted phrase being repeated completely out of the social context in whch it had been heard. This is called delayed echolalia.[26] These children often make requests by repeating what has been said to them in the interrogative form. For example, the child will say "you want to walk" rather than saying that he wants to go for a walk. Pronoun reversals using "you" or "he" for "I" or "me" are noted, and the object and subject of discourse are confused. The voice may sound atonal, arrhythmic, and hollow.

SYNDROME AND SUBCLUSTERS OF SYMPTOMS

The symptoms of early infantile autism and its variants have been described in the previous section in terms of their onset of occurrence. This multitude of symptoms will now be classified into certain related subclusters in order that a unified disease process can be delineated.

It is to be emphasized that the subclusters of symptoms are defined on the basis of observable behaviors. There is no a priori assumption that one subcluster of symptoms stands independently of another. In fact, it is one purpose of this paper to show that one of the subclusters (disturbances of perception) may underlie most of the other groups of symptoms which together make up the syndrome.

The subclusters are: (1) disturbances of perception, (2) disturbances of motor behavior, (3) disturbances of relating, (4) disturbances of language, and (5) disturbances of developmental rate and sequence.

It should be emphasized that the total syndrome characterized by these five subclusters of symptoms is based upon detailed observation of over 150 cases by us. It is not implied that in any particular case all symptoms will be seen nor will every subcluster of symptoms achieve full expression. In fact, we have observed individual autistic children who show primarily disturbances of relating and only minimal suggestion of the other subclusters. In contrast, we have seen an occasional child who shows primarily disturbances of perception, with minimal expression of the other subclusters and relatively intact ability to relate.

Disturbances of Perception

Heightened awareness, hyperirritability, and obliviousness to external stimulation all may occur in the same child. All modalities of sensation may be involved. While auditory changes are most often noted, unusual perceptual aberrations may be seen in the visual, tactile, gustatory, olfactory, proprioceptive, and vestibular senses.

Heightened Awareness of Sensory Stimuli

Auditory. Attention to self-induced sounds (e.g., scratching of surfaces), attention to background stimuli, ear-banging, ear-rubbing, and flicking of the ear are observed.

Visual. Prolonged regarding of writhing movements of the hands and fingers, brief but intense staring, and scrutiny of visual detail are noted.

Tactile. The auditory and visual scrutiny is paralleled by passing the hands over surfaces of varying textures.

Olfactory and Gustatory. Specific food preferences, according to taste and smell, and repetitive sniffing occur.

Vestibular. The children are unusually aware of things that spin and can become preoccupied with car wheels, phonograph records, or washing machines—far beyond the interest expressed transiently by normal children.

Heightened Sensitivity and Irritability

Auditory. Unusual fearfulness of sirens, vacuum cleaners, barking dogs, and the tendency to cover the ears in anticipation of such sounds are observed.

Visual. Change in illumination will occasionally precipitate fearful reactions.

Tactile. There may be intolerance for certain fabrics. The children often do not accept wool blankets or clothing against the skin, and show a preference for smooth surfaces.

Gustatory. A specific intolerance toward rough textured "junior" or table foods is observed.

Vestibular. A marked aversion to being tossed in the air or to ride in elevators occurs. Intense interest and pleasure in spinning objects may alternate with fearful, disturbed, and excited reactions to them.

Nonresponsiveness

Auditory. Most notable is the disregard of speech and the lack of detectable behavioral response to loud sounds.

Visual. These children ignore new persons or features in their environment. They may walk into or through things or people as if they did not exist.

Tactile. Early in the first year of life, they may let objects placed in the hand fall away, as if they had no tactile representation.

Pain. These children may not react with evidence of pain to bumps, falls, or cuts.

Disturbances of Motor Behavior

Motor behaviors can be divided into two groups, those that seem to be associated with sensory input and those that seem to be associated with discharge.

Motor Behaviors Apparently Associated With Sensory Input

Auditory. Scratching at surfaces is often accompanied by bringing the ear down as if to listen to the sound created. Banging of the ear or head may induce intense repetitive auditory and vibratory stimulation. Tooth grinding may have a similar effect.

Visual.   Both the regarding of the slow writhing movements of the hands and fingers and the more vigorous flapping of the hands within the visual field may provide visual input to the child.

Tactile.   Scratching at or rubbing of surfaces provides tactile sensation.

Vestibular.   Autistic children tend to whirl themselves or spend long hours spinning objects, such as tops, can lids, and coins. These activities may provide increased vestibular input. The children may whirl themselves in many ways, for example, while standing up or frequently while sitting on a smooth floor, swiveling around and around on their buttocks. They spin objects in many ways too and will become excited and preoccupied with spinning metal tops or take toys completely unrelated to spinning and find ways of spinning them. They seem to be able to make tops out of almost anything. Often bizarre ritualistic activities accompany the preoccupation with spinning. They will flap their hands and engage in excited, repetitive movements, lunging at the top as if to push against it and then pulling away from it only to repeat the activity again and again. At other times, the same child will appear frightened and run away from the top. The diagnosis was clarified in the case of a 3-year-old child with relatively intact capacity to relate when he was offered a top. He reacted with increasing tension and fearfulness, gesticulating as the top was spun faster. He stared at his hands and then ritualistically patted the floor while engaging in a stereotyped dance around the top. As his excitement increased, he became oblivious to reassurance, stared at the ceiling, and then began to flap his fingers while fixing his gaze intently on the top. When told that he could stop the spinning if he did not like it, he responded by making a "stop" gesture with his hand from a distance. Then he shot at the top with a toy gun, lay down to play "dead" and finally put the top in a cupboard out of sight.

Proprioceptive.   Hand-flapping deserves special mention, as it is an activity that is characteristic and almost pathognomic of the autistic child, although it may be seen occasionally in other syndromes. It may occur only transiently or may become a fixed behavior. It may be associated with states of excitement or occur over prolonged periods unassociated with external stimuli. The flapping of the arms has many modifications, such as wiggling of the fingers, flicking at surfaces, or oscillating of the hand while empty or while holding small toys. Flapping behavior often has an interesting evolution in individual children. In one case it was first noted at 11 months of age that while mouthing a small plastic airplane, the child would rhythmically flick at the wing with one hand while holding it to his mouth with the other. At the age of 5 years, this behavior evolved into a repetitive gesticulation wherein the child would start to put one hand and thumb into his mouth while flicking that hand away with the other. By 8 years of age, he had given up this activity, attempting to follow directions to suppress it; he was observed instead to repetitively flex his extended fingers at the metacarpophalangeal joints over long periods of time. Another child, 4 years old, whose variant of hand-flapping was a rapid oscillation (alternate pronation and supination) of the hand and forearm, developed a pruritic dermatitis and began scratching. As the dermatitis increased, the scratching took on the oscillatory nature of his hand-flapping, and for a period of time substituted in part for the hand movements. As the pruritus abated, he gave up the scratching and again oscillated. In some of the children hand-flapping does not occur spontaneously during examination, although a history of it may be elicited by detailed questioning. It may at times be elicited by specific stimulation, e.g., presentation of a top. However, under controlled conditions of observations, it is found to be a remarkably persistent behavior, neither increasing nor decreasing with time (Sorosky, A.; Ornitz, E.; Brown, M.; and Ritvo, E., unpublished data).

Other Motor Phenomena

Toe walking and periodic bursts of excited lunging, gesticulating, and darting movements do not seem especially related to sensory input. The lunging and darting may appear almost seizure-like. Toe walking may occur intermittently or may be the only mode of walking.

Disturbances of Relating

Poor eye contact, delayed or absent social smile, delayed or absent anticipatory response to being picked up, apparent aversion to physical contact, limpness or stiffening when held, disinterest in looking at, casting away, or bizarre use of toys, a lack of active response to the "peek-a-boo," "pat-a-cake," and "bye-bye" games, and the general preference to being alone are all characteristic. The use of people as an extension of the self, and the more pervasive lack of emotional responsiveness are additional manifestations of disturbed relating.

Disturbances of Language

Frequently, there is a complete failure of speech to develop. When and if speech does develop, it is often poorly modulated, atonal, arhythmic, and hollow sounding without communicative or affective content. The most prominent specific type of pathologic language is called echolalia.[26] Also, characteristic is pronoun reversal.

Disturbances of Developmental Rate

The rate of development may be disturbed, leading to discontinuities in the normal sequence. Altered rates of development involving motor and speech areas occur. The child may roll over precociously early and then may not sit without support until 11 months, or he may sit up without support at 5 months and not pull to a stand until 13 months. In the language area he may use a few words at 10 months and fail to use words again until 2 years old, or the early use of words may be followed by a long delay in joining them into phrases. Further, he may successfully perform some skill such as crawling and then may not ever do it again. Some of the children have been described on the one hand as slow and on the other hand as showing precocious motor and language development. The most characteristic finding on infant developmental testing is a marked scatter both between and within sectors of tests such as the Gesell.[27]

Other attempts to group the many symptoms of this disease have been made. Closest to our approach is the work of Creak.[28] She abstracted nine criteria from the descriptive literature on childhood schizophrenia and early infantile autism. These nine points overlap the five subclusters of symptoms described here. Impairment of emotional relations with people and preoccupation with objects have been included here with the other disturbances of relating. Speech disturbance, distortion in motility, and retardation are synonymous with the disturbances of language, motor expression, and developmental rate. Along with abnormal perceptual experience, we consider the unawareness of self-identity, the maintenance of sameness, and anxiety precipitated by change as derivatives of the disturbances of perception.

CHANGE IN SYNDROME AFTER EARLY CHILDHOOD

One of the most confusing aspects of this disease is that after the age of 5 or 6 years, symptom-complexes of early infantile autism and its variants tend to merge with other clinical entities, e.g., childhood schizophrenia (see above). The manifestations of the subclusters of symptoms as they appear past the age of 5 or 6 years will now be discussed.

Relationship to the Environment and Language

Disturbances of relating and disturbances of language are best considered together; as with increasing age, the capacity to relate depends markedly on the capacity to communicate with others. It has been observed that speech may not develop by the age of 5, in which case the autistic child becomes less and less distinguishable from the large group of severely retarded children.[15] Absence of speech has been correlated with low intelligence.[10] Those autistic children who develop noncommunicative speech and progress no further, when seen again at 10 to 15 years of age, tend to look much as they did when younger.

If they develop communicative speech by 5 years of age, then several possible courses of development are open. First, language capacity may be quite rudimentary. Communications are literal and concrete, with minimal capacity for abstract thought. Affect tends to be flat, and they do not become emotionally involved with others.

In a second course of development, characteristics typical of organic brain disease become manifest. There may be an impulsiveness, a lack of emotional control, hyperactivity, restlessness, and irritability accompanied by some degree of mental retardation and concrete thinking.

A third developmental course seen during the school years and in early adolescence is identical to that described by others as schizophrenia. This is often an insidious process wherein the child who is diagnosed earlier in life as being autistic becomes harder and harder to distinguish from those children who are called schizophrenic. Language is characterized by loose, free, or fragmented associations leading away from social contact and communication through tangles of irrelevancy and tangential thinking. Bizarre, illusory, or hallucinatory thinking may be present. A distorted fantasy life may be elaborated around some of the earlier behaviors which have been grouped as disturbances of perception or motor expression. For example, the child who evolved hand-flapping into a complex gesticulation wherein one hand and thumb was pushed back from the mouth by a flicking action of the other hand, elaborated the fantasy that his thoughts were falling out of his mouth and that he was pushing them back into his head.

A fourth course of development may evolve either from the schizophrenic stage or follow directly from the autistic syndrome itself. Such children superficially appear to have a relatively normal personality structure or neurotic or characterologic defects. However, careful attention to behavior and a detailed history of earlier development will reveal a clinical picture suggestive of residuals of an earlier autistic syndrome. Particularly, one sees a certain oddness in character and impaired empathy coupled with a lack of social judgment and discrimination. There may be excessive preoccupying interests in mechanical things coupled with a lack of interest in human relationships.

Perceptual and Motor Phenomena

The disturbances of perception and motor behavior may persist during the school years but usually dropout. Some of the children who suffer a schizophrenic outcome still toewalk, tend to whirl, and also may hand-flap. In the children who develop neurotic or personality disorders, one may under certain circumstances see hand-flapping or one of its variants. For example, one 10-year-old child was examined and purposely presented with a noisy spinning top; he commented that he used to get excited when he saw a top spin. While there was no overt hand-flapping, observation of his crossed hands, one pressing down on the other, revealed a rhythmic contraction of the tendons in the dorsum of the hand. It appeared that he was consciously suppressing the tendency to flap.

These relationships among diagnostic categories are illustrated in Figure 1. Increasing diagnostic specificity as the child gets older is evident.

DIFFERENTIAL DIAGNOSIS

The differential diagnosis of early infantile autism and childhood schizophrenia has been thoroughly reviewed by Reiser,[13] Rutter,[10] and Ekstein.[29] Discussion of differential diagnosis here will be limited to those syndromes wherein certain common symptoms suggest etiologic consideration.

In the syndrome of institutionalism,[30] not only are a certain limited number of symptoms common to early infantile autism, but certain aspects of the history may be common to both conditions, making differential diagnosis initially difficult. The child raised in an institution may suffer sensory, emo-

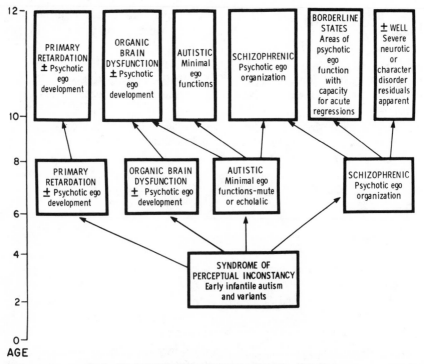

Fig 1.—Developmental relationships among diagnostic categories.

tional, and maternal deprivation, resulting in a developing state of apathy during the first year of life accompanied by a tendency to excessive rocking, transient preoccupation with looking at objects, and athetoid-like movements of the extremities. When followed later, some of these children showed unstable and particularly indiscriminate relating to others, failing to develop a meaningful one-to-one relationship with a mother figure. They also may show deficiencies in abstract thinking. Institutionalism can occur in home settings[31] and we have observed infants with this syndrome, particularly when the mother has suffered a prolonged but inadequately recognized postpartum depression. These infants, although at home, tend to be left alone and are therefore understimulated. The autistic child may also be left alone a great deal, and this can be in response to the mother's bewilderment at his lack of interest in her presence. Thus, the isolation of the autistic child follows rather than precedes the pathologic process. They apathy of the primarily understimulated child can superficially resemble the emotional deficiency of the autistic child, and the prolonged rocking, preoccupation with objects, and peculiar athetoid-like movements can mimic transiently some of their motor expressions. The indiscriminate relating superficially suggests the disturbed type of relating seen in early infantile autism. However, the children who suffer institutionalism either in the institution or at home do not develop the complete autistic syndrome. The myriad ways in which the autistic child expresses deviant development are not seen.

Loss of a maternal figure who has already become significant during the first year also leads to disturbed development. This has been referred to as anaclitic depression.[32] Here profound withdrawal is not accompanied by the other facets of the syndrome of early infantile autism or its variants.

The absence of development of early infantile autism in children suffering from institutionalism (S. Provence, MD, oral communication, November 1966) and following loss suggest that although early infantile autism is in part a profound disturbance of relating, etiologic factors must be looked for within the child. Such factors must lie within the central nervous system; sensory deprivation may at the most be a secondary component in the etiology of this condition.

Reiser[13] has commented on the variety of chronic brain damage syndromes with or without accompanying retardation which should be considered in the differential diagnosis of early infantile autism. While the behavioral disturbance in chronic brain syndromes includes irritability, emotional lability, hyperactivity, short attention span, and lack of impulse control, at times behavior more specifically suggestive of early infantile autism may occur. Berkson and Davenport[33] observed "hand flick-shake," "hand held before eyes," and "twirling" in severely retarded "mental defectives." As these behaviors which are probably identical with the handflapping, regarding, and whirling of autistic children are lumped with less specific "stereotyped movements," their incidence is unknown. Since diagnostic precision was limited to "mental defective," the number of possibly autistic individuals in the patient group is also unknown. Occasionally, in brain damage secondary to specific syndromes, we have seen whirling (tuberous sclerosis) and hand-flapping (phenylketonuria). However, it should be stressed that in all children suffering from these conditions we do not see these disturbed motor expressions which are so characteristic of autistic children. It is postulated, therefore, that in those cases with known brain damage and autistic behavior, certain specific functional systems of the central nervous system, pathology of which underlies early infantile autism, may become involved. No anatomical sites for these hypothesized functional systems are at present known. In those cases of early infantile autism which are not accompanied by evidence of brain damage, it is postulated that the same functional systems are involved on a congenital basis as suggested by twin studies.

Since early infantile autism can only be diagnosed as a behavioral syndrome,[34] it would seem that those cases of the syndrome where evidence of brain pathology, e.g., phenylketonuria, encephalitis, birth trauma exists should be referred to as "early infantile autism associated with . . ., e.g., PKU, encephalitis, birth trauma" rather than excluding those cases from the behavioral syndrome as is often done. Rutter[10] reports a high incidence of brain damage in a follow-up study of 63 autistic children.

The failure of speech development in both early infantile autism and aphasia creates diagnostic problems of both semantic and etiologic significance. While the autistic child without speech is by definition "aphasic" confusing cases of real differential diagnostic import are seen. The relationship between the two conditions has been thoroughly discussed by Rutter.[10,35] The fact that aphasic children may use gesture to communicate, while autistic children often do not, may help to separate the two conditions if the child is seen at an early age. If the child improves in all areas but speech, the diagnosis of aphasia is supported.

ETIOLOGIC CONSIDERATIONS

In the literature, the etiology of early infantile autism has been considered from several points of view: (1) hereditary tendency; (2) influence of parental personality or malignant family interaction; (3) critical or vulnerable periods in infancy; (4) possible disturbed neurophysiologic mechanism; and (5) underlying or concomitant developmental and neurologic pathology.

Various investigators have stressed different symptom subclusters as expressing the fundamental and basic nature of the disorder. For example, Kanner when first describing the disease process focused on disturbed relating to the environment. The coldness, aloofness, and withdrawal of the child was described in relationship to analogous though less severe behavior observed in the parents and even the grandparents in this particular patient sample. This lent itself initially to a genetically based interpretation wherein the autistic child was seen as the final expression of an innate tendency toward intellectualism and an associated lack of emotional expression.[1] The emphasis on the disturbed relatedness, however, also lent itself to an alternative etiologic notion, namely that the children were disturbed and emotionally "refrigerated" because they were raised in an emotionally refrigerated environment.[2,36] Therefore, the etiologic emphasis was changed from faulty genes to faulty parents. A more specific emphasis on the parents' role in the development of the syndrome was postulated by Szurek[37] and by Rank[38] and has been categorically stated by Reiser.[13] The emphasis shifted from the type of environment created for the child to the parent-child interaction; a state of emotional turmoil in the parents during the critical period of infancy was postulated to compromise the essential relationship. In our own experience, however, this has not been seen in all cases; moreover, in many families where great emotional turmoil has been present during the infancy of the child, that child has not become autistic. This experience has been confirmed by others.[10]

The concept of symbiotic psychosis was introduced by Mahler[6] and emphasized the parent as the etiologic agent in the development of psychosis in the child, but for opposite reasons than those of Kanner.[2] In the development of symbiotic psychosis, the parent was described as all-enveloping and never giving the child the opportunity to differentiate himself. However, we have seen both "symbiotic" clinging and complete physical and emotional fusion alongside of, and alternating with, emotional aloofness and cold, icy withdrawal in the same child. What is basic and common to these apparently opposite disturbances is the fluctuating capacity of such a child to perceive separateness between himself and the surrounding environment. The inability to maintain a distinction between self and nonself can be expressed as readily by fusion as by lack of awareness of the other person. Thus, both behaviors, which superficially appear to be opposites, are simply different expressions of a failure in these children to delineate the boundaries between themselves and their environment.

Emphasis on the disturbances of relating has led others to pin-point the period of differentiation from the mother between 6 and 18 months of age[34,39] as the critical period of vulnerability in development of the disease. However, our clinical experience and direct observation[40] show that the onset of the illness can be manifest at birth or in the first months of life when other symptom clusters are considered.

Another subcluster of symptomatology which has received particular consideration with reference to etiology has been that of disturbance of developmental rate. Bender has emphasized this aspect of the syndrome by postulating a maturation lag at the embryonic level as being characteristic of and fundamental to the development of the entire syndrome.[41]

The disturbances of motor expression which we have described have received mention in passing, but have not been related systematically to the syndrome as a whole. Some investigators have referred to the motor behaviors as self-stimulation.[42]

Disturbances of perception have been emphasized by several authors. Bergman and Escalona[5] observed abnormal sensitivities in a small group of children, some of whom became psychotic, and postulated a low barrier to external stimulation as being of etiologic import. Goldfarb[43] has studied perception from the point of view of receptor preference in these children and has pointed up their apparent preference for the use of near receptors (tactile sensation) over far receptors (vision and audition). Schopler[44] has attempted to use near receptor preference as evidence that early sensory deprivation due to inadequate reticular arousal mechanisms is a factor in etiology. Although the linkage between near receptor preference and sensory deprivation is not made clear, an overriding consideration is that infants actually suffering known sensory deprivation exhibit an entirely different syndrome than that of early infantile autism. Contrasting with the notion of reduced arousal functions is the postulation of a chronically high level of arousal as basic to the etiology.[45] Actual observation, however, of the behavior of autistic children, either individually or as a group, reveals them at times to be in apparent states of low arousal (posturing, immobility, and unresponsiveness), and at times in apparent states of high arousal (agitation, excitation, and fearfulness). Wing[46] stressed the autistic child's inability to make meaningful patterns out of sensory stimuli, thereby linking cognitive to perceptual disturbances.

Goldfarb[12, 47] has described both motility disturbances and disturbances of perception in a high percentage of schizophrenic (autistic) children whom he labels the "organic" subgroup. This subgroup is differentiated from "nonorganic" children who are relatively free of these disturbances. Goldfarb postulated a continuum of etiologic variables ranging from purely environmental to specific organic influences. These have been detailed by Sarvis and Garcia[39] who associated the illness with faulty family psychodynamics, traumatic environmental circumstances, severe physical illness, and temporal lobe and other neuropathology affecting perception. However, the absence of autistic behavior under conditions of severe environmental and organic insult, and the presence of the syndrome unassociated with such conditions suggests that a basic pathologic mechanism specific to the illness must be present. Environmental factors may determine in some cases the time at which the illness comes to clinical attention. Somatic factors may in some cases either trigger or replicate the expression of the basic pathology.

UNDERLYING MECHANISMS

Is it possible to relate the symptom clusters of early infantile autism to an underlying pathologic mechanism? All of the subclusters of symptoms can be seen as resulting from certain cardinal developmental failures occurring in the first year of life. First, many of the behaviors of an autistic infant stem from a failure to develop a distinction between himself and the outside world. Second, imitative behavior is fragmented, greatly delayed, or does not appear. Third, the autistic infant fails to develop the capacity to adequately modulate perceptual input; much of his behavior suggests that he is either getting too little or too much input from the environment. These three developmental failures can be associated and explained by assuming that autistic children do not have the ability to maintain *constancy of perception*. Thus, identical percepts from the environment are not experienced as the same each time. This is due, we further postulate, to an underlying failure of homeostatic regulation within the central nervous system so that environmental stimuli are either not adequately modulated or are unevenly amplified. This postulated failure to maintain perceptual constancy results in a random underloading or overloading of the central nervous system.

The autistic infant seems to get either too much or too little sensory input, and these states often alternate rapidly and without relation to the environment. Behaviors suggesting that sensory overload is being experienced include attention to inconsequential stimuli and scrutiny of tactile and visual detail. Such activities suggest that the trivial cannot be treated as trivial. More impressive is the tendency of so many of these children to respond with increased excitation, irritability, or apprehension bordering on panic to stimuli which may be either minimal or intense. Such stimuli may be in the auditory, visual, tactile, and proprioceptive modalities. Spinning objects may incite particularly intense reactions in these children. This suggests sensitivity in the vestibular modality as does the panic brought on by an elevator ride.

That these children also get too little external stimuli is inferred from their underresponsiveness.

What type of pathologic mechanism might interfere with the capacity to maintain perceptual constancy? While the failure of homeostatic regulation may represent a neurophysiologic deficiency, behaviors such as the tendency to rub surfaces, visual regarding of finger movements, hand-flapping, and whirling suggest a breaking through of a pathologic excitatory state or activating mechanism. Such a postulated state would have the characteristic of interfering with homeostatic regulation of perception.

Physiologic states can be characterized by degrees of excitation, facilitation, inhibition, or some combination thereof. In the behaviors which define early infantile autism and its allied conditions, we can discern expressions of both states of excessive excitation and inhibition. These states may occur independently in an individual child, may alternate rapidly with each other, or even appear to coexist. The hyperexcitatory state is manifested by hand-flapping, finger-fluttering, whirling, circling on tiptoes, sudden lunging and darting, accentuated startle, hypersensitivity to stimuli, and excited reactions to spinning objects. The overinhibitory state is manifested by posturing, prolonged immobility, and nonresponsiveness to external stimulation. To a considerable, though not complete extent, the symptoms indicative of the state of hyperexcitation include those behaviors which suggest that sensory input is not being adequately dampened. The symptoms indicative of the overinhibitory state, on the other hand, suggest excessive damping of sensory input whether from auditory, visual, proprioceptive, or other sources.

In Table 1, the symptomatology common to early infantile autism, childhood schizophrenia, atypical development, and the other related conditions is outlined for comparative purposes by chronological order of appearance, descriptive subclusters, developmental failure, and pathologic states of excitation and inhibition.

In summary, the behavior common to a group of related clinical entities, e.g., early infantile autism, childhood schizophrenia, and atypical children, suggests a common underlying pathologic mechanism. This mechanism involves the presence of states of hyperexcitation and inhibition which interfere with the normal capacity to maintain perceptual constancy. The presence of these states may indicate a dissociation of a physiologic equilibrium between facilitatory and inhibitory systems which regulate sensory input.

CLINICAL ILLUSTRATIONS

How do these postulated pathologic mechanisms find expression in the multivariant clinical entities under consideration and how do they lead to the major subclusters of the symptoms?

If the dissociated excitatory and inhibitory states are not too severe, then percepts are available for imitation and self can be distinguished from nonself. In such cases, symptomatology may be confined primarily to disturbances of perception and motor behavior.

Case 1

This 4-year-old boy has been under psychiatric observation since 2½ years of age. His older brother was diagnosed as having early infantile autism. His parents are nonprofessional people who did not complete college. Following an uneventful pregnancy, he was born three or four weeks postterm, weighing 3,714 gm (8 lb, 3 oz). The neonatal period was not remarkable. Between 3 and 19 months of age, he had asthmatic bronchitis.

Frequently, during the early months of life, his mother could not be certain when he was hungry. "Junior" foods were first introduced at 5 months, but were not accepted until 7 months.

Between 9 and 36 months, he was unusually aware of anything that would spin. He would go past the shower curtain, pressing his eyes very close to it, apparently preoccupied with the details in the printed pattern. At 36 months, he was particularly responsive to any change in his mother's appearance, such as a change in hair styling or make-up. From time to time, he would seem to stare as if he saw something that was not there. He was not excessively disturbed by auditory stimuli. Between 24 and 38 months he walked on his toes: when presented with a spinning top, he would flap his hands. Between 30 and 38 months he would whirl himself. The use of sounds, syllables, words, phrases, and sentences occurred on schedule. However, as he developed communicative speech, an excessive parroting of phrases and sentences also occurred. He particularly repeated questions directed to him rather than answering them. He developed a pleasant, responsive smile, an anticipatory response to being picked up, and good eye contact during the first half year of life. He was cuddly, affectionate, and always seemed to need his mother. His use of toys was limited, and he was preoccupied with any part of a toy that would spin. He played "peek-a-boo" and "patty-cake" and mimicked his parents' gestures and mannerisms. Motor development was not delayed.

He began psychotherapy at 3½ years of age. A relative paucity of fantasy was noted during the early phase of treatment. He tended to repetitively confuse the identities of persons, for example, calling his therapist "daddy" or "Dr. Smith Jones," a name combining that of his therapist and his father. He had some bizarre ideation: For example, when shown a microphone, he said, "Mommy is inside the microphone."

Such a case is often referred to as an *atypical child* or a *child with unusual sensitivities*.

In severe cases where perception is so unstable that imitation (and subsequent identification) and distinction between self and nonself is impossible, then disturbances of relatedness, language, and development are seen along with the disturbances of perception and motor expression.

Case 2

A 5-year, 7-month-old boy had his first psychiatric evaluation at the age of 3 years and 10 months. Since age 4 he has been an inpatient in a psychiatric hospital. He is the second child of parents whose formal education stopped at the end of high school. His father has been a truck driver and laborer. Following a normal pregnancy, he was delivered without incident at term, weighing 3,345 gm (7 lb, 6 oz). The neonatal period was not remark-

(continued on page 166)

Table 1.—The Symptomatology of Early Infantile Autism, Its Variants, and Certain Cases of Childhood Schizophrenia

CHRONOLOGICAL APPEARANCE OF SYMPTOMS	SUBCLUSTERS OF SYMPTOMS	DEVELOPMENTAL FAILURES EXPRESSED BY SYMPTOMS	EXCESSIVE EXCITATORY & INHIBITORY STATES EXPRESSED BY SYMPTOMS
Postnatal	**Disturbances of Perception**	**Failure to Distinguish**	**Excitatory States**
Hyperirritability	**Heightened awareness**	**Between Self and Nonself**	Hand-flapping
Failure to respond	*Auditory*	Lack of interest in eye contact	Whirling
Torpor	Attending to self-induced sounds,	Absent social smile	Circling
Flaccidity	ear-banging, & tooth-grinding	Failure to play "peek-a-boo"	Darting & lunging
First 6 mo	*Visual*	Let objects fall out of hand	Accentuated startle
Failure to smile	Regarding of hands, staring,	Use others as extension of self	Overreactivity to stimuli
No anticipatory response	& visual detail scrutiny	Pronoun reversal	in all modalities
Failure to vocalize	*Tactile*	**Failure of Imitative Behavior**	Excitation associated with
Hypersensitivity to stimuli	Rubbing surfaces	Failure to play "patty-cake"	spinning objects
Lack of eye contact	*Olfactory & gustatory*	Failure to say "bye-bye"	**Inhibitory State**
Second 6 mo	Bizarre food preferences, sniffing	Failure to mimic sounds	Posturing
Unwilling to chew or accept solids	*Vestibular*	& expressions	Prolonged immobility
Flicking at objects	Spinning objects	Lack of emotional expression	Nonresponsiveness to stimuli in
Casting away of toys	**Heightened sensitivity**	**Failure to Modulate Input**	all sensory modalities
Letting toys passively drop out	*Auditory*	*Sensory overload*	
of hands	Fearful reactions to noise;	Attention to trivial stimuli	
Irregular motor development	cover ears	Visual & tactile scrutiny	
Limp or rigid when held	*Visual*	Irritability or apprehension to incon-	
Unaffectionate	To change in illumination	sequential stimuli; cover ears, etc.	
Failure to discriminate mother	*Gustatory*	Panic in elevator	
Failure to play "peek-a-boo,"	Intolerance of "rough" foods	Intolerance of "rough" foods	
"patty-cake," or "bye-bye"	*Vestibular*	*Sensory Underload*	
Lack of words	Fearful of roughhouse,	Disregard of auditory &	
Failure to point	fright in elevators	visual stimuli	
Regarding of hands		Underreactivity to painful stimuli	
Intolerance of sensory stimulation;			
cupping ears			
May appear deaf			

Second-Third Yr
Attending to self-induced sounds
Ear-banging & flicking
Visual & tactile scrutiny
Ignoring meaningful or
    painful stimuli
Posturing & staring
Whirling
Hand-flapping
Darting, lunging motions
Spinning of objects
Deviant eye contact
Use others as extension of self
Early speech drops out
Prolonged tooth-grinding

Fourth-Fifth Yr
Failure to speak
Echolalia
Pronoun reversal
Atonal, arhythmic voice
Severe distress in novel situations

Nonresponsiveness
Auditory
Disregard of speech,
    ignoring loud sounds
Visual
Disregard of surroundings
Tactile
Let objects fall out of hand
Pain
Failure to react to bumps & falls

Motor Disturbances
Hand-flapping; finger-flicking
Bizarre gesticulations
Whirling
Toe-walking
Darting & lunging
Posturing

Disturbances of Relating
Deviant eye contact
Absent social smile
Delayed anticipatory response
Limpness or stiffness when held
Bizarre or stereotyped use of toys
Failure to play "peek-a-boo," etc.
Use others as extension of self
Lack of emotional responsiveness

Disturbances of Language
Lack of speech development
Echolalia
Pronoun reversal
Atonal, arrhythmic voice

Disturbances of Developmental Rate
Retarded development
Precocious development
Giving up of acquired skills
Scatter on developmental tests

Dissociated Motor Excitation and Inhibition
Excitation
Hand-flapping
Whirling
Circling
Darting & lunging
Inhibition
Posturing
Prolonged immobility

able, although he was described as "irritable and oversensitive." He developed chickenpox at 12 months. The parents were first concerned at 16 months as he did not seem to respond normally. However, they had noticed that he had been preoccupied with twirling beads in his crib at 4 months and twirling ashtrays at 8 months. Furthermore, he failed to show an anticipatory response to being picked up until after 12 months. He remained on baby foods until 36 months, as he had refused to chew earlier.

He was unusually aware of visual detail and spent considerable time regarding the movements of his fingers since 15 months. He completely ignored auditory stimulation and toys presented to him. If handed objects, he let them fall out of his hand or flicked them away. From 24 months, he whirled himself, walked on his toes, and developed a repetitive, rapid oscillation of the hands. From 4 months, he rolled his head rhythmically from side to side and could only be distracted from such activity with great difficulty. Although he had spontaneously used some sounds by 6 months and some syllables by 12 months, he did not imitate either sounds or syllables. By 36 months, he had developed a 10-word vocabulary, but after that age, he ceased using words. He never combined words into phrases. He never made eye contact, and he used others as an extension of himself. The parents have said, "he pushes us to his needs." He never played "peek-a-boo" or "patty-cake." Between 18 and 24 months, he occasionally waved "bye-bye" in imitation of his father, but then abandoned this activity. He sat without support by 7 months but did not walk alone until 16 months.

In the course of extensive observation in an inpatient setting, he was noted to sustain his oscillatory hand-flapping throughout the entire day. He was never observed to use toys or other objects in any appropriate way and would only spin them.

This case demonstrates a more severe manifestation of the same basic disease than does case 1 and is usually labeled *early infantile autism*. If the development of such a child remains static, particularly when speech fails to develop, while the motor and perceptual disturbances gradually abate, he may be relabeled *pseudoretarded*.

If a child such as case 2 develops speech, particularly echolalia and pronoun reversal, he will continue to be labeled autistic.

Case 3

This 6-year-old boy has been under psychiatric observation since 4 years of age. He is the third in a family of four children, and his parents are high school graduates. His father is a salesman. The pregnancy was not remarkable. He was delivered at term by breech presentation and weighed 3,970 gm (8 lb, 12 oz). His Apgar rating was 10, and the postnatal course was not remarkable.

He has been in good physical health with no illnesses other than chickenpox at age 2 years. The early feeding history revealed he was apparently unwilling to hold solid food in his mouth or to chew. He sat without support at 7 months, but did not walk until 21 months. He showed no excessive reaction to auditory, visual, tactile, or proprioceptive stimuli, but he would become excessively disturbed when given new toys or clothes. He consistently ignored people and did not respond to sounds or to painful stimuli, e.g., bumps and falls. He would let toys fall out of his hands. He maintained prolonged and unusual postures and between 2 and 3 years of age, whirled himself, flapped his hands, and walked on his toes. He never showed an anticipatory response to being picked up; he seemed to look through people, stiffened when held, and ignored affection.

He spontaneously made sounds such as "coos" and "babbles" by 4 months and later used syllables. He later ceased these vocalizations. He did not use phrases until after 36 months and never used complete sentences. Prior to 24 months, he failed to imitate sounds and words, but after 36 months, he would repeatedly parrot words and phrases he had heard in the past, but which had no relationship to the present situation. His speech was characterized by a flat tonal quality without inflection.

The echolalia and pronoun reversal are sequelae of the earlier failures to imitate and to distinguish between self and nonself.[26] If, in the early arrested autistic child, the failure to distinguish between self and nonself is manifested by persistent clinging to other people, then the label *symbiotic psychosis* may be applied.

Case 4

This 4-year-old girl has been under psychiatric observation since 30 months of age. She is the third child in her family. The mother, a teacher, had considerable experience with school-age children and was a warm and affectionate person. Following an unremarkable pregnancy, the patient was born several days after rupture of the membranes. At delivery, the umbilical cord was looped around the neck. She was kept in an incubator during the first postnatal day because of "congestion in the lungs." The first month of life was characterized by projectile vomiting until pyloric stenosis was diagnosed and corrected surgically. Following the surgery she thrived on bottle feedings and gradually accepted strained foods. She would not, however, accept any chopped foods, and at 30 months, eating was limited to strained baby foods or puddings. Paradoxically, she chewed on crinkly cellophane.

She failed to cry to be held or fed, from birth on, and by 6 months of age, it became apparent that she did not smile at others. During the first and second years, she never indicated wanting to be held by her mother. At 27 months she first seemed to be aware of changes in her surroundings and at such times began to cling tenaciously to the mother. By 33 months, she showed persistent clinging. She would throw severe temper tantrums if the mother refused to hold her on her lap. However, she accepted being held by any other person in the same way, and then would seem unaware of the mother's absence. She would kneel for hours at a time on her mother's lap, pressing her chest against her mother, or she would stand on her mother's lap, hanging onto her thumbs, vigorously rocking back and forth. She would press her fingers into her mother's eyes, with no apparent awareness that this caused pain. She would, on occasion, smile responsively when her hands were pushed together in the "patty-cake" game, but she did not actively imitate. By 33 months, she was saying "ring around" and "fall down" responsively to a "ring around the rosy" game, and she would also say "rock, rock the baby" while pantomiming rocking a doll in her arms. She would say "Mary, Mary" to her own image in the mirror but had no specific term for her mother. She would point to her nose and verbalize a word that sounded like a fusion between "nose" and "mouth" or mix up the words for "mouth" and "nose," and she often held her forearms flexed upward with her hands loosely waving in the air. She scratched at surfaces. In an elevator she would cry both at the beginning and at the end of the ride. From 15 months, she often engaged in peculiar posturing with her hands held in a "claw-like position." She did not sit without support until 12 months, but pulled herself to a standing position at that time and walked without support by 15 months.

Those cases in which communicative speech develops, the disturbance of relatedness is not too severe, and a thought disorder becomes manifest are usually referred to as *childhood schizophrenia*. In such cases, the perceptual inconstancy has not been so severe as to arrest the development of relatedness and language but results in distortion in these areas. This distortion is manifest in the thought disorder. The persistence of disturbances of motor behavior and perception are the pathologic sequelae of the abnormal or dissociated states of excitation and inhibition and reveal the fundamental developmental relationship between such cases of childhood schizophrenia and early infantile autism.

Case 5

This 11-year-old boy has been under continuous psychiatric observation since 4 years of age. His natural parents were high school graduates. Following a normal pregnancy, he was delivered at term, weighing 3,913 gm (8 lb, 10 oz). Examination at 8 days revealed good crying and color; the Moro reflex was described as "only fair." He was placed for adoption and was noted to be a quiet baby, not particularly responsive to stimulation. He entered the home of his adopting parents when 18 days old. Both adopting parents are college-educated, thoughtful, and affectionate people. The father is an engineer. A social work report at 4 months indicated a "happy and well-adjusted child." There were no early feeding problems and "junior" foods were introduced at 6 months without difficulty. He chewed well and ate everything offered until 24 months, at which time he limited his diet to liquids and soft foods. When 4 years old, he again accepted a regular diet.

From three months, he was panicked by any loud noise and startled repeatedly if one moved suddenly near him. The sensitivity to loud noises persisted until he was 6 years old. Until 15 months he became severely upset by any encounter with a strange person. He was markedly disturbed when brought into unaccustomed surroundings until 3 years old. Between 2 and 3½ years, he was panicked at any attempt to toss him in the air. He remained oblivious to any toy presented to him until he was 3 years old.

Photographs document a preoccupying interest in regarding his own writhing hand movements from 8 months and hand-flapping from 11 months. At first, he held a toy to his mouth with one hand and repetitively flapped his fingers against a part of it with the other hand. By 4 years this evolved into a stereotyped ritualistic gesticulation consisting of a rapid pushing of the fingers of the one hand against the other. At the same time, the thumb of one hand would be rhythmically pushed toward the mouth while it was pushed back by the pressure of the other hand. At 8 years of age he tried to consciously suppress this activity, but substituted a rhythmic stereotyped alternating extension and flexion of the fingers. He has always walked on his toes. When he was a baby, he would sit for hours content to be alone playing with a toy that he could spin. Later, he would say that he was inside the washing machine while he was preoccupied watching it spin.

From birth, he was described as being "very sober." When held he conformed without stiffening but did not snuggle or cuddle. He did respond to affection and to the "peek-a-boo" and "pat-a-cake" games. Although he was aware of his mother when she was present, separation evoked no response. He reacted to other children as if they were inanimate. By 4 years, he became interested in toys and began to use them functionally.

He first used syllables at 6 months and words at 9 months. He did not use speech for communication until after 4 years of age, but would parrot words and phrases up to that time. He was not able to use pronouns properly and characteristically confused and reversed the pronouns "you" and "I."

He never crawled, and while he started walking at 11 months of age, if he fell, he would not stand up again by himself. He never pulled himself up or cruised about the furniture prior to walking without support. He did not open doors or turn knobs until 3½ years old.

Once he began speaking, he revealed a preoccupation with fearful thoughts. Before the age of 6 years, he had a dream about a frightening chair and insisted on following his mother around so that he would be protected from it. He dreamed that his father or mother were in a chair costume chasing him. He became quite concrete and literal in his expressions, saying, for example, "There are so many chairs I have to be afraid of now." From 5 years to 9 years old, he thought of himself as being a car. Whenever he had to urinate, he would say that he was draining his tank. He believed that other people could control or actually think his thoughts. Between the ages of 7 and 10, he would ask his therapist, "Can you think my thoughts?" and, "Can you dream my dreams?" At 11 years, when his teacher tapped on her desk for attention he commented that her act "weakens my blood" and he often noted that everything around him seemed to grow smaller or larger.

This child experienced great difficulty in absorbing formal learning. Mastery of reading and writing was delayed and learning could only be accomplished in a special school.

The following case is presented to illustrate another clinical variant of the same basic syndrome. In this child, perceptual and motor disturbances are associated with precocious intellectual development.

Case 6

Case 6 is a 6-year-old boy. His parents, nonprofessional people, did not finish college. The child and a fraternal twin brother were born following a full-term pregnancy which was not remarkable except for a viral illness during the second trimester. The patient was the firstborn and was delivered by an easy breech extraction. He weighed 2,438 gm (5 lb, 6 oz). The neonatal period was not remarkable. The mother did not recall any early feeding difficulties. From the first months, he showed unusual awareness in all sensory modalities, including a tendency to stare at spinning objects such as the record player. He was easily upset by many types of stimuli. Hair clippers and vacuum cleaners were particularly disturbing to him. At 4 months, his sensitivity to noise was manifested by responding to his mother's voice with a startled reaction and scream. He flapped his hands and walked on his toes. Early motor development was not remarkable. While he smiled responsively, there were periods during his development when it was felt that he did not really look at people but rather looked through them, would stiffen when held, and seemed emotionally aloof. He would let objects fall out of his hands. His play with toys was limited, and he only became involved with toys that spin. He pointed to and gestured for what he wanted, and he communicated early with words, although his speech was described as being "a monotone with no inflection." He never confused pronouns and no echolalia was reported.

At 6 years of age, he had many fears and continued to panic at strange noises. He did not like to play with other children, apparently preferring to be alone and involved in fantasy. He became preoccupied with being able to name the capitols of all the countries of the world and with the relationship between the different species of animals in a nature book. He became fearful of things he had seen on television and reacted to them as if they were real. He learned to read early, read well, and was at the top of his class in a regular school.

Such a child may be labeled *autistic, atypical, borderline psychotic,* or *schizophrenic,* depending on the clinical setting in which he is seen.

These six cases illustrate the merging of clinical entities which have been described under different diagnostic rubrics.

The following case is an example of the clinical syndrome of early infantile autism in which specific neurological abnormalities were found.

Case 7

Both the mother and father of this 5-year-old boy held degrees in the physical sciences and their families had a long history of intellectual achievement. During the early years of the patient's life, his mother was depressed, agitated, and emotionally labile. The pregnancy, delivery, and postnatal course were not remarkable. During the first weeks of life, he was noted to lie very quietly, and he was described as being "apathetic." The mother felt that the baby did not want to be held. He was prop-fed and was not weaned until after his third birthday. No difficulties in chewing solid food developed. Prior to 24 months of age, he responded to many types of noise by "running and screaming" and putting his hands over his ears. He responded with equal distress to change in illumination and continued to show a sensitivity to auditory and visual stimuli throughout his life. He became preoccupied with spinning tops and pot covers before 36 months, and this behavior became a persistent activity. Before 48 months, he would often ignore both people and various forms of stimuli not related to people. At 36 months, he did not respond with pain to bumps and falls. From the time he could walk, he persistently whirled himself, flapped his hands, and walked around on his toes. He failed to imitate either sounds or words during his first 24 months, and he did not use words for communication until after 5 years of age. He also failed to communicate by gesture. He never used complete sentences. He did not show an anticipatory response to being picked up until 3 or 4 years of age and earlier he would stiffen when held. He used others as an extension of himself and actively withdrew from affection. He had not played "peek-a-boo" or "pat-a-cake."

Neurological examination revealed a spreading of the biceps reflex into the finger, active finger jerks, crossed adductor reflexes, and persistent plantar grasp reflexes at 5 years, 11 months. Two EEGs showed focal slowing appearing on the right side. A pneumoencephalogram revealed asymmetry of the frontal horns of the lateral ventricles with the right appearing slightly larger than the left. A bilateral carotid angiogram revealed the right lateral ventricle to be slightly larger than the left. The findings were felt to be consistent with focal cortical atrophy on the right side.

In this case, both the development of the child and the family history are consistent with the syndrome of early infantile autism as described by Kanner. The syndrome, however, is seen to occur in association with a specific cerebral abnormality.

The following case is presented as an example of children in whom careful history and observation does not reveal evidence of the symptoms characteristic of the syndrome of perceptual inconstancy (early infantile autism, its variants, and sequelae) yet who nevertheless have severe ideational and affectual distortion of psychotic proportions.

Case 8

This 7-year-old boy was admitted for inpatient evaluation because he refused to eat, saying, "bad people have touched my food." History revealed that at three months' gestation, the mother had a viral illness with high fever, vaginal hemorrhaging at four months, and that the patient was delivered five weeks prior to term, weighing just 2,268 gm (5 lb). He was reported to have had intermittent difficulty breathing from birth on, and at 6 months asthma was diagnosed. All motor developmental landmarks were normal. There was a good smiling response noted by 2 months, stranger anxiety at 6 months, words and phrases by 1½ years, and sentences were used by 2 years. No unusual sensitivities or mannerisms were noted. When the patient was 1½ years and 3½ years old, his mother was hospitalized for medical and surgical treatment. During these hospitalizations he was cared for by his grandfather. Six weeks following the mother's second hospitalization, the grandfather was killed in an automobile accident and the parents related the onset of his illness to this event. He refused to accept his grandfather's death, saying that he could see him and would speak to him. He wanted to die so that he could be with him and on one occasion released the car brake and rolled the car into the street in an attempt to get killed. He gradually withdrew interest from friends and family and evolved an elaborate fantasy world peopled by robots, devils, gods, and other powerful creatures. He became fixed in the belief that he was a mechanical robot, had switches on his body, and was impervious to pain. He was expelled from kindergarten because of unprovoked outbursts of severe hostile behavior to the other children. Psychiatric examination revealed loosening of associations, preoccupation with fantasies of being made out of steel and controlled by wires, and grossly inappropriate affect. Psychological testing revealed a psychotic ego organization with impairment of intellectual potential and no evidence of organic brain dysfunction. Prolonged observation has revealed no evidence of symptoms indicative of disturbed perceptual or motor development. Observation of his parents indicated that the mother had a severe thinking disorder; she, in fact, had frequently told her son that certain foods should not be eaten because they had been poisoned.

We consider such a case an instance where childhood schizophrenia is not related to the syndrome of perceptual inconstancy as are other cases of childhood schizophrenia (e.g., cases 5 and 6).

COMMENT

The basic pathologic mechanism underlying this syndrome is presumed to be on a neurophysiologic basis. A particular pathoneurophysiology will be postulated in a subsequent communication. The relationships between the basic dissociation of facilitatory and inhibitory influences, the resulting perceptual inconstancy, the major developmental failures, and the resulting symptom-complexes are illustrated schematically in Figure 2.

Early infantile autism, its clinical variants, and its sequelae can best be understood as a unitary disease with varying symptoms which are expressive of an underlying pathophysiology. With maturation the symptoms undergo certain vicissitudes. In those autistic children in whom the disease process severely limits development of intrapsychic organization, these symptoms may secondarily be utilized to modulate sensory input. For other autistic children, in whom more advanced intrapsychic organization occurs, these symptoms may secondarily serve as foci for the development of bizarre or psychotic fantasies. However, neither a "need" for self-stimulation nor the child's fantasy life explain the original development or the sustained activity level of these symptoms.

Since the symptoms of early infantile autism can be understood as expressive of a pathophysiologic mechanism related to dissociated states of excitation and inhibition, it may be possible to investigate the etiology from a neurophysiologic point of view. This seems to be hopeful since these behavioral states occur concomitantly with known brain pathology, disturbed environment, or completely independent of these factors. Therefore, such factors appear to be neither specific nor fundamental to the etiology of this disease. The overt expression of the pathologic mechanism may be triggered by some of the associated conditions. As the weight of clinical evidence sug-

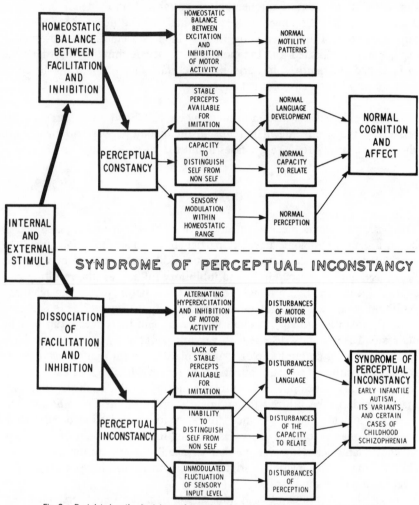

Fig 2.—Postulated pathophysiology of symptom formation in the syndrome of perceptual inconstancy compared with the regulation of sensory input in normal children.

gests that a schizophrenic thought and affect disorder may be one sequela of early infantile autism, the hypothesis suggested may have applicability to certain children and adults with this major psychiatric illness.

Since early infantile autism, its variants—atypical development and symbiotic psychosis—and its major sequela—some cases of childhood schizophrenia—are expressions of one disease process based on faulty homeostatic regulation of perceptual input, we could refer to children within this clinical spectrum as manifesting a *syndrome of perceptual inconstancy*.

SUMMARY

Early infantile autism and several related syndromes are described in terms of the natural history of the symptoms and their developmental relationships. Early infantile autism, atypical development, symbiotic psychosis, and certain cases of childhood schizophrenia are shown to be essentially variants of the same disease.

The symptoms of this disease have been grouped into five major subclusters: disturbances of perception, motility, relatedness, language, and developmental rate.

Disturbances of perception are shown to be fundamental to the other aspects of the disease and to be manifested by early developmental failure to distinguish between self and environment, to imitate, and to modulate sensory input.

It is suggested that these developmental failures are caused by a breakdown of homeostatic regulation of sensory input. This results in a condition of perceptual inconstancy.

The symptoms suggest that the illness is characterized by dissociated, uncoupled, and alternating states of excitation and inhibition. It is this pathophysiology which interferes with the adequate homeostatic regulation of perception and leads to a state of perceptual inconstancy.

Since the symptomatology is primarily expressive of an underlying pathophysiology, the symptoms may only secondarily in some cases come to be purposeful in the intrapsychic life of the afflicted child.

As this syndrome may be seen in children with specific organic brain dysfunction or may occur independently from birth, the pathophysiologic mechanism causing perceptual inconstancy is probably specific to the disease but may be activated in certain cases by particular neuropathologic conditions.

REFERENCES

1. Kanner, L.: Autistic Disturbances of Affective Contact, *Nerv Child* 2:217–250, 1943.
2. Kanner, L.: Problems of Nosology and Psychodynamics of Early Infantile Autism, *Amer J Orthopsychiat* 19:416–426, 1949.
3. Bender, L.: Childhood Schizophrenia: Clinical Study of One Hundred Schizophrenic Children, *Amer J Orthopsychiat* 17:40–56, 1947.
4. Putnam, M.C., et al.: Round Table, 1947: Case Study of an Atypical Two-and-a-Half-Year-Old, *Amer J Orthopsychiat* 18:1–30, 1948.

 5. Bergman, P., and Escalona, S.K.: "Unusual Sensitivities in Very Young Children," *Psychoanal Stud Child 3–4*:333–352, 1949.
 6. Mahler, M.S.: On Child Psychosis and Schizophrenia: "Autistic and Symbiotic Infantile Psychosis," *Psychoanal Stud Child 7*:286–305, 1952.
 7. Despert, J.L.: Some Considerations Relating to the Genesis of Autistic Behavior in Children, *Amer J Orthopsychiat 21*:335–347, 1951.
 8. Rank, B.: Adaptation of the Psychoanalytic Technique for the Treatment of Young Children With Atypical Development, *Amer J Orthopsychiat 19*:130–139, 1949.
 9. Wolff, S., and Chess, S.: A Behavioural Study of Schizophrenic Children, *Acta Psychiat Scand 40*:438–466, 1964.
10. Rutter, M.: The Influence of Organic and Emotional Factors on the Origins, Nature and Outcome of Childhood Psychosis, *Develop Med Child Neurol 7*:518–528, 1965.
11. Bender, L.: Schizophrenia in Childhood—Its Recognition, Description and Treatment, *Amer J Orthopsychiat 26*:499–506, 1956.
12. Goldfarb, W.: An Investigation of Childhood Schizophrenia, *Arch Gen Psychiat 11*:620–634, 1964.
13. Reiser, D.E.: Psychosis of Infancy and Early Childhood, as Manifested by Children with Atypical Development, *New Eng J Med 269*:790–798, 844–850, 1963.
14. Brown, J.L., and Reiser, D.E.: Follow-up Study of Preschool Children of Atypical Development (Infantile Psychosis): Latter Personality Patterns in Adaption to Maturational Stress, *Amer J Orthopsychiat 33*:336–338, 1963.
15. Eisenberg, L.: The Autistic Child in Adolescence, *Amer J Psychiat 112*:607–612, 1956.
16. Darr, G.C., and Worden, F.G.: Case Report Twenty-Eight Years After an Infantile Autistic Disorder, *Amer J Orthopsychiat 21*:559–570, 1951.
17. Tolor, A., and Rafferty, W.: Incidence of Symptoms of Early Infantile Autism in Subsequently Hospitalized Psychiatric Patients, *Dis Nerv Syst 24*:1–7, 1963.
18. O'Gorman, G.: *The Nature of Childhood Autism*, London: Butterworth Co., Inc., 1967.
19. Kamp, L.N.J.: Autistic Syndrome in One of a Pair of Monozygotic Twins, *Psychiat Neurol Neurochir 67*:143–147, 1964.
20. Ornitz, E.M.; Ritvo, E.R.; and Walter, R.D.: Dreaming Sleep in Autistic and Schizophrenic Children, *Amer J Psychiat 122*:419–424, 1965.
21. Vaillant, G.E.: Twins Discordant for Early Infantile Autism, *Arch Gen Psychiat 9*:163–167, 1963.
22. Schain, R.J., and Yannet, H.: Infantile Autism, *J Pediat 57*:560–567, 1960.
23. Kanner, L.: To What Extent Is Early Infantile Autism Determined by Constitutional Inadequacies, *Proc Assoc Res Nerv Ment Dis 33*:378–385, 1954.
24. Taft, L., and Goldfarb, W.: Prenatal and Perinatal Factors in Childhood Schizophrenia, *Develop Med Child Neurol 6*:32–43, 1964.
25. Fish, B.: Longitudinal Observations of Biological Deviations in a Schizophrenic Infant, *Amer J Psychiat 116*:25–31, 1959.
26. Griffith, R., and Ritvo, E.: Echolalia; Concerning the Dynamics of the Syndrome, *J Amer Acad Child Psychiat 6*:184–193, 1967.

27. Fish, B., et al.: The Prediction of Schizophrenia in Infancy: III. A Ten-Year Follow-up Report of Neurological and Psychological Development, *Amer J Psychiat 121*:768–775, 1965.
28. Creak, M.: Schizophrenic Syndrome in Childhood: Progress Report of a Working Party, *Cereb Palsy Bull 3*:501–503, 1961.
29. Ekstein, R.; Bryant, K.; and Friedman, S.W.: "Childhood Schizophrenia and Allied Conditions," in Belak, L. (ed.): *Schizophrenia: A Review of the Syndrome*, New York: Logos Press, 1958.
30. Provence, S., and Lipton, R.: *Infants in Institutions*, New York: International Universities Press, 1962.
31. Coleman, R., and Provence, S.: Environmental Retardation (Hospitalism) in Infants Living in Families, *Pediatrics 19*:285–292, 1957.
32. Spitz, R.A.: "Anaclitic Depression," *Psychoanal Stud Child 2*:313–342, 1946.
33. Berkson, G., and Davenport, R.K.: Stereotyped Movements of Mental Defectives, *Amer J Ment Defic 66*:849–852, 1962.
34. Garcia, B., and Sarvis, M.A.: Evaluation and Treatment Planning for Autistic Children, *Arch Gen Psychiat 10*:530–541, 1964.
35. Rutter, M.: "Behavioral and Cognitive Characteristics of a Series of Psychotic Children," in Wing, J.K. (ed.): *Early Childhood Autism*, New York: Pergamon Press, Ltd., 1966.
36. Eisenberg, L., and Kanner, L.: Early Infantile Autism 1943–1955, *Amer J Orthopsychiat 26*:556–566, 1956.
37. Szurek, S.A.: Psychotic Episodes and Psychotic Maldevelopment, *Amer J Orthopsychiat 26*:519–543, 1956.
38. Rank, B.: "Intensive Study and Treatment of Preschool Children Who Show Marked Personality Deviations, or 'Atypical Development,' and Their Parents," in Caplan, G. (ed.): *Emotional Problems of Early Childhood*, New York: Basic Books Co., Inc., 1955.
39. Sarvis, M.A., and Garcia, B.: Etiological Variables in Autism, *Psychiatry 24*:307–317, 1961.
40. Fish, B.: Involvement of the Central Nervous System in Infants With Schizophrenia, *Arch Neurol 2*:115–121, 1960.
41. Bender, L., and Freedman, A.M.: A Study of the First Three Years in the Maturation of Schizophrenic Children, *Quart J Child Behav 4*:245–272, 1952.
42. Simmons, J.Q., et al.: Modification of Autistic Behavior With LSD-25, *Amer J Psychiat 122*:1201–1211, 1966.
43. Goldfarb, W.: Receptor Preferences in Schizophrenic Children, *Arch Neurol Psychiat 76*:643–652, 1956.
44. Schopler, E.: Early Infantile Autism and Receptor Processes, *Arch Gen Psychiat 13*:327–335, 1965.
45. Hutt, S.J., et al.: A Behavioural and Electroencephalographic Study of Autistic Children, *J Psychiat Res 3*:181–197, 1965.
46. Wing, J.K.: "Diagnosis, Epidemiology, Aetiology," in Wing, J.K. (ed.): *Early Childhood Autism*, New York: Pergamon Press, Ltd., 1966.
47. Goldfarb, W.: *Childhood Schizophrenia*, Cambridge, Mass: Harvard University Press, 1961.

COMMENTARY by Fred R. Volkmar

This paper is an important, and widely cited, example of the "organic" theories of pathogenesis that began to appear more frequently in the late 1960s. Over the previous decade theoretical explanations had begun to shift in emphasis away from psychosocial factors to a focus on intrinsic, organic ones as investigators became increasingly aware of the frequency with which autistic children exhibited signs of central nervous system dysfunction and the frequency of autistic symptoms in children suffering from organic disorders.

The authors propose that autistic and other pervasively disturbed children exhibit an inability to maintain constancy of perception due to a failure of homeostatic regulation, which, in a later paper (Ornitz and Ritvo, 1968) they postulated as located in the lower central nervous system. Numerous studies have documented the difficulties of autistic children in selectively attending to and assimilating information (James and Barry, 1980).

In retrospect, it is apparent that the authors' assumptions about the unitary nature of the syndrome and its continuity with adult psychosis are not tenable. More importantly, autistic children tend to be consistently inconsistent in their performance and other brain centers appeared to be involved in the expression of the syndrome (DeMyer, Hingtgen, and Jackson, 1981). This theory focuses on one particular aspect of the syndrome and does not adequately address the divergent aspects of the disorder. This paper has, however, helped focus the attention of investigators on fundamental psychobiological mechanisms and has helped to deemphasize the role of parents in the pathogenesis of the disorder. Most investigators would now agree that fundamental organic deficits exist in autistic children but precise and testable theories remain to be developed.

REFERENCES

DeMyer, M. K., Hingtgen, J. N., & Jackson, R. K. Infantile autism reviewed: A decade of research. *Schizophrenia Bulletin*, 1981, 7, 388–451.

James, A. L., & Barry, R. J. A review of psychophysiology in early onset psychosis. *Schizophrenia Bulletin*, 1980, 6, 506–525.

Ornitz, E. M., & Ritvo, E. R. Neurophysiologic mechanisms underlying perceptual inconstancy in autistic and schizophrenic children. *Archives of General Psychiatry*, 1968, 19, 22–27.

9

Concepts of Autism:
A Review of Research

MICHAEL RUTTER

Psychotic or "schizophrenic" disorders in children have been recognized since the beginning of this century (Eisenberg, 1957), although it was not until the 1930s that the topic began to arouse much interest (Potter, 1933; Bradley, 1941; Bender, 1947), and it is only with Kanner's classical paper on infantile autism in 1943 that a major differentiation *within* the overall group of children with so-called "childhood schizophrenia" was attempted. The eleven children described in that paper were characterized by an inability to relate themselves to other people—what Kanner called "extreme autistic aloneness," a delay in the acquisition of speech together with abnormalities of language (particularly reversal of personal pronouns and echoing), an excellent rote memory, and an apparently obsessive desire for the maintenance of sameness. Kanner emphasized that the condition was first manifest in early infancy and concluded that in this respect autism differed from other cases of childhood schizophrenia. At that time, too, he put forward the view that autism represented an inborn disturbance of affective contact.

Different Views of Autism

Since then there have been a number of quite different trends in the literature and it is these that will be reviewed in this paper. In the first place, Kanner later came to place greater emphasis on the emotional coldness and obsessive qualities that he saw in the parents (Kanner and Eisenberg, 1955; Eisenberg and Kanner, 1956). He concluded that although the children had some inborn defect, nevertheless in part the disorder was due to lack of affection from the parents—that autism was partly a psychogenic disorder due to "emotional refrigeration." Other writers have taken this argument much further and have suggested that autism is mainly due to psychogenic factors. This view has been put forward, for example, by Despert (1951), Goldfarb (Goldfarb, 1961; Meyers and Goldfarb, 1961), Kaufman (Kaufman et al., 1957), and especially by Bettelheim (1967).

Reprinted with permission from *Journal of Child Psychology and Psychiatry* 9 (1968): 1–25. Copyright 1968, Pergamon Press, Ltd.

Secondly, Rank (1949) and Szurek (1956) under the term "atypical child," broadened the concept of autism to such an extent that it ceased to have much meaning. These writers have urged that autism, schizophrenia, mental subnormality, organic brain disease, and psychoneurosis should all be lumped together without any attempt at diagnosis or classification. The adherents of this viewpoint have also regarded as a psychogenic disorder (Szurek and Berlin, 1956; Boatman and Szurek, 1960).

Thirdly, this inclusion of all conditions under the same umbrella category has been paralleled by the opposite tendency to split autism and childhood schizophrenia into numerous distinct subcategories. Many of these received no general recognition but Mahler's concept of "symbiotic psychosis" (Mahler and Gosliner, 1949; Mahler, 1952) is still in general usage although its nosological status remains rather uncertain.

Most recently, behaviourist psychologists have added their own particular variety of hypothesis that autism is environmentally determined. It has been supposed that "a disease-health dichotomy . . . may not exist," and that "maladjustive behaviour is the result of differential reinforcement" (Krasner and Ullman, 1965). That is to say autism is due to faulty learning—it's just that the autistic child has not been conditioned properly by its parents (Ferster, 1961).

In sharp contrast to all these views, there has also been the claim by many writers that autism is basically due to organic brain disease. Bender (1947) has put forward the concept of a diffuse encephalopathy, and Knobloch and Pasamanick have gone on to suggest that brain damage may have originated in difficulties during pregnancy or the birth process (Knobloch and Grant, 1961; Knobloch and Pasamanick, 1962; Pasamanick and Knobloch, 1963).

In addition to these rather global views of autism as a "brain damage syndrome" there have been a number of more specific hypotheses concerning possible biological or physiological factors in the aetiology of autism.

The reticular system has been implicated by Rimland (1965) in the United States and by the Hutts and Ounsted (Hutt *et al.*, 1964 and 1965) working at Oxford. Rimland (1965) put forward the view that the reticular system is underactive while the Oxford group suggested that autism is due to over-arousal (Hutt *et al.*, 1964 and 1965; Hutt and Hutt, 1965).

Many writers have commented on the autistic child's abnormal response to sounds, sights, and smells and several workers (for example, Anthony, 1958; Schopler, 1965; Stroh and Buick, 1961) have suggested that there may be a basic defect in perception—that is in the integration of sensory stimuli. Opinions have differed on whether the defect is physiological or psychological.

Perhaps, most of all among the autistic child's abnormal responses to stimuli, his lack of response to sounds has been the subject of the greatest comment (Anthony, 1958; Goldfarb, 1961; Rutter, 1966a). This has led various writers (e.g., Hauesserman, 1962; Rutter, 1965a and b, and 1966a; Wing, 1966) to hypothesize that the main defect leading to autism may be a relative inability to comprehend sounds. That is, the autistic child's failure to develop a normal use and understanding of language is regarded as basically similar to the difficulties experienced by the child with a developmental language disorder—so-called "developmental aphasia."

Still other views have been put forward. Some have considered autism as a variety of mental subnormality (Van Krevelen, 1952). Others (particularly Goldfarb, 1961) have suggested that autism may be subdivided into organic varieties and psychogenic varieties. Most people have discussed the development of autism in terms of some kind of interaction between a basic defect in the child and maladaptive influences in the environment. However, the multifactorial viewpoint has perhaps reached its apogee in O'Gorman's idea (1967) that autism is a kind of schizophrenia, a psychosomatic disorder, a result of genetic over-breeding, the outcome of emotional disturbance, an exaggeration of normal selective withdrawal and also possibly a consequence of a defect in lead metabolism!

This sounds a hopelessly confused state of affairs but perhaps it is more confusing than it need be. Accordingly, the available evidence from recent clinical and experimental studies will be examined in an attempt to arrive at some kind of assessment of the relative merits and demerits of these various hypotheses which have been put forward.

Sub-classification of Psychotic Disorders in Childhood

The first consideration is that it is by no means clear that all these authors are talking about the same condition. Schizophrenia, psychosis, autism, atypical child and half a dozen other terms have been used interchangeably. It is necessary to begin, therefore, by defining the terms to be used.

The subclassification of psychotic disorders has been most ably discussed by Eisenberg (1967) and the scheme used here (Rutter, 1967a) is basically a simplification of that which he put forward. There appear to be three main broad groups of psychotic disorders which develop in childhood; these are most easily defined in terms of the age of onset. First, there is the variety which begins in early adolescence or in the year or so preceding the onset of puberty. This variety appears closely similar to schizophrenia as we know it in adult life. It will not be discussed any further in this paper.

Secondly, there is a type of psychosis which begins at about the age of 3, 4, or 5 yr. In this condition the child develops perfectly normally up to that age, then, often after a period of vague illness, he loses his speech, becomes incontinent, generally regresses and is often markedly overactive. A closer similar clinical picture may develop after a frank brain-disease such as encephalitis, and even in those cases where there is no overt brain disease the subsequent course often provides evidence of a degenerative condition of the brain (Anthony, 1958; Bender, 1942; Corberi, 1926; Creak, 1963; Kanner, 1949; Ross, 1959). Sometimes the disorder is rather similar to infantile autism and occasionally the differential diagnosis may be very difficult—if not impossible. But, in general, it seems that these disorders are basically a form of chronic brain disease and are different from autism as Kanner described it (although the two groups do share some problems). Again, this paper will not deal with this group.

Instead, it will concentrate on the last group—children whose disorder follows the description provided by Kanner in 1943 and in whom the disorder begins in infancy, usually very early infancy but occasionally as late as the second or rarely even the third year of life (Eisenberg and Kanner, 1956; Kanner and Lesser, 1958).

It should also be said there are a few other well-defined psychotic disorders which may rarely occur in childhood (Eisenberg, 1967)—for example manic-depressive psychosis (Anthony and Scott, 1960) and also *folie à deux* (that is a psychosis which has developed on the basis of imitation or sharing of symptoms with some other psychotic person, commonly a parent).

Characteristics of Infantile Psychosis

The rest of this paper, then, will be concerned with the infantile variety of psychosis. The term is used here to refer to children with a *severe* disorder beginning in *infancy* in which the chief features are "autism," profound abnormalities of language development, a variety of ritualistic and compulsive phenomena and, often, stereotyped mannerisms (Norman, 1954 and 1955; O'Gorman, 1967; Rutter, 1966a; Rutter and Lockyer, 1967; Wolff and Chess, 1965a and b). In this context, "autism" is used as a descriptive term for that particular variety of disturbance in interpersonal relationships shown by an impression of aloofness and distance, an apparent lack of interest in people, a failure to form enduring relationships, avoidance of eye-to-eye gaze, little variation of facial expression, a relative failure to exhibit feelings or appreciate humour, and a lack of sympathy or empathy for other people. It should be emphasized that these are the characteristics in early childhood and some features are greatly modified or not found at all in the older child (O'Connor, 1967; Rutter, Greenfeld and Lockyer, 1967).

This outline of the main features of "infantile autism" has much in common with the "9 points" put forward by the working party under the chairmanship of Creak (1961, 1964), although the "9 points" referred to child psychosis in general rather than specifically to the infantile variety. It differs principally in the requirement that the disorder begins in infancy, and also in the exclusion of those items, such as overactivity or excessive anxiety, which do not serve to distinguish the autistic child from children with *other* psychiatric disorders (Creak, 1964; Rutter, 1966a).

Terminology

A problem in terminology arises from the fact that the word "autism" has been used in the literature both to refer to a *syndrome* or *"disease"* (i.e., that described by Kanner using the term "infantile autism") and to a *symptom* (i.e., a particular kind of disturbance in inter-personal relationships). There is no entirely satisfactory resolution of this problem. "Psychosis" could be employed for the syndrome but this term has generally been used for a rather wider group of disorders than those considered in this paper. Furthermore, there are many reasons for regarding "psychosis" as an inappropriate term for the condition of "infantile autism" (Rutter, 1969), which, apart from the severity of disturbance, has little in common with the other disorders usually included in the psychoses. Accordingly, in line with common usage, throughout this paper the terms autism, infantile autism, and autistic child will be used interchangeably to refer to the syndrome.

This leaves the problem of what to call the symptom. A term is needed to differentiate this particular variety of disturbance in inter-personal relationships from the many other varieties which are not part of the syndrome of infantile autism. Social withdrawal will be used throughout the remainder of this paper to describe the symptom. It must be emphasized that, taken literally, this is a rather loose and inaccurate description of the relationship difficulty. Social withdrawal generally describes a wider variety of phenomena than that meant by the symptom of "autism" but in the sense that it is used in this paper it refers *only* to the symptom of "autism" as defined in the section of this paper headed "characteristics of infantile psychosis."

Autism as a Variety of Mental Subnormality

The first concept to be considered is the view that autism is simply a variety of mental subnormality. There can be no doubt that many autistic children function at a mentally subnormal level. Yet, Kanner (Kanner, 1943; Kanner and Lesser, 1958) and others (see Bettelheim, 1967, and Rimland, 1964) have claimed that, in spite of this, all autistic children are basically of normal intelligence. Unfortunately, there is no satisfactory evidence to support Kanner's claim. Well over half the autistic children in the Maudsley series obtained I.Q. scores in the mentally subnormal range (Rutter and Lockyer, 1967) and the findings with respect to other series are similar (Lockyer, 1967). It might be suggested that the low scores on the intelligence tests were due to social withdrawal and disturbed behaviour, but, if this were so, the I.Q. should vary greatly with the child's clinical state. This was not found. The I.Q. obtained in early childhood using objectively scored tests[1] proved to be highly stable and also a remarkably good predictor of intellectual functioning in adolescence and early adult life (Lockyer and Rutter, 1968). What is more important, the I.Q. remained much the same even in the small group of children who recovered or greatly improved (Rutter, 1966b). The I.Q. in autistic children exhibits the same qualities and carries the same implications as it does in any other group of children. Many autistic children are mentally subnormal as well as being autistic and the mental subnormality is just as "real" as it is in any other child who is mentally retarded.

But, in spite of this, autism *cannot* be regarded as merely another variety of mental subnormality. There are two important findings which are relevant in this connection. First, even on standard intelligence tests, between a quarter and a third of autistic children can be shown to have an I.Q. which is in the normal range (Rutter and Lockyer, 1967). As the behavioural characteristics of the children with low I.Q. are generally similar to those of high I.Q. (Rutter and Lockyer, 1967), it is evident on this fact alone that mental subnormality as a concept is insufficient to account for the autism. There is also a second point. The Maudsley study showed that to a much greater extent than in other children, the I.Q. in the autistic child differed widely according to what intellectual function was examined. Children might be above average on some tasks and yet at the severely subnormal level on others. Characteristically the autistic child did very poorly on verbal tasks or those which required abstract thought or logic, but relatively well on puzzle-type tests such as the block design and object assembly subtests of the Wechsler scales. This pattern of scores was found to be strongly related to the child's level of language development (Rutter, 1966a) and it may be concluded that to *some* extent the autistic child's poor level of intellectual attainment is related to specific defects in language rather than to a global deficiency of intellect.

Autism as a "Type of Schizophrenia"

Until the last year or two, perhaps the most widespread concept has been that of autism as a particularly early manifestation of schizophrenia. In fact, the British working party which produced the "9 points" used the terms "Schizophrenic syndrome in childhood" to describe the condition they were considering (Creak, 1961). The view that autism is essentially the same condition as adult schizophrenia is largely based on the observation that in both conditions a difficulty in interpersonal relationships is one of the key fea-

---

[1]In children with little or no speech, however, scores were based solely on the responses to nonverbal tests.

tures, but there are also some other similarities in symptomatology (O'Gorman, 1967).

On the other hand, the differences between infantile autism and adult schizophrenia are immense. First, the sex ratio is quite different. Autism is much commoner in males (Rutter, 1967a) whereas schizophrenia is about equally common in the two sexes (Mayer-Gross *et al.*, 1955). Second, the social class of the parents of autistic children is most unlike that of the parents of schizophrenics. A high proportion of the parents of autistic children are of above average intelligence and of superior socioeconomic status (Lotter, 1967). This is *not* an artefact of referral policies to clinics, as might be thought, as the findings have recently been confirmed by Lotter (1967) in an epidemiological study of all the autistic children living in one English county. In contrast the social background of schizophrenics is the same as that of the general population (Hare, 1967). Thirdly, the family history of schizophrenia in the two conditions is discrepant. All the major studies of infantile autism have shown that adult schizophrenia is rare in both the parents and the brothers and sisters of autistic children (Rutter, 1967a), whereas it is relatively common in the immediate families of schizophrenics (Brown, 1967; Shields, 1967). Fourthly, whereas mental subnormality is a common accompaniment of autism it is much less frequently associated with schizophrenia (Pollack, 1960). Fifth, the characteristic pattern of I.Q. subtest scores (high on visuo-spatial tasks and low on verbal tasks) found with infantile autism (Rutter, 1966a) is not a feature of schizophrenia. Sixth, whereas delusions and hallucinations are very common symptoms in schizophrenia (Mayer-Gross *et al.*, 1955) they are quite rare in autistic children, even after they reach adolescence and early adult life (Rutter, 1966b). Lastly, the course of the two conditions is rather different. Marked remissions and relapses are well recognized in schizophrenia but are decidedly uncommon in autism, where a relatively steady course is much more usual (Rutter *et al.*, 1967).

Some of these differences between autism and schizophrenia might be attributed merely to the difference in age of onset, but it is less easy to explain the dissimilarities in sex-ratio, social class and family history in this way. In view of the important features which differentiate the two conditions and the lack of convincing evidence for any meaningful association (apart from a resemblance in a few of the main symptoms), one can only conclude that the concept of autism as a variety of schizophrenia is very probably wrong (Rutter, 1965a).

The Genetic Basis of Autism

In his first description of the syndrome, Kanner (1943) laid emphasis on the inborn nature of the defect, and many other writers in the quarter of a century since then have discussed autism in relation to a basic constitutional defect or abnormality. Some writers, for example, Rimland (1965), have suggested that such a defect may be genetically determined. This hypothesis remains a possibility but so far the evidence is inconclusive.

That autistic children are rarely, if ever, born to frankly autistic parents is still compatible with a genetic hypothesis. Very few autistic children recover sufficiently for them to marry and have children, so if the parents possessed the relevant gene it would probably have to be in a heterozygotic or otherwise modified form. More problematical with respect to a genetic hypothesis is the low rate of autism in the brothers and sisters. If the three largest studies, those of Kanner (Kanner and Lesser, 1958), Creak (Creak and Ini, 1960) and Rutter (1965), are pooled, and if possible, as well as definite, cases are included, a rate of about 2 per cent is obtained. The rate of autism in the general population was found by Lotter (1966) to be 4.5 per 10,000 so the rate of autism in the sibs is higher than in the general public. On the other hand, the rate in the sibs is very low for a hereditary disorder (Rutter, 1967) unless (a) low penetrance of the gene is hypothesized or (b) it is assumed that genetically determined cases of autism form only a small sub-group of autistic disorders, or (c) nongenetic factors exert a powerful modifying influence. Van Krevelen (1962 and 1963) has suggested that the last possibility may in fact be the case, but the suggestion remains speculative.

It should be added that it is still possible for a condition to be genetically determined in spite of a very low rate of the disorder in the family. This is sometimes the situation with conditions due to chromosomal abnormalities—for example mongolism. But, so far the studies of chromosomes in autistic children have been entirely negative (Rutter, 1967a). Furthermore, there is an absence of any strong evidence which might give rise to the suspicion of a chromosomal abnormality. For example, increased maternal age and associated congenital anomalies of the heart made investigators suspect that mongolism might follow a chromosomal abnormality well before it was discovered that this was indeed the case (Penrose and Smith, 1966). But there is *no* such evidence with regard to autism; the maternal age is normal (Creak and Ini, 1960; Lotter, 1967) and structural congenital anomalies are fairly unusual.

Twin studies should be helpful in determining whether or not autism has a genetic basis. However, it is a rare condition and autistic twins are even rarer so that there have been few investigations and, unfortunately, the evidence from twin studies is rather limited and inconclusive (Rutter, 1967a).

The available data by no means rule out the possibility of a genetic basis for autism but neither do they offer much support for such a hypothesis. The Scottish verdict of "Not-proven" is appropriate.

Psychogenic Origin of Autism

The question of whether or not autism has a psychogenic basis has next to be considered. An evaluation of this question is complicated by the large number of different psychogenic hypotheses and by the ambiguity and vagueness with which some of them have been expressed.

Sometimes autism has been viewed as the child's response to general qualities in his parents' personality. Kanner (1949), Eisenberg (1957b), and many others (Rimland, 1964) have commented that most parents of autistic children appear detached, cold and obsessive. It is difficult to know how much weight to attach to these observations in that other workers have found a much greater variability in parental personality characteristics (Anthony, 1958; Creak and Ini, 1960; Rutter, 1967a). Perhaps many (but by no means all) of the parents are rather detached, organised, and meticulous people, although the adjective cold is probably inaccurate. But in this connection the high intellectual and social status of the parents needs to be kept in mind, and it is uncertain whether or not these characteristics are in excess in relation to the academic and professional circles from which the parents are drawn.

Supposing just for the moment that there may be a characteristic parental personality, it is still very questionable whether this suggests a psychogenic aetiology. What is important is that it is *general* abnormalities which have been described (not abnormalities directed against any one child). If these general abnormalities have caused the development of autism it would be expected that many of the sibs would also be autistic, or, at least, show some kind of psychiatric disorder. However, this is not the case (Rutter, 1967a; Rutter and Lockyer, 1967). Very few of the sibs are autistic and the majority do not have any kind of psychiatric disorder. It may be concluded that it is most unlikely that a *general* abnormality in parental attitudes or behaviour has led to the psychogenic development of autism.

The fact that the sibs are mostly psychiatrically normal would, of course, be irrelevant if it were supposed that the parental or family psychopathology was *specifically* concerned with the child who became autistic, rather than with all the children in the family. It is well known that mothers and fathers often have very different attitudes towards each of their children, and there is nothing out of the ordinary in the suggestion that there might be a specific kind of abnormality in the parental behaviour toward only *one* child in the family. This kind of hypothesis is implied in some of the views expressed in the literature (Rank, 1949; Boatman and Szurek, 1960; Meyers and Goldfarb, 1961; Singer and Wynn, 1963; Bettelheim, 1967).

There are several problems in relation to these concepts of psychogenic causation. In the first place, most writers have not carried out any kind of study to test their hypotheses. Where investigations have been undertaken, it has not been clear whether the children studied have had infantile autism or some other type of psychotic disorder (Meyers and Goldfarb, 1961; Singer and Wynn, 1963), or the differences found have been rather trivial (Goldfarb, 1961). Furthermore, there seems to be no agreement on what type of abnormality in parent-child interaction is supposed to be present. Nevertheless, it is apparent that many psychiatrists have thought that there is some kind of abnormality, so (although the evidence in support is by no means satisfactory) for the moment this observation will be taken for granted.

Three main objections may be made in relation to the suggestion that these supposed specific parental abnormalities have caused the autism. One, autism is a disorder which is first manifest very early in the child's life, in fact in early infancy, and it would seem that it must be a very severe parental abnormality indeed which could cause so quickly a disorder so gross as childhood autism. But, with the exception of Bettelheim (1967) whose views are considered below, most writers have described rather subtle abnormalities such as ambivalence or perplexity, which are quite common in all sorts of parents who do not have autistic children.

The second objection is that it is quite possible that the deviant parental behaviour may be due to the child's abnormalities rather than the other way round. In that the autistic child shows severe disturbances in the earliest and most basic interpersonal relationships with his parents, it is to be expected that many mothers feel that they lack a sense of intimacy and close rapport, and so become detached, ambivalent, or guilty (Escalona, 1948). Such parental abnormalities as do exist may well result in large measure from the pathology in the child rather than vice versa (Rutter, 1967a).

The third objection concerns the possibility that there is an "organic" variety of autism as well as a "psychogenic" variety, as suggested by many writers—for example Goldfarb (1961). If there are two varieties as Goldfarb (1961) maintains, the two types should differ in terms of parental or family psychopathology. However, this seems not to be the case. Anthony's "organic" and "environmental" groups were not differentiated to a significant extent by the Fels scales (Anthony, 1958), nor was there a significant difference in family adequacy between Goldfarb's (1961) organic and nonorganic groups, although both found nonsignificant differences in the expected direction.

Some clinicians have commented on the way in which autism may develop after some "stress" event such as admission to hospital or birth of a sib. "Stress" reactions may sometimes share some of the qualities of autism, but as Anthony (1958) observed, "backward development into infantile autism is not often complete unless there is gross cerebral disease." In any case, only a few autistic children show any regression, the majority appear abnormal from infancy (Kanner, 1943; Rutter, 1967a; Rutter and Lockyer, 1967) without there being a significant change at any one point in development, so that it is unlikely that any kind of "stress" can have been a *primary* aetiological influence.

That autism could develop in relation to more prolonged adverse situations in very early infancy is plausible. After all, delays in language and distortions in social relationships are two of the commonest consequences of long-term poor-quality institutional care (Ainsworth, 1962; Tizard, 1964) or severe deprivation in the home (Prince, 1967). Nevertheless, it seems highly improbable that such situations are responsible for the development of infantile autism. In the first place, these responses to deprivation are rather different from autism in a number of key respects (for example, obsessive features as described by Kanner are rare in institutional children). In the second place, autistic children only rarely have a history of such depriving circumstances in their lives.

It only remains to consider Bettelheim's view (1967) which constitutes the most clearly expressed psychogenic hypothesis so far available. He suggests that autism develops as a response to extreme negative feelings shown by the parent—feelings so marked that the child feels without hope, in the same way as did many inmates of concentration camps. He explains the severity of the child's response in terms of the critical periods in development at which he experiences these extreme situations (namely the first 6 months when real object relationships begin, at 6–9 months when language and locomotion are beginning to turn the infant into a child, and at 18–24 months when the child starts to shape his relations with the environment). Thus, the child lacks speech and lacks emotional expression because there is a lack of a receptive audience as perceived by the child. The autistic child's brothers and sisters are not affected because the parental reaction was specific to the one child, and because only the autistic child experienced the rejection at the critical period in development. While it is possible that Bettelheim's hypothesis is correct, it is improbable in that so far neither he nor anyone else have demonstrated that autistic children have in fact experienced these supposed extreme experiences. Furthermore, his argument takes little account of either the facts to be explained or alternative explanations. In addition, it is dependent on the existence of a "critical period" in development, and there is very little evidence in support of this idea (this is discussed in more detail later). The balance of evidence seems against the view that autism is psychogenically determined but there are no decisive findings one way or the other.

Autism as the Result of Faulty Conditioning

It is not necessary to spend long on the hypothesis that autism is the result of faulty conditioning. This view is based on the good response of some autistic children to operant conditioning methods of treatment. Certainly these techniques have had some striking successes but there have also been failures, and many of the results have been regrettably situation-specific and short-lived (Rutter, 1967a). In any case the history of medicine shows very clearly that it is hazardous in the extreme to argue from the type of therapy which is effective to the nature of the causal process. Bettelheim (1967) used a similar argument in relation to psychogenesis when he suggested that because some autistic children improve when treated with love and acceptance, therefore they must have lacked love and acceptance in earlier life. One might just as well suggest that because depression frequently responds to electric shock treatment, therefore the depression is due to a lack of electric shocks in childhood! It is conceivable that autism develops because of faulty conditioning, but there is a complete absence of supporting evidence for the supposed abnormalities in patterns of environmental reinforcement.

Social Withdrawal as the Primary Defect in Autism

In his first description of the autistic syndrome Kanner (1943) suggested that the primary defect was a disturbance in affective contact. Thus, he argued that the autistic child appears mentally retarded and does not speak only *because* of profound social withdrawal.

In favour of this view is the fact that abnormalities in social relationships are invariably present in infantile autism (by definition, however), and also the fact that the social difficulties are usually apparent right from infancy. On the other hand, it is striking that social withdrawal more than most symptoms tends to lessen considerably as the autistic child grows older. This is somewhat against the view that social withdrawal is the primary handicap.

Furthermore, if it is the basic handicap which underlies all the other symptoms, it should be possible to explain the I.Q. findings and also the language defects in terms of social withdrawal. The available evidence suggests that social withdrawal *cannot* account for these other symptoms.

In the first place it has been shown that the I.Q. of the autistic child is just as stable as in any other child. Also the I.Q. is a remarkably good predictor of the autistic child's intellectual, social, and behavioural adjustment in adolescence and adult life (Lockyer, 1967; Rutter, 1965; Rutter *et al.*, 1967). This is scarcely consonant with the view that the I.Q. is extremely unreliable in the autistic child (Anthony, 1958) and that the autistic child functions at a low I.Q. level only because he is socially withdrawn.

It could still be argued that the I.Q. is only measuring the effects of social withdrawal, but it has also been shown that loss of the symptom of social withdrawal has no effect on I.Q., and even the children with the best outcome in adolescence showed little change in I.Q.—on average an increase of only 7 or 8 points (Rutter *et al.*, 1967). This finding can be fitted into the social withdrawal theory only if it is assumed that the development of intelligence depends on the presence of normal social relationships at a critical period in early childhood, and that if the child is withdrawn at the time intelligence fails to develop regardless of what happens later. There is nothing to suggest that this is the case to any marked degree in human beings, and investigations of social deprivation in man indicate that even severe intellectual ill-effects are sometimes remarkably reversible (Clarke, 1965; Davis, 1947).

Even more damaging to the social withdrawal theory are the findings in relation to the autistic child's pattern of scores on the performance subtests of the Wechsler Intelligence Scales. The autistic child does very poorly on picture completion, picture arrangement, and digit symbol, but relatively well on block design and object assembly, the differences between subtests being large and statistically highly significant (Rutter, 1966a). The most likely explanation for this striking pattern of subtest scores is to be found in the *language* component of the subtests. None of the 5 "performance" subtests require that the child speak. However, picture arrangement (after the first few items), picture completion, and digit symbol all require concepts of abstraction, symbolization, and logic, concepts which require language but not speech. On the other hand, block design and object assembly require neither speech nor language, and have a much lower relationship with verbal skills, as shown, for example, in the results of factor analysis (Maxwell, 1959). That this may be the correct explanation is also suggested by the fact that the same pattern of subtest scores is found in developmental disorders of language which are unassociated with social withdrawal (so-called developmental aphasia) (Davies-Eysenck, 1966). An alternative, but similar, explanation may be derived from the observation that block design and object assembly require less in the way of verbal instructions than do the other subtests. Thus, the pattern might result from a defect in the comprehension of language which prevented the child from understanding what was expected of him in the tests (Rutter, 1965). Either way, an explanation in terms of language is suggested.

In contrast, it is very difficult to see how *current* social withdrawal could cause the child to do very poorly on 3 performance subtests yet well on 2 others. There are no grounds for suggesting that a higher level of social-interaction (other than in terms of language) is required for, say, picture completion or digit symbol than object assembly. Furthermore, profound social withdrawal in conditions other than autism is *not* associated with this pattern of subtest scores. For example, children with elective mutism show no particular weakness on verbal items as opposed to nonverbal items in intelligence tests (Reed, 1963). It may be concluded that the findings on the Wechsler Intelligence Scales strongly suggest not only that the autistic child cannot talk, but also that he is deficient in basic language skills. In contrast, it is very difficult to explain the findings in terms of a social withdrawal causing the child not to wish to speak.

A number of other, less plausible hypotheses to explain the pattern of subtest scores might be suggested, and although none offers any support for a social withdrawal hypothesis, it is convenient to consider them here. For example, it could be suggested that object assembly and block design require less social awareness than the other subtests. However, social awareness is just what the child with a receptive language defect lacks (Myklebust, 1954), and it is difficult to differentiate between poor social perception and a general impairment in symbolic functioning or language comprehension. Alternatively it might be thought that object assembly and block design are less perceptually complex than the other performance subtests. However, this is not the case if by perception something other than language comprehension is meant. Of the subtests, the object assembly and block-design subtests weigh most highly on the visuo-spatial factor (Maxwell, 1959 and 1960), and children with perceptual defects are most handicapped on these two subtests (Kinsbourne and Warrington, 1963). Lastly, it might be granted that the subtest pattern was due to an impairment of language and that this could not be due to *current* social withdrawal, but that, nevertheless, *previous* social withdrawal had prevented the development of language. This suggestion relies on the concept of "critical periods," otherwise if the child had ceased to show social withdrawal, language should still have developed. As this concept can be invoked to explain almost any current abnormality in terms of some hypothetical deficiency in the past (see several sections earlier and later in the paper), it is as well to consider it more closely now.

The concept of "critical period" implies that particular functions can *only* develop at a certain age or during a certain stage in maturation. It is, of course, obvious that for most skills and behaviours there is a stage in development at which they *usually* appear. Furthermore, it is clear that although learning plays a vital role in development, nevertheless a necessary stage of physiological maturity will be required before certain skills can develop (McGraw, 1946). The reason for this is readily seen in the major anatomical, histological, physiological, and chemical changes which take place in the brain after birth (Lenneberg, 1967). However, the concept of critical periods involves more than this, in that it supposes a limit at *both* ends, so that if a function fails to develop during a certain limited time-period, it will be impossible (or at least extremely difficult) for it to do so at any later point in time.

This is a concept which developed in relation to the study of birds, and there is no satisfactory evidence to suggest that the same kind of sharply defined critical periods occur in man (Hinde, 1962). Indeed, it has been shown that the periods are not as clear cut as once thought even in birds (Moltz,

1960; Sluckin, 1964). The testing of the concept in man is subject to immense practical difficulties in that it is very hard to find cases where individuals have failed to develop a skill at the usual time but yet where there is no neurological disorder which is still preventing the development of the function. In addition, testing is much complicated by the fact that the restoration of a function (such as sight) after years of deprivation may lead to profound emotional disturbance (Gregory and Wallace, 1962). (Also the learning of new skills may be hampered by the need to unlearn old skills.) Nevertheless, in spite of all these problems, on the rare occasions when it has been possible to test the concept of critical periods in man the results have been consistently negative (Cameron, 1968). In particular, it does not apply to speech development, with the possible exception of the situation of total deafness (Fry, 1966), which is irrelevant to the hypothesis of social withdrawal. In the Maudsley study there were several children who acquired speech for the first time well after 5 yr—in one case as late as 11 or 12 yr (Rutter *et al.*, 1967). Moreover, it was shown over 20 yr ago that it was possible for language to develop for the first time at 6 yr even after exceptionally prolonged and severe social deprivation (Mason, 1942). The best evidence suggests that the "critical period" for the development of language in man extends from about 2 to 12 yr (Lenneberg, 1967). This is much too long a period for it to be of the slightest support to any social withdrawal hypothesis.

The social withdrawal hypothesis may also be considered in relation to the developmental course of the symptom, particularly language. To a considerable extent social withdrawal and language impairment tend to improve or deteriorate together. However, the hypothesis of social withdrawal is tested in those cases where the course of the two symptoms does not run parallel. It was found in the Maudsley follow-up study that there may be marked improvements with respect to social withdrawal and yet no change in speech (Rutter, 1965; Rutter *et al.*, 1967). Whereas there was no child in the study who had normal speech and showed more than very slight social withdrawal, there were several children who remained completely without speech and yet had lost all evidence of social withdrawal. These findings run counter to the social withdrawal hypothesis in that, at least in those cases, there was *no* possibility of current social withdrawal preventing the child from speaking. Some other explanation for the language deficit must be provided. Of course, again, it could be suggested that *previous* social withdrawal during a "critical period" had permanently prevented language development but there is evidence that this does not happen (Mason, 1942), and the reasons for rejecting the idea of a narrowly defined critical period for language development have already been discussed. The problem of why language and social development often, but not always, run parallel, remains. This will be considered below in relation to the language hypothesis.

Finally, the results of studies of factors related to prognosis also, to some extent, argue against the social withdrawal hypothesis. The two most important items related to the prognosis in infantile autism are the level of I.Q. and the degree of language impairment (Rutter *et al.*, 1967). In contrast, the extent of social withdrawal shows only a weak association with outcome. As the reliability of different items was not compared, it is not possible to completely exclude the possibility that this might be explicable in terms of a lower reliability on the judgement of social withdrawal.

One may conclude that it remains uncertain whether or not autistic children have a primary defect in social relationships. There may be a basic social handicap but the available evidence suggests that if there is, it cannot account for the other major symptoms—namely the impairment in intellectual and language function.

Autism as a Brain Damage Syndrome

Autism has also been regarded by some workers as a brain damage syndrome. While the concept of brain damage is by no means as clear-cut as its name suggests (Rutter, 1967c), it is quite evident that there are a number of findings which point to the likelihood that some kind of organic brain lesion may be responsible for the development of at least some cases of infantile autism.

The main evidence in favour may be summarized as follows:

1. A clinical picture which is indistinguishable from infantile autism may develop after overt brain disease such as encephalitis when it occurs in infancy or early childhood (Rutter, 1967a).
2. Autistic children who have *no* abnormalities that are detectable on a neurological examination in early or middle childhood sometimes later develop evidence of organic brain dysfunction. In particular, epileptic fits develop in adolescence in up to one-sixth of cases (Rutter *et al.*, 1967). When considered in relation to evidence apparent at any time during childhood or adolescence it appears that about one in four autistic children probably has an organic brain disorder.
3. While the frequent occurrence of cognitive, language, and perceptual defects does not in itself necessarily indicate structural pathology of the brain, their presence is in favour of some kind of organic brain dysfunction. The chief alternative explanation is that these defects are functional abnormalities involving delays in maturation— like the developmental speech disorders of familial origin.

The main arguments against brain damage being a general explanation of autism are:

1. There is no evidence of brain damage in at least half the cases of autism.
2. All the types of brain damage found in association with autism are more usually found in association with nonautistic conditions, so the question remains as to why apparently the same kind of brain damage leads to autism in a few children but not in others (Bettelheim, 1967).
3. The impairment of cognitive, language, and perceptual function could just as well be due to environmental factors. Extreme social isolation can lead to even severe subnormality (Clarke, 1965), and language delays are very common in institutional children (Tizard, 1964). Furthermore, there is some evidence to suggest that profound lack of stimulation can occasionally even induce irreversible cell atrophy (Riesen, 1965).

Before discussing the pros and cons of these arguments it should be pointed out that much of the evidence which could be crucial is still missing. There are no published histopathological studies; the EEG studies in the literature are inadequate and contradictory; and metabolic investigations are still in their infancy (Rutter, 1967a).

Probably only two definite conclusions may be drawn. Firstly, many autistic children have no demonstrable evidence of brain damage. This does not necessarily mean that they have no organic brain pathology. Our tools to measure brain function are still very inadequate and it is well known that many children with proven brain disease appear quite normal on clinical examination. Nevertheless, the fact remains, in half the children with autism we cannot produce any satisfactory evidence of organic brain damage. The second conclusion is that in some cases there can be no doubt that frank brain disease is the main (but perhaps not the only) aetiological factor. Whereas profound environmental deprivation may occasionally produce lasting organic dysfunction, no-one has suggested that it can cause conditions like encephalitis (which sometimes lead to autism). Also, although it has been suggested that epileptic fits may be a form of psychogenic defence mechanism (O'Gorman, 1967), this suggestion is rather fanciful and most people would regard the development of fits as being in favour of some kind of organic aetiology.

However, even if it is accepted that autism may sometimes, or perhaps often, develop on the basis of brain damage, the explanation is too general to be of much help in understanding how autism develops. The term "brain damage" includes a wide variety of disturbances. The vast majority of children with brain damage are not autistic, and it remains to be explained why the minority who become autistic do so. More specific biological hypotheses are required.

Autism as an Abnormality of Physiological Arousal

One such hypothesis suggests that the autistic child's failure to respond to sensory stimuli (that is his "withdrawal") may be due to abnormalities in the brain's function in maintaining a state of normal alertness. For example, Rimland (1964) has suggested that the reticular formation in the brain stem may fail to work properly in autistic children, and that defective arousal is, to use his own words, "the secret of the veil of autism." This is a highly speculative proposal without much supporting evidence. However, more recently the Hutts and their colleagues have reported that the EEG's of autistic children show a low voltage irregular pattern without a dominant rhythm (Hutt *et al.*, 1964), which suggests a state of high physiological arousal. More circumstantial evidence in favour of high arousal is their finding that autistic children's stereotypes tend to be more frequent in complex than in simple situations (Hutt *et al.*, 1965), and Connell's observation (1966) that autistic children often require greater than usual doses of sedative drugs.

The matter remains undecided at the moment as very limited evidence is as yet available. However, if it is assumed, for the present, that autistic children are "overaroused," two main issues arise in the interpretation of this. First, the level of arousal is related to the child's level of maturation or development (Fountain and Lynn, 1966; Hermelin and O'Connor, 1968), and it is possible that the findings may be due in part to the low mental age of the children tested. Secondly, the high arousal may have developed as a secondary response rather than as a primary defect, and a recent investigation carried out by Hermelin and O'Connor (1968) suggests that this may indeed be the case. They examined the percent of alpha rhythm in the telemetred EEG records of autistic, mongol, and normal children in various conditions of light and sound stimulation. Few differences were found between the three groups of children, and only in a situation where there was continuous noise were the autistic children relatively more aroused. This suggests that high arousal may be a secondary response rather than a primary defect, but further studies are required before the issue can be settled one way or the other.

Autism as a Response to Language and Other Perceptual Abnormalities

Although there are several other hypotheses about the nature of autism, there is only one more which will be considered in any detail, namely the hypothesis that the basic defect in infantile autism is an impairment in the comprehension of sounds. According to this view, the language disorder in autism is the primary abnormality. Furthermore, it is thought that this abnormality in the development of language is closely similar to other developmental disorders of language involving defects in comprehension—

so-called "developmental receptive aphasia" or "congenital auditory imperception" (Rutter, 1965a, 1966a). As in these other developmental conditions the impairment in the comprehension of sounds may often be associated with other perceptual defects, and sometimes these may be the most important in the genesis of autism (Stroh and Buick, 1961).

There is now a considerable amount of evidence in support of this hypothesis. First, there is the well-established observation that retardation of speech development is an invariable, or almost invariable, manifestation in the condition of infantile autism, and that the speech abnormalities are very early symptoms and, indeed, are often the first to be observed (Rutter, 1966a). There are many aspects to the abnormalities of speech and language which might be emphasized, and elsewhere (Rutter, 1966a) the striking similarities between these and the abnormalities associated with severe developmental language disorders (so-called developmental "aphasia") have been commented upon. In the young child, however, there are three features which require particular mention. The first of these is the autistic child's often profound lack of response to sounds, reflected in his lack of startle response (Anthony, 1958), his nondistractibility (Rutter, 1966a), and the frequency with which he is suspected of deafness (Kanner, 1943; Rutter, 1966a). The audiometric responses of autistic children and of children with receptive aphasia are the same (Taylor, 1965). Difficulties in the comprehension of *spoken* instructions can often be demonstrated (Pronovost *et al.*, 1966; Rutter, 1965b) and it seems likely that the lack of response to sounds represents a failure or relative failure to *comprehend* sounds. Psychological experiments have also demonstrated abnormalities in the response to verbal stimuli (Hermelin, 1966). The second feature is the tendency to echo (echolalia) which is a characteristic of some three-quarters of those who gain speech. This, too, probably reflects a failure in comprehension (Myklebust, 1957; Stengel, 1964). The third feature is the tendency to reverse pronouns—particularly a confusion of "you" and "I." Although this has sometimes been regarded as possible evidence of unawareness of personal identity (Creak *et al.*, 1961), Kanner (Kanner and Eisenberg, 1955) thought it resulted from echolalia, which seems the more likely explanation in view of the close association between these two aspects of language (Rutter, 1966a).

It should also be noted that although there are similarities between the language deficit of autistic children and children with developmental language disorders, there are also differences. Echolalia and pronominal reversal, features of autism, are probably less frequently found in the uncomplicated language disorders. Similarly, a good short-term memory span may be more characteristic of autism than of "developmental aphasia" (de Hirsch, 1967). On the other hand, the use of gesture and mime to communicate is rare in autistic children but relatively common in "aphasic" children. The clinical significance of these differences remains uncertain and studies comparing the two conditions in more detail would be illuminating.

A study by Tubbs (1966) using the Illinois Test of Psycholinguistic Abilities (Kirk and McCarthy, 1961; McCarthy and Olson, 1964) has shown that not only is the autistic child retarded in language, but also his *pattern* of linguistic abilities is significantly different from that exhibited by either normal or mentally retarded children. The autistic child is particularly poor in his understanding of the meaning of spoken words, in his use of gestures, and in his transfer from one sensory modality to another.

The second piece of evidence in relation to the language hypothesis is provided by the results of follow-up studies (Rutter, 1960b; Rutter *et al.*, 1967). As already noted, apart from the level of intelligence, language is the most important prognostic factor. The autistic child who is not speaking by the age of 5 yr, or who had a profound lack of response to sounds in early childhood, may improve considerably, but he is unlikely to achieve a normal or near-normal level of social adjustment by the time of adolescence. Apart from language, no other single symptom (not even social withdrawal) had a significant association with outcome, although in general those with the mildest symptoms had the best outcome. Perhaps even more important with respect to the language hypothesis, there were several autistic children in the Maudsley study who ceased to show social withdrawal, who improved greatly in all other aspects of behaviour, but who remained entirely without speech in spite of normal intelligence on nonverbal tests (Rutter, 1965; Rutter *et al.*, 1967). All these children had considerable difficulties in the comprehension of *spoken* instructions although they complied readily if gesture or demonstration were used to convey the request, a finding also noted by Pronovost and his colleagues (1966). At least in these autistic children the language defect must be regarded as a primary phenomenon, not as a feature secondary to social withdrawal or any other abnormality. The language retardation may continue in spite of improvement in all other aspects of the autistic condition.

The third piece of evidence is provided by the autistic child's pattern of cognitive abilities (Rutter, 1966a; Lockyer, 1967). Characteristically, his immediate memory (as measured by digit span) is quite good, but his scores on all tests involving verbal concepts, abstraction, or symbolization, are very poor. This might merely reflect his lack of speech but what is highly significant is that this failure applies even *on tests which do not require him to speak* (such as a test which requires him to place a series of pictures in an order which conveys a story). Furthermore, it has been shown that this pattern of abilities is highly associated with the autistic child's level of speech development, and the pattern is the same as that found in children with severe developmental language disorders (Davies-Eysenck, 1966). It is clear that the autistic child's failure to speak is due to a basic impairment in language skills—not to an absence of motivation[2] to speak or to social withdrawal.

The fourth piece of evidence is provided by a series of ingenious and elegant experiments carried out by Hermelin and O'Connor in which they examined coding and immediate recall in autistic, subnormal and normal children matched for their scores on a vocabulary test (Hermelin, 1967; Hermelin and O'Connor, 1967; O'Connor and Hermelin, 1967). Ordinarily, verbal material tends to be remembered in terms of categories or concepts. For example, given the sequence "blue, three, red, five, six, white, green, eight," normal children will usually regroup the words into colours and into numbers when asked to recall the sequence they were asked to remember. But, autistic children did this significantly less often—they seemed not to use concepts in memorizing. A further experiment took this issue a stage further. Children were tested for their recall of eight word messages which consisted either of two nonsense phrases (such as: "half egg a pick; might got dress put") or two meaningful sentences (such as: "watch these green lights; eat bread and jam"). It was found that autistic children were more likely than other children to remember the last part of the message regardless of whether or not it made sense. Normal children were likely to remember the meaningful sentences. Thus the verbal recall of autistic children was relatively independent of the *meaning* of what they had heard. These results tend to suggest a hypothesis in terms of deficits in verbal coding and patterning (Hermelin, 1967).

Altogether, the evidence for the existence of a basic defect in the comprehension of language and in the utilization and organization of perception seems to be overwhelming. Moreover, the findings strongly suggest that this is a *primary* defect, and not one which is secondary to social withdrawal. The contrary evidence is mostly of an anecdotal kind but nevertheless it requires serious consideration. The two most weighty objections concern the selectivity of language deficits. Firstly, it has often been observed that the autistic child's response to sounds is inconsistent, and sometimes his failure to respond appears relatively selective toward certain individuals only, or towards certain types of stimuli only (O'Gorman, 1967). Inconsistency both in response to sounds and in production of speech is of course also characteristic of the aphasic person, or the child with a developmental language disorder. On the other hand, the selectivity does suggest the operation of

---

[2]Of course, there is no direct evidence regarding the motivation of these children, and in autistic children as well as other children, motivational factors will certainly influence communication (see below). The point is simply that there is no evidence that the mutism is in any way elective, and furthermore, that the lack of speech can be explained in language terms without the necessity to invoke hypothetical motivational factors as the cause of the *primary* defect.

psychogenic processes. The existence of such selectivity has not been adequately established but it may be accepted that in some autistic children it is probably present. The existence of a biological handicap in no way rules out psychogenic mechanisms and, indeed, it would be very surprising if motivational influences did not in part determine the way speech is used by autistic children as it does in any child. But it is very hard to see how motivation influences could explain *all* the language problems of the type outlined in considering the evidence in favour of a language hypothesis.

The second point concerns the child's use of personal pronouns. Bosch (1962) has suggested that the autistic child selectively avoids the use of "I," and Bettelheim (1967), making the same point, adds that autistic children never echo "I" although they will echo other personal pronouns. If this could be substantiated, it would unquestionably cast serious doubt on the relevance of a language hypothesis, at least with regard to the reversal of personal pronouns. The autistic child's echoing of personal pronouns is currently being investigated in a systematic and controlled fashion by Bartak (1967). The preliminary results of his study run completely counter to Bettelheim's claims. When the position of the pronoun in the sentence is controlled, and obviously this is essential, autistic children do echo "I" as often as they echo any other personal pronoun. The fact that "I" is rarely echoed in ordinary circumstances is simply a function of the fact that "I" normally comes at the beginning of a sentence, whereas other personal pronouns are more likely to come at the end, and the end of a sentence is much more commonly echoed than the beginning.

These objections based on selectivity of responses in no way invalidate the much stronger evidence in favour of the language hypothesis. Of course, the existence of a basic defect in language function does not explain how that defect was caused. Nor does it explain how the other symptoms arise. However, as argued previously (Rutter, 1966a), it seems likely that many of the key features of infantile autism can be explained on the basis of a perceptual and comprehension defect.

Some aspects of the disturbances in affective contact may stem fairly directly from an inability to comprehend the spoken word and especially the nuances and subtleties of abstract concepts, humour, and expression of emotions. An inability to understand humour, and failures in social perception, may result in a lack of empathy for other people and difficulties in interpersonal relationships. In addition, there may be a learned element in that because the child does not understand what is being said to him he may react to his perplexity by emotional withdrawal. Haeusserman (1962) put it like this: "We have little aphasic children who have grown to be afraid to look at faces, because their parents' faces have become more and more tense and desperate as they have spoken to the child . . . noises have come out of the parents' mouths which to the child who cannot interpret words do not mean anything . . . the voice has become louder and louder, the face has become more and more tense . . . then the child wanders away. You think you have an autistic child; in reality, you have an aphasic child who has been misunderstood by its parents, who have tried terribly hard to have the child speak."

Several difficulties arise with this type of explanation within the framework of the language hypothesis. Firstly, abnormalities in social relationships (such as the failure in infancy to adopt an anticipatory posture for picking up) might seem to be evident too early to be explained in terms of a language or perceptual defect. However, the relevant point here is that it is suggested that the social withdrawal arises in relation to the defect in comprehension of language, not in relation to the failure to speak. Comprehension of sounds plays an important part in development long before the child is ready to speak. By 16 weeks the normal child is already clearly responding to the human voice, and by 6 months the babbling of a deaf child is altering in quality in relation to the lack of auditory feedback (Lenneberg, 1967). This is probably early enough for a defect in comprehension to cause the first signs of social withdrawal. However, this naturally leads to a consideration of the second difficulty: if failure to comprehend causes social withdrawal, why does this not happen more often accompanying deafness? The probable explanation of this is that (a) *distorted* perception due to failure to understand what is heard may be more distressing and more perplexing than failure to hear at all, and (b) the deaf child has no general difficulty in comprehension. He can appreciate symbolic communications perfectly well through any sensory modality other than hearing, whereas the autistic child has a general defect of language and symbolization so that symbolic communications of any kind present some difficulty in comprehension (although the problem is most marked in the case of spoken language).

Thirdly, it remains to be explained why it is that only some children with these defects in the perception of sounds become autistic. In this respect it should be noted that all degrees of social withdrawal may be seen in relation to developmental language disorders which involve a failure in the comprehension of sounds. Some children show no social withdrawal and would not be called autistic by anyone, others show some withdrawal and terms like "autistic traits" are often employed, while yet others show the full syndrome of infantile autism (Myklebust, 1954). Similarly, in some cases the social withdrawal develops only after several years of language difficulties, in other cases it arises shortly after language retardation is evident, and in others the language retardation and social withdrawal are both evident from infancy (Rutter, unpublished data). But, autistic children virtually never show language difficulties arising only *after* the development of social withdrawal. Similarly, the social withdrawal (and, indeed, the full syndrome of infantile autism) may appear as a *transient* manifestation accompanying a developmental language disorder (Berg, 1961). In short, there seems to be a continuum from severe persistent social withdrawal to mild transient withdrawal, or no withdrawal at all, but most children with severe defects in language comprehension show some social difficulties for a time.

The reasons for this state of affairs may be found both in the child and in his environment. It may be that the added handicap of low intelligence (present in many but not all autistic children) increases the likelihood of social withdrawal. There is also some suggestion that the autistic child has more severe and more widespread perceptual defects than the child who does not develop social withdrawal. To what extent the differences between the type of language abnormality found in autism and in the uncomplicated developmental disorders of language (noted above) are relevant, remains unknown. That factors in the child are very important in relation to the development of social withdrawal is suggested by the finding that I.Q. and the degree of language impairment are the two most important prognostic features in autism. However, it may be that part of the reason for the development of social withdrawal also lies in the parents' response to the child's handicap. In support of this view is the marked improvement in social relationships which may sometimes follow daily attendance at a unit for autistic children, or counselling of the parents on how to deal with the child. How much improvement is possible, in what circumstances it most readily takes place, and what mechanisms are involved, remain quite unknown at present. Also, there is insufficient evidence to decide the relative importance of factors in the child and in his environment in the genesis of social withdrawal.

Fourthly, there is the related question of why social withdrawal sometimes ceases in spite of a persistence of the language handicap. Again, the answer probably lies both within the child and in the environment. If the handling of the child becomes more appropriate, social withdrawal should lessen regardless of what happens to the language handicap. However, it is important that the development of comprehension must precede the development of speech (Lenneberg, 1964), so that the comprehension defect, which, it is suggested, led to the social withdrawal, will improve before the child can speak, and the social withdrawal might be expected to do so also. Furthermore, the profound defect in comprehension found in children with the most severe developmental disorders of language during infancy shows a marked tendency to improve as the child grows older (Gordon and Taylor, 1964), so that other things being equal, social withdrawal should in any case diminish as the autistic child grows up.

Lastly, some symptoms, such as the ritualistic and compulsive phenomena, are less easily explicable in terms of a language defect. It appears most unlikely that they are a direct result of any perceptual abnormality. More probably, they arise as one means of the child's dealing with his handicaps—a maladaptive attempt to come to terms with his defects.

Other problems in relation to the language hypothesis could be mentioned and it is clear that, so far, it does not provide a complete or even an entirely satisfactory explanation. The nature of the basic language abnormality remains unknown, and the suggestions as to how social withdrawal and other symptoms develop as a response to failure in the comprehension of sounds are speculative. Nevertheless, a language hypothesis offers an explanation of the development of infantile autism that seems to account for most of the main findings and further research to confirm or refute these suggestions is indicated.

Summary

In the present state of knowledge only tentative conclusions are possible. However, it is suggested that contrary to earlier views, infantile autism is *not* anything to do with schizophrenia, and it is *not* primarily a disorder of social relationships. The presence of mental subnormality is not sufficient to account for autism and it seems unlikely that psychogenic or faulty conditioning mechanisms are *primary* factors in aetiology, although they may be important in the development of secondary handicaps. The importance of genetic factors remains unknown. The role of "brain damage" in the genesis of autism is also uncertain, but organic brain abnormalities appear to be primary influences in some cases—in how many is not known. In any case the concept of "brain damage" is too general to be of much help in understanding the genesis of autism. The determination of the relevance of abnormalities in physiological arousal awaits further research. Of all the hypotheses concerning the nature of autism, that which places the primary defect in terms of a language or coding problem appears most promising. It is suggested that many of the manifestations of autism are explicable in terms of cognitive and perceptual defects. This is an area of enquiry likely to reward further study.

REFERENCES

Ainsworth, M.D. (1962) The effects of maternal deprivation: a review of findings and controversy in the context of research strategy. In *Deprivation of Maternal Care: A Reassessment of its Effects*. Public Health Paper No. 14. WHO, Geneva.

Anthony, E.J. (1958) An experimental approach to the psychopathology of childhood: Autism. *Brit. J. Med. Psychol. 31*, 211–225.

Anthony, J. and Scott, P. (1960) Manic-depressive psychosis in childhood. *J. Child Psychol. Psychiat. 1*, 53–72.

Bartak, L. (1967) (Personal Communication).

Benda, C. E. (1952) *Developmental Disorders of Mentation and Cerebral Palsies*. Grune and Stratton, New York.

Bender, L. (1942) Childhood schizophrenia. *Nerv. Child 1*, 138–140.

Bender, L. (1947) Childhood schizophrenia: Clincial study of 100 schizophrenic children. *Am. J. Orthopsychiat. 17*, 40–56.

Berg, I. S. (1961) A case study of developmental auditory imperception: some theoretical implications. *J. Child Psychol. Psychiat. 2*, 86–93.

Bettelheim, B. (1967) *The Empty Fortress: Infantile Autism and the Birth of the Self*. Collier-Macmillan, London.

Boatman, M. J. and Szurek, S. A. (1960) A Clinical Study of Childhood Schizophrenia. In *The Etiology of Schizophrenia* (Edited by Jackson, D. D.). Basic Books, New York.

Bosch, G. (1962) *Der Fruekindliche Autismus*. Springer, Berlin. (Cited Bettelheim, 1967.)

Bradley, C. (1941) *Schizophrenia in Childhood*. Macmillan, New York.

Brown, G. W. (1967) The family of the schizophrenic patient. In *Recent Developments in Schizophrenia: A Symposium* (Edited by Coppen, A. J. and Walk, A.). R.M.P.A., London.

Cameron, H. (1968) Dysphagia in infancy: the critical period hypothesis and speech and emotional problems. D.P.M. Dissertation. Univ., London.

Clarke, A.D.B. (1965) Genetic and environmental studies of intelligence. In *Mental Deficiency: The Changing Outlook* (Edited by Clarke, A.M. and Clarke, A.D.B.). Methuen, London.

Connell, P.H. (1966) Medical Treatment. In *Childhood Autism: Clinical, Educational and Social Aspects* (Edited by Wing, J. K.). Pergamon Press, London.

Corberi, G. (1926) Sindromi die regressione mentale infantogiovanele. *Riv. Pat. Nerv. 31*, 6. (Cited Benda, 1952.)

Creak, E. M. (1963) Childhood Psychosis: a review of 100 cases. *Brit. J. Psychiat. 109*, 84–89.

Creak, M. (1961) (Chairman) Schizophrenic Syndrome in Childhood: progress report of a working party (April, 1961). *Cerebral Palsy Bull. 3*, 501–504.

Creak, M. (1964) (Chairman) Schizophrenic Syndrome in Childhood: further progress report of a working party (April, 1964). *Develop. Med. Child Neurol. 4*, 530–535.

Creak, M. and Ini, S. (1960) Families of psychotic children. *J. Child Psychol. Psychiat. 1*, 156–175.

Davies-Eysenck, M. (1966) Unpublished paper. Day Conference for Medical Officers. London, November 18th.

Davis, K. (1947) Final note on a case of extreme isolation. *Am J. Sociol. 52*, 432–437.

De Hirsch, K. (1967) Differential diagnosis between aphasic and schizophrenic language in children. *J. Speech Hearing Dis. 32*, 3–10.

Despert, J. L. (1951) Some considerations relating to the genesis of autistic behaviour in children. *Am. J. Orthopsychiat. 21*, 335–350.

Eisenberg, L. (1957a) The course of childhood schizophrenia. *A.M.A. Arch Neurol. Psychiat. 78*, 69–83.

Eisenberg, L. (1957b) The fathers of autistic children. *Am. J. Orthopsychiat. 27*, 715–724.

Eisenberg, L. (1967) Psychotic disorders in childhood. In *The Classification of Behaviour Disorders* (Edited by Eron, L. D.). Aldine, Chicago.

Eisenberg, L. and Kanner, L. (1956) Early infantile autism 1943–55. *Am. J. Orthopsychiat. 26*, 556–566.

Ferster, C. B. (1961) Positive reinforcement and behavioural deficits of autistic children. *Child Develop. 32*, 437–456.

Fountain, W. and Lynn, R. (1966) Change in level of arousal during childhood. *Behav. Res. Ther. 4*, 213–217.

Fry, D. B. (1966) The development of the phonological system in the normal and the deaf child. In *The Genesis of Language: A psycholinguistic Approach* (Edited by Smith, F. and Miller, G. A.). M.I.T. Press, Cambridge.

Goldfarb, W. (1961) *Childhood Schizophrenia*. Harvard Univ. Press, Cambridge, Mass.

Gordon, N. and Taylor, I. G. (1964) The assessment of children with difficulties of communication. *Brain 87*, 121–140.

Gregory, R. L. and Wallace, J. G. (1962) Recovery from early blindness: a case study. *Quart J. exp. Psychol. Monogr. 2*.

Hare, E. H. (1967) The epidemiology of schizophrenia. In *Recent Developments in Schizophrenia: A Symposium* (Edited by Coppen, A. J. and Walk, A.). R.M.P.A., London.

Hauesserman, E. (1962) In *Childhood Aphasia* (Edited by West, R.). Proc. Inst. Child Aphasia Conf., Stamford Univ., 1960.

Hermelin, B. (1966) Psychological Research. In *Childhood Autism: Clinical, Educational and Social Aspects* (Edited by Wing, J. K.). Pergamon Press, London.

Hermelin, B. (1967) Coding and immediate recall in autistic children. *Proc. Roy. Soc. Med. 60*, 563–564.

Hermelin, B. and O'Connor, N. (1968) Measures of the occipital alpha rhythm in normal, subnormal and autistic children. *Brit. J. Psychiat. 114*, 603–610.

Hermelin, B. and O'Connor, N. (1967) Remembering of words by psychotic and normal children. *Brit. J. Psychol. 58*, 213–218.

Hinde, R. A. (1962) Sensitive periods and the development of behaviour. In *Lessons from Animal Behaviour for the Clinician* (Edited by Barnett, S. A.). Little Club Clinic in Developmental Medicine No. 7, Wm. Heinemann, London.

Hutt, C., Hutt, S. J., Lee, D. and Ounsted, C. (1964) Arousal and childhood autism. *Nature, Lond. 204*, 908–909.

Hutt, S. J., Hutt, C., Lee, D. and Ounsted, C. (1965a) A behavioural and electroencephalographic study of autistic children. *J. Psychiat. Res. 3*, 181–198.

Hutt, C. and Hutt, S. J. (1965b) Effects of environmental complexity upon stereotyped behaviours in children. *Anim. Behav. 13*, 1–4.

Kanner, L. (1943) Autistic disturbances of affective contact. *Nerv. Child 2*, 217–250.

Kanner, L. (1949) Problem of nosology and psychodynamics of early infantile autism. *Am. J. Orthopsychiat. 19*, 416–426.

Kanner, L. and Eisenberg, L. (1955) Notes on the follow-up studies of autistic children. In *Psychopathology of Childhood* (Edited by Hoch, P. H. and Zubin, J.). Grune and Stratton, New York.

Kanner, L. and Lesser, L. I. (1958) Early infantile autism. *Ped. Clin. N. America.* 5, 711–730.

Kaufman, I., Rosenblum, E., Heims, L. and Willer, L. (1957) Childhood schizophrenia: treatment of children and parents. *Am J. Orthopsychiat.* 27, 683–690.

Kinsbourne, M. and Warrington, E. K. (1963) The developmental Gerstmann syndrome. *Arch. Neurol.* 8, 490–501.

Kirk, S. A. and McCarthy, J. J. (1961) The Illinois Test of Psycholinguistic Abilities—an approach to differential diganosis. *Am. J. ment. Def.* 66, 399–412.

Knobloch, H. and Grant, D. K. (1961) Etiologic factors in "early infantile autism" and "childhood schizophrenia." *Am. J. Dis. Childhood* 102, 535–536.

Knobloch, H. and Pasamanick, B. (1962) Etiologic factors in "early infantile autism" and "childhood schizophrenia." Unpublished paper. 10th Int. Congr. Pediat. Lisbon, Portugal. Sept. 9–15th 1962.

Krasner, L. and Ullman, L. (Eds.) (1965) *Research in Behaviour Modification.* Holt, Rinehart and Winston, New York.

Lenneberg, E. H. (1964) Speech as a motor skill with special reference to non-aphasic disorders. In *The Acquisition of Language* (Edited by Bellugi, U. and Brown, R. W.). Mon. Soc. Res. Child Dev. 29, No. 92.

Lenneberg, E. H. (1967) *Biological Foundations of Language.* John Wiley, New York.

Lockyer, L. (1967) A Psychological Follow-up Study of Psychotic Children. Ph.D. Thesis, Univ. of London.

Lockyer, L. and Rutter, M. (1968) A five to fifteen-year follow-up study of infantile psychosis. III Psychological aspects. *Brit. J. Psychiat.* (In press.)

Lotter, V. (1966) Epidemiology of autistic conditions in young children. I—Prevalence. *Soc. Psychiat. I*, 124–137.

Lotter, V. (1967) Epidemiology of autistic conditions in young children. II—Some characteristics of the parents and children. *Soc. Psychiat. I*, 163–173.

Mahler, M. S. (1952) On child psychosis and schizophrenia: autistic and symbiotic infantile psychoses. *Psychoanalytic Study Child VII*, 286–305.

Mahler, M. S. and Gosliner, B. J. (1955) On symbiotic child psychosis: genetic, dynamic and restitutive aspects. *Psychoanalytic Study Child 10*, 195–212.

Mason, M. K. (1942) Learning to speak after years of silence. *J. Speech Hearing Dis.* 7, 295–304.

Maxwell, A. E. (1959) A factor analysis of the Wechsler Intelligence Scale for Children. *Brit. J. educ. Psychol.* 29, 237–241.

Maxwell, A. E. (1960) Obtaining factor scores on the Wechsler Adult Intelligence Scale. *J. ment. Sci.* 106, 1060–1062.

Mayer-Gross, W., Slater, E. and Roth, M. (1955) *Clinical Psychiatry.* Cassell, London.

McCarthy, J. J. and Olson, J. L. (1964) *Validity Studies on the Illinois Test of Psycholinguistic Abilities.* Univ. of Illinois Press.

McGraw, M. B. (1946) Maturation of behaviour. In *Manual of Child Psychology* (Edited by Carmichael, L.). Wiley, New York.

Meyers, D. I. and Goldfarb, W. (1961) Studies of perplexity in mothers of schizophrenic children. *Am. J. Orthopsychiat.* 31, 551–564.

Moltz, H. (1960) Imprinting: empirical basis and theoretical significance. *Psychol. Bull. 57*, 291–314.

Myklebust, H. R. (1954) *Auditory Disorders in Children*. Grune and Stratton, New York.

Norman, E. (1954) Reality relationships of schizophrenic children. *Brit. J. Med. Psychol. 27*, 126–141.

Norman, E. (1955) Affect and withdrawal in schizophrenic children. *Brit. J. Med. Psychol. 28*, 1–18.

O'Connor, N. (1967) Visual input and social response in autistic children. *Proc. Roy. Soc. Med. 60*, 560–563.

O'Connor, N. and Hermelin, B. (1967) Auditory and visual memory in autistic and normal children. *J. Ment. Def. Res. 11*, 126–131.

O'Gorman, G. (1967) *The Nature of Childhood Autism*. Butterworths, London.

Pasamanick, B. and Knobloch, H. (1961) Epidemiologic Studies on the complications of pregnancy and the birth process. In *Prevention of Mental Disorders in Childhood* (Edited by Caplan, G.). Basic Books, New York.

Penrose, L. S. and Smith, G. F. (1966) *Down's Anomaly*. Churchill, London.

Pollack, M. (1960) Comparison of childhood, adolescent and adult schizophrenia. *A.M.A. Arch. Gen. Psychiat. 2*, 562–660.

Potter, H. W. (1933) Schizophrenia in children. *Am. J. Psychiat. 89*, 1253–1270.

Prince, G. S. (1967) Mental health problems in pre-school West Indian Children. *Maternal and Child Care* (June), 483–486.

Pronovost, W., Wakstein, M. P. and Wakstein, D. J. (1966) A longitudinal study of the speech behaviour and language comprehension of fourteen children diagnosed atypical or autistic. *Exceptional Children 33*, 19–26.

Rank, B. (1949) Adaptation of the psychoanalytic technique for the treatment of young children with atypical development. *Am. J. Orthopsychiat. 19*, 130–139.

Reed, G. F. (1963) Elective mutism in children: a re-appraisal. *J. Child Psychol. Psychiat. 4*, 99–107.

Riesen, A. (1965) Effects of early deprivation of photic stimulation. In *The Biosocial Basis of Mental Retardation* (Edited by Osler, S. F. and Cooke, R. E.). Johns Hopkins Press, Maryland.

Rimland, B. (1964) *Infantile Autism*. Appleton-Century Crofts, New York.

Ross, I. S. (1959) Presentation of clinical cases: an autistic child. Ped. Conf. The Babies Hosp. Unit. United Hosp., Newark, N.J. 2, No. 2.

Rutter, M. (1965a) The influence of organic and emotional factors on the origins, nature and outcome of childhood psychosis. *Develop. Med. Child Neurol. 7*, 518–528.

Rutter, M. (1965b) Speech disorders in a series of autistic children. In *Children with Communication Problems* (Edited by Franklin, A. W.). Pitman, London.

Rutter, M. (1966a) Behavioural and cognitive characteristics of a series of psychotic children. In *Childhood Autism, Clinical, Educational and Social Aspects* (Edited by Wing, J. K.). Pergamon Press, London.

Rutter, M. (1966b) Prognosis: Psychotic children in adolescence and early adult life. In *Childhood Autism: Clinical, Educational and Social Aspects* (Edited by Wing, J. K.). Pergamon Press, London.

Rutter, M. (1967a) Psychotic disorders in early childhood. In *Recent Developments in Schizophrenia: A Symposium* (Edited by Coppen, A. J. and Walk, A.). R.M.P.A., London.

Rutter, M. (1967b) Schooling and the autistic child. *Spec. Ed. 56*, 19–24.

Rutter, M. (1967c) Organic brain damage, hyperkinesis and mental retardation: Working paper for the WHO Third Seminar on Psychiatric Diagnosis, Classification and Statistics. *La Psychiatrie de l'Enfant*. (In press.)

Rutter, M. (1969) The description and classification of infantile autism. Proc. Indiana Univ. Colloquium on Infantile Autism. April 7–9th 1968. (In press.)

Rutter, M. and Lockyer, L. (1967) A five to fifteen-year follow-up study of infantile psychosis. I—Description of sample. *Brit. J. Psychiat. 113*, 1169–1182.

Rutter, M., Greenfeld, D. and Lockyer, L. (1967) A five to fifteen-year follow-up study of infantile psychosis. II—Social and behavioural outcome. *Brit. J. Psychiat. 113*, 1183–1199.

Schopler, E. (1965) Early infantile autism and receptor processes. *Arch. Gen. Psychiat. 13*, 327–335.

Shields, J. (1967) The genetics of schizophrenia in historical context. In *Recent Developments in Schizophrenia: A Symposium* (Edited by Coppen, A.J. and Walk, A.). R.M.P.A., London.

Singer, M.T. and Wynn, L. C. (1963) Differentiating characteristics of parents of childhood schizophrenics, childhood neurotics and young adult schizophrenics. *Am. J. Psychiat. 120*, 234–243.

Sluckin, W. (1964) *Imprinting and Early Learning*. Methuen, London.

Stengel, E. (1964) Speech disorders and mental disorders. In *Disorders of Language*. *Ciba Foundation Symposium* (Edited by De Reuck, A. V. S. and O'Connor, M.). Churchill, London.

Stroh, G. and Buick, D. (1964) Perceptual development in childhood psychosis. *Brit. J. Med. Psychol. 37*, 291–299.

Szurek, S. A. and Berlin, I. N. (1956) Elements of psychotherapeutics with the schizophrenic child and his parents. *Psychiatry 19*, 1–9.

Szurek, S. A. (1956) Psychotic episodes and psychotic maldevelopment. *Am. J. Orthopsychiat. 26*, 519–543.

Taylor, I. (1965) The deaf and the non-communicating child. In *Children with Communication Problems* (Edited by Franklin, A.W.). Pitman Med. Publ., London.

Tizard, J. (1964) *Community Services for the Mentally Handicapped*. Oxford Univ. Press, London.

Tubbs, V. K. (1966) Types of linguistic disability in psychotic children. *J. Ment. Def. Res. 10*, 230–240.

Van Krevelen, D. A. (1952) Early infantile autism. *Acta. Paedopsychiat. 19*, 91–97.

Van Krevelen, D. A. (1963) On the relationship between early infantile autism and autistic psychopathy. *Acta. Paedopsychiat. 30*, 303–323.

Van Krevelen, D. A. and Knipers, C. (1962) The psychopathology of autistic psychopathy. *Acta. Paedopsychiat. 29*, 22–31.

Wing, J. K. (1966) Diagnosis, epidemiology, aetiology. In *Childhood Autism: Clinical, Educational and Social Aspects* (Edited by Wing, J. K.). Pergamon Press, Oxford.

Wolff, S. and Chess, S. (1965a) A behavioural study of schizophrenic children. *Acta. Psychiat. Scand. 40*, 438–466.
Wolff, S. and Chess, S. (1965b) An analysis of the language of fourteen schizophrenic children. *J. Child Psychol. Psychiat. 6*, 29–41.

COMMENTARY by Marian K. DeMyer

Michael Rutter has had great impact on those who work to understand the basic nature of infantile autism. This theoretical article, appearing at the end of the 1960s, illustrates some of the reasons for his influence. He never lets "fanciful" ideas draw him away from sound evidence that he can marshal clearly for his audiences. One of the most dearly held ideas in the two decades following Kanner's first description of autism in 1943 was that defective nurture from the parents was the major, if not the sole, cause of autism. Rutter's masterful summation of the evidence for and against the parental defect hypothesis, in a few short pages, must certainly have swayed many readers to search for a biological defect in the child. In fact, in the 1970s major efforts were directed toward a search for biological deviations that might underlie the symptoms of autism. Well-conducted research later supported Rutter's contention that parenting defects were not a major cause of autism.

Another early and widely held idea was that "social withdrawal" was the core problem of autism. Rutter argued cogently that deficiency of language comprehension was a more likely candidate, an idea also given support by research of the 1970s. Rutter's well-reasoned writings may have influenced others to eschew publishing theories of autism that had little basis in fact as the quality of theorizing improved in the 1970s.

10

Psychological Studies of Childhood Autism: Can Autistic Children Make Sense of What They See and Hear?

BEATE HERMELIN
UTA FRITH

In 1943 the child psychiatrist Leo Kanner (1943) described a group of children he had encountered over the years who seemed to have certain unusual characteristics in common. The main symptoms he found were autistic aloneness, an obsessive desire for sameness, and severe disorder of language. He differentiated this group of children from the large, unspecified category of the childhood schizophrenias and named their condition "early infantile autism." The unusual pattern of symptoms captured the interest of many, despite the rarity of the disorder; however, it took approximately 20 years to arrive at reasonably precise diagnostic criteria, taking into account prognosis and prevalence. Controversies still persist on the question of etiology.

Only 4 in 10,000 children and three times as many boys than girls are afflicted with early infantile autism (Lotter, 1966). There appears to be an association with high parental socio-economic status, a finding which is not due to referral artefacts and which seems to be unique among the psychiatric childhood disorders (Lotter, 1967).

The illness first appears in early childhood, either at birth or before two and one-half years. The pattern of symptoms at this age may include a lack of response to sound or light, an apparent lack of recognition of the parents, and a lack of interest in the environment. Some children seem distressed for long periods and cry continuously, while others appear apathetic. Feeding and sleeping habits can be erratic and unpredictable. Subsequently the children show various obsessional features, aloofness and lack of interest in other people, abnormalities of language affecting speech as well as thought, and problems in the appropriate use of eyes and ears. The combination of symptoms may differ from child to child and the symptoms may differ in severity

Reprinted with permission from *Journal of Special Education* 5 (1971): 107–117.

and persistence. There are usually other handicaps, such as mental subnormality, which affect the majority of autistic children (Wing, 1970).

Though prognosis is not favorable, developmental changes do occur (Lockyer & Rutter, 1969; Rutter, Greenfeld, & Lockyer, 1967; Rutter & Lockyer, 1969), and various forms of treatment appear to lead to appreciable improvement (Rutter, 1967), particularly in the emotional and social spheres. Thus the symptom of autistic aloneness, with its concomitants of social withdrawal, gaze avoidance, lack of interest in people, and inability to form close relationships, may subside and no longer be markedly present in older, improved autistic children.

The features associated with Kanner's symptom of insistence on sameness, i.e., resistance to change and obsessional ritualistic phenomena, are also subject to developmental changes. Thus, while this symptom in very young children may take the form of extreme attachment to a useless object such as a piece of cloth or a tin container, or become manifest in extreme food fads, it may later become a preoccupation with certain events or thoughts. Resistance to changes in the order of familiar surroundings, adherence to rituals and fixed routines, and stereotyped play are common at all stages. Probably related to these obsessional phenomena are the characteristic motor mannerisms found in almost all autistic children: compulsive finger flicking, spinning, and other odd and repetitive movements. These motor mannerisms and stereotyped behavior sequences seem self-reinforcing, circular, and automatic. They also seem to be unrelated to, and inappropriate for, environmental demands.

The third major symptom of childhood autism—the abnormalities associated with language and thought—comprises a large variety of clinical features (Hermelin & O'Connor, 1970) including complete failure or delay of speech development; echolalia, i.e., the tendency to repeat verbatim the last words of another person's utterances; inability to understand meaning; lack of spontaneous communication in either talk or gestures; and phenomena reminiscent of developmental aphasia. Language abnormalities persist even if behavioral improvements have occurred. Thus even with good speech development, the language of autistic adolescents is recognizably odd, usually characterized by detachment, concreteness, and abundance of stereotyped utterances.

Apparent perceptual impairments without any detectable sensory defect are also often found in autistic children. In most cases this takes the form of an inability to interpret auditory or visual stimuli, frequently with a lack of orientation responses toward such stimulation (Hermelin & O'Connor, 1970). Occasionally young autistic children cover their eyes and ears with their hands. On the other hand, they often make extensive use of proximal receptor channels by licking or touching objects. Their movements are often described as graceful.

Not one of these symptoms is uniquely and exclusively associated with early infantile autism. Most of them can be found in other psychiatric disorders (Wing, 1969). However, the pattern of the combined symptoms and the course of the illness are very characteristic, and diagnosis is less problematic than it might appear.

There has been much speculation concerning the etiology of autism, especially about whether the cause is psychogenic or organic (Rutter, 1968). It is likely that the causes are manifold and varied, although they result in the same syndrome. No theory so far has factual substantiation; it seems unlikely that etiologic definition can be made before a more precise delineation of the symptoms. In this respect childhood autism is no exception to the range of psychiatric disorders, since causes for most such disorders are as yet unknown. Our research (Hermelin & O'Connor, 1970) has concentrated on an analysis and delineation of the perception, memory, and language pathology. The approach was empirical rather than theoretical, as even a behavioral description of these phenomena is not yet complete.

Procedure and Conclusions

The autistic children who took part in our experiments were between 7 and 15 years old. They were diagnosed by experienced psychiatrists according to the described criteria. Two control groups were used, i.e., normal and subnormal children of the same mental age (MA) as the autistic children. The MA was measured by standard IQ tests such as the Peabody Picture Vocabulary Test and the Wechsler scales. Owing to the MA criterion, the groups differed widely in chronological age (CA): the normal children were between 3 and 7 years old; the subnormal children were between 10 and 16 years old. The latter group included children presumably suffering from unspecified diffuse brain damage whose only common characteristic was severe mental retardation; they had no autistic symptoms. Because subnormality is also present in at least 75% of autistic children, it was important to control for this variable in investigations of cognitive processes. Since autistic children may be very difficult to test because of their various handicaps, experimental methods were chosen to take advantage of certain of their assets and to avoid elaborate verbal instructions. The intent was to present all tasks so as to spontaneously elicit the behavior to be analyzed.

In the first series of experiments, the tendency to echolalia in autistic children was utilized by selecting a recall task in which the subjects were required to repeat words spoken to them. In a first experiment a comparison was made between memory for words that formed an orderly sequence (such as a sentence) with memory for words randomly arranged. The number and kind of words in both conditions were the same; they differed only in their arrangement. All words were familiar and are frequently used even by very retarded children. The word messages to be recalled were, for example, "We went to town" (sentence message) and "light what leaf we" (nonsentence message). It is well known that memory for sentences in normal people is superior to memory for random word strings (Miller & Selfridge, 1953). This phenomenon is usually explained by assuming that a special ability exists that enables people to make use of their knowledge of and familiarity with language and the redundancies therein. This means, for example, that if a sentence is to be recalled, such as "The bear climbed up the tree to get some honey," what actually need be remembered are only the key words "bear-tree-honey." All other words in such a simple sentence can be guessed on the basis of one's knowledge of syntax. The load that has to be carried by the memory system is thus much smaller than if every single word had to be remembered.

This experiment confirmed that both normal children and subnormal children with the same MA (4 years) remembered more words in sentences than in nonsentences, and that therefore some principle of making use of redundancy (that is, an economical remembering) can be assumed to operate even in very young children. The autistic children with a MA of 4 years also recalled sentences better than nonsentences; however, the difference between the two conditions was significantly less marked for the autistic than for the control groups. When repeating a random string of words, the autistic children were at least as good as, and often better than, the normal and subnormal children. When repeating a sentence, however, they were much less proficient.

The autistic children had a marked tendency to recall the last words of any message. To find out whether this tendency could be overcome, a second experiment was carried out for which we made up word strings partially out of sentences and partially out of nonsentences, e.g., "wall long cake send where is the ship" or "read them your book way spoon here like." Half the time the sentence was at the beginning of the message and half the time at the end. There were more words in all the messages than the children could recall after hearing them only once. Which words would be recalled: the sentences in preference to the randomly connected words, or the last words regardless of whether they were meaningfully connected or not? We found that normal children recalled sentences better than nonsentences, independent of their position in the word list. On the other hand, autistic children recalled the last words better than those in the first part of the message, even if the first words were the meaningful sentence portion. It has often been clinically observed that autistic children parrot speech without understanding its meaning. The experiments indicate that these children used their excellent memory like an echo rather than reorganizing inputs.

A further experiment was undertaken to test this hypothesis of relative lack of active reorganization in autistic children. Special word messages were

Figure 1
Correct Recall of Word Messages

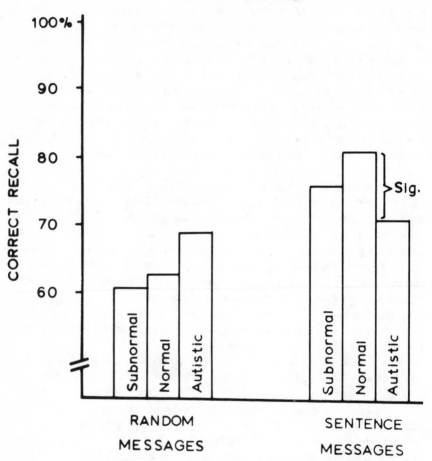

constructed consisting of words denoting two separate categories, for example, "cup white glass pink plate blue." It is an established finding that
normal subjects recalling messages of this type tend to cluster together words
of the same category (Bousfield, 1953), this strategy appearing to facilitate
recall. The results show that normal and subnormal children used the expected strategy of clustering. Thus in the cited example they would recall
all colors first, then the household objects, or vice versa. This was found to
a much lesser extent in autistic children, who tended to repeat the exact order of the words as they were presented. Thus the hypothesis was confirmed that autistic children do not actively reorganize material according to
its meaning.

Figure 2
Correct Recall of Mixed Messages

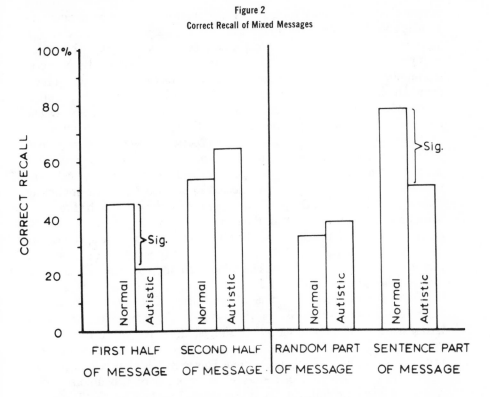

The results of all three experiments show that echo memory in autistic children is unimpaired. Even very young and very retarded children were able to process material by making use of structure and organization, whereas autistic children seemed to be much less efficient in this. Since very good immediate recall by autistic children can be obtained with unconnected words or digits, their main impairment may lie in those processes which categorize and organize material. Thus suitable means of investigating these processes had to be found. If some processing defect is present, this could be limited to an inability to apply grammatical rules. Alternatively the deficit could be more general, such as an inability to apply appropriate rules in various behavioral areas. The deficit might even consist in a failure to detect lawful sequential patterns in the environment.

To simplify the study of such deficit patterns it was opportune to restrict them to only one or two elements. Grammatical rules were considered far too complex for this study. The simplest sequential relationships of one word to another appeared to be repetitions, e.g., "one-one-one-one" and alternations, e.g., "one-two-one-two." Word lists of this type can be easily and immediately recognized by normal people as lawful and predictable. More

complex patterns in binary sequences can be created simply by mixing repetitions and alternations together, such as "one-one-two-one" or "one-two-
one-one-two." Sequences of this complex type cannot be so easily perceived
as lawful. In order to quantify the structure of the mixed word sequences,
the number of repetitions was counted within a repeating subunit of a message. The more often one is required to switch from one word to the other
in the mixed sequences, the more difficult the sequence is to remember. The
more repetitions there are in the sequence, the easier it is to remember.

In order to find out more about the processing mechanisms by which
people make use of such redundancy, our subjects were asked to recall word
sequences that varied in terms of repetitions and alternations. Normal, subnormal, and autistic children were selected and matched for their immediate
memory capacity. As in the previous experiments, the children had to recall
word lists that were longer than their immediate memory capacity. For example: "mouse-mouse-mouse-bag-bag-bag" or "spoon-horse-spoon-horse-
horse-spoon." All children could remember the two words in each list, and
they knew which one came first and which second. To obtain a high recall
score, it was necessary to remember the arrangement of the words.

The analysis of recall was done in two stages. First, the number of correctly recalled words (that is, the right word in the right place) was examined (Figure 3). The figure shows that simple, highly redundant patterns like
"mouse-mouse-mouse-bag-bag-bag" were recalled much better by the control groups than by the autistic children. However, with less redundant patterns of quasi-random arrangement, such as "spoon-horse-spoon-horse-horse-
spoon," the autistic children did at least as well as the controls. The result
is similar to the earlier findings in the comparison of sentences and random
word strings. In both studies the autistic children failed to make use of
structure. Since this structure was syntactical in the first experiments,
whereas in the second experiment it was not, it can be concluded that the
deficit in extracting rules is not specific to the rules governing grammar.

The second stage of the analysis was concerned with the type of errors
made. Just as key words alone, we observed, had to be stored in order to
remember the sentence, possibly predominant features alone, in the sequences discussed above, needed to be stored in order to remember the sequence. Such predominant features would be the rules which govern the
structure of the sequence, i.e., alternation or repetition. These rules could
be used to reconstruct the original sequence with minimal loss. For example, the sequence "one-two-one-one" contains predominantly alternations.
If this rule is used in recall, the sequence "one-two-one-two" is obtained,
which is almost correct except for one error. Since it was found that the relative proportion of alternations and repetitions in a given sequence determined the difficulty of recall, it seemed most likely that this was the key
feature. Thus it was assumed that the children who succeeded with these se-

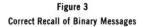

Figure 3
Correct Recall of Binary Messages

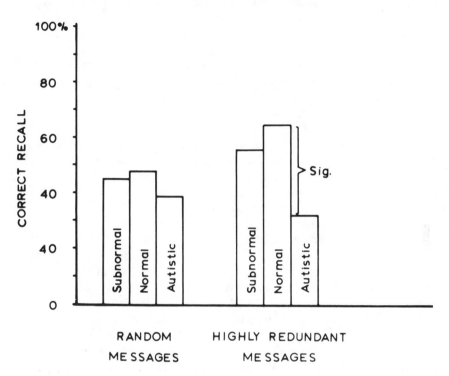

quences might have extracted the rule of whether a sequence contained predominantly repetitions or predominantly alternations.

The incorrectly recalled sequences were analyzed as follows: It was determined whether or not the dominant rule of the originally presented sequence was also the dominant rule of the recalled sequence. The results are illustrated in Figures 4 and 5. They show that the rules, "mainly repetitions" or "mainly alternations," were extracted and correctly retained by normal and by subnormal children even in otherwise incorrectly recalled messages. The results of the autistic children cannot be accounted for by the same strategy. It was found that errors made by normal children were in accordance with the dominant feature of the sequence. The rule which was correctly extracted was incorrectly applied, that is, applied in an exaggerated form. Instead of three repetitions besides one alternation ("one-two-two-two") there would be, say, four repetitions besides no or one alternation ("two-two-two-two" or "one-two-two-two-two"). On the other hand, if a given sequence contained predominantly alternations, the recalled sequence tended to contain even more alternations. For example, "one-two-one-one" was often recalled as "one-two-one-two." The nondominant rule was hardly ever exaggerated by the normal and subnormal children and was sometimes even omitted, as in the previous example.

Autistic children performed quite differently. They also showed rule exaggeration. However, they tended to apply almost exclusively the repetition rule, whether or not this was the dominant rule in the presented sequence. For example, the sequence "spoon-horse-spoon-horse-horse-spoon," containing four alternations and only one repetition, was recalled as "horse-horse-horse-spoon," containing only one alternation but two repetitions. In this case the nondominant rule was exaggerated.

Thus one might hypothesize that normal children are able to extract either one of the two important rules present in the input and that autistic children have a bias towards applying only one rule, that of repetition, regardless of the input. Similar results were found when nonverbal material was used, i.e., sequences of green and yellow counters, which the children had to reproduce from memory. However, in this case, the autistic children showed no bias towards repetition exclusively; the bias was towards producing simple strings of either repetitions or alternations which were never present in the input. As in recall of binary word lists, the autistic children showed little evidence of feature extraction with color sequences. These findings suggest that errors in recall can be the result of incorrect feature extraction or the result of some independent imposition of rules by the subject. These two processes, i.e., the extraction and the imposition of rules, may be relatively independent of each other. The reality of the two processes can be illustrated by concrete examples. Feature extraction is, for instance, the ability to recognize and reproduce tunes even when they are

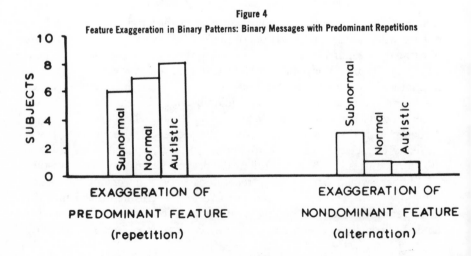

Figure 4
Feature Exaggeration in Binary Patterns: Binary Messages with Predominant Repetitions

Figure 5

Feature Exaggeration in Binary Patterns: Binary Messages with Predominant Alternations

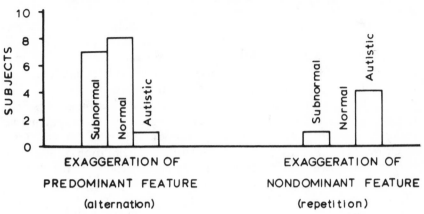

transposed or when their tonal qualities are changed. An example of pattern imposition is the tendency to perceive various definite rhythms in the objectively monotonous noise of an engine.

Patterning and structuring are basic properties of the way in which human beings deal with information. This is seen particularly in studies dealing with quasi-spontaneous response sequences. When people are required to produce binary sequences, they respond not in a random but in a patterned series, although they may be quite unaware of it. On the whole, investigators have found that in children the complexity of the resulting patterns increases with increasing age (Gerjuoy & Winters, 1968).

The stereotyped, rigid, and ritualistic phenomena in the behavior of autistic children might be regarded as an exaggerated form of pattern imposition. On the other hand, the unpredictable, often inappropriate, and seemingly random responses to environmental stimuli typical of autistic children may indicate an impairment in the feature-extracting process.

In the next study an attempt was made to investigate the nature of pattern-imposition tendencies on random input. Card guessing is a task where input is unstructured and where binary sequences can be elicited very naturally. The color, either red or black, is guessed for each card of an ordinary deck. The sequence of guesses can be analyzed in terms of response patterns. These response patterns might consist predominantly of repetitions or alternations or mixtures of the two. Such a guessing task was explained and carefully demonstrated to the children taking part in the experiment, i.e., autistic, subnormal, and normal children. Only those children who evidently understood the game were included as subjects. The age of the autistic and subnormal children ranged from 7 to 15 years. There were two groups of normal children, one group of 3-year-olds and one of 6-year-olds. Two hundred guesses were obtained from each child and were analyzed for significant response patterns.

The resulting sequence of guesses indicates highly significant pattern-imposition tendencies in all children tested. The rules governing the response sequences were either alternations or repetitions; only very rarely were they mixtures of the two. In line with other experiments of this type, a developmental progression appeared to be present: 90% of the 3-year-old normal children produced predominantly repetitions of color guesses (red-red-red . . . black-black-black . . .), and 80% of the 6-year-old normal children showed predominantly alternations of color guesses (red-black-red-black . . .). Autistic and subnormal children showed the same pattern-imposition tendencies as the normal children, the developmental change from repetitions to alternations being correlated with MA. Thus approximately half of the autistic and subnormal children showed perseveration tendencies like younger normal children, while the other half showed alternation tendencies, like older normal children.

It was concluded that in the absence of structured input, all children, including autistic ones, imposed simple patterns of their own. The pattern shown was similar in all groups; thus it seemed likely that autistic children did not function abnormally in this respect. Similar results were found when the children spontaneously constructed long rows of red- and green-colored counters.

The results of the experiments on spontaneous production of binary sequences show that all children of all groups imposed simple structures in situations where input was random or minimal. However, the groups differed in those experiments in which structured input was to be recalled or reconstructed. The normal and subnormal children reflected key input features even in otherwise incorrect reproductions. This was not true for the autistic children; they responded by producing the same simple patterns which they used when input was random or minimal. It thus seems that autistic children are largely insensitive to given sequential order and respond to such patterned input as if it were random. However, their responses themselves are not random, unlawful, and irregular; on the contrary, they are highly repetitive, predictable, and rigidly structured.

The experiments extended beyond the specific structure of language and it can therefore be assumed that the deficit found with autistic children may account for a wider area of cognitive dysfunctions. A lack of sensitivity to the inherent pattern of the input, combined with a tendency to impose simple patterns in different situations, might account for some of the stereotyped behavior of autistic children. A tendency towards pattern imposition may often be appropriate in apparently random situations, although it becomes inappropriate in situations governed by definite rules. The more complex and flexible those rules, as for instance in social interactions, symbolic play, and language, the more limiting and inappropriate stereotyped behavior becomes.

From this point of view, the behavior of the autistic child becomes less bizarre and mysterious and can be better understood in terms of a clearly delineated cognitive pathology.

REFERENCES

Bousfield, W. H. The occurrence of clustering in the recall of randomly arranged associates. *Journal of General Psychology*, 1953, *49*, 229–240.

Gerjuoy, I. R., & Winters, J. J. Development of later and choice-sequence preferences. In N. R. Ellis (Ed.), *International review of research in mental retardation*. Vol. 3. London: Academic Press, 1968.

Hermelin, B., & O'Connor, N. *Psychological experiments with autistic children*. London: Pergamon Press, 1970.

Kanner, L. Autistic disturbances of affective contact. *Nervous Child*, 1943, *2*, 217–250.

Lockyer, L., & Rutter, M. A five- to fifteen-year follow-up study of infantile psychosis. III. Psychological aspects. *British Journal of Psychiatry*, 1969, *115*, 865–882.

Lotter, V. Epidemiology of autistic conditions in young children. I. Prevalence. *Social Psychiatry*, 1966, *1*, 124–137.

Lotter, V. Epidemiology of autistic conditions in young children. II. Some characteristics of the parents and children. *Social Psychiatry*, 1967, *1*, 163–173.

Miller, G. A., & Selfridge, J. A. Verbal context and the recall of meaningful material. *American Journal of Psychology*, 1953, *63*, 176–185.

Rutter, M. Schooling and the "autistic" child. *Special Education*, 1967, *56*, 19–24.

Rutter, M. Concepts of autism: A review of research. *Journal of Child Psychology and Psychiatry*, 1968, *9*, 1–25.

Rutter, M., Greenfeld, D., & Lockyer, L. A five-to-fifteen-year follow-up study of infantile psychosis. II. Social and behavioural outcome. *British Journal of Psychiatry*, 1967, *113*, 1183–1199.

Rutter, M., & Lockyer, L. A five-to-fifteen-year follow-up study of infantile psychosis. I. Description of sample. *British Journal of Psychiatry*, 1967, *113*, 1169–1182.

Wing, L. The handicaps of autistic children—a comparative study. *Journal of Child Psychology and Psychiatry*, 1969, *10*, 1–40.

Wing, L. The syndrome of early childhood autism. *British Journal of Hospital Medicine*, 1970, *4*, 381–392.

COMMENTARY by Adrianna L. Schuler

The impact of this article authored by Hermelin and Frith is not easily overestimated. The findings and implications of a refreshing line of research are summarized in a clearcut and sensible manner. A changing view of autism as not primarily an emotional or perceptual, but rather, a central cognitive deficiency was thus articulated for an audience much larger than that reached by Hermelin and O'Connor's extensive report on their experiments published one year earlier. More specifically, the authors point out that the commonly observed idiosyncracies in perception and memory are not modality specific, but rather part of a more general limitation in restructuring stimulus input according to its meaning—a limitation most markedly observed when subjects were presented with sequential stimulus input. The authors' claim of autistic individuals being equally capable of recalling sense and nonsense has been a continuous source of quotation and insight ever since. The studies and views discussed explain the interrelations between cognitive and linguistic idiosyncracies, and continue to be invaluable in clarifying the complex, fragmented, and often paradoxical behavioral characteristics associated with the autistic syndrome. Hermelin and Frith were the first to link the observed perceptual/memory deficits to broader cognitive discrepancies. The view of autism as a generalized cognitive deficit has had an impact on the field that is best compared to the effects of the so-called pragmatic revolution on our current reappraisal of social deficits in autism.

11

Follow-up Study
of Eleven Autistic Children
Originally Reported in 1943

LEO KANNER

The June 1943 issue of the now extinct journal *The Nervous Child* carried a paper entitled "Autistic disturbances of affective contact"; the first 24 pages told about 11 children who had in common a pattern of behavior not previously considered in its startling uniqueness; this was followed by 9 pages of discussion and comment. An introductory paragraph concluded with the sentence: "Since none of the children of this group has as yet attained an age beyond 11 years, this must be considered a preliminary report, to be enlarged upon as the patients grow older and further observation of their development is made."

Twenty-eight years have elapsed since then. The periodical in which the article was printed has been out of circulation for a long time.

The patients were between 2 and 8 years old when first seen at the Children's Psychiatric Clinic of the Johns Hopkins Hospital. What has become of them? What is their present status?

Under the auspices of Dr. Alejandro Rodriguez, the present director of the Clinic, Miss Barbara Ashenden, head social worker since 1931, undertook the task of learning about their whereabouts, functioning levels, and interim destinies. The results will be presented in the sequence of the original presentation. . . .

Case 1: Donald T.

In 1942, his parents placed him on a tenant farm about 10 miles from their home. When I visited there in May 1945, I was amazed at the wisdom of the couple who took care of him. They managed to give him goals for his stereotypies. They made him use his preoccupation with measurements by

Reprinted with permission from *Journal of Autism and Childhood Schizophrenia* 1 (1971): 119–145. Copyright 1971 by Scripta Publishing Corporation.

Portions of Kanner's 1943 paper that were included in this article have been deleted here with permission of the publisher, V. H. Winston of Scripta Publishing Corporation. Readers should refer to chapter 2 of this book for background information on each case described in this chapter.

having him dig a well and report on its depth. When he kept collecting dead birds and bugs, they gave him a spot for a "graveyard" and had him put up markers; on each he wrote a first name, the type of animal as a middle name, and the farmer's last name, e.g.: "John Snail Lewis. Born, date unknown. Died, (date on which he found the animal)." When he kept counting rows of corn over and over, they had him count the rows while plowing them. On my visit, he plowed six long rows; it was remarkable how well he handled the horse and plow and turned the horse around. It was obvious that Mr. and Mrs. Lewis were very fond of him and just as obvious that they were gently firm. He attended a country school where his peculiarities were accepted and where he made good scholastic progress.

The rest of the story is contained in a letter from the mother, dated April 6, 1970:

"Don is now 36 years old, a bachelor living at home with us. He had an acute attack of rheumatoid arthritis in 1955. Fortunately, this lasted only a few weeks. Physically, since that time, he has been in perfect health. . . . Since receiving his A.B. degree in 1958, he has worked in the local bank as a teller. He is satisfied to remain a teller, having no real desire for promotion. He meets the public there real well. His chief hobby is golf, playing four or five times a week at the local country club. While he is no pro, he has six trophies won in local competition. . . . Other interests are Kiwanis Club (served as president one term), Jaycees, Investment Club, Secretary of Presbyterian Sunday School. He is dependable, accurate, shows originality in editing the Jaycee program information, is even-tempered but has a mind of his own. . . . He owns his second car, likes his independence. His room includes his own TV, record player, and many books. In College his major was French and he showed a particular aptitude for languages. Don is a fair bridge player but never initiates a game. Lack of initiative seems to be his most serious drawback. He takes very little part in social conversation and shows no interest in the opposite sex.

"While Don is not completely normal, he has taken his place in society very well, so much better than we ever hoped for. If he can maintain status quo, I think he has adjusted sufficiently to take care of himself. For this much progress, we are truly grateful. . . . Please give Dr. Kanner our kindest regards. Tell him the couple Don lived with for 4 years, Mr. and Mrs. Lewis, are still our friends. We see them quite often. Don has never had any medication for his emotional trouble. I wish I knew what his inner feelings really are. As long as he continues as he is now, we can continue to be thankful."

Case 2: Frederick W.

In September 1942, he was enrolled at the Devereux Schools, where he remained until August 1965. A close contact was maintained between the

Schools and our Clinic. In 1962, a report from Devereux stated: "He is, at 26 years, a passive, likeable boy whose chief interest is music. He is able to follow the routine and, though he lives chiefly within his own world, he enjoys those group activities which are of particular interest to him." He was a member of the chorus in the Parents' Day program and was in charge of the loud speaker at the annual carnival. He went on weekend trips to town unaccompanied and made necessary purchases independently.

Wikky, now addressed as Creighton, has been with his parents for the past 5 years. He is now 34 years old. After leaving Devereux, the family spent a year in Puerto Rico where "he picked up a lot of Spanish and worked out a schedule of studying language lessons on records at 4 o'clock every afternoon." The family then moved to Raleigh. The parents report: "We settled into a new home and he did his part in it. He has become acquainted with the neighbors and sometimes makes calls on them. We tried him out in the County Sheltered Workshop and Vocational Training Center. He took right to it, made friends with the teachers, and helped with some of the trainees. Through his relationship there, he took up bowling and he does pretty well . . . Creighton was suggested by the Workshop for a routine job in connection with running duplicating machines. Since November 25, 1969, he has been working in the office of the National Air Pollution Administration (HEW) every day, and all day." A letter from the Acting Director, dated April 29, 1970, says, "Creighton is an outstanding employee by any standard. Outstanding to me means dependability, reliability, thoroughness, and thoughtfulness toward fellow workers. In each case Creighton is notable."

Case 3: Richard M.

The mother felt that she was no longer capable of handling him, and he was placed in a foster home with a woman who had shown a remarkable talent for dealing with difficult children. After two changes of foster homes, he was placed at a State School for Exceptional Children in his home State in May 1946. A report, dated June 23, 1954, said: "The institution accepted him as essentially a custodial problem; therefore, he was placed with a group of similar charges."

Richard is now 33 years old. In 1965, he was transferred to another institution in the same State. The Superintendent wrote on September 19, 1970: "At the time of admission, tranquilizers were pushed to the point of toxicity. After about 3 months, he showed some awareness of his environment and began feeding himself and going to the toilet. He is now being maintained on Compazine, 45 milligrams t.i.d. . . . He now resides in a cottage for older residents who can meet their own personal needs. He responds to his name and to simple commands and there is some non-verbal communication with the cottage staff. He continues to be withdrawn and cannot be involved in any structured activities."

Case 4: Paul G.

When the mother came to this country, she deposited Paul with a lady who ran a small home for retarded children. She removed him some time at the end of 1941, wrote friendly sounding letters to the Clinic but did not keep return appointments. She consulted Dr. Walter Klingman in 1941, Dr. Samuel Orton in 1943, applied for Paul's admission to the Devereux Schools in 1945 but decided that this was not the proper place for him. This is where the trail ends. Mother and child could not be located since then.

Case 5: Barbara K.

Barbara was placed at the Devereux Schools in the summer of 1942 and remained there until June 1952, when she was admitted to the Springfield State Hospital (Maryland) where she is still residing. She is now 37 years old. A note written by her ward physician October 8, 1970, has this to say: "She still has the stereotyped smile, the little girl-like facial expression with a placid grin, the child-like voice when uttering her parrot-like repetitions. Whenever I pass the ward, she greets me as follows: 'Doctor, do you know I socked you once?' She then usually gets very close to the writer following her to the office. . . . She still shows a total absence of spontaneous sentence production; the same phrases are used over and over again with the same intonation. Her mind is fixed to the same subjects, which vary to some degree with the person she is communicating with. Besides all of this she is childish, impulsive, subject to temper outbursts with stamping her feet, crying loudly and upsetting other patients. Her memory is completely intact. She likes to hum some melodies monotonously; whenever she feels like it she bangs the piano with well-known songs."

Case 6: Virginia S.

Virginia will be 40 years old next September. She has been transferred to the Henryton State Hospital. "She is," the report from there, dated November 2, 1970, says, "in a program for adult retardates, with her primary rehabilitation center being the Home Economics Section. She can hear and is able to follow instructions and directions. She can identify colors and can tell time. She can care for her basic needs, but has to be told to do so. Virginia likes to work jigsaw puzzles and does so very well, preferring to do this alone. She can iron clothes. She does not talk, uses noises and gestures, but seems to understand when related to. She desires to keep to herself rather than associate with other residents."

Case 7: Herbert B.

After a short stay at the Emma Pendleton Bradley Home in Rhode Island, and another at Twin Maples ("a school of adjustment for the problem child") in Baltimore, he was placed by his mother with Mr. and Mrs. Moreland who had a farm in Maryland. He seemed happy there from the beginning. He followed the farmer around on his chores and helped him "making things in the barn." Mrs. Moreland reported in October 1950: "He knows his way around the area near the farm and can go for miles and come back without getting lost. He had learned to cut wood, uses the power mower, rakes the lawn, sets the table perfectly, and in his spare time works jigsaw puzzles. He is a manageable and nice child. Occasionally he get upset if there is a sudden change in plans. . . . When his mother comes to visit, he gets himself absorbed and does not come toward her." After Mr. Moreland's death, the widow opened a nursing home for elderly people. Herbert remained with her, took the old ladies out for walks, brought them their trays to their rooms but never talked.

His mother, after serving as a public health officer in Maryland, spent several years (1953–1958) abroad—in Iraq and in Greece. On her return, she took a position in Atlanta, Georgia. She died in 1965.

Herbert is now 33 years old. His father wrote on January 5, 1971: "He is still with the people in Maryland. It is several years since I have seen him but I have word that he is essentially unchanged. More than anything else, he seems to enjoy doing jigsaw puzzles which he can do with the utmost skill."

A letter from his mother, written shortly before her death, contained this lament: "Our marriage seems to have produced three emotionally crippled children. Dorothy, after a disastrous marriage, is at home with her little baby girl and is trying to get on her feet working part time as a nurse in a local hospital. Dave is on the West Coast and has cost me $450.00 monthly as he gets intensive psychiatric treatment."

Dorothy is Herbert's legally appointed guardian.

Case 8: Alfred L.

This ended the Clinic's contact with Alfred. The mother started him out on a tour of schools and hospitals, not informing them about preceding evaluations and taking him out after a time, not disclosing the next step she planned to take. We do know that he was at the V.V. Anderson School in Stratsburg-on-Hudson, N.Y. (1948–1950); the Taylor Manor in Ellicott City, Md. (July to October 1954); and the Philadelphia Hospital Department for Mental and Nervous Diseases (March 3 to April 20, 1955). Some time between the last two, he was for a time on Thorazine; then at a "school for brain damaged children" founded by his mother in October 1954.

Alfred is now 38 years old. So far as can be determined, he is at his mother's "school." Both at Sheppard-Pratt and Philadelphia Hospitals he was interested in the occupational therapy materials and did well with them. When this was brought to the mother's attention, she decided to take him out.

Case 9: Charles N.

Charles N. was brought by his mother on February 2, 1943, with the chief complaint: "The thing that upsets me most is that I can't reach my baby."

Charles was placed at the Devereux Schools on February 10, 1943. Early in 1944, he was removed, spent 3 months (from March to June) at Bellevue Hospital; was admitted on June 22, 1944, to New Jersey State Hospital at Marlboro; transferred to Arthur Brisbane Child Treatment Center on November 1, 1946; transferred to Atlantic County Hospital, February 1, 1951; transferred to the State Hospital at Ancora on October 14, 1955. He is still there, now 32 years old. This means that he has been a State Hospital resident from the age of 5 years and 10 months. Inquiries by the Clinic, if responded to at all, yielded meager general statements about continuing deterioration. One note of December 1953, said something about "intensive psychotherapy." The last note, dated December 23, 1970, said: "This patient is very unpredictable in his behavior. He has a small vocabulary and spends most of the time singing to himself. He is under close observation and is in need of indefinite hospitalization."

Case 10: John F.

After attending a private nursery school, John was at the Devereux Schools (1945–1949), then at the Woods Schools, then at Children's House (June 1950), and attended Town and Country School in Washington, D.C. An inquiry about him came from Georgetown Hospital in 1956.

Dr. Hilde Bruch, who saw him in 1953, remarked on his "exuberant emotional expression with no depth and variation and with immediate turnoff when the other person withdraws the interest."

John died suddenly in 1966 at 29 years of age.

Case 11: Elaine C.

Elaine was placed in a private school. The father reported "rather amazing changes: She is a tall, husky girl with clear eyes that have long since lost any trace of that wildness they periodically showed in the time you knew her. She speaks well on almost any subject, though with something of an odd intonation. Her conversation is still rambling, frequently with an amusing point, and it is only occasional, deliberate, and announced. She reads very well, jumbling words, not pronouncing clearly, and not making proper emphases. Her range of information is really quite wide, and her memory almost infallible."

On September 7, 1950, Elaine was admitted to Latchworth Village, N.Y. State School. While there, "she was distractible, assaultive, and talked in an irrational manner with a flat affect. She ran through wards without clothing, threw furniture about, banged her head on the wall, had episodes of banging and screaming, and imitated various animal sounds. She showed a good choice of vocabulary but could not maintain a conversation along a given topic. EEG did not show any definite abnormality." She was found to have an IQ of 83.

On February 28, 1951, she was transferred to the Hudson River State Hospital. She is still there. A report, dated September 25, 1970, says: "She is up and about daily, eats and sleeps well and is acting quite independent. She is able to take care of her personal needs and is fairly neat and clean. Her speech is slow and occasionally unintelligible and she is manneristic. She is in only fair contact and fairly well oriented. She cannot participate in a conversation, however, except for the immediate needs. If things do not go her way, she becomes acutely disturbed, yelling, hitting her chest with her fist, and her head against the wall. In her lucid periods, however, she is cooperative, pleasant, childish, and affectionate. She has epileptic seizures occasionally of grand mal type and is receiving antiepileptics and tranquilizers. Her general physical condition is satisfactory." She is now 39 years old.

DISCUSSION

Those were the 11 children who were designated in 1943 as having "autistic disturbances of affective contact." They were reported as representing a "syndrome, rare enough, yet probably more frequent than is indicated by the paucity of observed cases." The outstanding pathognomonic characteristics were viewed as (a) the children's inability from the beginning of life to relate themselves to people and situations in the ordinary way, and (b) an anxiously obsessive desire for the preservation of sameness. A year after the first publication, the term early infantile autism was added to psychiatric nomenclature.

Now, 28 years later, after early infantile autism has become a matter of intensive study, after dozens of books and thousands of articles, after active stimulation by concerned parent groups in many countries, after the crea-

tion of special educational, therapeutic, and research units, it may be of interest to look back and see how these few children have contributed to the
introduction of a concept that has since then stirred professional and lay
curiosity.

For quite some time, there was considerable preoccupation with the nosological allocation of the syndrome. The 1943 report had this to say: "The
combination of extreme autism, obsessiveness, stereotypy, and echolalia
brings the total picture into relationship with some of the basic schizophrenic phenomena. Some of the children have indeed been diagnosed as of
this type at one time or another. In spite of the remarkable similarities,
however, the condition differs in many respects from all known instances of
childhood schizophrenia." The "uniqueness" or "unduplicated nature" of
autism was emphasized strongly then and in subsequent publications.
Nevertheless, it has been just recently that this view has been generally accepted. The ultimate concession has come in 1967 from Russian investigators who had the courage to break through the officially sanctioned "line,"
according to which autism had been assigned the status of "schizoid psychopathy." The message, however, has not quite percolated to the framers
of the 1968 Diagnostic and Statistical Manual of Mental Disorders (DSM II)
adapted by the American Psychiatric Association. This is a widely used code
system in which autism is not included, and children so afflicted are offered
item 295.80 ("Schizophrenia, childhood type") as the only available legiti-
mate port of entry.

As for the all-important matter of etiology, the early development of the
11 children left no other choice than the assumption that they had "come into
the world with an *innate* disability to form the usual, biologically provided
contact with people." The concluding sentence of the 1943 article said, "here
we seem to have pure-culture examples of *inborn* autistic disturbances of affective contact." One can say now unhesitatingly that this assumption has
become a certainty. Some people seem to have completely overlooked this
statement, however, as well as the passages leading up to it and have referred to the author erroneously as an advocate of postnatal "psychogenicity."

This is largely to be ascribed to the observation, duly incorporated in the
report, that all 11 children had come from highly intelligent parents. Attention was called to the fact that there was a great deal of obsessiveness in the
family background. The very detailed diaries and the recall, after several
years, that the children had learned to recite 25 questions and answers of the
Presbyterian catechism, to sing 37 nursery songs, or to discriminate between 18 symphonies, furnish a telling illustration. It was noticed that many
of the parents, grandparents, and collaterals were persons strongly preoccupied with abstractions of a scientific, literary, or artistic nature and limited in genuine interest in people. But at no time was this undeniable and

repeatedly confirmed phenomenon oversimplified as warranting the postulate of a direct cause-and-effect connection. To the contrary, it was stated expressly that the aloneness from the beginning of life makes it difficult to attribute the whole picture one-sidedly to the manner of early parent-child relationship.

The one thing that the 1943 paper could neither acquire nor offer was a hint about the future. Everywhere in medicine, prognosis can be arrived at only through retrognosis. No empirical data were available at the time; the whole syndrome as such was a novelty as far as anybody was aware. Now we have information about the fate of the 11 children in the ensuing three decades.

We must keep in mind that they were studied before the days when a variety of therapeutic methods were inaugurated, based on a variety of theoretical premises: psychoanalytically oriented, based on operant conditioning, psychopharmacological, educational, via psychotherapy of parents, and combinations of some of them. Sufficient time has not elapsed to allow meaningful long-range followup evaluations. At any rate, no accounts are as yet available that would afford a reasonably reliable idea about the more than temporary or fragmentary effects of any of these procedures intended for amelioration.

Of the 11 children, 8 were boys and 3 (Cases 5, 6, and 11) were girls. It was, of course, impossible at the time to say whether or not this was merely a chance occurrence. A later review of the first 100 autistic children seen at the Johns Hopkins Hospital showed a ratio of 4 boys to 1 girl. The predominance of boys has indeed been affirmed by all authors since then. It may be added that the boys were brought to the Clinic at an earlier age (between 2 and 6 years) than the girls (between 6 and 8 years).

Nine of the children were Anglo-Saxon descent, two (Cases 9 and 10) were Jewish. Three were only children, 5 were the first-born of two, one was the oldest of three, one the younger of two, and one the youngest of three. Order of birth was therefore not regarded as being of major significance *per se*.

On clinical pediatric examination, all 11 children were found to be in satisfactory health physically. Two had large tonsils and adenoids, which were soon removed. Five had relatively large head circumferences. Several of the children were somewhat clumsy in gait and gross motor performances but all were remarkably skillful with regard to finer muscular coordination. Electroencephalograms were normal in all except John (Case 10), whose anterior fontanelle had not closed until he was 2½ years old and who, 3 years after his first visit to the Clinic, began having predominantly right-sided convulsions. Frederick (Case 2) had a supernumerary nipple in the left axilla. There were in the group no other instances of congenital somatic anomalies. All had intelligent physiognomies, giving at times—especially in the presence of others—the impression of serious-mindedness or anxious tenseness, at other times, when left alone with objects and with no anticipation of being interfered with, a picture of beatific serenity.

While there were, as is to be expected, individual nuances in the manifestation of some of the specific features, the degree of the disturbance, and in the step-by-step succession of incidental occurrences, it is evident that in the first 4 or 5 years of life the overall behavioral pattern was astoundingly similar, almost to the point of identity in terms of the two cardinal characteristics of aloneness and stereotype. Now, after 30 or more years, it is also evident that from then on, notwithstanding the basic retention of these two features, major differences have developed in the shaping of the children's destinies.

We do not know about the present status of Paul G. (Case 4) and of Alfred L. (Case 8). Paul's mother went shopping around to a number of specialists, dropping out each time after one or two appointments, and could not be located since 1945, despite many efforts worthy of a competent detective agency. Alfred's mother had him at first in rapid succession in 11 different public and private schools and then in several residential settings. He responded well to occupational therapy but the mother, not considering this adequate, took him out and kept him with her in a "school" founded and run by herself.

Two of the children, John and Elaine (Cases 10 and 11) developed epileptic seizures. John's began about 3 years after his first visit to the Clinic; after sojourns in several residential places, he died in 1966. Elaine's convulsions started in her middle to late twenties and she is now, at 39 years, still "on anti-epileptics and tranquilizers"; her EEG was reported normal in 1950, when she was admitted to the Latchworth Village, N.Y. State School. She was later transferred to the Hudson River, N.Y. State Hospital, where she still resides.

Richard M., Barbara K., Virginia S., and Charles N. (Cases 3, 5, 6, and 9), who spent most of their lives in institutional care, have all lost their luster early after their admission. Originally fighting for their aloneness and basking in the contentment that it gave them, originally alert to unwelcome changes and, in their own way, struggling for the status quo, originally astounding the observer with their phenomenal feats of memory, they yielded readily to the uninterrupted self-isolation and soon settled down in a life not too remote from a nirvana-like existence. If at all responsive to psychological testing, their IQ's dropped down to figures usually referred to as low-grade moron or imbecile.

This fortunately did not happen to the remaining three children. Herbert B. (Case 7), still mute, has not attained a mode of living that one can be jubilant about but has reached a state of limited but positive usefulness. He was placed on a farm, where, following the farmer around on his chores, he learned to participate in some of them. When the farmer died and the widow established a nursing home for elderly people, he learned to perform the functions of a kind, helpful, competent orderly, using his routine-consciousness in a goal-directed, dependable manner.

Donald T. (Case 1) and Frederick W. (Case 2) represent the two real success stories. Donald, because of the intuitive wisdom of a tenant farmer couple, who knew how to make him utilize his futile preoccupations for practical purposes and at the same time helped him to maintain contact with his family, is a regularly employed bank teller; while living at home, he takes part in a variety of community activities and has the respect of his fellow townspeople. Frederick had the benefit of a similarly oriented arrangement in the framework of the Devereux Schools, where he slowly was introduced to socialized pursuits via his aptitude for music and photography. In 1966, his parents took over. He was enrolled in a sheltered workshop and received vocational training, learning to run duplicating machines. He has now a regular job and is reported by his chief as "outstandingly dependable, reliable, thorough, and thoughtful toward fellow workers."

COMMENT

Such was the fate of the 11 children whose behavior pattern in preschool age was so very much alike as to suggest the delineation of a specific syndrome. The results of the followup after about 30 years do not lend themselves for statistical considerations because of the small number involved. They do, however, invite serious curiosities about the departures from the initial likeness ranging all the way from complete deterioration to a combination of occupational adequacy with limited, though superficially smooth social adjustment.

One cannot help but gain the impression that State Hospital admission was tantamount to a life sentence, with evanescence of the astounding facts of rote memory, abandonment of the earlier pathological yet active struggle for the maintenance of sameness, and loss of the interest in objects added to the basically poor relation to people—in other words, a total retreat to near-nothingness. These children were entered in institutions in which they were herded together with severely retarded coevals or kept in places in which they were housed with psychotic adults; two were eventually transferred from the former to the latter because of their advancing age. One superintendent was realistic enough to state outright that he was accepting the patient "for custodial care." Let it be said, though, that recently a few, very few, State Hospitals have managed to open separate children's units with properly trained and treatment-oriented personnel.

The question arises whether these children might have fared better in a different setting or whether Donald and Frederick, the able bank teller and the duplicating machine operator, would have shared the dismal fate of Richard and Charles in a State Hospital environment. Even though an affirmative answer would most likely be correct, one cannot get away from wondering whether another element, not as yet determinable, may have an influence on the future of autistic children. It is well known in medicine that any illness may appear in different degrees of severity, all the way from the so-called *forme fruste* to the most fulminant manifestation. Does this possibly apply also to early infantile autism?

After its nearly 30-year history and many bona fide efforts, no one as yet has succeeded in finding a therapeutic setting, drug, method, or technique that has yielded the same or similar ameliorative and lasting results for all children subjected to it. What is it that explains all these differences? Are there any conceivable clues for their eventual predictability?

At long last, there is reason to believe that some answers to these questions seem to be around the corner. Biochemical explorations, pursued vigorously in the very recent past, may open a new vista about the fundamental nature of the autistic syndrome. At long last, there is, in addition, an increasing tendency to tackle the whole problem through a multidisciplinary collaboration. Genetic investigations are barely beginning to be conducted. Insights may be gained from ethological experiences. Parents are beginning to be dealt with from the point of view of mutuality, rather than as people standing at one end of a parent-child biopolarity; they have of late been included in the therapeutic efforts, not as etiological culprits, nor merely as recipients of drug prescriptions and of thou-shalt and thou-shalt-not rules, but as actively contributing cotherapists.

This 30-year followup has not indicated too much concrete progress from the time of the original report, beyond the refinement of diagnostic criteria. There has been a hodge-podge of theories, hypotheses, and speculations, and there have been many valiant, well-motivated attempts at alleviation awaiting eventual evaluation. It is expected, with good justification, that a next 30- or 20-year followup of other groups of autistic children will be able to present a report of newly obtained factual knowledge and material for a more hopeful prognosis than the present chronicle has proved to be.

COMMENTARY by Linda Swisher

In 1943, Leo Kanner drew attention to a "common pattern of behavior" in 11 children under eight years of age. In this follow-up report, he describes their course of development over 28 years. Although the children had once appeared "very much alike," their outcomes ranged from "complete deterioration" to "superficially smooth social adjustment." In considering this range of outcomes, he commented that no one had succeeded in formulating an approach that benefited all children with autistic behaviors.

His first report led to the identification of *similarities* among children with autistic behaviors; the following report led to the next stage of investigation—a description of their *differences*. Thus, the need to address issues related to differential treatment for individual children became apparent.

12

Parents of Psychotic
Children as Scapegoats

ERIC SCHOPLER

Over the past several decades the most prevalent views of autism and child-hood psychosis have considered the parents to be the primary cause of the child's disturbance. Psychoanalytic theory has been used to identify inter-personal trauma, rejecting mothers, and destructive parental motives as pro-ducing the child's emotional withdrawal and ego disorganization. During the last few years, however, there has been growing evidence that autistic and psychotic children suffer from neurological, biochemical, or other organic impairments which predispose them to psychotic development. This new knowledge suggests that, regardless of what other adjustment problems they may have, parents also react with emotional and intellectual confusion to their problem child. The purpose of this paper is to examine some of the condi-tions and reasons why parents of autistic and psychotic children have been regarded as primary agents in their child's psychosis, and to see if these can be understood according to the age-old mechanisms of scapegoating. Ac-cording to Gordon Allport (1966), scapegoating may be defined as "a phe-nomenon wherein some of the aggressive energies of a person or a group are focused upon another individual, group or object: the amount of blame being either partly or wholly unwarranted."

Members of the mental health professions are usually not viewed as us-ing scapegoating in their professional activities. On the other hand, it is not at all uncommon in professional case discussions of family dynamics to hear the patient's psychosis or mental illness attributed to the scapegoating of his parents (see Bell and Vogel, 1960). Perhaps this selective use of the scape-goating device by clinicians is indicative of the clinician's projection of his own feelings and biases on the parents of severely disturbed children.

Parental and scientific indignation against such biases have been pub-lished with increased frequency in recent years (Park, 1967; Eberhardy, 1967; Kysar, 1968; May, 1958; Wilson, 1968). Recent research has reflected an accumulation of evidence suggesting that parents of autistic and psychotic children have often been mistakenly considered as the primary agent in their child's psychosis (Pitfield, M. and Oppenheim, A., 1964; Frank, G., 1965;

Reprinted with permission from *Journal of Contemporary Psychotherapy* 4 (Winter 1971): 17–22. Copyright 1971, Human Sciences Press, Inc., 72 Fifth Avenue, New York, N.Y. 10011.

Rimland, 1964; and Schopler, E. & Loftin, J., 1969). In his scholarly book on autism, Rimland attacks "the pernicious psychodynamic theories" which have been used to falsely accuse parents of having made their child autistic. Although Rimland has been criticized for taking an oversimplified position in the nature-nurture controversy, there appears to be smoke enough in arguments like his to investigate the fire hazard.

Allport's monograph on scapegoating suggests some helpful considerations. He defines quite precisely conditions and motives leading to scapegoating. He accurately characterizes the victims and the motives of scapegoaters. This paper presents some of Allport's dimensions of scapegoating and illustrates how they may apply to professional attitudes toward parents of autistic children.

Allport sees scapegoating in terms of stages or degrees of certain hostile relationships which represent a continuum. The mildest degree is simply a preference or predilection for certain human traits and characteristics. In the field of mental health this might simply be a preference for working with adults or children, neurotics or psychotics. In the second stage a predilection becomes rigid or exaggerated. It is a stereotyped judgment, hard to change, a prejudice. This attitude may be reflected in clinical evaluations in which children's pathology is consistently interpreted as a function of parental character and personality makeup, and any ambiguous clinical evidence is interpreted with the presumption that parental pathology was the primary agent in the child's adjustment problems. The next stages of scapegoating refer to prejudices which are acted out. In the third stage, discrimination is an act of exclusion prompted by prejudice. Generally it is not based on an individual's intrinsic qualities, but on a "label" branding the individual as a member of a discredited group. Some clinics and mental health workers label parents of autistic children as "refrigerator parents," "smothering mothers," or as "schizophrenogenic" parents. Even when parents do not consider themselves as patients they may be required to submit themselves to intensive psychotherapy with the threat that their child will be excluded from any help unless they do so. Allport's last stage of scapegoating involves full fledged aggression in word or deed. The victim belongs to a minority group weaker than ourselves and cannot fight back. Although parents of autistic children have not been awarded the treatment of Negroes and Salem witches, they have been subjected to distinctly unpleasant experiences. They have been told by clinicians like Bettelheim that the only hope for their child is a parentectomy—a complete and permanent separation of the autistic child from his parents. They have been told that our society has no obligation for the special education of their child, and the only way for them to partially discharge their guilt and responsibility is to undertake exorbitantly expensive private therapy with no guarantees of outcome of success.

I have indicated several common attitudes and actions typical of the relationship between mental health facilities and parents of autistic children, behaviors which appear consistent with scapegoating. Let us review some of the motives and underlying conditions which Allport describes as necessary in the process of scapegoating.

1. Thwarting and Deprivation. People are often frustrated in what they want or feel they need. The resulting aggression—scapegoating—may not be directed against the cause of the frustration, but against some other convenient object. Often the scapegoat is at least partially to blame, but he is usually made to pay for much more than his minor part. One of the chief frustrations in the field of mental health has been the pervasive lack of knowledge about the causes of psychosis, the course of the disorder, the descriptive classification, and the optimum treatment. This confusion is clearly reflected in the literature. In the Laufer and Gair (1969) chapter on Childhood Schizophrenia there are no less than 18 different diagnostic labels offered, all referring to overlapping conceptions of these primary disorders in childhood. This confusion and lack of knowledge in the field places a frustrating burden on the clinician.

2. Guilt Evasion. Guilt feelings arise from the omission or commission of certain deeds. The projection of guilt is as old as history. Allport observes that we never feel as innocent as when we see our own sins in other people. The confusion and lack of consensus regarding autism mentioned above tends to weigh heavily on those clinicians charged with the treatment of autistic children, charged with converting knowledge into practice. This burden is often experienced as guilt. Since the resulting aggression is not readily discharged against the child, his parents provide a most convenient substitute.

3. Fear and Anxiety. There are many sources of social strain generating more or less specific anxieties. These may involve threat of nuclear war, racial tensions, strains between generations and many others. These affect all of us. The clinician confronted with an autistic child has the additional burden of coping with the child's difficult interpersonal behavior. The child may be negativistic and irritable. He may say some advertising slogans, but does not use meaningful language. He does not relate well, acting as if he were alone. This interpersonal avoidance and disorganization is often communicated to the clinician. He feels unrelated and insignificant to the child. The resulting sense of helplessness in the adult is not easily expressed against the child, and considerable pressure develops to explain the child's impossible behavior in terms of his parents.

4. Self-enhancement. Feelings of inferiority may lead to scapegoating, so that the individual may convince himself of his own value and strength. When the basic causes for psychosis in a given child are not clear, and when the progress in treatment is uneven, the clinician's role as an authoritative expert is seriously threatened. If, in addition, he is working within a system that requires him to charge a high fee for his time, he is under considerable pressure to rationalize his role. The already existing traces of guilt, insecurity, and desperation in the parents form a convenient handle for explaining and rectifying the plight of both child and clinicians. The parents' perplexity may readily be interpreted as a primary cause of the psychosis.

5. *Conformity.* If everyone around us is given to scapegoating, particularly those held in esteem, then only by imitating their actions can we be fully accepted in the group whose approval we desire. If the predominant orientation of a clinic is the psychoanalytic framework, then the emphasis on parental pathology for explaining children's difficulties is a shared belief among the staff. The senior staff's working assumptions are reinforced by a wide array of social sanctions.

6. *Tabloid Thinking.* It is less trouble to think of "the bankers" or the army "brass hats" as responsible for war, than to figure out war's complex economic and cultural causes. Simplification of issues provides for economy and energy in directing aggression.

In the case of childhood psychosis, the clinician may be required to identify and consider organic causes: hard and soft signs; unusual sensory and perceptual processes in the child; the effects of traumatic experiences; genetic taint; dietary and glandular deficits; cold, guilty, and confused parents—to mention some of the more prominent suggested factors. Such an evaluation is difficult and time consuming. Critical thought is more easily replaced by simplifications and tabloid thinking as in cliches or labels.

Having discussed some of the motives behind the scapegoating, let us turn our attention to the victim. Allport defines four important characteristics of the victim.

1. *He has salient characteristics easy to identify.* The parent of an autistic child is often quite conspicuous in the waiting room and in public. Although his child generally looks quite normal, he engages in peculiar finger movements, noises, and is unresponsive to conversation directed to him. The parents are less conspicuous than other types of scapegoat victims, but they are embarrassed by their child's peculiarities, especially when exposed to strangers and well-meaning relatives.

2. *The victim has little possibility for retaliation because the scapegoater is stronger than he in terms of prestige and number.* Until recently, the parents of psychotic children had no organization through which to bring about legislation, funds, and resources for their children. Parents of retarded children, who appear not to have been scapegoated, have long been organized on a national level, thus effecting substantial support for their children's need.

This lack of social cohesion had kept parents of autistic children weak and disorganized in the past.

3. The victim's strength has been previously undermined through attack. The presence of an autistic child inhibits the family's social life. Their embarrassment and shame, coupled with their inability to account for their child's strange behavior, makes many parents withdraw from social life. The school system has not provided the appropriate special education, and the mental health facilities have lacked the necessary resources. Well-meaning relatives offer advice (which often takes the form of yet another criticism). The parents' confused and perplexed reactions to their child have often been turned around and presented as the primary cause of the autism. The resulting demoralization makes such parents ready and sometimes even willing victims for scapegoating.

4. The victim is accessible. In their desperate search for help, parents present themselves to any available mental health clinic. From the psychodynamic formulations which explain the child's disorder in terms of parental personalities, an equally adequate case might be made for the psychopathology of his grandparents. They are, of course, less accessible than the parents, who therefore remain as the most available target.

Following these four characteristics Allport cites various reactions of the scapegoat victim.

1. He may try to adapt through compliance, meeting the scapegoater's demands in his outward behavior. Some parents with necessary resources submit themselves to intensive psychotherapy with the hope that they can change those personality traits which are believed to have produced their autistic child. They spend a large percentage of the family's financial resources, or they try many different treatment techniques.

2. Resistance may take the form of assertive competition, striving by extra efforts, extra study, extra cleverness, to offset the artificial restrictions and handicaps imposed through prejudice. Parents of autistic children have written books, articles, and developed their own treatment programs. According to psychoanalytic theory, such intellectual efforts are often considered as the same defensiveness which was thought to have produced the autistic child in the first place. Perhaps it would be more accurate to describe these efforts as an effort to fill gaps of ignorance, than as a defense against scapegoating.

3. The victim may seek ameliorative legislation. After the publication of Rimland's book in 1964 in which he attacked the psychodynamic biases against parents of autistic children, he earned the prestige and leadership necessary for establishing the now growing National Society for Autistic Children, an organization which has spread throughout the United States.

I have attempted to document how parents of severely disturbed children have been scapegoated. In conclusion I will mention some methods for combatting scapegoating. These include: foremost, research and education; understanding our own motives in the light of changing scientific knowledge; and being open to the research which demonstrates that autism may be linked with genetic, constitutional and biochemical predispositions in the child. Such organic predispositions have long been recognized, but have failed to penetrate the actual psychological and psychiatric evaluations of autistic children. Far too little attention has been paid to the extent to which parents react to their autistic child's peculiarities, and the extent to which these perplexed and disaffected reactions have been confused with primary causes.

There are programs of behavior modification and special education like the one in our Child Research Project. In this project, parents of psychotic children have been effectively engaged as cotherapists in the successful socialization of their child. This symposium, devoted to the topic of parents as developmental agents in the rehabilitation of their impaired children, is perhaps the most immediate evidence that the scapegoating of parents is on the decline.

REFERENCES

Allport, G. W. *ABC's of Scapegoating*, Anti-Defamation League, 1966.

Bell, N. and Vogel, E. F. The emotionally disturbed child as the family scapegoat, in *The Family* (Bell & Vogel, ed.), pp. 382–397, The Free Press, 1962.

Eberhardy, F. The view from the couch, *J. Child Psychol. Psychiat.*, 1967, *8*, 257–263.

Frank, G. H. The role of the family in the development of psychopathology, *Psychol. Bull.*, *64*, 191–205.

Kysar, J. The two camps in child psychiatry; a report from a psychiatrist-father of an autistic and retarded child, *Amer. J. Psychiat.*, 1968, *125*, 103–109.

Laufer, M. D. and Gair, D. S. Childhood Schizophrenia, in *The Schizophrenic Syndrome* (Bellak & Loeb, ed.), Grune & Stratton, 1969.

May, J. M. *A Physician Looks at Psychiatry*, New York: John Day, 1958.

Park, C. *The Siege*, New York: Harcourt, Brace & World, Inc., 1967.

Pitfeld, M. & Oppenheim, A. Child rearing attitudes of mothers of psychotic children, *J. Child Psychol. & Psychiat.*, 1964, *1*, 51–57.

Rimland, B. *Infantile Autism*, New York, Appleton Century-Crofts, 1964.

Schopler, E. & Loftin, J. Thought disorders in parents of psychotic children—a function of test anxiety, *Arch. of Gen. Psychiat.*, 1969, *20*, 174–181.

Wilson, L. *This Stranger, My Son; A Mother's Story*, New York: G. P. Putnam Sons, 1968.

Wing, J. D. Diagnosis, epidemiology, aetiology in early childhood autism. J. K. Wing (Ed.) Pergamon Press, Long Island City, N. Y., 1966, 3–39.

COMMENTARY by Frank Warren

Eric Schopler's 1971 article, "Parents of Psychotic Children as Scapegoats," was received by many of us, who were scapegoat parents, as an explosive revelation—a consciousness-raising experience of the first order. It helped to strip away the curtain of mystery and power from the psychogenic establishment, and left us with feelings of relief (great burdens of guilt were lifted), appreciation (finally we found honest, helpful professionals), anger (how can it be that we, who went to them innocently for help, have been so brutally used?), and great energy to spend in our efforts to aid our children and all children with autism.

From my own experience, one instance after the other flashes into memory—examples of the arrogant scapegoating procedure that left confusion, pain, and demoralization. I remember in particular a meeting with mental health authorities in the late 1960s, as we sought help in developing programs. A mild-mannered and highly respected physician, leader of the "child advocacy" movement in North Carolina, turned on my wife in anger (she had expressed the desire for public education for our autistic son) and said: "What makes you think that you deserve a public education for your emotionally disturbed son? Why should state money be spent on your damaged child?" We were dealt with, almost to the word, as Schopler describes in his article: "They have been told that our society has no obligation for the special education of their child, and the only way for them to partially discharge their guilt . . . is to undertake exorbitantly expensive private therapy with no guarantees . . . of success."

Schopler's article suggested ways both parents and professionals could combat the problem of scapegoating: Parents could organize into chapters of the National Society for Autistic Children, Inc. Professionals could understand the tendency to scapegoat, and the insidious pressures that cause its occurrence. They could press for more research, and provide additional education. They could admit it when they lacked knowledge.

Both of these have happened, to varying degrees, since 1971. NSAC today has 172 chapters across the country working to create better education, human services, and an accurate understanding of autism. NSAC is a viable force. Few professionals publicly blame parents of autistic children today—but there are exceptions. Occasionally NSAC finds a parent labeled by ignorant members of the mental health professional as "schizophrenogenic."

The struggle continues, but the odds are better now.

13

Thirty Severely Disturbed Children: Evaluation of Their Language Development for Classification and Prognosis

THEODORE SHAPIRO
IRENE CHIARANDINI
BARBARA FISH

Communication by means of symbolic forms in grammatical arrangements is a uniquely human behavior. It is in the capacity for language that human beings can point to some discontinuity from lower phyletic levels.[1] Progress in this developmental line is central among the measure of human adaption, and information is available on the normal sequence of sound and word acquisition.[2-5]

When any global pathological state of the human condition occurs, as in childhood schizophrenia or early infantile autism, the disorder is apparent in those functions that converge on adequate language ability. The emergent distorted language provides the observer with a most accessible window to the defects and deviations of ego that have been detailed and inferred from more global clinical study. Furthermore, investigation of language acquisition of psychotic children is of practical importance because children who do not develop communicative speech by the age of 5 have been found to have the poorest prognoses.[6,7]

The earliest descriptions of childhood schizophrenia and early infantile autism describe variations in language behavior.[8-10] More recent quantitative studies attempt to pinpoint the characteristics of schizophrenic speech.[11-17] Utilizing existing norms and some principles of Piagetan cognitive psychology, these latter authors have succeeded in describing the immaturities and variations from normality of the children whom they studied. A recent review by Rutter and Bartak[18] suggests that speech abnormalities and an aphasic-type disorder are probably central to the development of childhood psychosis. Churchill and Bryson[19] argue even further that psy-

Reprinted with permission from *Archives of General Psychiatry* 30 (June 1974): 819–825. Copyright 1974, American Medical Association.

chotic children suffer from a central language disorder and that severity alone demarcates childhood psychosis from other aphasias.

Beginning in 1952, Fish[20-22] began to focus on the level of language development as a critical measure of initial severity and as a prognostic factor for improvement in young schizophrenic children. By 1966, Fish et al.[23] showed how behavioral rating scales weighted for language skills could be used in controlled studies of children under age 5, and by 1968, Fish et al.[24] reported on a classification of schizophrenic children under age 5 utilizing the language dimension as the critical measure in a behavioral rating scale that differentiated between subgroups with different prognoses as early as 3 years of age.

In 1968, Shapiro and Fish[25] presented their first study using a new method to classify speech events at a molecular level. The new scales included a measure of speech morphology (intelligibility) as did many prior scales, but also added a measure of communicativeness that had been estimated formerly only by clinical gestalt.

In an initial presentation of the new method, two children with communicative disorders were compared and the analyses distinguished between a child with a developmental speech lag and a child with schizophrenia. This initial clinical application was expanded to a cross-sectional study of imitation and echoing in psychotic children as compared to nonpsychotic children.[26] In that study, schizophrenic children at age 4 were significantly more likely to echo rigidly and use fewer creative constructions than even normally developing 2 year olds, thereby attesting to the fact that these children were developmentally deviant as well as immature.

In 1972, we reported a longitudinal study using the language data of 18 examinations of a single child between the ages of 2 and 6.[27] These language scales proved to be a sensitive measure of change as well as an indicator of cognitive skills, and pathological identification. Each study, whether cross-sectional or longitudinal, has illuminated the fact that the psychotic child's course is distinguishable from other language lags and retardation. Moreover, persistent attention to the microanalysis of a single function over time provides clues that are of practical clinical value.

In 1971 (*Infant Psychiatry*, in press),[28] we presented data on 11 of 30 children studied who were under 42 months of age at their first examination in order to show how our method aided in assessing prognosis. Data of our language examination three months after initial examination in children under 42 months provided an accurate indicator of subsequent school placement and language competence. Thus, our language measure enabled one to prognosticate, with reasonable accuracy, at 3½ years rather than having to await a child's fifth birthday.

We present here the data accumulated on 30 children studied using our language scales. In this investigation we attempted to uncover the structural and developmental precursors of poor prognosis reflected in speech and language development and, also, to arrive at functional subgroups based on language development that have prognostic importance. Such reproducible data, we believe, will provide a complement to and improvement on "good clinical judgment," and provide a more explicit index of a child's deviance and immaturity. A study of the reliability of our coding system and its relation to other methods of evaluation (validity) are also presented as well as theoretical comments that relate our results to broader clinical propositions regarding the structure and function underlying the behaviors that characterize childhood schizophrenia.

METHOD

Population

Thirty children under 7 years of age have been studied since 1965 by the method described by Shapiro and Fish.[25] All admissions to a special research nursery at the Bellevue Psychiatric Hospital were independently evaluated by two psychiatrists as severely withdrawn from social relationships and having gross retardation in speech function (most showed less than 70% of expected speech for their age according to Gesell norms). While in the nursery as inpatients or day-care patients the children were provided with a variety of treatments including drug therapy, milieu and educational techniques, and psychotherapy.

The group consisted of 24 severely impaired schizophrenic and autistic children and four children with severe behavior disturbances of the withdrawing type with borderline psychotic features (patients 21, 10, 14, 25) and one behavior disorder and one OMS without psychotic features (patient 15) (Table 1). Children with specific central nervous system signs were excluded except for one child (patient 15) who had a known history of meningitis with residual gross motor incoordination and tendency toward febrile seizures. Two children developed convulsions during their hospitalization that were controlled and one child was found to have a chromosomal picture consonant with Turner syndrome (patient 25). The 30 children (Table 2) ranged in age at initial examination from 27 months to 88 months with a mean age of 45.3 months. Eleven of the initial 30 were under the age of 42 months. There were 13 who were between 43 and 60 months. Twenty of the children were followed for more than one year and 18 children, who were initially under 5, were followed past age 5 when the former literature suggests that prognoses are more accurately predicted. There were nine girls and 21 boys (Table 1). Their placement at the time of study (February 1971) ranges from special schools for psychotic children to normal public schools.

Table 1.—Subjects, Age, and Diagnosis

Case	Exam 1, Age, mo	Exam 2, Age, mo	Exam 3, Age, mo	Length of Follow-Up	Diagnosis
6	27	31	74*	47	Childhood schizophrenia
29	32	35	39	7	Withdrawing reaction
8	34	34	40	6	Childhood schizophrenia severely retarded
17	35	39	66*	31	Childhood schizophrenia with aphasia
4	36	40	51	15	Developmental lag with withdrawing reaction†
15	38	40	55	17	OMS withdrawing reaction
16	38	40	66*	28	Childhood schizophrenia
14	39	41	81	42	Childhood schizophrenia
3	41	46	101*	60	Childhood schizophrenia
22	41	44	61*	20	Childhood schizophrenia
9	42	44	47	5	Childhood schizophrenia
18	44	47	78*	34	Childhood schizophrenia
23	46	53	64*	18	Childhood schizophrenia
27	46	49	58	12	Childhood schizophrenia
26	48	51	60*	12	Childhood schizophrenia
10	48	...	101*	53	Severe depression†
24	50	52	68*	18	Childhood schizophrenia
11	51	52	...	1	Childhood schizophrenia
13	51	...	114	63	Childhood schizophrenia
12	51	57	73*	22	Childhood schizophrenia
5	52	59	72*	20	Childhood schizophrenia
30	52	61	70	18	Childhood schizophrenia
28	54	57	60	6	Childhood schizophrenia
7	59	64	65*	6	Childhood schizophrenia
2	62	65	...	3	Childhood schizophrenia
25	62	66	77*	15	Childhood schizophrenia
21	62	65	71	9	Withdrawing reaction†
20	64	66	87*	23	Behav disorder†
1	76	78	...*	2	Childhood schizophrenia
19	88	90	...*	2	Childhood schizophrenia

Mean 45.3.
* ≥ 5 yr at final examination.
† Borderline psychosis.

Table 2.—Follow-Up by Age			
Age at Exam 1	N	Follow-Up 12 mo	Follow-Up Past Age 5 yr
≤ 3.6	11	8	6
3.7-5.0	13	10	12
5.1-7.4	6	2	6
Total	30	20	24

Procedure

Each child was seen at two- to four-month intervals by the examiner in a playroom for ten minute recordings of his speech. When the child was reticent there was a ten-minute warm-up period when the examiner did not interfere, followed by a second ten-minute period in which the examiner attempted to elicit speech. The structure of the session was open, but the same materials were used at each examination and the line of questioning was relatively constant for all children: The interviewer followed the child's lead or introduced material that included picture books, family figures, toy cars, and telephone as well as a doll and paper and pencil. As the child showed interest in a play thing, he was asked to name it, then to elaborate its qualities such as color and number, then its use and function were elicited, and finally general conversation or fantasy play.

The child's utterances were recorded using an audio tape recorder with a wide-range pick-up while his activities and the context in which the utterances occurred were recorded by a second observer who was also in the room. (See Shapiro and Fish, 1969,[25] for details of method.) Each taped ten-minute period was transcribed after the session and each utterance was numbered and correlated with notes about the context of the interview. The utterances were coded in two dimensions of morphology and function.

Speech morphology is divided between *prespeech* and *speech* utterances. The prespeech sector includes a spectrum of vocalizations according to their clarity ranging from vowel sounds through babbling and jargon. The speech consists of intelligible single-word through five-word utterances. Poorly formed agrammatic phrases are also noted.

Morphology (intelligibility) offers an index of speech development that may be compared to existing norms[29] and could indicate whether or not a specific subject functioned at age level.

Speech function is divided into two major categories and separates noncommunicative from communicative utterances. Noncommunicative utterances include *isolated expressive* speech, *echoes*, and speech that is completely or partially *out of context*. Isolated expressive speech may range in morphology from simple vowel sounds through longer monologues that are not directed to any observer in the room and are part of the isolated play of the child. Echoing represents immediate repetitions without additions or alterations from the examiner's model. Out-of-context speech includes the inappropriate rigid remarks for which the examiner could find no current reference in the room or common experience between him and the child.

Communicative utterances on the other hand include *appeal utterances* that are simple social openers, wishes and commands, and *signal-symbol speech* that include the simple naming of objects or sharing of events or such complex behaviors as asking questions, answering questions, metaphor, and role play. The communicativeness measure derived from the functional scale may be used to indicate deviance, because it segregates utterances that are echoes, isolated and poorly contextualized from appeal and symbolic utterances. Language use weighted toward the non-communicative sector is not like retarded functioning but represents a variant in the developmental pattern of language acquisition. While there are no published norms for this measure our pilot investigation of ten normal children indicates that at 3 years old, more than 90% of the utterances of normal 3 year olds are communicative.

Reliability

The morphological scale depends on judgments of intelligibility of an utterance, decided at transcription by two examiners, and length of utterance is the total number of words per utterance. The functional scale requires judgments achieved by matching utterance to context notes and the examiners prior communication.

The transcripts of 15 children were taken from the larger sample and scored for function by two independent raters (T.S. and I.C.). Each independent rater categorized each utterance into one of the five sectors of isolated speech and imitative speech, context disturbed speech, appeal-speech, or signal-symbol speech. The number of utterances in each group found by each examiner were analyzed by the Pearson correlation method: The raw score interobserver correlations were isolated speech .97, imitative speech .98, context disturbance .81, appeal speech .89, and signal-symbol speech .98. All are significant at $P < .001$.

RESULTS

Method of Data Analysis

This study reports on the analysis of 84 examinations. Of the 30 original children examined by the method described, 28 were examined from two to four months later for short-term follow-up, and six were evaluated at the final examination from 6 to 12 months later. Twenty of the original 30 were examined 12 to 63 months later (Table 1). The results of the initial examination are compared with examination two (short-term follow-up) and with the final examination done for each child by February 1971 (long-term follow-up). The three examinations provide an index of stability and short- and longer term outcome, according to the standards of this language coding procedure.

The analyses of each speech sample includes both an intelligibility and a communicativeness score. Each were used separately or in combination. When used together we have a more powerful classification that includes a *normative* as well as a *deviance* measure. We first segregated the less impaired from the more severely speech-retarded children and then used the functional score to separate the better from the poorer communicators. Group 1 includes those children who were more than 50% retarded in their intelligibility according to Sampson's[29] (1945) standards. The less retarded group, groups 2 and 3 were divided on the basis of their communicativeness. Group 2 have less than 75% communicative and group 3 have more than 75% communicative utterances.

RELATIONSHIP TO OTHER MEASURES (VALIDITY)

Correlation with Symptom Severity Scale (SSS)

During the period of observation in the nursery, the children of this study were also rated independently on a second scale (SSS) by another observer (B.F.). Observations were usually done in small-group interviews utilizing a symptom rating scale for 2 to 6 year olds developed by the NYU Children's Psychopharmacology Unit.[30] This scale is the only other objective measure that was used concurrently and available for comparison to our language rating.

The symptom severity scale (SSS) consists of four areas including (1) social symptoms with five items, (2) language symptoms with five items, (3) affective symptoms with two items, and, (4) motor symptoms with two items. Each symptom is scored on the basis of its severity from 0 to 6; 6 being very severe and 0 indicating that the symptom is absent. The total symptom score represents a global assessment of current disorders, the higher scores representing more symptoms of greater severity.

Examinations using the SSS done within two weeks of a language examination were compared to the percent of communicative utterances for examinations 1 and 2. There were insufficient numbers of final examinations using both scales to treat statistically. The Pearson correlation between total symptom score (SSS) and communicativeness (language scale) for the first examination was r=.68 and r=.81 for examination 2. (All are significant at $P<.001$ except r=.51 which is significant at $P<.01$ level.) Correlations using only the language subscore of the SSS and the communicativeness score were r=.51 for examination 1 and r=.62 for examination 2.

A number of factors may be considered to account for these correlations. (1) The children were not evaluated on the symptom rating scale at the same examination when the language study was done. The examinations were within one or two weeks of each other. The degree of correlation is surprising even at the level achieved given the fact that the children may also have been on and off pharmacological agents during the examination period. (2) The increasing correlation from the first to the second examination may be due to the fact that observers had gained in experience using the symptom rating scale that had been newly introduced. (3) The global score of the SSS correlates with the communicativeness scale better than the language subscale of the SSS because each measures different functions. The language scale of the SSS includes five items: (1) comprehension, (2) amount of speech, (3) vocabulary range, (4) psychotic disorganization, and (5) initiation of speech. On the other hand, the percent communicativeness on our molecular language study implies social appropriateness, affect as well as linguistic production, possibly explaining the better correlation with the total symptom score.

Correlation with Earlier Classification

An earlier classification of our children was based on a global evaluation of language skills relative to norms for language DQ (Gesell) and clinical estimates of comprehension and adaptive skills.[24,30] The children were divided into psychotic and nonpsychotic groups on the basis of their severity of withdrawal and then rated from A-E according to whether the child lacked speech (A, B, C) or had speech (D & E). The subgroupings of D and E depended on whether their DQ was 33% of expected norms; group B consisted of children with minimal adaptive skills and group C included children who in addition to adaptive skills showed some comprehension.

The final ratings using this earlier method were compared to our final speech performance ratings, groups 1, 2, and 3. (See "Method" for language grouping procedure presented here, Table 3.) The 26 children evaluated in both classifications show only a rough correlation. Of the five children who were nonspeaking in the earlier classification, four were in our most retarded group 1. (The apparent anomaly of a mute child who later fell into group 3 is accounted for by the fact that the last examination of this child

Table 3.—Relationship Between Earlier Clinical Classification and Language Classification					
New Language Classification	**Earlier Classification**				
	ABC	**D**	**E**	**Non-psychotic**	**Total**
Most retarded,* 1	4		3		7
Less retarded 2 <75% communicative		1	5		6
3 >75% communicative	1		8	4	13
Total	5	1	16	4	26

* Retardation refers to more or less than 50% intelligibility according to Sampson standards.

was a specific language study done on a revisit 2 months later when she had gained a substantial vocabulary of designative names. At discharge she was still mute though comprehending and was considered to have an expressive aphasia!)

Twelve of the 13 children in group 3 and all of the nonpsychotic group were in the best groups in the earlier classification including half of group E. The remaining children in class E despite DQs above 33%, function on a lower level according to the current detailed language scale because of their poor communicativeness score. The comparison suggests that both scales pertain to similar clinical judgments, but the current scale adds additional important information regarding *effective* language functioning as measured in our functional scale.

COMBINED LANGUAGE CLASSIFICATION

Each of the categories, 1—most retarded, 2—less retarded but poor communicativeness, and 3—most communicative, were represented during the three examinations (Table 4). The initial 16 who were most retarded dwindled to seven by the third examination and the initial seven children of group 3 who were most communicative increased to 13 indicating a trend toward better intelligibility with increasing age.

While there is a general group trend toward improvement each individual child's group (1, 2, and 3) tends to persist across examinations suggesting persistent typologic differences in impairment. (Pearson correlation: group types 1, 2, and 3 for each child and his group on successive examinations: exam 1 vs. 2, r=.84; exam 2 vs. 3, r=.72; exam 1 vs. 3, r=.63.)

Table 4.—Classification Based on Combined
Morphology-Function Score

	Examination Number		
	1	2	3
Most retarded 1	16 (7)*	14 (4)	7 (3)
Less retarded 2	7 (4)	11 (7)	6 (3)
3	7 (0)	3 (0)	13 (5)
Total	30	28	26

* Parentheses denotes those children under 42 mo old at first examination.

Thus, the grouping based on both retarded intelligibility and degree of communicativeness tends to withstand the developmental thrust associated with increasing chronological age.

Once a child achieves more intelligibility, the communicativeness of his speech is the factor that will mark his performance as deviant or not. The cutoff of 75% communicative used in our classification is only a rough dimension of social acceptability while *any* shift toward increasing communicativeness may be clinically noticeable. To avoid the restrictions of an arbitrary cutoff point and also to show the general maturation of our population, we compared the percent communicative utterances attained by each child among the three examinations regardless of their overall groupings. A one-way analysis of variance set up to determine whether the percent communicativeness scores were statistically different among the three exams was significant at $P<.01$ level (F=6.18 df 2,81) and the dependent t-tests between examinations were also significant (exam 1 and 2, $t=2.48\,P<.01$; exam 2 and 3, $t=3.35\,P<.001$; exam 1 and 3, $t=4.85\,P<.001$). This increasing communicativeness is presented in Fig 2 by the shifting median from 28 at examination 1 to 52 at examination 2, to 73 at examination 3.

The clinical meaning of this numerical analysis can only be understood in relation to other dimensions of social recovery. We used school placement as a prognostic post hoc index. We divided our population according to current school placement (as of February 1971) and retrospectively examined the segregation of their communicative speech at the second examination after having been on the ward for two to four months (Fig 2). Children who are currently placed at either a state hospital, state school and specialized school for schizophrenic children tend to cluster below the median communicativeness of the group. (Only three of this group are in classes offering special instruction for retarded.) Those who were in normal public school classes or classes for the retarded cluster above the median. The median for the entire 28 children was 52.5. Paradoxically, the one child who

Fig 1.—Relation of intelligibility and communicativeness to age (entire sample).

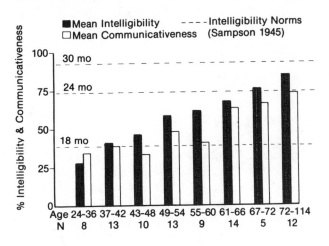

Fig 2.—Percent communicative utterances at second examination and placement.

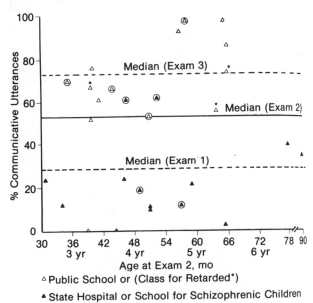

fell exactly at the median at 40 months of age was retarded at the second examination, but then joined our best group at the final examination when he was 66 months old. His development accelerated at 42 months when at a mean sentence length of 1.7 he showed a burst of echoing and subsequent better communicativeness.

A median test was used to test the significance of the relationship between percent communicative utterances and final placement and significance was at the $P < .01$ level.

Subgroup Under 42 Months

A former and more detailed analysis was done on the 11 children who were under 42 months old at the initial examination (*Infant Psychiatry*, 1973, Table 4, numbers in parentheses). The three children in that study in group 2 who remained noncommunicative during the third examination all showed more than 20% context disturbed speech on their last examination. Whereas echoing accounted for the poor communicativeness of these children initially, by the third examination their context problems predominated. The shift to context problems occurred when each child achieved a mean sentence length of approximately 1.9. By contrast, the five children who advanced to the best communicative group 3 showed a decrease in echoing with increasing sentence length without the context disturbance seen in group 2.

This suggestive finding was extended to the larger group of 26 children reported herein (Table 5). All of the six children who were in the poorly communicative group 2 had poor context scores ranging from 6% to 40%. (Patients 22 and 23 had 6% each and patients 7, 3, 14, and 6 ranged from 18%–40%.) Only three children of 13 in the best outcome group had more than 6% scores ranging from only 7% to 9% (patients 13, 28, and 20).

CONCLUSIONS

Ever since Kanner and Bender offered their unique descriptions of early infantile autism and childhood schizophrenia, clinicians have attempted to delineate relevant subcategories that are related to psychological structure, genetic developmental hypotheses, and prognosis.[24,31,32,33-35] Such subcategorization is a frequent step in the historical process of clinical science. Recently, more molecular attempts to study specific behaviors of deviant children have begun to appear in the study of autism and schizophrenia of childhood. This current study represents such a molecular approach to one dimension, speech behavior, which can be quantified from seminaturalistic observations that do not require the cooperation needed for formal testing. Moreover, these studies are clinically relevant because they describe deviance as well as retardation and provide a quantitative means of measuring

Table 5.—Significant Context Disturbance in Relation to Language Groups				
	Examination 2		Examination 3	
	Total	≥ 6% Context Disturbed	Total	≥ 6% Context Disturbed
Most retarded 1	14	2	7	2
Less retarded 2	11	2	6	6
3	3	1	13	3

prognosis. At the same time, the study of language permits inferences about psychic structure by analysis of the communicative forms and strategies used by these disturbed children.

The current study defines a spectrum of deviant language patterns and their course. There are children at the most retarded level who never are able to come up to age standards of intelligibility (group 1). There are those who become more consistently verbal, but retain deviant communicative patterns (group 2) showing speech behaviors such as echoing and contextual inappropriateness, which imply different cognitive and social strategies from normal children. Finally, there are children who develop largely communicative speech (group 3) from very retarded and difficult beginnings. Careful study of linguistic development can help to distinguish the differences in course that may distinguish the latter group with best outcome from those who remain more deviant.

These small as yet undeveloped children are not simply retarded, they are also different. Our groupings persist and attest to the possibility that we are distinguishing among important clinical types. No normally developing child or simple retardate shows the kind of communicative disorder that our group 2 children present. The early, clear preference for echoing, the later high complement of poorly contextualized utterances, the overall poor communicativeness remain striking examples of difference. Moreover, the data seem to challenge those who would consider childhood schizophrenia a mere variety of severe aphasia. Some of the difficulties in language shown by these children are shared with aphasic children, but such a designation is not sufficient. Indeed, it ignores the clinical advances that we owe to Kanner, Bender, and their followers. Aphasia, as a name, is less enlightening than is childhood schizophrenia or infantile autism. The latter permits us to segregate a clinical group with rather specific linguistic behaviors in a unique pattern associated with other social behaviors. We would hesitate, at this point in our knowledge, to suggest that the language behaviors determine the remainder of the clinical picture. Rather the language behavior is a part of a syndrome with some variability in its external form, which clearly involves a core cognitive and ego-disturbance that is distinguishable from retardation and aphasia. Geschwind's[36] enlightening review of the organization of language in relation to the brain offers a convincing argument for the anatomical bases of aphasic syndromes. Such specificity, as found in these defects, would demand that similar symptom complexes be found in children with schizophrenia. This does not seem to be the case.

The defects in coding complex relationships into grammatical forms and the difficulties using language for appropriate contexts came closer to recent cognitive[37-39] and linguistic models[1,40,41] than "simple" aphasias. By contrast our data suggest that our children show defects in coding experience in flexible linguistic forms. They do not seem to be able to match environmental change with the appropriate verbal forms. They can make grammatical relationships of the simplest type *but* seem stuck in the here and now. They are remarkable imitators but poor creators of new sentences fitted for use in human contexts. These integrations of inner and outer world and of language with the substantial world are not in evidence.

Our experience using this method suggests that closer evaluation of language behavior alone will not only serve to illuminate the structure of childhood schizophrenia but point to more apt models for understanding the disorder and its varying prognosis.

REFERENCES

1. Chomsky N: *Aspects of the Theory of Syntax*. Cambridge, Mass, MIT Press, 1965.
2. Irwin OC: Development of speech during infancy: Curve of phonemic frequencies. *J Exp Psychol* 37:187–193, 1947.
3. Lewis MM: *Infant Speech: A Study of the Beginnings of Language*. London, Routledge & Kegan Paul, 1951.
4. Nelson K: *Structure and Strategy in Learning to Talk*. Monographs of the Society for Research in Child Development 38 No. 1–2, Chicago, University of Chicago Press.
5. Lenneberg EH: *Biological Foundations of Language*. New York, John Wiley & Sons Inc, 1967.
6. Eisenberg L: The autistic child in adolescence. *Am J Psychiatry* 112:607–613, 1956.
7. Bender L: Schizophrenia in childhood: Its recognition, description and treatment. *Am J Orthopsychiatry*, 26:499–506, 1956.
8. Bender L: Childhood schizophrenia, clinical study of 100 schizophrenic children. *Am J Orthopsychiatry* 17:40–56, 1947.
9. Kanner L: Autistic disturbances of affective contact. *Nerv Child* 2:217–250, 1943.
10. Kanner L: Irrelevant and metaphorical language in early infantile autism. *Am J Psychiatry* 103:242–246, 1946.
11. Goldfarb W, Braunstein P, Lorge I: A study of speech patterns in a group of schizophrenic children. *Am J Orthopsychiatry* 26:544–555, 1956.

12. Weiland H, Legg DR: Formal speech characteristics as a diagnostic aid in childhood psychosis. *Am J Orthopsychiatry* 34:91–94, 1964.
13. Wolff S, Chess S: An analysis of the language of 14 schizophrenic children. *J Child Psychol Psychiatry* 6:29–41, 1965.
14. Cunningham MA, Dixon C: A study of the language of an autistic child. *J Child Psychol Psychiatry* 2:193–202, 1961.
15. Cunningham MA: A five year study of the language of an autistic child. *J Child Psychol Psychiatry* 7:143–154, 1966.
16. Cunningham MA: A comparison of the language of psychotic and nonpsychotic children who are mentally retarded. *J Child Psychol Psychiatry* 9:229–244, 1969.
17. Ward TF, Hoddinutt BA: The development of speech in an autistic child. *Acta Paedopsychiatrica* 35:199–215, 1968.
18. Rutter M, Bartak L: Causes of infantile autism: Some considerations from recent research. *J Autism Childhood Schizo* 1:20–32, 1971.
19. Churchill DW, Bryson CQ: Looking and approach behavior of psychotic and normal children as a function of adult attention or preoccupation. *Compr Psychiatry* 13:171–177, 1972.
20. Fish B: Involvement of the central nervous system in infants with schizophrenia. *Arch Neurol* 2:115–121, 1960.
21. Fish B: The study of motor development in infancy and its relationship to psychological functioning. *Am J Psychiatry* 117:1113–1118, 1961.
22. Fish B: Evaluation of psychiatric therapies in children, in Hoch PB, Zubin J (eds): *The Evaluation of Psychiatric Treatment*. New York, Grune & Stratton Inc, 1964, pp 202–220.
23. Fish B, Shapiro T, Campbell M: Long-term prognosis and the response of schizophrenic children to drug therapy: A controlled study of trifluoperazine. *Am J Psychiatry* 123:32–39, 1966.
24. Fish B, et al.: A classification of schizophrenic children under 5 years. *Am J Psychiatry* 124:109–117, 1968.
25. Shapiro T, Fish B: A method to study language deviation as an aspect of ego organization in young schizophrenic children. *J Acad Child Psychiatry* 8:36–56, 1969.
26. Shapiro T, Roberts A, Fish B: Imitation and echoing in young schizophrenic children. *J Acad Child Psychiatry* 9:548–567, 1970.
27. Shapiro T, Fish B, Ginsberg G: The speech of a schizophrenic child from 2 to 6. *Am J Psychiatry* 128:1408–1414, 1972.
28. Shapiro T: Language behavior as a prognostic indicator in schizophrenic children under 42 months. (Read before a panel on Primary Prevention, at the annual meeting of the American Academy of Child Psychiatry, 1971, Boston.)
29. Sampson OC: A study of speech development in children of 18–30 months. *Br J Educ Psychol* 20:144–201, 1945.
30. Fish B: Methodology in child psychopharmacology, in Efron DH, et al (eds): *Psychopharmacology: Review of Progress, 1957–67*, Public Health Publication No. 1836, 1970.
31. Mahler MS: One child psychosis and schizophrenia: Autistic and symbiotic infantile psychoses. *Psychoanal Stud Child* 7:286–305, 1952.

32. Goldfarb W: *Childhood Schizophrenia*. Cambridge, Mass, Harvard University Press, 1961.
33. Rank B: Adaptation of psychoanalytic technique for the treatment of young children with atypical development. *Am J Orthopsychiatry* 19:130–139, 1949.
34. Rutter M: Concepts of autism: A review. *J Child Psychol Psychiatry* 9:1–25, 1968.
35. Creak M, et al: Schizophrenic syndrome in childhood. *Cerebral Palsy Bull* 3:501–504, 1961.
36. Geschwind N: The organization of language and the brain. *Science* 170:940–944, 1969.
37. Piaget J: *The Psychology of Intelligence*. London, Routledge & Kegan Paul, 1950.
38. Bloom L: *Language Development: Form and Function in Emerging Grammars*. Cambridge, MIT, Press, 1970.
39. Brown R: Development of the first language in the human species. *Am Psychol* 28:97–106, 1973.
40. Miller W, Ervin S: The development of grammar in child language, in Bellugi U, Brown R (eds): *The Acquisition of Language*. Monographs of the Society for Research in Child Development, Chicago, University of Chicago Press, 1964, vol 24, No. 1, pp 9–34.
41. McNeill D: The creation of language in children, in Lyons J, Wales RJ (eds): *Psycholinguistic Papers*. Edinburgh, Edinburgh University Press, 1966, pp 99–132.

COMMENTARY by Beverly A. Kilman

In his original description, Leo Kanner defined language disturbance as one of the primary features of autism, and it has been understood that the disturbance represented more than a simple delay in development (Kanner, 1943). However, it was more than 30 years before the unique linguistic features were fully understood as part of the "core cognitive disability."

While the language deviance in autism is immediately apparent to any speaking partner, formal testing fails to define the depth and breadth of the handicap. Samples obtained in laboratory settings do not reveal the full nature of the deficits in language composition and communication or in use of contextual cues. Methods of study that provided not only phonological, morphological, and syntatic information but also a systematic framework for functional analysis, including analysis of context and communicative intent, made it possible to see the language patterns as more than merely exotic.

With analysis in seminaturalistic settings, Shapiro, Chiarandini, and Fish brought the functional and pragmatic features within the scope of formal study. This line of research revealed the relationship of the linguistic, social, and cognitive aspects of autism. It became possible to understand autistic language in terms of the underlying deficit; to study the pragmatic developmental progression, as for example the development of functional use of echolalic speech in some children (see Fay and Schuler, 1980); and to develop richer treatment approaches. The work of Shapiro, Chiarandini, and Fish provided a framework for analysis, a model for viewing the speech of autism in a communicative context, and a technique with which to approach the evaluation of the individual child within the environment. They were among the leaders in the development of the fruitful pragmatic approach to linguistic research in autism.

REFERENCES

Kanner, L., Autistic disturbances of affective contact. *Nervous Child*, 1943, 2, 217–250.

Fay, W. H., & Schuler, A. L. *Emerging Language in Autistic Children*. Baltimore: University Park Press, 1980.

14

Research in Infantile Autism:
A Strategy and Its Results

MARIAN K. DeMYER

INTRODUCTION

At the beginning of the work when the Clinical Research Center for Early Childhood Schizophrenia was started in the early 1960's there were few established or even consensually agreed upon facts concerning infantile autism. Most investigators agreed that autistic children were severely withdrawn socially and had severe disabilities in communicative speech. Three other generally accepted observations were the relatively high socioeconomic status of the parents, the scarcity of autism in siblings, and the relatively greater frequency in boys than in girls.

Nearly all other important facets of the condition were in dispute. There was disagreement about the relationship of infantile autism to childhood and adult schizophrenia (Freedman and Bender, 1957; Wing, 1963; Benda and Melchoir, 1959). The basic biological intelligence was considered normal by many (Kanner and Lesser, 1958; Rimland, 1964) even though the investigators who had obtained intelligence quotients reported them to be low (Souza, 1961; Pollack, 1958). There was disagreement about whether many autistic children had signs of neurological dysfunction and also about whether an autistic child with definite signs of neurological dysfunction truly merited the diagnosis of "infantile autism" (Baer, 1961; Mosse, 1958; Robinson, 1961). The parents were fully implicated, partially implicated, or fully exonerated as causing the condition (Tilton *et al.*, 1965).

BASIC TYPES OF CAUSATION THEORIES

Despite the varieties of opinions about so many aspects of the condition, the theories expressed in the literature could be coalesced into three basic types:

Reprinted with permission from *Biological Psychiatry* 10 (1975): 433–452. © 1975, Plenum Publishing Corporation.

This study was supported in part by U.S. Public Health Service grant MH05154, and also by LaRue C. Carter Memorial Hospital, State of Indiana, Indianapolis.

(i) defective parental nurture; (ii) defective biological system in the child ("nature") or (iii) defective "nature-nurture" interaction. See Tables I-III for some representative authors and thumbnail sketches of their theories during the 1950's and early 1960's.

Many versions of deficient parental nurture were proposed, but again, these could be grouped into two chief types. In the first variety, the parents were considered to have greater amounts of psychopathology than other parent groups. In the second variety, the parents were described as having extreme personality types or traits such as coldness, hyperintellectuality, or

Table I. Examples of Etiological Theories Extant in the Early 1950's and 1960's

Nurture	
Bettelheim (1959)	Parental rage and rejection.
DesLauriers (1962)	Theory within framework of psychoanalytic ego psychology. Inability to establish contact with reality.
Pavenstedt (1955)	Folie à deux between mother and child.
Rosenberger and Woolf (1964)	Children overwhelmed by affection from mentally ill parents.
Knight (1963)	Failure of establishment of oral primacy leads to shifting of cognitive development from exteroceptive to interoceptive ego.
Szurek (1956)	Both parents have disordered personalities. Child's reaction is a magnifier.
Clerk (1961)	Severe anxiety regarding management of agressive impulses in mother. Communication problem in mother and child.
Ferster (1961)	Parents reinforce development of symptoms.

Table II. Examples of Etiological Theories

Nature-Nurture	
Anthony (1958)	Psychotic child — organic and environmental causes.
Eisenberg and Kanner (1956)	Innate and experiential factors conjoin.
Garcia and Sarvis (1964)	Reaction between 6 and 18 months to a variety of psychological or physical factors.
Goldfarb (1961)	Organic and nonorganic cases. Organic children have more adequate families.
Rank (1955)	Hereditary and biological factors plus "as if" mother.
Mahler (1955)	Infant has a constitutional ego defect which may create a vicious circle of pathogenic mother-child relationships.
Bene (1958)	Mothers of I° Aut less able to establish social and emotional relationships than mothers of II° Aut.

Table III. Examples of Etiological Theories

	Nature
Bender (1955)	Disturb q. area of CNS function (schiz). Disturbance in maturational patterns using Gesell norms.
Colbert and Koegler (1958)	I° or II° dysfunction of vestibular pathway, mental deficiency, and abnormal EEG.
Rimland (1964)	Conceptual impairment due to malfunction in reticular formation.
Fish (1960)	Problem in uneven timing of perceptual-motor level due to neurological factors.
Macmillan (1961)	Defect in states of cortical inhibition and excitation (Pavlov).
Pasamanick and Knobloch (1963)	Many cases have CBS and negative feelings of mother result from illness in child rather than cause it.
Rees (1956)	Chemical imbalance exerting anesthesia like effect on brain.
Schain and Yannet (1960)	Limbic system likely locus of dysfunction.

full of rage. In either version the infant[1] was viewed as basically normal biologically, but normal identification was blocked or the parents failed to give optimum warmth and stimulation. This parental deficiency theoretically led to the infant's social withdrawal which in turn led to failure to acquire normal speech and other intellectual and social skills. Hence, the "nurture" theorists believed that normal biological intelligence was locked within the autistic child. If the right treatment key could be found, the child would accelerate in progress and eventually become normal or even supernormal in intelligence.

There were also two varieties of the "nature-nurture" interaction theory. In one version all autistic infants were seen as biologically deficient and the parents viewed as failing to give proper emotional support to a "vulnerable" infant. In the second version, some infants were viewed as "organically" damaged and others as biologically normal. In this second version, the parents of "nonorganic" infants were described as failing to a greater degree than parents of "organic" infants.

In the pure "nature" theory, the parents were viewed as contributing little more to the child's illness than symptom variations. The illness was considered basically the expression of a biological abnormality. As in the "nature-nurture" interaction theory, investigators disagreed about the kind of biological dysfunction that might be present in the infant.

---

[1] I use the word "infant" to emphasize that most investigators thought the seeds of infantile autism were sown during infancy and not childhood. Such would have to be the case in our population of autistic children for 95% were reported to be seriously disturbed before the third birthday and 75% before the second birthday.

Types of Consistencies in Theories

Through all the variations of parental deficiency theories ran a consistent thread of emphasis on the parental failure to adequately and warmly stimulate their autistic infants. In some theories, this adequate stimulation failure was implied, for some theorists dwelt on the greater degrees of psychopathology in the parents and did not state explicitly the mechanism of the developmental failure of the autistic child. Logically, such developmental failure could come from inadequate handling practices making life uncomfortable and incomprehensible to the infant. Alternatively, the infant could mimic the sick personality of the parents or, as Szurek (1956) stated, the psychotic child was a "magnified mirror" of the unhealthy parent personalities.

In the many theories concerning the kind of biological defect, there was rather consistent emphasis on the deficient nervous system. It is interesting to note that only a few authors (Fish, 1961; Pollack and Krieger, 1958) considered the deficiency to be the rather common neurological dysfunction such as might affect the infant's general intelligence as well as specifically the language centers. Most often some more esoteric and difficult to test biologic⍺ʹ deficiency was propounded concerning the reticular activating system (Rₐ-land, 1964), or the limbic lobe (Schain and Yannet, 1960), or the whole timing mechanism of somatic development (Fish, 1960).

Clearly, to test these three opposing theories and even a few of their variations, we needed to consider both the psychological nature of the parents and their child-rearing practices and the neurological status of the children. The reason it was logical to begin with such a homely biological procedure as a neurological evaluation was because of the proclivity for a maldevelopment or insult to any portion of the nervous system to be accompanied by other physical maldevelopments. These signs, small as they might be, such as deformed earlobes or cafe-au-lait skin spots, would be the outward tracks that would accompany the biological dysfunction in the brain. These kinds of outward tracks are common in other groups of neurologically dysfunctioning children such as the generally retarded (Kennard, 1960). Such a neurological study, in addition to giving us indirect evidence of CNS dysfunction, or of normal function, might also give us clues as to the nature of the insult in any given child or subgroups of children. It also might help us define neurologically normal and abnormal subgroups of autistic children.

Types of Control Groups Needed

Two sets of control groups were necessary to test the three theories: (i) parents whose children were all normal (Nr parents) and one of their normal children (Nr child), and (ii) parents who had at least one nonpsychotic child, subnormal in general intelligence or having a specific learning disability such as dysphasia (SNr parents and SNr children). The control parents would need to be matched to Aut parents on important demographic variables. The children should be age- and sex-matched. All the SNr children should have use of all four extremities and special senses so that the same developmental tests could be used on all child groups.

Findings That Would Prove or Disprove Theories

It was possible to outline a series of logical constructs of the findings that would prove or disprove each one of the opposing three theories (see Table IV, Parts A and B). If the pure nurture theory were correct, we should find that Aut parents in comparison to control parents mishandled their Aut infants or provided more inappropriate identification models. Unhealthy personality types, mental illness, or extreme character traits should be more common in Aut parents. Because 95% of the Aut children were disturbed before their third birthday, this parental deficiency would have had to occur before this time, and in 75% during infancy. We should find no more signs of neurological dysfunction in Aut children than in Nr children. The SNr children should have more signs of neurological dysfunction than either Nr or Aut children.

If the pure nature theory were correct, we should find that Aut children differed in some important biological way from Nr children and possibly also from the SNr children. There should be no important deficiency in the way Aut parents handled their Aut infants in comparison to parents of SNr infants.

If the nature-nurture interactionists were correct, then Aut and SNr children should be similar in neurological status but SNr parents should provide more adequate infant care practices than Aut parents. The alternate nature-nurture interaction theory was that there were two classes of Aut children—the neurologically normal and the abnormal; or as Goldfarb (1961) termed them, the "nonorganic" and the "organic." In this case, we should find that those Aut children who were normal neurologically would have had less adequate parenting than those who had signs of neurological dysfunction.

DIAGNOSTIC CRITERIA AND THE STUDY POPULATIONS

Over the 12 years of research, 155 Aut children were studied in various ways. The diagnosis of autism was a cross-sectional one and was based on the presence of three chief symptoms all of which were necessary in a given child for a diagnosis of autism: (i) extreme withdrawal; (ii) uncommunicative

Table IV. Logical Results Needed to Support Each of Three Basic Theories of Causation

Part A: Children

For Nurture theory to be correct	For Nature theory to be correct	For Nature-Nurture interaction theory to be correct:	
		Version A:	Version B:
1. Aut children should have no more signs of neurological dysfunction than Nr children but fewer signs than SNr children	1. Aut children should have more signs of neuropathology than Nr children 2. They could or could not resemble SNr children in overt neuropathology but should have some different modalities affected than SNr children	1. Aut children should have equal amounts and types of neurological dysfunction as SNr children 2. Nr children should have lesser amounts of neurological dysfunction than either Aut or SNr children	Parent type a should have a neurologically normal Aut child. Parent type b should have a neurologically abnormal child.

Part B: Parents

For Nurture theory to be correct	For Nature theory to be correct	For Nature-Nurture interaction theory to be correct:	
		Version A:	Version B:
1. Greater amounts of psychopathology or 2. More deficient child-care practices (during infancy especially) in Aut parents than Nr or SNr parents	1. Equal amounts of psychopathology or 2. Child-care practices should be insignificantly different in Aut vs. Nr and Aut vs. SNr parents	1. Greater amounts of psychopathology or 2. More deficient child-care practices (especially during infancy) than SNr parents who should be at least as good or better than Nr parents	1. There should be 2 classes of Aut parents with respect to amounts of psychopathology or adequacy of parenting: a. The emotionally ill or deficient parent b. The emotionally healthy or sufficient parent

speech or muteness; and (iii) nonfunctional object use. We defined three subcategories of autism based on symptom severity:

1. High Autism—some islands of emotional relatedness in a general background of withdrawal, a mixture of communicative and noncommunicative speech, and presence of splinter skills.
2. Mid Autism—severe emotional withdrawal, noncommunicative speech or muteness, and presence of splinter skills.
3. Low Autism—as Mid Autism except splinter skills were absent.

The nonpsychotic subnormal (SNr) children used as controls numbered 48. They had behavioral problems but were not severely emotionally withdrawn. They used objects functionally and used such speech as they had communicatively. The Nr children numbered 43 for the major studies. They were fully relating, exhibited no behavioral or learning problems severe enough to occasion professional evaluation, and related to a psychiatric examiner in a manner consonant with their chronological age and sex. A further requirement for all children was that they had the use of all four extremities and special senses. In Table V are displayed some descriptive data comparing the groups of children used for major studies.

One other important feature of our diagnostic system was the separation of the behavioral (psychiatric) diagnosis, the intellectual diagnosis, and the neurological diagnosis. Each child received not only a behavioral (psychiatric) diagnosis but also an intellectual diagnosis in the form of an intelligence quotient and also a guess about what his potential intelligence might be. The third diagnostic dimension was neurological. The latter eventually took the form of a brain dysfunction index but initially was a three-category diagnosis consisting of (i) no good evidence, (ii) equivocal evidence, or (iii) good evidence of organic brain dysfunction. The brain dysfunction index (BDI) eventually was used because it enabled us to compare each child with other children using weighted variables which were decided first on a logical basis and then on a statistical basis after applying the index to normal and sub-

Table V. Number, Ages, and Race of Nonpsychotic Subnormal and Early Onset Psychotic (Autistic) Children Evaluated at the Clinical Research Center (1959-1971)

Diagnostic group	Number evaluated	Evaluation mean age in months	Age range in years	% Black
Subnormal (SNr)	47	59.5	2-9	19.1
High autistic	26	79.5	5.5-10	11.5
Middle autistic	63	56.15	2-8	6.3
Low autistic	66	60.4	2-7	27.3
Total autistic	155			

normal populations of children. This eliminated much of the guess work that commonly contaminates the neurological diagnoses on psychiatric patients who commonly have no signs of focal neurological disease. The chief advantage of the BDI was in allowing us to make neurological diagnoses using clearly spelled out criteria applied in the same manner over the whole population of children.

For purposes of this report, only selected major studies of the Research Center will be reviewed. The studies selected for review are those that illustrated important results that linked infantile autism with neurologically based learning handicaps and in most cases mental retardation. The results of parental studies also lent strong support to the nature theory of causation of infantile autism. The parents of Aut children ran the gamut from being extremely adequate to highly inadequate in relating to their autistic children. Most of the parents were rated as being "average" in their personality structures and in their role as parents, the latter especially during the infancy of their Aut children when causes would have to be operating in the bulk of cases. In regard to the "nature" of the Aut children, we found far more signs of neurobiological dysfunction than in the Nr children, and we found some qualitative differences in the abilities of Aut and SNr children that may account for symptomatic differences of the two groups.

Thus, the bulk of evidence has pointed to neurobiological dysfunction in Aut children as necessary and sufficient cause of the clinical features of social withdrawal, noncommunicative speech, and nonfunctional object use. For fuller details of these and other studies, the original papers may be consulted. In Tables VI, VII, and VIII are listed selected major studies and thumbnail sketches of results.

EVIDENCE FOR ADEQUATE PARENTAL HANDLING DURING INFANCY

One of the most frequently expressed theories in the literature and in clinical practice is that Aut parents have been cold, aloof, and unstimulating. In fact, the one consistent thread running through the diverse "nurture" and "nature-nurture" interaction theories is parental mishandling of Aut children early in life, generally the first year. The pure nature theorists have held that Aut parents have fostered emotional distance so severe and pervasive that the infant failed to learn the basic trust in his parents that would in turn allow normal speech and social development. The interactionists have seen the deprivation as less severe and believe an abnormal "vulnerable" infant has failed to receive the extra stimulation that a normal infant would not need. Frequently, this lack of stimulation has been seen as stemming from the parental character traits of unusual intellectuality. The parents in this case have

Table VI. Selected Major Studies Showing Findings Supporting "Nature" Cause of Infantile Autism: Environmental

Name of study	Populations	N	Major findings
Parental practices and infant activity	Aut	33	Aut = Nr parents in warmth and stimulation to infants.
	Nr (matched on 8 variables)	33	
			SNr parents stimulated less and judged less warm than either Nr or Aut.
	SNr	30	
Psychopathology in parents as measured by MMPI responses	Aut	76	Aut = SNr and Child Guidance Clinic parents.
	SNr	18	Psychiatric patients more pathology than other parent groups.
	Child Guidance Clinic	37	
	Psychiatric patients with children	49	
Family adequacy in home	SNr	47	55% SNr homes rated as poor.
	Aut	155	33% Aut homes poor $p < 0.01$.

Table VII. Selected Major Studies Showing Findings Supporting "Nature" Cause of Infantile Autism: Neurobiological

Name of study	Populations	N	% Gross abn mean BDI	Major findings
EEG	Nr	13	0%	Nr differ from both SNr and Aut.
	SNr	47	39%	SNr fewer than Aut.
	Aut	155	65%	
Neurological evaluation from which a brain dysfunction index (BDI) was derived	Nr	48	11.6	Nr differ from SNr and Aut $p < 0.01$.
	SNr	47	52.5	SNr = Aut.
	Aut	155	45.9	

been viewed as possessing life styles that emphasized ideation rather than contact with people. Kanner's (1943) first description of Aut children prompted this widely held point of view.

Lotter (1967) reported that Aut parents were superior in socioeconomic status (SES), intelligence, and education to parents of SNr children. In contrast, Ritvo (1971) found no difference in SES between Aut parents and those of children with other psychiatric diagnoses admitted to the same institution. In our own population we found that parents of Mid-Aut children had

Table VIII. Selected Major Studies Showing Findings Supporting "Nature" Cause of Infantile Autism: Intellectual

Name of study	Populations	N	Major findings
Measurement of untestable autistic children	Aut	14	All Aut children are testable if suitable (i.e., low M.A.) items are used.
Measured intelligence of autistic children	Aut	155	Aut: Mean Vb IQ 35; Mean Perf IQ 54
	SNr	47	SNr-Mean Vb IQ 55; Mean Perf IQ 70
			Correlation of IQ at 6 yr. interval 0.700.
			Children with higher IQ at initial eval showed best adjustment at 6 year follow-up.
			Treated Aut child with initial IQ over 50 did better than untreated over 50. Treatment made no difference in children with initial IQ under 40.
Nature of the neuropsychological disability in autistic children (detailed verb, percept-motor and motor tests)	Aut	66	Hi Aut = SNr in verbal skills but have more difficulty in complex visual-motor integration (ball play and imitation in lower extremities).
	SNr	29	Mid and Low Aut = High Aut in fit-assemble tasks (objects remaining in visual field and demanding only infant motor skills) but have severe verbal expression and abstraction deficit plus more difficulties with visual memory and visual-motor skills (copying geometric forms and imitation in upper extremities).
Relationship of infantile autism to developmental language disorders of childhood	Aut	16	All Aut children demonstrated central language deficits closely related to those found in children with developmental aphasia but greater in severity.

a higher SES than SNr parents. Other groups did not differ in SES (unpublished data). Even if parents of Aut children were brighter, more affluent, and more successful than other diagnostic groups, the relationship between these observations and the autistic symptoms of their children was not satisfactorily explained. Rimland (1964) theorized that the parents' superior intelligence may have "backfired" by yielding an offspring with a high capacity for superior intelligence but also a high vulnerability to stress. A more commonly held view was that Aut parents were so "cold" and preoccupied with ideational matters that the normal identification of child with parents was blocked. There are still proponents of theories that Aut parents have molded their Aut child into a mechanistic individual preoccupied with objects instead of people.

In order to test these theories of relative parental inadequacy in both infant handling practices and character structure, we used interview methods and formal psychological tests on three groups of mothers and fathers: Autistic, nonpsychotic SNr, and those whose children all were developing normally.[2]

Parental infant care and stimulation were constructs defined by a series of 21 rating scales describing the parent's reported approach to the child during infancy. The rating items were designed to measure the amount of direct parental physical stimulation, such as cuddling, rocking, breast-feeding, bottle propping, talking/singing to the infant. The amount of appropriate care and stimulation the parents might be predisposed to give was measured by ratings on parental warmth, maternal feelings toward the newborn baby, and maternal energy level. The freedom given by the mother to the infant to investigate the environment and avail himself of varieties of self-stimulation was measured by the amount of time she restricted him to a playpen. Finally, we considered the infant's exposure to family social contacts. (For details see DeMyer *et al.*, 1972a.)

The results showed that Aut and Nr parents were about equal in overall infant stimulation scores but that SNr parents were significantly less stimulating than either Nr or Aut parents (see Table VI). SNr mothers reported significantly more abruptness and pressure on the infant to wean, were less appropriately responsive to infant crying, and were judged by the raters to show less general warmth. SNr mothers reported less cuddling, talking/singing, and rocking their infants. The fathers were rated for the overall feeling for the child during the child's entire life because of the proclivity for most fathers, Nr fathers included, to leave the greater amount of infant care to the mothers. Nr fathers were judged as warmer than both Aut and SNr fathers but Aut fathers were seen as warmer to the children than SNr fathers.

The study of how parents handled their infants, since it was done by parental report, was subject to differences in distortion of memory factors among the three parental groups. These differences, if they indeed did ex-

---

[2]The numbers of parents varied from study to study but extensive matching of the Nr and Aut samples was accomplished. Matching variables were age, sex, ordinal position, number and sex of sibs for the children and socioeconomic status and religion for parents. Because of the large pool of families required for matching by pairs for eight different variables, we could not match SNr parents to Aut and Nr families. The children were matched for age and sex. Over 1000 Nr families were contacted to match the Nr and Aut parents and children. Such a large pool for the SNr children in the appropriate age range (two to six and one-half years) did not exist in our locality. Consequently, the SNr parents differed in SES, education, race, and measured intelligence of fathers as well as in some important reported child care practices. The value of extensive subject matching in an investigation of parental personality and practices appears to have been demonstrated by our studies.

ist, were not possible to measure. The fact that SNr parents reported themselves to be less warm and stimulating may have been due to differences in important demographic variables as stated previously. Another feature limiting generalization of the findings was that important subtleties of infant-care practices might have been undetectable from rating direct parental reports. It could be postulated that infant social withdrawal might be induced by a parent who said he did all the right things but who in fact did them all wrong because of the presence of pervasive personality traits such as over-intellectualization or rage. These extreme personality traits might be detected through analysis of other portions of the interviews and from standardized personality tests.

One major problem of the parental trait theory of causation was the universally acknowledged observation of the scarcity of autism in siblings. If a parental trait were responsible for autism, this trait would have to be differently expressed toward the Aut child than to siblings. If the Aut child were similar biologically to his normal siblings, then a dissimilar "expression" of parental pathological character traits might be responsible for behavioral differences. If so, then we were back to the problem of measuring subtleties several years after the causal period. But if the Aut child were significantly different from his siblings (say, by virtue of neurological impairment), the pathological character traits of the parents might have affected adversely only the biologically impaired child who could be considered the most "vulnerable" child in the family. In that case, we should find that Aut parents would have more of the unhealthy character traits in question than the SNr parents.

Parental Intellectuality

Parental intellectuality was defined as a quality related to involvement or focus on some solitary intellective activity, such as thinking, reading, and solving abstract problems as opposed to feeling and relating to people. For analysis of the interviews, intellectuality was defined by a series of descriptive rating scales detailing parental preferences or disapproval of personal characteristics in themselves and other family members, importance of intellectual achievement in their children and spouses, reading material, father's occupation, and measured parent intelligence (for deatils see Allen, 1971).

Aut parents did not appear to be over-intellectualizers when the results were analyzed. They did not prefer an exceptionally intelligent spouse. All mothers' groups overwhelmingly wanted a husband who was kind and easygoing at home, and fathers wanted their wives to be "good mothers." Aut parents failed to emphasize high intellectual success for their children. Instead, like SNr parents, recognizing the Aut child's difficulties, they wished primarily for improvements in speech and social relationships. Thus, they set sensible and logical goals for their developmentally deviant children.

Amount of Parental Pathology

As measured by MMPI[3] responses, parents of Aut children did not appear to be psychiatrically disturbed. This self-administered test had the advantage of being relatively free from experimenter bias in administration and scoring and was standardized on a large sample of the general population. Aut parents' responses were no different than the original sample of "normal" adults used to standardize the MMPI. In addition, we compared the responses of 76 Aut parents with those of four other groups. The results of these analyses revealed that Aut parents had no more pathology than a group of extensively matched Nr parents and parents of nonpsychotic SNr children. Aut parents tended to have less psychopathology than parents of nonpsychotic emotionally disturbed children who were patients in a child guidance clinic ($p<0.1$). They had significantly less psychopathology than adult outpatients in a psychiatric clinic ($p<0.05$). This latter group was comprised of parents whose children were developing normally.

When the Aut children were divided into two groups "organic" and "nonorganic" on the basis of Goldfarb's criteria (1961), there were no differences in the MMPI scores of the respective parents. All of these results obtained whether the data were analyzed according to differences in the numbers of high MMPI scores (i.e., over 69) or according to group mean differences.

In summary, the only parent group that had more pathology as measured by the MMPI was the one comprised of adults who sought psychiatric treatment for themselves. The parents of Aut children had scores almost identical to those parents whose children were developing normally and who were themselves functioning normally. The number of signs of "organicity" (i.e., neurological dysfunction) in Aut children was not related to the parents' MMPI scores.

EVIDENCE FOR NEUROBIOLOGICAL DYSFUNCTION IN AUTISTIC CHILDREN

The evidence for neurobiological dysfunction in Aut children comes from several types of studies: the neurological evaluation, electroencephalo-

---

[3]Only the results of using the Minnesota Multiphasic Personality Inventory (MMPI) will be reported here. Further details and results of the parent studies will be reported later. These data were collected and analyzed by Gerald Alpern, Ellen Smith Yang, and Lois Hendrickson Loew.

graphic (EEG) studies, diagnostic-treatment testing, and from intelligence testing at evaluation and follow-up (see Table VII).

The Neurological Evaluation

There are in the literature relatively few reports of complete neurological assessments of psychotic children in which details of criteria for CNS dysfunction were given. Notable exceptions were the studies of Goldfarb (1961) and by Gittelman and Birch (1967) who found strong evidence of CNS abnormalities. In the neurological evaluation of children referred to the Clinical Research Center, thoroughness was the watchword and detailed histories were obtained from parents, hospital records, physicians, and in the neurological examination of the children. At least one and sometimes several EEG's were obtained on every patient referral. The neurologist applied a weighting system to positive findings. (Details of the weighting system and of differences in Aut, SNr, and Nr children are to be given in a forthcoming publication.) The aims of the neurological survey were to determine whether Aut children were more like SNr than Nr children in terms of overt signs and symptoms of CNS dysfunction and to determine any possible organic causes of infantile autism. In essence, our findings showed that Aut children had significantly more signs of neurological dysfunction than Nr children. There was no significant difference between SNr and Aut children in *total* numbers or *sums* of weighted signs.

The clinical electroencephalogram revealed that 65% of the Aut children had abnormal brain rhythms in contrast of 51% of SNr children ($p < 0.05$). This was the one finding of neurobiological import in which the Aut children exceeded the SNr children. It is important to note that for this study, only those abnormal rhythms found in about 2% of a normal population of children (Eeg-Olofsson, 1971) were counted as abnormalities. These were focal spike, paroxysmal spike and wave, and independent spikes.

The cause or causes of the neurological dysfunction proved to be as elusive in the Aut group as in the SNr group, just as is reported for other kinds of known organic conditions such as cerebral palsy. In a large percentage of cases at lease a putative cause could be located. However, when we examined the medical histories of the well-matched Nr control children, we found to our surprise that a similar number of Nr children had putative causal medical events similar to both Aut and SNr children. The one difference was that Nr mothers gave histories of fewer total medical illnesses than the Aut and SNr mothers. No one illness was more prevalent than others. Surprisingly, the Nr children had nearly as high incidence of abnormal labor as the Aut and SNr children. However, the SNr and Aut neonates had a higher incidence of neonatal distress than the Nr group. These kinds of findings indicate strongly the need for prospective research to locate the biological causes of all kinds of child developmental failure. Retrospective research is too inexact to yield much knowledge about causative factors especially those that occur during gestation.

Evidence of Neurobiological Dysfunction from Training-Testing Procedures

Hingtgen and Churchill (1969) and Churchill (1969) demonstrated conclusively that reliable and consistent performances can be elicited from every autistic child they worked with "even the most negative and uncooperative." In a series of experiments, Churchill (1972) demonstrated using a nine-word language that all 16 of the Aut children he tested had a disability in language processing. The disabilities involved the processing of auditory or visual information or in making those association or groupings "which would seem logically prerequisite to language competence. While each child showed a unique error pattern, the pattern within each child was stable and could be reliably reproduced." This systematic and detailed training-testing of Aut children in precision language skills provided direct evidence of the similarity between handicaps of Aut children and those diagnosed as having *central language disorder*. Churchill pointed out: (These two diagnostic groups) "share not only the more obvious deviations of echolalia and pronominal reversal but also more subtle difficulties, such as sequencing problems and special problems with the meaning of words." Most disabling languagewise was Churchill's finding of the Aut child's "inability to relate the word elements of a sentence independently to each other which gives language its power and permits an individual to understand and generate an infinite variety of sentences." Churchill then proposed that Aut children share a central language disorder with "other children who are given only the latter term as a diagnosis and that the fundamental difference between the two groups is severity of involvement."

The Measured Intelligence of Autistic Children

Lengthy intelligence testing at initial evaluation and follow-up periods has added to our knowledge of the severity of the verbal disability and also pin-pointed some of the perceptual-motor disabilities frequently found in Aut children. In an empirical survey of the measured intelligence of 155 Aut children, mean age 65 months, DeMyer et al. (1974) found that the overwhelming number (94%) had IQ's in the retarded ranges (67 and below). Low verbal IQ's accounted most heavily for the skew to the moderately to severely retarded end of the IQ spectrum.

Many other details about the measured intelligence of Aut and SNr children (see DeMyer et al., 1974) could be reported but for purposes of this communication only a few items of the most compelling significance will be given. These have been chosen to illustrate the testability of the Aut child, the value of the IQ in prognosis, and the import of various relatively low and high scores in understanding the nature of the Aut child's symptoms (see Table VIII).

In the past, most clinicians have tended to view low measured IQ's as spurious and not reflecting the basic biological intelligence of the Aut child. The prevailing view of the past was that the negativism of the Aut child prevented him from being "testable." On the contrary, all of our studies show the Aut child is "testable." The intelligence of Aut children can be measured reliably and validly. Alpern (1967) showed that nonperformance on standard intelligence tasks was related to task difficulty. Aut children performed tasks designed for infants and demonstrated high test-retest reliability on infant items.

Clinicians also pointed to some test performances that seemed to reflect higher ability in Aut children. DeMyer (1975b) investigated the most common types of splinter abilities and splinter disabilities by using items from various standardized intelligence tests (DeMyer *et al.*, 1975a). The most common perceptual-motor splinter ability in Aut children was found to be in fitting and assembly tasks; e.g., WISC Object Assembly and Block Design, Seguin Formboard, and matching color and sizes. In this type of perceptual-motor task the visual cues were in the child's view at all times and the motor component was not beyond that of a 12 to 15-month-old infant (picking up and releasing an object). When either the visual component or the motor component was made more complex (i.e., demanded more complex integration skills) then the Aut child generally performed at a relatively lower mental age level. His perceptual-motor splinter disabilities involved those visual-motor tasks that required him to imitate the body motion of another individual (DeMyer *et al.*, 1972b).

In verbal performance the most common splinter ability was rote repetition of words or digits, but this was far less common than splinter abilities in object assembly. The most common verbal disability, indeed it was universal in Aut children, was the low performance in verbal abstraction items or the inability to express and use symbolic language. If we were to estimate the Aut child's general intelligence by using only his splinter abilities as an IQ figure, as is a common clinical practice, then we would miss the Aut child's abysmally low intelligence in verbal abstraction and his disability in imitating body motion.

We still must deal with the question of measuring the Aut child's general intelligence. We have found the most useful procedure was to administer to the Aut child a large group of intelligence test items taken from 13 different tests covering a span of mental ages from infancy to late childhood (DeMyer *et al.*, 1972c). This allowed us to develop a profile of scores in children whose performances may scatter widely from which we can then compute both a verbal and performance quotient and then, finally, a general IQ.

How useful were these IQ estimates? In a follow-up study, mean 6 years follow-up time, we found that the IQ was the best single predictor of the child's outcome at follow-up. It was also strongly related to severity of symptoms. A major question we wanted to answer was how stable was the IQ in Aut children? Would treatment procedures alter it substantially? How did the passage of time affect the IQ independent of treatment? The answers to these questions are discussed at length in DeMyer *et al.*, 1974.

Essentially, we found the following:

1. The IQ of Aut children over a period of six years had nearly the same stability as that of the normal child ($r=0.7$).
2. Treatment had no differential effect on IQ's in children whose initial IQ's were <40. In the children whose IQ's were >50 at initial evaluation, treatment raised their IQ's more than the IQ's of their IQ>50 counterparts who were not treated.
3. While the mental ages of nearly all the children, treated or untreated, increased over the passage of time, their IQ's generally did not increase significantly. The meaning of this finding is that the passage of time would allow the brain to increase in growth (i.e., myelinization and dendritic branching) but that this growth was not an accelerated process and neither was the behavioral progress of the child accelerated. The Aut child's intellectual and perceptual-motor development thus progressed, as did that of the SNr child, but in only rare instances was this progress accelerated as would be expected if the deficiency were primarily functional and not organic.

One might argue that our treatment was not effective enough to bring about the child's accelerated progress or that his trauma at the hands of his parents was so severe that his potential for normal development was irrevocably blunted. Again, the evidence of high incidence of neurological signs and gross EEG abnormalities refute these arguments. The extensive follow-up studies of Rutter and Lockyer (1967a; 1967b), in England, gave results very nearly like our own studies. They, and we, found that most Aut children, like most other neurologically disabled children, had a general intelligence in the moderately to profoundly retarded ranges. Also, like other retarded children, they may have splinter skills which do not reflect their low general intelligence. The studies of Hingtgen and Churchill (1969) have demonstrated that even with high motivation, most Aut children do not overcome their specific and general learning disorders which, while they vary from child to child, are remarkably consistent over time in the same child.

A present working theory is that nearly all Aut children have a neurobiologically based language dysfunction which interferes seriously with the acquisition of expressive speech and abstract language competence. In addition, Aut children have a visual-motor imitation deficiency akin to dyspraxia which interferes with the acquisition of normal body language so important to human communication. Having neither of the two principal avenues of communication open to them, Aut children would logically refrain from paying much attention to other humans, the phenomenon known as social withdrawal.

Differences in symptomatology among the High, Middle, and Low Aut groups can be explained as follows: The severity of verbal (Vb) abstraction disability exists on a continuum of severely retarded in the Low and Mid Aut groups to moderately retarded in the High Aut group. For the two lowest groups, the severe central language disability may be enough to explain all three major symptoms of infantile autism. However, the High Aut children have Vb abstraction disabilities similar to the SNr children who are not socially withdrawn. High Aut do have more deficient visual-motor integration problems. They do not imitate body motion with the lower extremities or play ball as well as SNr children. Thus, in Aut children with relatively higher Vb abstraction capacity, the dyspraxia-like visual-motor dysfunction may be a necessary disability that tips the child into psychotic social withdrawal.[4]

REFERENCES

Allen, J., DeMyer, M., Norton, J., Pontius, W., and Yang, E. (1971). Intellectuality in parents of psychotic, subnormal and normal children. *J. Autism Child. Schizo.* 1: 311.

Alpern, G. D. (1967). Measurement of "untestable" autistic children. *J. Abnorm. Psychol.* 72: 478.

Anthony, J. (1958). An experimental approach to the psychopathology of childhood. *Brit. J. Med. Psychol.* 31: 211.

Baer, T. E. (1961). Problems in the differential diagnosis of brain damage in childhood schizophrenia. *Am. J. Orthopsychiat.* 31/IV: 728.

Benda, C., and Melchoir, J. (1959). Childhood schizophrenia, childhood autism, Heller's disease. *Intern. Rec. Med.* 172/3:137.

Bender, L. (1955). Twenty years of clinical research on schizophrenic children with special reference to those under six years of age, in *Emotional Problems of Early*

---

[4]For more detailed results and discussion of the neuropsychological mechanism of infantile autism, see DeMyer (1975a; 1975b).

Childhood, Caplan, G. (ed.), Basic Books, New York, pp. 503–515.

Bene, E. (1958). A Rorschach investigation into the mothers of autistic children. *Brit. J. Med. Psychol.* 31:226.

Bettelheim, B. (1959). Joey: a mechanical boy. *Sci. Am.* 200/3: 117.

Churchill, D. W. (1969). Psychotic children and behavior modification. *Am. J. Psychiat.* 125:1585.

Churchill, D. W. (1972). The relationship of infantile autism and early childhood schizophrenia to development language disorders of childhood. *J. Autism Child. Schizo.* 2: 182.

Clerk, G. (1961). Reflections on the role of the mother in the development of language in the schizophrenic child. *Can. Psychiat. Assoc. J.* 6: 252.

Colbert, E. G., and Koegler, R. R. (1958). Toe-walking in childhood schizophrenia. *J. Pediat.* 53:219.

DeMyer, M. K. (1975a). The nature of the neuropsychological disability in autistic children, in *Proceedings of First International Kanner Colloquium on Child Development, Deviations, and Treatment*, Schopler, E. (ed.) (in press).

DeMyer, M. K. (1975b). Motor, perceptual-motor and intellectual disabilities of autistic children, in *Early Childhood Autism*, 2nd ed., Wing, L. (ed.), Pergamon Press, London (in press).

DeMyer, M. K., Pontius, W., Norton, J. A., Barton, S., Allen, J., and Steele, R. (1972a). Parental practices and innate activity in normal, autistic, and brain-damaged infants. *J. Autism Child. Schizo. 2: 49.*

DeMyer, M. K., Alpern, G. D., Barton, S., DeMyer, W. E., Churchill, D. W., Hingtgen, J. N., Bryson, C. Q., Pontius, W., and Kimberlin, C. (1972b). Imitation in autistic, early schizophrenic and non-psychotic subnormal children. *J. Autism Child. Schizo.* 2:264.

DeMyer, M. K., Barton, S., and Norton, J. A. (1972c). A comparison of adaptive, verbal, and motor profiles of psychotic and non-psychotic subnormal children. *J. Autism Child. Schizo.* 2: 359.

DeMyer, M. K., Barton, S., DeMyer, W. E., Norton, J. A., Allen, J., and Steele, R. (1973). Prognosis in autism: A follow-up study. *J. Autism Child. Schizo.* 3: 199.

DeMyer, M. K., Barton, S., Alpern, G. D., Allen, J., Yang, E., and Steele, R. (1974). The measured intelligence of autistic children. *J. Autism Child. Schizo.* 4: 42.

DesLauriers, A. M. (1962). *The Experience of Reality in Childhood Schizophrenia*, International Universities Press, New York.

Eeg-Olofsson, O. (1971). The development of the electroencephalogram in normal children and adolescents from the age of 1 through 21 years. *Acta Paediat. Scand. Suppl.* 208: 46.

Eisenberg, L., and Kanner, L. (1956). Early autism—childhood schizophrenia symposium. *Am. J. Orthopsychiat.* 26: 556.

Ferster, C. B. (1961). Positive reinforcement and behavioral deficits of autistic children. *Child Develop.* 32: 437.

Fish, B. (1960). Involvement of the central nervous systems in infants with schizophrenia. *A.M.A. Arch. Neurol.* 2: 115.

Fish, B. (1961). The study of motor development in infancy and its relationship to psychological functioning. *Am. J. Psychiat.* 117: 1113.

Freedman, A. M., and Bender, L. (1957). When the childhood schizophrenic grows up. *Am. J. Orthopsychiat.* 27: 553.

Garcia, B., and Sarvis, M. A. (1964). Evaluation and treatment planning for autistic children. *Arch. Gen. Psychiat.* 10: 530.

Gittelman, M., and Birch, H. G. (1967). Childhood schizophrenia: Intellect, neurologic status, perinatal risk, prognosis, and family pathology. *Arch. Gen. Psychiat.* 17:16.

Goldfarb, W. (1961). *Childhood Schizophrenia*, Harvard University Press, Cambridge, Massachusetts.

Hingtgen, J. N., and Churchill, D. W. (1969). Identification of perceptual limitations in mute autistic children. Identification by the use of behavior modification. *Arch. Gen. Psychiat.* 21: 68.

Kanner, L. (1943). Autistic disturbances of affective contact. *Nervous Child* 2: 217.

Kanner, L., and Lesser, L. (1958). Early infantile autism. *Pediat. Clin. N. Am.* 5/ 3:711.

Kennard, M.A. (1960). Value of equivocal signs in neurologic diagnosis. *Neurology* 10: 753.

Knight, E. H. (1963). Some considerations regarding the concept "autism." *Diseases Nervous System* 24: 224.

Lotter, V. (1967). Epidemiology of autistic conditions in young children. II. Some characteristics of the parents and children. *Soc. Psychiat.* 1: 163.

Macmillan, M. B. (1961). A Pavlovaian approach to symbiotic psychoses. *J. Nervous Mental Disease* 132: 397.

Mahler, M. S. (1955). On symbiotic child psychosis: Genetic, dynamic, and restitution aspects. *Psychoanal. Study Child.* 10: 195.

Mosse, H. L. (1958). The misuse of diagnosis childhood schizophrenia. *Am. J. Psychiat.* 114/9: 791.

Pasamanick, B., and Knobloch, H. (1963). Early feeding and birth difficulties in childhood schizophrenia: An explanatory note. *J. Psychol.* 56: 73.

Pavenstedt, E. (1955). History of a child with an atypical development, and some vicissitudes of his treatment, in *Emotional Problems of Early Childhood*, Caplan, G. (ed.), Basic Books, New York, pp. 379–405.

Pollack, M. (1958). Brain damage, mental retardation and childhood schizophrenia. *Am. J. Psychiat.* 115:422.

Pollack, M., and Krieger, H. P. (1958). Oculomotor and postural patterns in schizophrenic children. *Arch. Neurol. Psychiat.* 79(1): 720.

Rank, B. (1955). Intensive study and treatment of preschool children who show marked personality deviations or "atypical development," and their parents, in *Emotional Problems of Early Childhood*, Caplan, G. (ed.), Basic Books, New York, pp. 491–501.

Rees, E. L. (1956). Metabolism of the schizophrenic child: Etiological hypothesis. *J. Am. Med. Wom. Assoc.* 11: 11.

Rimland, B. (1964). *Infantile Autism*, Appleton-Century-Crofts, New York.

Ritvo, E., Cantwell, D., Johnson, E., Clements, M., Benbrook, F., Slagle, S., Kelly, P., and Ritz, M. (1971). Social class factors in autism. *J. Autism Child. Schizo.* 1: 297.

Robinson, J. F. (1961). The psychoses of early childhood. *Am J. Orthopsychiat.* 31: 536.

Rosenberger, L., and Woolf, M. (1964). Schizophrenic development of two children in the 4-6 age group. *Psychoanal. Rev.* 57: 469.

Rutter, M., and Lockyer, L. (1967a). A five to fifteen year follow-up study of infantile psychosis. I. Description of the sample. *Brit. J. Psychiat.* 113: 1169.

Rutter, M., and Lockyer, L. (1967b). A five to fifteen year follow-up study of infantile psychosis. II. Social and behavioural outcome. *Brit. J. Psychiat.* 113: 1183.

Schain, R. J., and Yannet, H. (1960). Infantile autism: An analysis of 50 cases and a consideration of certain relevant neurophysiological concepts. *J. Pediat.* 57: 560.

Souza, D. S. (1961). Schizophrenic syndrome in childhood. *Brit. Med. J.* 5256: 889.

Szurek, S. A. (1956). Childhood schizophrenia symposium, 1955. Psychotic episodes and psychotic maldevelopment. *Am. J. Orthopsychiat.* 25: 519.

Tilton, J. R., DeMyer, M. K., and Loew, L. H. (1966). *Annotated Bibliography on Childhood Schizophrenia 1955–1964*, Grune and Stratton, New York and London.

Wing. J. K. (1963). Epidemiology of early childhood autism. *Develop. Med. Child. Neurol.* 5: 646.

COMMENTARY by Patricia L. Mirenda

This article reviews the results of twelve years of research designed to investigate the etiology of autism. These studies are notable for their thoroughness and meticulous attention to methodological detail. DeMyer and her colleagues were among the first autism researchers to incorporate features such as multiple control groups and multiple matching variables in their research design. An unusually extensive test battery was used to measure parent pathology, personality, and caregiving skills, and to assess the neurological status and intelligence levels of the children.

DeMyer's results are significant in that they offered strong support to the "nature" theory of causation of infantile autism. The bulk of DeMyer's evidence points to a neurological dysfunction in autistic children as the *necessary and sufficient* cause of their social withdrawal, noncommunicative speech, and nonfunctional object use. Thus, the evidence effectively absolves the parents of autistic children of blame for the disorder through the accumulation of sound empirical data.

15

Issues in Teaching
Communicative Skills

ADRIANNA L. SCHULER
ANNE M. DONNELLAN-WALSH

Introduction

When trying to design language teaching programs for autistic children, you should realize that we are not just dealing with cases of slow or incomplete development. Exposure to everyday instances of spontaneous language use has not led these children to develop even the most rudimentary forms of language. A remedial effort, therefore, cannot just consist of stimulating and encouraging normal development. Strict application of a developmental model will not suffice. This is not to say that a developmental model is not at all applicable to your autistic students. You will find that some of the procedures suggested in this chapter coincide with procedures that follow from a developmental model (for example, the move from one-word to two-word utterances). But, in determining training procedures, you will have to rely on actual observation and analysis of your students' speech and language performance and on their cognitive and perceptual skills, not on inferences from a hypothetical developmental model alone. This is particularly important since our understanding of very early language or pre-language behaviors in general is still very limited.

Autistic children differ from other children with language acquisition problems in that they generally do not display any type of communicative initiative. Children with, for example, childhood aphasia, Down's Syndrome, and even elective mutism, will tend to make their demands and desires clear through some type of gesturing, signing, or speech approximation (such as use of grunts, appropriate intonations, etc.). In spite of a sometimes uncanny ability to echo the speech of others, autistic children will seldom use speech in a communicative way. Emphasis should therefore be placed on making autistic children experience language, in whatever form,

Reprinted with permission from *Teaching Makes a Difference—A Guide for Developing Successful Classes for Autistic and Other Severely Handicapped Children*, by A. Donnellan-Walsh, L. D. Gossage, G. W. LaVigna, A. L. Schuler, and J. D. Traphagen (Sacramento, Calif.: California State Department of Education, 1976), 149–157.

as a means of effecting their environment. Autistic children should learn that speaking, signing, gesturing or use of written words, pictures or chips can be a tool for having their needs met. Communicative intent is, therefore, a teaching priority.

Autistic children are known for their robot-like, stereotyped speech patterns. If they speak at all, they tend to only reproduce rote phrases that they have heard before. They do not seem to be able to put words together and form their own sentences. Our teaching efforts should therefore be directed toward developing productive use of grammatical rules such that the children can begin to make up their own utterances rather than being limited to borrowing the phrases of others.

Some autistic children appear to have a very difficult time trying to produce sounds or sound combinations; others just do not seem able to tune into auditory stimuli. This means that understanding and production of spoken words may sometimes be too much to ask. It may be more realistic to have a child sign, hold up a picture, or read. Sound production is not crucial to human language. The essentials of human language are *referentiality*—words, signs, pictures, or whatever, stand for something else, and *producitivity*—a limited set of words and linguistic rules allow for the production of an enormous number of sentences. The language system that we happen to use is arbitrary and very elaborate and complex, which is unfortunate for children with language problems. To produce even the simplest syllable, strings of sounds have to be precisely analyzed and muscle movements intricately coordinated. Fortunately, the establishment of communicative intent is not dependent upon the spoken word; other systems of communication may therefore be more useful for you to start with. Later on in this chapter, we will discuss these other systems in greater detail.

Communicative Intent

In teaching autistic children any type of speech, sign, gesture, written or pictorial language response, you should start out with those forms of language that have the greatest direct impact. Make sure that every response is immediately met by tangible and reinforcing consequences. If you teach a child to say or sign "drink," "juice," "water," or to point to the faucet when he is thirsty, or to hold up a picture of water, he is likely to find out what communication is all about. The consequences of this kind of language usage are directly relevant to the child and also natural rather than contrived. You should realize that many other language functions do not provide for such clear consequences. When you are teaching the child to say "juice" when showing a picture of a glass of orange juice or "boy is running" when looking at a picture, you do not provide for such clearcut consequences. In everyday speech those types of labeling responses are followed by social consequences, such as nods or smiles, which are too subtle to be picked up by autistic children. In a structured teaching situation, you could provide clearer consequences and teach the child to respond, but the consequences would be contrived, arbitrary, and not inherent to the particular situation. The child could perform in the teaching situation but would probably not generalize the response to real life situations. In order to establish communicative intent, therefore, initially avoid teaching labeling responses. Labeling functions (also referred to as *"tacts"* or *"identification"*) are used in many syntax teaching programs and will probably be more appropriate for autistic children once communicative intent has been established and specific syntactic exercises seem desirable. When you do work on syntax, you should always make sure that what the child says is being put into a meaningful context. By having them link phrases to irrelevant features of a picture presented, you may be promoting the meaningless, rote language in which these children tend to be masters. When starting out, have the child describe what you or other children are doing rather than the action in a picture. It is possible, of course, for a child to attend to irrelevant features of what another person is actually doing or role playing. But, attending to irrelevant stimuli is more likely to occur when a child is presented with a picture than when he is presented with live action.

In order to help you select appropriate first teaching goals, Table 1 lists a sample of single words that seem easily used in a functional manner.

These words (often referred to as *"mands"*) can be used in a direct, *interrogative* sense. You can use them to ask a child about her desires or needs. The child can use them to tell you what she wants, to ask you for a particular item or for access to a particular activity. The listed words only serve as examples of words that may be selected. Obviously, decisions about which words to select are dependent upon a careful analysis of the child, her needs, and the characteristics of her particular environment. In order to select relevant words, it may be helpful to identify the activities the child is most likely to engage in. These activities can then be made contingent upon the child's expressing her wants through speaking, signing or whatever. In this manner, you are directly teaching communicative intent.

Do not waste time perfecting articulation, or in putting elaborate sentences together. It is the experience of communication that is essential in working with autistic children. The response form that you select should be as uncomplicated as possible. Simple, single words or word approximations (such as those given above) will often suffice. Function, not structure, should be your concern in early language training.

Generalization and Productivity

When you are dealing with echolalic children who exhibit remarkable memory skills, it may be tempting to teach elaborate responses such as, "May I have a cookie, please?" in a specific stimulus context. Such a phrase will

---

TABLE 1

**EXAMPLES OF SINGLE WORD UTTERANCES THAT
MAY BE USEFUL AS FIRST TEACHING OBJECTIVES**

Food		Clothing		Playtime	
Lunch	Eat	Pants	Put on	Ball	Ride
Cookie	Drink	Shirt	Take off	Truck	Jump
Juice		Sweater		Car	
Ice Cream		Coat		Doll	
Candy		Shoes		Bike	
Milk		Pajamas		Blocks	
Etc.		Etc.		Book	
				Etc.	

People/Socialization			Things Around Home			Body Parts
Own Name	Hug	Hi	TV	Sit	In	Nose
Mommy	Sit	Thanks	Bed	Look	Out	Face
Daddy		Help	Table	Sleep	Up	Eye
Jimmy			Chair			Ear
Debby			Toilet (potty)			Tummy
Etc.			Cup			Arms
			Door			Etc.
			Home			

Movement	Requesting	
Walk	Give me	more
Go	Want	
Come		
Etc.		

---

most likely be processed as one single string of sounds rather than as composed of several elements (may have—a cookie—1—please). It will probably only occur in that particular form and only in that particular context because the autistic child will not have been able to detect the structure of the response. Research (Hermelin and Frith, 1971; Hermelin, 1971; Hermelin, 1976) has shown that autistic children tend to be unable to detect structure and ordering rules. If they are, for example, asked to retain the following random sequence of visual stimuli:

$$\bigcirc\circ\bigcirc\bigcirc\bigcirc$$

they will do just as well as when asked to retain an ordered set of visual stimuli, such as:

$$\circ\circ\bigcirc\circ\circ\bigcirc$$

Normal children find the second series easier. Similarly, these same researchers found that autistic children will do as well recalling a random series of sounds as a meaningful sentence. As with the visual stimuli, their normal peers do better on the sentences which have order and structure.

This research suggests that teaching such phrases as "May I please have a cookie?" may not help your student to discover the structure of the sentence. The chances of his coming up with phrases such as "May I please have a piece of candy?" or "Can Johnny have a crayon?" are minimal. He will not be able to generate similar sentences to express similar requests. Generalization is not very likely to occur. . . . You will find it more functional to teach simple two-word combinations such as "Want cookie." From that first combination, you will be able to teach a whole class of compositions of "want" and "x." Whatever the child's level of speech production and degree of communicative intent, it is essential to teach *constituency*: that is, teach him words and word combinations (whether in sign, speech, pictures or written words) which he can recombine by himself.

Not only should you avoid teaching elaborate phrases which do not encourage generalization, you should also avoid using these phrases yourself. Address the child with simple word combinations.

In order to further promote generalization, you will have to vary the stimulus settings in which you teach specific responses. "Want cookie" should be used at home and in the classroom and at varying times in both of those settings. The response should be required by teachers as well as aides, parents, siblings, friends, etc. You do not want the child to associate the response with only one person, place or time.

In your concern for generalization, you must also deal with the major attentional deficit of autistic children, *stimulus overselectivity*. . . . Generalization requires the child to be able to tune into a variety of stimuli simultaneously and to have the attentional flexibility to tune out the less relevant stimuli. Let us suppose, for example, that you want to teach a child "cup." You present a cup and say, "What is this? . . . *cup*"; he learns to say "cup." You would assume that he has learned the concept of cup, i.e., all of the component parts which make a cup different from a chair. In fact, however, with an autistic child you may have only taught him to say "cup" when he sees the blue line across the cup. Even worse, he may only give the correct response when you raise your eyebrows, use a certain intonational pattern or show other idiosyncratic mannerisms. This is a major problem because it is not at all uncommon for autistic children to learn to respond to an irrelevant stimulus feature. Stimulus overselectivity thwarts generalization since stimulus generalization involves responding to various components of a stimulus complex, not to only one element.

We still know very little about the nature and remediation of such problems but there are things which can be done to reduce them. . . . [We have] stressed the need for absolute consistency when teaching new things to autistic children. This structure is essential because we know that the children characteristically fail to attend to "rich" stimulus settings. Paradoxically, however, this very structure which the children need is exactly what hampers generalization. What you must do, therefore, is start out with "over-consistency" but plan to gradually move to a less controlled stimulus presentation. When, for example, you are teaching "cup," you will begin by presenting the same cup until you are confident that he is responding consistently. At that point, you will want to present many differently colored and shaped cups (or pictures of them). In the same way, you will want to be very consistent, in fact artificial, in the way you use your voice, intonation or facial expression and in the words you use. Gradually you can move in the direction of a more natural presentation of the S^D. This process will require very subtle judgments on your part and you will have to carefully monitor both your behaviors and those of your student. Careful attention to data will be necessary to ensure that the child is not "losing" what he has already learned because you have made too dramatic a change in the S^D. Keep in mind, too, that having successfully generalized on one item does not mean that your student will necessarily be able to make the same transition on the next. You will probably have to go through the process many times before you begin to see that the child is getting the idea of generalization. It is an arduous, though fascinating, process. Nonetheless, it is essential to attempt to overcome these difficulties in *stimulus control/generalization* if the autistic child is going to make any real progress. . . .

Alternative Systems of Communication

In selecting a system of communication to teach a student, keep in mind that you want your child and his family to be able to quickly experience some success. Setting unrealistic teaching goals only creates frustration. The different communicative systems you may consider are:

SPOKEN WORDS: preferable in terms of provision for the broadest usage.
SIGN LANGUAGE: rapidly becoming more popular as a "full-grown" language system with rich opportunities for expression.
TOTAL COMMUNICATION: a combination of spoken and signed language such that signed and spoken words are simultaneously presented. For these purposes only *signed English* can be used, since the grammar of spoken English has to be followed, not the grammar of *American sign language*.

Each of these three systems has been commonly used to teach communication to autistic children and all have been shown to have some degree of success. Nonetheless, they are not the complete answer for every autistic child because, even with intensive efforts to teach these children to communicate using one or a combination of these systems, some children have not progressed. Perhaps part of the reason is that the effective use of these systems requires the ability to analyze and store sequences of stimuli over time. The words or signs, by their very nature, are presented and then disappear. Because some of the children you teach may have major deficits in the areas of *temporal sequencing* and *temporal retention skills*, you should be familiar with those systems of communication where stimuli are patterned across space rather than time. In the following examples, stimuli are permanent rather than transient:

PICTORIAL SYSTEMS: instead of speaking or signing, a child can be asked to hold up a picture or even a series of two or more pictures. Only a very simple manual response is required.

CODED CHIPS: chips of various colors and shapes can be used to convey a particular meaning (e.g., "red and round" for juice, "yellow and hexagonal" for sandwich) or neutral chips can be coded with different pictures or symbolic representations. Form boards can be used in a similar manner.

READING: written words can be used instead of, or conjointly with, pictures.

These last three systems are useful because elaborate vocal or manual responses are not essential to language. Referentiality and productivity are not tied to speaking and signing. Many autistic children may be able to learn to express themselves through simplified language systems. Language, no matter how simple, gives children the opportunity to expand their symbolic and conceptual thinking. Intellectual development will be stagnated if language does not develop (Hollis and Carrier, 1975; Meadow, 1968). Therefore, simplified language systems may be of help for those autistic children who are unable to learn to speak or to sign. Premack's work with chimpanzees (1970, 1971, 1972) provides us with an example of the use of a simplified response form. He demonstrates that remarkable results can be obtained when a language system, i.e., colored chips of different shapes, is used which requires responses that are of only minimal complexity. The simplification of language responses is necessary in working with chimpanzees because chimps seem (due to their differently shaped vocal tracts) to be unable to produce human-like speech sound (Lieberman, 1975). Carrier's work (1974a, 1974b) demonstrates that similar simplifications of the response form may be fruitful in teaching the basics of language to retardates who have previously failed to learn language. McLean and McLean's work with autistic children (1974) utilizing similar principles suggests that these systems are worth further application and study.

Chip systems are used by Premack, Carrier and McLean are all arbitrary, and their resemblance to human language limited. While chips function as words and can have meanings identical to spoken words, and even can be combined together just like spoken words, one has to be specifically trained in order to understand the code used. This limits the chances for spontaneous functional use.

A further limiting factor is that chips or form boards have to be carried around. These limitations are not important when chips are used specifically to develop initial communicative intent and/or to practice syntax by combining chips in various orders. A chip system can be particularly helpful when initial progress with speech and signing is slow and the chips are used mainly in a supportive manner.

As pointed out by LaVigna (1975, 1976), the major advantages of color and shape coded chips are, to a large degree, shared by the written word. Both are patterned across space and do not require temporal sequencing skills because the stimuli presented are permanent. The major advantage of the written word over chips, and in fact signs, is that it ties the children into a communication system which is shared by the rest of our society. A second advantage is that the response of holding up a word card is relatively easy and rapidly taught. You do not need five thousand trials to accomplish this. In addition, there have long been reports of autistic children who have failed to develop speech, but who appear fascinated with the written word and tend to develop a sight word vocabulary on their own (Elliot and Needleman, 1975). This suggests that use of the written word may be particularly valuable when attempting to teach a communicative system to autistic children.

To use the written word, the child has to be able to make rather fine visual discriminations. If this is problematic, use of a pictorial system may be considered. Holding up an appropriate picture to express a need is progress when compared to a child's being unable to show intentions at all. Favorite activities or objects can be portrayed through pictures or simple drawings and thus be used to stimulate communicative initiative.

You should realize that there is no simple "cure-all" solution in terms of selecting a system of communication. Decisions will depend on the individual child and his needs in terms of his environment. In attempting to make a choice, you should consider the following factors:

AGE OF CHILD: The chances of acquiring speech are greatly reduced as a child gets older. Many researchers report that acquisition of speech is confined within a critical span of years ending at approximately the sixth year (Lenneberg, 1967). This position is, however, being challenged by case studies which indicate that children may be able to learn language after age six (Fromklin et al., 1974). This latter position is supported by our own experiences across a variety of classrooms. Therefore, one should not automatically discontinue attempts at speech based on the age of the child.

AMOUNT AND TYPE OF SPONTANEOUS VOCALIZATION: If a child produces many speech-like sounds, perhaps when engaged in self-stimulatory behavior, tape and/or transcribe those sounds. Sounds that have any resemblance to vowels and consonants can then be used to construct the first target words for you to teach the child. If a child has a high rate of vocalization, the acquisition of words formed by those sounds will be facilitated (Traphagen, 1976).

USE OF SIGNS OR GESTURES: If a child has initiated the use of some type of signing or gesturing in the absence of any vocalization, he is demonstrating communicative intent. By using a series of gestures or signs, the child shows a grasp of the referential function of language as well as an intent to communicate. Such effective use of gestures or signs is rare in autism (Wing, 1974; Ricks and Wing, 1975). But, if a child is signing spontaneously, it may be preferable for you to select signing as the system of communication to teach, at least as a start.

PRE-VERBAL PERFORMATIVES: If a child tries to express wishes, emotions, etc., through grunts or vowel-like sounds (non-verbal signs accompanied by reaching and attending behavior), this indicates some notion of speech as a means of communication. In general, the presence of such *pre-verbal performatives* is a first step toward the development of a language system (Bates, 1976; Dore, 1975; Greenfield and others, 1976). Presence of such rudimentary vocal communication may mean that it is preferable for you to teach an oral system of communication. You should consequate all purposeful vocalization and gradually shape in more elaborate vocal behavior. However, if speech is produced in a laborious manner and progress is slow, signing may be preferable to oral language.

AMOUNT OF SELF-STIMULATION: If a child shows a high rate of self-stimulation it is likely that little of his attention is directed toward the acquisition of speech and language. Suppression of self-stimulation may very well lead to the increase of many positive behaviors, including appropriate speech. A high frequency of manual self-stimulation may indicate that it would be difficult to teach the child signing. Discrete response systems, such as written language or the use of a sign board, may be preferable in those instances.

IMITATIVE SKILLS—VERBAL AND NON-VERBAL: An ability to imitate a series of movements is a prerequisite for both speaking and signing. If you find that your student is much more capable of manual imitation than of imitating sounds, or tongue, lip and other facial movements, this suggests that signing may be more appropriate.

RECEPTIVE SKILLS: If a child's receptive skills appear to be much greater than his expressive skills, he probably has more of a notion of communication than it would seem. If his verbal imitation skills are very poor, a visual system of communication may be the way to go. In the long run, his prognosis for spoken language may be good once initial problems in sound production are eliminated or overcome. In the meantime, he is learning about the value of communication.

STIMULUS OVERSELECTIVITY: If a student selectively responds, is excessively prompt dependent, shows extreme lack of generalization, or is completely unable to learn in the presence of multiple stimulus input, this will have implications for your selection of a communication system to teach. For instance, if the child continuously fails to attend simultaneously to an auditory and a visual stimulus, the acquisition of meaningful, spoken language will be greatly hampered (see Lovaas and Schreibman, 1971; Schreibman and Lovaas, 1973). If a child is also overselective within one modality (Koegel and Wilhelm, 1973), and has problems in the areas of stimulus discrimination and generalization as well, it will probably be most useful to select the easiest response mode, i.e., a pictorial system.

It is this characteristic of overselectivity which makes the use of total communication questionable with autistic children. Newsom (1975), in his discussion of learning and attentional characteristics of autistic children, expresses reservations about the use of total communication, because the child may be unable to combine the signed and spoken words and will be confused rather than helped by such simultaneity.

MODALITY PREFERENCE: Some children respond much better to visual than auditory stimuli, or the other way around. If your student shows such definite modality preference, it seems logical to start working to his strengths. You would not want to start out with a visual system if a child performs better with auditory stimuli.

VISUAL DISCRIMINATION ABILITIES: If you want to work with a visual system, it is important for you to know to what extent the child can make visual discriminations. The various communication systems require differing amounts of discrimination ability. Signing not only requires refined visual discrimination but also intact temporal sequencing and retention skills. Use of a reading system requires refined visual discrimination skills. As pointed out by Elliot and Needleman (1975), it is not unusual to find great fascination with the written word in children who are otherwise mute. In such cases, reading may be preferable. So, be sure to evaluate a child's visual discrimination skills in relation to the system to be selected.

OPPORTUNITIES FOR PRACTICE AT HOME AND IN THE CLASSROOM: The teaching of any communicative system is only going to be effective if there are numerous opportunities for practice, generalization, and reinforcement. Obviously, these opportunities are most easily and naturally provided through the use of oral language. On the other hand, given the abilities and disabilities of a child, you may feel that you should put your efforts into teaching him to sign. Part of that decision making process requires that you take into consideration the fact that, if he is to communicate through signing, he will have to have parents, teachers, siblings and friends who are willing to learn along with him. Similarly, chips, picture boards and, to a lesser extent, the written word are limited in terms of a variety of opportunities for practice because they either require others to have learned a specialized set of skills or they have a finite number of words available for the child at any given time. Any decision about which system of communication to teach has to be made in the context of the child's communicative environment as well as the abilities of the child.

While the choice of an appropriate communicative system is of extreme importance, you must remember that these choices are not necessarily mutually exclusive. It is, for example, conceivable that you might be teaching a child to speak at one time while in another teaching session you would be using a pictorial manual, or written system. This would provide for the opportunity to put words together and to learn about syntax without having to wait until articulation skills are perfected. Once communicative intent has been established within the system that is easiest for that child, you can then decide to either shift to another, more practical system, or to continue to develop the child's skills in the modality. In any case, choosing a communication system to start with does not sentence either you or the child to the use of that system forever.

One final word regarding the choice of a communicative system. We have discussed some of the strengths and weaknesses of various systems. For example, oral language would be the mode of choice because it can be universally understood; but it is extremely complicated and particularly difficult for children who have specific problems producing sounds or with auditory analysis. Chips, picture boards, and written words should be considered within the limitations that we have mentioned. We feel, however, that signing deserves a special comment because its recent rise in popularity in the field of autism has reached the level of fadism. It is our belief that, while sign seems to hold great promise for some children, it is not a "cure-all."

Because it is a language system just like spoken English or any other language, it requires abstraction, generalization ability, a comprehension of linguistic rules and temporal sequencing skills. Therefore, you may find it as difficult to move a child from imitative signing to spontaneous and creative signing as you do in trying to develop spontaneous oral language in the autistic child. Total communication ought to be viewed with the same kind of hesitancy and, more particularly, you must monitor the child's responding carefully to see if his stimulus overselectivity problems prevent him from learning as effectively when he is simultaneously presented with two different types of stimuli. Within the context of these hesitations, we take hope in the anecdotal reports, as well as the recent literature (Bricker and Bricker, 1972; Fulwiler and Fouts, 1976; Creedon, 1973; Schaeffer et al., 1975) which give examples of children who start with signing and eventually acquire speech.

REFERENCES

Bricker, W., & Bricker, D. (1974). An early language training strategy. In R. Schiefelbush and L. Lloyd (Eds.), *Language perspectives: Acquisition, retardation and intervention.* (pp. 430–468). Baltimore: University Park Press.

Carrier, J. K. (1974-a). Application of functional analysis and a non-speech response to teaching language. Developing systematic procedures for training children's language. *Monograph 18, American Speech and Hearing Association,* Washington, DC.

Carrier, J. K. (1974-b). Non-speech noun usage training with severely and profoundly retarded children. *Journal of Speech and Hearing Research, 17,* 510–518.

Creedon, M. P. (1973). "Language Development in Non-verbal Autistic Children Using a Simultaneous Communication System." Paper presented to the Society for Research in Child Development, Philadelphia.

Elliot, D., & Needleman, R. (1975). "Hyperlexia." Paper presented to the Linguistic Society of America, San Francisco.

Fulwiler, R. L., & Fouts, R. S. (1976). Acquisition of American Sign Language by a Non-communicating Autistic Child, *Journal of Autism and Childhood Schizophrenia, 6,* 1.

Hermelin, B., & Frith, U. (1971). Psychological studies of childhood autism: Can autistic children make sense of what they see and hear? *Journal of Special Education, 5,* 107–117.

Hermelin, B. (1976). Coding and the sense modalities. In L. Wing (Ed.), *Childhood Autism* (2d ed.). London: Pergamon Press.

Hermelin, P. (1971). Rules and language. In M. Rutter (Ed.), *Infantile autism: Concepts, characteristics and treatment* (pp. 113–131). London: Churchill Livingstone.

Hollis, J., & Carrier, J. K. (1975). Research implication for communication deficiencies. *Exceptional Children, 41* (6), 405–412.

La Vigna, G. (1976). *Itardian Reading Program.* Adolescent Unit, Camarillo State Hospital, P.O. Box "A", Camarillo, CA 93010.

La Vigna, G. (1976). "Language Training in the Mute Autistic Adolescent." Paper presented to the Western Psychological Association, Los Angeles, CA.

Lieberman, P. (1975). *On the Origins of Language.* New York: MacMillan.

Meadow, K. P. (1968). Early manual communication in relation to the deaf child's intellectual, social and communicative functioning. *American Annals of the Deaf, 113,* 9–41.

McLean, L. P., & McLean, J. E. (1974). A language training program for non-verbal autistic children. *Journal of Speech and Hearing Disorders, 39* (2), 186–194.

Premack, A. J., & Premack, D. (1972). Teaching language to an ape. *Scientific American, 277,* 92–99.

Premack, D. (1970). A functional analysis of language. *Journal of Anal. Behavior, 14,* 107–125.

Premack, D. (1971). Language in chimpanzees, *Science, 172,* 808–822.

Schaeffer, B., Kollinzas, G., Musil, A., & McDowell, P. (no date). "Signed Speech: A New Treatment for Autism." Unpublished paper, University of Oregon.

COMMENTARY by Edward G. Carr

The significance of this article is twofold. First, it translates scientific research into a form that is usable by parents and teachers—the "consumers" of behavioral technology. Second, it focuses on the core issue in language development for autistic children, namely, communicative competence.

With respect to the first issue, we now take for granted the idea that research will only benefit autistic individuals when it is presented in a form that can be understood and used by practitioners. Thus, today, there exist excellent tracts on effective teaching techniques (e.g., Koegel, Rincover, and Egel, 1982; Lovaas, 1981). The picture was different seven years ago with relatively few sources available. The contribution of this paper lies primarily in translating available research for widespread dissemination, particularly to teachers, and convincing such individuals that empirically based techniques do have an impact on language development.

The second issue is critical in the field, specifically, the notion that what ultimately counts is the development of language *use* rather than language forms per se, and this is true whether the language is taught in the vocal, sign, or graphic modality. Much effort is expended in the typical classroom on labeling objects or verbs. Yet, such efforts are wasted unless the child is taught to use these skills in order to influence another person. This is the notion of functionality or communicative competence and it is a basic idea that runs through much current research and clinical practice.

REFERENCES

Koegel, R. L., Rincover, A., & Egel, A. *Educating and Understanding Autistic Children.* San Diego: College Hill, 1982.

Lovaas, O. I. *Teaching Developmentally Disabled Children.* Baltimore: University Park Press, 1981.

16

The Motivation
of Self-Injurious Behavior:
A Review of Some Hypotheses

EDWARD G. CARR

Self-injurious behavior is perhaps the most dramatic and extreme form of chronic human psychopathology. Self-injurious behavior involves any of a number of behaviors by which the individual produces physical damage to his or her own body (Tate & Baroff, 1966). Some individuals engage in scratching, biting, or head banging to the point at which bleeding occurs and sutures are required. Others may engage in self-inflicted punching, face slapping, or pinching, thereby producing swellings and bruises over large areas of their bodies.

Self-injurious behavior is most frequently reported in individuals labeled autistic, schizophrenic, retarded, or brain damaged. The frequency of occurrence of such behavior has been reported to be about 4–5% in psychiatric populations (Frankel & Simmons, 1976; Phillips & Alkan, 1961). Interestingly, self-injurious behavior, particularly head banging, is also seen in young normal children (Ilg & Ames, 1955). Here, the frequency of occurrence has been reported to be 11–17% at ages 9–18 months and 9% at 2 years of age (Shintoub & Soulairac, 1961). De Lissovoy (1961) reported the incidence of self-injurious behavior to be 15.2% in a normal population aged 19–32 months.

Despite the relative infrequency of self-injurious behavior, the behavior has commanded a great deal of attention from clinicians because of its life-threatening nature and because of the barrier it poses to normal social and intellectual development. Treatment efforts, which have been numerous, have been summarized in comprehensive review articles by Smolev (1971), Bachman (1972), and Frankel and Simmons (1976).

The focus of the present article is on the motivation, rather than the treatment, of self-injurious behavior. The major reason for this focus stems

Reprinted from *Psychological Bulletin* 84 (1977): 800–816. Copyright 1977 by the American Psychological Association. Reprinted by permission of the publisher and author.

The preparation of this manuscript was supported by National Institute of Mental Health Grant 11440 and a Medical Research Council of Canada Postdoctoral Fellowship.

from the fact that treatment interventions have not always been successful (e.g., Romanczyk & Goren, 1975; Seegmiller, 1972). It is very likely that self-injurious behavior, like most complex human behavior, may be under the control of a number of motivational variables and that different treatment interventions may be required to eliminate each source of motivation. For this reason, it would be important to identify what the different motivational variables might be. With this consideration in mind, a review of several hypotheses pertaining to the motivation of self-injurious behavior is undertaken.

A search of the literature indicates that the most noteworthy hypotheses, in terms of frequency of citation and/or amount of empirical support, are the following: (a) self-injurious behavior is a learned operant, maintained by positive social reinforcement (positive reinforcement hypothesis); (b) self-injurious behavior is a learned operant, maintained by the termination or avoidance of an aversive stimulus (negative reinforcement hypothesis); (c) self-injurious behavior is a means of providing sensory stimulation in the absence of adequate levels of tactile, vestibular, and kinesthetic input (self-stimulation hypothesis); (d) self-injurious behavior is the product of aberrant physiological processes (organic hypothesis); and (e) self-injurious behavior is an attempt to establish ego boundaries or to reduce guilt (psychodynamic hypotheses). The evidence bearing on each of these hypotheses is reviewed and evaluated, and some directions for future research are discussed.

Positive Reinforcement Hypothesis

This hypothesis states that self-injurious behavior is a learned operant, maintained by positive social reinforcement, which is delivered contingent upon performance of the behavior (Lovaas, Freitag, Gold, & Kassorla, 1965). This hypothesis suggests that the frequency of self-injurious behavior should decrease when the social consequences that presumably maintain the behavior are withdrawn. There is a substantial body of literature indicating that the complete removal of social consequences can in fact greatly reduce or eliminate self-injurious behavior (Bucher & Lovaas, 1968; Ferster, 1961; Hamilton, Stephens, & Allen, 1967; Jones, Simmons, & Frankel, 1974; Lovaas & Simmons, 1969; Tate & Baroff, 1966; Wolf, Risley, Johnston, Harris, & Allen, 1967; Wolf, Risley, & Mees, 1964). In a representative study, Hamilton et al. (1967) treated several severely retarded institutionalized individuals, using a time-out procedure. This procedure prescribes that access to all forms of reinforcement be removed from an individual for a fixed period of time, contingent upon the emission of a response. In the present example, the procedure consisted of confining the individual to a chair for a fixed period of time, contingent upon each instance of self-injurious behavior. Because the chair was located in an isolated area of the ward, the procedure effectively removed all opportunity for reinforcement (including social reinforcement) for the fixed period. Under these conditions, self-injurious behavior decreased precipitously to negligible levels. One interpretation of these data is that self-injurious behavior decreased because social reinforcement, the variable maintaining the behavior, was removed each time the behavior occurred. Curiously, in this study and others like it, there was no measurement of the frequency of occurrence of social reinforcement. There was thus no demonstration that ward staff, for example, were in fact attending to such behavior at any time. Yet, when self-injurious behavior occurs at a high frequency, the assumption is often made that somebody must be attending to such behavior, thereby reinforcing it. Because this assumption is a prevalent one, it would be important, in future research, to include measures of the frequency of adult social reinforcement before, during, and after treatment intervention. In this manner, the role of social reinforcement in maintaining self-injurious behavior could be more adequately assessed.

Another methodological point pertaining to time-out studies relates to the possibility that time-out procedures may actually constitute aversive stimuli, that is, self-injurious behavior decreases, not because of the removal of social reinforcement, but because of the punishing aspects of being confined to a chair or being forced to wait in a barren room. From this standpoint, time-out studies are poor tests of the positive reinforcement hypothesis because reinforcement withdrawal and punishment are confounded. A purer test can be found in those studies involving the use of extinction. Extinction is a procedure in which the reinforcement for a previously reinforced behavior is discontinued. In the present example, extinction would involve the brief discontinuation of social reinforcement contingent upon each occurrence of self-injurious behavior. Since the extinction procedure does not involve placing the individual in a physically aversive situation, punishment effects are presumably minimized, and any reduction in self-injurious behavior can be attributed directly to the removal of social reinforcement. Interestingly, Lovaas et al. (1965) and Tate and Baroff (1966) found that simple extinction had no effect on the frequency of self-injurious behavior. Superficially, it would thus appear that social reinforcement is not an important variable. The results are difficult to interpret, however, because no measure of adult attending behavior was reported in either study. It is entirely possible that the adults inadvertently attended to the self-injurious behavior on an intermittent basis. This situation is likely because of the difficulty of ignoring an individual when that individual is engaging in dangerous high-frequency head banging or face slapping.

Because of the above problems, many researchers have employed a noncontingent time-out procedure to study self-injurious behavior. In this procedure, the individual is placed in an isolation room. The isolation, however, is not contingent upon the occurrence of self-injurious behavior. Instead, each day, a period of time is set aside during which the individual is physically and socially isolated. Since the procedure is noncontingent, the punishment aspect is controlled for, while at the same time, inadvertent social reinforcement (such as might occur during simple extinction) is eliminated because no adult is present. Using this procedure, several investigators (Jones et al., 1974; Lovaas & Simmons, 1969) have reported that self-injurious behavior gradually declined to negligible levels. Corte, Wolf, and Locke (1971), however, reported that noncontingent social isolation did not change the rate of self-injurious behavior for their two subjects. But, as the authors themselves pointed out, the procedure was in effect for a sum total of 12 hours, probably too short a time for any effect to show. On balance, then, the above evidence is consistent with the hypothesis that social reinforcement may play a role in maintaining self-injurious behavior.

Finally, on the topic of noncontingent social isolation, Lovaas and Simmons (1969) and Romanczyk and Goren (1975) presented data, both anecdotal and experimental, showing that at the beginning of isolation, there was an increase (over pretreatment levels) in the intensity and frequency of self-injurious behavior. This increase is apparently identical with the *extinction burst* phenomenon, frequently reported in the animal literature (Skinner, 1938, p. 74). Skinner noted that in rats, following the discontinuation of reinforcement for a previously reinforced response, there was typically an initial but temporary increase in the frequency and/or magnitude of that response. Thus, the demonstration of a self-injurious behavior extinction burst at the start of the isolation procedure may also be taken as support for the positive reinforcement hypothesis. Parenthetically, it might be noted that a frequent byproduct of extinction is aggressive behavior (Azrin, Hutchinson, & Hake, 1966). The occurrence of aggressive behavior during the extinction of self-injurious behavior would thus be noteworthy, since such a finding would tend to support the positive reinforcement hypothesis. Such research remains to be done.

Another corollary of the positive reinforcement hypothesis is that self-injurious behavior should increase when positive reinforcement is made contingent upon the behavior. Lovaas et al. (1965) and Lovaas and Simmons (1969) demonstrated that when comforting remarks or preferred activities were made contingent on the occurrence of self-injurious behavior, self-injurious behavior increased dramatically. Such evidence supports the above hypothesis. In addition, the fact that activities may also serve to reinforce self-injurious behavior suggests that social reinforcement is not the only variable maintaining self-injurious behavior. Thus, the positive reinforcement hypothesis may have to be broadened to include activity reinforcers or perhaps even material reinforcers as sources of motivation for self-injurious behavior.

Another property of self-injurious behavior, consistent with the positive reinforcement hypothesis, is that such behavior can come under rather powerful stimulus control. Several studies have shown, for instance, that self-injurious behavior rates may be rather low when the child is alone but very high when adults are present (Bucher & Lovaas, 1968; Romanczyk & Goren, 1975; Hitzing & Risley, Note 1). These findings are predictable within the framework of the positive reinforcement hypothesis: The children, over time, discriminate that self-injurious behavior results in positive reinforcement in the presence of adults but not in their absence and thus engage in self-injurious behavior primarily when adults are present. This notion might be tested further by measuring self-injurious behavior rates in the presence of familiar versus unfamiliar adults. One expectation would be that the rates might be higher in the presence of the familiar adults, since the child presumably has a history of social reinforcement for self-injurious behavior in their presence (but not in the presence of the unfamiliar adults).

Several other studies in the literature are pertinent to a discussion of the stimulus control of self-injurious behavior. Lovaas et al. (1965) demonstrated that for one child, the withdrawal of positive social reinforcement (i.e., adult attention) for singing and dancing to a set of songs was discriminative for high rates of self-injurious behavior. Similarly, Corte et al. (1971) and Peterson and Peterson (1968) demonstrated that high rates of self-injurious behavior occurred when a blanket or mittens were taken away from the children whom they were treating. There was some indication that the blanket and mittens functioned as positive reinforcers. These three studies taken together suggest that the operation of reinforcement withdrawal can be discriminative for high rates of self-injurious behavior. Lovaas et al. (1965) suggested a way to understand this type of stimulus control in the context of the positive reinforcement hypothesis. They speculated that, over time, a child can learn that when a positive reinforcer is withdrawn, it may be possible to get the reinforcer reinstated, simply by emitting a bout of self-injurious behavior. Parenthetically, it might be noted that such speculation has a close conceptual similarity to the notion that self-injurious behavior is a learned response to frustration, frustration being operationalized in terms of reinforcement withdrawal (Baumeister & Forehand, 1973; Dollard, Miller, Doob, Mowrer, & Sears, 1939, pp. 46-49). To test the hypothesis, it would be necessary to arrange experimentally for a variety of positive reinforcers to be reinstated each time a child engaged in self-injurious behavior. The child should soon learn to engage in high rates of self-injurious behavior in the reinforcement withdrawal situation. Such a demonstration has never been made because, of course, it is ethically indefensible. Perhaps the relationship between frustration and self-injurious behavior could best be studied experimentally by using lower organisms, such as monkeys. In this regard, recent demonstrations that self-injurious behavior occurred in some monkeys following frustration produced by extinction of a lever-pressing response are noteworthy (Gluck & Sackett, 1974).

If self-injurious behavior depends on positive social reinforcement for its maintenance, one would expect that deprivation and satiation of social reinforcement should influence the rate of self-injurious behavior. The small amount of data pertaining to this question is equivocal. Lovaas and Simmons (1969) found that following 1-day periods of either social reinforcer satiation (the child had been given continuous attention) or social reinforcer deprivation (the child had been left alone in his room), no systematic changes in the rate of self-injurious behavior were observed. On the other hand, Lovaas et al. (1965) found that following several sessions of social extinction (a deprivation operation), reinstatement of social attention contingent on self-injurious behavior produced the highest rates of that behavior recorded in their study. This situation presumably arose because the deprivation operation enhanced the potency of the social reinforcement. Perhaps the conflicting results obtained in these two studies were a function of procedural differences. In the Lovaas and Simmons (1969) study, the effects of the deprivation and satiation operations on self-injurious behavior were studied while the child was in isolation. No adult was present. By contrast, in the Lovaas et al. (1965) study, the child's self-injurious behavior was examined while an adult was present. Thus, it may be that the sensitizing effects of the deprivation and/or satiation operations are not apparent unless an adult is present to dispense social reinforcement.

If the positive reinforcement hypothesis has merit, the reinforcement schedule applied to self-injurious behavior might also be expected to influence the rate of this behavior. As a test of this notion, Lovaas et al. (1965) delivered supportive remarks on either a continuous reinforcement schedule (each instance of self-injurious behavior was reinforced) or on a variable-ratio schedule (every fifth instance of self-injurious behavior, on the average, was reinforced). There was some indication that the variable-ratio schedule generated higher rates, but no direct comparisons of the two schedules were made. Other studies have demonstrated that the differential reinforcement of behavior other than self-injurious behavior (i.e., a DRO schedule) can produce a decrement in the rate of self-injurious behavior (Corte et al., 1971; Peterson & Peterson, 1968; Repp, Deitz, & Deitz, 1976; Weiher & Harman, 1975). Weiher and Harman, for example, delivered reinforcement only after a given amount of time had elapsed during which there were no instances of self-injurious behavior. They found that on the DRO schedule, the rate of self-injurious behavior decreased dramatically to negligible levels, a finding that parallels the effects of DRO reported in the animal learning literature (Reynolds, 1961). One possible danger of using a DRO schedule should be noted: This schedule does not specify that a particular, desirable response should be reinforced, but only that reinforcement must be withheld until a given time period has elapsed during which self-injurious behavior has not occurred. Therefore, it is conceivable that on this schedule one could potentially reinforce some other undesirable high-frequency behavior, such as tantrums, a behavior that might well be occurring after the specified DRO time interval has elapsed. The clinician must be wary of this pitfall when using DRO to treat self-injury.

A potential avenue for future research might be to explore the use of differential reinforcement of low rates (DRL) schedules to produce decreases in self-injurious behavior frequency. That is, one might explicitly reinforce only low rates of self-injurious behavior, with the goal of making the behavior occur so infrequently as to be relatively innocuous. This strategy might be particularly desirable when the complete elimination of self-injurious behavior by other means has proven impossible. DRL schedules have already been used successfully to control various classroom misbehaviors in retarded and normal populations (Deitz & Repp, 1973, 1974). Extending the use of DRL schedules to the control of self-injurious behavior would have clear clinical and theoretical significance. Taken as a whole, then, the literature reviewed above does suggest that the rate of self-injurious behavior can be influenced by changes in the reinforcement schedule applied to that behavior. This fact is consistent with the positive reinforcement hypothesis.

There is evidence that the topography of self-injurious behavior, at least in the case of lower organisms, can be shaped by using positive reinforcement (as one might expect if reinforcement were an important controlling variable). Schaefer (1970), for example, successfully shaped head hitting in two rhesus monkeys by using food reinforcement. The only attempt at influencing the topography of self-injurious behavior in humans was reported by Saposnek and Watson (1974). By utilizing positive reinforcement procedures, these investigators were able to shape a child's head slapping into the more benign behavior of slapping the therapist's hands. Of course, hand slapping can be an aggressive behavior and might well become a clinical problem in itself. An alternative tactic that might be clinically useful (as well as providing data on the validity of the positive reinforcement hypothesis) would be to shape the intensity of self-injurious behavior into a low-magnitude and therefore less dangerous response. Herrick (1964) and Notterman and Mintz (1962) have shown that with lower organisms, the intensity of an operant can be shaped by differential reinforcement procedures. Perhaps it might also be possible to alter the intensity of self-injurious behavior, that is, low-intensity self-injurious behavior would be reinforced while high-intensity self-injurious behavior would be subjected to extinction. Such research remains to be done.

In summary, the positive reinforcement hypothesis receives considerable empirical support from studies demonstrating that (a) self-injurious behavior rates can be reduced when social reinforcers are withdrawn, (b) self-injurious behavior rates can be increased when positive reinforcement is made contingent upon the behavior, and (c) self-injurious behavior can come under the control of stimuli in whose presence self-injurious behavior is positively reinforced. Data on the effects of deprivation and satiation variables, reinforcement schedules, and shaping procedures on the rate of self-injurious behavior are equivocal or incomplete. Considerable additional experimentation (possibly utilizing lower organisms when ethically required) therefore remains to be done.

Despite the power of the positive reinforcement hypothesis in accounting for much self-injurious behavior, there remain many instances in which the behavior appears to be a function of different variables. Some of these motivational variables are discussed next.

Negative Reinforcement Hypothesis

This hypothesis states that self-injurious behavior is maintained by the termination or avoidance of an aversive stimulus following the occurrence of a self-injurious act (Carr, Newsom, & Binkoff, 1976). The small amount of literature on this topic centers almost exclusively on the role of escape motivation in the maintenance of self-injurious behavior, and the present discussion therefore focuses on escape factors.

There are several anecdotal reports concerning children who injure themselves, presumably to terminate an aversive situation. Freud and Burlingham (1944, pp. 74–75), for example, described one institutionalized girl who would bang her head against the bars of her crib when put to bed against her wishes. She did so presumably to escape from the crib. Similar cases have been cited by Goodenough (1931, p. 139). More recently, Jones et al. (1974), Myers and Deibert (1971), and Wolf, Risley, Johnston, Harris, and Allen (1967) noted that demands were very likely to set off self-injurious behavior in children. Following such behavior, the adult therapists who were working with the children would typically stop making demands. Reports such as these imply that demands may constitute aversive stimuli and that self-injurious behavior may be an escape response, maintained by the termination of such stimuli. The experimental evidence relevant to this problem is reviewed next.

Carr et al. (1976) demonstrated that levels of self-injurious behavior were high in demand situations (such as a classroom) and low in conversational and free-play situations (which did not contain demands). If demands are aversive stimuli and self-injurious behavior is an escape response, one would expect that (a) self-injurious behavior should cease upon the onset of a stimulus correlated with the termination of demands (i.e., upon the presentation of a so-called safety signal) and (b) self-injurious behavior should, under certain circumstances, show the schedule properties exhibited by other behaviors under aversive control. Both of the above features were observed by Carr et al. First, when the child was presented with the safety signal, "O.K., let's go," a stimulus that normally terminated the classroom (i.e., demand) period, the child abruptly stopped hitting himself. In contrast, when the child was presented with a neutral stimulus such as, "The sky is blue" (a stimulus that was never used to terminate the classroom sessions and therefore could not have become a safety signal), the child's rate of self-injurious behavior remained high. Second, the child's rate of self-injurious behavior during the demand sessions showed a scalloped pattern, that is, the rate gradually increased during the course of a given session. This is the pattern of responding that is generally obtained on fixed-interval schedules of escape with lower organisms (Azrin, Hake, Holz, & Hutchinson, 1965; Hineline & Rachlin, 1969). The scalloping was thought to evolve as follows: Each demand session was of fixed length (10 min.); hitting that occurred at the end of the session would be negatively reinforced, since such hitting would be correlated with the termination of the demands. Conceptually, this situation corresponds to a fixed-interval schedule of escape, a schedule that typically generates a scalloped pattern of responding.

Demands may not be the only aversive stimuli that can function to maintain self-injurious behavior. Ross, Meichenbaum, and Humphrey (1971) reported a case in which an adolescent girl would wake herself up each night, whenever she was having nightmares, by banging her head against the bed. (Oswald, 1964, cited a similar case). Ross et al. assumed that the self-injurious behavior was maintained by the negative reinforcement that resulted from the termination of the aversive dreams. On the basis of this assumption, they proceeded to desensitize their patient to the content of her nightmares and by this procedure were able to eliminate her self-injurious behavior altogether. It should be noted that covert stimuli other than dreams, for example, hallucinations or compulsive thoughts, might also play some role in escape-motivated self-injurious behavior. At present, however, this remains an unresearched area, except for a brief report (Cautela & Baron, 1973) of an individual whose self-injurious behavior was always preceded by a compulsive thought that he must poke or bite himself.

The above studies support the hypothesis that self-injurious behavior can be motivated by escape factors and also suggest several additional studies for future research. First, if the frequency of self-injurious behavior is controlled by the termination of aversive stimuli, one would expect that counterconditioning and desensitization procedures that were applied with respect to such stimuli should reduce the rate of self-injurious behavior. The desensitization study by Ross et al. (1971) was a preliminary test of this notion. In addition, Carr et al. (1976) reported that counterconditioning procedures (e.g., presenting the demand stimuli in the context of a positive, entertaining conversation known to be discriminative for appropriate social behaviors) could also be used to reduce escape-motivated self-injurious behavior. These two studies, though preliminary, suggest that additional research with these procedures might yield effective management techniques. Second, if self-injurious behavior is escape behavior, then it should be possible to eliminate it by ensuring that the occurrence of self-injurious behavior no longer has the consequence of terminating the aversive stimulus. That is, the demands would not be withdrawn as long as the child was engaging in self-injurious behavior. This procedure corresponds to *escape extinction* as reported in the animal literature (Catania, 1968, p. 187). Finally, the notion of self-injurious behavior as escape responding suggests some plausible research that is relevant to the role of restraints in the control of self-injurious behavior. Many children exhibiting self-injurious behavior are put in physical restraints to protect themselves from injury. Removing such a child from restraints usually sets off a bout of self-injurious behavior (e.g., Romanczyk & Goren, 1975; Tate, 1972). It is plausible that restraints could, over time, become a safety signal for such children, indicating that few or no demands will be placed on them. Typically, a child in restraints is allowed to lie passively, spread-eagled on a bed, or to sit alone, hands bound. Although such a child is unlikely to receive much social reinforcement, the social isolation is, in a sense, more than compensated for by the absence of even the most minimal demands. It is only when demands need to be made on the child (e.g., the child must be fed, clothes must be changed, or he must be taken to the washroom) that the child is taken out of restraints. An important research problem, with clear treatment implications, centers on the question of whether the safety signal value of the restraints could be altered by making them discriminative for high levels of demands. That is, as long as the child is restrained, he would be showered with demands; when unrestrained, he would be permitted to sit or lie passively, free to do anything he wished. Under this condition, one might predict that the restraints should lose their positive value. The above three questions, though not exhausting the research possibilities relevant to the negative reinforcement hypothesis, would provide some significant tests of such a hypothesis.

Self-Stimulation Hypothesis

This hypothesis holds that a certain level of stimulation, particularly in the tactile, vestibular, and kinesthetic modalities, is necessary for the organism, and that, when such stimulation occurs at an insufficient level, the organism may engage in stereotyped behaviors, including self-injurious behavior, as a means of providing sensory stimulation (Baumeister & Forehand, 1973; Cain, 1961; Cleland & Clark, 1966; Green, 1967, 1968; Kulka, Fry, & Goldstein, 1960; Lourie, 1949; Rutter, 1966, p. 80; Silberstein, Blackman, & Mandell, 1966). Kulka et al. (1960) postulated the existence of a kinesthetic drive and on this basis predicted that overrestriction of motoric acitivity would result in self-injurious behavior. In support of this prediction, Levy (1944) noted several cases of head banging among institutionalized orphans who were restricted to their cribs without toys. When the infants were given toys to play with, self-injurious behavior disappeared, presumably because of the increased tactile and kinesthetic stimulation. Similarly, Dennis and Najarian (1957), working with a group of institutionalized orphans left to lie alone in their cribs because of understaffing, observed self-injurious behavior, such as self-slapping, in several children and attributed such behavior to "stimulation hunger" (p. 11). Collins (1965) reported head banging in a restrained, isolated, retarded adult. Treatment consisted of exposing the adult to a great deal of sensory stimulation in the form of toys, activity, and radio. The consequent elimination of self-injurious behavior was attributed to the increase in tactile and kinesthetic stimulation during treatment. De Lissovoy (1962) and Kravitz, Rosenthal, Teplitz, Murphy, and Lesser (1960) noted that the normal young children in their sample banged their heads primarily at bedtime, before falling asleep. To the extent that lying in bed in a dark room, alone, and without anything to do, represents a state of diminished stimulation, the above observations are consistent with the self-stimulation hypothesis. The studies cited thus far, though suggestive, are limited by the fact that they are based solely on anecdotal or correlational accounts. The experimental evidence bearing on the self-stimulation hypothesis provides a more meaningful test and is reviewed next.

Some of the more interesting data relating to the hypothesized self-stimulatory nature of self-injurious behavior come from the animal analogue experiments conducted by Harlow and his associates (Cross & Harlow, 1965; Harlow & Griffin, 1965; Harlow & Harlow, 1962, 1971). Monkeys were studied under two rearing conditions. One group was reared with their mothers, in a playpen situation in which other young monkeys were also present. A second group was reared in partial social isolation. They could see and hear other monkeys but could not make physical contact with them. They were thus deprived of the opportunity to play with their peers and to cuddle with their mothers. In addition, they were raised in small cages and thus had limited opportunity to move around. The typical finding was that many of the partially isolated monkeys engaged in a variety of repetitive, stereotyped acts, such as rocking, cage circling, staring into space, and most importantly, self-injurious behavior in the form of self-biting. Monkeys reared with their mothers in the playpen situation rarely exhibited such behaviors. One interpretation fo the anomalous behaviors is that the cage-reared isolates, being deprived of tactile and kinesthetic stimulation, generated their own stimulation through self-injurious behavior and other repetitive, stereotyped behaviors.

An implication of the self-stimulatory hypothesis, supported by the animal literature cited above, is that a barren unstimulating environment would be much more conducive to the maintenance of self-injurious behavior and other stereotyped behaviors than would an environment that provided opportunities for stimulation in the form of play activities. Several studies with mental retardates are relevant to evaluating this implication. Berkson and Mason (1964) studied the stereotyped behaviors (e.g., head banging, rocking, and complex hand movements) of mental retardates under two conditions. In the no-objects condition, the subject was brought into a room, barren except for an observer, and his behavior was recorded for a period of 400 sec. The objects condition was identical with the preceding, except that several objects (e.g., a rubber ball, plastic train, string, furry toy dog) were left lying on the floor of the room. Stereotyped behaviors (including head banging) occurred at a higher level in the no-objects condition than in the objects condition. Furthermore, there was a negative correlation between frequency of object manipulation and frequency of stereotyped behaviors. This negative correlation, which has been found in several other studies as well (Berkson & Davenport, 1962; Berkson & Mason, 1963; Davenport & Berkson, 1963), led Berkson (1967) to conclude that such stereotyped behaviors may be self-stimulatory in nature, occurring primarily in the absence of adequate stimulation. When adequate stimulation is provided (e.g., in the form of play activities), the stereotyped behaviors are no longer required as a source of stimulation, and disappear.

The self-stimulation hypothesis is, on occasion, evoked as an explanation of self-injurious behavior when no other explanation is available. It should be clear that this argument by exclusion does little to advance our understanding. An adequate evaluation of the self-stimulation hypothesis must take into consideration several methodological problems inherent in the above research. First, the data on self-injurious behavior were typically grouped together with the data on other stereotyped behaviors, and we therefore do not know how self-injurious behavior per se changed as a function of the different experimental conditions. In the few studies in which data on self-injurious behavior have been reported separately from data on other stereotyped behaviors (Hollis, 1965a, 1965b), the frequency of self-injurious behavior did not change as a function of the different conditions of stimulation. We cannot be certain whether or not this relationship was also obtained in the other studies noted above. Second, in all of the reported studies, only group data on self-injurious behavior were presented, and we therefore do not know how an individual subject's self-injurious behavior changed across stimulus conditions. Third, the self-stimulation hypothesis is particularly open to the criticism of circularity. If a subject is engaging in self-injurious behavior, there is said to be a lack of adequate stimulation, but if the subject is not engaging in self-injurious behavior, the amount of stimulation is said to be adequate. One way out of this tautology is to define adequate stimulation in terms of the physical parameters of the stimulus rather than in terms of the occurrence or nonoccurrence of self-injurious behavior.

Myerson, Kerr, and Michael (1967), for example, studied the effects of vibration (as a source of sensory stimulation) on the level of self-injurious behavior of their autistic patient. They suggested that the child engaged in self-injurious behavior because he was deprived of tactile stimulation. They reasoned that if an alternative form of tactile stimulation (such as vibration) were provided, self-injurious behavior would decrease. There was some indication that the sensory stimulation that they used decreased the duration of self-injurious behavior from what it was at baseline, but their results were inconclusive because they ran only two treatment sessions. The study is noteworthy, however, in that the authors defined the level of sensory stimulation provided in physical terms (i.e., the amount of vibratory stimulation), as opposed to inferring the level of stimulation from the level of self-injurious behavior. Finally, in many of the reported studies, social attention from adults was introduced simultaneously with toys and other sources of physical stimulation. Such a procedure, of course, confounds the effects of social reinforcement with the effects of sensory reinforcement. These two sources of reinforcement must be separated for an adequate test of the self-stimulation hypothesis.

The review of the literature thus suggests that future research should (a) stress the measurement of self-injurious behavior independently of other stereotyped behaviors, (b) attempt to present data on individual subjects rather than continuing to report only group means, (c) specify the level of sensory stimulation provided in terms of physical parameters, and (d) separate social reinforcement effects from sensory reinforcement effects. Until such research is carried out, the self-stimulation hypothesis of self-injurious behavior remains plausible but untested.

Organic Hypothesis

The organic hypothesis states that self-injurious behavior is the product of aberrant physiological processes. Available evidence implicates either a genetically produced aberration (as in the Lesch-Nyhan and de Lange syndromes) or a nongenetic aberration (possibly involving elevated pain thresholds or such medical problems as otitis media, a middle ear infection). Data bearing on each of these conditions are reviewed next.

Lesch-Nyhan syndrome is a rare form of cerebral palsy that is X linked and found only in males (Nyhan, Pesek, Sweetman, Carpenter, & Carter, 1967; Seegmiller, 1972). The syndrome results from a genetic flaw in purine metabolism that results in a deficiency of the enzyme hypoxanthine–guanine phosphoribosyltransferase. Manifestations of the disease include muscle spasticity, choreoathetosis, mental retardation, and hyperuricemia (Lesch & Nyhan, 1964). More pertinent to the present review is the observation that self-injurious behavior is also part of the syndrome and almost invariably takes the form of compulsive, repetitive biting of the tongue, lips, and fingers (Dizmang & Cheatham, 1970; Hoefnagel, 1965; Hoefnagel, Andrew, Mireault, & Berndt, 1965; Lesch & Nyhan, 1964; Nyhan, Oliver, & Lesch, 1965; Nyhan, Pesek, Sweetman, Carpenter, & Carter, 1967; Seegmiller, Rosenbloom, & Kelley, 1967). Because of the homogeneity of symptoms across cases, it has been proposed that the self-injurious behavior is directly produced by the specific biochemical abnormality (Seegmiller, 1972; Seegmiller et al., 1967). On this basis, one might expect that a chemical cure would be possible. In support of this viewpoint is a recent report (Mizuno & Yugari, 1975) of the apparently successful elimination of self-injurious behavior in Lesch-Nyhan disease with L-5-hydroxytryptophan. Unfortunately, the report had several methodological flaws: There was no measurement of interobserver reliability, the recording procedure was inadequately specified, and the nurses who acted as observers were not blind to the drug condition in effect. Further, there was considerable variability in the frequency of self-injurious behavior during the treatment intervention. Finally, Nyhan (1976) reported discouraging results using L-5-hydroxytryptophan to control self-injurious behavior. More promising results were obtained using a combination of carbidopa and L-5-hydroxytryptophan, but no systematic data were presented. Successful treatment using the combination of drugs would tend to support the organic hypothesis.

Also relevant to the organic hypothesis is a proposal by Hoefnagel (1965) that the proximal cause of self-injurious behavior in the Lesch-Nyhan syndrome may be the irritation produced by an elevated uric acid level in the saliva, a fact that might explain why the self-injurious behavior is directed to the area of the mouth. Hoefnagel's hypothesis seems unlikely, however, in light of data demonstrating that prevention of elevated uric acid levels through early administration of allopurinol did not block the eventual appearance of self-injurious behavior (Marks, Baum, Keele, Kay, & MacFarlen, 1968).

Several lines of evidence mitigate against a purely organic explanation of the motivation of self-injurious behavior. First, there are reports that self-injurious behavior may be lacking altogether in Lesch-Nyhan (Nyhan, 1968; Seegmiller, 1969, 1972) or that it may take atypical forms, such as head banging or eye gouging (Dizmang & Cheatham, 1970; Duker, 1975; Hoefnagel et al., 1965). Second, operant treatment techniques such as extinction, time-out, and differential reinforcement of behavior other than self-mutilation can be effective in eliminating the self-injurious behavior (Duker, 1975; Anderson & Herrmann, Note 2). One would not expect such procedures to be effective if self-injurious behavior were directly controlled by a biochemical abnormality. Finally, there are observational reports that self-injurious behavior can be brought under stimulus control, becoming more likely in the presence of certain adults (Duker, 1975; Anderson &

Herrmann, Note 2). These authors intimated that the children learned to mutilate themselves more frequently in the presence of adults who attended to such behavior. The organic hypothesis would have predicted that, since self-injurious behavior is biochemically determined, its occurrence should therefore be relatively independent of external stimulus conditions. It is possible, of course, that a behavior can be brought under stimulus control and yet still have organic involvement. Nevertheless, these observations on stimulus control, if verified experimentally, would be significant insofar as they are consistent with the other evidence cited above, evidence that suggests that self-injurious behavior, even in Lesch-Nyhan syndrome, may have an operant component.

Another organic condition, of possibly genetic origin (Jervis & Stimson, 1963) and involving self-injurious behavior (Bryson, Sakati, Nyhan, & Fish, 1971), is the de Lange syndrome. The self-injurious behavior in the two cases reported by Shear, Nyhan, Kirman, and Stern (1971) took the form of self-scratching and biting of the fingers, lips, shoulders, and knees. One child could dislocate his hips while standing. Shear et al. (1971) reported that for one of the children, an operant therapy program including aversive stimulation was useful in controlling the self-injurious behavior. On this basis, it seems again unlikely that self-injurious behavior is simply the product of aberrant physiological processes.

Several reports in the literature have described an association between self-injurious behavior and certain other problem conditions. Goldfarb (1958), for example, reported on the pain reactions of 31 schizophrenic children observed over a 1- to 3-year period. Twenty-three of the children showed aberrant pain reactions (e.g., failing to show defensive behavior when a finger was caught in the door and bleeding). Seven of the children also exhibited self-injurious behavior with no evidence of apparent pain behavior. One child would bite his hand until it bled and another mutilated his hand using scissors, but neither child gave any indication of a pain reaction. It was suggested that perhaps such children had elevated pain thresholds. This hypothesis seems unlikely in view of the fact that the children's pain reactions to a pin prick test were normal. Also, it is clear that even if such children have elevated pain thresholds, that fact alone would not explain what motivates self-injurious behavior, but only why there is an absence of pain reaction.

A study involving nongenetic organic pathology was carried out by de Lissovoy (1963). He compared the incidence of painful middle ear infection (otitis media) in a group of 15 head bangers with that in a control group (matched for age, sex, etc.) of 15 children who did not engage in self-injurious behavior. There was a higher incidence of otitis in the headbanger group (6 out of 15) than in the control group (1 out of 15). De Lissovoy (1963, 1964) concluded that head-banging was a form of pain relief. The data are difficult to interpret, however, because the question remains as to why nine of the children in the head-banger group, who did not have otitis, banged their heads anyway. Despite this difficulty, a recent study of self-mutilation in mice lends some credibility to de Lissovoy's hypothesis. Harkness and Wagner (1975) found that many mice in their colony produced severe head lacerations as a result of self-scratching. They discovered that all mice engaging in such behavior suffered from otitis media. The interpretation was somewhat complicated by the fact that some additional mice who had otitis did not mutilate themselves. The authors suggested that self-injurious behavior was most likely to occur when the otitis was severe enough to inflame sensory nerve fibers. Such inflammation acted as a painful stimulus that elicited self-injurious behavior, a behavior that functioned as a form of pain relief. Parenthetically, it might be noted that this suggestion, if verified by further research, would lend additional support to the negative reinforcement hypothesis discussed above. This study also serves to emphasize the utility of animal research in testing hypotheses concerning the motivation of self-injurious behavior.

Taken as a whole, the evidence reviewed above indicates that self-injurious behavior is sometimes correlated with a number of conditions of demonstrated or plausible organic origin. The available studies on humans have suffered from too heavy a reliance on subjective, anecdotal, or retrospective accounts. There have been no conclusive demonstrations of a causal relationship between organic pathology and self-injurious behavior. Where systematic observations have been made, the evidence suggests that self-injurious behavior may be an operant. Adequate experimental analyses of self-injurious behavior that is correlated with organic conditions have yet to be made. Perhaps when they are made, the organic pathology may turn out to be a contributing factor to the initial development of self-injurious behavior, a behavior that, at a still later period in its development, is maintained by social reinforcement in the form of adult attention.

Psychodynamic Hypotheses

A number of hypotheses concerning the motivation of self-injurious behavior can best be grouped together under the term psychodynamic. Several theorists, for example, have suggested that some individuals have difficulty in distinguishing the self from the external world (Hartmann, Kris, & Loewenstein, 1949) and that self-injurious behavior arises as an attempt to establish "body reality" (Greenacre, 1954, p. 38) or to trace the "ego boundaries" (Bychowski, 1954, p. 67). No attempt is made here to review such viewpoints in depth. The interested reader can consult Cain (1961) for a review of the psychoanalytic literature on self-injurious behavior. The major problem with such theories lies in the difficulty of operationalizing constructs such as "body reality" or "ego boundaries." This difficulty might account for the lack of empirical tests of these hypotheses. One exception to this lack of testing comes from a study by Lovaas et al. (1965) that sought to evaluate the psychodynamic hypothesis that individuals attempt to alleviate their guilt through self-injury (Beres, 1952; Frankl, 1963). Lovaas et al. (1965) reasoned that on the basis of the guilt hypothesis, it should be possible to reduce self-injurious behavior by making guilt-alleviating statements such as, "I don't think you're bad," each time that the child hit herself. What they found, however, was that such statements actually increased the frequency of self-injurious behavior, a fact that suggests that the comments were functioning as social reinforcers. The guilt hypothesis would thus seem to be disconfirmed. Of course, it could be argued that such statements as those mentioned above are not adequate to alleviate guilt. Such arguments, however, only serve to emphasize the difficulties inherent in operationalizing constructs such as guilt or guilt alleviation. Until some consensus can be reached on how best to operationalize these constructs, empirical testing of psychodynamic hypotheses remains all but impossible. In the absence of such tests, the utility of these hypotheses in understanding the motivation of self-injurious behavior is moot.

Treatment Implications

This review of the literature on self-injurious behavior suggests that such behavior is multiply determined, that is, it seems unlikely that a single factor is responsible for the motivation of all self-injurious behavior. Instead, one could profitably make a distinction between two broad sets of motivational factors underlying the maintenance of self-injurious behavior. On the one hand, there are several forms of *extrinsic reinforcement* for the behavior. Both social and negative reinforcement, as described in this article, are examples of extrinsic reinforcement. The occurrence or nonoccurrence of such reinforcers are controlled by individuals other than the client. On the other hand, there are several forms of *intrinsic reinforcement* for self-injurious behavior. Specifically, the self-stimulation and organic hypotheses seem to imply that the source of reinforcement for self-injurious behavior may be inherent in the behavior itself. Individuals other than the client himself cannot directly control the occurrence of such sources of reinforcement.

The dichotomy between extrinsically and intrinsically motivated self-injurious behavior has several important treatment implications. First, to the extent that self-injurious behavior appears to be extrinsically motivated, treatment would consist largely of redefining the contingencies of reinforcement. For example, if the self-injurious behavior is being maintained by social reinforcement, then one might expect that techniques such as extinction or time-out would be effective, in that these techniques result in a removal of the social reinforcers maintaining the behavior (Hamilton et al., 1967; Lovaas & Simmons, 1969). These same techniques, however, should be ineffective in dealing with intrinsically motivated self-injurious behavior, for which the maintaining variables are presumably biochemical or sensory. As a further example, if the self-injurious behavior is an escape behavior in response to demands, the treatment would again consist of redefining the reinforcement contingencies, in this case, so that the client would not be permitted to escape from demands simply by engaging in self-injurious behavior (Carr et al., 1976). In this manner, the extrinsic negative reinforcement resulting from escape would be terminated.

Whereas the treatment strategy for dealing with extrinsically motivated self-injurious behavior would center largely on redefining the contingencies of reinforcement as described above, the strategy for dealing with intrinsically motivated self-injurious behavior would consist of an attempt to negate or attenuate the reinforcers themselves. Thus, if it is thought that a child is injuring himself in an attempt to reduce the pain inherent in a middle ear infection (otitis media), one might expect that a direct medical intervention designed to cure the infection and thereby attenuate the pain should result in a decrease in self-injurious behavior. Sometimes, of course, it is not possible to attenuate the reinforcers for self-injurious behavior. For example, some children might be hitting themselves to generate tactile and kinesthetic stimulation (Berkson, 1967). A technology does not currently exist for attenuating the reinforcement inherent in such stimulation. In such cases, the therapist could consider an alternative tactic, one that would involve providing reinforcers to compete with the reinforcers maintaining the self-injurious behavior. The use of toys as a source of competing tactile and kinesthetic reinforcement has been explored by Berkson and Mason (1964). Presumably, toys might be effective in two ways: first, by providing a competing source of reinforcement, and second, by setting the occasion for play behaviors that compete with the occurrence of the self-injurious behavior itself.

Clearly, the treatment issues described above are complex, but the present review of the literature does suggest a plausible sequence of steps that the clinician may wish to follow in determining the possible motivation (and therefore the treatment) of self-injurious behavior. Table 1 lists the screening sequence. As the psychodynamic hypotheses do not currently rest on a firm data base, they have not been included in the table.

The outlined screening procedure is by no means definitive, but it does reflect our current, rudimentary state of knowledge. As a guide for assessment, it should provide a useful beginning and a basis for deciding which treatment procedures might be appropriate. Reviews of some current treat-

Table 1
*A Screening Sequence to Determine the
Motivation of Self-Injurious Behavior*

Step 1

Screen for genetic abnormalities (e.g., Lesch-Nyhan
and de Lange syndromes), particularly if lip,
finger, or tongue biting is present.
Screen for nongenetic abnormalities (e.g., otitis
media), particularly if head banging is present.
If screening is positive, motivation may be organic.
If Step 1 is negative, proceed to Step 2.

Step 2

Does self-injurious behavior increase under one or
more of the following circumstances:
(a) When the behavior is attended to?
(b) When reinforcers are withdrawn for behaviors
other than self-injurious behavior?
(c) When the child is in the company of adults
(rather than alone)?
If yes, motivation may be positive reinforcement.
Does self-injurious behavior occur primarily when
demands or other aversive stimuli are presented?
If yes, motivation may be negative reinforcement.
If Step 2 is negative, proceed to Step 3.

Step 3

Does self-injurious behavior occur primarily when
there are no activities available and/or the environment is barren?
If yes, motivation may be self-stimulation.

---

ment interventions for dealing with self-injurious behavior have been provided by Azrin, Gottlieb, Hughart, Wesolowski, and Rahn (1975), Bachman
(1972), Frankel and Simmons (1976), Seegmiller (1976), and Smolev (1971).

Summary and Evaluation

This review has suggested the possibility that self-injurious behavior may
be multiply determined. One important direction for future research would
seem to center on the question of what, if any, are the relationships between
the different motivational sources of self-injurious behavior. De Lissovoy
(1962, 1963, 1964) observed that a large percentage of head bangers had,
early in life, engaged in certain rhythmical activities such as rocking and head
rolling. Green (1967) hypothesized that during the course of such activities,
the infant might accidentally strike his head. In this manner, the sensory
stimulation of rocking, for example, would become associated with self-in-

jurious behavior, endowing the latter with self-stimulatory properties. However, as Green noted, other factors soon come into play: Parents observing the head banging are likely to attend to the child. Over time, the behavior may come under the control of social stimuli and the associated positive reinforcement (i.e., adult attention). Empirical studies should be carried out to determine if such sequential relationships, as described above, do indeed exist between the various motivational sources of self-injurious behavior.

Yet another example implying a sequential progression is that concerning the organic control of self-injurious behavior. Children suffering from the Lesch-Nyhan syndrome may, at least initially, mutilate their fingers and lips as part of a reaction to a biochemical abnormality (Seegmiller, 1972). In time, however, such behavior evokes much attention from parents and nursing staff. At this point, the behavior may be, at least partially, under social control (Dizmang & Cheatham, 1970; Duker, 1975; Anderson & Herrmann, Note 2). Again, a sequential relationship among the different sources of motivation is intimated. Developmental studies, now lacking, could provide information on such relationships.

Research into the motivation of self-injurious behavior could also profit from an increased use of animal analogue experiments. Such studies avoid the ethical problems stemming from human experimentation and at the same time provide useful information on motivational hypotheses. A start has already been made in this direction. For example, head banging in monkeys has been shaped, brought under stimulus control, and extinguished using operant conditioning procedures (Schaefer, 1970). Pigeons have been taught to peck a key in order to receive mild punishment, provided that such punishment has, in the past, been correlated with food reinforcement (Holz & Azrin, 1961). (Here, the analogy to humans is clear: Perhaps some individuals engage in self-injurious behavior because such behavior has, at one time, been correlated with positive reinforcement.) Frustration in monkeys (Gluck & Sackett, 1974) and certain organic factors in mice (Harkness & Wagner, 1975) have been demonstrated to be potentially important in the control of self-injurious behavior. Finally, a number of bizarre and stereotyped behaviors (including self-injurious behavior) have been observed in monkeys who have had a history of prolonged social and sensory isolation (Cross & Harlow, 1965; Harlow & Harlow, 1971). It should be possible to manipulate positive reinforcement variables, level of sensory stimulation, and length of social deprivation, as well as organic and frustrative factors, to study the effects of each of these variables on the frequency, intensity, and topography of self-injurious behavior in lower organisms. The results of such studies could help to form a basis for assessing the validity of the various hypotheses pertaining to the motivation of self-injurious behavior and thereby bring us closer to eradicating this dangerous form of human psychopathology.

Reference Notes

1. Hitzing, E. W., & Risley, T. *Elimination of self-destructive behavior in a retarded girl by noxious stimulation.* Paper presented at the meeting of the Southwestern Psychological Association, Houston, April 1967.
2. Anderson, L. T., & Herrmann, L. *Lesch-Nyhan disease: A specific learning disability.* Paper presented at the meeting of the Association for the Advancement of Behavior Therapy, San Francisco, December 1975.

REFERENCES

Azrin, N. H., Gottlieb, L., Hughart, L., Wesolowski, M. D., & Rahn, T. Eliminating self-injurious behavior by educative procedures. *Behavior Research and Therapy*, 1975, *13*, 101–111.

Azrin, N. H., Hake, D. F., Holz, W. C., & Hutchinson, R. R. Motivational aspects of escape from punishment. *Journal of the Experimental Analysis of Behavior*, 1965, *8*, 31–44.

Azrin, N. H., Hutchinson, R. R., & Hake, D. F. Extinction-induced aggression. *Journal of the Experimental Analysis of Behavior*, 1966, *9*, 191–204.

Bachman, J. A. Self-injurious behavior: A behavioral analysis. *Journal of Abnormal Psychology*, 1972, *80*, 211–224.

Baumeister, A. A., & Forehand, R. Stereotyped acts. In N. R. Ellis (Ed.), *International review of research in mental retardation* (Vol. 6). New York: Academic Press, 1973.

Beres, D. Clinical notes on aggression in children. In R. S. Eissler (Ed.), *The psychoanalytic study of the child* (Vol. 7). New York: International Universities Press, 1952.

Berkson, G. Abnormal stereotyped motor acts. In J. Zubin & H. F. Hunt (Eds.), *Comparative psychopathology—Animal and human.* New York: Grune & Stratton, 1967.

Berkson, G., & Davenport, R. K. Stereotyped movements of mental defectives: I. Initial survey. *American Journal of Mental Deficiency*, 1962, *66*, 849–852.

Berkson, G., & Mason, W. A. Stereotyped movements of mental defectives: III. Situation effects. *American Journal of Mental Deficiency*, 1963, *68*, 409–412.

Berkson, G., & Mason, W. A. Stereotyped movements of mental defectives: IV. The effects of toys and the character of the acts. *American Journal of Mental Deficiency*, 1964, *68*, 511–524.

Bryson, Y., Sakati, N., Nyhan, W. L., & Fish, C. H. Self-mutilative behavior in the Cornelia de Lange syndrome. *American Journal of Mental Deficiency*, 1971, *76*, 319–324.

Bucher, B., & Lovaas, O. I. Use of aversive stimulation in behavior modification. In M. Jones (Ed.). *Miami Symposium on the Prediction of Behavior, 1967: Aversive stimulation.* Coral Gables, Fla.: University of Miami Press, 1968.

Bychowski, G. Problems of infantile neurosis: A discussion. In R. S. Eissler (Ed.), *The psychoanalytic study of the child* (Vol. 9). New York: International Universities Press, 1954.

Cain, A. C. The presuperego turning inward of aggression. *Psychoanalytic Quarterly*, 1961, *30*, 171–208.

Carr, E. G., Newsom, C. D., & Binkoff, J. A. Stimulus control of self-destructive behavior in a psychotic child. *Journal of Abnormal Child Psychology*, 1976, *4*, 139–153.

Catania, A. C. (Ed.). *Contemporary research in operant behavior*. Glenview, Ill.: Scott, Foresman, 1968.

Cautela, J. R., & Baron, M. G. Multifaceted behavior therapy of self-injurious behavior. *Journal of Behavior Therapy and Experimental Psychiatry*, 1973, *4*, 125–131.

Cleland, C. C., & Clark, C. M. Sensory deprivation and aberrant behavior among idiots. *American Journal of Mental Deficiency*, 1966, *71*, 213–225.

Collins, D. T. Head-banging: Its meaning and management in the severely retarded adult. *Bulletin of the Menninger Clinic*, 1965, *4*, 205–211.

Corte, H. E, Wolf, M. M., & Locke, B. J. A comparison of procedures for eliminating self-injurious behavior of retarded adolescents. *Journal of Applied Behavior Analysis*, 1971, *4*, 201–213.

Cross, H. A., & Harlow, H. F. Prolonged and progressive effects of partial isolation on the behavior of Macaque monkeys. *Journal of Experimental Research in Personality*, 1965, *1*, 39–49.

Davenport, R. K., & Berkson, G. Stereotyped movements of mental defectives: II. Effects of novel objects. *American Journal of Mental Deficiency*, 1963, *67*, 879–882.

Deitz, S. M., & Repp, A. C. Decreasing classroom misbehavior through the use of DRL schedules of reinforcement. *Journal of Applied Behavior Analysis*, 1973, *6*, 457–463.

Deitz, S. M., & Repp, A. C. Differentially reinforcing low rates of misbehavior with normal elementary school children. *Journal of Applied Behavior Analysis*, 1974, *7*, 622. (Abstract)

de Lissovoy, V. Head banging in early childhood. *Journal of Pediatrics*, 1961, *58*, 803–805.

de Lissovoy, V. Head banging in early childhood. *Child Development*, 1962, *33*, 43–56.

de Lissovoy, V. Head banging in early childhood: A suggested cause. *Journal of Genetic Psychology*, 1963, *102*, 109–114.

de Lissovoy, V. Head banging in early childhood: Review of empirical studies. *Pediatrics Digest*, 1964, *6*, 49–55.

Dennis, W., & Najarian, P. Infant development under environmental handicap. *Psychological Monographs*, 1957, *71*(7, Whole No. 436).

Dizmang, L. H., & Cheatham, C. F. The Lesch-Nyhan syndrome. *American Journal of Psychiatry*, 1970, *127*, 671–677.

Dollard, J., Miller, N. E., Doob, L. W., Mowrer, O. H., & Sears, R. R. *Frustration and aggression*. New Haven: Yale University Press, 1939.

Duker, P. Behavior control of self-biting in a Lesch-Nyhan patient. *Journal of Mental Deficiency Research*, 1975, *19*, 11–19.

Ferster, C. B. Positive reinforcement and behavioral deficits of autistic children. *Child Development*, 1961, *32*, 437–456.

Frankel, F., & Simmons, J. Q. Self-injurious behavior in schizophrenic and retarded children. *American Journal of Mental Deficiency*, 1976, *80*, 512–522.

Frankl, L. Self-preservation and the development of accident proneness in children and adolescents. In R. S. Eissler (Ed.), *The psychoanalytic study of the child* (Vol. 18). New York: International Universities Press, 1963.

Freud, A., & Burlingham, D. T. *Infants without families.* New York: International Universities Press, 1944.

Gluck, J. P., & Sackett, G. P. Frustration and self-aggression in social isolate rhesus monkeys. *Journal of Abnormal Psychology,* 1974, *83,* 331–334.

Goldfarb, W. Pain reactions in a group of institutionalized schizophrenic children. *American Journal of Orthopsychiatry,* 1958, *28,* 777–785.

Goodenough, F. *Anger in young children.* Minneapolis: University of Minnesota Press, 1931.

Green, A. H. Self-mutilation in schizophrenic children. *Archives of General Psychiatry,* 1967, *17,* 234–244.

Green, A. H. Self-destructive behavior in physically abused schizophrenic children. *Archives of General Psychiatry,* 1968, *19,* 171–179.

Greenacre, P. Problems of infantile neurosis: A discussion. In R. S. Eissler (Ed.), *The psychoanalytic study of the child* (Vol. 9). New York: International Universities Press, 1954.

Hamilton, J., Stephens, L., & Allen, P. Controlling aggressive and destructive behavior in severely retarded institutionalized residents. *American Journal of Mental Deficiency,* 1967, *71,* 852–856.

Harkness, J. E., & Wagner, J. E. Self-mutilation in mice associated with otitis media. *Laboratory Animal Science,* 1975, *25,* 315–318.

Harlow, H. F., & Griffin, G. Induced mental and social deficits in rhesus monkeys. In S. F. Osler & R. E. Cooke (Eds.), *The biosocial basis of mental retardation.* Baltimore, Md.: Johns Hopkins Press, 1965.

Harlow, H. F., & Harlow, M. K. Social deprivation in monkeys. *Scientific American,* 1962, *207*(5), 136–146.

Harlow, H. F., & Harlow, M. K. Psychopathology in monkeys. In H. D. Kimmel (Ed.), *Experimental psychopathology.* New York: Academic Press, 1971.

Hartmann, H., Kris, E., & Loewenstein, R. M. Notes on the theory of aggression. In R. S. Eissler (Ed.), *The psychoanalytic study of the child* (Vols. 3 and 4). New York: International Universities Press, 1949.

Herrick, R. M. The successive differentiation of a lever displacement response. *Journal of the Experimental Analysis of Behavior,* 1964, *7,* 211–215.

Hineline, P. N., & Rachlin, H. Notes on fixed-ratio and fixed-interval escape responding in the pigeon. *Journal of the Experimental Analysis of Behavior,* 1969, *12,* 397–401.

Hoefnagel, D. The syndrome of athetoid cerebral palsy, mental deficiency, self-mutilation, and hyperuricemia. *Journal of Mental Deficiency Research,* 1965, *9,* 69–74.

Hoefnagel, D., Andrew, E. D., Mireault, N. G., & Berndt, W. O. Hereditary choreoathetosis, self-mutilation, and hyperuricemia in young males. *New England Journal of Medicine,* 1965, *273,* 130–135.

Hollis, J. H. The effects of social and nonsocial stimuli on the behavior of profoundly retarded children: Part I. *American Journal of Mental Deficiency,* 1965, *69,* 755–771. (a)

Hollis, J. H. The effects of social and nonsocial stimuli on the behavior of profoundly retarded children: Part II. *American Journal of Mental Deficiency,* 1965, *69,* 772–789. (b)

Holz, W. C., & Azrin, N. H. Discriminative properties of punishment. *Journal of the Experimental Analysis of Behavior*, 1961, *4*, 225–232.

Ilg, F. L., & Ames, L. B. *Child behavior.* New York: Harper, 1955.

Jervis, G. A., & Stimson, C. W. De Lange syndrome. *Journal of Pediatrics*, 1963, *63, 634–645*.

Jones, F. H., Simmons, J. Q., & Frankel, F. An extinction procedure for eliminating self-destructive behavior in a 9-year-old autistic girl. *Journal of Autism and Childhood Schizophrenia*, 1974, *4*, 241–250.

Kravitz, H., Rosenthal, V., Teplitz, Z., Murphy, J. B., & Lesser, R. E. A study of head-banging in infants and children, *Diseases of the Nervous System*, 1960, *21*, 203–208.

Kulka, A., Fry, C., & Goldstein, F. J. Kinesthetic needs in infancy. *American Journal of Orthopsychiatry*, 1960, *30*, 562–571.

Lesch, M., & Nyhan, W. L. A familial disorder of uric acid metabolism and central nervous system function. *American Journal of Medicine*, 1964, *36*, 561–570.

Levy, D. M. On the problem of movement restraint: Tics, stereotyped movements, and hyperactivity. *American Journal of Orthopsychiatry*, 1944, *14*, 644–671.

Lourie, R. M. The role of rhythmic patterns in childhood. *American Journal of Psychiatry*, 1949, *105*, 653–660.

Lovaas, O. I., Freitag, G., Gold, V. J., & Kassorla, I. C. Experimental studies in childhood schizophrenia: I. Analysis of self-destructive behavior. *Journal of Experimental Child Psychology*, 1965, *2*, 67–84.

Lovaas, O. I., & Simmons, J. Q. Manipulation of self-destruction in three retarded children. *Journal of Applied Behavior Analysis*, 1969, *2*, 143–157.

Marks, J. F., Baum, J., Keele, D. K., Kay, J. L., & MacFarlen, A. Lesch-Nyhan syndrome treated from the early neonatal period. *Pediatrics*, 1968, *42*, 357–359.

Mizuno, T., & Yugari, Y. Prophylactic effect of L-5-hydroxytryptophan on self-mutilation in the Lesch-Nyhan syndrome. *Neuropaediatrie*, 1975, *6*, 13–23.

Myers, J. J., & Deibert, A. N. Reduction of self-abusive behavior in a blind child by using a feeding response. *Journal of Behavior Therapy and Experimental Psychiatry*, 1971, *2*, 141–144.

Myerson, L., Kerr, N., & Michael, J. L. Behavior modification in rehabilitation. In S. W. Bijou & D. M. Baer (Eds.), *Child development: Readings in experimental analysis.* New York: Appleton-Century-Crofts, 1967.

Notterman, J. M., & Mintz, D. E. Exteroceptive cueing of response force. *Science*, 1962, *135*, 1070–1071.

Nyhan, W. L. Lesch-Nyhan syndrome: Summary of clinical features. *Federation Proceedings*, 1968, *27*, 1034–1041.

Nyhan, W. L. Behavior in the Lesch-Nyhan syndrome. *Journal of Autism and Childhood Schizophrenia*, 1976, *6*, 235–252.

Nyhan, W. L., Oliver, W. J., & Lesch, M. A familial disorder of uric acid metabolism and central nervous system function: II. *Journal of Pediatrics*, 1965, *67*, 257–263.

Nyhan, W. L., Pesek, J., Sweetman, L., Carpenter, D. G., & Carter, C. H. Genetics of an X-linked disorder of uric acid metabolism and cerebral function. *Pediatric Research*, 1967, *1*, 5–13.

Oswald, I. Physiology of sleep accompanying dreaming. In J. P. Ross (Ed.), *The scientific basis of medicine: Annual reviews.* London: Athlone Press, 1964.

Peterson, R. F., & Peterson, L. R. The use of positive reinforcement in the control of self-destructive behavior in a retarded boy. *Journal of Experimental Child Psychology*, 1968, *6*, 351–360.

Phillips, R. H., & Alkan, M. Some aspects of self-mutilation in the general population of a large psychiatric hospital. *Psychiatric Quarterly*, 1961, *35*, 421–423.

Repp, A. C., Deitz, S. M., & Deitz, D. E. D. Reducing inappropriate behaviors in classrooms and in individual sessions through DRO schedules of reinforcement. *Mental Retardation*, 1976, *14*, 11–15.

Reynolds, G. S. Behavioral contrast. *Journal of the Experimental Analysis of Behavior*, 1961, *4*, 57–71.

Romanczyk, R. G., & Goren, E. R. Severe self-injurious behavior: The problem of clinical control. *Journal of Consulting and Clinical Psychology*, 1975, *43*, 730–739.

Ross, R. R., Meichenbaum, D. H., & Humphrey, C. Treatment of nocturnal headbanging by behavior modification techniques: A case report. *Behaviour Research and Therapy*, 1971, *9*, 151–154.

Rutter, M. Behavioral and cognitive characteristics of a series of psychotic children. In J. K. Wing (Ed.), *Early childhood autism*. London: Pergamon Press, 1966.

Saposnek, D. T., & Watson, L. S. The elimination of the self-destructive behavior of a psychotic child: A case study. *Behavior Therapy*, 1974, *5*, 79–89.

Schaefer, H. H. Self-injurious behavior: Shaping headbanging in monkeys. *Journal of Applied Behavior Analysis*, 1970, *3*, 111–116.

Seegmiller, J. E. Diseases of purine and pyrimidine metabolism. In P. K. Bondy (Ed.), *Duncan's diseases of metabolism* (6th ed.). Philadelphia: Saunders, 1969.

Seegmiller, J. E. Lesch-Nyhan syndrome and the X-linked uric acidurias. *Hospital Practice*, 1972, *7*, 79–90.

Seegmiller, J. E. Inherited deficiency of hypoxanthine-guanine phosphoribosyltransferase in X-linked uric aciduria (the Lesch-Nyhan syndrome and its variants). In H. Harris & K. Hirschhorn (Eds.), *Advances in human genetics* (Vol. 6). New York: Plenum, 1976.

Seegmiller, J. E., Rosenbloom, F. M., & Kelley, W. N. Enzyme defect associated with a sex-linked human neurological disorder and excessive purine synthesis. *Science*, 1967, *155*, 1682–1684.

Shear, C. S., Nyhan, W. L., Kirman, B. H., & Stern, J. Self-mutilative behavior as a feature of the de Lange syndrome. *Journal of Pediatrics*, 1971, *78*, 506–509.

Shintoub, S. A., & Soulairac, A. L'enfant automutilateur. *Psychiatrie de l'Enfant*, 1961, *3*, 111–145.

Silberstein, R. M., Blackman, S., & Mandell, W. Autoerotic head banging. *Journal of the American Academy of Child Psychiatry*, 1966, *5*, 235–242.

Skinner, B. F. *The behavior of organisms*. New York: Appleton-Century-Crofts, 1938.

Smolev, S. R. Use of operant techniques for the modification of self-injurious behavior. *American Journal of Mental Deficiency*, 1971, *76*, 295–305.

Tate, B. G. Case study: Control of chronic self-injurious behavior by conditioning procedures. *Behavior Therapy*, 1972, *3*, 72–83.

Tate, B. G., & Baroff, G. S. Aversive control of self-injurious behavior in a psychotic boy. *Behaviour Research and Therapy*, 1966, *4*, 281–287.

Weiher, R. G., & Harman, R. E. The use of omission training to reduce self-injurious behavior in a retarded child. *Behavior Therapy*, 1975, *6*, 261–268.

Wolf, M. M., Risley, T., Johnston, M., Harris, F., & Allen, E. Application of operant conditioning procedures to the behavior problems of an autistic child: A follow-up and extension. *Behaviour Research and Therapy,* 1967, *5,* 103–111.

Wolf, M. M., Risley, T., & Mees, H. Application of operant conditioning procedures to the behavior problems of an autistic child. *Behaviour Research and Therapy,* 1964, *1,* 305–312.

COMMENTARY by Richard A. Mesaros

Edward Carr's article, "The Motivation of Self-Injurious Behavior: A Review of Some Hypothesis," is an excellent review of five major motivational hypotheses reported in the literature of self-injurious behavior. That focus is its strength. Rather than a concentration on treatment procedures per se, Carr makes a thorough case for the importance of identifying various motivational variables that can assist researchers and practitioners in developing appropriate treatment interventions.

Carr's article helps to lay the foundation for subsequent research and articles examining the functions of self-injurious behavior as well as other so-called aberrant behaviors (e.g., Carr, Newsom and Binkoff, 1980; Iwata, Dorsey, Slifer, Bauman, and Richman, 1982; Lovaas, 1982; Schuler and Goetz, 1981). In addition, the article is an important contribution to the ecobehavioral literature and other research exploring the impact of environmental variables on behavioral problems (e.g., Baker, 1980; Center, Deitz, and Kaufman, 1982; Etzel and LeBlanc, 1979; Rogers-Warren and Warren, 1977; Schroeder, Mulick, and Rojahn, 1980; Volkmar and Cohen, 1982; Weeks and Gaylord-Ross, 1981). Carr's work is a testimony to researchers' and practitioners' continued and growing interest in understanding antecedent and ecological factors that can ultimately assist in the development of appropriate, longitudinal educational programs and interventions for individuals with handicaps.

REFERENCES

Baker, D. B. Applications of environmental psychology in programming for severely handicapped students. *Journal of the Association for the Severely Handicapped,* 1980, *5,* 3.

Carr, E., Newsom, C. D., & Binkoff, J. A. Escape as a factor in the aggressive behavior of two retarded children. *Journal of Applied Behavior Analysis,* 1980, *13,* 10–17.

Center, D. B., Deitz, S. M., & Kaufman, M. E. Student ability, task difficulty and inappropriate classroom behavior. *Behavior Modification,* 1982, *6,* 3.

Etzel, B. C., & LeBlanc, J. M. The simplest treatment alternative: The law of parsimony applied to choosing appropriate instructional control and errorless-learning procedures for the difficult to teach child. *Journal of Autism and Developmental Disorders*, 1979, *9*, 4.

Iwata, B. A., Dorsey, M. F., Slifer, K. J., Bauman, K. E., & Richman, G. S. Toward a functional analysis of self-injury. *Analysis and Intervention in Developmental Disabilities*, 1982, *2*, 1.

Lovaas, O. I. Comments on self-destructive behaviors. *Analysis and Intervention in Developmental Disabilities*, 1982, *2*, 1.

Rogers-Warren, A., & Warren, S. F. *Ecological perspectives in behavior analysis*. Baltimore: University Park Press, 1977.

Schroeder, S. R., Mulick, J. A., & Rojahn, J. The definition, taxonomy, epidemiology, and ecology of self-injurious behavior. *Journal of Autism and Developmental Disorders*, 1980, *10*, 4.

Schuler, A. L., & Goetz, L. The assessment of severe language disabilities: Communicative and cognitive considerations. *Analysis and Intervention in Developmental Disabilities*, 1981, *1*, 3–4.

Volkmar, F. R., & Cohen, D. J. A hierarchical analysis of patterns of noncompliance in autistic and behavior disturbed children. *Journal of Autism and Developmental Disorders*, 1982, *12*, 1.

Weeks, M., & Gaylord-Ross, R. Task difficulty and aberrant behavior in severely handicapped students. *Journal of Applied Behavior Analysis*, 1981, *14*, 444–463.

17

Genetic Influences
and Infantile Autism

SUSAN FOLSTEIN
MICHAEL RUTTER

In his original description of infantile autism, Kanner suggested an "inborn defect," because symptoms were often present from early infancy. Despite the rarity of a family history of autism and lack of a known increase in parental consanguinity, there are two reasons for suspecting hereditary influences: the 2% rate of autism in siblings is 50 times that of the general population,[1] and a family history of speech delay is found in about a quarter of families.[2] Reports of single pairs of twins with autism have not added much to our knowledge of genetic effects because of a bias toward reporting monozygotic (MZ) concordant pairs and because few reports contain both adequate clinical descriptions and evidence of zygosity.[1] We therefore undertook a study of a systematically collected sample of 21 pairs of same-sexed twins, one or both of whom had autism as diagnosed by the criteria of Kanner[3] and Rutter.[4] The results reported here indicate the importance of hereditary influences in the aetiology of autism.

The names of twins were collected from consultants, schools and units for autistic children, the National Society for Autistic Children and two hospital twin registers. Apart from two pairs in which dermatoglyphics were used, zygosity was determined by blood grouping in all cases not markedly different in physical appearance. Case notes of the 33 pairs thus obtained were reviewed and eight pairs were rejected on diagnostic grounds. The remaining 25 pairs and their families were extensively interviewed, tested and examined at home or in hospital. Obstetric records and case notes were also studied. On the basis of all information, a further four pairs were excluded as not meeting diagnostic criteria.

The adequacy of our sampling is shown by the MZ:DZ ratio (11:10) which was about that expected for same-sexed twin pairs surviving the first year (6:7); and by the number of autistic twin pairs found. In the English twin population of school age who would meet our diagnostic criteria, between 19 and 27 autistic children would be expected and 20 were found. Our

Reprinted by permission from *Nature* 265 (February 24, 1977): 726–728. Copyright © 1977, Macmillan Journals Limited.

sampling of children over school age was less complete, but not likely to be biased as to zygosity or concordance since most cases came from twin registers.

The diagnoses were made from case summaries, numbered randomly to prevent sorting by pair, and from which name, exact age, and zygosity had been deleted.

At least one member of 21 same-sexed pairs of twins met the diagnostic criteria for autism. In all, the 11 MZ and 10 DZ pairs gave rise to 25 autistic children. Apart from being twins, these were similar to other reported series of autistic children with respect to sex ratio (3.4:1), social class (57% from I and II), and IQ (about 1/2 severely retarded but 1/4 with normal nonverbal IQ). Affective disorder was described in four families, but schizophrenia did not occur. One sibling suffered from autism (a rate of 2.8%). Delayed speech was reported in three families (table 1).

Four of the 11 MZ pairs but none of the 10 DZ pairs were concordant for autism ($P=0.055$). All concordant pairs were male. Because autism is a rare condition (about 4 per 10,000 children), the MZ concordance rate is equivalent to a very high correlation in liability (over 0.9) using the multifactorial model.[5,6]

If, using this model, it is hypothesised that autism reflects some form of continuously distributed, abnormal characteristic, the question arises whether the non-autistic co-twins showed any other abnormality. We found that very few did in the DZ pairs but in most MZ pairs the co-twins showed some form of cognitive disorder (see tables 1 and 2).

Thus, in addition to the autistic twins, 6 non-autistic co-twins (5 MZ and 1 DZ) showed a cognitive abnormality as defined by the criteria of no phrase speech until 3 yr (three cases), IQ 70 or below (two cases), severely abnormal articulation after 5 yr (two cases), or scholastic difficulties requiring special schooling (two cases). Four non-autistic twins showed only one of the above features and none were severely handicapped. All the autistic twins met at least two of the criteria. Thus, 9 (82%) of the 11 MZ pairs were concordant for cognitive disorder/autism compared with only 1 (10%) of the DZ pairs ($P=0.0015$). The findings strengthen the suggestion of genetic determination and indicate that what is inherited is a form of cognitive abnormality which includes but is not restricted to autism.

Table 1	Pair-wise concordance by zygosity		
	MZ pairs ($n=11$)	DZ pairs ($n=10$)	MZ−DZ difference (exact test)
Concordance for autism	36%	0%	$P=0.055$
Concordance for cognitive disorder (including autism)	82%	10%	$P=0.0015$

Table 2 Summary of findings for MZ pairs

	First-born twin	Second-born twin
1	Autism + severe MR	Autism + severe MR
2	Autism + mild MR	Autism
3	Autism + severe MR	Autism + severe MR
4	Autism	Autism + mild MR
5	Mild MR	Autism + severe MR
6	Autism	Educational difficulties (ESN school)
7	Severe articulation defect	Autism
8	Autism + severe MR	Language disorder
9	Mild MR	Autism + severe MR
10	Autism + mild MR	Normal
11	Normal	Autism

MR, Mental retardation.
ESN, Educationally subnormal.

Twins have a raised rate of perinatal difficulties leading to brain injury and it was necessary to check that the concordance was not an artefact of these. We found that it was not. In none of the four pairs concordant for autism did both twins have a history of brain injury. Furthermore, no twin with cognitive disorder in the absence of autism showed evidence of perinatal brain injury (table 3).

Brain injury was, however, relevant to discordance regarding autism. We identified five features known to be associated with brain injury: kernicterus, perinatal apnoea of more than 6 min, neonatal convulsions, multiple

Table 3 Summary of biological hazards in discordant pairs

Hazard	MZ pairs	
	Autistic twin	Non-autistic twin
Definite	Multiple congenital anomalies	—
	Neonatal convulsions	—
Possible	Severe febrile illness	—
	Pathologically narrow cord	—
None	—	—
	—	—

Hazard	DZ pairs	
	Autistic twin	Non-autistic twin
Definite	Apnoea	—
	Delay second birth	—
	Delay second birth	—
	Delay second birth	—
Possible	Severe haemolytic disease + apnoea	Delay second birth
or		
Difference in severity	Severe haemolytic disease + apnoea	Mild haemolytic disease
	Birth weight 1 and ¾ pounds lower	—
	Birth weight 1 and ¾ pounds lower	—
None	—	—
	—	—

congenital anomalies, and a second birth delayed by at least 30 min. In 6 of the 17 pairs discordant for autism, the autistic child but not the non-autistic co-twin had experienced one or more of these biological hazards in the perinatal period.

A wider definition of biological hazard was then applied to the 11 cases not differentiated on the stricter criteria. Using the wider definition (lower birth weight by 1 pound or more, pathological narrow umbilical cord, a more severe kernicterus with apnoea and a severe febrile illness—possibly encephalitis—just before onset), a further six discordant pairs were differentiated. Thus, in 12 of 17 pairs discordant for autism, the autistic member probably or possibly suffered a brain injury, whereas in none of the discordant pairs did this occur only in the non-autistic member.

To summarise the results: the markedly higher rate of concordance in MZ, compared with DZ, pairs for both autism and cognitive abnormalities indicates the importance of genetic factors in the aetiology of autism. Indeed, the concordance rates in conjunction with the very low prevalence of autism in the general population point to a strong genetic determination. Nevertheless, the finding of an association between biological hazards in the perinatal period and autism also demonstrates the important role of environmental influences for the causation of autism (but not cognitive disorder).

In some cases, genetic factors seem to be both necessary and sufficient causes. Among the eight autistic children in the four concordant MZ pairs, biological hazards (even using the broader criteria) occurred in only one child. He was more severely affected than his twin. On the other hand, brain injury alone seems to be a sufficient cause in some cases. In one of the two completely discordant MZ pairs, the autistic twin had experienced neonatal convulsions, whereas the non-injured co-twin was normal in every way. The importance of brain damage is also indicated by the finding in other studies of autism in children with congenital rubella or infantile spasms.

Finally, some cases seem to result from the combination of an inherited cognitive defect plus brain damage. In three of the five MZ pairs discordant for autism but concordant for cognitive deficit, the autistic child had experienced a biological hazard whereas the cognitively impaired non-autistic co-twin had not.

Determining the mode of inheritance is difficult since autistic children rarely reproduce. It would be helpful to know what happens to the offspring of the non-autistic twins with cognitive impairment, but no such information is available.

In summary, we conclude that this systematic study of 21 same-sexed twin pairs in which at least one twin showed the syndrome of infantile autism, indicates the importance of a genetic factor in the aetiology of autism. It also indicates the importance of brain injuries, especially during the perinatal period, which may operate either by themselves or in combination with a genetic predisposition involving language. Both the mode of inheritance and exactly what is inherited remain uncertain.

We thank our many colleagues whose collaboration made the study possible.

REFERENCES

1. Rutter, M. in *Recent Developments in Schizophrenia* (ed. Coppen, A. J. & Walk, D.) (Royal Medico-Psychological Association, London, 1967).
2. Bartak, L., Rutter, M. & Cox, A. *Br. J. Psychiat.* 126, 127–145 (1975).
3. Kanner, L. *Nervous Child* 2, 217–250 (1943).
4. Rutter, M. in *Infantile Autism* (ed. Churchill, D. W. *et al.*) (Charles C. Thomas, Springfield, Illinois, 1971).
5. Smith, C. *Am. J. Hum. Genet.* 26, 454–466 (1974).
6. Curnow, R. N. & Smith, C. *J.R. Statist. Soc.*, A138, 131–169 (1975).

COMMENTARY by David L. Pauls

The twin study reported in this paper represents an important step in our understanding of the etiology of infantile autism. The results suggest several important facts that if replicated need to be incorporated into subsequent studies:

1. The higher concordance rate among monozygotic twins compared with the rate among dizygotic twins suggest genetic factors are important etiologically.
2. The occurrence of some cognitive disorder in the non-autistic co-twin of many of the MZ and several of the DZ twins suggest that the same etiologic factors may be contributing to a milder or different expression of the disorder.
3. By examining discordant MZ twin pairs some potentially important non-genetic etiologic factors are identified.

These are important results. However, they do not identify specific genetic factors that may be important nor do they suggest anything about the mode of transmission. Twin studies do not allow complete answers to those questions. Other types of studies (e.g., family studies) are needed that will incorporate what we have learned from this study (e.g., the existence of possible milder forms and non-genetic etiologic factors) and expand on it. These new studies need to employ the same approach as described here: All family members need to be examined and tested so that the information will be of the highest quality. With this type of information, hypotheses about specific genetic mechanisms can be tested.

18

Symbolic Play
in Severely Mentally Retarded
and in Autistic Children

LORNA WING
JUDITH GOULD
SYBIL R. YEATES
LORNA M. BRIERLEY

The relationship of symbolic play to the development of language has been discussed and investigated by Piaget (1962), Lunzer (1959), Sheridan (1969, 1975) and Singer (1973). Lowe (1975) described the stages in the development of representational play in children under three years of age.

Play is usually considered to be part of the educational programme in nursery and infants' schools for normal children. The results of the Brooklands' experiment (Tizard, 1960a, 1960b) suggest that play is also important for the development of language and social behaviour in severely mentally retarded children. In Tizard's study a group of severely retarded children were moved from a subnormality hospital into an environment where learning through play (both gross motor activity and imaginative games) was encouraged in an educational approach modelled on nursery school lines. During 2 years residence in the Brooklands' unit, the children gained an average of 14 months in verbal mental age as measured on the Minnesota pre-school test, compared with 6 months average gain by matched control children remaining in the hospital.

It is not possible to generalize from Tizard's results to all severely retarded children, because this term covers many different syndromes, including a group that could be classified as having early childhood psychosis, some of whom are classically autistic. The Brooklands' experiment excluded psychotic children and those who were non-ambulant. One of the clinical features of early childhood autism is poverty or absence of symbolic play (Kanner, 1943, 1973), even when good opportunity for such play is provided. Ricks and Wing (1975) put forward the hypothesis that the central problem in this condition is a severe impairment of the normal human ability to abstract concepts from experience, to give these abstractions symbolic

Reprinted with permission from *Journal of Child Psychology and Psychiatry* 18 (1977): 167–178. Copyright © 1977, Pergamon Press, Ltd.

labels, to store the concepts in symbolic form and to draw on them for relevant associations when thinking of the past, reacting to the present and planning for the future. This problem occurs in varying degrees of severity, ranging from the child who cannot form any concepts at all to the child who is able to abstract sufficiently to cope with practical everyday tasks, but who cannot hold a conversation beyond the exchange of stereotyped remarks and who is gauche and naïve in social situations. In children, lack of symbolic play is the outward sign of this central problem.

This hypothesis, if correct, has implications for the planning of educational programmes for the children concerned. It is, therefore, of interest to see if lack of symbolic play is confined to autistic children or whether there are other types of children who share this impairment.

A survey of the prevalence of early childhood autism (Wing et al., 1976), using a rating scale for defining the autistic syndrome devised by Lotter (1966, 1967), provided an opportunity for studying symbolic, imaginative activity among a complete population of mentally handicapped children of school age.

METHOD

Identification of Children to Be Included in the Study

The 108 children to be considered here had home addresses in the former London borough of Camberwell and were aged 5-14 on the chosen census day (31 December 1970). They were identified from the Camberwell Register (Wing and Hailey, 1972) and included: (a) children who, on the census day, were in any kind of school, hospital or home for severely retarded children (N=90); (b) one child with Down's syndrome attending an ESN (mild) school, included in order to have a complete population of Down's syndrome children of school age; (c) children not in (a) or (b) but who were recorded in their educational case notes as having an intelligence quotient below 50 (N=5); (d) children not in (a) (b) or (c) but who had, at some time had a diagnosis recorded of autism, psychosis, or severe language disorder (N=9); (e) children not in (a) (b) (c) or (d) who attended any kind of special school, tutorial or remedial class, or a speech therapy clinic, who were found, from a brief, screening interview with the teacher or speech therapist, observation in the classroom and inspection of all available case records, to have some items of behaviour seen in early childhood autism (N=3). The brief interview schedule included questions on symbolic activities. The details of the methods used are described in Wing et al. (1976). At the time of the census there were approximately 23,500 children aged 5-14 with home addresses in Camberwell.

Rating of Symbolic Play and Other Symbolic Activities

For each of the children selected as above, a teacher, nurse or child care worker and, where possible, a parent were interviewed (by J.G. or L.W.) using a detailed structured schedule concerning behaviour over the past month. This schedule covered many aspects of behaviour (Wing, 1975) and contained questions on the child's level of symbolic activity with toys and with other children, or where appropriate, his interest in and understanding of stories, television programmes, or films, and his ability to contribute to a conversation on topics needing ready access to associations in symbolic form for their comprehension.

In addition to the interviews with parents and teachers, each child was observed by the investigators at his school or other unit, and, where possible, in his own home. Also, during psychological testing, symbolic play with the test materials and other toys was noted. Use was made of Sheridan's technique for fairly standardized observations of the play behaviour of young children (Sheridan, 1969).

On the basis of this information, each child's level of play or other relevant activity could be placed in one of three categories, as follows:

1. *Symbolic play or other relevant activity.* At the lowest level a child was rated as showing symbolic play if for example, he made appropriate noises while pushing a toy car along, or pretended to drive it into a garage to fill up with petrol. Symbolic play with dolls involved at least holding them as if they were real babies and brushing their hair, or tucking them up in bed. The upper end of the scale included active participation in pretend games with other children, the invention of stories, lively discussion of past experiences, or modelling or drawing pictures with imaginative themes. Flexibility and variety of activity was necessary. Endless repetition of the same symbolic themes, to the exclusion of other ideas, was included in the next category.

2. *Stereotyped play.* Some children used toys symbolically or had other apparently "pretend" games, but they stood out from the rest because of the narrow range and stereotyped quality of their play, which seemed to be a repetitive copy of certain aspects of other children's play, or of the child's own experiences. One child's only play activity was to load and unload a toy truck in imitation of his father at work. Another repetitively copied the voice and movements of a robot from a television series. A third acted out and drew scenes of aeroplanes crashing, with lively detail, but was preoccupied with this to the exclusion of all else.

Stereotyped play was not modified by suggestions from other children, nor by the demands of any particular social setting.

Children with this type of play certainly showed some symbolic, representational activity, but this stood out as a special preoccupation and not as part of a general ability to engage in a variety of imaginative pursuits appropriate for the child's level of mental development. The content of stereotyped symbolic activity can range from, at its simplest, pouring pretend tea into toy tea cups, up to a preoccupation with physics or space travel, but, at all levels, it is characterised by repetitiveness and lack of the capacity for innovation, development and change that is found in true symbolic play.

3. *No symbolic play.* In this category, "play," if present at all, consisted of repetitive manipulation of toys or other objects regardless of what they represented. Thus, a child would spin the wheels of a miniature car, but never use it to represent a real car.

A few children were on the borderlines between categories. For example, one child repeatedly made identical three-dimensional models of lorries, but, when they were completed, he lost interest in them. He never used them in any way that suggested they represented real lorries for him. He did not push them along, or load and unload them, unlike the child with stereotyped play. He was therefore rated as having no symbolic play, although there was clearly a fine distinction between his "play" and that placed in the "stereotyped" category.

Physical and Behavioural Problems

The interview schedule also contained sections dealing with the following:

Mobility
Simple stereotypies, such as finger or object flicking, spinning, tapping
    and scratching, fascination with simple sensory stimuli, repeated self
    injury
Repetitive routines of a more elaborate kind, involving some organiza-
    tion of materials and the environment
Social responsiveness, initiation of social contact and social communica-
    tion
Behavioural and emotional disturbances

This information was supplemented by observation of the children at school, during psychological testing and, where possible, at home.

Tests of Non-verbal Skills and Language Development

Each child was observed and, if appropriate, tested by one of the present authors (J.G.) or, in a minority of cases, by psychologists at the Hilda Lewis Unit, Bethlem Royal Hospital. The tests were selected according to the child's level of ability. They included the Bayley scales of infant development (Bayley, 1969), Merrill-Palmer scale of mental tests (Stutsman, 1931), the Wechsler intelligence scale for children (Wechsler, 1949), the Reynell developmental language scales (Reynell, 1969), and the Illinois test of psycholinguistic abilities (McCarthy and Kirk, 1961). Details are given by Gould (1976).

Mental ages on non-verbal skills, and language comprehension ages were calculated for each child. The Wechsler scale does not provide a direct measure of mental age, but all the children who could do this test were performing well above the crucial cut-off point of 20 months used in the analysis of the results.

Timing of the Interviews, Tests and Observations

The children considered here formed part of a larger population of 743 children who were screened by means of a short interview with a teacher, and another 171 who were investigated in detail. Owing to the large numbers of children studies, the interviews and the psychological tests were completed over a period of 4 yr. The intervals between interviews and psychological testing varied between 1 day and 4 yr, but, in 85%, the gap was less than 2 yr. In all but 8 cases, the testing was carried out after the interview. When the children were tested, their level of symbolic play was rated again and compared with the findings from the interviews.

The investigators, because of clinical as well as research commitments, were in frequent contact with the children over the four years of the study, so were able to observe any changes from one category of behaviour to another.

Recording of Problems of Educational Placement

Two of the present authors (L.B. and S.Y.) were, during the time period of the study, responsible for recommending placements in, respectively, units for autistic children and in ESN (severe) schools. They provided details of the children's previous educational histories and of the educational and medical problems each child presented.

RESULTS

Reliability and Stability of the Ratings of Symbolic Play

The between-informant reliability of the full interview schedule will be discussed elsewhere (Wing and Gould, to be published).

Ratings of symbolic play were available from two informants for 64 of the 108 children in the present study. Using the three categories described above, there was agreement in 55 cases (86%). Two children showed good symbolic play at home, but were so shy and inhibited in the presence of their teachers that they were rated as having no symbolic activity at school. The other 7 children for whom there was disagreement were in the group described by one informant as having stereotyped play. Six of them showed this type of play at home only and were rated as having no symbolic activity at school. The seventh child played in a stereotyped way at school, but not at home.

The investigators' observations of each child's play gave the same rating as the informants where the latter were in agreement with each other. Where they differed, the investigators made the final decision on the basis of their own observations. Thus one final rating for each child was arrived at for use in the analysis of results.

It was found that no child changed his category of play between interview and psychological testing, though those with symbolic play showed increasing elaboration and involvement with other children. It should be noted that the youngest age at interview was 6 yr 6 months and the majority of children were over 10 yr when first seen (see Table 1).

Mental Age on Non-verbal Tests

The relationship between symbolic play and mental age based on the non-verbal items of the intelligence tests used (that is those items not requiring the ability to manipulate symbols in speech or in thought) is shown in Table 1, variable no. 3.

Free symbolic play is not seen in children of non-verbal mental age below 20 months and stereotyped play occurs in one child only at that low level of performance. On the other hand, there are 11 children with no symbolic play who perform at a mental age of 20 months or more. It was decided to consider this last group separately.

Children with No Symbolic Play and Non-Verbal Mental Age Below 20 Months (N=31)

As can be seen from Table 1, there is a somewhat higher proportion of girls in this group as compared with the whole sample, though the difference is not significant. There is no tendency for children in this group to be younger than the others.

All the children have language comprehension ages below 20 months. All but one are catered for by the services for severe retardation, whether in day schools, hospitals or residential homes. Only 10% of the group have Down's syndrome, compared with 20% of the total sample.

TABLE 1. TYPE OF PLAY BY SEX. CHRONOLOGICAL AGE, MENTAL AGE, EDUCATIONAL PLACEMENT AND DIAGNOSIS (ABSOLUTE NUMBERS OF CHILDREN)

	None (Non-verbal M.A. < 20 months)	None (Non-verbal M.A. 20+ months)	Stereotyped	Symbolic	Total
1. Sex					
Male	18	10	16	27	71
Female	13	1	7	16	37
2. Chronological age at interview					
5–9 yr	9	3	6	15	33
10+ yr	22	8	17	28	75
3. Non-verbal mental age					
0–19 months	31	—	1	—	32
20–60 months	—	7	9	14	30
61 + months	—	4	13	29	46
4. Language comprehension age					
0–19 months	31	9	3	—	43
20–60 months	—	2	11	29	42
61 + months	—	—	9	14	23
5. Educational placement on census day (31.12.70) ESN (severe) services					
(day or residential)	30	9	15	36	90
Other	1	2	8	7	18
6. Diagnosis					
Down's syndrome	3	—	2	16	21
Other	28	11	21	27	87
Total	31	11	23	43	108

Table 2 shows that, while only 2 children have the complete autistic syndrome, characterised by both social aloofness and elaborate repetitive routines, the simple stereotypies often seen in autism, combined with very poor social contact, occur in about 60% of the children. Five are too severely physically handicapped to show these behaviour problems, and a further 5 do not have any aspects of the autistic syndrome, when their behaviour is considered in the light of their very low mental ages. About one-third are aggressive, have temper tantrums or injure themselves.

All the non-mobile children in the study are in this group.

Children with No Symbolic Play, and Non-verbal Mental Ages of 20 Months or Above (N=11)

In this group there is a marked excess of boys (see Table 1) although this does not reach statistical significance. There is no bias in the age distribution.

Nine of the children have language comprehension ages below 20 months, but 2 function at a higher level.

The majority of the group are in the services for ESN (severe) children. None of the group has Down's syndrome.

TABLE 2. TYPE OF PLAY BY BEHAVIOURAL AND PHYSICAL PROBLEMS (ABSOLUTE NUMBERS OF CHILDREN)

	None (Non-verbal M.A. < 20 months)	None (Non-verbal M.A. 20+ months)	Stereotyped	Symbolic	Total
1. Autistic syndrome, and related problems					
Too handicapped to show following problems	5	—	—	—	5
Complete autistic syndrome (Lotter's rating scale)	2	6	4	—	12
Simple stereotypies, and little or no social contact	19	5	—	1†	25
No initiation of social contact, but passively accepts social approaches	—	—	7*	1	8
Repetitive speech	—	—	11	—	11
None of above problems (general mental retardation only)	5	—	1	41	47
2. Physical, behavioural and emotional problems					
Non-mobile	15	—	—	—	15
Physical agression/temper tantrums/self injury	10	7	5	—	22
Stubborn/pestering/rebellious/anti-social	—	—	3	10	13
Anxious/shy/emotional distress	—	—	—	6	6
None of the above problems	6	4	15	27	52
Total	31	11	23	43	108

*Four of these children also have simple stereotypies and all have abnormalities of language development.

†This child withdraws from large groups of his peers, but interacts well with one or a few children or adults.

From Table 2 it can be seen that 6 of the 11 children have early childhood autism. The rest have simple stereotypies and very poor social contact, but not the elaborate routines necessary for a diagnosis of autism.

The 2 children with language comprehension ages above 19 months have the classic autistic syndrome. Both make stereotyped 3-dimensional models but do not play with them. These 2 children score above the 19 month level on the Reynell comprehension test because they understand a large number of nouns, some verbs and can follow simple instructions. Their comprehension is limited to familiar situations, and they cannot cope with new ideas or experiences. Their non-verbal skills are at a higher level than their language comprehension.

Children with Stereotyped Play (N=23)

The sex distribution in this group is similar to that in the total sample. There is no significant bias in the age distribution (see Table 1).

All but 1 of the group have non-verbal mental ages of 20 months or above. Only 3 have language comprehension ages below 20 months. These 3 repetitively copy a few of the low level symbolic activities of other children, such as washing a doll and putting it to bed, but do not initiate such play on their own.

Approximately one-quarter of this group are placed outside the ESN (severe) services in contrast to 7% of those with no symbolic play. Only 2 of the group have Down's syndrome.

Table 2 shows that the group includes 4 children with the complete autistic syndrome, and a further 7 who do not initiate social contact though they join in passively if pulled into games. All of these seven have marked abnormalities of language development; one has no executive speech, three have echolalia only, two have developmental receptive or executive speech problems, and one has the limited use of speech for social communication found in autistic children (Bartak et al., 1975). Of the rest of the group, 11 have repetitive, stereotyped speech, sometimes with repetitive questioning, that continues regardless of the social situation. The 1 child who does not show any of these problems has a language comprehension age around 18 months. He copies other children's play and uses language at a level appropriate for his language age.

Aggression, temper tantrums, or rebellious, stubborn behaviour occur in about one-third of the group.

Children with Symbolic Play (N=43)

There are no particular biases in the sex and age distributions in this group (see Table 1).

All the children have non-verbal and language comprehension ages of 20 months or above. Most of the group are in the ESN (severe) services.

Sixteen of the 43 children with symbolic play have Down's syndrome, compared with only 5 of the 65 children with either no symbolic play or with stereotyped play. This difference is significant ($\chi^2 = 12.57$, $d.f. = 1$, $p < 0.001$).

No child with symbolic play has the complete autistic syndrome (see Table 2). One child with visuo-spatial problems has simple stereotypies. One child does not initiate social contact but the rest communicate freely with their peers in speech or gesture appropriate for their language comprehension ages.

The behaviour problems shown by about one-third of the children in this group are of the "socially aware" kind—that is, stubborn, rebellious, antisocial behaviour, or anxiety and emotional distress.

History of Service Placement

Each child's history of placement in different services was traced up to the end of 1975, as shown in Table 3.

The children without any symbolic play are more likely to be in residential care than those with stereotyped and symbolic play (20 out of 42 of the former, against 9 out of 66 of the latter, $\chi^2 = 13.41$, $d.f. = 1$, $p < 0.001$). More than half of those with no symbolic play but with a non-verbal mental age above 19 months are in hospital or residential homes.

Almost half (11 out of 23) of the children with stereotyped play have changed schools during the five years following the census day, compared with one-sixth (14 out of 85) of the rest of the children ($\chi^2 = 8.32$, $d.f. = 1$, $p < 0.01$). The former have tended to move among a variety of kinds of schools including those for autistic, maladjusted and delicate children. The children with symbolic play, if they change schools, tend to have moved from ESN (mild) to ESN (severe) perhaps after an initial period in a school for normal infants.

DISCUSSION

In the present study, it is likely that almost all children with no symbolic play, in the relevant age range, were identified, since this abnormality of behaviour is strikingly obvious once the child enters school. It is less certain that all children with stereotyped play were included. The existence of this problem among children not receiving any form of special education was not investigated.

Symbolic representational play that is flexible and varied in theme does

TABLE 3. TYPE OF PLAY BY HISTORY OF SERVICE PLACEMENT (ABSOLUTE NUMBERS OF CHILDREN)

History of placement on 31 December 1975	None (Non-verbal M.A. < 20 months)	None (Non-verbal M.A. 20+ months)	Stereotyped	Symbolic	Total
In residential care	13	7	3	6	29
Remained in same type of school	16	3	9	26	54
Infants school ↓ ESN (Mild) ↓ ESN (Severe)	1	—	4	8	13
Other school changes	1	1	7	3	12
Total	31	11	23	43	108

not seem to occur in retarded children below a mental age of around 20 months. This fits in with Lowe's (1975) and Sheridan's (1975) findings on the development of symbolic play in young normal children, but awaits confirmation from observations of pre-school severely retarded children. Language comprehension age is probably the more important factor, since 9 children with non-verbal ages of 20 months or above, but language comprehension below that level, had no symbolic play.

Stereotyped play is found mostly in children whose language comprehension is above 19 months, although there are 3 children with this type of play whose comprehension is below this level. Sheridan (1975) points out that, in the small child, imitation usually precedes comprehension of his everyday experiences, but, until there is comprehension based on concept formation, there can be no meaningful re-creation of these experiences. It could be suggested that the child with stereotyped play has achieved the precursor of true symbolic play, but has not developed beyond that level. In a few of the children, this type of play appears to be related to their having a mental age just around the level at which symbolic play has hardly emerged from copying activities. The majority of those with stereotyped play have mental ages on language comprehension and non-verbal tasks above this level, but have marked abnormalities of language development, or of the way in which language is used. The explanation for the peculiarly narrow and limited development of symbolic activities remains obscure.

The complete absence of symbolic play is, in most cases, linked to a mental age below 20 months on all types of skills. The 11 children with no symbolic play but mental ages on non-verbal tasks of 20 months or above are of particular interest. The Merrill-Palmer scale was standardized over 40 years ago and probably gives a higher estimate of a child's mental age as compared with tests standardized more recently. However, this is not sufficient to explain the very large discrepancies between language and non-verbal development found in some of the children. The important point is that the non-verbal skills tested are fitting and assembly tasks not demanding symbolic language for their performance.

The apparent excess of boys in this group with higher non-verbal skills needs further investigation, using larger numbers of subjects.

It is clear from the results that, as would be predicted from the formulation put forward by Ricks and Wing (1975), complete absence of symbolic play is closely linked to the presence of typical early childhood autism, or of simple stereotypies combined with poor social contact. The full autistic syndrome is found more often in children with non-verbal skills at the 20 month level or above. There is a small minority of children with no symbolic play and very low levels of skill in all areas who do not show any aspects of the autistic syndrome. Study of this group might help elucidate the nature of infantile autism. This is discussed more fully elsewhere (Ricks and Wing, 1975; Wing, 1977).

The results from the present study, linking both repetitive speech and the autistic syndrome to abnormalities of symbolic play, plus the fact that some autistic children develop repetitive speech in later childhood, suggest a connection between these conditions, the exact nature of which needs to be explored.

The autistic children in this study who have stereotyped play have intelligence quotients on both verbal and non-verbal tests in the mildly retarded or normal ranges. They appear, from their development to date, to have a much better prognosis for achieving some degree of independence as adults than the autistic children with no symbolic play. Among the latter are a small number of children with non-language dependent skills in the mildly retarded range, but their lack of ideas in symbolic form severely impairs their ability to use these skills in constructive occupations.

The Brooklands' experiment (Tizard, 1960a, 1960b) showed that the development of symbolic play can be retarded by an environment, such as that found in large, understaffed institutions, that does not provide appropriate stimulation, social interaction, or sufficient material for play. The present findings suggest that some children do not develop symbolic play even when given ample opportunity. Although a number of children in the study with no symbolic play were in residential care, about half of these were in small homes run on family lines. Those living at home attended special schools in which play and social activities were emphasized as an integral part of education, as advocated by Tizard.

Children with Down's syndrome are especially likely to have symbolic play. Many of the children with no symbolic play, or with stereotyped play had identifiable organic abnormalities, other than Down's syndrome, likely to be associated with mental retardation, such as a history of infantile spasms, encephalitis, or maternal rubella (Wing, 1977). It would be of great interest to know what pathological processes can produce, on the one hand, general retardation with a pattern of behaviour that is reasonably similar to a normal child of the same mental age, as in most cases of Down's syndrome, or, on the other hand, marked discrepancies between different aspects of cognitive function, leading to behaviour that cannot be predicted from the child's mental age.

Educational Implications

A child who has developed symbolic play, even if mentally retarded, is able to join in school activities needing imagination and can, at least to some extent, add what he learns to his mental store of symbolic concepts, allowing him to generalize to other situations.

Total lack or marked limitation of symbolic activity presents many educational problems. Aggressive behaviour is especially likely to occur in the group of children without symbolic play whose non-verbal level is higher than their language comprehension, perhaps because of the frustration induced by good mobility and practical skills combined with poor ability to understand and communicate needs.

Those without any symbolic play are severely limited in their ability to learn. Basic self care and practical tasks can be taught by techniques of operant conditioning (Carr, 1976). Some children learn to understand and say some words through operant language training, but there is no convincing evidence that any child without spontaneous symbolic activity has managed to acquire more than a limited vocabulary (Kahn, 1975). The reduction of disturbances of behaviour is also possible (Carr, 1976). The type of teaching needed by children with the autistic syndrome has been described by Elgar (1966), Rutter and Bartak (1973) and Schopler et al. (1971). The main problem is the lack of generalization and the dependence on continuation of the programme for maintenance of the skills and behaviour (Lovaas et al., 1973). Presumably the child who is good at practical tasks, but has no symbolic play, can store what Sheridan (1975) calls "lively perceptual memoranda, e.g., kinetic, visual, auditory, tactile," which are not coded. This is an extremely inefficient way of storing information and limits the quantity and quality of the data in the memory bank (Hermelin, 1976), but it can be put to some practical use.

Children with stereotyped play present particular problems, as shown by the many changes of school that some of them undergo. Part of the difficulty seems to be that parents and teachers have too high expectations of these children's potential for achievement. They appear to fall between those with symbolic play and those without, possibly needing a more structured and organized approach than the former, but more flexibility than the latter. However, detailed studies are needed to clarify the nature of stereotyped play and to find appropriate educational methods for children with this form of symbolic activity.

There is much to be said for including in teacher training information concerning symbolic development and the abnormalities that can occur. This knowledge would help to counteract both unrealistic expectations and total pessimism in teachers of mentally handicapped children. These attitudes, though at opposite extremes, are equally incompatible with good teaching that can be sustained over a long period of time.

SUMMARY

Children aged 5-14 on one census day, known to the services for severe mental retardation, or having items of behaviour found in early childhood autism, were identified from the Camberwell register. The children can be divided into 3 groups: (a) 42 with no symbolic play; (b) 23 with stereotyped, repetitive, copying play; (c) 43 who have flexible, varied symbolic play. The last occurs only in children with language comprehension age above the 19 month level, and is seen in less than half of the school-age severely retarded children.

The majority of children with no symbolic play, or with stereotyped play, have marked autistic features or the full autistic syndrome. Only 2 of those with true symbolic play have any behavior like that found in autism and none has the full syndrome. A small group of children with "repetitive" speech and stereotyped play is identified and the relationship with childhood autism is considered.

The educational implications of the findings are discussed.

REFERENCES

Bartak, L., Rutter, M. and Cox, A. (1975) A comparative study of autism and specific developmental receptive language disorders—I. The children. *Br. J. Psychiat. 126*, 127–145.

Bayley, N. (1969) *The Bayley Scales of Infant Development.* Psychological Corporation, New York.

Carr, J. (1976) The severely retarded autistic child. In *Early Childhood Autism*, 2nd Edition (Edited by Wing, L.). Pergamon Press, Oxford.

Elgar, S. (1966) Teaching autistic children. In *Early Childhood Autism*, 1st Edition (Edited by Wing, J.K.). Pergamon Press, Oxford.

Gould, J. (1976) Language development and non-verbal skills in severely mentally retarded children: an epidemiological study. *J. ment. Defic. Res.* (in press).

Hermelin, B. (1976) Coding and the sense modalities. In *Early Childhood Autism*, 2nd Edition (Edited by Wing, L.). Pergamon Press, Oxford.

Kahn, J.V. (1975) Relationship of Piaget's sensorimotor period to language acquisition of profoundly retarded children. *Am. J. ment. Defic. 79*, 640–643.

Kanner, L. (1943) Autistic disturbance of affective contact. *Nerv. Child. 2*, 217–250.

Kanner, L. (1973) *Childhood Psychosis: Initial Studies and New Insights.* Winston, Washington.

Lotter, V. (1966) Epidemiology of autistic conditions in young children—I. Prevalence. *Soc. Psychiat. 1*, 124–136.

Lotter, V. (1967) The prevalence of the autistic syndrome in children. PhD. thesis, University of London.

Lovaas, O.I., Koegal, R., Simmons, J.Q. and Long, J.S. (1973) Some generalisations and follow-up measures on autistic children in behaviour therapy. *J. appl. Behav. Anal. 6*, 131–166.

Lowe, M. (1975) Trends in the development of representational play in infants from one to three years—an observational study. *J. Child Psychol. Psychiat. 16*, 33–48.

Lunzer, E.A. (1959) Intellectual development in the play of young children. *Educ. Rev. 11*, 205–217.

McCarthy, J. and Kirk, S.A. (1961) *The Illinois Test of Psycho-linguistic Abilities: Experimental Edition.* University of Illinois Press, Urbana, Ill.

Piaget, J. (1962) *Play, Dreams and Imitation in Childhood.* Routledge & Kegan Paul, London.

Reynell, J. (1969) *Reynell Developmental Language Scales.* N.F.E.R., Slough, Bucks.

Ricks, D.M. and Wing, L. (1975) Language, communication and the use of symbols in normal and autistic children. *J. Autism Child. Schizophrenia 3,* 191–221.

Rutter, M. and Bartak, L. (1973) Special educational treatment of autistic children: a comparative study—II. Follow-up findings and implications for services. *J. Child Psychol. Psychiat. 14,* 241–270.

Schopler, E., Brehm, S., Kinsbourne, M. and Reichler, R.J. (1971) Effect of treatment structure on development in autistic children. *Archs Gen. Psychiat. 24,* 415–421.

Sheridan, M.D. (1969) Playthings in the development of language. *Health Trends 1,* 7–10.

Sheridan, M.D. (1975) The Stycar language test. *Dev. Med. Child Neurol. 17,* 164–174.

Singer, J.L. (1973) *The Child's World of Make-Believe.* Academic Press, New York.

Stutsman, R. (1931) *Merrill-Palmer Scale of Mental Tests.* Harcourt, Brace & World, New York.

Tizard, J. (1960a) Residential care of mentally handicapped children *Br. med. J. 1,* 1040–1046.

Tizard, J. (1960b) The residential care of mentally handicapped children. Paper given to London Conference on the Scientific Aspects of Mental Deficiency, July 1960.

Wechsler, D. (1949) *Wechsler Intelligence Scale for Children: Manual.* Psychological Corporation, New York.

Wing, J.K. and Hailey, A.M. (Eds.) (1972) *Evaluating a Community Psychiatric Service.* Oxford University Press, London.

Wing, L. (1977) Social and behavioural characteristics of autistic and other psychotic children: a preliminary report of an epidemiological study. Paper given at *International Symposium on Autism: Reappraisal of Concepts and Treatment,* St. Gallen, July 1976 (in press).

Wing, L. and Gould, J. (to be published) The between informant reliability of an interview schedule of children's handicaps, behaviour and skills.

Wing, L., Yeates, S.R., Brierley, L.M. and Gould, J. (1976) The prevalence of early childhood autism: a comparison of administrative and epidemiological studies. *Psychol. Med. 6,* 89–100.

COMMENTARY by June Groden and Gerald Groden

This paper presents a descriptive study of symbolic imaginative activity among a complete population of mentally handicapped children. The purpose of this study was to inquire as to whether the lack of symbolic play is confined to autistic children or whether there are other types of children who share this impairment. It makes a significant contribution to the field in several areas:

1. *Assessment.* In addition to the finding that complete absence of symbolic play is closely linked to the presence of typical early childhood autism, the study provides the reader with operational definitions of relevant categories of play behavior. This information is valuable in the assessment of play behavior in natural environments. Wing et al. found that 16 of the 43 children who *had* symbolic play had Down's syndrome. Of the 65 children with either no symbolic play or with stereotyped play only 5 had Down's syndrome. No child with symbolic play had the complete autistic syndrome and of the children with no symbolic play and non-verbal mental age of 20 months or above (N=11), 6 of the 11 had autism.

2. *Developmental.* This study explored the relationship between language development, cognitive functioning, and play behavior. The complete absence of symbolic play was in most cases linked to a mental age below 20 months on all types of skills. The article also emphasized the importance of symbolic play for its value in prognosis. The children with symbolic play have a much better prognosis for achieving some degree of independence as adults than the children with no symbolic play.

3. *Generalization.* One of the major problems in teaching autistic children is their lack of generalization. This paper points out the relationship between symbolic play and generalization. Wing states, "Without symbolic activity, the quantity and quality of the storage of information is inefficient." In other words, the autistic child may not be able to add what he learns to his mental store of symbolic concepts that allow him to generalize to other situations.

4. *Communication.* In describing the severe deficits that autistic children have with symbolic play (even those with some language), it should be pointed out that there is a need for language therapists to focus more on the importance of play as a field of therapeutic intervention. This article was written in 1977, but to date there has been a dearth of literature in the field of autism describing programs to increase play behavior and particularly symbolic play. Although Wing states, "The present findings suggest that some children do not develop symbolic play even when given ample opportunity," this writer has found that introducing the teaching of symbolic play into a curriculum for autistic children can be fruitful and needs further exploration.

19

Neurochemical and Developmental Models of Childhood Autism

DONALD J. COHEN
BARBARA K. CAPARULO
BENNETT A. SHAYWITZ

Contemporary achievements in neurochemistry, psychology, and linguistics provide clinical researchers with new strategies for investigating the most enigmatic behavioral disorders of childhood and clarifying the relations between normal development and its disabilities. Understanding facets of normal development, such as the acquisition of the first language, may illuminate the problems of children with severe difficulties e.g., developmental aphasia. On the other hand, clarification of the underpinnings of developmental handicaps—e.g., severe attentional disorders—may highlight preconditions for normal development or associations between areas of development (such as between cognitive and social development). We have conducted systematic, multidisciplinary, multimethod studies of developmentally disabled children, attempting to explicate principles of biological and cognitive development which can clarify normal maturation and the ways in which various types of difficulties may emerge. Our emphasis has been on children with early onset childhood psychosis (autism and autistic-like disorders), with and without mental retardation; children with central language impairments (aphasia); children with severe learning disabilities; and the interface between biology and competence in normal children (Cohen, 1974). This chapter focuses on clinical and neurochemical studies of autism and similar developmental disturbances.

CLINICAL PHENOMENOLOGY

Clinical Examples

Biologically-oriented clinical research must be firmly based on rigorous behavioral studies and knowledge of natural history. Thus, the description

Adapted with permission from *Cognitive Defects in the Development of Mental Illnesses,* ed. Geroge Serban (New York: Brunner/Mazel, 1978), 66–100.

These studies were supported by the William T. Grant Foundation, Mr. Leonard Berger, the Schall Family Trust, and NIH grants HD-03008 and NS 12384-01.

343

of several children will illustrate the basic dimensions for which neurochemical models are required.

Henry was the third of four children. His mother and father, quiet and thoughtful people, were in good health, as were his siblings. On his mother's side, his grandmother and great-grandmother had mild depressive episodes, and two cousins had seizures with fever. There was no other family history of neurological or psychiatric disorder, and the family considered itself to be relatively healthy.

Henry's gestation and delivery were uncomplicated, and, as a newborn weighing 7 pounds and 14 ounces, he appeared perfectly healthy. He was a quiet, non-demanding infant, but he did not enjoy being held or lifted by his parents and seemed unresponsive to their smiling and affection. His mother felt that something was wrong when he was three weeks old.

Motor development was normal: He reached for objects at four months, sat unsupported at eight months, pulled himself to standing at 13 months, and walked at 16 months. He never babbled or mimicked sounds. At 18 months, he said something which sounded like "no" but then stopped talking.

At age two years, Henry was hospitalized for an adenoidectomy. On returning home, he was extremely active, constantly darting about purposelessly from one part of the house to another. By age two and a half years, Henry showed a total lack of concern at separation from his parents, no language, inability to deal with any changes in his environment, and a complete absence of social relatedness. His next years were marked by a series of developmental and physical examinations, and lack of progress emotionally or intellectually. He remained easily distracted, mute, and very hyperactive. There were periodic mood swings from extreme anxiety to lethargy, and periods of self- and other-directed aggressiveness.

At seven and a half, Henry was an attractive, bright-eyed, thin boy, whose only attempts at communication were aggressive lunges toward adults and whining to his mother to indicate hunger. At age eight, a course of phenothiazine medication led to decreased activity and increased social contact. For the first time, he followed simple instructions. After four months on medication, his behavior deteriorated radically and his activity and destructiveness increased to such an extent that he required inpatient hospitalization, to which he responded positively. However, after four months in residential treatment, another mood swing left him uncontrollable, banging his head all day and bruising himself. Restraints were required to prevent Henry from hurting himself. Following this period of agitation, he entered a state of sitting for hours, holding a nurse's hand, apparently in great distress, and muttering "uh, uh." He pulled out clumps of hair, leaving wide areas of baldness. Thorough re-evaluation revealed no organic basis for these dramatic transitions, agreeing with the repeated neurological, physiological, and metabolic evaluations done in the past.

Bruce was delivered by an emergency Caesarean section necessitated by prolapse of an arm and a transverse lie. At birth, he weighed 7 pounds, 7 ounces, and appeared healthy; there were no immediate signs that he suffered from his difficult delivery. His first months of life were entirely normal. By six months, he said "Mama" and "Dada" and soon after he was able to meaningfully use "car." Between six and nine months, for no apparent reason, his development suddenly stopped. He no longer babbled and he lay motionless in his crib, totally uninterested in surrounding events. At nine months, a child developmentalist diagnosed autism.

During the next years, Bruce was involved in psychotherapy, nursery school education, and parental guidance, yet he remained mute, socially isolated, and bizarre. Every evening he wandered throughout the house, breaking windows and pulling out drawers; he suffered from nightmares which did not respond to calming. He recognized no one in the family until well over age three years and then distinguished immediate relatives but would go anywhere with a stranger.

Everything had to remain perfectly stable in Bruce's life. Because of a family history of allergy, Bruce was started on a milk substitute as an infant. When he was one and a half years old, a mental health worker told his mother to discontinue the milk substitute and give him a full glass of milk. Bruce drank the milk, made a face, and refused to drink liquids for the next seven and a half years.

When Bruce was seven, his mother, unwilling to accept the fact that there were no services available for her child, took special courses in education and became her child's teacher. Using various methods for language instruction, she taught Bruce 100 words. However, he never used words voluntarily. His vocabulary was restricted to words directly related to his experience; he was able to use simple signs to volunteer basic information and indicate basic needs or feelings. Through gestures and pictures, his family learned to communicate with him. A trip to the bakery, for example, was indicated by pointing to a picture in the book which his mother assembled for him. Red shoes meant "school day," sneakers meant "no school," and dress clothes meant "party." His eye-hand coordination was brilliant and sometimes a cause of distress to his family. His ability to hit a bird in flight with a piece of bread or a stone led strangers to feel that his aggressiveness was encouraged. He assembled puzzles more quickly than his older siblings. Yet, when he was not engaged in very structured activities, he would rock, twirl a stick in front of his eyes, and gaze blankly into space.

At age 20, Bruce was a physically healthy young man with deep-set eyes, jutting jaw, high palate, and thrusting gait. No abnormalities were present on physical or metabolic evaluation. He remained mute but used some signs to express wishes or respond to direct questions. His ability with puzzles, noted during the first years of life, persisted, and the perceptual abilities were an asset in pre-vocational training. When left alone, he rocked for hours, twirled a leaf in front of his face, and made unintelligible noises in a socially distant, other-worldly fashion, much as he had as a preschooler.

Henry and Bruce are autistic children with pervasive disturbances in social attachment and language acquisition. Introducing other children will indicate difficulties in defining the criteria for the autistic syndrome.

Peter's first years of life were similar to Henry's, but while he remained odd, socially detached, and hyperactive, by age five years he was able to use language in a meaningful way. Many years of special education resulted in improved social behavior and revealed his good intellectual potential. At age 16, Peter was a husky adolescent who looked much like his father, a man with a professional degree who chose to work as a plant manager. With clear directions, Peter could work on a puzzle or remain involved in limited discussion. His language comprehension was far better than his production.

During one office visit, Peter produced a list with two columns. In one were adjectives describing "Good Peter"; in the other, "Bad Peter." The "good" list contained "talks sensibly, plays with toys, sees the doctor, listens to his parents, is a big boy." In the other, "talks nonsense, scratches his neck, bites people, makes funny noises, doesn't look in your eyes, does things twice, gets nervous, is a baby." Peter, thus, showed awareness of his abnormalities and the pain of struggling against what he felt he could scarcely control. Once he was finishing a puzzle when the clinician accidentally made a squeaking noise with a drawer. Peter asked him to repeat this, but when he could not make exactly the same sound, Peter screamed, tried to break the desk, and ran about wildly. During catastrophic episodes such as this, one could observe the same necessity for maintaining everything unchanged which had dominated Peter's life 14 years earlier and the rage and terror which were always close to the surface.

Daryl's hyperactivity, excitement, and poor speech development led to the diagnosis of autism at age three years. During the next several years he was unsuccessfully involved in intensive psychotherapy. At age 6, he suffered a dislocation of the lens in his left eye and secondary glaucoma. Following surgery, he was able to see well enough to learn to read. Six months later, the condition recurred in the right eye, and a hemorrhage was observed in the left. Following removal of the right lens, a fibrinous membrane formed and his vision was reduced to discriminating light and dark. Re-examination of his urine revealed the diagnosis of homocystinuria, an inborn deficiency of cystathionine synthetase which results in decreased brain cystathionine and increased blood and tissue homocystine and methionine.

No school was appropriate for a blind, "autistic" child, and Daryl was moved from one to another. As an only child, he became the center of his parents' life and his mother was his sole social contact. His central interest was collecting records, which led to little real satisfaction. At age 16, Daryl would repetitively ask, for hours on end, one question after another about recording stars and radio announcers: "Who was the singer?" "What is the title?" "When will it be on the air?" And his mother would answer, wearily, with a mixture of anger and sadness. Daryl's discussions with his father about the same topics elicited a combination of banter and rage, with both father and son feeling hurt, bewildered, and trapped.

Except for his thin, elongated fingers and his blindness, Daryl looked no different from Peter, and his language was far better than Henry's or Bruce's. He was quite silly, and talked incessantly of his records, but even this could be interrupted by a direct question which might be answered in a moving and clear manner. "I am sad about my body, but it's no good to be sad," Daryl would say, and then suggest, "You should try making jokes sometimes when you're feeling sad." While touching on issues in his life, he fought to keep himself distracted with questions to which he knew the answers and endless talks leading nowhere.

Of the four children we have introduced, only one had a known metabolic defect. All the others received intensive evaluations without evidence of a specific organic diagnosis.

Natural History

We have studied over 30 children like Henry and Bruce, and many like Daryl. A syndrome such as childhood autism has been associated with a variety of metabolic disturbances, including homocystinuria and phenylketonuria, and with many other types of brain damage, including congenital rubella, brain damage from lead, measles encephalitis, craniosynostosis, and structural malformations of the brain. With the arrival of new diagnostic procedures, some children whose autistic syndrome was of unknown aetiology (primary autism) have been moved into more specific diagnostic categories (autism secondary to a defined aetiology).

For what we believe to be deep, biological reasons, the emotional and behavioral disturbances of children with primary autism and some forms of secondary autism are remarkably alike (Cohen and Caparulo, 1975; Cohen, 1976). These disturbances may be apparent from the first week of life, when the child's attention fades in and out, or when he becomes uncomfortable being held. He may cry inconsolably or be unusually good. By age one year, the autistic child may become preoccupied with one object or toy and spend hours looking at his fingers or banging his head against the crib. The parents' persistent, but vague feeling that something has gone wrong becomes certain as the child grows older and fails to socially babble or learn to use language. Because of his social inaccessibility, lack of language, and unresponsiveness to noises, the child may be thought to be deaf. But often he responds violently to certain sounds, such as the noise of the washing machine, and appears unable to hear others, even his own name or his parent's voice. By age three years, the child's increasing hyperactivity, aloofness, difficulties with language, and odd mannerisms contrast so sharply with normal toddlers' behavior that specialized consultation is sought.

The preschool autistic child is unable to play imaginatively or to share with other children. He seems driven or may be sluggish or underaroused. He may become panicked with small changes in routine or rearrangement in the physical environment. Sleeping patterns are often abnormal, allowing the child and family only three or four hours of uninterrupted sleep. The most devastating symptom, and the central criterion for the diagnosis, is the child's inability to relate to other human beings in a normal, affectionate way. Parents may be used as objects for the satisfaction of basic needs, but the autistic child shows no closeness or mutual enjoyment and concern. A devoted mother, who spent every day with her child for the first 17 years of his life, described her feelings when she brought him to a residential center for the first time. "I knew that as soon as I brought him there," she said, "he would be as happy as he was at home. He didn't seem to miss me for a minute."

Many autistic children have limited vocabularies or no language at all (Caparulo and Cohen, 1977). For those who speak, there may be a variety of peculiarities, including the immediate or delayed repetition of words or phrases, difficulties with pronouns, and other syntactic and semantic peculiarities. The autistic child's speech is usually socially inappropriate or intrusive, and the content tends to be silly or out of context. The odd, mechanical quality of speech makes it sound as if the child is repeating memorized sentences rather than creating new ones. In contrast with their profound disturbances of behavior, many autistic children have limited, "splinter" areas of competence. Sometimes, this intellectual ability is expressed negatively, through mischief or by figuring out how to take a lock off the door or when to throw a glass when not observed. One autistic boy memorized lists of birthdates. Another could assemble radios but could not follow a simple verbal command or say one meaningful sentence.

While the literature is rich in description of appealing young autistic children, who become the subjects for parents' books and movies, far less is known about the less appealing adolescent and adult autistic individuals. The fortunate 10% or 15% of autistic individuals with language and improved social relations may seem odd, eccentric, or very immature as young adults (Wing, 1976). Their behavior in social situations usually lacks spontaneity and reflects the hard work they and their parents and teachers have put into education. They must be taught social conventions, for example, how to say "fine, thank you," instead of honestly responding with a discussion of their daily lives when asked "How are you?" In school, such autistic individuals show areas of high intellectual ability and learn to read well. Yet, their comprehension may be limited and the information they acquire of limited value. The speech of older autistic individuals remains deliberate and stiff, often with the tone of speech-making. They may have odd mannerisms or flap, especially when they are upset or excited, and they are unable to engage in imaginative activities or work or play in mutually meaningful ways with peers. In spite of their major improvements, or because of them, they may be depressed and disheartened, fully aware of their unconquerable handicaps. One very intelligent 21-year-old autistic man described his plight movingly, "I still seem to have some autism . . . my major problem is with initiative."

For the less fortunate children whose language does not progress, behavior during the school-age and adolescent years remains continuous with that of the preschool years. While the child's activity may decrease spontaneously or come under control through precision training, his ability to communicate, understand language, use abstract symbols, follow commands, or relate with peers or adults remains extremely limited. Rocking, flapping, and twirling may be preferred activities, and the appearance and disappearance of parents and others may evoke little response. Sometimes, patterns of behavior may become crystallized and driven. A child may twirl a string, hold a stick, play with straws, bang his nose, bite himself—for hours, without stop. Perhaps the most dramatic example of such driven, repetitive behavior was offered by Daniel, a 16-year-old autistic boy who often broke his nose by banging it with his hand. Daniel was an adequate swimmer and one day began to bang his hand against his nose while standing in the shallow end of the swimming pool. His counselor decided that one way of interrupting the repetitive behavior would be to force Daniel to swim and dragged Daniel to the deep end of the pool. Daniel continued to bang his nose and sank to the bottom of the pool. The counselor dove in and watched Daniel slowly sink while continuing to bang his nose with his hand. The counselor pulled him to safety and quickly revived him. We know what the counselor experienced, but what was occurring inside of Daniel's head remains a dark mystery.

DIFFERENTIAL DIAGNOSIS

Research on the basis of primary childhood autism has been impeded by disagreements on differential diagnosis (Kanner, 1973; Fish and Ritvo, 1977; Rimland, 1964; Ritvo, 1976; Bartak et al., 1975; Creak, 1961, 1964). Unless diagnostic groups can be clearly differentiated and relatively homogeneous, it is unlikely that even the most sophisticated methods can reveal interesting psychobiological correlations.

Mental Retardation

At times, autism has been considered a form of mental retardation. Yet, there are important ways in which primary childhood autism differs from most other forms of organic (or idiopathic) mental retardation. While most retarded children with chronic encephalopathy are more competent socially than intellectually, the opposite is usually true of autistic children. Generally, even those autistic children with relatively more intact expressive language and manual skills are much less capable in social than in non-social situations, and are more interested in mechanical than human stimulation. Also, the majority of profoundly retarded children present clinical and laboratory evidence of central nervous system dysfunction, morphological abnormalities, and impairment in motor development—stigma far less often observed in autistic children with equivalent intellectual deficits. However, as with Daryl, even very experienced clinicians may overlook a secondary form of autism in the absence of appropriate laboratory tests, as was often the case with phenylketonuria or homocystinuria before the availability of techniques for detecting inborn errors of metabolism.

Atypical Development

Children with profound "atypical development" share many features with autistic children—difficulties in perceptual functions, in the modulation of anxiety, in social relations, attention, and the regulation of state. Yet, their disabilities are less severe and may appear later, during the second or third years of life; motor skills may be more slow to develop or more impaired; and social relations may be characterized more by immaturity than by aloofness and disturbance in primary attachment. For these children, an array of diagnostic labels has been proposed, highlighting one or another aspect of impairment: early-onset psychosis, borderline personality, childhood schizophrenia, or childhood psychosis. From one perspective, atypical children may be conceptualized as the "milder' region of the autistic spectrum; from another, as forming the more extremely deviant region of the "minimal cerebral dysfunction" ("minimal brain dysfunction," MBD) phenotype in which children have difficulties in attention, cognitive processing, motor organization, and personality development.

Historical factors, too, account for controversy and disagreement. For example, the clinical distinctions between childhood autism, symbiotic psychosis, atypical personality development, and childhood schizophrenia may rest more upon the clinician's theoretical orientation than on objective, definable clinical criteria. For all of these clinical syndromes, transitions during the course of development may obscure the initial justifications for differentiation. For example, as a nonverbal autistic child develops language, underlying cognitive disturbances and bizarre ideation, more typically associated with childhood schizophrenia, may more clearly emerge. Or, on the other hand, as a nonverbal autistic child moves into adulthood, the social inaccessibility and apparent areas of negativistic intelligence may fade in emphasis as the global retardation moves into greater prominence.

Primary Aphasia

For biological studies, simple diagnostic labels are far less valuable than detailed clinical reports and a range of measurements. The distinction between the psychoses of early onset (autism, atypical development, schizophrenia) and the central language disorders is an example of the value of clinical differentiation (Cohen, Caparulo, and Shaywitz, 1976). Children with developmental or primary aphasia may have histories similar to those of the psychotic children, or their first year or two of life may be more normal. Usually, aphasic children are able to form warm, natural social attachments during infancy and they become worrisome only as they fail to develop language or progress linguistically past short phrases during the second year of life.

As language becomes the primary means for social relations and cognitive tasks increasingly require linguistic mediation for their solution, aphasic children develop serious behavioral disturbances. They become hyperactive, anxious, and difficult to control. At age four or five years, a child with a central language disorder may be intensely attached to his mother, who may be the only person who can understand his modes of communication. At this time, only very careful evaluation will distinguish the aphasic child from autistic children or those children who are sometimes referred to as symbiotic. Careful observations show, however, that the aphasic child has relatively far more intact capacities for inner language, as revealed in spontaneous and structured play, the creation of symbolic gestures, language comprehension, and warm, meaningful social relations. Aphasic children may develop rich repertoires of mime and gesture, using their signs for making declarative and imperative assertions and combining three or four signs in syntactically explicable patterns to convey more complex thoughts (Caparulo and Cohen, 1977).

In contrast with autistic children, the electroencephalograms of aphasic children are typically abnormal, often displaying focal, paroxysmal features.

In the absence of firm, biological markers or correlates, it is almost speculative to postulate whether this spectrum of disorders—autism, schizophrenia, certain forms of central language dysfunctions—represents phenotypic variations on an underlying common genotype, or whether each represents a cluster of phenotypes reflecting a large set of different genotypes (Fish, 1975). Are they more alike than different? Are they the "same disorder" expressed differently, perhaps because of interactions with other aspects of genetic endowment or environmental provision? Are they really heterogenous groups—such as "fevers"—lumped together because of ignorance? None of these questions can be answered definitively, and we believe their resolution will await biological advances. However, extremely fine diagnostic delineation is essential for systematic biological investigation and for the construction of meaningful neurochemical models and correlations. Precision in the biochemical laboratory is meaningful to the degree to which we are precise in the clinic.

DEVELOPMENTAL MODELS

The phenomenological descriptions of autistic and similar children have defined major sectors of deviance affecting social attachment, creative language, and emotional growth. To provide intellectual coherence and guide treatment, clinical investigators have proposed cognitive, psychological, and behavioral models for the "underlying disturbance" in childhood autism. These models may be helpful in organizing diverse types of clinical information and in suggesting methods for biological inquiry, as will be described later. As with adult schizophrenia, however, there has been no shortage of models or any universally acceptable one. Most often, models of autism have emphasized one or another facet of the clinical syndrome or have elevated a symptom cluster (observed as one aspect of the disorder in some children) into an explanation (for the entire spectrum of disabilities) (Rutter, 1971; Churchill et al., 1971; Ritvo, 1976; Cohen et al., 1976).

An adequate model of primary childhood autism must address both the most consistent, enduring handicaps (failure in normal social and language development), as well as areas of functioning which are more closely normal (perceptual abilities, short-term memory, rote memory, and cognitive activities involving calculation and well-learned rules). For the most fortunate autistic children, remarkable intellectual feats may coexist alongside primitive understanding of the human nature of social encounters. How is this possible?

Normal Developmental Mechanisms

During normal development, especially during the first months of life, there is a close interdependence between various psychological subsystems.

The formation of primary social attachments and the creation of concepts about the physical world develop in tandem (Piaget, 1952; DeCarie, 1965; Fraiberg, 1969). This synchrony results, in part, from the dependence of both spheres of competence on the normal unfolding of basic psychological functions—the capacity to attend to aspects of the environment; to modulate arousal; to perform visual, auditory, tactile, and other discriminations; to have normal capacity for experiencing comfort and discomfort from internal and external sources; to form associations and perceive relations; to form action schemata; to store perceptions and sensations in memory and retrieve information on cue; and to use and refine strategies for searching for information (Gibson, 1969; Gibson and Levin, 1975; Neisser, 1976). These basic functions involve processes, which, from the perspective of later psychological organization, could be defined in terms of perceptual, motivational, cognitive, and motoric systems. During the first days and months of life, however, these systems are in the process of emergence and are closely tied to congenitally organized patterns of behavior ("instincts"), innate mechanisms guiding initial adaptations, such as visual orientation and motor quieting during sucking and the organized search for information (Bowlby, 1969; Hinde, 1966; Gregg et al., 1976; Bruner, 1973; Cohen, 1967; Mendelson and Haith, 1976).

The set of basic psychological functions which underlies the unfolding of social and cognitive competence is demonstrable in the behavior of the healthy six-month-old infant. As revealed by clinical histories, the first symptoms—the "basic faults"—in primary childhood autism are often already apparent during this pre-linguistic, sensorimotor phase of development. These symptoms include abnormalities of attention ("looking through" or "looking past" the mother during feeding), arousal (unusual placidity or irritability), social relatedness (absent social smile and lack of pleasure in being cuddled), and motivation (resistance to being comforted by another person or apparent displeasure in normal parent-child dialogue). Thus, a model of the basic dysfunctions in primary childhood autism naturally is concerned with processes or functions represented during the first months of life and which seem, at least in part, to express innately organized, psychobiological systems.

Desynchronization

The unfolding of competence often is not globally or evenly disturbed in childhood autism as it is in some forms of organic brain disorders—e.g., Down's syndrome, in which the unfolding of social and cognitive competence remains closely associated and evenly retarded (Cicchetti and Sroufe, 1976). In primary childhood autism social relatedness may be far more seriously impaired than other areas of development. Even autistic children who differ considerably in general intellectual abilities may present similar types of social impairment (aloofness, detachment, lack of concern) (e.g., see Bartak and Rutter, 1976). Thus, while primary childhood autism presents dysfunctions in basic psychological functions, the areas of major impact and the areas of sparing require specific delineation in a model. As an example of this need for specificity, we will focus primarily on autistic detachment.

Because of the long dependence of the human newborn, it is vital for young infants to perceptually and motorically orient themselves to their caregivers—to stay close, to reach out toward and grasp their mothers. Similarly, for the human newborn, there are no more important cognitive tasks than those involved with understanding people's behavior: how mother (or father) feels now, why she acts the way she does, when to expect her to come, how to please her, how to call for help, and how to display gratification. Social orientation and an interest in social action may be the leading edge in the progress of creating flexible cognitive strategies and structures of other types, e.g., physical object constancy (Bell, 1970; Humphrey, 1976).

Autistic children's social orientation and attention to social interchange are areas of perhaps permanent impairment. Unlike normal children, autistic children show profoundly more "thing" than "person" orientation: They are either *congenitally unable* to become engrossed in the cues and puzzles presented by human relations or they *turn away* from them. Both hypotheses deserve discussion.

Various clinical examples can be cited to illustrate the hypothesis that autistic children are innately not interested in other people. An autistic child was cared for by devoted parents and an unusually involved father for the first 10 years of life. Her father died of a painful illness, and the child showed no signs of missing him. She did not search for him, cry, appear upset or in any other way indicate she suffered his loss. An 11-year-old boy talked about his therapist when separated from her and enjoyed being with her to eat. One day he simply punched her in the stomach when she offered a suggestion about a change in routine. A 16-year-old boy threw his small mother to the floor when she made a simple request. These, as well as the examples previously described, suggest that the autistic children behaved as if they were unable to perceive or appreciate the essence of other people, as if they suffered from a defect no less physiological than color blindness.

The failure of autistic children to display normal social interests in infancy, and their continuing lack of empathic social relatedness, led Kanner (1942, reprinted 1973) to the concept that autism is an inborn disorder of affective relationships similar to inborn errors of metabolism. This model would suggest that autistic children, suffering from a specific mutation affecting the genome underlying social orientation, are congenitally unable to digest caregiving nutrients and use them as building blocks in the synthesis of social structures of attachment and affiliation.

From another perspective, the social disturbances in childhood autism may be seen to reflect dysfunctions in more pervasive psychological functions which are not essentially related to socialization. In this conception, the autistic child—unable to understand social cues, overly stimulated by them, or in a state of constant confusion—turns to the more dependable, stable, and simpler world of physical objects. In fact, the autistic child's cognitive dysfunctions are as enduring as his social limitations. These cognitive impairments are most clear in relation to rule extraction, integration, and elaboration, with auditory processes, short-term memory, and rule-governed problem-solving relatively spared (Hermelin and O'Conner, 1970; Caparulo and Cohen, 1977). It may be hypothesized that because these impairments also emerge during the pre-linguistic phase of development, the autistic child cannot create normal social structures (the concept of the mother as an enduring, caregiving other person) or normal physical world structures (the concept of regularity in events and predictable, natural laws, moving from animistic to more refined epistemologies).

The autistic child's language difficulties are of special interest in this respect since they may, in part, reflect the autistic child's problems in the formation of pre-linguistic concepts upon which explicit language concepts are mapped during the second year of life (Huttenlocher, 1974). The language problems may thus reveal the basic, deep cognitive disturbances. From another angle, the language patterns of autistic children may be studied to understand compensatory mechanisms which the autistic child may develop. For the verbal autistic child, atypicalities of language provide the best illuminated road to understanding the child's competence and handicaps (Caparulo and Cohen, 1977). Syntactic and especially semantic and pragmatic atypicalities reveal the child's disturbance in creating stable internal representations (of self and others), in analyzing and manipulating symbolic representations (especially those which call upon language).

Models

The present stage of knowledge suggests a modest, two-factor model of childhood autism. In this model, congenital disturbances of both social orientation and cognitive maturation may be depicted as playing mutually compounding roles. In neither sphere is the child, even the more intelligent, verbal autistic child, able to move flexibly and intuitively from one hypothesis to another, or to react to barriers or alterations with zestful involvement in problem solving. Cutting across both spheres are major limitations in the creative use of language, a deep disturbance which reflects underlying conceptual difficulties and which prevents the child from becoming empathically assimilated into the social and emotional world of normal peers.

In support of this model, we have noted the enduring impairments in social attachment and feelings of human connectedness and have reviewed clinical histories which highlight not only the child's lack of affiliation but his continued negativism and apparent active resistance to the usual forces of socialization (modeling, reinforcement, effectance motivation, wish to gain and maintain love). On the other side, cognitive difficulties have been shown to persist in the context of areas of intellectual ability and even when behavior is well modified. Such cognitive impairment may become most clear, in fact, when the child is motivated to learn in the course of precision education and when secondary characteristics—e.g., hyperactivity and distractibility—are ameliorated.

In devising models of autistic children's disturbances, we must remain alive to the exceptions—the phenomena which cast doubt upon fundamental premises (Caparulo and Cohen, 1977). During hundreds of hours of observation, parents, teachers, and investigators will be struck by phenomena at apparent odds with their previous understanding of the child's competence: a day or two when the child seems remarkably more in tune with the world and eager to please, perhaps when he has a cold; the sudden use of a sentence, never to be repeated; an absolutely brilliant piece of mischief, planned with precision and executed flawlessly. The investigation of no other syndrome is more burdened by the disparity between competence and performance, by the overwhelming effects of shifting motivation, by the need for patient-watching calling upon the gifts of the anthropological field worker or ethologist. The apparently rigorous laboratory experiment unguided by clinical insight can distort phenomena and yield data consistent with any favored theory.

In summary, the basic faults of childhood autism may be seen as the resultant of several vectors: genetic failure, mutation, or congenital dysfunction involving the psychobiological system which underlies social orientation (and the ability to metabolize parental provisions) and disruptions in the unfolding of those basic psychological processes and competencies which make cognitive creativity possible. The impairments of a child's interest or ability in loving or in his ability to create flexible conceptual schemas (and to find pleasure in confronting ever more varied dilemmas) interact with each other; refinement of cognitive, perceptual, and social structures depends on healthy, mutual interaction between social and intellectual spheres. In the absence of integrated development, autistic children are exposed to incomprehensible social phenomena, perplexing environmental events, and unpredictable shifts in internal state and external responses.

Each autistic child responds to his handicaps with a unique blend of adaptations, based on his endowment, environmental provisions, and fortune. These adaptations consist of combinations of using what he can do best, often heavily relying upon the use of rote and fixed cognitive structures; struggling to learn; withdrawing; and disorganizing. The details of an autistic child's life provide opportunities for understanding the relations between social and cognitive domains, as they appear during the first years of life and are increasingly structured by maturation and education throughout the life cycle.

Psychological models of this type can help locate the significance of neurochemical models, suggesting where they intersect with clinical phenomena. In turn, we will now assess the degree to which neurochemical models—standing on quite different grounds—can highlight clinical phenomenology by casting beams from a new perspective.

NEUROCHEMICAL MODELS

For decades, the psychoses of early onset—childhood autism, schizophrenia, and similar atypicalities of development—have been associated with a hypothesized biological predisposition, perhaps catalyzed by traumatic experiences in early caregiving provisions. However, metabolic research on this predisposition has been highly unsystematic; investigators have focused on one compound at a time, knowledge has not been cumulative or closely related to theory, and suggestive findings have not been intensively followed. At the present time, the most promising area for metabolic study appears to be the neurochemical basis of central nervous system (CNS) signal transmission: Theory has been advanced, knowledge in adult psychiatry has been cumulative, and suggestive findings have emerged (for certain neurological and psychiatric disorders) and have been pursued (Barchas and Usdin, 1973; Goodwin and Post, 1975; Snyder et al., 1974; Schildkraut, 1970).

However, there are major methodological limitations in the path of neurochemical studies in children (Cohen et al., 1977a). Chief among these is the inaccessibility of the brain to direct chemical assessment, and the need for reliance on various indirect methods. Also, understanding of pathological deviations is dependent on the clarification of normal developmental processes, and this enterprise is still very much in its infancy. Clinical researchers are able to study only a restricted range of neurophysiological or neurochemical events in children, and most research has focused on several compounds (substrates, metabolites, and enzymes) in the catecholamine and indoleamine pathways. These compounds constitute only several fragments of what is already known to be a much more complex biological mosaic, and the findings which we will report in this area must, therefore, be interpreted with considerable caution.

CSF Metabolites of Dopamine and Serotonin

The most direct, currently available method for studying biogenic amine metabolism in the human brain involves sampling of cerebrospinal fluid (CSF) for catecholamines (such as dopamine) and indoleamines (serotonin) found in low concentration or their major metabolites, homovanillic acid (HVA) and 5-hydroxyindoleacetic acid (5-HIAA), respectively. HVA and 5-HIAA are actively excreted into the CSF, where their concentration appears to reflect the turnover rate of parent compounds in the brain mass. Diseases and medications which alter brain amines lead to changes in CSF findings; however, the relation between brain physiology and CSF metabolites is far from simple.

Interpretation of metabolite concentrations in the CSF is hazardous. First, the CSF dynamically undergoes replenishment and active re-uptake, and the momentary value of a metabolite is the vector of several processes (brain turnover, excretion, pooling, re-uptake). Second, metabolites differ in concentration at various points of sampling, e.g., the 5-HIAA concentration of the lumbar CSF reflects spinal cord metabolism. Third, the function of all parts of the brain are not equivalently represented in CSF, since areas closer to the ventricles (e.g., basal ganglia) are more likely to affect CSF concentrations than more distant areas (e.g., medial forebrain bundle). Fourth, to obtain CSF, it is necessary to perform a procedure (lumbar puncture) which is both uncomfortable and sometimes frightening and which may affect CSF metabolites, obscuring an underlying trait by an acute state change. And, fifth, alterations in brain physiology in quite limited areas (e.g., locus coeruleus) may have dramatic effects on CNS functioning but lead to only small changes in CSF metabolites.

Several major methodological difficulties, such as momentary variability and low initial concentration of metabolites, are in part overcome by the use of the probenecid blockade method. Probenecid is a benzoic acid derivative used in clinical medicine to inhibit active membrane transport in the kidney to reduce the excretion of penicillin or the reabsorption of uric acid (in gout). In the CNS, probenecid limits egress of the acid metabolites from the CSF, leading to elevations in concentration of HVA, 5-HIAA, and MHPG (Extein et al., 1973; van Praag et al., 1973). When probenecid is administered over 10–18 hours, limiting the reabsorption of the metabolites, the CSF concentrations increase and more closely reflect the amine turnover in brain during a specified period of time (Bowers, 1972; Bowers et al., 1969; Korf and van Praag, 1971; Post et al., 1975; Roos and Sjöström, 1969).

The probenecid method for studying biogenic amine metabolism poses its own methodological difficulties. First, most patients experience gastric distress, nausea, and vomiting toward the end of the loading period. More importantly, the blockage produced by probenecid appears to be progressive (rather than a simple threshold phenomenon) and the concentrations of metabolites remains a function of the probenecid concentration which is achieved. To interpret HVA and 5-HIAA values, these concentrations must be expressed in relation to simultaneously determined CSF probenecid. This relationship may be statistically considered by analysis of covariance or by a ratio of metabolite to probenecid (ng. HVA or 5-HIAA/μg. probenecid in the CSF). On theoretical grounds, the probenecid blockade may be viewed as a dose-response model expressed as a logarithmic relationship; if so, the adjustment for CSF probenecid may best be expressed as ng. metabolite/log μg. probenecid (Cohen et al., 1974, 1977a, 1977b).

Clinical Studies of CSF Metabolites in Children

The probenecid method for studying the physiology of biogenic amine metabolism has been used with children with a spectrum of psychiatric and neurological disorders: autism, aphasia, severe atypical development (early onset, non-autistic psychosis), multiple tic syndrome (of Gilles de la Tourette), epilepsy, minimal cerebral dysfunction, Reye syndrome, and movement disorders (Cohen et al., 1974, 1977b, 1977c; Shaywitz et al., 1975a, 1975b). Ethical and practical restrictions prevent obtaining CSF from normal children. Instead, we have relied on contrast groups and children suffering from various neurological difficulties (such as headache and disc disease). The need for an extended period of probenecid loading has precluded the use of children receiving lumbar punctures for emergency evaluations (for example, to diagnose meningitis).

Early Childhood Psychosis (Autism)

Without probenecid loading, the concentrations of the two major metabolites of dopamine and serotonin (HVA and 5-HIAA, respectively) in autistic children are low, closely clustered, and within the range roughly defined for adults. Determined in six school-age children (ages 6-15, mean=8 years, all male) with classical, primary childhood autism, HVA ranged from 45-100 ng./ml. (mean + SE = 65 ng./ml. $\pm$ 7.7) and 5-HIAA ranged from 36-60 ng./ml. (mean + SE = 41.2 ng./ml. $\pm$ 4.2). Without probenecid loading, there appeared to be a negative relation between HVA and 5-HIAA in the autistic children (r = − .52), most evident in the values of the two extreme cases whose HVA and 5-HIAA concentrations were as follows: (1) 100 ng./ml. HVA, 37 ng./ml. 5-HIAA, and (2) 45 ng./ml. HVA, 60 ng./ml. 5-HIAA. . . .[1]

---

[1]The figures and tables providing raw data in the original article were deleted by the senior author because of space limitations in this volume.

Following 10–12 hours of probenecid loading, the accumulations of the amine metabolites increased significantly. For 12 children with primary autism, HVA following probenecid ranged from 60–414 ng./ml. (mean + SE = 184.2 ng./ml. ± 28.8) and 5-HIAA ranged from 54–182 ng./ml. (mean + SE = 90.5 ng./ml. ± 12.0. . . . The acid metabolites correlated highly with the levels of probenecid achieved in the CSF: .47 for HVA (not statistically significant) and .72 (p< .05) for 5-HIAA. . . .

We have studied 34 other children with aphasia, cognitive processing disturbances, early onset non-autistic psychosis, and non-specific neurological difficulties (pediatric contrast children), all of whom received probenecid (Cohen et al., 1977a, 1977b). . . . For this group, the correlation between metabolites is around .60, significant at p<.001. . . . Within individual diagnostic groups, the product-moment correlation of HVA-5-HIAA is positive, varying from .41 to .80. The relationships of the two metabolites to probenecid for this group of non-autistic, developmentally disabled and medical contrast children are statistically significant. . . .

The functional relations between HVA and 5-HIAA may differ between diagnostic groups, reflecting differences in the balance between serotonergic and dopaminergic systems. To assess this, regression curves may be compared or, more conveniently, a ratio of 5-HIAA/HVA may be constructed for individuals and for groups. The importance of this ratio is underscored by the observation of the possible negative relation between the metabolites without probenecid (discussed in greater detail later) which is obscured by the probenecid method. Most studies of adult schizophrenic and depressed patients using the probenecid method have reported a ratio of 5-HIAA/HVA between 0.5 and 0.7; for autistic children, the ratio is at the lower end of this range, reflecting, in part, our finding of relatively higher HVA levels in child patients and a weak, but statistically significant, negative relation between CSF HVA/log probenecid and age in years (between three and 21 years).

Since CSF metabolite concentrations span such a considerable range within the autistic and non-autistic early childhood psychosis groups, the detection of between-group differences is quite difficult. Thus, we have utilized alternative strategies involving (a) delineation of subpopulations within diagnostic groups and (b) correlation of metabolites with explicit dimensions of behavior, within and across diagnostic groups. Similar approaches have been applied in adult psychiatry, e.g., in relating CSF metabolites and motor activity levels in adult depression (van Praag et al., 1975). In studies of childhood psychosis, we have scored dimensions such as language comprehension and expression, activity, movement abnormalities, and social relatedness, using rating scales completed by clinicians, parents, and teachers (such as adaptations of the Behavior Rating Instrument for Autistic and Atypical Children, Ruttenberg, 1974). These ratings and rank orderings of ratings are related to the concentrations of metabolites found with the probenecid method, across and within groups.

One intriguing finding across diagnostic groups is a difference between children with childhood autism and children (matched for age) with non-autistic, early onset psychosis (severe atypical development or childhood schizophrenic-like youngsters). The autistic children had lower levels of CSF 5-HIAA (Cohen et al., 1977b). More noteworthy, however, was the finding of a subgroup within the autistic population with especially elevated levels of HVA, both absolutely and in comparison with 5-HIAA (as reflected in 5-HIAA/HVA ratios). This subgroup was behaviorally distinguished by the greatest degree of stereotypic, repetitive behavior (flapping, twirling, finger flicking, and the like) and locomotor activity, and was overall the most severely afflicted group.

A special opportunity for investigating these relations was offered by a set of monozygotic twins concordant for primary childhood autism. In this twinship, one twin consistently was rated as more hyperactive and stereotypic. Both with and without the use of the probenecid method, the more active, repetitive child had higher CSF HVA levels than his twin. For therapeutic reasons, both children were treated with haloperidol, a potent inhibiter of dopaminergic activity. The more stereotypic, active child, with the higher concentrations of CSF HVA tolerated a larger dose of haloperidol before displaying toxicity. Interestingly, for both children toxicity was manifested by walking in circles and heightened irritability.

Dopamine, Serotonin, and Behavior

The most convincing evidence, to date, about CNS catecholamine functions in psychotic and attentionally disturbed children relates to the effects of pharmacological intervention. The therapeutic response of autistic and similar children to psychoactive medication is similar in type, although unfortunately different in degree, to the response of adults with schizophrenia. Medications which inhibit dopaminergic functioning (phenothiazines and buytrophenones) reduce the severity of the autistic syndrome in certain children, manifested by decreased self-destructive repetitive actions (such as hand-biting), decreased stereotypic behavior, reduced bizarre behavior, and reduction in overall anxiety; with treatment, social relatedness and availability to behavior modification and special education may improve.

Dopamine releasing medications (dextroamphetamine and methylphenidate) also evoke similar responses in autistic and schizophrenic patients: marked exacerbation of symptomatology (Janowsky et al., 1973). Within minutes after their second or third dose of a stimulant medication, many autistic and severely atypical children become extremely agitated and hypersensitive to sensory input. They will cry, moan, hold their hands over their ears, blink their eyes, complain of spots in front of their eyes, rush about, lunge at people, and literally "climb the walls." One child had to be restrained to control his incessant head-banging; another, because it appeared that he was going to throw himself down the stairs. A third autistic child received about 20 mg. of methylphenidate over the course of three days; following the fourth 5 mg. dose, he suddenly developed jerking movements of one arm, weakness in that arm and the ipsilateral leg, and loss of depth perception (evidenced by behavior such as walking into walls and misjudging steps); these behaviors lasted three weeks.

On the basis of CSF studies, described above, we have postulated that certain manifestations of the autistic syndrome (such as stereotypic behavior) are positively related with dopaminergic overactivity and that there is a reciprocal relation between dopaminergic and serotonergic functioning. In this reciprocal relation, serotonin, which generally plays an inhibitory role in CNS metabolism, appears to modulate catecholamine activity, a relationship which has been observed in various experimental paradigms involving both specific surgical lesions and neurochemical interventions (Kostrzewa et al., 1974; Samanin and Garattini, 1975). In addition, serotonin appears to be responsive to environmental input, with increased sensory intake leading to increased serotonin turnover (Aghajanian et al., 1975; Sheerd and Aghajanian, 1968). Thus, relatively higher serotonin turnover may be associated with a child's greater responsivity to the environment or relatively less tuning out of external sensory bombardment (Cohen and Johnson, 1977).

In summary, the roles of dopaminergic and serotonergic systems in childhood psychosis are suggested by a confluence of basic and neuropsychopharmacological observations, as well as by theoretical considerations: relatively lower CSF 5-HIAA in autistic, as compared to less impaired non-autistic, early onset psychotic children; relatively higher HVA concentrations (in relation to 5-HIAA) in the autistic children with greater stereotypy and activity; the negative relation between CSF HVA and 5-HIAA in children who were studied without probenecid loading; the improvement in certain children treated with dopamine-inhibiting medication; and the dramatic exacerbation of symptomatology following treatment with medications which increase dopaminergic functioning.

These observations on children with early onset psychosis (autistic and non-autistic) can be augmented, we believe, by (a) increased understanding of brain mechanisms in other types of developmental and neurological disturbances and (b) study of specific syndromes which share important features with the psychoses but which are less globally handicapping. Paroxysmal disorders (epilepsy and tic syndromes) and attentional disorders seem especially promising models for dimensions of disturbance found in autism and similar types of early onset psychosis. . . .

Chronic Multiple Tics

The syndrome of Gilles de la Tourette was classically described in the 1880s in Charcot's clinic in Paris (Tourette, 1885). Dozens of publications since then have amply documented the presence of a highly replicable clinical disorder with an onset during the early school years, when tics are quite prevalent, and a generally lifelong duration. The typical clinical presentation in normally intelligent patients involves many years of multiform *movements*: lightning-fast and spasmodic tics (eye blinking, facial jerks, shoulder jerks, full body spasms) and more organized, compulsive movements (hand tapping, gyrations, pacing, foot tapping, touching, finger snapping, etc.). In addition, either early or in more advanced cases, there is the appearance of symptoms involving *vocalization*: repetitive phonic productions (hissing, coughing, hawking, grunting) and verbalizations (parts of words, small words, foul words, repetitions, sudden interjections). Increased psychological tension exacerbates symptomatology, but there is no evidence of neurological or mental deterioration except for the depression and social withdrawal experienced because of the interpersonal difficulties posed by the affliction. The only laboratory evidence of structural CNS pathology is the increased prevalence of non-specific electroencephalographic abnormalities, perhaps associated with the increased prevalence of birth trauma.

The syndrome of chronic multiple tics is a useful partial model for one aspect of the autistic syndrome: Unusual, extremely frequent repetitive movements are characteristic of both. The value of the model is supported by its neuropharmacological properties. All aspects of .the syndrome of chronic multiple tics may be ameliorated by haloperidol, all aspects markedly exacerbated by stimulants. The role of dopaminergic activity in stereotypic and repetitive behaviors is also supported by a range of laboratory and clinical observations, involving administration of amphetamines (in monkeys and man) and localized injections of stimulants into brain substance (Garver et al., 1975; Randrup and Munkvad, 1970). We have studied adolescents with chronic multiple tics of eight or nine years' duration, who have had almost total suppression or amelioration of vocal symptoms with quite small doses of haloperidol (4–6 mg. daily). They can titrate their own need for medication by the degree to which they experience the impulse to emit a tic or compulsive action or sound.

On the basis of the apparent relation between dopaminergic functioning and stereotypic behavior, it would be predicted that patients with chronic multiple tics would have markedly elevated levels of CSF HVA following probenecid administration. The hypothesis, however, was not confirmed in the children. Instead, the levels of CSF HVA were, if anything, slightly reduced; surprisingly, what was observed was a marked, significant reduction in CSF 5-HIAA. In addition to an overall reduction in 5-HIAA, two lines of evidence connected the relation between 5-HIAA and HVA to the severity of the chronic tic disorder. First, severity of the tic disorder was associated with the degree of 5-HIAA reduction relative to HVA, with the most severely impaired patients having the highest levels of HVA relative to 5-HIAA. Second, there was a consistent response of CSF metabolites to treatment with dextroamphetamine in one adult patient. With a short course (48 hours) of treatment, the 28-year-old patient, who had suffered from the syndrome of chronic multiple tics since childhood, experienced marked exacerbation of symptomatology accompanied by increased levels of CSF 5-HIAA and decreased levels of CSF HVA. We have interpreted these findings to suggest that the medication increased dopaminergic functioning, which led to feedback inhibition of presynaptic dopaminergic neurons and to compensatory augmentation of inhibitory serotonergic systems (Cohen et al., 1978).

There are occasional patients with the syndrome of chronic multiple tics who do not respond to haloperidol or who require such large doses that the side-effects of medication interfere to an unacceptable degree with activities. For an occasional patient, treatment with the serotonin precursor, 5-hydroxytryptophan, has been found to be beneficial (van Woert et al., 1977b), as would be predicted from our neuropharmacological observations. The great range of response to haloperidol, the variance in symptomatology and in severity of disturbance, and the range of CSF findings all suggest the heterogeneity of the syndrome of chronic multiple tics. Future research may better delineate subgroups, based on CSF and pharmacological findings, just as it has in studies of adult depression (Maas, 1975; Åsberg et al., 1976). . . .

CONCLUSIONS

In this chapter, we have described the array of psychological dysfunctions presented by children with primary childhood autism and similar, pervasive developmental disturbances which appear during the first years of life. The pervasive cognitive, social, emotional, motivational, linguistic, and motoric difficulties of children with autism are related to each other in complex ways. Whether the various syndromes which have been described (such as autism and childhood schizophrenia) are intrinsically or genotypically similar or are merely phenotypic cousins cannot be determined by the type of behavioral studies which are available. In the future, behavioral markers may help organize the syndromic diversity, but it appears to us that neurochemical parameters will be more likely to bring about syndromic clarity. However, biological research and clinical studies must proceed in tandem, each helping to define the appropriate domain for the other.

At our current level of methodological competence, only a highly restricted range of metabolic parameters has been investigated. In this chapter, we have reviewed studies on cerebrospinal fluid metabolites of dopamine and serotonin, only two of the many already identified neurotransmitter substances. It may be that the autistic syndromes will be related to disturbances in one or another metabolic pathway concerned with neurotransmitter regulation; it is just as likely that the genetic predisposition to the autistic syndrome, and similar disorders, is expressed in the mapping of neuronal circuits (wiring diagrams) or in some other aspect of CNS integration. If so, the network of neuropsychopharmacological observations which we have outlined (e.g., concerning stereotypic behavior and dopamine or the relations between dopaminergic and serotonergic mechanisms) will be seen to be only of peripheral interest. The biological study of childhood autism, and similar developmental disorders, however, will progress to the degree to which we can (a) remain aware of the complexity of the phenomena which our child patients present and (b) systematically define simple, testable hypotheses which can be related to relevant clinical dimensions. From this perspective, we see the study of CSF metabolites as a model of the type of investigations which remain ahead in the study of the most devastating disorders of childhood.

REFERENCES

Aghajanian, G. K., Haigler, H. J., and Bennett, J. L.: Amine receptors in CNS. III. 5-Hydroxytryptamine in brain. In: L. L. Iverson, S. D. Iverson, & S. H. Snyder (Eds.), *Handbook of Psychopharmacology*, Vol. 6. New York: Plenum Publishing Corporation, 1975, pp. 63-96.

Åsberg, M., Thoren, P., Traskman, L. I., Bertilsson, L., and Ringberger, V.: "Serotonin depression"—A biochemical subgroup within the affective disorders? *Science*, 1976, 191:478-480.

Barchas, J. and Usdin, E.: *Serotonin and Behavior*. New York: Academic Press, 1973.

Bartak, L. and Rutter, M.: Differences between mentally retarded and normally intelligent autistic children. *J. Austism Childhood Schizoph.*, 1976, 6:109-120.

Bartak, L., Rutter, M., and Cox, A.: A comparative study of infantile autism and specific developmental receptive language disorder. I. The children. *Brit. J. Psychiat.*, 1975, 126:127-148.

Bell, S. M.: The development of the concept of object as related to infant-mother attachment. *Child Develpm.*, 1970, 41:291-311.

Bowers, M. B., Jr.: Clinical measurement of central dopamine and 5-hydroxytryptamine metabolism: Reliability and interpretation of cerebrospinal fluid acid monoamine metabolic measures. *Neuropharmacol.*, 1972, 11:101-111.

Bowers, M. B., Jr., Henninger, G. P., and Gerbode, F. A.: Cerebrospinal fluid 5-hydroxyindoleacetic acid and homovanillic acid in psychiatric patients. *Int. J. Neuropharmacol.*, 1969, 8:255-262.

Bowlby, J.: *Attachment and Loss*, Vol. 1, *Attachment*. New York: Basic Books, 1969.

Bruner, J. S.: Organization of early skilled action. *Child Develpm.*, 1973, 44:1-11.

Campbell, B. and Randall, P. J.: Paradoxical effects of amphetamine on preweanling and postweanling rats. *Science*, 1977, 195:888-891.

Cantwell, D. P.: *The Hyperactive Child: Diagnosis, Management, Current Research*. New York: Halsted Press, 1975.

Caparulo, B. K. and Cohen, D. J.: Cognitive structures, language, and emerging social competence in autistic and aphasic children. *J. Amer. Acad. Child Psychiat.*, 1977, 16(4):620-645.

Churchill, D., Alpern, G., and de Myer, M. (Eds.): *Infantile Autism.* Springfield, Ill.: Thomas, 1971.

Cicchetti, D. and Sroufe, L. A.: The relationship between affective and cognitive development in Down's syndrome infants. *Child Developm.*, 1976, 47:920-929.

Cohen, D. J.: The crying newborn's accommodation to the nipple. *Child Develpm.*, 1967, 38:89-100.

Cohen, D. J.: Competence and biology: Methodology in studies of infants, twins, psychosomatic disease, and psychosis. In: E. J. Anthony & C. Koupernik (Eds.), *The Child in His Family: Children at Psychiatric Risk.* New York: Wiley, 1974, pp. 361-394.

Cohen, D. J.: The diagnostic process in child psychiatry. *Psychiatric Annals*, 1976, 6(9): 404-416.

Cohen, D. J. and Caparulo, B. K.: *Childhood autism. Children Today*, 1975, 4:2-6, 36.

Cohen, D. J., Caparulo, B. K., and Shaywitz, B. A.: Primary childhood aphasia and childhood autism: Clinical, biological and conceptual observations. *J. Amer. Acad. Psychiat.*, 1976, 15:606-645.

Cohen, D. J., Caparulo, B. K., Shaywitz, B. A., and Bowers, M.B., Jr.: Assessment of cerebrospinal monoamine metabolites in children using the probenecid method. *Israel Ann. Psychiat. Related Disc.*, 1977, 15 (1):47-57.

Cohen, D. J., Caparulo, B. K., Shaywitz, B. A., and Bowers, M. B., Jr.: Dopamine and serotonin in neuropsychiatrically disturbed children: Cerebrospinal fluid homovanillic acid and 5-hydroxyindoleacetic acid. *Arch. Gen. Psychiat.*, 1977, 34(5):561-567. (b)

Cohen, D. J., Shaywitz, B. A., Caparulo, B. K., Young, J. G., and Bowers, M. B., Jr.: Chronic multiple tics of Gilles de la Tourette: CSF acid monoamine metabolites after probenecid administration. *Arch. Gen. Psychiat.*, 1978, 35:245-250.

Cohen, D. J., Johnson, W. T., and Bowers, M. B., Jr.: Biogenic amines in autistic and atypical children: Cerebrospinal fluid measures of homovanillic acid and 5-hydroxyindoleacetic acid. *Arch. Gen. Psychiat.*, 1974, 31(6):845-853.

Creak, M. (Chairman): Schizophrenia syndrome in childhood: Progress report of a working party. *Cerebral Palsy Bull.*, 1961, 3:501-504.

Creak, M. (Chairman): Schizophrenia syndrome in childhood: Further progress report of a working party. *Dev. Med. Child Neurol.*, 1964, 6:530-535.

DéCarie, T. G.: *Intelligence and Affectivity in Early Childhood.* New York: International Universities Press, 1965.

Dews, P. B. and Morse, W. H.: Behavioral pharmacology. *Ann. Rev. Pharmacol.*, 1961, 1:145-174.

Extein, I., Korf, J., Roth, R. H., and Bowers, M. B., Jr.: Accumulation of 3-methoxy-4-hydroxyphenylglycol-sulphate in rabbit cerebrospinal fluid following probenecid. *Brain Res.*, 1973, 54:403-407.

Fish, B.: The "one child, one drug" myth of stimulants in hyperkinesis: Importance of diagnostic categories in evaluating treatment. *Arch. Gen. Psychiat.*, 1971, 25:193-203.

Fish, B.: Biologic antecedents of psychosis in children. In: D. X. Freedman (Ed.), *Biology of the Major Psychoses. Res. Publ. Assoc. Res. Nerv. Ment. Dis.*, Vol. 54. New York: Raven Press, 1975, pp. 49-83.

Fish, B. and Ritvo, E.: Childhood psychosis. In: J. Noshpitz (Ed.), *Handbook of Child Psychiatry* (in press).

Fraiberg, S.: Libidinal object constancy and mental representation. *The Psychoanalytic Study of the Child*, 1969, 24:9-47.

Garver, D. L., Schlemmer, R. F., Maas, J. W., and Davis, J. M.: A schizophreniform behavioral psychosis mediated by dopamine. *Amer. J. Psychiat.*, 1975, 132:32-38.

Gibson, E. J.: *Principles of Perceptual Learning and Development.* New York: Prentice-Hall, 1969.

Gibson, E. J. and Levin, H.: *The Psychology of Reading.* Cambridge, Mass.: MIT Press, 1975.

Goodwin, F. K. and Post, R. M.: Studies of amine metabolism in affective illness and schizophrenia. In: D. X. Freedman (Ed.), *Biology in the Major Psychoses. Res. Publ. Assoc. Res. Nerv. Ment. Dis.*, Vol. 54. New York: Raven Press, 1975, pp. 299-332.

Gregg, C. L., Haffner, M. E., and Korner, A. F.: The relative efficacy of vestibular-proprioceptive stimulation and the upright position in enhancing visual pursuit in neonates. *Child Develpm.*, 1976, 47:309-314.

Hermelin, B. and O'Connor, M. A.: Rules and language. In: *Infantile Autism: Concepts, Characteristics and Treatment.* London: Churchill Livingstone, 1970, pp. 98-111.

Hinde, R.: *Animal Behavior.* New York: McGraw-Hill, 1966.

Humphrey, N.: Personal communication. University of Cambridge, 1976.

Huttenlocher, J.: The origins of language comprehension. In: M. Solso (Ed.), *Theories in Cognitive Psychology.* Loyola University Press, 1974.

Janowsky, D. S., El-Yosef, M. K., Davis, J. M., and Sekerke, H. J.: Provocation of schizophrenic symptoms by intravenous administration of methylphenidate. *Arch. Gen. Psychiatry*, 1973, 28(2):185-191.

Kanner, L.: *Childhood Psychosis: Initial Studies and New Insights.* Washington, D.C.: Winston & Sons, 1973.

Korf, J. and van Praag, H. M.: Amine metabolism in the human brain: Further evaluation of the probenecid technique. *Brain Res.*, 1971, 35:221-230.

Kostrzewa, R. M. and Jacobowitz, D. M.: Pharmacological actions of 6-hydroxydopamine. *Pharmacol. Rev.*, 1974, 26(3):200-288.

Kostrzewa, R. M., Samanin, R., Bareggi, S. R., Marc, V., Giarattini, S., and Valzelli, L.: Biochemical aspects of the interaction between midbrain raphe and locus coeruleus in the rat. *Brain Res.*, 1974, 82:178-182.

Maas, J. W.: Biogenic amines and depression. *Arch. Gen. Psychiatry*, 1975, 32:1357-1361.

Mendelson, M. and Haith, M. M.: The relation between audition and vision in the human newborn. *Monographs of the Society for Research in Child Development*, 1976, 167. Whole issue.

Neisser, U.: *Cognition and Reality.* San Francisco: W. H. Freeman & Co., 1976.

Piaget, J.: *The Origin of Intelligence in Children.* New York: International Universities Press, 1952.

Post, R. M., Fink, E., Carpenter, W. T., and Goodwin, F. K.: Cerebrospinal fluid amine metabolites in acute schizophrenia. *Arch. Gen. Psychiat.*, 1975, 32:1063-1069.

Randrup, A. and Munkvad, I.: Biochemical, anatomical and psychological investigations of stereotyped behavior induced by amphetamines. In: E. Costa and S. Garratini (Eds.), *Amphetamines and Related Compounds.* New York: Raven Press, 1970, pp. 695-713.

Rimland, B.: *Infantile Autism.* New York: Meredith Publishing, 1964.

Ritvo, E. (Ed.): *Autism: Diagnosis, Current Research, and Management.* New York: Spectrum Press, 1976.

Roos, B. E. and Sjöström, R.: 5-Hydroxyindoleacetic acid (and homovanillic acid) levels in the cerebrospinal fluid after probenecid application in patients with manic-depressive psychosis. *Pharmacologia Clinica*, 1969, 1:153-155.

Ruttenberg, B.: *Behavior Rating Instrument for Autistic and Other Atypical Children.* Philadelphia: The Developmental Center for Autistic Children, 1974.

Rutter, M. (Ed.): *Infantile Autism.* London: Whitefriars Press, 1971.

Samanin, R. and Garattini, S.: The serotonergic system in the brain and its possible functional connections with other aminergic systems. *Life Sciences*, 1975, 17:1201-1210.

Schildkraut, J. J.: *Neuropsychopharmacology and the Affective Disorders.* Boston: Little, Brown, 1970.

Shaywitz, B. A., Cohen, D. J., and Bowers, M. B., Jr.: CSF amine metabolites in children with minimal brain dysfunction (MBD)—Evidence for alteration of brain dopamine. (Abstr.) *Periat. Res.*, 1975, 9(4):385. (a)

Shaywitz, B. A., Cohen, D. J., and Bowers, M. B., Jr.: Reduced cerebrospinal fluid 5-hydroxyindoleacetic acid and homovanillic acid in children with epilepsy. *Neurology*, 1975, 25:74-79. (b)

Shaywitz, B. A., Cohen, D. J., and Bowers, M. B., Jr.: CSF amine metabolites in children with minimal brain dysfunction (MBD)—Evidence for alteration of brain dopamine. *J. Pediat.*, 1977, 90:67-71.

Shaywitz, B. A., Yager, R. D., and Klopper, J. H.: Selective brain dopamine depletion in developing rats: An experimental model of minimal brain dysfunction. *Science*, 1976, 191:305-307.

Sheerd, M. H. and Aghajanian, G. K.: Stimulation of midbrain raphe neuron: Behavioral effects of serotonin release. *Life Sciences*, 1968, 7:19-29.

Snyder, S. H., Banerjee, S. P., Yamamura, H. I., and Greenberg, D.: Drugs, neurotransmitters, and schizophrenia: Phenothiazines, amphetamines, and enzymes synthesizing psychotomimetic drugs aid schizophrenia research. *Science*, 1974, 184:1243-1253.

Tourette, de la, G.: Clinique Nerveuse. Étude sur une affection nerveuse caractérisée par de l'incoordination motrice accompagnée d'écholalie et de coprolalie (jumping, latah, myriachit). *Arch. Int. de Neurol. des Maladise*, 1885, 9:19-42.

van Praag, H. M., Flentge, F., Korf, J., Dols, L. C. W., and Schut, T.: The influence of probenecid on the metabolism of serotonin, dopamine and their precursors in man. *Psychopharmacologia (Berl.)*, 1973, 33:141-151.

van Praag, H. M., Korf, J., Lake, J. P. W. T., and Schut, T.: Dopamine metabolism in depressions, psychoses, and Parkinson's disease: The problem of the specificity of biological variables in behavior disorders. *Psychol. Med.*, 1975, 5:138-146.

van Woert, M. H., Rosenbaum, D., Howieson, J., and Bowers, M. B., Jr.: Long-term therapy of myoclonus and other neurologic disorders with L-5-hydroxy-tryptophan and carbidopa. *New Engl. J. Med.*, 1977, 296:70-75. (a)

van Woert, M. H., Yip, L. C., and Balis, M. E.: Purine phosphoribosyltransferase in Gilles de la Tourette syndrome. *New Engl. J. Med.*, 1977, 296:210-212. (b)

Weiss, B. and Laties, V. G.: Enhancement of human performance by caffeine and the amphetamines. *Pharmacol. Rev.*, 1962, 14:1-36.

Wing, J. K.: *Early Childhood Autism.* Oxford: Pergamon Press, 1976.

COMMENTARY by Theodore Shapiro

This complex, comprehensive discussion sums up the state of the art at the turn of the new decade, 1980. The authors skillfully pull together the problems of differential clinical distinction on behavioral grounds, and then they turn to biological discriminations on the basis of new neurochemical approaches using neurotransmitter research. There are difficulties in both approaches, but there are grounds for hope for continued development of testable hypotheses and studies of both behavior and neurochemistry that are complementary.

The authors are careful and sensitive to the complexity of the human problems in these "most devastating disorders of childhood" and thus do not oversimplify the answers. This paper is a contribution of broad significance; a summing up of the art of integrative approaches, with modest suggestions for new directions. It is clear that new technology is available, but it also seems true that the answers to the problem of autism will not be a one-to-one simple biological-behavioral correlate—at least not at the present state of understanding. The links suggested on biological grounds between autism and dysphasia, Tourettes and Attention Deficit Disorder (A.D.D.) open new vistas for speculation.

20

The Autistic Syndromes

MARY COLEMAN

In 1971, infantile autism was briefly reviewed by Rutter as a small portion of a review of psychiatry for volume III of *Mental Retardation*. In the seven years since that time, a large new body of data has been published about autistic children and we know a great deal more about them. Now there is enough information to fill an entire chapter—in fact, a great deal more than that. And autism, in spite of the psychiatric symptoms of the patients, is now regarded as an organic disease that belongs in a review of mental retardation entities. Although there is agreement that there is an organic etiology to this syndrome, the anatomical location or neurophysiological system or biochemical system involved still has not been specifically identified in most cases.

Symptoms Seen in Patients with the Autistic Syndromes

The diagnosis of a patient with the classical autistic syndrome is made when there is an onset before 36 months of age of a disease process involving:

1. A profound inability to relate to other people (Kanner's "extreme autistic aloneness" (35) or Chess et al.'s "lack of affective human contact" (13)).
2. Often profound language retardation, including impaired comprehension of language appropriate for age and unusual use of language.
3. Other abnormal perceptual responses to sensory stimuli, including non-language auditory processing as well as visual and tactile modalities. These disturbances of perception include both hypersensitivity and hyposensitivity to the same external stimuli in the same child at different times, called "perceptual inconstancy" (44). The olfactory perceptions often appear to be spared.
4. Ritualistic and compulsive behavior patterns.
5. Disturbances of motility (particularly hand flapping and appearances of stereotypies).

Reprinted with permission from *Mental Retardation and Developmental Disabilities*, vol. 10, ed. Joseph Wortis (New York: Brunner/Mazel, 1978), 65–76.

A sixth criterion seen in some autistic children is "areas of excellence," or "islands of competence," or "splinter skills." These are isolated superior levels of intellectual functioning in a child functioning at a much lower level in most other areas. When present, this sixth criterion is useful in differentiating autistic children from mentally retarded youngsters.

The first criterion of autistic aloneness, originally described as the hallmark of the syndrome, improves with age in patients and is less apparent in some older autistic children, adolescents and adults. When young, these patients usually are described as "isolated," "withdrawn," "unresponsive to people," or having "selective inattention" to other human beings.

The language pattern or lack of language in autistic patients is a major area of research focus at present, particularly in Britain. Autistic children have been compared to patients with developmental dysphasia (1, 4) and to mentally retarded patients (3). In one comparative study, 80% of the control patients, 60% of the mentally retarded, and only 8% of the autistic children had mastered the past tense (2). In these early studies, autistic children appear to be more impaired in the receptive language area than dysphasic patients and have a more global delay in language development than retarded children of comparable mental age. There is clear evidence that these children lack the ability to extract the components of structured auditory input.

Some investigators have felt that autism is primarily a language disorder with the other symptoms stemming from this disability. For example, Michael Rutter has written that the evidence at this time suggests that what he calls a "cognitive defect" has a central role in all of the symptomology in autistic children (55). Specifically, he appears to be referring to their receptive language disorder and often profound incomprehension of language and concepts so that there is even impairment in their understanding and use of gesture. He points out that these patients have a "paucity of inner language" (54). He notes that verbal sequencing is particularly impaired in these patients who perform poorly on most verbal subtests such as comprehension, similarities and vocabulary.

The main difficulties with this concept are that "cognitive defect" is not a meaningful or exact term in a neurophysiological sense and there is no convincing reason at this time to suppose that any one critical feature (such as language impairment) of these multifaceted syndromes of autistic behavior disorders is primary (5). Also, if this concept is true, it is puzzling that blind children are more likely to have "autistic" symptoms than deaf children.

In addition to difficulty with perceiving language, autistic patients have problems with other auditory and, in fact, most perceptual responses to sensory stimuli. An explanation of the underlying mechanisms causing these symptoms is a failure of consistent processing of sensory input or failure of "perceptual constancy" (44). Ornitz and Ritvo have noted that identical sensory input from the environment appears not to be experienced the same way each time by the autistic child. They postulated an underlying failure of homeostatic regulation within the central nervous system so that environmental stimuli are either not adequately modulated or are unevenly amplified—a failure to maintain perceptual constancy. They suggested there may be a non-physiological state of the central nervous system or an imbalance in regulation of the usually finely tuned facilitative and inhibitory influences of the resting level of excitation of the brain. The result is inappropriate amplification or actual distortion of apparently innocuous stimuli followed, perhaps, at another time by loss or diminution of such stimuli.

Except for olfactory processing, all the other sensory modalities may be involved in the perceptual inconstancy of these patients. Autistic patients may smell a toy rather than feel, look at or listen to it. They may have inconstant responses to a variety of sounds beside language, and deafness is usually considered when an autistic child is young. Yet they often hold their hands over their ears, perhaps to diminish sounds during some periods. The reports of infant patients stiffening in their mothers' arms or crying when touched may be related to aberrant tactile functioning in younger children. Also, autistic children are masters of the fleeting glance. Gaze aversion, a common symptom of autistic children, has been clearly documented by a number of objective observations (48). Hutt and Ounsted (33) interpreted this aversion as having the function of minimizing arousal or cutting off sensory receptors from stimulating activity in an autistic child whose level of arousal is already overactive. They note that gaze aversion in animals is an "appeasement posture" which serves to inhibit aggression on the part of others. We have noted the apparent emotional pain seen in some autistic children while they look at an examiner's eyes after having learned to do so for a fixed period of time by behavior conditioning techniques.

Another symptom of autism is ritualistic and compulsive behavior patterns (59). These patients have an obsessive desire for sameness (47). They may eat exactly the same limited foods each day, insist on wearing the same clothes, be troubled by a slight change in furniture arrangement in their home. A change in their schedule, normally difficult for many young children for a day or so, may trigger a developmental regression in autistic children. This imposition of rigid rules and structure on their life experiences can also be seen in testing situations where they differ from normal children in their structuring of recall of material and spontaneous pattern-making (27).

The fifth criteria of the autistic syndromes are motility disturbances and stereotypies. Hand flapping is the most common adventitious movement in these patients. Their hand clapping or clasping may be a suppressed form of hand flapping (68). Hand posturing, including choreic movements, jumping, rocking, and facial grimacing are also seen. One theory suggests that these movements are an attempt to make sense out of both exogenous and endogenous sensations by kinesthetic feedback (45). It is interesting that stereotypies are greatest in the presence of a stranger and least often observed when the child is alone (34).

Classification of Patients with the Autistic Syndromes

How many autistic patients are there with this constellation of symptoms? There have been two studies which estimate the frequency of autistic patients to be roughly one out of every 2,200 live births or between four or five out of every 10,000. One of these studies was done in England (42) and one in the United States (66).

Patients who present the symptoms of autism can be classified into three separate syndromes (Table 1). First is the classical autistic syndrome as originally described by Kanner in 1943. These patients have the classical symptoms described above with no observable signs of neurological or electroencephalographic impairment. However, if such a patient develops a seizure disorder after adolescence, this does not exclude him as a Class I patient. One-third of autistic patients who test as retarded develop a seizure disorder after puberty. Some of the patients with this syndrome can be further subdivided into several subgroups, which will be discussed later. However, the majority of patients with the classical autistic syndrome, at this time, do not have a specific sub-category of diagnosis.

The second class of patients are those who have the childhood schizophrenic syndrome with the autistic type of symptoms. These patients also have the symptoms mentioned above except that their age of onset is usually past 30 or 36 months of age. Also, they are more likely to have other psychiatric symptoms in addition to the classical autistic symptoms. Whether these children have a late onset of some of the etiological agents causing infantile autism or have completely separate disease entities is unknown and remains to be investigated in the future.

The third group of patients, Class III—the neurologically impaired autistic syndrome—are children who have a number of autistic symptoms and are also neurologically impaired. These patients are children with identifiable organic disease of the brain who are occasionally misdiagnosed as clas-

TABLE 1

The Autistic Syndromes

I. The classic autistic syndrome

II. The childhood schizophrenic syndrome with autistic-type symptoms

III. The neurologically impaired autistic syndrome

* From M. Coleman (Ed.), *The Autistic Syndromes* (North Holland, 1976).

sical autistic patients until careful examination or the clinical course reveals the correct diagnosis (Table 2). This group may have evidence of organic brain disease on neurological examination or on electroencephalographic examination, or evidence of a deteriorating, degenerative clinical pattern. With rubella autistics, there is a definite correlation between the number of physical defects and the presence of psychiatric disorders (13).

Most research and interest in autistic patients are centered on those children who have Class I, the classical autistic syndrome. These are patients with the full syndrome. It appears that there may be several specific disease entities among such patients with the classical syndrome, although studies are so preliminary that no entity can be considered as established at this time.

One subgroup of autistic patients appears to have familiar etiology to their illness, most likely genetic in origin. Of 131 siblings of Kanner's first 100 cases of infantile autism, three, or 3%, could be regarded as probably autistic (36). Of the 79 families reported by Creak and Ini (20), two families (less than 3%) had one other autistic child. Rutter (51) reported two siblings with "disorders which might be termed autistic" in his group of 63 patients (less than 2%). A somewhat higher percentage was reported by Spence et al. (61), who found five affected siblings in their sample of 47 families (9%). There are several reports of three affected children in the same family (43, 49, 53, 57).

In the recent study of 78 patients with the classic autistic syndrome and age/sex matched controls, 8% of the autistic children had a relative who also had the same diagnosis (17). Patient pedigrees suggested that the genetic pattern may be autosomal recessive. Two-thirds of these families were Jew-

TABLE 2

The Neurologically Impaired Autistic Syndrome

Disease Entity	References
Metabolic	
Phenylketonuria	Friedman (26)
Tuberous Sclerosis	Valente (67)
Mucopolysaccharidoses	Knobloch and Pasamanick (37)
Infectious	
Rubella	Chess et al. (13)
Lues	Rutter and Bartak (55A)
Non-specific	
Hydrocephalus	Schain and Freedman (56)
Infantile spasms syndrome	Taft and Cohen (64)
Sensory deprivation syndromes (blindness, deafness)	Fay (24)

* From M. Coleman (Ed.), *The Autistic Syndromes* (North Holland, 1976).

ish in contrast to only 18% of the total sample of 78 autistic patients. There are not yet enough families with two or more autistic children described in detail in the literature, so this initial study of a possible genetic pattern remains to be confirmed.

A twin study by Folstein and Rutter (25) has shown an increased concordance rate for autism of 36% in monozygotic twins but no concordance rate in dizygotic twins (25). These authors point out that the non-autistic twin in the monozygotic sets was likely to have another central nervous system diagnosis, such as mental retardation, articulation defect or language disorder. This pattern was not seen in the dizygotic pairs.

Twins share the same intrauterine environment so evidence from twin studies can apply to gestational insults as well as patterns of genetic inheritance. However, the difference between monozygotic and dizygotic pairs suggests genetic influences could be one factor in this twin study.

Another possible subgroup among patients with the classical autistic syndrome are children with malabsorption or a type of gastrointestinal disease (19, 29). Also reported are possible patients with unusual urine turnover (18). There is speculation that autistic symptoms without gross neurological abnormalities could be caused by viral agents other than rubella (such as varicella (37), toxoplasmosis, or herpes) (46) perhaps as an early manifestation of an initially progressive chronic panencephalitis that becomes static with age. These possibilities have taken on added weight since the reports of a relative T cell deficiency, decreased lymphocyte responsiveness (63) and altered immune responses in autistic children (66). Also, it has been suggested that an autoimmune mechanism may be implicated in the classical autistic picture (18).

Postulated Anatomical Substratum of Autistic Symptoms

Thus, it is clear that "autism" is not a disease entity. It is a constellation of symptoms, i.e., a syndrome, one of the limited patterns the infant's central nervous system has in reaction to injury or genetic misinformation. Since autopsy and neuropathology studies are pitifully inadequate (21), even the most elementary questions have yet to be answered.

One basic question is—can there be an anatomical location for these syndromes? A number of locations have been suggested by various authors because of the patient's symptoms. One location could be possible bilateral lesions of the temporal lobe or specifically the hippocampal area. This area has been suggested by several different disciplines—psychological testing (6), pneumoencephalographic studies (31), and viral studies identifying the herpes virus as a possible etiology (46). (This virus has a predilection for the temperal lobe.) However, autistic patients differ from developmental dyslexics who may have bilateral temporal lobe lesions (39). Another way station in the auditory pathway that has been suggested as a site of lesions is the inferior colliculus (or acoustic tectum) (58). Again bilateral lesions would be needed to explain the symptoms and, again, such a lesion specific to the language pathway would be inadequate to explain the other symptoms of autism. The association areas of the brain, particularly those serving language centers, have also been suggested as site of the lesion. More impressive is the evidence in favor of the thalamus, a grey matter substation serving auditory, visual and tactile pathways. The only sensory system not processed through the thalamus—the olfactory pathway—is also the only system intact in many young autistic children.

A very interesting hypothesis has been suggested by Tanguay (65). He has proposed that autism is a failure of the process of specialization and differentiation of the left and right hemispheres that occurs in normal children. The normal lateralization of cerebral function could fail to occur at all or to occur normally. Recent studies showing unusual patterns of right and left handedness in these patients (7, 66), adds to the relevance of Tanguay's observations.

The brainstem, particularly the reticular activating system, has been suggested by a number of investigators (15, 49). Evidence from studies of alertness, arousal levels, and biochemical studies of biogenic amines (Table 3) have led to these suggestions.

A specific gross anatomical lesion in autistic patients may never be identified. The lesion could be at the cellular or molecular level. The attempt to correlate specific symptoms with specific anatomical locations in the human central nervous system has been less than clarifying in many diseases of the brain, often in spite of devastating and overwhelming symptomatology. But, at this time, the basic neuropathological studies remain to be completed in the autistic syndromes.

Treatment and Prognosis

Adequate treatment depends upon understanding the etiology of a syndrome, rather than on attempts to suppress symptoms. Treatment of autism remains, at present, in the latter category.

Methods used today vary. Many are controversial, such as the use of electric shock in some of the types of behavior conditioning, or extremely expensive, such as the use of a computer for a self-training keyboard. Educational techniques are gradually being developed specifically for autistic children; sign language can now be taught to nonverbal children. Pharmacological studies are in adjunct in some cases to make a child more amenable to other therapies, but a satisfactory drug treatment for most autistic children has not been developed (12). Metabolic treatments are still in their infancy (18).

TABLE 3

Abnormalities of biogenic amine pathways reported in patients with symptoms of autism

Biochemical	Abnormality reported	Medium	Authors
5-hydroxytryptamine (serotonin)	elevated endogenous level	whole blood	Schain and Freedman, 1961
	reduced uptake	platelets	Sivo Sankar et al, 1963
	elevated endogenous level plus increased platelet count	whole blood	Ritvo et al, 1970
	abnormal efflux	platelets	Boullin et al, 1970
	elevated endogenous level	whole blood	Yuwiler et al, 1970
	abnormal efflux	platelets	Boullin et al, 1971
	elevated endogenous level	platelets	Campbell et al, 1974
	elevated endogenous level	whole blood	TAS, 1976, Chapter 6
5-hydroxyindole acetic acid	low level after probenecid	cerebral spinal fluid	Cohen et al, 1977
Dopamine	uptake and loss both abnormally high	platelets	Boullin and O'Brien, 1972
Dopamine-beta-hydroxylase	decreased level	serum	TAS, Chapter 6
	decreased level	plasma	Lake et al, 1977
Homoprotocatechuic acid	present in 88% of patients	urine	TAS, Chapter 7
Norepinephrine	higher level	plasma	Lake et al, 1977
Bufotenin	present	24-hour urine collection	Hinwich et al, 1972

* From M. Coleman (Ed.), *The Autistic Syndromes* (North Holland, 1976).

The prognosis in autistic patients is very guarded. In one series, only 1% to 2% recovered and can be classified as normal. Five to 15% have a borderline prognosis, 16-25% a fair prognosis and 60-75% a poor prognosis (22). The patients' rating at five years of age has prognostic implications. In other series, 75% of patients have been classified as mentally retarded all of their lives (30, 52).

At our present level of knowledge, we do not know either the etiology, neuropathology or neurophysiological mechanisms causing autistic symptoms. Much research lies ahead.

REFERENCES

1. Bartak, L., Rutter, M., and Cox, A.: A comparative study of infantile autism and specific developmental receptive language disorder. *Brit. J. Psychiat.* 126: 127-48, 1975.
2. Bartolucci, G. and Albers, R. J.: Deictic categories in the language of autistic children. *J. Aut. Child. Schiz.* 4:131-141, 1974.
3. Bartolucci, G., Pierce, S., Streiner, D., and Eppel, P. T.: Phonological investigation of verbal autistic and mentally retarded subjects. *J. Aut. Child. Schiz.* 6:303-316, 1976.
4. Boucher, J.: Articulation in early childhood autism. *J. Aut. Child. Schiz.* 6:297-302, 1976.
5. Boucher, J.: Is autism primarily a language disorder? *Brit. J. Dis. Commun.* 2:135-143, 1976.
6. Boucher, J. and Warrington, E. K.: Memory deficits in early infantile autism: Some similarities to the amnesic syndrome. *Br. J. Psychol.* 67:73-87, 1976.
7. Boucher, J.: Hand preference in autistic children and their parents. *J. Aut. Child. Schiz.* 7:177-187, 1977.
8. Boullin, D. J., Coleman, M., and O'Brien, R. A.: Abnormalities in platelet 5-hydroxytryptamine efflux in patients with infantile autism. *Nature* 226:371-372, 1970.
9. Boullin, D. J., Coleman, M., O'Brien, R. A., and Rimland, B.: Laboratory predictions of infantile autism based on 5-hydroxytryptamine efflux from blood platelets and their correlation with the Rimland E-2 score. *J. Aut. Child. Schiz.* 1:63-71, 1971.
10. Boullin, D. J. and O'Brien, R. A.: Uptake and loss of 14-C-dopamine by platelets from children with infantile autism. *J. Aut. Child. Schiz.* 2:67-74, 1972.
11. Campbell, M., Friedman, E., DeVito, E., Greenspan, L., and Collins, P.: Blood serotonin in psychotic and brain damaged children. *J. Aut. Child. Schiz.* 4:33-41, 1974.
12. Campbell, M.: Pharmacotherapy in early infantile autism. *Biolog. Psychiat.* 10:399-423, 1975.
13. Chess, S., Korn, S. J., and Fernandez, P. B.: *Psychiatric disorders of children with congenital rubella.* New York: Brunner/Mazel Inc., 1971.

14. Cohen, D. J., Caparulo, B. K., Shaywitz, B. A., and Bowers, M. B.: Dopamine and serotonin metabolism in neuropsychiatrically disturbed children. *Arch. Gen. Psychiat.* 34:545-550, 1977.
15. Cohen, D. J., Caparulo, B., and Shaywitz, B.: Primary childhood aphasia and childhood autism. *J. Amer. Acad. Child. Psychiat.* 15:604-645, 1977.
16. Colby, K. M. and Parkinson, C.: Handedness in autistic children. *J. Aut. and Child. Schizo.* 7:3-9, 1977.
17. Coleman, M. and Rimland, B.: Familial autism. In Coleman, M. (Ed.), *The Autistic Syndromes.* Amsterdam: North Holland, pp. 175-182, 1976.
18. Coleman, M., Landgrebe, M. A., and Landgrebe, A. R.: Purine autism. Hyperuricosuria in autistic children; does this identify a subgroup of autism? In Coleman, M. (Ed.), *The Autistic Syndromes.* Amsterdam: North Holland, pp. 183-195, 1976.
19. Coleman, M., Landgrebe, M. A., and Landgrebe, A. R.: Celiac autism. Calcium studies and their relationship to celiac disease in autistic patients. In Coleman, M. (Ed.), *The Autistic Syndromes.* Amsterdam: North Holland, pp. 197-205, 1976.
20. Creak, M. and Ini, S.: Families of psychotic children. *J. Child Psychol. Psychiat.* 1:156-175, 1960.
21. Darby, J. K.: Neuropathologic aspects of psychosis in children. *J. Aut. Child. Schizo.* 6:339-352, 1976.
22. DeMeyer, M. K., Barton, S., DeMeyer, W. E., Norton, J. A., Allen, J., and Steele, R.: Prognosis in autism: A follow-up study. *J. Aut. Child. Schizo.* 3:199-246, 1973.
23. DeMeyer, M. K., Barton, S., Alpern, G. D., Kimberlin, C., Allen, J., Yang, E., and Steele, R.: The measured intelligence of autistic children. *J. Aut. Child. Schiz.* 4:42-60, 1974.
24. Fay, W. H.: On the echolalia of the blind and of the autistic child. *J. Speech and Hearing Dis.* 38:478-489, 1973.
25. Folstein, S. and Rutter, M.: Genetic influences and infantile autism. *Nature* 265:726-728, 1977.
26. Friedman, E.: The "autistic syndrome" and phenylketonuria. *Schizophrenia,* 249, 1969.
27. Frith, U.: Cognitive mechanisms in autism: Experiments with color and tone sequence production. *J. Aut. and Child Schiz.* 2:160-173, 1972.
28. Goldstein, M., Mahanand, D., Lee, J., and Coleman, M.: Dopamine-beta-hydroxylase and endogenous total 5-hydroxyindole levels in autistic patients and controls. In Coleman, M. (Ed.), *The Autistic Syndromes.* Amsterdam: North Holland, pp. 57-63, 1976.
29. Goodwin, M. S., Cowen, M. A., and Goodwin, T. C.: Malabsorption and cerebral dysfunction: A multivariate and comparative study of autistic children. *J. Aut. Child. Schiz.* 1:48-62, 1971.
30. Havelkova, M.: Follow-up study of 71 children diagnosed as psychotic in preschool age. *Am. J. Orthopsychiat.* 38:846-847, 1968.
31. Hauser, S. L., DeLong, G. R., and Rosman, N. P.: Pneumographic findings in the infantile autism syndrome. A correlation with temporal lobe disease. *Brain* 98:667-688, 1975.

32. Himwich, H. E., Jenkins, R. L., Fujimori, M., Narasimhachari, N., and Ebersole, M.: A biochemical study of early infantile autism. *J. Aut. Child. Schiz.* 2:114-126, 1972.

33. Hutt, C. and Ounsted, C.: The biological significance of gaze aversion with a particular reference to the syndrome of infantile autism. *Behav. Sci.* 11:346-356, 1966.

34. Hutt, C., Forrest, S. J., and Richer, J.: Cardiac arrhythmia and behaviour in autistic children. *Acta Psychiat. Scand.* 51:361-372, 1975.

35. Kanner, L.: Autistic disturbances in affective contact. *Nervous Child*, 2:217-250, 1943.

36. Kanner, L. and Lesser, L. I.: Early infantile autism. *Pediat. Clin. N. Amer.* 5:711-730, 1958.

37. Knobloch, H. and Pasamanick, B.: Some etiologic and prognostic factors in early infantile autism and psychosis. *J. Pediat.* 55:182, 1975.

38. Lake, C. R., Ziegler, M. G., and Murphy, D. L.: Increased norepinephrine levels and decreased dopamine-beta-hydroxylase activity in primary autism. *Arch. Gen. Psychiat.* 34:553-556, 1977.

39. Landau, W. M., Goldstein, R., and Kleffner, F. R.: Congenital aphasia: A clinicopathologic study. *Neurol.* 10:915-921, 1960.

40. Landgrebe, A. R. and Landgrebe, M. A.: Urinary catecholamine studies in autistic children. In Coleman, M. (Ed.), *The Autistic Syndromes*. Amsterdam: North Holland, pp. 65-72, 1976.

41. Lelord, G., Laffont, F., Jusseaume, P., and Stephant, J. L.: Comparative study of conditioning of averaged evoked responses by coupling sound and light in normal and autistic children. *Psychophysiol.* 10:415-425, 1973.

42. Lotter, V.: Services for a group of autistic children in Middlesex. In Wing, J. K. (Ed.), *Early Childhood Austim*. Oxford: Pergamon Press, 1966.

43. Murphy, R. C. and Preston, C. E.: Three autistic brothers. Paper presented at the 1954 Annual Meeting of the American Orthopsychiatric Association.

44. Ornitz, E. M. and Ritvo, E. R.: Perceptual inconstancy in early infancy. *Arch. Gen. Psychiat.* 18:76-98, 1968.

45. Ornitz, E. M.: The modulation of sensory input and motor output in autistic children. *J. Aut. Child. Schizo.* 4:197-215, 1974.

46. Peterson, M. R. and Torrey, E. F.: Viruses and other infectious agents as behavioral teratogens. In Coleman, M. (Ed.), *The Autistic Syndromes*. Amsterdam: North Holland, pp. 23-42, 1976.

47. Prior, M. and MacMillan, M. B.: Maintenance of sameness in children with Kanner's syndrome. *J. Aut. Child. Schiz.* 3:154-167, 1973.

48. Richer, J. M. and Coss, R. G.: Gaze aversion in autistic and normal children. *Acta Psychiat. Scand.* 53: 193-210, 1976.

49. Rimland, B.: Infantile Autism. New York: Appleton-Century-Crofts, 1964.

50. Ritvo, E. R., Yuwiler, A., Geller, E., Ornitz, E. M., Saeger, K., and Plotkin, S.: Increased blood serotonin and platelets in early infantile autism. *Arch. Gen. Psychiat.* 23:566-572, 1970.

51. Rutter, M.: The influence of organic and emotional factors on the origins, nature and outcome of childhood psychosis. *Develop. Med. Child Neurol.* 7:518, 1965.

52. Rutter, M.: Autistic children: infancy to adulthood. *Seminars in Psychiat.* 2:435-450, 1970.
53. Rutter, M.: The description and classification of infantile autism. In Churchill, D., Alpern, G., and DeMyer, M. (Eds.), *Infantile Autism.* Springfield: C. C. Thomas, 1971.
54. Rutter, M.: Clinical assessment of language disorders in the young child. In Rutter, M. and Martin, J. A. M. (Ed.), *The Child with Delayed Speech.* London: Heineman, pp. 33-47, 1972.
55. Rutter, M.: The development of infantile autism. *Psycholog. Med.* 4:147-163, 1974.
55A. Rutter, M. and Bartak, L.: Causes of infantile autism: Some considerations from recent research. *J. Aut. Childhood Schizo.* 1:20-32, 1971.
56. Schain, R. J. and Freedman, D. X.: Studies on 5-hydroxyindole metabolism in autistic and other mentally retarded children. *J. Pediat.* 58:315-320, 1961.
57. Seidel, 1970, cited by Rutter et al., 1971.
58. Simon, N.: Echolalic speech in childhood autism. *Arch. Gen. Psychiat.* 32:1439-1445, 1975.
59. Simons, J. M.: Observations on compulsive behavior in autism. *J. Aut. Child. Schizo.* 4:1-10, 1974.
60. Siva Sankar, D. V., Cates, N., Broer, H., and Sankar, D. B.: Biochemical parameters of childhood schizophrenia (autism) and growth. In Wortis, J. (Ed.), *Recent Advances in Biological Psychiatry.* New York: Plenum Press, p. 76, 1963.
61. Spence, M. A., Simmons, J. Q., Brown, N. A., and Wikler, L.: Sex ratios in families of autistic children. *Amer. J. Ment. Defic.* 77:405, 1973.
62. Stubbs, E. G.: Autistic children exhibit undetectable hemagglutination-inhibition antibody titers despite previous rubella vaccination. *J. Aut. Child. Schizo.* 6:269-274, 1976.
63. Stubbs, E. G., Crawford, M. E., Burger, D. R., and Vanderbark, A. A.: Depressed lymphocytes responsiveness in autistic children. *J. Aut. Child. Schiz.* 7:49-67, 1977.
64. Taft, L. T. and Cohen, H. J.: Hypsarrhythmia and infantile autism: A clinical report. *J. Aut. Child. Schiz.* 3:287, 1971.
65. Tanguay, P.: A tentative hypothesis regarding the role of hemispheric specialization in early infantile autism. BIS report #34, University of California, Los Angeles, pp. 27-29, 1974.
66. Torrey, E. F., McCabe, K., and Hersh, S.: Early childhood psychosis and bleeding during pregnancy. *J. Aut. Child. Schiz.* 5:287-297, 1975.
67. Valente, M.: Autism: Symptomatic and idiopathic- and mental retardation. *Pediatrics,* 43:495-496, 1971.
68. Walker, H.: Characteristics of adventitious movements in autistic children. In Coleman, M. (Ed.), *The Autistic Syndromes.* Amsterdam: North Holland, pp. 135-144, 1976.
69. Yuwiler, A., Plotkin, S., Geller, E., and Ritvo, E. R.: A rapid accurate procedure for the determination of serotonin in whole human blood. *Biochem. Med.* 3:426-436, 1970.

COMMENTARY by David Boullin

Mary Coleman is an acknowledged expert in the field of infantile autism and has written a number of articles on the subject and a book. In this brief chapter she has covered the salient features of the autistic syndrome with a considered account of the relative importance of various factors, including biochemical factors, which may be involved in the aetiology of this disorder; it is one of her best efforts.

The article is clearly written and much of it could be assimilated by the educated layman.

Coleman rightly divides the autistic syndrome into three separate categories, thus highlighting the difficulty of making a diagnosis of autism and the slow rate of progress in determining its cause. An account of the autistic syndrome is difficult to encompass in a few pages and these are emphasized by contradictions; in the first paragraph it is stated: "Autism . . . is now regarded as an organic disease. . . ."; later contradicted by, "It is clear that 'autism' is not a disease entity."

In spite of Coleman's interest in the biochemical aspects of autism, these are not given undue emphasis and she points out the inadequacy of hard scientific data on autistic subjects; in this regard she says, "Even the most elementary questions have yet to be answered."

This article, written in 1977, is still valid in many respects, particularly the descriptive aspects of autistic signs and symptoms. At the time of writing, Coleman, in her concluding sentence, points out that we know virtually nothing of the cause of autistic symptoms. Sadly, the situation has not changed in the last half decade. Further research progress will not be made until clinical material, including autopsy material, is obtained from autistic subjects in order to define any brain lesions or peripheral abnormalities.

Since the article was written some progress has been made in the drug therapy of autism, still without any information on the aetiology, but the true nature of the disease has been thrown into question. There is now some doubt as to whether autism *per se* really exists and in this regard the article remains slightly archaic as representing opinion in the middle 1970s.

In general, this article stands the test of time and probably is as good a brief introduction to the subject as any other that has been written. It is right that it should be included in *Classic Readings in Autism*.

21

A Neurological Model for Childhood Autism

ANTONIO R. DAMASIO
RALPH G. MAURER

Failure to develop normal social relationships, developmental disturbances of verbal and nonverbal communication, and ritualistic and compulsive behaviors (resistance to change in routine or surroundings, abnormal preoccupations, morbid attachments, morbid collections) are the distinctive behavioral abnormalities characterizing childhood autism.[1,2] Other important clinical signs are disturbances of motility (stereotyped movements, abnormalities of gait and posture) and of attention (abnormal responses to auditory, visual, and vestibular stimulation).[1-13] This investigation is concerned with explaining these abnormalities and their interrelationships in neurologic terms and is based on our own observations and on observations previously published.

The syndrome, also known as infantile autism and as early childhood autism, was first recognized by Kanner in 1943.[14] It is not a form of schizophrenia, [9,10,15-20] although it frequently has been so classified, and it is distinguishable from other disorders characterized by developmental disturbances of language[21,22] and from mental retardation.[8,19,23-34] In the last 15 years, autism has been demonstrated to have a characteristic age of onset, prevalence, and sex distribution.* But, the clinical courses and prognosis have been found to be variable and so have the signs that may appear together with the core manifestations.† Such studies support the notion of autism as a distinct syndrome, but raise doubt as to its status as a distinct clinical entity with a single etiology and characteristic pathologic substrate.

Autism can be associated with established neurological syndromes such as phenylketonuria, hypsarrhythmia, or rubella encephalitis, but usually is not, although often, there is evidence of brain dysfunction such as seizures

Reprinted with permission from *Archives of Neurology* 35 (December 1978): 777–786. Copyright 1978, American Medical Association.

*References 2, 9, 10, 16, 23, 24, 35-38.

†References 2, 9, 10, 16, 23, 24, 39-46.

and EEG abnormalities.‡ In 1974, Rutter, reviewing 30 years of research on autism, concluded that "although there is good reason to suppose that infantile autism may well arise on the basis of some type of organic brain disorder . . . there are no good grounds for placing the lesion in any one particular area of the brain."[20(158-159)] We suggest that the latter part of this statement is no longer true.

Our analysis of the patterns of abnormal behavior seen in autism indicates that in many ways, they are comparable to those seen in adults with certain forms of brain damage, particularly damage to the frontal lobe or to the closely related structures of the basal ganglia or limbic system. Furthermore, our analysis of the disturbances of motility seen in autism also shows them to be similar to those seen in patients with disease of the basal ganglia or frontal lobes. These resemblances have led us to conclude that autism is consequent to dysfunction in a complex of bilateral CNS structures that includes mesial frontal lobes, mesial temporal lobes, basal ganglia (in particular, the neostriatum), and thalami (dorsomedial and anterior nuclear groups). A detailed discussion of our reasoning, as it applies to the major manifestations of autism, is presented.

Disturbances of Motility

Disturbances of motility are an important aspect of the clinical picture of autism and constitute a clear indication of CNS involvement in autism. Although changes in motor behavior traditionally have been mentioned, the disturbances generally have not been considered primary and only rarely have they been described from a neurological point of view.[55] In our observations of a group of autistic children, all of whom met Rutter's criteria,[56] varying degrees of dystonia, bradykinesia and hyperkinesia, involuntary movements, and an emotionally related facial asymmetry were frequent disturbances (A. Damasio, MD, R. Maurer, MD, unpublished data).

Dystonia of the extremities was an almost constant finding. Patients often had bilateral or unilateral "striatal" toes, a spontaneous upward movement of the big toes similar to that in the Babinski reflex and commonly seen in parkinsonism.[57,58] They also exhibited dystonic posturing of the feet, hands, and fingers, with noticeable agonist-antagonist imbalance.

We occasionally noted involuntary dyskinesias of the mouth and extremities or complex involuntary synergies involving the head and the proximal segment of the limbs. In the dystonic extremities, we observed other types of involuntary movements, some rhythmic and tic-like, such as flapping, some nonrhythmic and best described as a variation of chorea, or athetosis,

---

‡References 2, 18, 23, 24, 38, 40, 41, 43, 46-54.

or both, and some repetitive, stereotyped, and composed mostly of complex hand movements and postures.

We also observed abnormalities of muscular tone. Some patients exhibited mild degrees of rigidity and hypotonia. None had spasticity. "Psychomotor" signs such as Gegenhalten (counterpull), grasp reflex, and avoidance reaction often were present.

Posture and gait have been described as abnormal in autism.[59] Our own observations confirm this. In some cases, the abnormalities were like those seen in specific neurologic disorders. One autistic child had a typical parkinsonian gait, which featured short steps, festination, and a flexed posture of limbs and trunk. Other autistic children had some of these features in isolation.

An interesting motor defect was the inability of some of these children to handle two motor tasks at the same time. One of our patients interrupted his hand movements whenever he started to speak. We considered this impairment in execution of simultaneous motor programs a sign of akinesia.

All of the disturbances described here are classical neurological signs indicative of dysfunction in the basal ganglia, particularly the neostriatum, and in closely related structures of the frontal lobe, particularly in its mesial aspect.[60-66] These disturbances commonly are seen, with varying intensity and variable syndromatic arrangement, in human disease processes of degenerative, inflammatory, vascular, neoplastic, or drug-induced nature, involving those structures. They also are seen in experimental animals (rodents, felines, and primates) with surgically or chemically induced dysfunction of the basal ganglia.[67-71] In addition, it should be noted that patients with disorders of motility consequent to dysfunction of the basal ganglia or the frontal lobes also exhibit, clinically as well as in an experimental setting, a variety of behavioral disturbances.[60,72-77] The same is true of experimental animals.[67-69,78-84]

The most interesting disturbances of motility were related to the face. One was akinesia that contrasted with the dyskinesia of the extremities. Another, which was all the more remarkable considering that these children had symmetrical and often expressionless faces, was an occasional but striking asymmetry of the lower portion of the face, noticeable when the children smiled or spoke spontaneously, but not when they voluntarily moved their facial musculature at our request. This phenomenon, an emotionally determined facial asymmetry that is known as emotional facial paralysis or reverse facial paralysis, departs from the commonly seen association of impaired voluntary movement of the lower half of the face with symmetric movement on smiling or crying, which is the hallmark of lesions of the corticobulbar system.[85-87] This reverse paralysis traditionally has been interpreted as a sign of damage to the basal ganglia[88,89] or to the thalamus.[90] The phenomenon has not been thoroughly studied, but recent investigations indicate that it is related to dysfunction of the older, sensorimotor cortex, which integrates nonpyramidal motor systems located in the mesial frontal lobe.[91-93] Although the motor nature of this cortex often is neglected, clinical evidence[94] and the results of experimentation with electrical stimulation[95,96] show that it indeed is concerned with primitive motility and thus, may be the expression of limbic system activity and therefore intimately linked with affective states and emotional control. The recent discovery in man of a small but highly differentiated area of motor cortex deep in the cingulate sulcus[97] further strengthens the view that this region is the primordial motor outlet of the limbic system. A reverse facial paralysis can also be the result of lesions in the basal ganglia[98] and has been observed in patients with psychomotor epilepsy,[99] suggesting that it is related to dysfunction in mesial regions of the temporal lobe. It never has been described in association with the far more common lesions of the neocortical areas. Consequently, it is our impression that it is associated with dysfunction in the transitional periallocortical structures that are located in the mesial aspect of both frontal and temporal lobes ("mesolimbic cortex" or "mesocortex"), as well as with dysfunction in structures of the basal ganglia and thalamus that are intimately related to them. We presume that the lesions that produce the phenomenon are bilateral but asymmetrical (e.g., as in parkinsonism) and that the facial imbalance reflects that asymmetry.

In regard to the above, it is of interest to note that monkeys, who do not possess voluntary control of facial expression, but who do have emotionally related mimicry, lose this capacity as a result of ablations of frontal and temporal cortex encompassing the mesocortical structures.[100] Furthermore, the same surgical preparations cause impairment of social behavior. When "frontotemporal" monkeys return to the colony, they tend to isolate themselves, exhibit decreased and inappropriate social signaling, fail to participate in group activities, and are ultimately rejected by the colony.[101,102] This set of behaviors, which in some ways comes close to representing an animal model of autism, is not seen in animals with lesions in the neocortex, even if the lesions involve visual association areas causing major perceptual defects, or the motor areas producing major paralysis. Thus, signs such as emotional facial paralysis are explainable on the basis of dysfunction in the same structures, dysfunction of which explains the remaining motor disturbances and accounts for changes in communication and social behavior.

Disturbances of Communication

Verbal defects in autism vary according to the stage of development of the patient and the severity of the syndrome.[2,14,24,43,103-111] Mutism is common. Speech, if present, is variably abnormal in terms of amount, content, and grammatical structure. In some high functioning patients, it can be relatively normal, except for unusual concreteness and dysprosody. A considerable amount of speech production is based on repetition, either immediate ("classic" echolalia) or deferred ("delayed" echolalia, in which phrases are repeated verbatim some time after they are heard, often with well-imitated stress and intonation). Non-echoed speech usually is sparse, poorly structured, and commonly exhibits immature and abnormal syntax and lexicon. It may consist mostly of stereotyped repetitive phrases. Respiratory control during speech is often defective and not integrated with grammatical structure, so that phrase markers occur at inappropriate points in an utterance. Some degree of verbal aspontaneity usually is present and there may be a tendency to reduce the number of words to the minimum needed to convey meaning. Defects in aural comprehension range from complete failure to understand or attend to speech, to a good understanding of practical, everyday speech with impaired ability to comprehend abstractions and complex associations. Written language is often better processed than spoken, as indicated by an interest in reading and ability to read aloud, to the point of hyperlexia.[44,112-114] But, reading comprehension is usually defective, regardless of the level of adequate visuo-oral "transcoding."

The presence of defects in nonverbal communication differentiates autistic children from children who are deaf or who have developmental aphasia.[21,22,59,105,109] These defects occur in all forms of nonverbal communication (gesture, facial expression, posture) and are characteristic of autistic children regardless of their verbal ability. Both comprehension and expression are impaired and unlike deaf or aphasic children, autistic children make no attempt to compensate by gesture or facial expression for what they cannot communicate verbally. Nonverbal communication often is limited to circumstances in which rather gross movements are concretely related to the intent of the message and can be used to convey it, such as leading an adult by the hand in order to obtain a given object or food.

The verbal disabilities in autism are distinguishable from most of the acquired aphasias. Specifically, they do not resemble any of the fluent or nonfluent aphasias related to perisylvian lesions of the dominant hemisphere, eg, Broca's aphasia, conduction aphasia, Wernicke's aphasia, or anomic aphasia.[115-117] Two prominent features of the verbal defects of autism, mutism and echolalia, are seen only in a set of syndromes that constitutes the borderland between disturbances of language and disturbances of thought, the so-called transcortical aphasias that result from a more or less complete anatomical "isolation of the speech areas."[116,118,119] Two syndromes have been described under this designation: transcortical sensory aphasia and transcortical motor aphasia. The former is characterized by severe defect in aural comprehension and by spontaneous, often abundant, fluent, and semantic paraphasic speech with echolalia. It does not resemble the verbal defects of autistic children.

    The latter, transcortical motor aphasia, is distinguished by a normal
ability to repeat speech, with or without echolalia, by marked aspontaneity
that may reach the point of mutism and by relatively preserved aural comprehension. It is associated with a lesion of the lateral aspect of the dominant frontal lobe outside of the anterior speech center (Broca's area). Its
general features bear a superficial resemblance to the verbal defects of autism, but it is distinguishable from autism by the preserved ability to communicate nonverbally.
    On the other hand, there is a great resemblance between the verbal de-
fects of autism and the syndromes of mutism or relative speech inhibition
that appear during the recovery from mesial frontal lobe lesions and that, as
in autism, are always accompanied by profound defects of nonverbal communication.[92,120-122] These are defects in communication that do not derive
from an impairment of primary linguistic processing and are, accordingly,
unrelated to damage to the primary language processing area of the brain.
Rather, these defects seem to derive from a lack of initiative to communicate and from a lack of "orientation" towards stimuli and are suggestive of
an underlying impairment in higher motor or perceptual control, or, more
generally, in overall cognitive organization. Unilateral or bilateral lesions of
the mesial aspects of the frontal lobe, particularly in regions such as the
supplementary motor area or the cingulate gyrus, may produce these defects. Lesions in the left or right hemisphere may produce the defect,[123,124]
testifying to the lack of a lateralized linguistic bias. Bilateral lesions cause
more severe mutism and akinesia, although some recovery is generally possible if the pathogenic cause stabilizes. Unilateral lesions of the supplementary motor area produce a milder syndrome in which patients are
spontaneous, and yet are able to repeat words and sentences quite appropriately and to understand simple utterances of the examiner.[92,93,121,125]
These patients have a concomitant impairment of nonverbal communication
and they never resort to gesture to compensate for their obvious verbal
weakness. Their lack of mimicry, their placidity, their failure to attend to
stimuli in the environment and properly orient to them, and their ability to
repeat speech are remarkable parallels of many features of childhood autism. Even when recovery takes place, these patients are unable to regain
creative use of language. Regardless of how good the previous vocabulary,
the propositional organization of speech is always impaired and speaking or
writing in a creative fashion is not possible. Creative use of gesture is impaired to the same extent and these patients show a marked inability to use
gesture or miming or body posture for communication. Other defects commonly seen in these patients include inability to control speech volume and
pitch, and repetitive vocalizations resembling palilalia.[126]
    The association between relative or absolute mutism and dysfunction of
the mesial frontal cortex has also been demonstrated by direct electrical
stimulation of this region, which commonly produces phenomena such as

speech inhibition (which consists of the involuntary omission of the utterance the subject intends to make), speech arrest (involuntary interruption of the utterance at the time of stimulation), palilalia (involuntary iteration of groups of phonemes), and disturbances of control of volume of speech and breathing.[96,97] It is important to note that, just as in the case of the disturbances of motility discussed above, a similar set of phenomena can be elicited with electrical stimulation of closely related structures of the basal ganglia, such as the caudate,[127,128] a finding that is in keeping with palilalia and the well-known disturbances of speech initiative, speech volume, and pitch that accompany many diseases of the basal ganglia.

The developmental defects of communication in autism, both verbal and nonverbal, can be related to a primary, predominantly motor dysfunction and are distinguishable from the acquired aphasias and apraxias, characterized by a primary linguistic disability. These developmental defects are not accompanied by signs characteristic of lesions of the lateralized "language area" of the dominant hemisphere. We propose that the defects result from dysfunction in interrelated structures of the periallocortex of the mesial frontal lobe and of the neostriatum. Experimental data suggest that lesions of the latter, sustained in infancy, may produce permanent defects not compensated by CNS plasticity.[129] That possibility, combined with the fact that dysfunction would have its onset prior to the process of normal language acquisition, could explain the severity of the disturbances and the appearance of cognitive nonverbal defects secondary to the language impairment.

Disturbances of Attention and Perception

An example of a defect in the attentional sphere is that in visual scanning. Autistic children have a shorter visual inspection time than controls, their scanning seems less comprehensive and systematic, and they exhibit a less sustained orientation towards visual stimuli than do normal children or retarded controls.[4,8] Furthermore, the way they orient to visual stimuli is quite unpredictable. Autistic children seem to use peripheral vision more than they do central vision; they may repeatedly avoid focusing their attention on a target, as when after refusing to look at an examiner or at a given object in the environment, they suddenly may fixate on an object or person and do so for a considerable time. It appears that the children are occasionally able to produce a normal performance, but usually they do not. Often, the children may stop entirely, for a brief period, and stare into space. Such episodes can be distinguished from seizures, both clinically and electroencephalographically. The closest parallel in the clinical neurology of adults is with the similar episodes of brief suspended attention that are seen in patients with damage to mesial frontal lobe regions and described as "intermittent interruptions of behavior."[130]

The results of recent primate experimentation on the production of visual saccades directed towards stimuli placed in the periphery of the visual fields are relevant as an explanation of the phenomenon of inattention. The process apparently serves the purpose of updating visual information so that appropriate motor programs can be organized in relation to the environment and is the result of the action of parietal lobe "command" cells.[131,132] But, there will only be a saccade if the stimulus is of special interest to the animal at a given time and the monkey will "foveate" food or water when he is hungry or thirsty, but not when he is satiated,[131] indicating that even if the parietal command cells and visual perception that feeds into those cells are intact, the actual orientation towards a given object will only be carried out after the organism has determined that the object is of importance for future behavior. Experimental evidence[133-138] supports the notion that the responses of an organism to a given stimulus depend on the set of "goals" of that organism and on a hierarchically organized "executive control" that will modulate the response according to the "goals" and the "cortex" of stimulation. "Limbic" system marking is necessary for this operation and the determination and marking of the importance of a given stimulus takes place at different levels of limbic processing, according to the nature and complexity of the stimuli involved.[139] The marking of complex stimuli that involve the comprehension of, for instance, a social situation most probably will require frontal lobe functioning, which, as a result of appropriate weighing of the value of the stimulus, will release or inhibit parietal command function. We propose that one of the causes of inattention in autism may be the inappropriate control of parietal command function.

The observation that, in general, autistic children are less responsive to sound than nonautistic children[1,59] is quite compatible with a defect in attention and should not be taken to indicate impairment of auditory perception. Not only can autistic children at times become hyperresponsive, but also, there is often evidence that their auditory perception is intact.[1,59] Unlike normal children, they cannot be conditioned to respond preferentially to a sound source, although, like nonautistic children, they respond to light in preference to sound.[8] They show no difference in their response to intelligible speech as opposed to noise, although, when presented with material that is randomly organized or organized solely by phonological stress, their auditory rote memories are better than those of retarded controls and as good as or better than those of normal children.[8] But, when the material is meaningful, their auditory rote memory is worse than those of both normal children and retarded controls.[8] These findings are consistent with the notion that their potential for normal perception and normal memory of perceived material is intact and that the defect is of a higher order, in the process of governance of perception, memory storage, and memory retrieval.

Autistic children also exhibit several abnormalities of vestibular function, such as diminished postrotatory nystagmus.[6,11,12] Autistic children have increased tolerance to spinning and twirling and will actually enjoy it.[60] These manifestations have been interpreted on the basis of a defect in sensory integration at a brain stem level.[12] While a defect in overall control of sensory integration may be a good description of the mechanism underlying this defect, the primary dysfunction could certainly reside at a higher level of control, such as basal ganglia or the cerebral cortex. Support for the latter contention comes from observations by Mettler and Mettler,[140] who showed that cats with bilateral removal of the frontal lobe or of the caudate and frontal lobe would disregard labyrinthine stimulation. (The lesioned animals differed from normal animals in showing less obvious distress during rotation and diminished postrotatory nystagmus.) This and other observations by Mettler and Mettler[67] can be adduced to explain the finding that autistic children seem to depend inordinately on somatosensory clues in order to perceive instructions and learn how to carry out a task that also involves visual or auditory stimulation.[8] In fact, unlike mentally retarded controls, autistic children show a preference for somatosensory stimulation over auditory and in general, prefer somatosensory stimuli over visual ones.[8,141] On the basis of his observations in animals with lesions of the basal ganglia, Mettler[142] suggested that a striatally deprived organism would come under primary "proprioceptive domination."

Except for occasional blindness or deafness often secondary to rubella, autistic children do not show primary defects of perception. But, they have behavioral abnormalities, both in clinical terms and in specific neuropsychologic testing, that indicate a defective ability to maintain optimal conditions for ongoing perceptual processes. When such an impairment pertains to complex stimuli, it hallmarks dysfunction in higher integrative and decision-making neural structures, such as those of the frontal lobe and basal ganglia.[139,143-146]

Ritualistic and Compulsive Behaviors

Rituals, compulsions, and negative reaction to changes in routine or surroundings occur in the behavior of normal children. In autistic children, however, these are marked by their severity, abnormal content, and tendency to form a large part of the child's behavioral repertoire.[1,59] Particularly characteristic is the distress with which the young autistic child often responds when even minor changes are made in familiar settings or when he is prevented from carrying out activities to which he is accustomed. This is the source of the "intense desire for the preservation of sameness" that was originally described by Kanner.[14] With age, this and other ritualistic and compulsive behaviors tend to diminish in severity, although they may become more complex and organized and rarely disappear altogether.[24,42-45]

In our view, most of these behaviors represent adaptive responses of an individual with brain dysfunction to the demands of the environment. They reflect the tendency of the organism to perform what it can perform adequately.[147] The modification of these behaviors with age is a result both of changes in the environment and of changes in the repertoire of learned responses with which the autistic child copes with external stimuli. The tantrums and distress that result when accustomed activities are prevented or familiar settings changed are similar, in nature, frequency, severity, and resistance to modifiability to the "catastrophic" reactions that have been described in some patients with acute and chronic frontal lobe syndromes[148-150] and that occur when these patients are confronted with situations for which they lack an adequate learned response and in which they are unable to create a new and appropriate response. In this light, "maintenance of sameness" becomes a form of adaptive behavior aimed at avoidance of "catastrophe." Compulsive, stereotyped, ritualistic behaviors may be viewed as ways in which that avoidance is enacted and homeostasis of a disturbed biological system achieved.

Like catastrophic reactions, all of these stereotyped and ritualistic avoidance strategies may be seen in frontal lobe patients, particularly in those in whom, having sustained lesions early in life or having stabilized them, an evolving equilibrium has developed with their environment.[151,152] What autistic children and patients with some frontal lobe syndromes seem unable to do is to teach themselves ways of adapting to modified environmental contingencies. Presumably, this teaching ability depends on normal frontal lobe function, since it is in structures of the frontal lobe that the process of organizing appropriate responses to complex aspects of the environment in relation to the more complex goals of the organism probably takes place. Consequently, autistic children, as well as patients with some frontal lobe syndromes, are bound to patterns of behavior that were either previously learned, or explicitly taught to them. In a way, "perseveration," another behavioral characteristic that is common to both autistic children and frontal lobe patients, is an aspect of this inability to organize and consolidate new forms of response. The perseverative tendency permeates tasks of every type and complexity and can be demonstrated in clinical as well as experimental settings.[8,153-157]

Near-normal autistic individuals strikingly resemble patients with some types of frontal lobe defects. They share a similar lack of initiative, a similar concreteness in thought and language, an inability to focus attention, shallowness of affect, and lack of empathy. An example of this similarity is to be found in the patient described by Ackerly and Benton.[152] This patient, on the other hand, differed from an autistic child in his occasional antisocial conduct, an inconstant behavioral feature in frontal lobe patients. This difference may be explained in a variety of ways, among them the age at which damage took place and the anatomical structures preferentially involved, the latter being of particular importance, since damage to orbital aspects of the frontal lobe, in addition to mesial and lateral, may correlate with the additional psychopathic features of some frontal lobe syndromes, while relative preservation of this region may correlate with their absence.[158] Finally, the fact that lesions of the striatum (and apparently, also of the mesolimbic structures) in experimental animals have been associated with stereotyped and stimulus-bound behavior[71,84] suggests that dysfunction of this system in man might provide the motor substrate on which ritualistic and compulsive behaviors could be modeled.

Failure to Develop Normal Social Relationships

The autistic child's abnormalities in social behavior vary with age and severity of the illness, but generally seem to involve deficits in those interactions that require initiative or reciprocal behavior on the part of the child. Autistic children are not usually physically withdrawn and they often enjoy tickling and rough-and-tumble play. However, they generally lack cooperative play and are almost always devoid of imaginative play, while autistic adolescents and adults lack the skills and the sense of social appropriateness necessary for making and maintaining personal friendships.*

Kanner[14] regarded the autistic child's abnormalities in social behavior as a primary defect. Contemporary authorities have considered them secondary to other defects, particularly those of verbal and nonverbal communication.[20,59,161] We agree that most, if not all, of those abnormalities are of a secondary nature, but we consider them consequent to an organized collection of primary defects that we described under disturbances of motility, disturbances of attention, and ritualistic and compulsive behaviors, as well as under disturbances of communication.

Etiology and Pathogenesis

We have explained how the manifestations of autism can be accounted for on the basis of dysfunction in one neural system and have noted that some are the direct signs of dysfunction, while others reflect the result of the interaction between a child with a specific brain disorder and the environment.

The manifestations of autism best correlate with dysfunction of the ring of phylogenetically older cortex located in the mesial aspect of the frontal and

---

*References 24, 34, 39, 42-46, 59, 159, 160.

temporal lobes (supplementary motor area, cingulate gyrus, entorhinal area, perirhinal area, parahippocampal gyrus, subicular and presubicular region), and dysfunction in the neostriatum. The former set of structures is cytoarchitectonically distinctive, in that it is mainly formed by neither neocortex nor allocortex, but rather, by a transitional type of cortex, commonly known as periallocortex,[162] proisocortex,[163] or mesocortex (G. Van Hoesen, Ph.D., personal communication, 1978). It is also distinctive in terms of angioarchitecture.[164]

It is of particular interest that both groups of structures (the ring of mesocortex and the neostriatum) together constitute the entire area of termination of the dopaminergic neurons arising in the mesencephalon, making this system also neurochemically distinctive. The mesocortex is the principal target of the so-called mesolimbic axon terminals whose cell bodies are located in the ventral tegmental area (area A10 of Dahlström and Fuxe)[165] and in the medial one third of the pars compacta of the substantia nigra, while the neostriatum is the well-known terminating point of the axons originating in the lateral two thirds of the pars compacta of the substantia nigra (area A9), the nigrostriatal pathway.[165-172] Consequently, the possibility that the neural dysfunction that causes autism is produced or at least accompanied by changes in dopamine content in these target structures deserves consideration. These changes would be in the direction of deficiency, rather than excess, and might also reflect regional imbalance between dopamine and other neuromediators. Such a disturbance could be the result of different mechanisms. One could be direct damage either to target cells in the mesocortex, or to cells of the dopaminergic pathway, at their mesencephalic origin or in transit in the diencephalon. Another mechanism could be an inborn neurochemical abnormality, possibly of genetic nature, localized to these specific target regions without obvious histological or cytological changes.

Dysfunction in structures of the mesocortex could account for some features of autism. Evidence from experimental work demonstrates that the mesocortex is a relay point for information coming from the perceptual neocortex on its way to allocortical structures such as the hippocampus, or to subcortical limbic system structures such as the amygdala.[173-177] Perhaps more important, mesocortical structures also relay limbic system information back to the neocortex,[178-183] as is the case with the output of the hippocampus, which is in good part conveyed to the mesocortical subiculum and, from there, either to temporal and parietal neocortex, or to frontal neocortex via the mesocortical cingulate gyrus.[184] Thus, appropriate affective labeling of stimuli in the process of learning, as well as appropriate affective recognition of the same stimuli later in life, may depend on the integrity of this cortical way station. The intimate connection of the mesocortex with the neostriatum,[185-188] the other major target of dopaminergic neurons, further reinforces the concept of an integrated system.

It is not possible at present to predict which of these structures is predominantly affected. In order to account for the considerable clinical variability of the autistic syndrome, different causes and different mechanisms need be postulated. Among the possible causes of autism, we would include perinatal infection, a process that could not only explain the age of onset, but also the increased incidence in twins.[189] Evidence that autism is associated with viral diseases is already available, as autism has been described in patients with congenital rubella, measles encephalitis, and cytomegalovirus infection itself[38,52,190] (the last commonly involves deep structures of the brain, namely, those of the basal ganglia[191]). Perinatal cardiorespiratory distress is another possible cause. Hypoxia can cause damage to specific areas of the brain, including the basal ganglia[192] and the areas affected are different from the ones involved as a consequence of anoxia. It is conceivable that, under certain circumstances, the damage would be less severe than the damage that produces cerebral palsy. It would involve neural structures both macroscopic and microscopic, different from the ones involved in cerebral palsy, and instead, would determine the syndrome of autism. Deficient perfusion of the brain is also a cause to consider. By producing damage to the deep watershed area that surrounds the ventricles, it impairs the function of periventricular structures such as the caudate or the medial nuclei of the thalamus.[193] Such mechanism is made likely by the fact that the deep watershed region is not matured at the time of birth and is therefore prone to insult.[194] A genetically determined variation of the architecture of the periventricular vascular supply or of its rate of maturation might be a factor and explain the occurrence of autism in siblings. Again, evidence is available that severe perinatal distress and autism can be related.[18,49,189,195,196] Moreover, several cases of autism have been described in patients with arrested hydrocephalus[107,197] and there is pneumoencephalographic evidence that autistic children can have bilateral dilation of the lateral ventricles,[198] a finding possibly indicative of previous pathologic process in the periventricular structures. Finally, a genetic disturbance could cause autism by producing preferential functional impairment of certain CNS structures. This could result from deficient maturation of neurons in regions such as the mesocortex, abnormalities in mesencephalic neural loci concerned with the production of neuromediators or neuromodulators essential for the functioning of those target regions, abnormal angioarchitectural patterns of the same regions, or increased susceptibility of those regions to a variety of neuropathologic agents (e.g., infection, metabolic changes). The syndrome of autism has a relatively consistent symptomatic core that results from the impairment, by one mechanism or another, of the function of a given system. The causes of that impairment vary in nature and intensity and as a result, produce variants of the syndrome with different clinical course, outcome, and accompanying signs.

REFERENCES

1. Rutter M: Behavioural and cognitive characteristics of a series of psychotic children, in Wing JK (ed): *Early Childhood Autism: Clinical, Educational and Social Aspects,* ed 1. Oxford, England, Pergamon Press, 1966.
2. Rutter M, Lockyer L: A five to fifteen year follow-up study of infantile psychosis: I. Description of sample. *Br J Psychiatry* 113:1169–1182, 1967.
3. Wolff S, Chess S: A behavioural study of schizophrenic children. *Acta Psychiatr Scand* 40:438–466, 1964.
4. Hutt C, Hutt SJ, Lee D, et al: A behavioral and electroencephalographic study of autistic children. *J Psychiatr Res* 3:181–197, 1965.
5. Ritvo ER, Ornitz EM, LaFranchi S: Frequency of repetitive behaviors in early infantile autism and its variants. *Arch Gen Psychiatry* 19:341–347, 1968.
6. Ritvo ER, Ornitz EM, Eviatar A, et al: Decreased post-rotatory nystagmus in early infantile autism. *Neurology* 19:653–658, 1969.
7. Sorosky AD, Ornitz EM, Brown MB, et al: Systematic observations of autistic behavior. *Arch Gen Psychiatry* 18:439–449, 1968.
8. Hermelin B, O'Connor N: *Psychological Experiments with Autistic Children.* London, Pergamon Press, 1970.
9. Kolvin I: Studies in the childhood psychoses: I. Diagnostic criteria and classification. *Br J Psychiatry* 118:381–384, 1971.
10. Kolvin I, Ounsted C, Humphrey M, et al: Studies in the childhood psychoses: II. The phenomenology of childhood psychoses. *Br J Psychiatry* 118:385–395, 1971.
11. Ornitz EM, Forsythe AB, de la Pena A: The effect of vestibular and auditory stimulation on the REMs of REM sleep in autistic children. *Arch Gen Psychiatry* 29:786–791, 1973.
12. Ornitz EM, Brown MB, Mason A, et al: The effect of visual input on vestibular nystagmus in autistic children. *Arch Gen Psychiatry* 31:369–375, 1974.
13. Hutt SH: An ethological analysis of autistic behavior, in van Praag HM (ed): *On the Origin of Schizophrenic Psychoses.* Amsterdam, De Erven Bohn, 1975.
14. Kanner L: Autistic disturbances of affective contact. *Nerv Child* 2:217–250, 1943.
15. Rutter M: Concepts of autism: A review of research. *J Child Psychol Psychiatry* 9:1–25, 1968.
16. Kolvin I, Ounsted C, Richardson LM, et al: Studies in the childhood psychoses: III. The family and social background in childhood psychoses. *Br J Psychiatry* 118:396–402, 1971.
17. Kolvin I, Garside RF, Kidd JSH: Studies in the childhood psychoses: IV. Parental personality and attitude and childhood psychoses. *Br J Psychiatry* 118:403–406, 1971.
18. Kolvin I, Ounsted C, Roth M: Studies in the childhood psychoses: V. Cerebral dysfunction and childhood psychoses. *Br J Psychiatry* 118:407–414, 1971.
19. Kolvin I, Humphrey M, McNay A: Studies in the childhood psychoses: VI. Cognitive factors in childhood psychoses. *Br J Psychiatry* 118:415–419, 1971.
20. Rutter M: The development of infantile autism. *Psychol Med* 4:147–163, 1974.
21. Bartak L, Rutter M, Cox A: A comparative study of infantile autism and spe-

cific developmental language disorder: I. The children. *Br J Psychiatry* 126:127–145, 1975.

22. Bartak L, Rutter M, Cox A: A comparative study of infantile autism and specific developmental receptive language disorders: III. Discriminant function analysis. *J Autism Child Schizophr* 7:383–396, 1977.

23. Lotter V: Epidemiology of autistic conditions in young children: I. Prevalence. *Soc Psychiatry* 1:163–173, 1967.

24. Rutter M, Greenfeld D, Lockyer L: A five to fifteen year follow-up study of infantile psychosis: II. Social and behavioural outcome. *Br J Psychiatry* 113:1183–1199, 1967.

25. Lockyer L, Rutter M: A five to fifteen year follow-up study of infantile psychosis: III. Psychological aspects. *Br J Psychiatry* 115:865–882, 1969.

26. Lockyer L, Rutter M: A five to fifteen year follow-up study of infantile psychosis: IV. Patterns of cognitive ability. *Br J Soc Clin Psychol* 9:152–163, 1970.

27. DeMyer MK, Alpern GD, Barton S, et al: Imitation in autistic, early schizophrenic, and non psychotic subnormal children. *J Autism Child Schizophr* 2:264–267, 1972.

28. DeMyer MK, Barton S, Norton JA: A comparison of adaptive, verbal, and motor profiles of psychotic and non psychotic subnormal children. *J Autism Child Schizophr* 2:359–377, 1972.

29. DeMyer MK, Barton S, Alpern GD, et al: The measured intelligence of autistic children. *J Autism Child Schizophr* 4:42–60, 1974.

30. Bartak L, Rutter M: Special educational treatment of autistic children: A comparative study: I. Design of study and characteristics of units. *J Child Psychol Psychiatry* 14:161–179, 1973.

31. Bartak L, Rutter M: Differences between mentally retarded and normally intelligent autistic children. *J Autism Child Schizophr* 6:109–120, 1976.

32. Rutter M, Bartak L: Special educational treatment of autistic children: A comparative study: II. Follow-up findings and implications for services. *J Child Psychol Psychiatry* 14:241–270, 1973.

33. Wing L: A study of language impairments in severely retarded children, in O'Connor N (ed): *Language, Cognitive Deficits and Retardation*. London, Butterworth & Co, 1975.

34. Wing L, Gould J, Yeates SR, et al: Symbolic play in severely mentally retarded and in autistic children. *J Child Psychol Psychiatry* 18:167–178, 1977.

35. Lotter V: Epidemiology of autistic conditions in young children: I. Prevalence. *Soc Psychiatry* 1:124–137, 1966.

36. Makita K: The age of onset of childhood schizophrenia. *Folia Psychiatr Neurol Jpn* 20:111–121, 1966.

37. Prior MR, Gajzago CC, Knox D: An epidemiological study of autistic and psychotic children in the four eastern states of Australia. *Aust NZ J Psychiatry* 10:173–184, 1976.

38. Wing L, Yeates SR, Brierley LM, et al: The prevalence of early childhood autism: Comparison of administrative and epidemiological studies. *Psychol Med* 6:89-100, 1976.

39. Eisenberg L: The autistic child in adolescence. *Am J Psychiatry* 112:607-612, 1956.

40. Creak EM: Childhood psychosis: A review of 100 cases. *Br J Psychiatry* 109:84-89, 1963.
41. Lotter V: Factors related to outcome in autistic children. *J Autism Child Schizophr* 4:263-277, 1974.
42. Lotter V: Social adjustment and placement of autistic children in Middlesex: A follow-up study. *J Autism Child Schizophr* 4:11-22, 1974.
43. Rutter M: Autistic children: Infancy to adulthood. *Semin Psychiatr* 2:435-450, 1970.
44. Kanner L: Follow-up study of eleven autistic children originally reported in 1943. *J Autism Child Schizophr* 1:119-145, 1971.
45. Kanner L, Rodriguez A, Ashenden B: How far can autistic children go in matters of social adaptation? *J Autism Child Schizophr* 2:9-33, 1972.
46. DeMyer MK, Barton S, DeMyer WE, et al: Prognosis in autism: A follow-up study. *J Autism Child Schizophr* 3:199-246, 1973.
47. Goldfarb W: *Childhood Schizophrenia.* Cambridge, Harvard University Press, 1961.
48. Goldfard W: *Growth and Change of Schizophrenic Children: A Longitudinal Study.* New York, Winston/Wiley, 1974.
49. Gittelman M, Birch HG: Childhood schizophrenia: Intellect, neurologic status, perinatal risk, prognosis, and family pathology. *Arch Gen Psychiatry* 17:16-25, 1967.
50. Creak M, Pampiglione G: Clinical and EEG studies on a group of 35 psychotic children. *Dev Med Child Neurol* 11:218-227, 1969.
51. Gubbay SS, Lobascher M, Kingerlee P: A neurologic appraisal of autistic children: Results of a Western Australia survey. *Dev Med Child Neurol* 12:422-429, 1970.
52. Chess S, Korn SJ, Fernandez PB: *Psychiatric Disorders of Children with Congenital Rubella.* New York, Brunner/Mazel Inc, 1971.
53. Taft LT, Cohen HJ: Hypsarrhythmia and infantile autism: A clinical report. *J Autism Child Schizophr* 1:327-336, 1971.
54. Small JG: EEG and neurophysiological studies of early infantile autism. *Biol Psychiatry* 10:385-397, 1975.
55. Walker HA, Coleman M: Characteristics of adventitious movements in autistic children, in Coleman M (ed): *The Autistic Syndromes.* New York, American Elsevier Publishing Co Inc, 1976.
56. Rutter M: Infantile autism and other child psychoses, in Rutter M, Hersov L (eds): *Child Psychiatry: Modern Approaches.* Oxford, Blackwell Scientific, 1977.
57. Duvoisin RC, Yahr MD, Lieberman J, et al: The striatal foot. *Trans Am Neurol Assoc* 97:267, 1972.
58. Duvoisin RC: Problems in the treatment of parkinsonism, in Messiha FS, Kenny AD (eds): *Parkinson's Disease, Advances in Experimental Medicine and Biology.* New York, Plenum Press, 1977, vol 90.
59. Wing L: Diagnosis, clinical description and prognosis, in Wing L (ed): *Early Childhood Autism: Clinical, Educational and Social Aspects,* ed 2. Oxford, England, Pergamon Press, 1976.
60. Kleist K: *Gehirnpathologie.* Leipzig, J Barth, 1934.
61. Rylander G: *Personality Changes After Operations on the Frontal Lobe.* Copenhagen, Munksgaard, 1940.

62. Martin JP: *The Basal Ganglia and Posture*. London, Pitman Medical Publishing Co Ltd, 1967.

63. Denny-Brown D: Clinical symptomatology of diseases of the basal ganglia, in Vinken PJ, Bruyn GW (eds): *Handbook of Clinical Neurology: Disorders of the Basal Ganglia*. Amsterdam, North-Holland, 1968, vol 6.

64. Schwab R, England AC: Parkinson syndromes due to various specific causes, in Vinken PJ, Bruyn GW (eds): *Handbook of Clinical Neurology: Disorders of the Basal Ganglia*. Amsterdam, North-Holland, 1968, vol 6.

65. Weingarten K: Tics, in Vinken PJ, Bruyn GW (eds): *Handbook of Clinical Neurology: Disorders of the Basal Ganglia*. Amsterdam, North-Holland, 1968, vol 6.

66. Yahr M, Duvoisin R: Drug therapy of the extrapyramidal disorders, in Vinken PJ, Bruyn GW: *Handbook of Clinical Neurology: Diseases of the Basal Ganglia*. Amsterdam, North-Holland, 1968, vol 6.

67. Mettler FA, Mettler CC: The effects of striatal injury. *Brain* 65:242-255, 1942.

68. Mettler FA, Thompson RL, Hovde CA, et al: The striatal syndrome. *Trans Am Neurol Assoc* 82:24-31, 1957.

69. Denny-Brown D: Experimental lesions of the basal ganglia in the monkey, in *The Basal Ganglia and their Relation to Disorders of Movement*. London, Oxford University Press Inc, 1962.

70. Randrup A, Murkvad I: Stereotyped activities produced by amphetamine in several animal species and man. *Psychopharmacologia* 11:300-310, 1966.

71. Iverson SD: Striatal function and stereotyped behavior, in Cools AR, Lohman AHM, van den Bercken JHL (eds): *Psychobiology of the Striatum*. Amsterdam, North-Holland, 1977.

72. Denny-Brown D: The frontal lobes and their functions, in Feling A (ed): *Modern Trends in Neurology*. New York, Paul B Hoeber Inc, 1951.

73. Milner B: Some effects of frontal lobectomy in man, in Warren JM, Akert K (eds): *The Frontal Granular Cortex and Behavior*. New York, McGraw-Hill Book Co Inc, 1964.

74. Hecaen H: Mental symptoms associated with tumors of the frontal lobe, in Warren JM, Akert K (eds): *The Frontal Granular Cortex and Behavior*. New York, McGraw-Hill Book Co Inc, 1964.

75. Bowen FP: Behavioral alterations in patients with basal ganglia lesions, in Yahr M (ed): *The Basal Ganglia*. New York, Raven Press, 1975.

76. Teuber HL: Complex functions of the basal ganglia, in Yahr M (ed): *The Basal Ganglia*. New York, Raven Press, 1975.

77. Damasio A, Castro-Caldas A: Neuropsychiatric aspects of parkinsonism, in Stern G (ed): *The Clinical Uses of Levodopa*. Baltimore, University Park Press, 1977.

78. Gomez JA, Thompson RL, Mettler FA: Effect of striatal damage on conditioned and unlearned behavior. *Trans Am Neurol Assoc* 83:88-91, 1958.

79. Battig K, Rosvold HE, Mishkin M: Comparison of the effects of frontal and caudate lesions on discrimination learning in monkeys. *J Comp Physiol Psychol* 55:458-463, 1962.

80. Pribram AH, Ahumada A, Hartog J, et al: A progress report on the neurological processes disturbed by frontal lesions in primates, in Warren JM, Akert K (eds): *The Frontal Granular Cortex and Behavior*. New York, McGraw-Hill Book Co Inc, 1964.

81. Teuber HL, Proctor F: Some effects of basal ganglia lesions in subhuman primates and man. *Neuropsychologia* 2:85-93, 1964.
82. Divac I, Rosvold HE, Szwarebart MK: Behavioral effects of selective ablation of the caudate nucleus. *J Comp Physiol Psychol* 63:184-190, 1967.
83. Bailey P, Davis EW: The syndrome of obstinate progression in the cat. *Proc Soc Exp Biol Med* 51:1841, 1942.
84. Villablanca JR, Marcus RJ: Effects of caudate nuclei removal in cats: Comparison with effects of frontal cortex ablation. *UCLA Form Med Sci* 18:273-311, 1975.
85. Gowers WR: *A Manual of Diseases of the Nervous System,* ed 2. Philadelphia, Blakiston, 1893.
86. Brain WR: *Diseases of the Nervous System,* ed 6. London, Oxford University Press Inc, 1962.
87. Adams RD, Victor M: *Principles of Neurology.* New York, McGraw-Hill Book Co Inc, 1977.
88. Monrad-Krohn GH: On the dissociation of voluntary and emotional innervation in facial paresis of central origin. *Brain* 47 (pt 1), 1924.
89. Monrad-Krohn GH: *The Clinical Examination of the Nervous System,* ed 7. New York, Paul B Hoeber Inc, 1938.
90. Nothnagel H: *Traité Clinique du Diagnostic des Maladies de l'Encephale Basé sur l'Etude des Localisations.* Paris, Delahaye et Lecrosnier, 1885.
91. Laplane D, Orgogozo JM, Meininger V, et al: Paralysie faciale avec dissociation automaticovolontaire inverse par lesion frontale. *Rev Neurol* 132:725-734, 1976.
92. Laplane D, Talairach J, Meininger V, et al: Clinical consequences of corticectomies involving the supplementary motor area in man. *J Neurol Sci* 34:301-314, 1977.
93. Damasio AR, Kassel NF: Transcortical motor aphasia in relation to lesions of the supplementary motor area. *Neurology* 28:396, 1978.
94. Penfield W, Jasper H: *Epilepsy and the Functional Anatomy of the Human Brain.* Boston, Little Brown & Co, 1954.
95. Penfield W, Welch K: The supplementary motor area of the cerebral cortex. *Arch Neurol Psychiatry* 66:289-317, 1951.
96. Van Buren JM, Fedio P: Functional representation on the medial aspect of the frontal lobes in man. *J Neurosurg* 44:275-289, 1976.
97. Braak H: A primitive gigantopyramidal field buried in the depth of the cingulate sulcus of the human brain. *Brain Res* 109:219-233, 1976.
98. Selby G: Parkinson's disease, in Vinken PJ, Bruyn GW (eds): *Handbook of Clinical Neurology: Diseases of the Basal Ganglia.* Amsterdam, North-Holland, 1968, vol 6.
99. Remillard GM, Andermann F, Rhi-Sausi A, et al: Facial asymmetry in patients with temporal lobe epilepsy. *Neurology* 27:109-114, 1977.
100. Myers RE: Comparative neurology of vocalization and speech: Proof of a dichotomy. *Ann NY Acad Sci* 280:745-757, 1976.
101. Myers RE: Neurology of social behavior and affect in primates: A study of prefrontal and anterior temporal cortex, in Zülch K, Creutzfeldt O, Galbraith GC (eds): *Cerebral Localization.* New York, Springer-Verlag, 1975.

102. Franzen EA, Myers RE: Neural control of social behavior: Prefrontal and anterior temporal cortex. *Neuropsychologia* 11:141-157,1973.
103. Kanner L: Irrelevant and metaphorical language in early infantile autism. *Am J Psychiatry* 103:242-246, 1946.
104. Rutter M: Speech disorders in a series of autistic children, in Franklin AW (ed): *Children with Communication Problems*. London, Pitman Medical Publishing Co Ltd, 1965.
105. Rutter M: Clinical assessment of language disorders in the young child, in Rutter M, Martin JAM (eds): *The Child with Delayed Speech*. London, William Heinemann Ltd, 1972.
106. Wolff S, Chess S: An analysis of the language of fourteen schizophrenic children. *J Child Psychol Psychiatry* 6:29-41, 1965.
107. Wing L: The handicaps of autistic children: A comparative study. *J Child Psychol Psychiatry* 10:1-40, 1969.
108. Ricks DM: Vocal communication in pre-verbal normal and autistic children, in O'Connor N (ed): *Language, Cognitive Deficits and Retardation*. London, Butterworth & Co, 1975.
109. Ricks DM, Wing L: Language, communication, and the use of symbols in normal and autistic children. *J Autism Child Schizophr* 5:191-221, 1975.
110. Simmons JQ, Baltaxe C: Language patterns of adolescent autistics. *J Autism Child Schizophr* 5:333-351, 1975.
111. Walker HA: Language behavior in a sample from an autistic population, in Coleman M (ed): *The Autistic Syndromes*. New York, American Elsevier Publishing Co Inc, 1976.
112. Mehegan CC, Dreifuss FE: Hyperlexia: Exceptional reading ability in brain-damaged children. *Neurology* 22:1105-1111, 1972.
113. Huttenlocher PR, Huttenlocher J: A study of children with hyperlexia. *Neurology* 23:1107-1116, 1973.
114. Simon N: Echolalic speech in childhood autism: Consideration of possible underlying loci of brain damage. *Arch Gen Psychiatry* 32:1439-1446, 1975.
115. Geschwind N: Disconnexion syndromes in animals and man. *Brain* 88:237-294, 585-644, 1965.
116. Benson DF, Geschwind N: The aphasias and related disturbances, in Baker AB, Baker LH (eds): *Clinical Neurology*. New York, Harper & Row, 1971.
117. Goodglass H, Kaplan E: *The Assessment of Aphasia and Related Disorders*. Philadelphia, Lea & Febiger, 1972.
118. Goldstein K: *Die Transkortikalen Aphasien*. Jena, Gustav Fischer, 1917.
119. Geschwind N, Quadfasel F, Segarra J: Isolation of the speech area. *Neuropsychologia* 6:327-340, 1968.
120. Foix C, Hillemand P: Les syndromes de l'artere cerebrale anterieure. *Encephale* 20:209-221, 1925.
121. Critchley M: The anterior cerebral artery and its syndromes. *Brain* 53:120-165, 1930.
122. Cushing H, Eisenhardt L: *Meningiomas*. Springfield, Ill, Charles C Thomas Publisher, 1938.
123. Penfield W, Roberts L: *Speech and Brain Mechanisms*. Princeton, Princeton University Press, 1959.

124. Kaplan LR, Zervas NT: Speech arrest in a dextral with a right mesial frontal syndrome. *Arch Neurol* 35:252-253, 1978.
125. Rubens AB: Aphasia with infarction in the territory of the anterior cerebral artery. *Cortex* 11:239-250, 1975.
126. Alajouanine T, Castaigne P, Sabouraud O, et al: Palilalie paroxystique et vocalisations iteratives au cours de crises epileptiques par lesion interessant l'aire motrice supplementaire. *Rev Neurol* 101:685-697, 1959.
127. Van Buren JM: Evidence regarding a more precise localization of the posterior frontal-caudate arrest response in man. *J Neurosurg* 24:416-417, 1966.
128. Van Buren JH, Ojemarin GA: The frontostriatal arrest response in man. *Electroencephalogr Clin Neurophysiol* 21:117-130, 1960.
129. Goldman PS, Rosvold HE: The effects of selective caudate lesions in infant and juvenile rhesus monkeys. *Brain Res* 43:53-66, 1972.
130. Fisher CM: Intermittent interruption of behavior. *Trans Am Neurol Assoc* 93:209-210, 1968.
131. Mountcastle VB, Lynch JC, Georgopoulos A, et al: Posterior parietal association cortex of the monkey: Command functions for the operations within extrapersonal space. *J Neurophysiol* 38:871-908, 1975.
132. Yin TCT, Mountcastle VB: Visual input to the visuomotor mechanisms of the monkey's parietal lobe. *Science* 197:1381-1383, 1977.
133. Olds J: Effects of hunger and male sex hormone on self-stimulation of the brain. *J Comp Physiol Psychol* 51:320-324, 1958.
134. Olds J: *Drives and Reinforcements: Behavioral Studies of Hypothalamic Functions.* New York, Raven Press, 1977.
135. Valenstein ES: The anatomical locus of reinforcement, in Steelar E, Sprague J (eds): *Progress in Physiological Psychology.* New York, Academic Press Inc, 1966, vol 1.
136. Valenstein ES: Behavior elicited by hypothalamic stimulation: A prepotency hypothesis. *Brain Behav Evol* 2:295-316, 1969.
137. Valenstein ES: Stability and plasticity of motivational systems, in Schmitt FO (ed.): *The Neurosciences: Second Study Program.* New York, Rockefeller University Press, 1970.
138. Rolls ET: *The Brain and Reward.* Oxford, England, Pergamon Press, 1975.
139. Damasio AR: Frontal lobe dysfunction, in Heilman K, Valenstein E (eds): *Clinical Neuropsychology.* Oxford, England, Oxford University Press, 1979.
140. Mettler FA, Mettler CC: Labyrinthine disregard after removal of the caudate. *Proc Soc Exp Biol Med* 45:473-475, 1940.
141. Schopler E: Visual versus tactual receptor preference in normal and schizophrenic children. *J Abnorm Psychol* 71:108-114, 1966.
142. Mettler FA: Perceptual capacity, functions of the corpus striatum and schizophrenia. *Psychiatry Q* 29:89-111, 1955.
143. Artemieva EY, Homskaya ED: Changes in the asymmetry of EEG waves in different functional states in normal subjects and in patients with lesions of the frontal lobes, in Pribram K, Luria AR (eds): *Psychophysiology of the Frontal Lobes.* New York, Academic Press Inc, 1973.
144. Baranovskaya OP, Homskaya ED: Changes in the electroencephalogram fre-

quency spectrum during the presentation of neutral and meaningful stimuli to patients with lesions of the frontal lobes, in Pribram K, Luria AR (eds): *Psychophysiology of the Frontal Lobes*. New York, Academic Press Inc, 1973.

145. Luria AL: The frontal lobes and the regulation of behavior, in Pribram K, Luria AR (eds): *Psychophysiology of the Frontal Lobes*. New York, Academic Press Inc, 1973.

146. Simernitskaya EG: Application of the method of evoked potentials to the analysis of activation processes in patients with lesions of the frontal lobes, in Pribram K, Luria AR (eds): *Psychophysiology of the Frontal Lobes*. New York, Academic Press Inc, 1973.

147. Goldstein K: Abnormal mental conditions in infancy. *J Nerv Ment Dis* 128:538-557, 1959.

148. Goldstein K: The significance of the frontal lobes for mental performances. *J Neurol Psychopathol* 17:27, 1935.

149. Goldstein K: The mental changes due to frontal lobe damage. *J Psychol* 17:187-208, 1944.

150. Brickner RM: *The Intellectual Functions of the Frontal Lobes: A Study Based upon Observation of a Man after Partial Bilateral Frontal Lobectomy*. New York, Macmillan Co, 1935.

151. Hebb DO, Penfield W: Human behavior after extensive bilateral removal from the frontal lobes. *Arch Neurol Psychiatry* 44:421-438, 1940.

152. Ackerly SS, Benton AL: Report of a case of bilateral frontal lobe defect. *Res Publ Assoc Res Nerv Ment Dis* 27:479-504, 1948.

153. Frith U: Studies in pattern detection in normal and autistic children: Reproduction and production of colour sequences. *J Exp Child Psychol* 10:120-135, 1970.

154. Frith U: Studies in pattern perception in normal and autistic children: Immediate recall of auditory sequences. *J Abnorm Psychol* 76:413-420, 1970.

155. Frith U: Cognitive mechanisms in autism: Experiments with colour and tone sequence production. *J Autism Child Schizophr* 2:160-173, 1972.

156. Boucher J: Alternation and sequencing behaviour, and response to novelty in autistic children. *J Child Psychol Psychiatry* 18:67-72, 1977.

157. Prior MR: Conditional matching learning set performance in autistic children. *J Child Psychol Psychiatry* 18:183-189, 1977.

158. Faust C: Different psychological consequences due to superior frontal and orbito-basal lesions. *Int J Neurol* 5:410-421, 1966.

159. Dewey MA, Everard MP: The near-normal autistic adolescent. *J Autism Child Schizophr* 4:348-356, 1974.

160. Gajzago CC, Prior M: Two cases of "recovery" in Kanner syndrome. *Arch Gen Psychiatry* 31:264-268, 1974.

161. DeMyer MK: Research in infantile autism: A strategy and its results. *Biol Psychiatry* 10:433-452, 1975.

162. Filimonoff IN: A rational subdivision of the cerebral cortex. *Arch Neurol Psychiatry* 58:296-310, 1947.

163. Sanides F: Functional architecture of motor and sensory cortices in primates in the light of a new concept of neocortex evolution, in Noback CR, Montagna W

(eds): *The Primate Brain*. New York, Meredith Press, 1970.

164. Lazorthes G, Gouaze A, Salamon G: *Vascularisation et Circulation de L'Encephale*. Paris, Masson et Cie, 1976.

165. Dahlström A, Fuxe K: Evidence for the existence of monoamine containing neurones in the central nervous system: I. Demonstration of monoamines in the cell bodies of brain stem neurons. *Acta Physiol Scand* 62(suppl 232):1–55, 1964.

166. Beckstead RM: Convergent thalamic and mesencephalic projections to the anterior medial cortex in the rat. *J Comp Neurol* 166:403–416, 1976.

167. Lindvall O, Björklund A, Divac I: Organization of mesencephalic dopamine neurons projecting to neocortex and septum, in Costa E, Gessa GL (eds): *Nonstriatal Dopaminergic Neurons*. New York, Raven Press, 1977, pp. 39–46.

168. Hökfelt TA, Ljungdahl A, Fuxe K, et al: Dopamine nerve terminals in the rat limbic cortex: Aspects of the dopamine hypothesis of schizophrenia. *Science* 184:177–179, 1974.

169. Mishra RA, Demirjian C, Katzman R, et al: A dopamine-sensitive adenylate cyclase in anterior limbic cortex and mesolimbic region of primate brain. *Brain Res* 96:395–399, 1975.

170. Berger B: Histochemical identification and localization of dopaminergic axons in human cerebral cortex, in Costa E, Gessa GL (eds): *Nonstriatal Dopaminergic Neurons*. New York, Raven Press, 1977, pp 13–20.

171. Tassin JP, Stinus L, Simon H, et al: Distribution of dopaminergic terminals in rat cerebral cortex: Role of dopaminergic mesocortical system in ventral tegmental area syndrome, in Costa E, Gessa GL (eds): *Nonstriatal Dopaminergic Neurons*. New York, Raven Press, 1977, pp 21–28.

172. Farley IJ, Price KS, Hornykiewicz O: Dopamine in the limbic regions of the human brain: Normal and abnormal, in Costa E, Gessa GL (eds): *Nonstriatal Dopaminergic Neurons*. New York, Raven Press, 1977, pp. 57–64.

173. Pandya DN, Kuypers HGJM: Corticocortical connections in the rhesus monkey. *Brain Res* 13:13–36, 1969.

174. Jones EG, Powell TPS: An anatomical study of converging sensory pathways within the cerebral cortex of the monkey. *Brain* 92:793–820, 1970.

175. Van Hoesen GW, Pandya DN, Butters N: Cortical afferents to the entorhinal cortex of the rhesus monkey. *Science* 175:1471–1473, 1972.

176. Seltzer B, Pandya DN: Some cortical projections to the parahippocampal area in the rhesus monkey. *Exp Neurol* 50:146–160, 1976.

177. Herzog AG, Van Hoesen GW: Temporal neocortical afferent connections to the amygdala in the rhesus monkey. *Brain Res* 115:57–69, 1976.

178. Van Hoesen GW, Pandya DN: Afferent and efferent connections of the perirhinal cortex (area 35) in the rhesus monkey. *Anat Rec* 175:460–461, 1973.

179. Van Hoesen GW, Pandya DN: Some connections of the entorhinal (area 28) and perirhinal (area 35) cortices in the rhesus monkey: I. Temporal lobe afferents. *Brain Res* 95:1–24, 1975a.

180. Van Hoesen GW, Pandya DN: Some connections of the entorhinal (area 28) and perirhinal (area 35) cortices of the rhesus monkey: III. Efferent connections. *Brain Res* 95:39–59, 1975b.

181. Rosene DL, Mesulam MM, Van Hoesen GW: Afferents to area FL of medial

frontal cortex from amygdala and hippocampus of the rhesus monkey. *Neurosci Abstr* 2:203, 1976.

182. Mesulam MM, Van Hoesen GW, Pandya DN, et al: Limbic and sensory connections of the inferior parietal lobule (area PG) in the rhesus monkey: A study with a new method for horseradish peroxidase. *Brain Res* 136:393–414, 1977.

183. Jacobson S, Trojanowski JT: Prefrontal granular cortex of the rhesus monkey: I. Intrahemispheric cortical afferents. *Brain Res* 132:209–234, 1977.

184. Rosene DL, Van Hoesen GW: Hippocampal efferents reach widespread areas of cerebral cortex and amygdala in the rhesus monkey. *Science* 198:315–317, 1977.

185. Nauta WJH: Some projections of the medial wall of the hemisphere in the rat's brain (cortical areas 32 and 25; and 24 and 29). *Anat Rec* 115:352, 1953.

186. Carman JB, Cowan WM, Powell TPS: The organisation of the corticostriate connections in the rabbit. *Brain* 86:525–562, 1963.

187. Kemp JM, Powell TPS: The cortico-striate projection in the monkey. *Brain* 93:525–546, 1970.

188. Yeterian EH, Van Hoesen GW: Corticostriate projections in the rhesus monkey: The organization of certain cortico-caudate connections. *Brain Res* 139:43–63, 1978.

189. Folstein S, Rutter M: Infantile autism: A genetic study of 21 twin pairs. *J Child Psychol Psychiatry* 18:297–321, 1977.

190. Stubbs EG: Autistic symptoms in a child with congenital cytomegalovirus infection. *J Autism Child Schizophr* 8:37–43, 1978.

191. Bell W, McCormick W: *Neurologic Infections in Children.* Philadelphia, WB Saunders Co, 1975.

192. Myers RE: Two patterns of perinatal brain damage and their conditions of occurrence. *Am J Obstet Gynecol* 112:246–276, 1972.

193. DeReuck J, Chattha AS, Richardson EP: Pathogenesis and evolution of periventricular leukomalacia in infancy. *Arch Neurol* 27:229–236, 1972.

194. Takashima S, Tanaka K: Development of cerebrovascular architecture and its relationship to periventricular leukomalacia. *Arch Neurol* 35:11–16, 1978.

195. Lobascher MD, Kingerlee PE, Gubbay SS: Childhood autism: An investigation of aetiological factors in 25 cases. *Br J Psychiatry* 117:525–529, 1970.

196. Ornitz EM, Guthrie D, Farley AH: The early development of autistic children. *J Autism Child Schizophr* 7:207–229, 1977.

197. Schain RJ, Yannet H: Infantile autism: An analysis of 50 cases and a consideration of certain relevant neurophysiologic concepts. *J Pediatr* 57:560–567, 1960.

198. Hauser SL, DeLong GR, Rosman NP: Pneumographic findings in the infantile autism syndrome: A correlation with temporal lobe disease. *Brain* 98:667–688, 1975.

COMMENTARY by Edward M. Ornitz

Childhood autism is the most severe behavioral disorder of childhood, and presumably reflects fundamental alterations in brain function and maturation. However, in spite of the broad range of handicaps shown by autistic children, it has as yet been impossible to localize any specific neurological basis for the condition. Routine laboratory tests, such as the electroencephalogram and head X-rays, are often normal, even in children who go on to develop seizures; even more sophisticated laboratory procedures, such as computed brain tomograms, have failed to reveal major or consistent abnormalities. Many autistic children have some abnormal findings on clinical neurological examination, including peculiarities of gait and posture, but no pattern has clearly emerged to define a single neurological substrate or clear subgroups of neurological signs that pinpoint a specific brain system.

Sophisticated methods for studying brain electrophysiological processes, such as vestibular functioning, combined with clinical observation, have suggested areas that are likely to be implicated in the pathogenesis of the disorder. Because of the importance of trying to define the neurological basis of autism, various investigators have suggested brain areas that are most likely to be involved.

The paper by Damasio and Maurer represents an attempt to understand the neurological basis of autism by using analogies with known neurological diseases, particularly as manifested in adults. Arguing by analogy may be both useful and dangerous. At its best, an analogy can suggest hypotheses that are amenable to further experimental investigation and serve as a model for clinical inquiry; at its worst, analogies may obscure important details and provide a semblance of knowledge that may impede further search. The study of autism has provided examples of both types of results of analogical thinking. It is my impression that, while the goals of the Damasio and Maurer paper are laudable, the results fall short of what is needed.

Damasio and Maurer describe autistic behavior in a neurologic vocabulary and draw analogies between the redefined behavior and deficits observed in adult neurological patients. This argument by analogy only is not supported by experimental evidence. Autistic children are said to show "classic neurological signs" of disease in parts of the cerebral cortex and associated subcortical motor control areas of the brain. The communication deficiencies and the verbal spontaneity of autistics are said to resemble that of patients recovering from lesions in some of these structures. Staring is compared with "intermittent interruptions of behaviors" seen in patients with such damage. Autistic rituals and compulsions are described as defensive responses in neurologically vulnerable patients, and the disturbances of social relating are considered as "consequent to an organized collection of primary defects. . . ." In this theory, a concept of "inattention" in autistics is derived from an analogy between autistic attentional problems and neurological disease.

Other attentional aberrations, e.g., the apparent preference for tactile over visual stimuli, are explained by analogy to the behavior of animals with lesions of these areas. However, the processing of sensation occurs in circuits linking these areas to more primitive parts of the core of the brain. Thus, attentional deficits attributed to dysfunction of one part of the brain could as readily be explained by dysfunction of another part. In addition, the neurologic signs mentioned by Damasio and Maurer may not be accurate descriptions for autistic motility. Applying a neurologic vocabulary to autistic behavior may be misleading. Unless autistic motility is rated blindly and scored quantitatively for neurologic signs, it seems prudent to stay with nonneurologic descriptive terms.

Despite these limitations, the paper serves a purpose by suggesting that autism can be understood within the range of neurologic disorders. It also provokes us to try to define better models that more closely satisfy the clinical and research data. My own attempts in this direction, which will no doubt generate their own share of criticism, have led to an alternative model (Ornitz, 1983).

REFERENCE

Ornitz, E.M. The functional neuroanatomy of infantile autism. *International Journal of Neuroscience*, 1983, *19*, 85–124.

22

The Effect of High Doses
of Vitamin B₆ on Autistic Children:
A Double-Blind Crossover Study

BERNARD RIMLAND
ENOCH CALLAWAY
PIERRE DREYFUS

In a previous study of 200 children with autistic symptoms treated with an experimental vitamin regimen (C, B₆, niacinamide, and pantothenic acid), Rimland (1, 2) noted that B₆ (pyridoxine) appeared to be the key factor in some of the observed behavioral changes. He also reviewed the literature on vitamin treatment in autism and found additional support for the idea that B₆ may be beneficial in certain cases. Subsequently, some of the parents participating in the study reported to Rimland that their children had relapsed on withdrawal of B₆ and improved when the vitamin was again given.

Having identified B₆ as the vitamin most likely to be effective and having a group of children who appeared to be responsive to B₆, we undertook evaluation of the effectiveness of megavitamin amounts of B₆ by conducting a double-blind withdrawal of B₆ from autistic-type children who were believed to be behaviorally responsive to it. Specifically, we predicted that during B₆ withdrawal behavior would deteriorate.

METHOD

Subjects

From the files of the children who had participated in Rimland's original megavitamin/cluster analysis study (1, 2) we located 20 children who had apparently improved on B₆, relapsed on withdrawal of B₆, and improved

Reprinted from *American Journal of Psychiatry* 135:4 (1978), pp. 472–475. Copyright 1978, the American Psychiatric Association. Reprinted by permission.

This research was supported by Alcohol, Drug Abuse, and Mental Health Administration grant MH-25235 and Biomedical Research Support grant RR--05755 from the National Institute of Mental Health.

again when B₆ was instituted. None of the children was taking B₆ alone. All were taking other vitamins and minerals, and some were also taking drugs. Although all of these children were considered improved by their megavitamin regimes, none was considered cured. In some cases the informal withdrawal-relapse experiences reported by the parents had involved the withdrawal of other vitamins, minerals, and drugs in addition to the withdrawal of B₆. Letters of inquiry to the 20 families brought responses from 16 who agreed to participate.

One parent declined to participate because of the observation that after each restart it took the child longer than before to achieve maximum behavioral improvement. Rees (3) also observed that some children respond less well to the megavitamin treatment when it is reinstated than they did on its initiation.

Procedure

Each of the 16 children who participated in the study was put through a five-phase procedure as follows: phase one—baseline 1; phase two—test period A, B₆ or placebo; phase three—baseline 2; phase four—test period B, B₆ or placebo; and phase five—baseline 3. Thus, all subjects took B₆ through four out of five phases.

Although all the children were uniformly assigned to the five phases described above, the experimental procedure was individually tailored to fit each child as follows:

1. Each child was continued on the same vitamins, minerals, or drugs he or she had been taking routinely before the study.
2. The B₆ and placebo given in phases two and four were specially prepared as a tablet, capsule, or vitamin mix powder so as to be indistinguishable from each other and to be in the form that the child was accustomed to.
3. The duration of the five experimental phases was based on the parents' experience of the time it took their child to respond to the initiation or withdrawal of the megavitamin regime.
4. The child's behavior was recorded by parents and teachers using both narrative notes and individually developed target symptom checklists (TSCLs) (4). The TSCLs were prepared after several telephone and mail contacts with the child's parents and teachers. In most instances the families, which were widely spaced geographically (California to Florida), were also personally visited by a project research assistant who went over the details of the study design and the TSCL with the parents and teachers. Sometimes the same TSCL could be used both at home and at school. In other cases different checklists were needed.

Once the content of the TSCL was satisfactory to the parents and teachers, a supply of each was printed and sent to the families and schools for completion and return to us on a prearranged schedule, either daily or biweekly depending on the duration of the child's participation in the study. Enclosed in the packets addressed to the families was a schedule telling them the length of each of the five phases and instructions for conducting the experiment, as well as self-addressed envelopes for returning the completed TSCLs. Teachers also received this packet.

The parents were asked to adhere closely to the instructions. However, they were told they could terminate phase two or four if there was severe deterioration in their child's behavior. In such cases they could go on to the next phase (that is, to phase three or phase five). Thus, the parents could reinstate the usual B_6 dose themselves if their child seemed to respond badly to the unknown supplement.

At the conclusion of phases two and four a morning urine sample was collected from each child and frozen. The remaining contents of the B_6 and placebo bottles from phases two and four were also saved for laboratory analysis as a final check on the identity of the materials and the bioavailability of the B_6 (5).

RESULTS

The results are summarized in Table 1. After all data were collected on all subjects, Callaway, Rimland, and a research assistant studied the TSCL ratings and the narrative material. Each then rated test periods A and B for each child to indicate the child's behavior during the rated period compared with behavior during the baseline periods. Callaway and Rimland then jointly assigned a single overall behavior rating based on an 11-point scale on which +5 indicated that the child's behavior during test period A (phase two) was markedly better than during test period B (phase four); a score of −5 meant that the child had done markedly better during test period B than during test period A. After Callaway and Rimland had assigned ratings to all 16 cases, Dreyfus disclosed the contents of the bottles, i.e., which had contained B_6 and which had contained placebo. As can be seen in Table 1, the raters, using the hypothesis that behavior would deteriorate on withdrawal of B_6, correctly classified the placebo periods for 11 of 15 children.

In the case of the 16th child, the raters were unable to discern a behavioral difference between the A and B test periods. According to the code, bottle B should have contained the B_6. On analyzing the contents of the remaining capsules in the A and B bottles for child 16, it was discovered that

TABLE 1
Data for 16 Subjects in a Double-Blind Crossover Study of Vitamin B_6

Child	Age	Sex	Autism Score*	Behavior Ratings**	Dose of B_6/Day mg	mg/kg	Number of Days to Relapse Previous Study	Current Study	Pyridoxic Acid Level in Urine (µg/ml) Test Period A	Test Period B
1	14	Male	+18	−5	400	7.3	7	1	0.7	2.5
2	11	Male	+16	−1	75	2.4	42	—	1.0	2.0
3	13	Male	−32	−4	450	8.6	28	16	2.4	73.5
4	13	Female	+24	−3	200	3.5	10	6	1.4	130.7
5	18	Female	0	+5	300	6.6	14	—	4.8	57.7
6	14	Female	−4	+3	500	6.3	14	—	1.4	361.7
7	11	Male	+42	−4	800	25.1	3	3	1.0	47.9
8	10	Male	+33	−3	150	5.4	7	5	1.0	2.2
9	17	Male	−25	+1	450	9.4	28	—	58.8	1.9
10	19	Male	−3	+3	450	9.4	28	10	17.1	2.0
11	8	Female	+29	−2	300	9.4	6	—	25.7	5.1
12	4	Male	+24	+5	100	5.5	7	1	44.8	1.4
13	12	Male	+9	+5	100	3.7	7	9	13.4	6.5
14	10	Male	+26	−1	150	4.9	2	—	5.9	18.1
15	14	Male	+16	+1	450	5.8	28	—	61.7	1.9
16	11	Male	0	0	3,000	94.3	14	—	181.5	272.3

*A score of +20 indicates definite presence of infantile autism (6, 7).
**For patients 1–8, placebo was administered during test period A and B_6 during test period B; the mean behavior rating for this group was −1.50±3.63. For patients 9–16, B_6 was administered during test period A and placebo during test period B; the mean behavior rating for patients 9–15 was +1.71±2.75. Student's one-tailed t test for the difference between means was 1.79 (p<.05).

both bottles contained B₆. Furthermore, the urine samples taken from this child at the end of test periods A and B both showed high loadings of pyridoxic acid in the urine. The source of this error is unknown, but the data for child 16 were removed from subsequent analysis.

Another discrepancy appeared in the case of child 14. This is 1 of the 4 whom the raters had misclassified as being on placebo when, according to the code, he was actually on B₆. Laboratory analysis of the tablets in bottle A indicated that they were, in fact, B₆ as expected. However, the pyridoxic acid level in the urine sample collected at the end of test period A was only 5.85 μg/ml, compared with 18.11 μg/ml in the urine collected after test period B. Despite this discrepancy, it was decided to leave the data for child 14 in the data analysis because leaving them in militated against rather than supported our hypothesis and because it is possible that the laboratory or parents had mislabeled the urine sample.

The mean of all behavior ratings was 0, indicating no consistent difference between first and second test periods. However, when the mean for the group that received placebo first was compared with the mean for the group that received placebo second, the two measures differed significantly, by one-tailed t test in the predicted direction (t=1.91, p<.05, df=13).

Comment

The results show the predicted change in the children's behavior at an acceptable level of statistical significance. This is true even with the inclusion of a case in which analysis of the child's urine raised questions as to whether the parents gave the materials to the child in the proper order. It is also interesting to note that although there were only 4 girls in the study, 3 of the 4 patients whose reactions were contrary to prediction were girls.

Certain problems with this study need to be kept in mind. This was a heterogeneous group of children. Their ages ranged from 4 to 19 years, and only half of the cases showed scores above the level Rimland uses to separate out the classical cases of Kanner's syndrome from other childhood psychoses (6, 7). The B₆ doses varied widely, as did the amount of time taken for relapses on previous occasions when B₆ had been withdrawn. A withdrawal study such as this does not rule out the possibility that something like pyridoxine addiction exists and that worsening on withdrawal might occur even though no improvement had occurred initially. This alternative seems unlikely. The largest effects of withdrawal in our study were seen in children receiving only 100 mg of B₆ a day. Nevertheless, this possibility does need to be ruled out experimentally.

All of the children were receiving a variety of other agents, including usual doses of vitamins, minerals, and drugs as well as megadoses of ascorbic acid and niacin. The roles of these other agents remain completely un-investigated.

Finally, a study carried out in such widely scattered locations leaves many variables uncontrolled. The ratings made by parents and teachers were of unspecified reliability. Indeed, the clinical judges found the narrative summaries generally more useful than the TSCLs for evaluating the children's clinical changes. Children living in a home environment are also subject to many uncontrolled factors that might influence their behavior. These include visitors in the home, changes in school routine, and intercurrent illness.

Therapeutic responses to B₆ in children with autism and related disorders should not be surprising. Boullin and associates (8, 9) reported a marked increase in serotonin efflux from the platelets of children with classical infantile autism as compared with those of both nonautistic psychotic and normal control groups. Large doses of B₆ will elevate serotonin levels (10, 11). These findings as well as the work of Heeley and Roberts (12) a decade ago make it plausible that supplemental B₆ may correct, or partially correct, a tryptophan-related metabolic error.

More recently, Goldstein and associates (13) found and Lake (14) confirmed that the level of dopamine β-hydroxylase is low in children with some subtypes of autism. These and other investigators (15) also reported low plasma serotonin levels in other subgroups of autistic children. Theoretically, both of these metabolic errors might be helped by supplementation with additional B₆. Rosenberg (16) also noted that vitamin B₆ is required in large amounts in about half of the dozen or so disorders known to be due to genetic vitamin dependencies.

As far as we have been able to determine, there is no evidence that massive doses of B₆ have been or can be harmful. Wilcken and Turner (17) reported a decrease in the level of blood folate in homocystinuric children receiving megadoses of B₆ for an extended time but reported no anemia, morphological changes in blood cells, or other problems. They recommended accompanying the B₆ with a small supplement of folate in order to avoid any problems that might be associated with a folate deficiency. Rimland (2) noted that some children experienced increased irritability, sound sensitivity, and enuresis when B₆ was given in large amounts, but these problems promptly disappeared when increased amounts of magnesium were added to these children's dietary intake.

In short, B₆ seems a safe agent of potential value in the management of autistic-type children. In view of accumulating evidence for metabolic disorders in such cases, further investigations seem merited.

REFERENCES

1. Rimland, B.: High-dosage levels of certain vitamins in the treatment of children with severe mental disorders, in *Orthomolecular Psychiatry*. Edited by Hawkins, D., Pauling, L. San Francisco, WH Freeman & Co. 1973, pp 513-539.
2. Rimland, B.: An orthomolecular study of psychotic children. *Journal of Orthomolecular Psychiatry* 3:371-377, 1974.
3. Rees, E.L.: Clinical observations on the treatment of schizophrenic and hyperactive children with megavitamins. *Journal of Orthomolecular Psychiatry* 2:93-103, 1973.
4. Arnold, L.E., Wender, P.H., McCloskey, K., et al.: Levo-amphetamine and dextroamphetamine: comparative efficacy in the hyperkinetic syndrome. *Arch Gen Psychiatry* 27:816-822, 1972.
5. Miller, O.H.: Bio-availability of common vitamin mineral products. *Journal of Applied Nutrition* 27:52-59, 1975.
6. Rimland, B.: *Infantile Austism*. New York: Appleton-Century-Crofts, 1964.
7. Rimland, B.: The differentiation of childhood psychoses: an analysis of checklists for 2,218 psychotic children. *J Autism Child Schizo* 1:161-174, 1971.
8. Boullin, D.J., Coleman, M., O'Brien, R.A.: Abnormalities in platelet 5-hydroxytryptamine efflux in patients with infantile autism. *Nature* 226:371-372, 1970.
9. Boullin, D.J., Coleman, M., O'Brien, R.A., et al.: Laboratory predictions of infantile autism based on 5-hydroxytryptamine efflux from blood platelets and their correlation with the Rimland E-2 score. *J Autism Child Schizo* 1:63-71, 1971.
10. Coleman, M.: *Serotonin in Down's syndrome*. Amsterdam, North-Holland Publishing Co., 1973.
11. Bhagavan, H.N., Coleman, M., Coursin, D.B.: The effect of pyridoxine hydrochloride on blood serotonin and pyridoxal phosphate contents in hyperactive children. *Pediatrics* 55:437-441, 1975.
12. Heeley, A.F., Roberts, G.E.: A study of tryptophan metabolism in psychotic children. *Dev Med Child Neurol* 3:708-718, 1966.
13. Goldstein, M., Mahanand, D., Lee, J., et al.: Dopamine-beta-hydroxylase and endogenous total 5-hydroxyindole levels in autistic patients and controls, in *The Autistic Syndromes*. Edited by Coleman, M. Amsterdam, North-Holland Publishing Co., 1976, pp 57-63.
14. Lake, C.R., Ziegler, M.G., Murphy, D.L.: Increased norepinephrine levels and decreased dopamine beta hydroxylase activity in primary autism. *Arch Gen Psychiatry* 34:553-556, 1977.
15. Ritvo, E.R., Yuwiler, A., Geller, E., et al.: Increased blood serotonin and platelets in early infantile autism. *Arch Gen Psychiatry* 23:566-572, 1970.
16. Rosenberg, L.E.: Vitamin-dependent genetic disease. *Hospital Practice*. July 1970, pp. 59-66.
17. Wilcken, B., Turner, B.: Homocystinuria: reduced folate levels during pyridoxine treatment. *Arch Dis Child* 48:58-62, 1973.

EDITOR'S NOTE: Following the completion of the above paper, two studies have been conducted in France confirming the positive behavioral effects of B$_6$ on autistic children, and also showing both electrophysiological and metabolic effects of B$_6$ on autistics that differentiated them from normal control children.

G. Lelord, E. Callaway, J. P. Muh, J. C. Arlot, D. Sauvage, B. Garreau, and J. Domenech. Modifications in urinary homovanillic acid after ingestion of vitamin B$_6$: Functional study in autistic children. *Rev. Neurol. (Paris)*, 1978, *134*, 12, 797-801.

G. Lelord, J. P. Muh, J. Martineau, B. Garreau, and S. Roux. Electrophysiological and biochemical studies in autistic children treated with vitamin B$_6$. In D. Lehman and E. Callaway (Eds.), *Human Evoked Potentials: Applications and Problems*. New York: Plenum, 1979.

COMMENTARY by Ralph G. Maurer

For years Rimland has championed the use of high doses of certain vitamins as a treatment of autism. This has been controversial, and in this study he and his colleagues undertake to obtain data that will support their point of view. The study, though adequate in many ways, is flawed in others, and the net result has been to fuel the controversy rather than dampen it. In the paper there are arguing points for proponent and opponent alike.

The authors took children who already were on high doses of vitamin B$_6$ and who seemed to deteriorate whenever it was stopped. Then they stopped it in a controlled way. They found that although the majority of the children did deteriorate, there were some who showed little change, and even a few who improved.

What do these findings mean? One cannot infer from them that the vitamin is beneficial, any more than one could infer that coffee is good for me because I have a headache on days I fail to drink it. The authors are aware of this logical difficulty and try to reason around it by asserting the equivalent of: my neighbor, who drinks far more coffee than I, seldom has a headache when he stops; therefore coffee withdrawal is not the cause of mine. There *are* alternative hypotheses, but even if the conclusion is true, it does not prove the case for coffee drinking and does not necessarily even strengthen it.

All in all, there is so much variability in the data in the study that the strongest inference that can be made is probably a simple restatement of the findings: most do worse, some stay the same, a few improve, all for unknown reasons. This leaves us with many interesting questions for future study, but few or no answers.

ABOUT THE EDITOR
EDITORIAL PANEL
NAME INDEX
SUBJECT INDEX

About the Editor

Professor Anne M. Donnellan is a member of the Department of Studies in Behavioral Disabilities at the University of Wisconsin–Madison. Her interest in autism began in 1970 when she founded Los Ninos Center in San Diego, one of the first programs in the country for preschoolers with autism. She is a long-time member of the Professional Advisory Board of the National Society for Children and Adults with Autism (NSAC) and for three years directed the NSAC National Personnel Training project, which developed in-service training capabilities in more than a dozen states and provinces.

Dr. Donnellan received her Ph.D. from the University of California at Santa Barbara. She is a member of Phi Beta Kappa, serves as an editor of several journals in the field of special education, and is active nationally with the Association for Persons with Severe Handicaps (TASH). She has written numerous articles on the topics of nonaversive behavior management, community-based instruction, and teacher training. She is co-author with Gary W. LaVigna of *Alternatives to Punishment: Non-Aversive Strategies for Solving Behavior Problems* (Irvington Press) and co-editor with Donald J. Cohen of *The Handbook of Autism and Disorders of Atypical Development* (John Wiley & Sons). With a grant from the U.S. Department of Education, Office of Special Education and Rehabilitation Services, she is developing nonaversive strategies to enable persons with severe behavior problems to work in integrated employment.

Editorial Panel

Name Index

Page numbers followed by *n* refer to footnotes or references.

Subject Index

Adaptation, 69
Affective development
  autistic characteristics and, 146–49
  disturbances of, 153
  empathy in, 155
  linguistic development and, 200–1
Age
  autistic characteristics and, 146–49
  at onset of autism, 117–18, 123
  prevalence of autism and, 121–22
  reinforcement by parents and, 70
  speech development and, 288
  of walking, 116
Allopurinol, 307
Anaclitic depression, 157
Anencephaly, 91
Anticipatory posture, 41–42, 48–49
Aphasia, 158, 191, 197, 199, 351–52
  cerebrospinal fluid metabolites and, 359,
    360
  as elective disability, 89
  schizophrenia as form of, 255–56
  verbal defects of autism versus, 387–89
Atavisms
  parental role in development of, 56, 62–64
  symbolic play and, 335, 338–39
Attention, parent, 65–66
Attentional disorders, 362
  neurological factors in, 389–91
Atypical development, 143, 161–63, 180,
    350–51
Auditory perception, 390
Autism
  causes of. *See* Etiology
  diagnosis of. *See* Diagnosis
  prognosis for, 378
  schizophrenia versus, 143–44, 154, 155,
    156–58, 161–62, 180, 181, 184–85, 210,
    230, 350–51, 373
  of siblings, 145–46, 271, 321, 374. *See*
    also Twins
  symptoms of. *See* Symptoms
  as term, 2
Autocatalysis, 63–64
Aversive control

by child, of parent, 62, 63
  role of, in performance deficits, 71

Bayley scales of infant development, 331
Birth order, 86, 91–92, 231
Birth trauma, 146, 180, 323–24, 395
  tic syndromes and, 363
Birth weight, 116
Blindness, 391
Brain function
  as basis of autism, 194–95
  birth trauma and, 146, 180, 323–24, 363,
    395
  diagnosis of autism and, 157–58, 373–74
  difficulty of measuring, 86, 195
  electroencephalographic studies of,
    272–73, 351
  etiology of autism and, 393–95
  5-hydroxyindole metabolism and, 74–83,
    358–64
  lesions and, 375–76, 384, 388–89, 392–93
  measurement of, 266–67
  motility disturbances and, 384–86
  organic factors in, 100, 272–77
  ritualistic behavior and, 392.
  See also Neurological factors

Carbidopa, 307
Cerebral palsy, 395
Chemical factors, 6, 357–64
  homovanillic acid metabolism, 358–64
  5-hydroxyindole metabolism, 74–83,
    358–64
  in tic syndromes, 362–64
  vitamin therapy, 408–15
Child Research Project, 241
Chips, coded, 287–88, 291
Chlorpromazine, 78
Coded chips, 287–88, 291
Cognitive development, 6, 47, 108
  models of, 352–57
  rote memory in, 42, 49, 198–99, 390
  testing for disturbances in, 219–21
  of twins, 322–24.
  See also Intelligence

435